To the Lyme Public
Library, as a
sign of continuing
interest and

concern.

Wright and Mary
Bakke

Private Services Friday For Prof. E. Wight Bakke

WOODBRIDGE — Private funeral services for E. Wight Bakke of 55 Rimmon Road, one of the nation's leading authorities on industrial and personnel relations, will be held Friday. Mr. Bakke, 68, died Tuesday morning in his home after a sudden illness.

Mr. Bakke, Sterling Professor of Economics at Yale University, had been teaching his regular classes and had been in his Yale office on Monday.

The service, for members of the family only, will be held at 11 a.m. in Dwight Chapel, Yale University. Burial will be private. The Hawley Lincoln Memorial, New Haven, is in charge of arrangements. Contributions in his memory may be made to the General Scholarship Fund of Quinnipiac College.

A member of the Yale faculty since 1932, he was director of Yale's Labor and Management Center, which operated for 15 years after World War II as an interdisciplinary research and advisory group.

While a student at the Yale School of Religion, he served for two years as the pastor of the former Park Methodist Episcopal Church in Morris Cove.

Mr. Bakke. husband of Mary Sterling Bakke, was born in Onawa, Iowa, Nov. 13, 1903, son of Oscar C. Bakke and the late Harriet Francis Bakke.

E. WIGHT BAKKE

For his exceptional contributions in the field of human relations, he was cited in 1948 by the American Society for the Advancement of Management.

He received his B.A. degree in 1926 from Northwestern University in Evanston, Ill.. and attended the Yale Graduate School and School of Religion, where he received his M.A. and Ph.D degrees. During his college career, he won wide reputation as an orator and debater.

In addition to his service as a pastor, he was also an instructor of public speaking at New Haven College and assistant director of interpersonal relationships for the Department of Commerce during these years.

He joined the Yale faculty as instructor in sociology and a supervisor of research on unemployment problems of the Yale Institute of Human Relations. He was promoted to assistant professor in sociology in 1934 and was named professor of economics in 1938.

He became interested in the problems of employment during the economic depression of the 1930's. He was appointed Sterling professor in 1944 and in the 1950's he helped reorganize Yale's new department of Industrial Administration.

In 1965 he was named to the board of overseers of the Tuck School of Business Administration at Dartmouth College, Hanover, N.H. In 1964, he received an honorary Doctor of Laws degree from Northwestern University.

He wrote or co-authored more than ten books and has written many magazine articles. He had served as chairman of the board of trustees of Quinnipiac College, Hamden. He was a former director of the National Bureau of Economic Research, a former member of the Corporation of Haverford College, Haverford, Pa. and a Fellow of the American Association for the Advancement of Science.

He was a consultant for the U.S. Department of Labor and a consultant to the Foreign Operations Administration of the State Department on the development of management training programs abroad.

In 1948, he was a member of the Emergency Board created by President Harry Truman to investigate the dispute that year between the Pennsylvania Railroad and its employes.

From 1943-1946, he was co-chairman of the appeals committee of the National War Labor Board and from 1947-1949 was a consultant to the U.S. Navy.

Besides his wife, he leaves one daughter, Mrs. Albert S. Bacdayan of Lexington, Ky.; two sons, Karl E. Bakke of Falls Church, Va., and William W. Bakke of Woodbridge; two brothers, Clarence and Maurice Bakke, both of Onawa; and six grandchildren.

CAMPUS CHALLENGE

STUDENT ACTIVISM IN PERSPECTIVE

E. WIGHT BAKKE
MARY S. BAKKE

Archon Books
1971

A Project of the Inter-University
Study of Labor Problems in
Economic Development

14, 580   gift

ISBN 0-208-01205-2
Library of Congress Catalog Card No. 77-150394
Printed in the United States of America

Contents

Preface

The student rebellion at Berkeley in 1964 initiated a period of traumatic experiences for American students, for their families, for university faculties and administrators, for public officials, and for responsible citizens. The experiences came to a tragic climax, but not to an end, in the senseless killing of students at Kent State and Jackson State in 1970. It appeared to many that a sizeable portion of the students had suddenly gone beserk, intent on destroying the institutions of which they were supposedly the chief beneficiaries. Even those who credited the activists with courageous idealism were concerned about the violent methods they used.

The explosive events of those years took many by surprise, particularly when the current highly activist attitudes and actions of the students were contrasted with those of the so called "apathetic student generation" of the fifties. Some of these people reacted angrily to the events, castigating the students involved as everything from "spoiled brats" to the "dupes of those plotting revolution." Others, many of whom had themselves become critical of the features of university and public life against which the students proclaimed they were in rebellion, were more generous in their evaluations. Those whose vocations place upon them the responsibility, and provide them with the opportunity, to study and analyze the behavior of people in society, directed their attention to explaining the phenomenon of student protest. Some of these produced careful and insightful empirical studies of particular American situations and of the activists involved. Others, aware that in other parts of the world students had long played a significant role in university and public affairs, sought for clues to events at home in the records of student activism abroad.

vii

We began our investigation of this subject in 1962 with study tours to Mexico and Colombia. This was followed by two study tours to Japan in 1964 and again in 1965, to India in 1965, and a return to Mexico and Colombia in 1968.

Our original objective was a comparative study of student movements in these countries. However, signs were beginning to appear that American student dissatisfaction with many aspects of university, social, and political affairs, and an interest in having a larger voice in "setting things right," was increasing in intensity. In anticipation that this interest would continue to escalate, we hoped that insights gained from the studies abroad would prove useful in interpreting the phenomena at home. The escalation exceeded our anticipations, and the secondary objective became dominant. The result is this book and the conclusions presented in Section V, "Student Activism in Perspective."

We have tried to identify, from our field investigations and from study of the literature recorded in the bibliographical appendix the variables which clearly have been universally present in producing among students a predisposition to activism, in bringing those predispositions to an action producing focus, and in contributing to its escalation. "Universal" in this context is, of course, defined by reference to those variables present and observed in Mexico, Colombia, Japan, India, and the United States, although we have explored, albeit less exhaustively, major studies and commentaries concerning student movements in other countries, as well. We have suggested in the chapter on "Roots and Soil of Student Activism," if not a theory, at least a model of a syndrome of essential variables which have had a positive impact resulting in overt student activism in every case which has come to our attention.

The gathering of data for a study of this geographical, population, and substantive scope presents the researcher with methodological problems not present in more discrete and focused studies of a particular campus, or of a specific group of subjects. Experimental, survey, questionnaire, and participant observer methods, which we have used in a number of organizational studies during the past 40 years, are not practical approaches for an individual researcher working on a problem of the scope indicated. Briefly the method used was as follows.

Primary dependence was placed on first hand observation and

on 1517 interviews. The interviews were held with 1002[1] students, 104 of whom were present or former leaders among the activists, 224 faculty members, and 86 university administrators, on 65 campuses. These campuses included those of the major public and private universities and colleges in Mexico, Colombia, and Japan. Those in India were chiefly in and near Delhi, Agra, Calcutta, Hyderabad, Madras, Trivandrum, and Bombay. In the United States we had the same kind of first hand contact with 3 major campuses, including of course our own university. But we have examined the several investigations, and/or the specific studies made by academic researchers, of student activism at Berkeley, Chicago, Northwestern, Colombia, Harvard, San Francisco State, Kent State, Wisconsin, and Swarthmore.

In addition to the above named campus-centered interviews were those conducted with national and local government officials associated with education, youth affairs, and police activities, and with knowledgeable public figures and representatives of the press who had displayed an analytical interest in the subject, 205 in all.

The approach in these interviews was that employed by ethnologists in field research. The responses sought were primarily those germane to the societal role of the informant, and those interviewed were encouraged to respond as informants depicting the situation as it appeared to them, not only as individuals, but as reporters for the social group of which they were members. The questions used in these interviews are set forth in Appendix A. Emphasis, of course, was placed in each interview on those matters with which the instant informant was most knowledgeable. Prior to study tours to the several countries the questions were pretested in interviews with students from those countries doing work at Yale, Berkeley, and Cornell.

The findings from the study tour interviews were then checked against the findings reported by others in documents or systematic studies; were related to data concerning the institutional and other cultural features of the country and the particular university; and most importantly, were tested for significance by reference to whatever understanding of social, political, and psychological factors and processes had been acquired during a

[1]Interviews with students were both with individuals and with small groups of two to six.

career devoted to research and study in the social sciences. But the major intial touchstone for our conclusions was the observations made and our systematization and analysis of the responses received in these interviews.

A primary draft was then prepared and returned for comment to those in the several countries whose awareness of issues had been most apparent. Corrections in the draft were made. Return visits were made to Latin America and Japan for the purposes of clarifying or rechecking and correcting any inconsistencies or inadequacies that had been pointed out in our findings and conclusions.

We then explored those documents recorded in the bibliographical appendix under "General and American," which we had not already examined, in order to be clear about the reported nature of the activism in the United States and interpretations of it which we desired to view in the perspective of our studies in the other four countries.

It is obvious that we are greatly indebted to a host of informants each of whom gave hours of time to our questioning, and in many cases on repeated occasions. The limits of space forbid listing all their names. But when they read these pages they will recognize their contributions. To all of them we extend our heartfelt gratitude.

Our thanks go also to John Dunlop, Fred Harbison, Clark Kerr, and Charles Myers, who contributed to the framing of the design for the studies, read and criticized parts of the manuscript, and gave constant and stimulating encouragement to our efforts. We are most appreciative of the financial support given by the Interuniversity Study of Labor Problems in Economic Development. We also acknowledge our indebtedness to Edna Vreeland, Doris Boveé, and Judi Stringer for their secretarial and clerical labors during the eight years in which this book has been in preparation.

New Haven, Connecticut
January, 1971

SECTION I
STUDENTS ON THE MARCH

Students on the March

Since World War II, dramatic and frequently violent student demonstrations all over the world have aroused the interest and the sympathetic or unsympathetic reaction of university and public officials and of the general public. Until 1964, Americans generally viewed these demonstrations from afar as something which "couldn't happen here." Such undisciplined student rebellion was looked upon as peculiar to countries where in one way or another society itself was in upheaval and its system of governance unable to control the turbulent forces at work. The occasional examples in the United States of students getting out of hand in "panty raids," "football weekend riots," "town and gown clashes," and the like, were not taken as indicators that anything fundamental was out of joint in the universities and the colleges or in the society itself.

Then came the explosion at Berkeley followed by six years of escalating student demonstrations, strikes, the occupation of buildings, attacks on university officials, which could not be passed off with the complacent explanation, "boys will be boys." The incidents that ricocheted across the country like a crazy billard ball were obviously not instigated just for fun. They were launched to protest conditions and arrangements and relationships in the universities and in society about which a large number of students were very clearly disturbed and angry. And in many cases the form of protest was a challenge to the very legitimacy of the governance of the universities and of the nation itself. Even when such a challenge was not made explicit, the action taken brought a number of the universities to a halt, and some of the demands presented would, if granted, introduce revolutionary changes into the traditional mission, organization, and governance of the universities. Moreover, the forces of law and order in the community were confronted with unprecedented difficulties in preserving the public peace at home, and the government was faced with mounting opposition to conducting war abroad. The student movement had become a force to reckon with.

A natural reaction for many was to charge that the demonstrations were instigated, or at least encouraged, by foreign or domestic anti-Establishment revolutionaries who were using the students as pawns in their efforts to undermine the American system of life and government. Many more were concerned that we were witnessing a breakdown of respect for law and authority and of a concern for societal order and civility. Some bemoaned the "irresponsibility" of the students and their "lack of appreciation" for the costly efforts of their elders to provide them with more economic security and educational advantages than any previous generation had enjoyed. A widespread sentiment developed that the activist "minority," who were stirring up the great majority of students, who had no other desire than to go on with their education, should be "put in their place before things got completely out of hand." Even those who expressed sympathy for the objectives which the students alleged they were seeking, decried the extra-legal methods they frequently employed.

There were some, however, who welcomed such student activity as evidence of deep concern among youth for the critical problems of our time and of their readiness, if not their competence, to throw themselves into efforts to seek solutions their elders had obviously failed to devise. In a limited few cases, the activism and particularly the violence of the students have shaken the confidence of responsible adults that their own policies, decisions, and actions are soundly conceived or that their efforts provide a viable basis for order and progressive development in the internal and external affairs of the nation. The assumption that such events were simply the irrational and undisciplined expression of "kids" who had little grasp of the complexities of carrying on the social, political, and economic affairs of the world did not appear to them to be completely dependable as a clue to interpretation. A gnawing suspicion grips the minds of the more thoughtful adults responsible for the direction of public affairs, that they themselves are not masters of those complexities. The actions of the students sharpen that suspicion.

But even a superficial consideration of the issues around

which the demonstrations are organized in the United States and abroad indicates that those issues are important to large numbers of conservative people interested in security-providing stability as well as to those interested in radical change. A sizeable portion of the population in any country might still be inclined to "let well enough alone." These people are likely to consider the agitation and protest of any individuals or groups irrational and even, at times, revolutionary. But knowledgeable persons in places of responsiblility for determining public policy cannot afford to neglect the possibility that the agitations of students may reveal not only the areas where changes are desired and needed, but the intensity of the desire and the seriousness of the need. In any case the students will in the near future be shouldering the duties of office in private and public effort, and the character and adequacy of the training for such roles, particularly in the universities, is of unquestionable significance for the future. A stimulus to the reassessment of the strengths and the shortcomings of the university experience as producers of human resources for future economic, social, and political stability, change, and development is one of the possible results of student activism.

The study of the nature and of the roots and soil of student activism in Japan, India, Mexico, and Colombia here recorded was begun in 1962, when evidences of increasing concern of and protest by American students with respect to university and public affairs was beginning to appear on the horizon, in the hope that such study would be an aid to understanding that concern and protest when it became a critical element in American student life. We have attempted to focus the findings from the study of these four student movements on the American scene in Section V.

The nature of student activism and the factors stimulating and encouraging that activism, in these countries are significant for other reasons also.

Of particular interest to Americans is the fact that a recurrent characteristic of student demonstrations since World War II, in South America, Asia, and Africa, has been its anti-United States emphasis. By reference to the "students are pawns of the extremists" hypothesis, one could agree with Governor Rockefeller, whose recent (1969) visits to South America as the representative of President Nixon were met in every South American country with such "Yankee-go-home" demonstrations, that such an expression was unrepresentative of the *general* popular sentiment in the countries. But closer study of the phenomenon of student activism abroad makes it necessary to assign a supportive rather than an initiating role to extremist influences, and suggests that the students are reflecting in overt behavior a general attitude toward the United States which less active or more diplomatically responsible elements in the population do not express, or feel it unwise to express, openly.

The interest shown by journalists, visiting statesmen, and others in such demonstrations has brought to light, moreover, that student activism has a potential impact on university and public policy that is noteworthy. The results of the demonstrations are not merely that, through such explosive protests, the students get something off their chests, but, frequently, that public opinion is galvanized, that public and university policy is modified, that governors and prime ministers are toppled from office, and that professors, vice-chancellors, and rectors lose their jobs. Student activism must be taken seriously as one of the factors influencing the policy and practice of many nations.

At a time when our relations with the internal affairs of these countries was less intimate and our own future was assumed to be less influenced by what happens there, we could afford to be distant and disinterested observers of these matters. Like the fiesta and the bullfight and periodic palace revolutions, student demonstrations could be considered an interesting and exciting aspect of the domestic life of these countries, but really no concern of ours, save as they provided us with subjects for after dinner conversation.

That time is past. We are now aware that nothing which can give us an insight into the way of life and thought and action of our neighbors is no concern of ours. Especially is a phenomenon like the student demonstration, which apparently is a more than a casual ingredient in local and national political affairs, likely to be symptomatic of an underlying set of factors and relationships which influence the development of these countries and our relations with them. In the light of our close involvement with them, we may be observing something which will have an impact on our own future as well. The investigation of student activism may introduce us to the underground currents of social and political and economic affairs in these countries (and in the United States as well) which periodically burst through the crust of normal life like an explosive geyser or volcano.

Moreover, among those who participate in these student demonstrations are unquestionably young men and women whose future decisions and actions will shape the economic, social, and political development of these countries. That development is one major objective of our foreign policy and practice in relation to them. Do the direct action tendencies of students have any bearing on that development and the character of their participation in it?

There are, in the countries whose student activism is the subject of this book, few roads to vocations which influence, in a major way, the course of economic, political, and social development which do not pass through one of the universities. Agrarian and labor leadership are possible exceptions. The reason for this is not merely the need for the training acquired for one of the "careers," for the pursuit of which the several faculties (or schools)[1] are organized. Indeed one is frequently inclined to suspect that such vocational or professional "training" is secondary to gaining the prestige of a university degree, to having participated in a socially approved ritual, and to acquiring the personal contacts, social skills, and influence which facilitate the entrance to a position or career and the solving of operating problems presented by that career. In all countries it is true that technical abilities and skills are "not enough." In countries which are in transition from a feudal or colonial system (with its emphasis upon class rule, personal contacts, influence, power, and loyalties) to a bureaucratic and managerial state and industrial organization, this is particularly true.

The universities are very naturally expected by those who attend them to provide an experience helpful in the kind of a world in which they will live and work. In any case, the impact of the university experience upon the potential participants in decisions and action affecting economic, social, and political development is an important intervening vari-

[1]Following the European tradition, it is customary in these countries to use the designation "faculty" where North Americans would use "school," e.g. Law *Faculty* instead of Law *School*. In Mexico, the divisions of the universities which grant the doctorate are designated as "faculties," the others as "schools."

able between the manpower potential of youth and the contributions, either positive or negative, they later make to the
life and destiny of their countries.

That experience can be compared to, but it is far from
identical with, that to which students in the United States
are subjected. In considering, therefore, the impact of university life on economic, political, and social development
in the several countries, we need to understand the nature
and potential effect of the experience of the students *in
these countries.* We cannot safely infer from our knowledge
of American higher education, student life, and public affairs
what the effect is likely to be.

But neither is it desirable to interpret such phenomena
solely as a reflection of particular problems, circumstances,
institutions, and the character of people in particular countries. While recognizing the dangers of generalization, we
may seek for common factors that could help us to understand the important bearing student activism is likely to
have on the developing countries whose future is bound
up with our own.

Nor would such clues to the activism of students in other
parts of the world be irrelevant to understanding the increasing tendency of American students to make the affairs of
their universities and of their country the objects of their direct
action. In the final section of this book we shall summarize
these clues and relate them to current explanations of student
activism in the United States.

That summary and analysis in Section V is based on
the observations set forth in Sections II, III and IV, each
of which considers student activism in each of the countries
from the point of view of a particular aspect of the phenomenon, and is introduced by a discussion of the dimensions of that aspect.

Chapters 1 through 3 in Section II report the major features
and chacteristics of the so called student movements in Japan,
India, and in Latin America (Mexico and Colombia).

Sections III and IV set forth the evidence, pertaining to
each of these countries, concerning factors which can plausibly be considered as encouraging and generating, if not
causing, student activism of the type observed.

In Section III (Chapters 4-6) those factors are related to
the plausible possibility that student activism is a function
of the universal search of youth for a self-identity and for

social integration, and of their predisposition to self-assertion, with peer group support, at this stage in the maturation process.

In Section IV (Chapters 7-9) those factors are related to the plausible possibility that the type and degree of student activism (1) is suggested and reinforced by the image of the "Student" held by students and others, (2) is stimulated by the inadequacies in the university and societal systems for personalizing that image, (3) is intensified by the student's perception of the inconsistencies between the moral imperatives associated with that image and the actual morality of those who manage and govern their university and society, and (4) is amplified both by public opposition to, and permissiveness with respect to, their efforts to remove those inadequacies and resolve those inconsistencies, and by the attempt to create new roles for students not implied in the traditional image of the Student.

The latter possibility is particularly significant when the image of the Student is characterized basically by the expectancy that he is one who has an active concern about societal problems affecting all citizens and is an important instrument of change, and that he has a responsibility to assert in action his conception of a resolution of the contradictions between his own or his elders' expressed ideal premises and what is actually being done about these problems.

Only against the background of the evidence relative to these possibilities does it become meaningful to ask to what degree student activism is a function of the stimulus from groups with revolutionary axes to grind.

Section V, as indicated above, focuses the findings from the investigation of student activism in Japan, India, and Latin America upon the analyses made and explanations given of student activism in the United States by suggesting the answers to three questions: Are there dimensions of student activism which are strikingly similar in all of these countries, including the United States? Are there present in all cases where student activism occurs similar factors which encourage, activate, and reinforce it, suggesting a universally applicable explanation of the activism? What accounts for the universally observable tendency of student activism to escalate from relatively peaceful and orthodox expressions of dissent to civil disobedience and violent direct action? In other words, Section V considers student activism from the point of view of a broader perspective than that provided by the examination of that phenomenon within the boundaries of any one country.

SECTION II

THE CHARACTER OF STUDENT ACTIVISM

The Character of Student Activism

Student activism has been given many names: student unrest, student indiscipline, student protest, student rebellion, student politics, student movement. We choose the term student activism as defining best the nature of the thing we are trying to describe, analyze, and interpret. It is the most comprehensive and relatively neutral of the foregoing terms. The first term suggests a state of mind, the second a mode of behavior, both characterizing some manifestations of student activism. The next two suggest reactions to circumstances and experience which lead to student activism. The last two suggest analogies with well known manifestations of social action and organization which provide an analytical approach to a part, but not all, of the modes of student activism. The aspects of student activism suggested by all the terms are, however, significant clues to its roots in and impact on persons and institutions. Continued study leads one eventually to a consideration of the relevance of the aspects of student activism suggested by all of these terms.

The kind of student behavior which we shall consider under the term "student activism," however, is not synonymous with "student activity." The largest portion of the behavior of persons in any social group is of the normal routine variety appropriate to carrying on their life and work within the framework of opportunities and constraints offered or imposed by the existing folkways and mores and institutions of the group. Implicit in their behavior is a predisposition to accept, or at least to tolerate, that framework and to seek whatever satisfaction of their desires and aspirations it is possible to realize within it.

The kind of behavior in which we are interested implies no such predispositions. On the contrary it reveals a predisposition to change that framework. It reveals a dissatisfaction with the status quo, a desire for a change, and commitment to actions which would effect that change. It implies that the actor conceives of himself as an instrument of change. The behavioral manifestation of this self-conception will range from civil and orthodox dissent to antagonistic confrontation and violent direct action. The end sought may be reform or revolution.

In all the countries in which we have made firsthand observations, student activism reveals certain similarities. The cast of characters is composed of youth, most of whom are registered students, predominantly between the ages of 16 and 23, give or take a couple of years at either extreme. All examples have a collective dimension, and most have some kind of organization (or organizations) with officers and, frequently, headquarters offices. All engage in group activities the most dramatic of which is the mass demonstration, the strike, or forceful interruption of normal orthodox societal processes, in which the activists are protesting something they don't like or the absence of something they are asserting they would like. All are led by a few initiating activists who propose certain targets for action and the kind of action to be taken, and whose continuing problem is to mobilize a following large enough to make the action effective. All of these collective actions raise problems of public order and institutional stability and continuity for university and public authorities.

There are, of course, observable differences in the several countries: (a) in the degree to which student activism can be characterized historically and currently as a "movement;" (b) in the relative emphasis given to the objectives toward which action is directed, to the operational field chosen for activity (i.e. campus, community, nation), and to political or non-political issues; (c) in the kinds of tactics and strategies which predominate; (d) in the character and stability of organizational structure; (e) in the relationship of student activists to other pressure and action groups; (f) in the characteristics of the activist leaders, including their ideological orientation and the intensity of their commitment to the objectives they allegedly seek.

The Initiators of Student Activism

The last named aspect of student activism is so significant

in determining its character and direction that it is desirable to give it further emphasis before we turn to the description, with reference to the above named dimensions, of student activism in the several countries. Explanations of student activism considering it as a mass phenomenon are probably most accurately designated as hypotheses with respect to factors which produce a *readiness* for activism among large numbers of students, rather than as hypotheses with respect to the *causes* of that activism. Those factors result in overt activism only when their potential is activated by a dynamic leader.

The group activity of students, like that of workers, professionals, businessmen, and politicians is seldom the result of a simultaneous consensus on objectives among folk and a spontaneous combustion of joint activity directed toward those objectives. Even if a latent consensus is present as to objectives and how to achieve them, the spark of leadership is normally necessary to set action ablaze. Action is promoted by individual activists whose personal, but not necessarily selfish, purposes can be served by enlisting their fellows in a collective endeavor. So obvious is this that the explanation of student activism usually places heavy, if not exclusive, emphasis upon the purposes and ambitions of leaders. Commentaries on student direct action in all the countries visited make this emphasis. Three such personal purposes are widely referred to.

First there is the desire of particularly ambitious young students to stand out among their fellows as leaders and to acquire the personal prestige which goes with such leadership, the desire to be "number one." Colombian, Mexican, Japanese, and Indian students do not differ from their counterparts in the United States in this desire. There are, of course, differences in the demonstrated qualities of leadership which appeal to the students in the different countries. Seldom, however, is the evidence that of capacity for patient, organized, and systematic activity. More normally it is that of the manly heroic deed in a crisis situation, the sort of dramatic act that distinguishes "the men from the boys."

Moreover university life in these countries offers opportunities for the realization of that ambition different from those in the United States. In the United States a large amount of this ambition has normally been supported by the opportunities for leadership, influence, and prestige provided by participation and captaincies in the several "prestige" sports, by the editorship and management of the student publications, by the extracurricular activities of various voluntary associations, clubs, fraternities, dormitory or "college" units, by membership on committees in charge of university events, by the election to a number of academic honor societies, by the receipt of prizes for academic and student-citizenship excellence, and by election to student advisory and governing bodies concerned with student (rather than university administration) affairs.

In Colombia and Mexico, at least in the public universities, the search for satisfaction of this leadership ambition can, on the whole, focus in the participation in university management and in the opportunity to stimulate, organize, and inspire student group action. Membership on university governing boards amplifies this opportunity, but the operational field is provided for a larger number by office in the autonomous student societies and in the federations of which they are the constituent units.

The opportunities for extracurricular organization leadership in Japan are more similar to those in the United States than is the case in the other countries. The Japanese students organize for any and all kinds of purposes, and with administrative and faculty approval, if not active participation. No one of the eleven colleges or universities in which we had extensive interviews with student, faculty, and administrators has less than 25 such student groups. In Keio University (one of the universities least troubled by student agitations, though there are other reasons for this) there are claimed to be 400 student groups on the campus; these include 80 which are oriented toward cultural, music, and hobby interests; 10 are academically related study groups; 60 are athletic associations (40 athletic teams); 200 which are recreational, religious, or regional. One university had erected 20 Quonset huts, each housing two student organization headquarters. The search for activist leadership tendencies in Japan must go beyond the assumption that the paucity of on-campus student leadership opportunities is responsible. Moreover the events and crises of life in Japan were collectively responded to by national as well as by campus oriented student organizations. This development provided an opportunity for activists to become visible as leaders both national, and, on occasion, international. For those students with an urge to personal leadership, the Japanese situation offers unusual opportunities.

In India, by comparison, the normal and non-political opportunities for leadership of student groups, the grasping of which would satisfy the ego aspirations of would-be leaders, are minimal. The same thing is true in Latin America. In these countries the tradition of university experience for all but the select and fortunate few is so recent that the organization of specific purpose student associations on an ongoing basis has not had adequate chance to develop.

A second stimulus to student leadership frequently mentioned is the possibility that such activity will attract the attention of political leaders, and thus become a prelude to an offered opportunity for a political career. Such a career frequently means "pure" political party or factional activity, but not necessarily so. In countries in which a non-political civil service is of comparatively recent origin and has not yet achieved the stability of institutionalized autonomy, almost any government job is highly involved in political maneuverings, and the politically skillful have a superior chance of survival. But even in business, industry, and the professions (including medicine), the operations are clearly influenced by political considerations, political personalities, organizations, and agencies. The man who can double as a liason man or "fixer" in relations with politicians has a capacity valuable to such enterprise.

It is not surprising, therefore, to find that some ambitious young people, calculating the "main chance," consider that training and a reputation as a political student leader is one of the major contributions a university experience can make to a successful career. Interviews with student and also with government officials and businessmen underscored the probability of this as a stimulus to student leadership in direct action.

It is clear that once the possibility of students serving their political "apprenticeship" in the university is established, the process feeds on itself. University life attracts those with political ambitions and *for this purpose*. Registration as a student becomes *the*, or at least a major, accepted way of preparing for and entering political life. Virtually every political leader of note in Latin America has been a student leader, and among the promient political figures in all the countries will be found some who have served their apprenticeship as organizers of political action in their student days. Only in Latin America, however, does this stimulus to activist student leadership have major significance.

The allegation is frequently heard in all the countries visited that politicians of all parties take an active interest in the elections to the student unions, and that they support, in various ways, the candidates who are likely to be "cooperative" when needed in mustering mass demonstrations for their particular purposes, and that they see the demonstrated qualities of leadership in student affairs as indicative of potential capability for future party leadership.

The most controversial of the alleged stimuli to student leadership in direct action is the desire to promote factional political interests either as a fellow traveler or as an actual "agent" employed by one of the political factions desirous of having student support. In one sense this is simply amplification of the previously mentioned stimulus to leadership. It is, however, a tendency to seek not merely a "prelude" to a political career in general, but the specific engagement in political activity at the moment as representative or agent of a particular political faction or party. The belief is widespread that student leaders in communist, left wing, conservative, and liberal groups are approved, if not selected by their senior counterparts, that they are employed to support senior strategy, and even paid for this purpose, that they meet regularly to coordinate their efforts, and that many of them "graduate" into formal party positions.

Such a relationship is difficult if not impossible to verify, and its extent can only be guessed. It is set forth as an unverified hypothesis concerning stimulants to leadership in student direct action because of the frequency of its assertion by well-informed residents of these countries and because no denial from any source was made of such assertions. It is certainly not unlikely under the political circumstances existing in Colombia, Mexico, Japan, and India. We shall refer to these circumstances in more detail later. Any or all of them might well encourage an energetic and active politically inclined student, with developed sympathy for the philosophy and program of a particular political faction or a conviction about its ability to ride the wave of the future, to accept a relationship as "representative" of that faction among the university students. These encouraging circumstances include the high visibility and obvious significance and importance for the life of the country of the intense and frequently bitter and violent factional political rivalries, the exclusiveness and non-cooperation of the "ins" and the "outs" which heightens the tension, the emphasis on political action as an instrument of change, the presence in the student bodies of a growing number of students from the middle classes who have much to gain from such change, and the presence in these countries of active communists dedicated to "winning the world for Communism in this generation." These latter have their counterparts on the right, seeking to return to Catholicism in Latin America, to communalism in India, and to the Emperor System, or some equally ultra-nationalist concept, in Japan.

It is the alleged presence, among the student activists, of dedicated communists, however, which makes this matter so controversial.   And indeed most of the assertions made in Mexico, Colombia, and Japan, merely use the word "com-munistic" where we would use "factional."   To observers from the United States accustomed to think of "political" rivalry in terms of the long time institutionalized competi-tion in electoral and pressure group methods between the Republican and Democratic parties appealing to all groups in the population with essentially the same promises, differing only in emphasis, the identification of "factionalism" with "Communism" suggests stimulus from a foreign source, those who provide the stimulus as the agents of a foreign power, and the characterization of "fellow travelers" as the "dupes" of an alien philosophy, purpose, and program, if not com-pensation.

No one except the communists denies that such "foreign" influence is present in the political rivalries in Colombia and Mexico and few deny that it is present in Japan and India.   It is commonly believed that the Communist Party "plants" in the universities young men whom they have trained locally or in Moscow for this service.   Actually, therefore, these young men would be Party agents, whose function is to work themselves into positions of leadership and exert their influence to instigate direct action favorable to the interests of the Communist Party. We obtained, without any persistent probing, admissions from a few student leaders in Mexico, Colombia, Japan, and in India that they had served as paid agents of the Communist Party.

It is the sober judgment of thoughtful people among students, faculty, school administrators, businessmen, several labor leaders, and government officials that such directly employed communist agents are present among student leaders.

Even the lowest estimates (obviously guesses) we could get of the proportion of dedicated and radical communists in the universities, 2% in Mexico and in Colombia, would provide those universities with a communist core of over 2,800 in Mexico and 1,000 in Colombia among which it should be possible to find candidates for such service as agents.   Informed guesses in India range from 1% to 3%. In Japan the proportion most frequently mentioned ranges from 1% to 2%.

If it is pointed out that the issues with respect to which direct action is instigated by these "agents" are, in the majority of cases, related to student intra-university relations and have little reference to purely political objectives, and that those issues which do have political relevance (such as, for example, the objection to the raising of bus fares, nuclear submarine visits, Vietnam military action, or anti-Yankee or pro-Castro enthusiasm) are not the exclusive concern of communists, the answer is that such direct action, producing, as it does, confusion and uncertainty, and emphasizing the ineptitude, stupidity, or evilness of existing authorities, is favorable to the advancement of communist interests. Furthermore, whatever the issue, it is said, mass action provides a training ground for revolutionary activity and habituation to the tactics which eventually will serve the purposes of revolutionary activists when comes "The Day."

It is commonly acknowledged that *all* factions both left, middle, and right, have on occasion sought this kind of arrangement with student leaders in all countries.   In the light of the recognized power of the students to influence university and public affairs, it is difficult to see why any intelligent and capable political leader would fail to enlist the services of such student agents.   Failure to utilize such a tactic might almost be set down as a dereliction in an obvious duty to his party or faction.

The possibility of making a career out of being a student over an extended period by moving from one practically autonomous faculty (or school) to another, and the extended periods of study chosen by many students, so that the presence of students over 30 years of age does not cause any lifted

eyebrows, is a circumstance favorable to the unremarkable
continuous presence among the students of such agents who
have motives other than to get an education.   There were
reports of "professional" student movement organizers in Latin
America and India who had passed through four or five
different faculties already, thus retaining their student status
in public universities for political work for which they had
been specially trained.   Such perpetual student status is less
possible in Japan.   Under public university regulations in
Latin America, however, a student's studies cannot be discontinued as long as he remains in fair standing.   The
fact that factions among students promoting the candidacy
of particular students for election to the Faculty, Academic,
and Superior Councils, which are governing boards of the
universities, frequently duplicate the factions in the national
political life would also appear to indicate the possibility
that, not only the communists, but the other political factions,
might well have an interest in the assignment of "representatives" or agents to this "university" service.

Whatever their ideological orientation, these leaders are the
essential actors in the student movement.   Indeed in a very
real sense they *are* the student societies which form the
constituent units in the organized student movement.   They
are the ones who are in more or less continuous consultation,
discussing campus, city, national, and international affairs
and who from time to time decide that the time is ripe
for the mobilization of a mass student support for some
"action" on an issue deemed by them to be important to
the students', the university's, or the country's interest.   They
are the ones who focus attention on an issue about which
they, in their assumed role as the molders of student opinion,
have decided the students need to be "educated" or "radicalized," and a student "position" made clear to the university
or government authorities or to the public generally.   It
is they who prepare the content of the posters and the newspaper ads, who appear on behalf of an action they have
decided upon where students have gathered for classes or
(on important issues) for the assemblies they have called.
It is they who plan the strategy and tactics for securing
the support of societies from other faculties or schools, for
"marshaling" the students for demonstrations or strikes when
these are deemed appropriate, for obtaining the help of interest or political groups beyond the campus. It is they who

draft the resolutions which are to be submitted to a vote of a called "democratic" assembly, or a congress. In case of multiple society gatherings they determine what the position of their society shall be. It is they who plan and implement any ongoing services for, or communications adressed to, the students, either as a duty of office or as measures laying the ground work for a positive response from large numbers of students when direct action is called for as an expression and instrument of student power.

In other words, this nucleus of ambitious, concerned, and often committed student leaders *is the movement* in the same way that the professional politicians *are the party or the faction.* The students generally may either support or fail to support, when mass action is essential to the realization of the objectives and initiatives of the activist nucleus, the proposals and program of that nucleus. This political role of the students is consistent with the role which citizens generally are predisposed to play in community and national politics.

It is for this reason that explanations of "student activism" cannot be based simply on sample surveys of the demographic characteristics and opinions and predisposition of the *total* student body. Such factors are, of course, relevant to the probabilities of student response to initiatives of the "professional" nucleus, but are only indirectly and partially relevant to what those intiatives are. The ideological tendencies and loyalties of the inner circle, the things *they* believe are important and critical as objectives for student power plays, the deals *they* need to make among themselves and with other groups in order to get a particular action in motion, *their* estimate of the advantages or disadvantages to them personally, now and in the future, of particular policies and actions, any idealistic commitments *they* may have concerning the welfare of the students, the future of the university and the nation, these are the factors which shape the initiative and direction of student activism. The probable tendency of the students to accept or reject, to give or withhold mass support to the activism necessary to implement their initiative is essential to, but not the source of, a so-called movement.

As stimuli to student leadership, then, these three: the drive of individuals for personal prestige and leadership for which the major if not the only outlet is in arousing the student group to activism; the search for a promising prelude to a political career; and the promotion of factional or party political interests, are by definition limited to the *instigators* and *promoters* of direct action.   They cannot explain the actual occurence of that direct action.   For, however strongly motivated the instigators may be, their efforts would die aborning were it not that they gained a following.   In order to do that there must be present, in the cases of both instigators and followers, common motivations and circumstances which cause the initiative of the leaders to be supported by the action of the followers.   There may be differences between them in intensity and concern for the factors, and differences which create among followers varying degrees of a predisposition to see the leaders as the champions of "causes" which are the concern of both. But there must, of course, be a degree of sharing the same motivations in order that the spark from leaders shall light fire to the flammable dispositions of students generally.

Chapter 1
Student Activism in Japan

It is doubtful whether student activism in many countries is appropriately given the label, "a student movement." There is no doubt about the appropriateness of that label in Japan. Among the over 1,200,000 students in institutions of higher education there is an active minority who plan and direct nationwide as well as local organized collective action in protest against, and for the reform of, certain aspects of their universities and of Japanese society. During the postwar years one organization, Zengakuren, dominated the activism, although it was not the only one involved. It stood at the national apex of a hierarchy of autonomous local campus student self-government societies, the size of its membership dependent upon the number and vitality of the local organizations it could bring into the federation. The number of local organizations affiliated waxed and waned during the postwar years.[1] After 1948, there was never a time, however, when there was no active national core organization (or organizations) striving to make the voice of the students heard in the land.

[1]There is no single source of reliable information on the number of local societies choosing to affiliate with Zengakuren, but estimates can be made (chiefly from claims made by the organization itself) as to the numbers affiliated in the 12 years prior to the year of greatest activity 1960. The estimates follow:

Year	No. of Schools	No. of Societies	No. of Students
1948	145		300,000
1949		394	350,000
1950	40		
1951			81,000
1952	57	150	130,000
1953	72	149	151,000
1955	130		180,000
1959-60	170	250	296,000

24

The activism had many of the characteristics normally associated with protest and reform *movements*. It inherited a *tradition* of student interest in and agitation for reform and also a tradition of the persecution of those who participated in that agitation. Postwar activism became manifest in periodic regional and national conventions and rallies, in the publication of stated objectives for the planned spring and the fall "struggles" each year, and in the explosive centrally organized and managed mass demonstrations set in motion to promote those objectives. It associated itself as an organization with other domestic and international organizations with which it had a community of interest on some issues. Its leaders were much concerned to develop an ideology which would stimulate, motivate, make logical, and justify its activism, which would provide an integrating focus for the interest and activities of its members, and which would give that activism the character of a crusade directed toward future as well as present achievement.

The tradition of prewar activism which the postwar actors inherited was one of sporadic collective action and organization rather than one related to the varied experiences of a continuing particular organization. It was a tradition of a minority protest against the political and economic arrangements provided by the Establishment, and of aspiration for and effort toward such arrangements as would provide a greater freedom and opportunity for participation in self governance by those not numbered among the governing classes. It was a tradition of a search for ideological foundations chiefly in the writings of foreign socialists, Marx in particular, and in the writings of the few Japanese intellectuals who dared to examine the premises of Japanese political and economic arrangements, some of them liberals, most of them socialists. It was a tradition of facing, and

The 1948 and 1949 number of students include those from senior high schools. Since affiliation was by societies rather than by individuals, all students in the societies whatever their degree of commitment to the national organization, are counted as belonging to it. On the eve of the widespread activism in 1960, it is evident that somewhat less than one-half of Japanese students could by most liberal estimates be considered as members of Zengakuren since there were at that time 600,000 students in institutions of higher learning. The splintering of Zengakuren during the sixties makes estimates today even less reliable. See below pp. 62ff.

suffering from, counter measures and repression, and persecution from the governors of the state who saw in such
activity a threat to the order and progress of the nation
which they governed.

The ground work for later activism was laid in the nine-
teenth century after the translation into Japanese of the
works of Marx and Engels, and of a number of representatives
of the Western liberal tradition.   Students formed study
groups, sometimes among themselves, sometimes under the
leadership of a professor.   Greatest interest appears to have
centered in Marxist writings.

The democratic ideals proclaimed by President Wilson and
the communist revolution in Russia stirred many persons,
among them students, in Japan, as was the case in many
other countries of the world in the early 20's.   In many cases,
under the leadership of faculty members, renewed and widened
interest was aroused in the formation on local campuses of
student organizations primarily for the study of Marxism.
Some of these societies had informal contacts with each
other, on a regional and even national basis.   Some of the
students participated individually in active efforts of labor
and communist groups.   But there are few reported cases
of the student organizations as such taking part in such
activity. In 1922 a national Student Federation was formed. Its
name was changed to the Student Social Science Federation
in 1924.

Such student activity was frowned on by the authorities.
In the same year, the Ministry of Education took serious
note of the leftist tendencies among the students and began
to take counter measures to undermine the attractiveness
of Marxism.   The next year the Peace Preservation Law provided an instrument for restricting the opportunity of students
(and others) to associate and to engage in study or action
considered dangerous to the status quo.   In some of the
university centers the attention of the students shifted to
what at first seemed less dangerous ground, the effort to
gain a greater voice for all students in the management
of their own student affairs and in the solution of the
daily problems of student life.   This effort was to have
a rebirth in the days immediately following World War II.
That such prewar student self-government activity was influenced by those who had previously advocated leftist ori-

ented objectives is indicated by the fact that one of the objectives of student self-government declared in resolutions of student congresses was to make student activities one important aspect of "the proletarian movement in its struggle for political freedom."

Communists were searched out and arrested in the spring of 1929, and thereafter a purge was started of teachers who were suspected of having leftist sympathies. With the forced dissolution of the Student Social Science Foundation in 1929, open and organized collective action by students became impossible.

From then on until the end of World War II, only the most defiant and daring of students were willing to face the repressive measures of the increasingly militaristic and fascist government. Not merely overt protest action (such as protest against conscription and military training) but the holding of "dangerous ideas," was considered a threat to the State. And the dangerous ideas included almost any liberal or democratic (as well as, of course, communistic) ideas which departed from those supporting the Emperor System and the concept of the divine national identity and destiny. A Thought Control Bureau was set up in the Ministry of Education. With the aid of the police, those holding "dangerous" ideas were ferreted out; around a thousand were arrested in each of the years 1931 and 1932. By 1937 practically all leftist students had been put out of the universities and the most active and vocal were in jail.

Government action was not limited to the *suppression* of spontaneous and "promoted" unorthodox thought and action. The inclination of the Japanese students to group activity was used positively by the government to establish patriotic groups and societies to inculcate the nationalistic principles and virtues supportive of the ultra-nationalistic and expansionist program on which Japan embarked in the 30's. Indoctrination was centrally planned and directed, and was supervised on each campus by a government representative. By 1940 the organization of students and other youths was thoroughly and completely regimented in a fascist type monolithic Japan Youth Corps designed to mold the thought and action tendencies in youth favorable to absolute commitment and service to the Emperor and to the ultra-

nationalism and militarism then manifest in the national
policy and program. Against such regimentation, rebellious
actions were necessarily few and far between, and when they
occurred their sponsors were quickly silenced.

The traditions of student activism contained, therefore,
these elements: As an expression of protest and reform, it
had involved a very small minority of very daring students.
Its ideological stimulus and justification was definitely, and
all but exclusively, Marxist. It had enjoyed a very few
years of relatively free expression in the early twenties, and
thereafter had been the object of overwhelming government
opposition, repression, and of counter measures to control
all student thought and action in the interests of an increasingly fascist national policy and program. The few daring
students who continued their commitment to leftist ideology
and action were forced to become conspirators and underground operators. As such they came into contact with
professional communists and were frequently their companions in prison.

The end of the war brought their release, the abolition
of the repressive policies, and the positive encouragement
of self-initiated student organization and action. The dam
holding back free action was broken down and the flood
waters of student response to the new freedom swept over
the campuses and the nation.

Objectives of Activism

Any interpretation of Japanese student activism must recognize the definiteness and clarity with which objectives were announced by its leaders. What happened in Japan was no mere
expression of adolescent revolt against authority, the decline of
disciplined morality among youth, or an egotistical emotional
outpouring of a generalized conviction that they could build a
better world than their elders. All such factors may have been
involved, but they were not exclusively responsible for the
planned and organized and goal-directed characteristics of that
activism.

The issues to which the activism of the Japanese students
were directed in the postwar period can be classified as follows:

University and Japanese government educational policy and
practice

Student participation in university government at particular places

Freedom of action

International relations policy and practice, and in particular those involving dependency on, and collaboration with, the United States

Avoidance of involvement in war and contact with the instruments of war (such as nuclear weapons)

The objectives associated with the "rehabilitation", and later the "defense", of education embodied in the first classification were dominant chiefly in the years before the organization of Zengakuren (late 1948). Thereafter much greater emphasis was placed on the objectives associated with the last four classifications.

From 1965 on, rebellion against university policy and practice increased although political objectives were also much in evidence.

There is no detailed survey for the whole period from 1945 to the present which reveals the specific objectives students hoped to accomplish by the actions they took. To be sure, the spring and fall "struggles" were in support of a number of alleged objectives. The records of where the action took place, how many students were involved, the nature and length of the action are most untrustworthy. If we limit ourselves, however, to reported events which were either countrywide in character, or which involved a large number of students in large universities, and which were the result of planned and organized effort, we get some idea of the scope of the problems substantial numbers of students felt impelled to do something about.

The general declarations in the resolutions of national conventions are not very revealing of the specific foci for student activism, but they do indicate the general objectives about which they were concerned. Here are some of the main slogans used to make a declaration of purpose:

For rehabilitation and defense of education

For national unity among student organizations

For cooperation with national labor unions on all issues of economic nature (Last convention of Kokugakuren, the predecessor of Zengakuren)

For defense of national culture
For defense of racial culture
For defense of peace and racial emancipation
For defense of peace and democracy
For defense of freedom and democracy
Against imperialism and monopoly capitalism
Against war and imperialism

More important are the specific issues which allegedly lay at the root of particular actions:

Japanese Government Education Policy (at first subsumed under "rehabilitation of education" later under "defense of education")

Against raise in tuition fees
Against inadequate educational budget
Against a government sponsored student section of the Bureau of Higher Education
Against discrimination between public and private schools
For equal educational opportunities for all
For increased financial assistance to students
Against increase in transportation costs
Against University Administration Bill
Against Local Board of Education Act
For participation of students in administration of state universities
For removal of "fascist" professors
Against military education and for "racial" education

Student Participation in University Government on Particular Campuses

For dismissal of reactionary and "incapable" professors and administrators
For dissolution of the old prepeace student societies and their replacement by democratic self-governing societies
For control of student union building
For voice in election of unversity president
For participation of students in screening of university personnel

For correction of university poor housing and food

Freedom of Action

Against government restrictions on political activities and party organizations of students on campus

Against requirement that student organizations engaging in political activity must register with the government

Against classification of Zengakuren as political

Against arrest and disciplining of students who participated in strikes or demonstrations

Against purge of communist professors and teachers and against a United States representative (Dr. Walter Eells) who asserted universities and schools were hot beds of Communism

Against police espionage work on campuses

Against Subversion Activities Prevention Bill

Against organizational changes in Ministry of Education alleged to be leading to reintroduction of "thought control"

Against requirements that students had to go home to vote

Against Yoshida's two education bills to neutralize education and insulate it from political influence of individuals and groups

Against public safety regulations (increasing police control)

Against Police Duties Execution Law (1958)

Japanese Government International Policy

Against "partial" peace treaty (should include Russia as well as Western Allies)

Emperor incident at Kyoto (popularly interpreted as derogatory of Emperor)

For ouster of Premier Yoshida

For ouster of Premier Kishi and against Diet "undemocratic" procedures in Security Pact renewal

Against "depurge" of war criminals

Against Ikeda cabinet

For restoration of diplomatic relations with China

For withdrawal of occupation forces

Against administrative agreements between United States

and Japan alleged to place Japan in colonial status (both before and after peace treaty)

Against peace conference and later against ratification of peace treaty

For return of Okinawa to Japanese rule

Against negotiations about and resolution of Japanese-South Korean problems

Against renewal of security pact

Against visits of U. S. official Haggerty to arrange for the visit of President Eisenhower

Avoidance of War

Against revision of "Peace" Constitution which would weaken Article IX (renunciation of war)

Against collaboration with United States in Korean War

For sabotage of Japanese support of United States in Korea

Against buildup of "defense forces"

Against conscription

Against renewal of security pact with United States and involvement of Japan in world power struggle

Against enlargement of United States air force bases

Against United States H-bomb tests

Against Soviet and American resumption of nuclear tests

Against visits of Polaris submarines

Against nuclear armament for Japan

Against building of atomic piles and nuclear and atomic power research effort in Japan

Hiroshima anniversary rallies against nuclear weapons

Against United States policy in Cuba, Laos, and Vietnam

Many of the convention resolutions were also the slogans used in announcing the objectives of mass demonstrations. A summary of the government reports on demonstrations for which police had been called out, for the period of most intensive student activity, January 1958 to June 1963, reveals something of the extent of this type of student activism and the issues on which it concentrated. Table 1 reports the number of demonstration incidents by reference to the place where they occurred and to the major issue which was alleged to be the "cause" in this period.

Nearly 2500 incidents were involved over the 5 year period, 973 involving students from more than one school, and 1523 additional reported as pertaining to the students of a single school. Incidents related to the renewal of the Security Pact with the United States (1315), related to government education policy and action (405), related to nuclear weapons (301), and related to freedom of action (135), appear in that order of numerical importance. The issue of war and peace, especially as associated with Japan-United States relations, clearly dominates. The total incidents related to such issues (items 1, 2, 3, and 4 in the table) comes to 1644.

Demonstrations with political objectives continued throughout the 60's accompanied by increasing violence. Violence was a deliberate policy of one of the factions in the student movement. Shin Sampa Rengō (Sampa Zengakuren, after 1966) declared its objective was to destroy the existing social order by violence. The riots it instigated in 1968 at Sasebo, ostensibly to protest the visit of the nuclear submarine, Enterprise, and at Haneda airport in 1967, ostensibly to prevent the departure of Prime Minister Sato on a good will tour of South East Asia, appeared to many Japanese observers as directed toward such a revolutionary objective. Both affairs involved pitched battles with the police.

Beginning in 1964-65 a wave of tuition increases in the private universities ranging from 20% to 70% sparked sit down strikes, class boycotts, and occupation of university buildings in Kyoto, Osaka, Kobe, Nara, and Tokyo, and in other regions. The years 1968 and 1969 witnessed a nationwide explosion of student activism directed against university authorities. The chronicle of events of that violent period is recorded in Table 2. The initial stimuli to student activism are seen to be predominantly dissatisfaction with university oriented conditions and the rising cost of an education. But political issues were injected into the confrontations particularly by the radical and revolutionary (anti-Japanese-Communist) factions in Zengakuren. The degree of disorder and violence characterizing the activism was heightened by the struggle for power among the warring factions within the student movement. It was apparent to informed observers that a major objective of the far left factions was to achieve a radicalization of the students and in particular to ready them for the action to be taken in the year of

TABLE 1

Japanese Student Demonstration Incidents
By Primary Issue and Place
January 1958—June 1963[2]

Issue	In Tokyo Major Multi-School	In Tokyo Single School	Outside Tokyo Major Multi-School	Outside Tokyo Single School	Total Multi & Single School
1. Vs. Security Pact & undemocratic Diet actions	50	44	304	917	1315
2. Vs. U. S. bases & for return of Okinawa	3				3
3. Vs. Nuclear weapons	22	52	44	183	301
a. U.S. H-bomb tests	(5)	(52)	(34)	(82)	
b. Nuclear armaments	(3)		(10)	(42)	
c. Resumption of Soviet tests	(5)		(a)		
d. U.S. tests in space	(1)				
e. Resumption of tests both by U.S. & Soviet	(6)			(39)	
f. U.S. Navy Polaris submarine visits	(2)\(b)			(20)(b)	
4. Vs. Revision of peace constitution & anti-war	6		19		25
5. Vs. Police policy & action	13		35	(c)	48
6. Vs. Political violence bill	16		37	34 (d)	87

7. Vs. government educational policy	19	59	193	134	405(e)
8. Miscellaneous	30	8	182	92	312
a. In support of labor strikes, etc.	(4)		(91)		
b. Protest vs. assassination of Asanuma	(6)		(21)		
c. Vs. Japan-Korea negotiations	(5)		(37)		
d. Vs. Ikeda Cabinet	(6)		(1)		
e. For diplomatic relations with China			(1)		
f. Zengakuren vs. Communist Party	(2)				
g. Mass funeral for student	(1)				
h. Vs. U.S. blockade of Cuba	(1)		(17)		
i. General—May Days, etc.	(5)	(8)	(14)	(92)	
Total	159	163	814	1360	2496

(a) Numbers only = 7600.
(b) Reported to June 1963 but demonstrations were just beginning.
(c) Numbers only = 56,000. In addition to these cases were many others in which police brutality was alleged as a secondary issue.
(d) Additional with numbers only = 28,710.
(e) The issue also a secondary one in numerous cases.

[2]The demonstrations listed as "major" are those that are identified on police reports by names of cities or places. Those listed as schools are those whose number is reported by reference to incidents at schools, presumably not communitywide. In a few instances of demonstrations occurring outside Tokyo only the total numbers participating throughout the country are given in the reports. In any case the figures in each column are *unduplicated* by those in the other columns.

decision, 1970, when the renewal, modification, or abrogation
the Security Pact with the United States would once more
dominate the political scene as it had in 1960.

TABLE 2

Major Japanese University Struggles,
January 1968-February 1969*

S after the name of university stands for "State Controlled"
whereas P means "Private Controlled."

January 1968

Kobe University (S), Tokyo Medical College (S): Students opposed the revision of the professional regulations on medical
doctors and refused to take graduation exams.

Chuo University (P): Students temporarily closed down the University administration buildings protesting against another
tuition raise.

Seinan Gakuin University (P): Students boycotted all classes protesting against consecutive tuition increases.

Tokyo University (S): Department of Medical Science students,
interns, and assistants went on to a strike protesting the "irrational" disciplinary actions upon seventeen students and
interns of the department.

February 1968

Niigata University (S)., Nagoya University (S)., Chiba University
(S)., Kyoto University (S)., Osaka University (S)., Kanazawa
University (S):   Students of Dept. of Medical Sciences of
these universities protested against the revision of the profes-
sional regulations for medical doctors and boycotted classes.
Some of them refused to take graduation exams.

Tokyo Medical College (S): Students openly accused seven professors of irrational disciplinary actions.

*Compiled from *Asahi*, Japan's leading newspaper, and from the
Japan Times by Kanoh Wada, for this study.

Saga University (S): Students accused seventeen professors and staff members of restricting self-government of dormitories. Professors were confined in a room by force and required to apologize to the students.

Shibaura Institute of Tech. (P), Hokkai Gakuen University (P): Students boycotted classes and final exams protesting consecutive tuition increases.

Nippon University (P): Government Tax Office made a special inspection on the financial management of the university on the suspicion of tax evasion.

Hiroshima University (S): Students confined the President in a room and challenged his cancelling of scholarships.

March 1968

Saga University (S): Police entered the university in search of evidence relative to the violence in February. Students protested.

Hiroshima University (S): Students protested the disciplinary actions taken by the authorities relative to the February incident and confined a student advisor in a room forcing him to attend the "mass-bargaining" or "mass-negotiation."

Kansei Gakuin University (P): Students confined the President in a room and opened a "mass-negotiation" asking him to cancel disciplinary actions for students who boycotted classes. Riot police mobilized, and the scheduled commencement ceremony was cancelled.

Tokyo University: Faculty Meeting of the Dept. of Medical Science announced that there would be no change in the disciplinary action relative to seventeen students and interns.

April 1968

Komazawa University (P): Students went on a hunger-strike protesting against disciplinary actions for unauthorized gathering. Some class rooms were closed down by the students.

Waseda University (P), Kyoto University (S), Ritsumeikan University (P): Students partly boycotted classes to observe what they called the "International Anti-War Day."

Nippon University (P): Faculty members' union demanded the resignation of Chancellor Furuta and other members of the Board of the Trustees for sharing secretly five million dollars among themselves.

May 1968

Saitama University (S): Students opened a "mass-negotiation" with the deans about the school bus service.

Tokyo Medical College (S): Students and Assistants closed down the hospitals attached to the college.

Nippon University (P): Students organized an All-Campus Joint Struggle Committee. Nippon University struggle against authoritarianism and alleged corruption of administrators started.

June 1968

Kyushu University (S): U.S.A.F. jet fighter fell down on the campus creating a significant damage to the computer center of the university. Students and faculty members demanded that the Government evict all U.S. bases from Japan.

Waseda University (P): Students went on strike protesting the procedure for the election of the President.

Doshisha University (P): Students closed down classrooms to stop the procedures for the election of a President.

Nippon University (P): All departments (11 in all) went on strike. Bloody confrontations between the protesting students and ultra-rightist students, the latter financed by the university authorities.

Tokyo University of Education (S): Students protested against the relocation of campus. The students of the Dept. of Literature closed down the administrative building.

Keio University (P): Students protested the research funds supplied by the U. S Army for bio-chemistry studies, claiming the research projects were connected with military purposes. All freshman and sophomore classes were suspended.

Toyo University (P): Students occupied administrative building protesting the curtailed construction of the Student Center. Riot police were called in and occupying students were evicted.

Tokyo University (S): Anti-JCP Students groups occupied Yasuda Auditorium (6/15). University administrators evicted the occupants by calling police squad onto Hongo Campus (6/17). Department of Literature went on a strike (6/26). President Okochi met representatives of students and promised to withdraw the disciplinary action unconditionally. Department of Economics went on a strike (6/29). Department of Jurisprudence went on a strike (6/29).

July 1968

Kanto Gakuin University (P): Students protested the long-delayed construction of dormitories and closed down the administrative building.

Sophia University (P): Students protested the university authorities' use of plainclothesmen in a case involving theft on the campus. Classes were suspended. Students occupied main buildings.

Yamaguchi University (S): Students and faculty members went on strike protesting the planned relocation of the campus.

Tokyo University (S): Yasuda Auditorium was again occupied by students (7/2). Department of Engineering went on strike (7/4). Department of Arts and Sciences went on a strike. All-campus Struggle committee (Zen Kyoto) was organized by students (7/5). Representative Committee of Zen Kyoto announced "Seven-item Request to the University" (7/15).

August 1968

Kyushu University (S): Pro-JCP groups and anti-JCP groups fought one another violently about the strategy of protesting against the jet plane incident.

Sophia University (P): University authorities announced the disciplinary actions for thirteen students leaders. Students ignored the announcement.

Tokyo University (S): University Administrative Board announced their "final" conclusion as "8/10 Notice to the Students." Students ignored this notice (8/10). Department of
Medical Science building was closed down by the students
(8/28).

September 1968

Nippon University (P): Riot police were called in to evict
the occupying students from the buildings. Bloody fight
between police and the students. One police platoon
commander was killed by stones thrown by the students.
Mass-negotiation was held between Mr. Furuta and other
trustees and the All-Campus Struggle Committees. Mr.
Furuta and others admitted that they had been unqualified
as university administrators and had acted inappropriately,
signed a written statement to that effect, and promised to
resign to settle the chaotic situation.

Kobe Nautical College (S): Students went on strike protesting
against the construction of an express-way which cuts
through a part of the campus.

Tokyo Medical College (S): Students ceased strike.

Rissho University (P): Students occupied administrative building protesting against what they called "unilateral" disciplinary actions.

Keio University (P): Students occupied main administrative
building.

Sagami Women's College (P): Students went on strike protesting against the procedure for electing a president.

Tokyo University: Administrative building was closed down by
the students (9/16). Department of Education went on a strike
(9/29).

October 1968

Keio University (P): Classes were resumed in freshman and
sophomore courses.

Toyo University (P): Pro-JCP students and anti-JCP students started fighting on campus about the strategy of direct action, and riot police were called to settle them.

Meiji Gakuin University (P): Students occupied the administrative building protesting disciplinary actions.

Nippon University (P): Riot police were called in to evict the occupying students from detached Department of Engineering at Koriyama (northern part of Japan). Students furiously resisted and set fire to the Department building.

Tokyo University: Department of Science went on a strike (10/1). Department of Agriculture went on a strike (10/5). Department of Pharmacology went on a strike (10/7).

November 1968

Nippon University (P): Chancellor Furuta and other trustees ignored their promise to resign. Nation-wide parents' association of Nippon University students held a general conference in Tokyo and demanded the immediate resignation of these administrators. Riot police were called in to evict the occupying students from the Department of Arts building. More than a hundred policemen and students were badly injured.

Hitotsubashi University (S): Students opened a mass-negotiation with the president concerning the procedures for electing a departmental chairman.

Tokyo University: President Okochi resigned (11/1). Professor Katoh (Department of Jurisprudence) nominated as the acting President (11/4). Student protesters at Nippon University (mainly anti-JCP groups) joined the Zen-Kyoto of the University of Tokyo and held a general conference at Hongo Campus (11/22).

December 1968

Chuo University (P): Students demanded the abolishment of university disciplinary committee and went into an unlimited strike.

Sophia University (P):   Riot police were called in to evict the students occupying the administrative building.   University authorities announced a closing of the university for the coming six months to repair the damages to the main building as well as to cool off the situation.

Tokyo Metropolitan University (S):   University authorities admitted students to participation in the election of the president.

Tokyo University of Education (S):   Entrance examinations for the academic year 1969-1970 officially suspended.

Tokyo University (S): Mr. Katoh, acting President, announced new proposals to ease the situation (12/2). Departments of Economics and of Jurisprudence discontinued strike (12/26). Suspension of spring entrance examination in 1969 (March) became almost inevitable (12/29).

January 1969

Yokohama University (S): Students protested the integration of detached departmental buildings into the main-campus, and occupied the administrative building.

Nagasaki University (S):   Students demanded more academic freedom and improvement of the quality of education; they confined the president in the auditorium and opened a mass-negotiation.   Riot police were called in and rescued the exhausted president.

Kyoto University (S):   Anti-JCP groups temporarily occupied main administrative building.   Students confined president in a class room and held a mass-negotiation.

Tokyo Institute of Technology (S):   All departments went on strike protesting the procrastinated construction of dormitories.

Shibaura Institute of Technology (P):   University authorities accepted all demands from the students including the withdrawal of tuition increase and an improvement of laboratory facilities.

Nippon University (P): Riot police evicted students from three major departmental buildings.

Tokyo University (S): Anti-JCP groups and JCP groups (Minsei) started a violent fighting of one another on Hongo Campus and university administrators introduced police squads to settle the violence (1/9). Seven Departments (7,000 students and 1,000 faculty) held a mass negotiation at Prince Chichibu Memorial Athletic Field and exchanged a letter of confirmation with Acting President Mr. Katoh which contained ten major items emphasizing students' autonomy and academic independence and freedom within the university[3] (1/10). Eight departments except Department of Medical Science and Department of Literature discontinued the strike (1/11). Anti-JCP groups and JCP groups respectively called a general meeting on Hongo Campus. Anti-JCP groups occupied the Yasuda Auditorium and constructed barricades (1/15). Metropolitan Police Riot Squads of 8,500 started the elimination of occupying students from Yasuda Auditorium using gas grenades and tear gas. Students resisted for three days throwing molotov cocktails, stones, and acids. On 20th of January police finally completely cleared out the students from Hongo Campus (1/18—1/20). Suspension of entrance examination for academic year 1969-1970 formally decided upon by the Ministry of Education. Normal commencement in Spring cancelled because there would be few students eligible for graduation due to the long-continued stoppage of academic activity (1/22).

February 1969

Osaka University (S): Freshmen and sophomores boycotted classes protesting disciplinary actions taken by the university.

[3]Among the items acceding to student demands which caused the Government to ask Mr. Katoh for further explanation were (1) agreement to take "appropriate" action on the discharge of two professors in the Department of Medical Science; (2) refusal to cooperate with police unless they came with an arrest warrant and unless a definite public law had been broken; (3) agreement that university would not cooperate with Japanese industry in research which would serve the interest of "monopolistic capital"; (4) agreement that students could exercise the right of collective bargaining over certain university policies through mass bargaining sessions.

Nagoya University (S): University authorities announced that they would officially admit the students to participation in solving major administrative problems.

Kwansei Gakuin University (P): Conduct of entrance examinations for 1969-1970 was heavily guarded by the riot police.

Kyoto University (S): All-Campus Struggle Committee was organized and they declared their intention to prevent the entrance examinations for 1969-1970 academic year.

Tokyo University: Ten point letter of confirmation, exchanged between the students and acting President Mr. Katoh (1/11), was endorsed by the faculty meeting as well as by the Board of Trustees (2/11).

Characteristics of Objectives

Examination of the issues which were alleged to stimulate student direct action indicates a concern, certainly among the leaders, with much more than changing the circumstances and conditions of their educational environment. They gained experience in group action in the three years immediately following the end of the war in demands for the improvement of their facilities and for keeping the costs of educational opportunities within range of their limited resources. Such issues continued to be included in the platforms of Zengakuren, and were heavily emphasized by minority student groups who did not favor the involvement of Zengakuren in political affairs. After 1948, however, great stress was laid upon attention to issues linked with, and threatening to, their desire for peace, for independence and autonomy for Japan as a nation, for non-involvement in a worldwide power struggle in which nuclear weapons held the clue to national power, and for the avoidance of any return to restrictions on free expression, expecially for those harboring leftist ideas.

The students were not alone in these desires. The great majority of people in Japan were sympathetic to the desire for peace, and it would be strange if they did not share the desire for independence and autonomy for their nation, and the avoidance of involvement in a nuclear supported power struggle. School teachers, intellectuals, and labor leaders had much at stake in the avoidance of infringements on freedom of association and expression, especially since the leftist ideological orientation of these groups was well recognized. Over all hung the memory of the prewar repression of unorthodoxy in thought and action and the intensive concentration of government action on insuring the inculcation of and commitment to a single concept of the national entity and polity. Moreover, action directed against obstacles to every single one of these objectives was consistent with the strategy of the Communist Party in its struggle for greater power in Japanese society. If leaders of the student movement were inclined to hold to revolutionary goals—as many of them certainly did—action with respect to such issues would be entirely compatible with the pursuit of those goals.

It will be noted that the great majority of these objectives are negative in character, that is they declared very specifically what the students were against and toward which an attack could be directed. This is not unusual in popular protest and reform movements, and it does not reduce their contribution to the achievement of positive objectives like peace, freedom, democracy, and independence. That negative characteristic is pointed out here, because one of the sources of frustration to some of the student leaders, after nearly a score of years devoted to the removal of obstacles to their positive objectives, was the realization that they had had no positive program for the creation of institutional values, the plausible obstacles to which they had struggled to destroy. Before criticism is leveled at any movement on the grounds that it is more destructive than constructive, it might be well to consider the degree to which in human history the working concept of what is "good" in societal arrangements and processes has developed as an implied opposite to what was considered "bad" enough to challenge protesting and reforming activists.

It has been observed by some commentators that the objectives of student activism were "event," rather than "issue," oriented. The inference is that the activism of the past 20 years has no steady and basic core of purposefulness that will provide a continuing stimulus to student activism in

Japan; that it will wax and wane with events, as indeed it
did in the period reported on, as critical events become
numerous or minimal.   That is probably generally true.
For example, the intensity and extent of student activism
began to decline after 1960 until the visits of the nuclear
submarines provided a renewed surge of activism in 1963.
It might be observed, however, that the efforts of Japan and
other nations to find a stable adaptation to and resolution of
the increasing tensions and disequilibria in the world's affairs
are often stimulated by events which will continue to challenge the achievement of the positive, though unclearly defined, objectives implicit in the negative efforts of the Japanese
students. Having established as an aspect of the image of the
Japanese Student, "a challenger of threats to peace, to personal
freedom, to Japanese independence, and to non-involvement in
power bloc politics," the predisposition of students to political
activism may be expected to manifest itself when such threats
appear in the future. There seems little likelihood that such
threats will not occur.

The impression gained from examining the *declared* objectives is that student activism was directed toward advertising
the students' opposition to certain political and educational
policies and practices and toward bringing the pressure of
public opinion to bear on the relevant authorities to modify
them.   In other words the activism would appear to be reform
oriented.   The volume of active support for such declared
objectives, not only among students, but among faculty
members and members of the general public as well, reveals
a widespread concern about the issues involved and a willingness to engage in mass direct action in the hope of achieving
the reforms indicated.

But discussions with the activist leaders of such manifestations of protest revealed other objectives more radical in
character which could be, they believed, accomplished by
getting the students to commit themselves, through personal
participation in such unorthodox change-effecting tactics,
to widely approved purposes. Among these less openly stated
objectives were the following: to radicalize the masses of students and to develop in them a consciousness of their power
to effect change in educational and political decisions made
by the relevant Establishments; to develop a mechanism for
student power to influence and even determine the mode of

their governance; to demonstrate the ineptitude and the autocratic character of their educational and political governors and the stubborn intransigence of these in the face of demands for reform; to test the limits of the tolerance of those governors; to induce confrontations in which force would have to be used by university and public authorities; and, among the most radical, to light and cause to spread the fires of political revolution and to make habitual the kinds of mass action suited to this purpose.

If the *declared* objectives were the only ones operative, then direct action would be undertaken and could be justified as a *last resort* when more orthodox means were unavailable or had failed to produce results. In such case, violent and illegal direct action would occur only when more peaceful direct action led to intolerable frustration or was escalated under the impact of unanticipated and unplanned for circumstances. If, however, the objectives of the leaders included those undeclared aims named above, direct action, especially violent and illegal direct action of the kinds indicated in Table 2, would have a value in itself quite apart from the progress it might conceivably produce toward achieving the declared objectives. That value would not even be destroyed if the reaction of university and public authorities was of a kind which raised higher barriers against free expression, dissent, and protest. For such a reaction would lend credence to the contention of the revolutionaries that the Establishment could maintain its power to govern, ultimately only by the use of force and that revolution was the only way to achieve the "legitimate" ends on which their sights were fixed.

The objectives named in the immediately foregoing discussion can be summed up in two words, "student power." That objective reflects more than a protest against the traditional exclusion of students from the decision making process in the determination of the university and public policies, practices, and system of governance to which they are expected to conform. It reflects more than dissatisfaction with the quality of the education and political opportunities and restraints which they experience. It reflects a growing awareness of the potential capacity which students possess, when implemented by their collective activism, to have a decisive impact on those policies and practices and on the shaping and administration of that system of governance. Moreover, it reflects a determination to transform that potential power into actual power by actions which *force* the authorities to recognize the de facto legitimacy of their claims to participation in the decision making process and to admit students to such participation through mechanisms of the students' own choosing (such as mass bargaining and the negotiation of terms on which an occupying contingent of students will evacuate the building they have seized).

There are those who contend, on the basis of evidence of the intransigence of student leaders in the negotiations they instigate through such tactics, that the demand for student power is not merely a demand for *participation* in, but for *dominance* of, the decision making process.

The confrontation relative to this objective is more than a confrontation of a particular group of students with a particular group of university and public officials and police. It is a confrontation between two philosophies and systems of governance, between two sets of habitual predispositions and values. The one system and set are supported by those whose experience has been acquired in accommodating their roles to the authoritarian and hierarchical character of traditional relations between the governors and the governed. The other system and set are supported by those who refuse to accommodate their roles to any such pattern of relationship.

All three of the major factions of the student movement claiming to be the "true" Zengakuren in 1968 were ideologically committed to revolution. The largest faction, Heimingakuren, however, really a student arm of the Japanese Communist Party, which at the moment is Moscow oriented, while looking forward to ultimate revolution is more concerned with establishing itself as a radical pressure group within the present structure of Japanese society and government. It opposed the extreme ideological radicalism as well as the outright confrontation policy of the other two factions (Kakumaru and Shin Sampa Rengō) and the violent and destructive confrontation tactics of Shin Sampa Rengō. These latter two factions consider Heimingakuren (JCP Zengakuren), and indeed the Japanese Communist Party itself, as revisionists and traitors to the cause of national and world revolution.

Types of Activities

The activity most familiar to those whose chief source of

information is the press is the mass demonstration involving confrontation with the police. Such direct action is indeed predominant, especially during the annual spring and fall "struggles."[4] Direct action is also prominent among activities organized to take place simultaneously in different parts of the country and stimulated by the national leadership. Mass demonstration is not, however, the only operational definition of student activism.

Other countrywide activities were the annual conventions resulting in long lists of well-publicized resolutions; the signing of petitions for presentation to the government; statements and open letters addressed to various people like President Truman, President Johnson, General Ridgway, Secretary Dulles, and Secretary Rusk, as well as to Japanese leaders; the organization of mass singing groups; and the Return-to-the-Native Places Movement.

The Group Singing Movement between 1950 and 1955 was originally communist inspired and as such focused on Russian, anti-war, anti-American, and pro-Red Chinese songs. It spread sufficiently widely among students and labor organizations to raise the apprehensions of the Ministry of Education, which initiated a similar singing group project in 1955 and appropriated one million yen for the printing and distribution of popular and easy-to-sing "safe" songs. Also Zenro, a conservative labor federation, and the second largest in Japan, promoted singing groups among its members alternative to the ones with a leftist orientation.

The Back-to-the-Native Places Movement was relatively short-lived. It was initiated by Zengakuren in the summer of 1952 with help from within the Communist Party. A successful effort was made to recruit students returning to rural areas in the summer for political missionary work. But the reaction of the provincials was disappointing. Lectures with slides, handbill distribution, personal talks, picture-plays, etc. were employed to work up opposition chiefly to the perpetuation of United States military bases on Japanese soil. The issue was not one close at hand for people in most regions. The social distance between students and the rural population, as well as the allegations from rightist groups that the students were

---

[4]During the 5½ years for which we were able to obtain police records, major demonstrations were recorded for 139 days, 67 of these days in the April-June quarter and 45 in the September-November quarter. The remaining months were relatively quiet.

taking part in a communist inspired activity were also factors in producing an apathy toward and a suspicion of the students. Little is heard of the movement after 1954. With respect to the result of their failure to establish influential contacts one student leader remarked, "That was the begining of our losing confidence in the people as a revolutionary force."

When the focus of activity was on campus issues, the chief early form of activity was negotiation, although sometimes the efforts of the negotiators were supported by student rallies and parades, as well as by boycotts of examinations and classes. Prior to 1949, efforts were made to negotiate also with the Ministry of Education on matters such as tuition rates. When such negotiations brought no success, the students turned to demonstrations as a way of calling attention to their needs and demands. During that immediate postwar period, when educational facilities and living accommodations, and even food supply arrangements were in disarray, a considerable amount of mutual aid and self-help efforts was organized to make student life as comfortable and meaningful as possible under the circumstances.[5] Student organized lectures and discussions on the full range of issues named above were frequent and widespread. They must have consumed a far greater number of student hours than demonstrations either on or off campus.

Yet the time consumed in demonstrations was a major factor in the lives of large numbers of students. This is clearly evident in the police reports referred to above. By multiplying the numbers of students reported as involved by the number of days on which demonstrations were reported as taking place (some incidents lasted several days) we can calculate the student-days which were devoted to this sort of activism. Over the 5½ years between 1958 and 1963, a total of 1,110,334 days of student time were spent in demonstrations. Over half of this time was spent in the single year, 1960, chiefly in relation to the agitation opposing the renewal of the Security Pact and the handling of that matter by the Kishi government.

In view of the extent of these demonstrations, the numbers involved, and the violence which was reported to characterize them, the number of arrests made by the police was surpris-

[5]Students in many Japanese universities have traditionally been in charge of the governance of dormitory life.

ingly small, 31 in 1958, 44 in 1959, 306 in 1960, 88 in 1961, and 193 in 1962. Seventy-two percent of the arrests occurred in Tokyo. These numbers can be compared with those of an earlier period. In the year 1931 and 1932 an average of over 1,000 arrests were made each year in the efforts of the government to control the far less extensive unrest of those years.

By the end of the 60's, the violent and destructive tactics which had occasionally characterized student activism during the past 20 years became the norm. Street demonstrations became not so much mere collective expressions of dissent and protest as deliberate confrontations challenging the legitimacy of the constituted authorities and seeking immediate capitulation of those authorities to the demands of the demonstrators. Inevitably police action was required to quell the politically oriented disturbances, and the confrontations were in fact pitched battles the like of which had not been seen since the invasion of the Diet grounds in 1960. Both students and police came to the scene armoured and prepared for battle.

The activism with respect to campus issues also took an ugly turn. Overt disobedience of campus rules and regulations; boycotting of classes and examinations; and physical restraint of students who were "uncooperative" with respect to the boycott; restraining of university officials from performance of their duties including in some case physical attacks on them; the insistence on "mass bargaining" in which thousands of students and faculty would participate in "deciding" issues (8000 were involved in one case); damage to property; the occupation of university buildings and their reconstruction as virtual fortresses in a small scale civil war when riot police were sent to evict the students; these became the typical operational definitions of student activism. The struggle for power among the three factions seeking to be recognized as the "real" Zengakuren complicated the situation. Many of the most destructive disturbances involved pitched battles between these factions.

All such activities had taken place before in particular universities at particular times. What stirred the deep concern, frustrations, and, frequently, the anger and fears of university and public authorities and many segments of the general public was not simply the continuation of such examples of direct action. Nor was it simply that the disturbances were country-wide, although that fact intensified the reactions.

The startling message delivered by the volcanic student activism in the late 60's was that the students had the power to challenge effectively not only the system of university governance but the traditional concept of the role of the university in society. Students not only were able to make that challenge, but to bring the governors of the universities, in which the challenge was raised, to their knees in capitulation to the terms they demanded as their price for releasing their strangle hold on the operation of the educational process for all students. Even then organized students had the power to disrupt that process so that, in major universities, students were robbed of a whole year of educational opportunity.

In the face of that disruption the university authorities were helpless. Only by calling on the student-hated police could the violent and illegal tactics of the student forces be countered. Such a move symbolized the inability of the universities to control their internal relationships consistently with the premise of reasonableness, humanity, and community which were assumed to characterize university life. Especially disturbing to those committed to maintaining the freedom of the universities to carry on their functions unconstrained by political pressure was the cloud cast over their claim to the right to exist as autonomous institutions.

Moreover, serious doubt was cast on the assumption that the roots of the student protests lay in the rebelliousness of a small minority of dissident students and that the traditional "low posture" attitude of, and respect for the learned by students in relation to their mentors could be counted on to short circuit the escalation of minority agitation into a widespread rebellion.

Although it was still possible to blame a small minority of radical and revolutionary activists for sparking the direct action and for managing the invasion and occupation of campus buildings, the numbers who responded to the boycotting of classes and examinations, and who assembled for the mass bargaining sessions (on one occasion over half of the students at the University of Tokyo) indicated that the virus of student power and of actual disrespect for their educators had infected far more that the minority instigators of revolt.

During 1968 and 1969 activities protesting university conditions and governance of the sort recorded in Table 2, were reported in at least 67 universities in all parts of

Japan.   That   protests   in   Tokyo   University   overshadowed
all others was a shock to leaders in all areas of Japanese
life.   For Todai[6] was peculiarly *their* university.   Since
its founding as an Imperial University in 1875 it had been
the "West Point" in the Japanese educational system producing the "Generals" for the operation of the governmental,
educational, and to some extent industrial tasks of the nation.
Its graduates occupied the posts where power lay in the governing of affairs of state and education. The prestige of their
university degree assured graduates of such positions. They
were considered to be the elite corps upon which the strength,
growth and stability of the nation depended.   Such a mass
rebellion, directed at the university authorities and faculty and
which resulted in the reduction of the numbers available
for eventual occupation of elite positions from two classes[7]
just couldn't happen at Todai, or so they had assumed. Yet
it did.

Tokyo University students had been prime movers in the
many politically oriented demonstrations mounted by Zengakuren since 1948. But the activism of 1968-69 challenged
either directly or by implication the system of governance of
the university not only with respect to the relationship of the
university authorities to the students, but with respect to the
hierarchical relation of professors to those of lower rank and
to the system of decision making and the locus of power and
discretion in the determination of university policy.   Moreover, a. challenge was raised to the system by which graduates
(particularly in the Medical School) found their way into their
careers, and to the research relations between the university
and industry.

Although the direct action manifestations of student activism
exemplify reliance on a primitive form of political methods,
the Japanese students have also used methods which are consistent with stable and democratic government. Particularly in
their early protests related to the policies and actions of university administrators was negotiation a tactic frequently
used. Even when demonstrations and strikes were organized

[6]Popular abbreviation for Tokyo University.

[7]The interruption of classes because of student strikes was disastrous
for the class of 1969, and entrance examinations for the class which
would normally have entered in 1970 were not held.

to support demands, the negotiation was a major focus of effort. In a number of cases, direct action was employed to get an issue, previously considered inappropriate for joint discussion and decision making by students, faculty, and administrators, on to the agenda for the more orthodox method of issue resolution.

Several former student leaders now practicing law have continued as advisors of the current student leaders. Their counsel has caused the students in some cases to turn to the support (and on several occasions to the initiation) of court cases to forward their interests. For example, the protest against the arrest of students who attacked a detective who was taking notes while attending an on-campus radical play was in the form of a court defense of the students on the grounds that they were reacting to an invasion of the campus by the police, a violation of the constitutional right of academic freedom. Those arrested for an attack on a military base and sabotage of war supplies were defended on the grounds that the maintenance of the bases and war supplies was a violation of Article IX of the "Peace Constitution." When election rules made it necessary for students to return to their homes to vote, court action was undertaken against this alleged denial of their voting rights. The results of these actions have not been entirely satisfactory, but such legal challenges are now at least possible, and hence are, in one sense, a testing of the significance and substantially of the constitutional guarantees provided the Japanese people by the 1947 constitution.

It is unlikely that the orthodox methods of negotiation and self-government in campus affairs and of electoral and pressure group political party influence in community and national affairs will provide adequate channels for protest and participation by students in all matters that touch their interest. It is hardly to be expected that a judicial system concerned for generations with protecting the State and its agents from attacks from the people will overnight become an effective protector of the people from an infringement on their individual and common rights by the State and the agents of the State. But such possibilities are in process of development. The students are playing a role, albeit a minor role, in that development. Upon the success of that form of student activism depends the possibility that direct action politics may become less predominant as it is slowly replaced by a type of activism which can be integrated with the processes of stable and democratic popular expression and self-government.

Characteristics of Direct Action

The direct action aspects of student activism in Japan are characterized by a lack of restraint and of concern for the maintenance of social order and stability. Eye witness accounts of the demonstrations suggest that the deliberate intent of a substantial number of the participants was to invite police confrontations and to test the limits of public tolerance. The testimony of former leaders of the student movement indicates that a challenge to governmental police, and academic authority, including the employment of violence, was accepted as a matter of policy by the Marugakudo faction, in 1960.

However non-violent may have been the intention of many of the participants, some of the leaders indicated that violence was not entirely a matter of "things getting out of hand." One 1960 leader explained, for example, that the purpose of their "spy system" for learning where the police would be concentrated, was not the desire to avoid such an area, but to mobilize their forces in that place in order to make sure a confrontation would occur.   Disobedience to regulations as to the line of march, the linked arms, and snake dancing obstruction of traffic was planned, with full knowledge of, not in ignorance of, those regulations.   Mass demonstrations were planned and carried out without concern for the degree to which they interfered with either the effective conduct of the educational process or the orderly pursuit of community and public affairs by other Japanese citizens and by government officials.   Demonstrations were intended to have shock impact upon both officials and the public.   The student leaders were not seeking public approval.   They were on some occasions seeking a conflict with the police who stood as a barrier between them and access to those whose policy and action they were protesting.

The planning, organization, and direction of these demonstrations, in the early 50's, around 1960, and in the late 60's were carried on in an atmosphere of conspiracy and underground, extralegal activity.

The conspiratorial aspect was encouraged and given a boost in 1950 by the McArthur promoted-and-insited-upon red

purge.   Apparently some important leaders of Zengakuren
felt they were likely to be caught in the net.   Student movement activities for a time resembled, or actually were, of the
underground variety. The Communist Party also went underground at that time, and there were enough associations
between JCP leaders and Zengakuren leaders, so that the
second could be reenforced by the first, and feel the zest of
conspiratorial activity.   It is possible of course that, without
this support and example, the student leaders would in any
case have moved in this direction.   Eventually, in 1960 the
students were, out of experience, to come to consider the
socialists and even the communists as temporizers and even
"softies."   But at the earlier stage they had the Communist
Party model and example to be inspired by and to learn from.

The influence on the student activism of the conspiratorial
core among the student leaders was to be strengthened by the
violent incidents of 1951 and 1952.   The more conservative
students just withdrew from participation in the public oriented activities of Zengakuren.   This left the dedicated activists to develop tactics appropriate to a small group poorly
supported by a popular following until the issues centered in
the renewal of the Security Pact in 1960 aroused masses of
students and gave them a sense of urgency concerning those
issues.

To some extent the conspiratorial aspect of student activism
was encouraged and intensified during the 60's.   Until the
tuition increases and deterioration of educational facilities, in
relation to the size of the task of providing an education for
escalating numbers of students, produced an issue of deep
concern to all students, student activism was in reality made
manifest in the conspiratorial efforts of the hard core activists
of the several warring factions to gain control of the organized
student movement.   The transformation of student protest
respecting educational issues into organized open and violent
confrontations with university, police, and public authorities
has all the marks of well planned strategy and tactics by a
nucleus of determined radical activists.   The designation of
Sampa Rengo as subject to the Riot Act and the consideration
given to outlawing that faction of the student movement are
obviously based on the government's interpretation that it is
a subversive organization of dedicated revolutionaries.   With
that interpretation many Japanese, including other leftist
student activists, would agree. If reports of activities of Sampa

Rengō are correct and its declared intention to destroy the existing social order by violence can be taken at its face value, there can be little doubt that, were it to be outlawed, its members would go underground and continue their conspiratorial activism.

Another feature of the direct action, which had on occasion characterized student activism in the past but which could be anticipated as normal in the late 60's, was the "improvement" in the armour and weaponry of participants in the confrontations. Crash helmets (of differing colors for differing factions) and the four foot long squared and lead weighted sticks, and molotov cocktails became standard equipment.

Finally as a characteristic of the most recent direct action can be noted the increased, although not completely new, emphasis upon tactics which involve masses of students in collective tactics directed to *forcing* compliance with their demands. Unlike demonstrations, which were chiefly effective as mechanisms for *advertising* dissent and protest, the mass boycotting of classes and examinations, the "mass bargaining", and the occupation of buildings, place the university authorities upon whom the demands are made under compulsion to accede to the demands or face the consequences in terms of their inability to keep in operation the universities for whose operation and governance they are held responsible. A demonstration may *proclaim* student power, The tactics indicated *implement* that power.

Scope and Organization of Japanese Student Activism

It is frequently asserted that student activists are not *typical* students and that their activism is not therefore a true indicator of the attitudes and action predisposition of students generally. The plausibility of the assertion is self-evident, for the very connotation of the term "activist" suggests one who is sufficiently dissatisfied by the status quo, which is supported by the positive or apathetic predispositions of the vast majority, to devote thought and effort to making changes. Although the significance of student activism is not truly represented by the minority status of activists in a given population, their numerical strength is of interest.[8]

[8]Japan is the only one of the countries visited concerning which even approximately reliable data could be obtained to make possible such an estimate. The subject is treated, therefore, only for Japan.

As indicated above, the university student population of Japan in 1960 was 600,000, about half of whom were, in that year of greatest activity of Zengakuren (prior to 1968), members of student self-governing societies affiliated with that organization.   There are no statistics available as to how many students participated in the campus *non-demonstration* activities organized by Zengakuren or, of course, in those sponsored by the unaffiliated societies.   Nor is it possible to measure the extent of student activism undertaken by student groups organized for specific social service reform, action, or "missionary" purposes, for example Soka Gakkai or other new religious groups, political party youth groups, and reactionary rightist groups.[9]   Moreover, organized activism, particularly that concerned with the peace issue, was initiated also from sources other than the leadership of Zengakuren, and others than students were caught up in such activities.

In 1952 the First Japanese Peace Conference was held with 318 delegates from 77 universities, representatives from over a dozen other organizations such as the Y.M.C.A., the Y.W.C.A., and Buddhist associations.   In 1954, the Second National Student Peace Conference was held, composed of 1600 representatives from an even broader number of non-Zengakuren associations, although Zengakuren played a prominent part. The roster of participant associations included Y.M.C.A., and Y.W.C.A., and UNESCO Student Leagues, the Christian Society for Peace, the Society for Mutual Assistance, the Woman's Student Society, the Korean Students League, the Okinawa Student Society, the Buddhist Student Society, as well as two associations (the National Council of Pedagogical College Students and the anti-war association, Wadatsumi Kai) in which the communists were very active.   The leadership and activists in both Zengakuren and the Communist Party partic-

[9]During the Occupation until 1950 there was, according to Battistini, no rightist student movement as such, although some students were associated with what general rightist groups could be organized during a period of the Occupation's drive to eliminate all ultra-nationalistic elements from Japanese society.   With the termination of the Occupation in 1952 rightist groups mushroomed.   Battistini identifies 18 such groups.   Most of them, however, were local organizations, a relatively small group of followers of an enthusiastic nationalistic anti-communist leader.   Battistini, L.H., *Postwar Student Struggle in Japan*, Tokyo and Rutland,Vt.: C.E. Tuttle Co., 1956

ipated in, but did not initiate or completely control, the nature or direction of such activities. The last above named association (Wadatsumi Kai) grew out of the Memorial Society for Japanese War Dead Students. It continued to mount an active anti-war campaign throughout the 50's, on the whole employing non-violent and non-demonstration methods. Two other organizations which attracted the support of groups other than the leadership of Zengakuren were the Society of Peace Supporters and the Defense of the Peace Constitution Movement. Toward the end of the decade a National Council for Joint Struggle Against the Security Pact (Kokumin Kaigi) was organized of which Zengakuren and Sohyo, the largest labor federation, were the largest affiliated groups. Under the aegis of this organization a large number of demonstrations were carried on. The Communist Party was not formally an affiliate, but Communist Party "observers" were permitted at the executive committee meetings and the Party announced in the press that it was an ally of Kokumin Kaigi. But with respect to Zengakuren itself it is possible to estimate to some degree the extent of its potential to involve students in its activism.

If any year prior to 1968 is to be selected in which the activism of students was of acknowledged significance in the national life of Japan, that year would be 1960. In that year there were 600,000 students in Japanese universities. On the day of most widespread demonstrations (June 18) in that year, the police reported 83,800 engaged in the entire country (37,500 in Tokyo and environs). An unknown number of these were high school students and youthful non-students. Police, or any other, estimates in the midst of a major mass disturbance are, of course, not entirely reliable. If the reported number (83,800) is taken, however, as the number of students sufficiently predisposed to activism to participate in a major direct action effort, we can say that about 15% were potential activists.

Had each of the 600,000 enrolled students devoted 150 days during 1960 to academic pursuits, Japanese students would have spent 90,000,000 student days in the activity assumed to be the normal "business" of students. During that year student demonstrations are reported by the police to have occurred on 46 days, or on nearly one-third of the normal school days. The number of students reported by police records as participating was such that at least a portion of 654,214 student-days can be calculated as having been spent in demonstrations.   In the year of greatest activity, then, 7/10 of 1% of the student-days available for academic pursuits by the 600,000 students (654,214÷90,000,000) were voluntarily spent by students in demonstrations.

In 1968-69, however, the student strikes, occupation of buildings, destruction of university property, boycott of examinations, pitched battles between students and police, etc. resulted in such an interruption to academic work that, for a large portion of the students in many universities (including Tokyo University) nearly a whole year's education was lost.

The student organization, Zengakuren, whose leaders instigated this sort of activism, has had an organizational structure which has continued since 1948 as a visible core of activism in the midst of the rise and fall of other organizations, some of them of a competitive or oppositional nature.   Until 1960 that organization, in most years, held a National Conference of delegates from local campus student self-government societies, who elected officers and a Central Committee which met four or five times a year.   The Central Committee in turn elected an Executive Central Committee, who in turn employed a Secretariat.   Objectives, plans, and slogans were set for public spring and fall "struggles" by the Central Committee.   The identification of Zengakuren as *the* Japanese student movement is, therefore, in many respects justified.   It was formally organized and continuously engaged in planning and carrying out specific "struggles."   Nationally it had a grassroots base in the local campus student self-government societies in all parts of the country.   It assumed the right to speak for the Japanese students in several international student organizations and congresses.[10]   But it was not the only manifestation of student activism.

Organized Opposition to Zengakuren

A potentially disturbing factor in the attempt to achieve organized national student unity was the fact that a majority of students in Japan attend private universities. Indeed the first ap-

[10]Zengakuren sent delegates to several communist dominated international conferences of the International Union of Students, the World Democratic Youth League, the Asian-Pacific Peace Liason.

proximation to a national student movement was a National Federation of the Self-governing Societies of Private Schools. The leadership of Kokugakuren and its successor Zengakuren came largely from the public universities, although students from some private universities, particularly Waseda, were active also. In 1949 an objection to the lack of attention of Zengakuren leadership to the affairs of the private schools, plus the tendency toward violence and the suspected (and actual) connections with the Communist Party, was manifest in the organization of Shingakuren as an anti-Zengakuren movement concerned with the student problems in the private schools.[11] Many societies in private schools associated themselves with Zengakuren, however.

Opposition to violence, to communist domination, and to lack of focus on specifically student problems were motivations for a number of attempts on the part of students to organize reform movements, all of which were shortlived, although they probably exerted a certain restraining influence on Zengakuren leadership. In 1950 a General Council of Student Activities was organized emphasizing concentration on moves for student welfare and the rejection of interference by the Communist Party. Its membership, probably not over 500, was limited to six universities. Also in 1950 two other shortlived anti-Zengakuren groups were formed: the League for the Preservation of Student Autonomy and the League for Democratization of the Student Movement, both of them raising objections to the influence of the Communist Party on Zengakuren and to the violent forms of direct action, as well as insisting that the improvement of student welfare was the primary legitimate objective of student activism.

With the onset of the Korean War in 1950 government action to weaken communist influence in all areas of Japanese life, including the universities, supplemented and strengthened these student initiated moves. Zengakuren (as a national movement) was for a time under the shadow of probable government dissolution, and during this period around 1951, the Anti-War Student League carried the torch of activism against war, a partial peace, and the de-purge of those previously branded as "war criminals." In 1955 the Central

[11]Another "branch" of the private school federation, Shigakuyo, was organized in 1953 as a rival to Shingakuren, stressing the importance of attention to private school students' problems, but pro-Zengakuren on other matters.

Executive Committee of Zengakuren undertook a critical self-examination, concluding that the organization had degenerated into an ultraleftist organization, that its activities had been oriented too exclusively to political objectives to the neglect of matters pertaining to student welfare, and that the Secretariat had assumed control in a way destructive of democracy. The Tokyo branch of Zengakuren (Togakuren) even suggested that Zengakuren was no longer necessary, but it remained affiliated to the national organization.

Until 1958, these oppositional moves did not destroy at least the appearance of a unified student movement.

Internal Factionalism

The chief threat, however, to the viability of Zengakuren, was internal factionalism, and the reasons for that factionalism are closely related to the friction within the communist movement not only in Japan but among communists in other parts of the world. Had the world-wide communist movement been able to remain unified with respect to its interpretation of the action implications of Marxist ideology, and had the Japanese Communist Party been able to reflect that unity, it is entirely possible that Zengakuren would have been able to avoid the factionalism which developed. For the schismatic tendencies in the student movement were closely related in time to such tendencies within the communist and socialist camps.

A split developed in 1950-51 between Zengakuren leaders committed to "the true international working class revolution" and the "coexistence" Marxists. The rupture was temporarily healed in 1951, but in 1952, 21 "internationalist" student leaders were expelled from the Communist Party and the Antiwar Student League was dissolved.

In 1958 a majority of the leadership of Zengakuren and the Japanese Communist Party came to a parting of the ways, an event which resulted in the fact that Zengakuren leadership entered in 1960 struggles divided into the Mainstream faction (those who had revolted against Japanese Communist Party domination and who charged the Party leadership with lack of revolutionary emphasis, and had been expelled from the Communist Party[12]) and the anti-Mainstream faction which

[12]The numbers expelled are variously estimated as from 100 to 200. As is indicated below this did not mean they ceased to adhere to Marxism. Indeed one of the points of disagreement (in addition to the attempt of

continued its adherence to the existing emphasis in the Japanese Communist Party on a united front with other Japanese liberal and leftist forces.   Both factions, however, were strong and they instigated independent actions during the 1960 period.

After the failure to prevent the renewal of the Security Pact with the United States in 1960, organizational chaos ensued.   Some indication of the schismatic developments is found in the police records which designate the sponsors of demonstrations which came to their attention. From 1958 through 1959 the designation is either "Zengakuren" or "Zengakuren Mainstream."   Beginning on January 16, 1960 the designations are "Zengakuren Mainstream" and "Zengakuren Anti-Mainstream."   In January 1961 the designation of the Anti-Mainstream is "Zenjiren", which was in many respects a student arm of the Communist Party.   In September 1961 begin to appear the names of organizations described as Zengakuren splinter groups: Marxist Student League, Socialist Student League, Kokai faction, Socialist Youth, the League of Three Factions, Heimin Gakkyo, and the Democratic Student League.

In 1963 there were identifiable at least five groups of student leaders vying for control of the local self-government associations and the national Zengakuren.[13]   Four of these were anti-Japanese Communist Party, i.e. were more radical in ideology and more violent in tactics than the Party.

1. Kōkai Ha and Kaihō Ha, two factions descended from Shaseido (The League of Socialist Youth) and its successor Sampa Rengō (an early three faction coalition.)   Later in the year Kaihō Ha affiliated with Shin Sampa Rengō (The Three Faction Federation.)

2. Kansai Ha, Toitsu Ha, Marx-Lenin Ha, three factions remaining after a number of dissolutions and mergers of the organization Sagakudō (League of Socialist Students.)   The first two affiliated later in the year with Shin Sampa Rengō.

3. Chūkakū Ha and Kakumaru Ha, two factions descended

---

the Japanese Communist Party to dominate the choice of Zengakuren leadership) was the adherence of the expelled student leaders to a "purer" and more revolutionary form of Marxism than was at that time the basis of the mainstream Japanese Communist Party program.

[13]Usami Sho, "Zengakuren," *Japan Quarterly*, June 1968, p. 234

from the organization Kakukyōdō (The League of Revolutionary Communism) and its successor Marugakudō (League of Japanese Marxist Students.) Chūkakū Ha later in the year affiliated with Shin Sampa Rengō.

4. Kyōseidō (The League of Communist Youth) which had separated from the JCP dominated Zenjiren as "true" revolutionaries.

Rapidly growing in 1963 and the largest single faction was:

5. Heimingakuren, (The National Liason Council for Students to Oppose the Security Pact and Safeguard Peace and Democracy.) This faction was closely allied with and supported by the Japanese Communist Party. It was a direct successor to Zenjiren and the earlier Minsei Student Corps[14] both of which were closely related to the Japanese Communist Party.

As we have already indicated, the struggle among these factions for power and for control of the local campus societies and the national student movement was, from 1960 on, a major stimulus to campus unrest and disturbance as they vied with each other to demonstrate that they were the true and legitimate manifestations of a revolutionary student movement, the only authentic inheritor of the mantle of the once powerful Zengakuren. By 1966, three of the groups had attached the name "Zengakuren" to their factional titles, Heimingakuren had become "JCP Zengakuren," Shin Sampa Rengō had become "Sampa Zengakuren," and Kakumara Ha had become "Kakumaru Zengakuren." In 1969, JCP Zengakuren claimed the affiliation of 310 university and college associations compared with the 114 whose affiliation all the other factions claimed. Police estimate that this relatively non-violent JCP leadership has by far the greatest influence in the local student self government associations, and that they "lead" the numerically largest group of Japanese students. The Tokyo Metropolitan Police Board estimates that there are only about 12,000 leading activists in the anti-JCP groups and that they can marshal in the neighborhood of 40,000 students for demonstrations. But Sampa Zengakuren

[14]The pro-Communist Party faction of Zengakuren is referred to in many current commentaries as "The Minsei faction."

because of the violence of its tactics and the absolutism of its revolutionary goals held the center of public attention.

The continuous and frequently violent competition for leadership nationally and locally during the sixties led to much confusion (and in many cases disgust) among the students. The result for nearly a decade, was a weakened movement and reduced interest of the students as a whole. No great national issue of widespread concern among the students as great as the combination of issues in 1960 was present to arouse the interest of students generally and to stimulate their mass commitment to direct action under the leadership of student activists whose number-one concern was apparently to win factional battles. It was anticipated by many, however, that when the renewal of the Security Pact once more became an issue upon which not only students but all Japanese citizens could focus, there would occur a temporary need for collaboration in action which would override the ideological differences and disputes over tactics, at least temporarily, until the issue once more became an item of history. The year of renewal, 1970, did witness increased anti-Security Pact demonstrations but not on a scale comparable to that of 1960. Nor did the experience bring unity to the student movement.

In September 1969, several of the anti-JCP student factions opposing the renewal of the Security Pact gathered to establish Zenkoku Rengō (all Japan Federation of Student Associations). Eight groups joined. Time only can tell whether this effort will result in a viable coalition or whether it will suffer the fratricidal fate of other attempts to get ideological radical groups to work in harness.

The student leaders who replace those now engaged in factional struggles are likely to find themselves, however, facing a threat from university and public authorities to the effective activity, and indeed the survival, of all their factional organizations, and furnished therefore, with a protest-stimulating issue of deep concern to all students. The pragmatic necessity for unity to meet that threat and to marshal widespread student support for effective protest could well weaken the predisposition to maintain ideological and tactical purity. That threat and that issue are being created out of the reaction of university and public authorities to the escalating internecine warfare of the past decade. Public tolerance also has been strained to the breaking point. Even the Communist and Socialist Parties have denounced the violent tactics of Shin Sampa Rengō (Sampa Zengakuren), the group committed openly to the destruction of the social order by violence.

The measures taken by governmental agencies to meet the disturbances to public order are understandable. But they are reminders of government action characterizing an earlier era in Japanese history when the exercise of a freedom to dissent was counted as disloyalty and treason. In April 1968 Shin Sampa Rengō was designated as subject to the Riot Act, and the government was known to be considering outlawing it as a subversive organization. The government was also forced to take notice that on many campuses the university authorities had lost control of the situation. Early in 1969 two government actions were taken, Those university authorities were served notice that, if they failed to put their houses in order, the government would take "appropriate" steps including ultimately the permanent closing of the institutions. The police were informed that the campuses were no longer to be considered sanctuaries into which the police could enter only on invitation of the university authorities. The quick and well planned response of the riot police to the Sasebo confrontation in 1968 and to the mass actions to prevent the departure of the Prime Minister for conferences with President Nixon in the fall of 1969 indicated a considerable strengthening of the government's determination and readiness to counter with force any direct action which sought to interfere with a course of action which the government had decided to pursue. Viewed against the memories of near fascistic controls of dissenting thought and action in the past, it is not difficult for students to interpret these emergency measures as preludes to a return to those restrictions on civic freedom and in particular on that related to autonomous university life and governance. Do universities deserve to be left free whose governors are unable to maintain, against minority attacks, institutional processes and values conducive to making the contribution to the common life which, in free societies, has justified their status as free and autonomous institutions? That issue seems irrelevant to the students and faculty and administrators who could find common cause in opposing any infringement on that freedom. The defense of that freedom when it is perceived to be under attack will be the kind of an issue which will cement the interests and the action commitments of all members of the academic community, conservative, reformist, revolutionary, and reactionary alike, at least temporarily.

And necessary as determined and force-wielding police action may be in the preservation of a minimum level of public order, the action itself symbolizes for students generally the ultimate basis in force of the power to govern. Negative restraining action is continuously on the margins of, and plausibly interpreted as positive police brutality by those whose heads are cracked, or eyes and lungs are stung by tear gas, and by their sympathizers. Protest against police brutality can be counted on to recruit a far larger number for direct action than were enlisted on behalf of the original issue.

The reactions to the violence of the late 60's and 1970 on the part of a large number of students themselves raises another challenge to the leaders of the divided factions among the organized student movement. In 1968 in the midst of the violent disruption of academic life at Tokyo University, some students formed the United Council of All-Campus Student Bodies to seek a non-violent solution to the issues alleged to be at the root of the struggle which were depriving them of the opportunity to get an education. Calling themselves "nonpori" students because they renounced any political orientation, they fixed their sights upon the correction of educational inadequacies and inequities within the universities themselves and denounced the efforts of the more radical Zengakuren factions to "capture" protest induced by these genuinely student problems for political ends. The organizers of this movement like their predecessors who proclaimed the same ambitions in 1950, are attempting to develop a viable collective vehicle for student participation in determining the conditions influencing their educational experience. While efforts would necessarily be focused on particular problems in particular universities, the organizers hope to coordinate their local efforts through regional and a national organization. Whether this attempt to institutionalize the voice of the "silent majority" will be more successful than previous similar attempts remains to be seen. In any case it is a competitor for student interest and commitment of which the leaders of the warring factions of Zengakuren must take account.

The violent disturbances of the 60's also brought to the fore, in some private universities, organizations of "cheer-leaders" and athletes as the defenders of university administrators who were under attack from militant activists. The observation that on several occasions they served as "body guards" for university administrators during "mass bargaining" and were employed in the attempt to clear radical activists from the university buildings they had occupied led radical activists to label them as "storm troopers" in the pay of the governors of the university. Whatever the degree of truth in this allegation, their form of "reactionary" activism is unlikely to do anything but intensify the violent predispositions and tactics of the activists.

Leadership

During 1964 and 1965, we were able to interview twenty-nine current and former leaders of Zengakuren both at the national and at the local campus level, and 279 members of the student self government associations affiliated with Zengakuren. The picture of the organization's leadership which emerges from the testimony obtained in those interviews is, of course impressionistic. Yet there is clear evidence that certain characteristics were present among a large number, especially among the national leaders.

The leaders we interviewed were clean-cut, sincere young men, sharp in mind, able in debate, and forceful in expression. They were well-versed in Marx and Lenin, but not in writings critical of the thought of these men. Nor were they well-versed in comparative economic and political theory. They had a hazy notion of the institutional facts of life in socialist, or for that matter in capitalist, countries. Their arguments were couched in theoretical rather than in empirical terms, their reasoning deductive rather than inductive, dogmatic rather than analytical. Without much reference to empirical data, they had a tendency to accept any act of capitalist regimes as exploitive, imperialistic, and warmongering and those of socialist countries as democratic and peace-loving. Yet they acknowledged an honest difficulty in interpreting the meaning of the Hungarian revolt and its suppression, the denouncement of Stalin, and the mutual recrimination between the Chinese and Russian communists. They were critical of the conservatism and lack of activism and revolutionary fervor in both the Communist and the Socialist Parties. Their family backgrounds were middle-class: they were sons of lawyers, small businessmen, doctors, professors, teachers, and government officials, etc. They found it unneccessary to demonstrate their self-images by means of sartorial and tonsorial symbolism.

They were undoubtedly young men with a genuine commitment to a mission, and that mission was during their student years to serve as an elite vanguard of a Marxist revolution. That revolution would begin, they believed, among Japanese students, involve the working classes in Japan, and spread to the working classes of other nations. It would wrest power both in the universities and in the nation itself from the existing governing Establishment in Japan. Particular targets in the Establishment were liberal-democrats, higher class members of the bureaucracy, owners of the large industries and banks, and leaders of the "self-defense" forces. Moreover, the revolution would free Japan from the control of both Japanese and foreign (particularly American) exploiters, imperialists, and militaristic "warmongers" at home and abroad whose governing was moving the powerful nations of the world toward war. They were interested in Marxism primarily as providing a methodology, and a justification for the reconstruction of society and the destruction of those institutions they considered exploitive and unjust. That methodology, including violent demonstrations, provided an opportunity both for "awakening" and educating the masses, for the development of group solidarity, and for confrontations with the police without whom the nation's existing governors would, as one former leader remarked, be "naked."

Like Marxist revolutionists everywhere they engage in fratricidal disputes about what is "genuine" Marxist methodology. The most radical heap abuse upon the reformers and the "revisionists" in the present Communist and Socialist Parties as well as upon the leaders of the JCP Zengakuren, whose efforts to develop a temporary coexistence with other leftist and liberal forces they assert, would only shore up the existing system and lull the masses into acceptance of a capitalistic order that is doomed to eventual destruction. Even among the anti-JCP leaders there are ideological divisions. There are Trotskyites whose objective is international rather than one-country Socialism, but who consider neither Russia nor China a true socialist State. There are Maoists who consider the ideas of Mao and Lenin the genuine guides to the carrying through of both a Japanese and a world revolution. And there are the one-stage revolutionists whose objective is an immediate and one-stage overthrow of Capitalism and Imperialism in Japan. The factional strife within the leftist camp then, characterizing the political life of many nations, was mirrored in the Japanese student movement especially after 1960 and until the present. Whether to "go it alone" as pure revolutionaries or to join and maintain a "united front" for the time being with liberal or even capitalist forces was, and still is, a hotly disputed question.

Until 1960 there had been a sufficient number of successful conclusions to their exercise of power politics in the streets to buoy up the confidence of many of the leaders that the students' independent activism was or could be politically effective. For example, their "struggles" such as agitation against the purge of Communist Party professors, their efforts to get the directive against political activities modified so that academic freedom and the right of students to be members of political parties would be acknowledged, their demonstrations against the enlargement of an air force base in the suburbs of Tokyo, were sufficiently successful, although carried on in collaboration with other action groups, to convince some of the leaders that they were on the right track, and that student power was a force with which political leaders must reckon. They were encouraged by the fact that the press on the whole reacted to their "struggles" in a sympathic way.

It was a rude awakening for student leaders, therefore, when, in spite of the great and violent storm which was whipped up in 1960, and the participation of so many from the more conservative ranks of society in the action, the Security Pact was nevertheless renewed, and the mass effort to block Prime Minister Kishi's departure for the United States was to no avail. After 1960 there appears to have been among some of them a reexamination of objectives and methods and an increased emphasis on getting back to Marxist fundamentals and a loss of confidence in the possibility of involving the Japanese "proletariat" in revolutionary activity. Some of those with whom we spoke frankly admitted that their total concern had been negative toward, and destructive of, the existing Establishment and that they had little concept of what a reconstructed and positive set of societal arrangements, institutions, and policies should be.   Interest in exploring and debating such matters was evident by 1965.

A notable characteristic of the post-1960 leaders was their conception of their role as part-time and temporary, rather than full-time leaders. There is much testimony from both students, university faculty and administrators, and police reports that prior to 1960 a number of leaders looked upon their leadership role as a full-time occupation.   Their role as students acquiring an education was distinctly secondary and covered a much longer span than is normally required to achieve a degree, if indeed they ever completed the requirements.

Both present and past leaders, moreover, appear to conceive of their activism in the student movement as a temporary matter rather than the opening phase of a career in radical politics. We are aware of no investigations of the careers of former student leaders, but those with whom we talked could think of only two prominent leaders during their student days who had continued to operate as political activists with the Communist or Socialist parties, or who were active promoters in public life of the kinds of protest action they had led or the revolutionary doctrine they had espoused as students.

Impact of the Communist Party

There can be little doubt that the Communist Party exerted a direct influence on the leadership of Zengakuren in the decade following its organization in 1948.   Even after 1958, when the membership in the Communist Party of over 100 Zengakuren leaders was terminated, the Party continued direct influence on the anti-Mainstream leadership, and, at this time (1970), the faction among the leadership which works closely with the Communist Party is unquestionably the largest of any single faction.   It claims that 70% of the self governing student associations in Japan are subject to its leadership.

The influence of the Party on the students as a whole was indirect, exerted through the committed student leader communists in Zengakuren and in a number of other leftist student and youth organizations in which these leaders participate.

There is no extensive commitment to the Communist Party on the part of the students generally. Many are Marxists, but every survey of student attitudes and activity with which we are familiar indicates that, in expressing a choice among the several parties, the great majority prefer the Socialist Party. Two estimates were made by the Ministry of Education of the number of Communist Party "members" and "sympathizers." The first, made in 1952 at one of the peaks of student activism, reported that, of the 360,000 four year students, 5,500 or 1½% could be classified in this way, and that even in Tokyo the percentage was less than 2%. In 1959 the membership of Zengakuren was estimated at 290,000 among whom 2,000 were communists and an additional 2-3,000 were sympathizers. It was further estimated that possibly 900 of the members of the Association of Socialist Students were communist.

The Communist Party tactic of organizing communist cells in particular groups, including students, was early employed, and, by the year in which Zengakuren was organized (1948), the Party was sufficiently on its feet to undertake their widespread organization. These cells were, of course, composed of a small number of committed and normally dedicated members, usually from 10 to 20 members. According to police reports based on registration of these cells, amplified by estimates of unregistered cells, the number in several years was:

1948	106
1949-50	125 (with 1534 members)
1962	808 (listed as "school" cells)

After 1949, a large number of universities presumably regulated these cells out of existence as violating the political neutrality of the campus, but this did not eliminate the possibility of their establishing headquarters off campus.

According to college administrators, the students we interviewed, and police sources, an unknown but a considerable number of students participate in youth organizations in which committed communists play influential roles.

Such estimates of the extreme minority status of Communist Party members and sympathizers among the students are, of course, completely misleading if from them is drawn the conclusion that the Communist Party influence on Zengakuren was minor. It is through the *leaders* of a social movement that outside action groups can give direction and emphasis to the programs and activities launched by that movement. And here the evidence is irrefutable. At the organization of Zengakuren in 1948, the student-elected Chairman, Vice Chairman, and Chief Secretary of the Central Executive Committee were all communists. The platform drawn up by the Executive Committee for the second national convention contained these words, "On the eve of the overall collapse of world Capitalism, the international monopoly capitalists, who are warmongers seeking to maintain their prosperity through war production, are now thrusting into Japan." Zengakuren joined the International Union of Students which was communist dominated. A communist cell was established in the secretariat. In 1950 the Communist Party Central Committee ordered dissolution of this cell in the light of its tendency to depart from the Party line.

The strategy of the Party was to assist student members to gain important roles within the organization. Students we interviewed at Kyoto, Tokyo, and Waseda Universities declared that many of the most important of these career revolutionists were, in the early sixties on the Communist Party payroll. An interview with Professor Juitsu Kitaoka reported by Battistini in his *The Post-war Student Struggle in Japan* supports that declaration:

> According to Professor Kitaoka the "career revolutionists" at one time received monthly stipends of 10,000 yen while lesser agents generally received about 3,000 yen monthly from the Communist Party. Professor Kitaoka also maintains that during the flourishing period of Zengakuren, the Communist Party had about a hundred students on its payrolls as "career workers."

The most clear-cut evidence of the relation of the leadership of Zengakuren to the Communist Party is that from 1952 on student leaders were expelled from the Party on grounds of opposition to the Party line or failure to observe Party discipline. In 1958 the Party leadership called the leadership of Zengakuren to their offices to account for themselves, and attempted to replace several of the leaders. It is noteworthy that the students felt impelled to answer that summons. Over a hundred ot them, however, responded by violently asserting their independence and were promptly expelled from the Party.

They thereupon organized to promote an even purer brand
of Marxism and a more "no-compromise" and violent form
of revolutionary brand of direct action than the Communist
Party could accept. This faction was the core of the Mainstream element of Zengakuren during the disturbances of 1960,
those still remaining submissive to the position and direction
of the Communist Party became the anti-Mainstream faction.

During the decade from 1948 to 1958, the foci of Zengakuren's
spring and fall struggles paralleled in the political field those
of the Communist Party. Differences on tactics and on
positions with respect to revolutionary strategy within the
Communist Party were duplicated within Zengakuren. It
is true that the extremely militant and "pure" Marxist revolutionary group who were ejected from the Party in 1958 became
increasingly disdainful of what they called the "bureaucratic,"
"swivel chair," "timid" leaders of the Party. But the disdain
centered in their judgment that the Party was betraying
its revolutionary mission. They saw in the leaders of the
Japanese Communist Party the same weaknesses which had
resulted in the failures of the German, the Spanish, the
French Communist Parties. And some saw in the party
line emphasis on using even liberal and capitalist talent
to develop strong national movements the tendencies toward
national statism exhibited by Stalin. To push the international working class revolution into the background, to
abjure the use of violence, to tolerate the compromises inevitable in the building of a united front, such action tendencies
were, in the judgment of these expelled student leaders, a
betrayal of true Marxist Communism.

It is probably true, however, that the student leaders who
shaped a Zengakuren program so similar in many respects
to that of the Communist Party would have needed no
"directives" from the Party to stimulate them toward that
program. The ultimate values to the students and to the
Communist Party of opposition to military involvement with
the United States, of fighting against the legal and police
restrictions on freedom of expression and assembly, of opposition to the recentralization of education and the police
forces, and to extension of military bases, of resisting revision
of the "Peace Constitution," of preventing visits of nuclear
submarines, may have been different. But the achievement
of those different values was served by activism directed in

the same channels. Directives from the Communist Party to
student leaders who were members or sympathizers may well
have been acceptable to the latter, not on grounds of the
necessity to submit to Party discipline, but as an obviously
appropriate indication of ways to achieve goals of interest
to students. Moreover, those ambitious but inexperienced
students who wished to lead a social movement must have
been impressed with the value to them of help from experienced and apparently sympathetic organizers and directors
of direct action politics. And in the light of the intensity
of concentration on, and concern about, the preservation
of peace, there were few adult Japanese who could be sought
as allies who were more dynamic, organized and devoted,
and whose record promised more effective anti-militarism in
Japan than that of the communists.

That the "career" in the phrase applied by Battistini to
certain student leaders, namely, "career revolutionaries" was
not a "life career" but a "student days career" is suggested
by our informants who were former student leaders when
they could think of only two who had continued in active
service to the Communist and Socialist Parties. There may
have been more, and one of the most important insights
into the basic motiviation for student activism could be
provided by research into the continuing life patterns of
one time leaders of these student movements.

What appears here is a coincidence among students and
Communist Party leaders of concern about and the desire
to do something about many of the same issues, and a
recognition by both of the reciprocal advantage to each
of working in harness with the other, though the immediate
objectives to be achieved by each were of a different order.

The question which can be raised is, whether had there
been no Communist Party influence, how much of the activity
carried on would have been undertaken in any case? How
many issues toward which demonstrations were directed would
have been so important and significant to students that they
would have provided an entirely adequate self-generated stimulus to activism and direct action politics?

In our judgment the following issues would have done so:
the improvement in education and in educational opportunities; participation in the governance of the universities;
protests against the violations of free speech and association,

Chapter 2
Student Activism in India

A major generalization which can be made about student activism in India is that in no sense has it even been a self-generated social movement exclusively of, by, and for the students. Moreover, until the Chinese border incidents of 1962 it was only during the post-World War I, pre-independence period, that is the quarter of a century from 1920 to 1945, that one could find anything resembling an organized marshaling, over a large part of the nation, of substantial student forces for the achievement of commonly acknowledged objectives. On-campus life was politically active during this period. Students did provide large numbers of recruits for the anti-British independence struggle, but they were not the primary initiators of that struggle. Any traditions which presently affect student activism in India are rooted in the experiences of that pre-independence period. The tradition of stimulation and sponsorship by political, communal, and cultural public action groups; the tradition of direct action and violent tactics disruptive of public order; the tradition of attacks launched against the established university and public authorities; the tradition of internal factionalism; such traditions color tendencies which still characterize student activism.

History

It is practically impossible to find original records on which a systematic history of student movements in India can be based.[1] Much of the pre-independence (1947) activism was of an underground nature, and, throughout the period when student activists have played a role in the campus and national life of India, the number of organizations, most of which

[1]P. G. Altbach's chapter, "Student Politics and Higher Education in India", in the volume which he edited, *Turmoil and Transition*, Basic Books, 1968, is an excellent concise summary of available materials including several previously unpublished documents.

kept no available records, has been so great that the task, even with good records, would be monumental. Nevertheless, the picture of Indian student activism since 1920 can be painted with broad strokes in a way which will distinguish it from that in other countries here considered.[2]

Pre-independence students were widely and deeply involved in the nationalist or independence movement. There were several allegedly all-India federations with varied political orientations which attempted to establish communication and a degree of coordination among groups of student activists on the several campuses. The goal of independence and of participation in any action which would weaken the hold and authority of England was sufficiently widespread to give the appearance of a nationwide student movement. The objective of independence was of such obvious significance and was so emotionally appealing that the standing of the activists among their fellow students was high and the acceptance of their leadership was natural. Political study groups and action groups became a popular and exciting aspect of college life.

The 1920's saw the emergence of Gandhi as the charismatic leader of a mass nationalist movement. He appealed to

[2]Sources for the following are, first of all, interviews with Indian government officials and leaders of political parties who have had contact with the twistings and turnings of the student activism over the years, a number of whom were active in student organizations during their student years; with members of the U.S. Embassy and Consulate staffs with assignments to keep abreast of this aspect of Indian society; with faculty and administrators in the universities; and with present and former student leaders. Two graduate students prepared unpublished papers, the one on Communist and the other on Congress Party activities relative to the students in India. Several students who became interested in our data gathering in India in 1965 have continued to send us summaries of student activism from Indian journals and newspapers. The following published sources have also been helpful: Altbach, P. G., "Transformation of the Indian Student Movement," in *Asian Survey*, August 1966, pp. 448ff; and *Turmoil and Transition*, N. Y.: Basic Books, 1968; Chandra, Prabadh, *Student Movement in India*, Lahore, All India Students Federation, 1938; Weiner, Myron, *The Politics of Scarcity*, University of Chicago Press, 1961; Bureau of Social Science Research, *The Indian Student Movement*, American University, 1955; Reddy, M. Muni, *The Student Movement in India*, Lucknow, K.S.R. Acharya, 1947; Shah, A. B., *Higher Education in India*, Bombay: Lalvani, 1969.

students as well as to the masses. The success of the Russian revolution not only fired the imagination of many students about chances for throwing off English rule, but suggested Socialism as a type of societal organization which could provide India with progress toward modernization. Moreover, large numbers of students returning from their education in England were familiar with that nation's brand of Fabian Socialism, and many of these were employed as teachers and professors.

Already in the 1920's, Indian leaders representing the political emphases which are still dominant in India were interested in influencing the students. These leaders included the Indian National Congress (particularly its more socialistic elements) the Hindu Nationalists, and the Communists. Congress leaders established Youth Leagues and inaugurated in 1920 a series of annual All-India Conferences designed to marshal students for the nationalist struggle. These All-India Student Conferences became excellent platforms for the increasingly active leaders of the Indian National Congress. These leaders were much in evidence at student gatherings giving direction and emphasis to them.

The Hindu nationalists, emphasizing the values of traditional Hindu religion and culture, so obviously threatened by western influences, also sponsored the organization of Rashtriya Swayamsevak Sangh (RSS). This organization made efforts to enlist the interest and enthusiasm of the students.

The Indian communist movement was not yet strong enough in the 20's to sponsor an all-India organization, but communists were active on a number of local campuses.

Ideological, communal, and choice-of-tactics conflicts early arose to such an extent that a series of attempts was made under the auspices of the Indian National Congress to organize a student, non-politically oriented, Congress Seba Dal. Its allegedly non-political character was shortlived, and in 1928 it affiliated with the League Against Imperialism, an international communist front organization, and thus became the first organizational link of the youth movement in India with international Communism.

Two other student gatherings. ambitious to have an all-India character, came to life during the 20's, the All-India Youth Congress and the First Socialist Youth Congress, both in 1928. The latter was under the chairmanship of Nehru.

There was in the midst of these politically and communally
inspired efforts an insistence from a number of liberal politicians on the need for a truly independent and non-political
student movement.   Many of these attempts were local to
particular campuses and resulted in local cultural associations
sponsoring extracurricular activities and off-campus social
service. As such they provided some outlet to student energies
alternative to political activities. Also regional student associations, originally independent of political party influences,
were formed in Bengal, Bihar, and Punjab. So obvious did
this liberal pressure become that the Indian National Congress
in 1931 appointed a committee to plan for the organization
of an independent all-India student federation which would
be one truly and solely representative of student interests.
The committee was under the chairmanship of Nehru. The
result of this committee's work was the establishment in 1936
of The All-India Student Federation. But note that even
this allegedly "independent" student federation was not the
creation of spontaneous student initiative; it was initiated
by leaders of the Indian National Congress.

The phrase "All-India" in the name of this, and a number
of subsequent federations, was brave assertion of national
unity of student interest which never reflected reality. Within
a year, Muslim students in Bengal launched in Calcutta
the organization soon labeled the All-India Muslim Students
Federation with the declared intention of "supplying a good
cadre to the Muslim League."   Incidentally, it did this
successfully.   A number of other more localized attempts
were made at the organization of communal student associations, supporting interests of Hindus, Muslims, Sikhs, and
particularly those of the disadvantaged castes.

The Hindu traditionalists were uneasy participants in any
all-India student association. The R.S.S., however, continued
to gain support for its emphasis on militant *Hindu* nationalism. In addition, and drawing support from those committed
to the preservation of peculiarly Hindu values, there was
organized the Hindu Students Federation.

The Congress-supported All-India Student Federation continued its annual conferences, but under increasing communist
domination. In 1940 the communists, who favored support
of England in World War II, and the nationalists who were
of course anti-British, could find no common ground. The

nationalists called a convention at Patna in 1941 and formed the Nationalist Students Federation. The communist dominated A.I.S.F. went its own way through experiences closely paralleling those of the whole communist movement in India.

The N.S.F. was banned by the government after the Indian National Congress made its "quit India" challenge to the British rulers. When the ban was lifed in 1944, the N. S. F. convened in Bombay, castigated the A.I.S.F. for its support of the English in the war and christened itself the All-India Students Congress.

At the end of the Second World War, therefore, there were two all-India student organizations with roots in traditions neither of which had much to do with the educational problems of Indian youth. The one (A.I.S.F.) was oriented to the support of Indian and international Communism, the other (A.I.S.C.) had its roots in the nationalist and now increasingly strong independence movement. In 1945 both sent delegates to the World Student Congress at Prague and to the International Union of Students, a communist front organization. Acting in accord with the then Communist Party line for united front action, the International Union of Students tried to bring the two organizations together. The attempt failed. For all practical purposes the early political activism of students as Indians, rather than as communists, came to an end with the achievement of Independence in 1947, and intensive participation had ceased at least a year earlier.

The post-independence period has witnessed attempts on the part of the political and communal national organizations to sponsor student organizations claiming to be national in scope, and to stimulate several so-called non-partisan, but really multi-partisan, all-India student organizations. The result is a multiplicity of student organizations, no one of which until very recently gave any unity and coherence to the activism of students on anything resembling a national front.

The All-India Students Congress was disbanded in 1948, its chief function having been to support the nationalist independence activities in India.

Congress Party leaders and Socialists sponsored the organization of a so-called non-political National Union of Students. It was non-partisan chiefly in declaration of intent, and its political in-fighting utilized most of the energies of its leaders.

With the decision to have a nominally non-political student organization, the parties, particularly the Congress, and Praja Socialist parties, activated their own youth sections, which of course were not limited to a student membership.

In 1955, a nominally independent federation was formed called the Federation of Indian Youth. It was soon under heavy influence from the communists. They, together with a number of other leftist groups, withdrew and formed the All-India Youth Federation in 1959.

Another attempt (1958) to establish a non-partisan movement, undertaken under the stimulus of the several parties, was the organization of the National Council of University Students of India. The communists who soon infiltrated this organization, along with a few members of the Socialist Party and students supporting Mr. V. K. Krishna Menon, withdrew in 1962 to form the National Union of University Students of India. These two organizations continued to vie with each other to obtain the affiliation of college and university student unions. It is alleged that both of these organizations receive foreign support, the first from the West, the second from Russia.

By November of 1964, the 11th National Student Congress of N.C.U.S.I. had representatives from 17 universities, an increase from the 12 at the 10th Congress. To the 12th National Student Congress held by N.C.U.S.I. in December 1965-January 1966, 21 of the 30 student unions sent representatives. Observers were also present from the All-India Student Congress (the youth wing of the Congress party) and the All-India Catholic Student Federation. But aside from its periodic congresses to which come leaders of less than half of local student societies it has no program of national scope.

The communist-dominated All-India Student Federation still exists, but has a highly concentrated influence in Bengal and Kerala.

Three other youth organizations not limited to students, by 1968 were indirectly exerting influence on the student organizations particularly when representation to international youth conferences was the issue involved. These were the All-India Youth Federation (A.I.Y.F.), pro-Moscow communist; The Democratic Youth Federation (D.Y.F.) pro-Peking communist; and Indian Youth Congress (I.Y.C.), the youth wing of the Congress Party.[3]

The only other student organization which can lay claim to nationwide influence is Akhil Bharatiya Vidyarthi Parishad (All-India Students Organization). Nominally non-partisan, its members appear to be drawn largely from students with Hindu communalist backgrounds, and its programs lay heavy stress on the development of understanding of and respect for traditional Hindu values. Its strongest hold is in north India. Its cooperative attitude toward school administrators and faculty have made it a welcome influence for order and stability in the midst of the unrest and violence characterizing much of the student activism in India.

From 1920 on, then, student activism has been predominantly stimulated and sponsored and supported by political, communal, patriotic, and cultural groups who sought, and still do seek, student support for their particular objectives. It has not been a spontaneous welling-up of widespread initiative of students to achieve primarily student objectives.

Since these groups themselves experienced a history of constant factionalism, it was natural that the student activism should have a tradition of being subject to the same centrifugal tendencies.

Moreover, the tradition is one of repeated attempts of a particular group to claim national coverage and the right to speak for all Indian students by prefixing their names with the words "all-India" or "national." Such labeling, however, has never mirrored the reality, since communal, political, cultural, linguistic, and regional concepts of "national" and "all-India" supplied a multidimensional concept of India itself. As indicated above, however, the N.C.U.S.I. is increasingly earning the right to claim national leadership, and had by 1966 obtained the affiliation of two-thirds of the university student unions in India.

Tradition also emphasized the tactics appropriate to rebellion and violence and the relegating of educational con-

[3]In June 1970, the Indian Youth Congress called a two day all-India student convention. Here it was decided to form an all-India student front loyal to the socialistic policies of Indira Gandhi's faction of the Congress Party. It is, in effect, a revival of the India Student Congress which was dissolved in 1947. But it is now serving the political need of a faction of the Congress Party.

siderations to a subordinate place. In the early 1920's Gandhi called on students to boycott the English sponsored colleges they were attending, and to support the shortlived "national" colleges with which the Indian National Congress, in nationalistic fervor, sought to replace the historical colleges and universities. In the 1930's, civil disobedience tactics of the Gandhi movement caught up and involved the students. They were developed by students as well as others beyond the borders of nonviolence to which Gandhi, at least philosophically, would have held. The printing and distribution of illegal papers, strikes, riots, demonstrations, deliberate confrontations with the police, massed attacks on centers of British administration, and destruction of government property were standard tactics of the independence movement. Participation resulted in the dismissal from college and in the imprisonment of many students. College administrators also learned to rely on closing the colleges to provide a cooling off period, leaving the students with even more free time to gain experience and training in such tactics.

The high-water mark of this training was reached in student participation in the quit-India campaign directed against the British in the early 1940's. Daily demonstrations, sabotage, strikes which closed the colleges, underground conspiracies, interruption of train movements, invasion and disruption of the work of government agencies, anything to embarrass the English, were the kinds of operations in which popular heroes, including student heroes, were made. Appraised in terms of nationalistic ideals, this was a tradition of education in the sacrificing of immediate personal self-interest for long range ideal national goals, the most immediate and pressing of which was self-determination. Appraised in terms of means to an end, it was a tradition of education in the "creative joy of destruction."

It is difficult to assess to what extent this tradition suggests the present pattern of student activism. Today's students were not born during that period, and the patriotic and idealistic fervor for glorious objectives, which was widespread in those days, was not currently present to justify such tactics until the threats to national stability involved in the Chinese "invasion" incidents of 1962 and the confrontation with Pakistan over Kashmir. To whatever degree a heroic tradition suggests current tactics, the thrust of that suggestion is clear. But our concern here is with the character of present-day student activism.

Objectives and Activities

It is possible to define the objectives of Indian student activism during the 25 years from 1920 to 1945. The most extensive activity involving the largest number of students was directed toward collaboration with the revolutionary efforts to embarrass English governance and to further the cause of India's independence. Those students who were influenced by communist leadership also directed their activism toward this objective until 1940, when they refused to make non-cooperation with Britain in the war a part of their program, and to an expected degree were concerned about advancing the cause of international Communism, Moscow style. A strong, but distinctly minority, Muslim sector of the activism was directed toward providing support for and providing activists for the separatist efforts of the Muslim League.

The testimony of those who were involved in that period of struggle for independence is all but unanimous that the majority objective was implemented enthusiastically and effectively even to the extent that the students took over the leadership of the anti-British forces at times when the adult leaders of the independence movement were imprisoned.

After World War II, and the achievement of independence, the objectives of student activism take on a crazy quilt pattern to such an extent that most commentators have given up the attempt to find any consistent or logical relationship between what the students do and any reasons they give for doing it. Even the objectives of the communist and rightist Hindu sectors of student activism are largely defined by commentators by reference to what is assumed to be respectively the revolutionary emphasis in world Communism and the communal nationalistic emphasis among Hindu militants. To derive any generalizations about objectives from a categorization of the alleged "reasons" for, or stimuli to, the myriad cases of direct action launched by students in many parts of the country is most difficult.

There are some who contend that it is useless to seek

the objectives for Indian student activism in the interests of the students, since the dominant stimulus for that activism in India, they allege, comes from political and communal off-campus groups who support, if they do not instigate, student organizations and activities.   There is ample evidence that such off-campus forces have a significant interest in utilizing student organizations and activities for their own purposes.   But this is not to say that student participation may not be directed to purposes which, though not clearly defined, are held by students themselves. What evidence is it possible to marshal for the latter conclusion?

Not all activism manifest by Indian students and student organizations can be characterized as "indiscipline" or "unrest" which is so fully reported in the press.   That type is the most dramatic and attracts most attention.   It presents the greatest threat to the nation's stability and development, and dealing with it has high priority among university and government officials.   Before examining such events from the point of view of what, if anything, it is desired to accomplish, let us take note of other types of activism the objective of which is all but self-evident.   These are of four types: (a) on campus extracurricular cultural and educational activities, (b) participation in electoral activity, (c) participation in generating support for national defense, (d) activity in connection with an unquestionably critical national issue.

The organization and carrying through of orderly and useful extracurricular activities which provide students with conceivably valuable educational experiences receives little publicity in the press or in public discussion about the problems of higher education. Although on each of the forty campuses we visited few such examples of educationally or even recreationally meaningful activities were to be observed, in sum, over the whole of India such activities might possibly provide as great an outlet for student interests and energies as the more dramatic direct action affairs. For the kind of direct action which is so much in the public eye is not universal in all of the universities and colleges.   Discussion groups on public questions, lectures to students by prominent citizens, social get-togethers, projects of on-campus and off-campus social service, performance of musical, dance, and dramatic companies, collection of funds to improve the college library, cultural study groups, religious meetings, linguistic associations, literary societies, film societies, debating clubs, all are to be found in many campus communities, frequently sponsored by the same student unions and their leaders more widely known as the instigators of direct action, as well as by local groups organized for one such specific purpose.

The National Student Scheme launched by the government in January 1970 is expected to involve 40,000 students from 38 universities (200,000 by 1974) in various service projects, such as literacy campaigns, promotion of family planning, reductions of the stigma of untouchability, disaster relief, construction of school buildings, etc. While this plan was initiated in 1968 by the government as a compulsory National Service Corps alternative to the National Cadet Corps (military training), student opposition to its compulsory nature and to lack of student participation in its operation led to the present plan for a voluntary National Service Scheme in which students will participate as members of the administrative committees on the several campuses. Although such nation building "activism" as results from the operation of this scheme is not, properly speaking, a part of the student "movement", it has had the support of many student leaders, and could provide an outlet for idealistic energy, some of which would have become manifest in less constructive forms of student activism.

Since independence, India has held four general elections, the last in 1967. As students normally begin their university experience at 16, the large majority are too young to vote. But they are not too young to participate in election campaigns by doing campaign chores and taking part in political meetings and demonstrations. In 1967 older students actively campaigned in several states against Congress candidates. The disillusionment of youth with the elder statesmen of the Congress Party was alleged by a number of political observers to be an important ingredient in the setback suffered by that party.[4] Student voters under the age of 26 would have been only 5 years of age at the time many of the present Congress Party members were being hailed as heroes for their successful

[4]Although receiving 40% of the overall popular vote the party's numbers in the Lok Sabha were reduced from 364 to 273 (261 is a majority) and control over state legislatures was reduced from 17 to 8. Long time party leaders, including the president of the party and seven former cabinet members, were not returned.

challenge to English rule. The students of voting age we interviewed in India shared the disillusionment with the Congress Party leadership, almost to a man, and were looking forward to the election of 1967 as an opportunity to express their dissatisfaction through their vote and frequently through campaign activity.

It would, of course, be unwise to overemphasize the numerical weight of students in this campaign since so large a proportion are not of voting age, and since even the youth wings of the Congress and opposition parties, which involve, not primarily students, but all youth under 35 or so, are estimated to have an active membership of only about 2% of the electorate.

In recent years India has faced two national crises to which the student organizations have given attention.

In December 1962 the N.C.U.S.I. organized an All-India Student Convention on National Defense to discuss the nation's defense needs and what students could do in the face of the military assault of China on India's borders. They drew up a program of action for Indian university students, urging upon them the duty to volunteer for the armed forces. They also urged the modernization of military training of students in the National Cadet Corps. Students were challenged to take an active part in civil defense programs, and in voluntary social work in rural areas, particularly those along the border subject to direct Chinese threat.

Calling upon the traditions of pre-independence student activity, the convention declared:

Students, who played a heroic role in the struggle for independence, are once again called upon to defend our country's freedom. We in this Convention dedicate ourselves to the purpose of safeguarding the security of the nation at all costs.

They also took the opportunity to criticize the National Union of University Students (the leftist oriented dissenters from the N.C.U.S.I.) for its inaction in the crisis.

At the 1964 All-India Conference of the N.C.U.S.I., a resolution was adopted condemning the Chinese nuclear explosion. In a national student conference sponsored by this organization the next year the condemnation was repeated, the production of atomic weapons by India was favored, and a resolution was passed urging that anti-national political parties such as the pro-Chinese sector of the Communist Party should be banned.

In the confrontation of India and Pakistan over Kashmir in 1965, the N.C.U.S.I. asked the International Student Conference (Leiden), with which it is affiliated, to make a statement condemning Pakistan for starting the war.   Student newspapers and organizations promoted rallies and pledges of support for the Indian government.   Once again a national crisis focused the attention and activism of the students on an all-India issue.

One of the clearest examples of the participation of students in the struggle over an issue of national significance was the part they played in the language bill crisis, which from 1965 through 1967 agitated the nation and at times, in particular localities, verged on civil war.[5]   The issue is central both to Indian nation building and to the development of India's system of higher education.   Student activism in relation to the issue was not merely "unrest" or "indiscipline" but purposeful and well organized.   It is also an excellent example of the violent methods which frequently characterize Indian student activism.

We were present in India in 1965 at the beginning of that conflict and sensed the intensity of the concern both in the north and the south of the country.   Here was an issue which combined the interests of the country in all institutional and cultural areas with the very special concerns of the university community.   The question of a link language which would enable the universities all over India to profit from an exchange of personnel and their intellectual products was obviously important to the development of university facilities and intellectual growth.   Moveover the students looking forward to civil service examinations could not but anticipate the inequality of opportunities as between those whose native language was related to Hindi and those whose native language was not so related.

The original agitation against the elimination of English and the "imposition" of Hindi took place in the South and particularly in the Tamil language area of Madras.   The violence of the activity surprised many observers of student

[5]cf. Shah, B., (ed.), *The Great Debate: The Language Controversy and Higher Education*, Bombay: Lalvani, 1969.

affairs accustomed to think of the "more volatile" students
of north India as the chief instigators of student strikes and
riots.   Many could only declare that the students must have
been stirred to action by the D.M.K., the locally patriotic
political party.   Their agitation was no doubt influential,
but the students were not dependent on the D.M.K. for
stimulation.

An excellent short summary of the corresponding activity in
north India on the opposite side of the issue was reported in
News Features of the Institute for International Student Affairs
on December 19, 1967. Following is a part of that report.

> Students in many cities of India are embroiled in a bitter contro-
> versy over the Government's desire to maintain both Hindi and En-
> glish as official languages. Demonstrations first began at the Bana-
> ras Hindu University and as they rapidly spread to other university
> centers, so did violence and vandalism.
>
> The country's 1950 constitution stipulated that English would
> lose its official status on January 26, 1965, leaving Hindi as the
> sole "link" language for the country's 14 linguistic regions each of
> which has a different official language of its own. When the day
> came, violent rioting in the non-Hindi speaking southern part of
> India led the late Prime Minister Shastri to pledge a constitutional
> change.
>
> Last July it was decided to use the regional languages in higher
> education. Then, on November 27, the Government introduced in
> Parliament what sparked the current violence, the Official Lan-
> guages (Amendment) Bill. According to the provisions of the Bill,
> English is to be retained with Hindi as an official language on a
> national level until all of the constituent states of the country agree
> to drop it and all agree to accept Hindi.
>
> But Hindi-speaking Indians, about 40 per cent of the population
> mostly in the central and northern parts of the country, feel that the
> development, acceptance and use of their language on a national
> level will be retarded by the retention of English and therefore want
> it removed altogether from an official status at once.
>
> Even before the Bill was officially introduced, some 200 militant
> Banaras Hindu University students staged a demonstration against
> it on November 25. On November 28, students of the University ab-
> stained from classes and some 5,000 of them marched to the railway
> station and damaged its property, the reasoning being that to punish
> the railway would be to punish the Government, the "owner" of the
> national railways and the originator of the Bill.
>
> Government property—especially the railways—continued to bear
> the brunt of the students' ire. In Lucknow, on December 6, S. P.

Rana, President of the Lucknow University Students' Union, was arrested for holding up the Lucknow-Delhi mail train. On the same day, police tear-gassed a violent crowd at the railway station in Agra. On December 8, in Lucknow—where railway property had been damaged earlier—students set fire to three post offices, completely gutting one of them.

Delhi, India's national capital, was also hit by the agitation. A group of Delhi University students called for a strike to observe "Remove English Day." The Delhi University Students' Union (D.U.S.U.), however, disassociated itself from the strike move and appealed to students to desist from any agitational approach on the language issue and not to participate in the strike.

But on December 6, anti-English demonstrators went on a rampage tearing down or blacking out English shop nameboards and direction and other signboards, smashing neon advertising signs and otherwise violently proclaiming their opposition to the Government's Bill. For its anti-strike stand, D.U.S.U.'s office was ransacked and Union spokesmen claimed that all telephones were pulled out, newspapers and periodicals in the office's reading room burned and all furniture destroyed. On December 14 the University closed early for its winter vacation. It is scheduled to reopen on January 3.

Meanwhile, on December 12, Prime Minister Indira Gandhi denounced the violence and appealed for passage of the Bill. Mrs. Gandhi pointed to the need for India to have both a national "link" language, Hindi, and an international one, English: "We want our languages to progress. But there is also need for an international link. If we want English today, it is not because we want it to take the place of Hindi, Bengali, Tamil or other languages." It is a drawback in today's world, she continued, not to know at least one other foreign language and pointed to the example of the world's major powers which teach one or more foreign languages to their students. In the Soviet Union, Mrs. Gandhi asserted, most of the students selected English as their foreign language. The Prime Minister spoke in Hindi.

Student agitation and violence continued as on December 13 the lower house of Parliament approved the controversial Bill 224 votes to 75.

In a nation in which both the federal and state governments play so large a role in the planning and implementation of economic and social affairs and in seeking to structure university arrangements to meet the nation's manpower needs, and in which appropriations and personnel for the universities are so subject to political objectives, student action focused on correcting circumstances in the universities which they consider damaging to their interests can quite naturally take on the character of action directed at the government.

The violent upheaval at Osmania in October 1966 began when students joined in a faculty protest against the violations of the university's autonomy when a new Vice Chancellor was appointed against the wishes of the faculty.

In 1970 medical students joined with medical graduates, house surgeons, and interns in Tamilnad demanding a reduction in the number of admissions to the nation's medical colleges. Unemployment among medical graduates has become a serious problem. Sympathy strikes among medical students in other parts of the country followed. Government policy is involved in the establishment of medical colleges, in admissions, and in recruitment of doctors.

Almost any issue of concern to students relative to university governance, facilities, finance, policy, personnel appointment can quickly become one in which the government itself is the focus of student action.

The great majority of the activities which symbolize "student activism" in the public mind in India, however, are, at least apparently, stimulated by localized "causes". Edward Shils has portrayed a representative list of some of the incidents which spark such activism.[6]

> The lecture halls attended by Indian undergraduates and aspirants for the M.A. and LL.B. are often scenes of disorder—not always the organized rampageousness which attracts the worried attention of the President of the Republic, the Prime Minister, Governors and Chief Ministers of States, journalists, the University Grants Commission, Vice-Chancellors, Gandhian social workers, et al.—but the random individual disorder of shuffling feet, audible conversation, note-passing, and gestures of fearful bravado. Outside the lecture hall, but still within the academic compound, there are violently contested campaigns for election to office in the Student Union, tuggings to and fro, breathless denunciations, squabbles, scuffles, and even assassinations. "Student leaders" constantly present memorials to university and college authorities, regarding themselves as rulers of sovereign realms and as entitled to treat as equals or superiors with Deans and Vice-Chancellors. Closer to the public surface, and hence engaging wider attention, are the strikes, the screaming demonstrations, the banner-carrying processions and picketing, the hunger strikes, the physical combats with the police, the de-railing

[6]From *Turmoil and Transition*, edited by Philip G. Altbach, Basic Books, Inc., Publishers, New York, 1969.

of tramcars and overturning of buses, the smashing of furniture in examination halls, the cordons around the residence of the Vice-Chancellor, connivance with revolver journalists and local politicians, the organization of scandal-mongery against teachers and administrators, and physical assaults on teachers.

These drastic actions are undertaken on behalf of a variety of causes, many of which seem disproportionately slight in comparison with the passion and fashion of their espousal. The size of concessions on cinema or on bus, tram, or railway tickets; the refusal of university authorities to admit an unqualified person or the general admissions policy of the university; particular examination questions or the general severity of examination standards; the behaviour of a college porter or watchman; the alleged sexual conduct of teachers; the quality of food and service in college or university refectories; a statement by a teacher about the quality of an Indian poet; the fees to be paid by students; disciplinary measures taken by college or university authorities against particular students who have infringed a university or college rule; the conduct of the police in dealing with student demonstrations; the once projected Bihar-Bengal merger; the attachment of Bombay to Maharashtra—all and any of these can stir the students into remonstrances, slight or extreme. These are the pretexts for the outpouring of clamour and excitation. What actually makes the Indian student so responsive to these occasions, which are often grounds of reasonable grievance, is another matter. These are matters which lie more deeply in the nature of the present-day Indian university system, and the situation of the young male in present-day Indian society.

Stated Objectives

Have the organizations claiming, or ambitous for, national influence made any declaration of their objectives which could provide a framework for analyzing the activism which is so prominently labeled simply as student "unrest" or "indiscipline"? Two of them have.

The National Council of University Students of India (N.C. U.S.I.) declares in its constitution that its objectives are: (1) to maintain academic freedom and student rights; (2) to stimulate and improve democratic student union; (3) to promote better educational standards, facilities, and teaching methods; (4) to promote interuniversity student activities for the social, cultural, and educational advancement of the student community; (5) to represent Indian students on the national as well as the international plane. The Constitution further declares that the "N.C.U.S.I. shall be a nonpartisan body and shall work toward

the fulfillment of its aims and objects without reference to any
political or religious considerations."

The leftist oriented National Union of University Students of
India during its lifetime declared its objectives to be: (1) to safeguard the rights of the students of India; (2) to promote students' welfare and standards of education; (3) to prepare students for their tasks as free citizens; and (4) to build a better
world desirous of liberty, peace, and progress.

The Hindu communal influenced All-India Students Organization (Vidyarthi Parishad) could, to judge from the campus
programs it sponsors, agree with these very general objectives.
Interest in the perpetuation of and in extending the hold of
traditional Hindu culture and values could be inferred from
the educational efforts sponsored on a number of campuses by
this organization.

The differences in the purposes of these organizations would
become obvious only in the comparison of the operational content given to these highly generalized objectives. That these objectives are related to what takes place as a manifestation of
student activism should not be dismissed offhand because of
the unpredictability, variety, and seemingly ad hoc and imme-
diate-situation-related character of events which spark overt activity. Although the leader-stimulated or spontaneous action
may not have been launched for a stated reason clearly recognized by the instigators as deducible from the objectives set forth
above, it may be that such stated reasons nevertheless provide
the material for operational definitions of what is meant by at
least two of these objectives, namely:

> To meet the challenge to "academic freedom and student
> rights."
>
> To reduce the threat to students' welfare, to standards of
> education, to adequate facilities, and to teaching, or to job
> opportunities.

Perhaps the best way to approach this matter would be to describe the activity of Indian students reported in the press in
the years which saw such activity reaching a violent peak, 1966-
67. The *Hindustan Times* for February 12, 1968 contains the
following article entitled "Second Bad Year for Education."

The academic year 1967-68 will be remembered as one of the most
disturbed years in the recent past, a survey has revealed.

For several States such as West Bengal, Uttar Pradesh, Madhya Pradesh and Kerala, it was the second year of almost continuous disturbances.

. . . In some States during 1967-68 hardly a month has passed without students staying away on one pretext or another.

No cause was too small or unimportant for the agitators . . . . One Lucknow correspondent says that agitations have become more regular than convocations, for students have found that stones and slogans may get them degrees sooner than by burning the midnight oil.

The ring-leaders of agitations in U.P. have found that political leadership was the prize for successful agitators, and the size of the halo depended on how serious the confrontation with the arm of the law was—whether there was a lathi-charge, firing and some deaths.

According to a Rajasthan educationist, students never cared what place Hindi or English had in the national life; they only wanted their degrees without having to put in much effort.

In Madhya Pradesh discontented students campaigned against the the Congress candidates in the general elections and helped opposition parties to a great extent in routing the Congress.

In Madras the language issue provided the spark to many agitations. Just as in the north students tried to delay a parliamentary decision by brandishing the fire-brand, students in the South are trying to change the decision by the same method. Reports from Andhra Pradesh last week showed how rail services were being interfered with.

In Kerala, students some years ago went on a prolonged strike over a quarter-anna increase in ferry-boat fares, but strikes this year were prompted by food shortage. Closure of schools posed a problem for parents, for children at school needed only two meals; at home they asked for three.

In Delhi engineering students burned college property on the ground that their laboratories were ill-equipped. There have been riots on the ground that the city bus service was inadequate. The language issue proved inflammable, and there were some incidents of arson at the university. There was a strike in at least one college to press the demand that no student should be detained.

Maharashtra was the only State in which agitations did not disrupt academic life.

The number of working days lost varies from state to state, and each institution is trying to make up for the losses in its own way. Schools and colleges in Bengal and Rajasthan have cut their holidays. Madras and Kerala have postponed their examinations. U.P. has neither cut holidays nor postponed examinations. The argument appears to be that time lost can never be regained.

It is not possible to assess how much the agitations have prevented students from availing themselves of the new opportunities

in the field of education during the last 20 years, but at least one
Rajasthan educationist is uneasy over the fact that so many decisions, academic and other, are being taken under the threat of
agitations.

This statement of the situation in very generalized terms can
be made more specific by examining the daily reports of events
for a single month from the middle of September to the middle
of October 1966 in three States in North India, Uttar Pradesh,
Madhya Pradesh and Bihar, at least the part of the record
which is available in news published in the *Hindustan
Times, The Times of India,* and *The Statesman.*

In the news reports for this 30 day period there are recorded
68 incident-days on which newsworthy student action took
place in 38 different communities in these three states. Thirty-
three different reasons are alleged for these incidents. To what
extent can the alleged reasons be considered approximations
to operational definitions of the kinds of obstacles to realization of student objectives set forth above? The analysis
follows.

Challenge to academic freedom and student rights

> Express sympathy and support for demands of students at
>   another university (9 incidents)
> Protest against police brutality (8 incidents)
> Demand for release of arrested students
> Demand for judicial investigation of police brutality and
>   invasion of campus
> Protest against invasion of campus by police
> Protest killing of a student by police
> Charge that government is indifferent to student problems
> Charge of maladministration and harassment by Principal
> Objection to rustication of certain student leaders
> Demand for right to form a college union
> Demand for right to form an all-university union
> Observance of student "martyrs" day

Threat to student welfare, adequate education, etc.

> Demand for abolition of year's apprenticeship and Bar ex-

aminations for law students[7]

Demand for restoration to the Ayurvedic (traditional Indian medicine) students of the degree of M.B.B.S. (Bachelor of Medicine and Bachelor of Surgery) or making their degree of equivalent status

Objection to postponement of abolition of English

Protest against closing the university

Demand for better sports and library facilities

Demand for abandonment of American system of teaching and course examinations

Protest against alleged immoral conduct of a faculty member

Demand for dismissal of Vice Chancellor

Demand for change in type of examination

Resentment at delay in distribution of exam papers

Demand for more water taps

The other alleged reasons for incidents do not lend themselves to classification as logically related to any one of the declared objectives. They are as follows:

Resentment that businessmen and cinema owners refused to close up shop in support of a student strike

Failure of a newspaper to publish a statement submitted by students

Opposition to visit of Prime Minister Gandhi

Protest against showing of an atlas indicating parts of Kashmir in Pakistan

Protest against United States Vietnam action

Protest against change in train schedules

Dissatisfaction with performance of a dance troupe

Demand to hospital for delivery of the body of student killed by police

[7]If any initiating "reason" is to be assigned to the succeeding agitations here recorded, this objection by law students to the imposition on law graduates, by the so-called Advocates Act, of the requirement of a year's apprenticeship and of a bar examination, is it. The trouble apparently started at the University of Delhi, whose law students went on strike. Other students from neighboring states assembled in support of the Delhi action. These students continued the "action" in their own universities.

Protest against lateness of trains
Altercation of student with a shoeshine boy
Altercation of student with a taxi driver

There were no violent incidents during this particular month in these three states, the reasons for which would indicate the determination to realize the other declared objectives of the student organizations' ambitions to be all-India in character. The objectives "to prepare students for their tasks as free citizens," "to build a better world desirous of liberty, peace and progress" (with the possible exception of the protest against U.S. Vietnam action), "to stimulate and improve democratic student union," "to promote interuniversity student activities for social, cultural, and educational advancement of the student community" do not appear in the list of reported reasons for student activism at this time in this area.

It must be remembered, however, that not only is the data limited in time and place, but the data source was newspaper reports. These would naturally be biased in favor of what is considered "newsworthy." Activism designed to achieve these other declared objectives would for the most part take the form of local campus affairs, associations, and projects which, because of their peaceful and unexciting nature, do not provide the type of newspaper copy which sells newspapers. Leaders of the three major organizations with whom we spoke were most positive in declaring that such objectives were very much their concern. Even in the larger colleges, however, reported activities relevant to such objectives were not numerous. Nevertheless, on every one of the forty campuses we visted some such "extracurricular" activities which could be considered an implementation of these objectives had recently taken place or were planned for the near future.

It is possible, therefore, by viewing the cumulative character of many of the occasions and circumstances which spark direct action incidents, to infer objectives which students might believe were being advanced. But few of the *specific* causes have relevance to issues of general concern to the students all over India. Simultaneous local demonstrations, although uncoordinated on a national scale, have occasionally been widespread, those for example either for (in the north) or against (in the south) the elimination of English as a link language, those in support of a teachers' movement for higher wages, those expressing patriotic fervor for marshaling resources against the threatened Chinese invasion, those protesting corruption in the administration of government affairs (as in the case of Orissa where student demonstrations had an influence in forcing the resignation of the Chief Minister charged with corruption), those protesting the violation of university autonomy, those demanding stronger action against the movement of Pakistani troops into Kashmir, and strikes against tuition increases, and against limitations on entrance to the universities.

Particular actions conceivably having a negative impact on such a long range declared objective as improvements in the educational system were not, in our discussions with student leaders, however, evaluated in terms of such an impact. The tuition increases against which students struck, for example, were not appraised or criticized in terms of the relevance of increased revenues to the amplification of university facilities, or the need for greater economic rewards to attract better candidates into the academic profession. The limitation on numbers of entrants to the universities against which active criticism was leveled were not concerned with the negative impact on quality of the increasing number of students pressing upon already overextended educational resources.

Yet student leaders we met were aware that a viable student movement would have to focus its concern and its action on something of continuing importance to the academic and national community, something more substantial than the response to sporadic and unpredictable dissatisfactions of students in particular universities and colleges. Is it possible that the efforts to reach consensus on resolutions in national student conferences is a signal indicating the direction in which more substantial student concerns are moving?

It is dangerous to take the resolutions of a student convention or congress as an indication of the objectives or interests either of students generally or of the leadership of student organizations. Yet against the background of the often minor and petty "causes" of student unrest and the lack of consistent and meaningful, and nationally important, policy and practice of student organizations in the post World War II era, it is a ray of hope to observe what could be the beginning of such policy and practice.

In February of 1965 the N.C.U.S.I. in cooperation with the Delhi University student union, held a three day convention in which attention was given to matters of unquestioned national importance. Among the results in resolutions of that convention were the following:

On Education: The present system of higher education in India, based on the archaic British model, needs radical change. It needs to be changed to reduce the overemphasis on the humanities and the bureaucratic system of examinations. Teaching methods and curricula do not prepare students for effective roles in national development. The State should not only finance the facilities for higher education but the students as well. The language problem should be handled in a way which makes possible the mobility of students and teachers, and the prevention of the fractionalization of the talent for the development of the nation as a whole. Coeducation at all levels and more facilities for women in subjects like domestic science should be encouraged. The Government Education Commission should include student representatives.

National Politics: Favored were a policy of peaceful coexistence and the production of atomic weapons by India. The Chinese atomic bomb test was condemned. Anti-national political parties such as the pro-Chinese sector of the Communist Party should be banned.

Anti-Hindi riots in the South: Sympathy was expressed for the rebellious attitude of the Tamil-speaking students, but their acts of violence were deplored and their decision to call off the demonstrations applauded.

Student participation in politics: The students, it was declared, are inevitably involved in politics as voters and intellectuals concerned with the general problems of society.

Student Unions: The formation of student unions was declared essential and necessary and the Conference on Education proposal that membership be entirely voluntary was deplored. (Only about half of the Indian universities have student unions).

Social Changes: Students should contribute to slowing down population increase by taking a pledge against early marriage. They also should pledge themselves not to give or accept dowries. Students should contribute to achieving an ultimate goal of social equality by participating in N.C.U.S.I. organized literacy and adult education drives.

Representatives were present at this convention from only 17 of the 65 universities and 20 of the over 2000 colleges. The resolutions are not world shaking, but they point in the direction of student concern for national problems, both those concerning education and national life generally.

But one is not completely dependent on conference resolutions for indicators that demands which students seek to have satisfied through direct action are showing more definite focus on specific issues related to educational experiences. Recently the objectives of specific actions in a number of places appear to be directed toward modifications in the educational system and frequently toward the policies of state or federal government educational ministers and administrators, since matters of national educational policy are involved. The outstanding example, of course, is the demonstrations which took place over the question of elimination of English as a link language and designation of Hindi for that purpose and especially as the language used for civil service examinations. The year long strike of the Students of the Ayurvedic (traditional medicine) College in Lucknow to insist on the restoration of the M.B.B.S. (Bachelor of Medicine and Bachelor of Surgery) degree was another such example. The strikes of the law school students in Delhi and in Uttar Pardesh against the requirement of Bar examinations and a year's apprenticeship is another. In the Union Territory of Chandigarh, technical and engineering students went on strike to press for jobs for unemployed engineers and for a reduction in the seats in colleges so that the number would be in closer balance with the job opportunities available. Students in engineering and medical colleges in other parts of the country are being aroused to activism by this problem also. In Maharashtra, where student agitations have in recent years been mild or nonexistent, the convocation at Nagpur University was disrupted by demonstrations (in which some teachers joined). Demands included reduction of the minimum percentage marks required for passing examinations, and raising the eligibility limit for educational concessions. In Madhya Pradesh the location of a medical college provided an issue for demonstrations in several competing areas.

Student direct action, moreover, though often diffuse, sporadic, unplanned, and situation stimulated has had one result which future historians with the benefit of hindsight may point to as evidence that the students did act in pursuit of the major objective of improving their educational opportunuties. That activism has kept the problem of higher edu-

cation before the public and governmental authorities in a
negative sort of way, and has led to the appointment of
numerous task forces and commissions, and to widespread
soul-searching by intellectuals, particularly those associated
with the universities and the press, as to "what is wrong with
the educational system." That is of course a necessary, though
not sufficient, move in the process of improvement. In the
past there has been little indication that this possible impact
of student activism has, however, been the conscious and
avowed objective of student leaders and their political and
communal supporters, or that their choice of strategy and
tactics has been shaped and evaluated in accordance with
the greatest possibility for making this objective realizable.

Kinds of Action

The same news reports from which the foregoing generalizations about the objectives of student action were derived can
be analyzed to give an indicaton of the range of tactics
employed. Again we must warn that direct action is not the
only manifestation of student activism. Yet it is the direct
action which is the cause of public concern and the best
indicator of serious and frustrating inadequacies in the conduct of educational affairs. A listing of the kinds of action
carried on in the period and places already referred to reveals
how serious the problem is.

Non-violent expression
   Orderly demonstration before relevant government office or
   court
   Hunger strike, individual and group
   Torchlight procession

*Actions primarily designed to generate student enthusiasm for
action*
   Mass meeting
   Circulation of inflammatory leaflets
   Calls for united action

Orthodox efforts to influence official action
   Deputation of student leaders to university or government
   administrators
   Resolutions sent to legislature condemning police brutality
   and demanding an investigation

Resolution demanding resignation of Vice Chancellor
Resolution demanding resignation of state ministers, including Chief Minister
Visit of student leaders to State Chief Minister and Educational Minister
Delegation to Federal Prime Minister

Unorthodox attacks on university and government officials
Burning of university and government officials in effigy
Heckling of Prime Minister at meeting
Breaking into compound of state legislature
Confining the Vice Chancellor to his home and then to the campus

Actions of spontaneous anger related to student affairs
Abstain from going to classes
Boycott of library
Walk out from examinations

Acts of vandalism
Destruction of college flowerbeds
Set fire to buses
Cut telephone wires
Loot shops[8]
Stone shops and cinema
Damage railroad property, including cars
Hold up trains (because late) by pulling emergency brake cord
Stone buses
Set fire to college and municipal records
Turn over several taxicabs
Raid office of newspaper and damage press
Raid cobbler's shop

Action against police
Deliberate flaunting of Section 144 (which prohibits, when

[8]Sarkar reports in *The Unquiet Campus* that "the townspeople's image of the student in the mass is also interesting. Shopkeepers, cinema proprietors, and newspaper officers have learned through painful experience that it is wise to keep in their (the students') good graces because arson, assault, and rioting can be as likely as hunger strikes. There is no end to the variety of such images one encounters in Lucknow and Allahabad. The only thing common to them is that they are all depressing and far removed from what images in a university should be, and they make it difficult for a real university to emerge."

invoked, the assembly of more than five persons)
Stone and brick battle with police
Mobbing local police station
Set fire to police station

Actions in the first three categories with the exception of
hunger strikes are likely to be planned and organized by
leaders of the local student union or council.   The rest are
more likely to be spontaneous outbursts which frequently run
amuck without much organized direction.   Students leaders
at local, state, and national levels, however, frequently attempt
to extend the scope of the activity.   For example, in the month
under consideration here, the following broadening of the
scope and field of action was carried out.   Such actions were
taken primarily by leaders of the A.I.S.F. but also in some
cases by leaders of the N.C.U.S.I.

> Call for complete strike of all business houses in the city in sup-
> port of a student strike
> State student action committee calls on unions in all colleges in
> the State to carry on daily strikes and demonstrations in support of
> Lucknow students and advocates meeting violence with violence
> Local Branch of the All-India Student Federation (A.I.S.F.) warns
> municipal authorities not to provoke students by invoking Section
> 144
> National A.I.S.F. issues a call for students all over India to ob-
> serve a "National Day of Solidarity" with students in Uttar Pradesh
> with strikes and demonstrations
> National A.I.S.F. officers visit Chief Minister and Education Min-
> ister asking for inquiry into police handling of the direct action
> National Council of University Students of India issues a call for
> a national meeting of students to discuss the situation
> Representatives of the several all-India organizations send delega-
> tion to the Home Minister in Delhi with a series of demands for cor-
> rective action

There is apparent in these actions a minimum of rational
or logical relation of specific means to declared specific ends.
What then justifies such actions in the minds of leaders and
students generally? It is simply that such means are the only
ones that get results. It is the all but universal experience of
student leaders whom we interviewed that neither university
authorities nor government officials paid much attention to
student protests or suggestions unless a disturbance disruptive
of university or public order was launched.

Moreover, it is clear to these leaders that a substantial number of students agree that such direct action is necessary and that they can count on the approval of that action by a sufficient number to mount an attention getting demonstration or strike.   A well designed and carefully analyzed survey conducted under the direction of David Bayley in 1965-66 underscores the correctness of the leaders' perception.[9]

The attitude toward strikes and demonstrations revealed by the student replies to the Bayley questionnaire goes far to suggest why it is so easy to generate such activism on the campuses on which the survey was conducted.   The attitudes on the four campuses varied, and it is dangerous to consolidate the results into a single conclusion.   But even the lowest proportions on the individual campuses who responded in a way indicating the probability of support for, if not participation in, such activism would suggest a substantial student population readied for recruitment to action.

To the question, "Do you think public demonstrations are or are not a useful way of getting authorities to do the right things or to correct some wrong?"   58% responded "Useful" (range 42% to 69%).   To the question, "Are student agitations necessary in order to get university/college authorities to take notice of student grievances and needs?"   57% responded, "Yes" (range 41% to 66%).   To the question, "Are student strikes a proper means of putting pressure on university/college authorities?"   45% responded, "Yes" (range 32% to 57%).   Moreover, a substantial proportion of the students judged the demonstrations they were aware of in their own university to be stimulated by real and serious, rather than by artificial concerns, the overall proportion being 55% (range, 29% to 68%).   Nevertheless, the students were not uncritical of the use of direct action, 47% (range 41% to 50%) responding that they felt this form of protest was used too often or frivolously. Their judgment of the readiness of their student

[9]The Institute of Public Opinion in India conducted a survey for Bayley involving the questioning of 2,400 citizens generally and 1,200 students in 4 universities (Osmania, Bangalore, Allahabad, and Delhi). The questions for the students included several relevant to their appraisal of direct action as an effective means of meeting their needs and seeking redress of their grievances.   Bayley, David H., *The Police and Political Development in India*, Princeton, 1969, pp. 331 ff.

peers generally to participate in demonstrations contrasts with
their own declared extent of participation.   57% (range 52%
to 63%) felt that students generally were eager to participate.
Yet 76% (range 63% to 81%) had never participated in a demonstration or a strike.   5% had participated in both, 11%
(range 6% to 23%) in a strike only, and 9% (range 5% to 12%)
in a demonstration only.[10]

Public Reaction

As far as could be judged from the editorials in the English
language press and journals, and from discussions with leaders in academic, industrial, and public life, the reaction to
student activism of the kind here recorded is one of outrage
against "student indiscipline" coupled with frequent observations that the system, or lack of system, of higher education
itself is to blame.   Nevertheless, there is little sympathy expressed, by those who have access to facilities for expression,
for what appears to most commentators to be an irrational
and restless rebelliousness of students.

Those responsible for public order on the university campus and in the community are faced with what appears to
them as mob action and mob psychology, and they react
accordingly.   Charges of police brutality come not only from
the students but from leading citizens, and (with possibly
an eye to political advantage) from members of opposition
parties.

However necessary the methods used by the police may seem
to be in the light of the violent and undisciplined action of students, they are bound to be the basis of additional protests, as
they are in every country where mass direct action is employed
as a tactic of student or popular expression. The record of the
events in the three states in the period in 1966 referred to above
discloses the following number of occasions on which the
police used the following methods:

Cane charges	9 cases
Tear gas	7 cases
Firearms	8 cases

[10]Incidentally the proportion of students participating in demonstrations was not significantly larger than the proportion of the public
generally. As Bayley remarks, "This evidence supports the view that
demonstrational politics is not peculiar to students but is part of a society wide pattern of political behavior".

Breaking down main college gate with a heavy truck	1 case
Invasion of dormitories	4 cases
Beating of faculty members	2 cases

The student activism whose character we have been discussing also stimulated action outside the university community. On several occasions it was reported that there were more "townies" and loiterers involved in the melee than students, a circumstance underscored by the fact that in those cases three to four times more of these persons than of students were arrested.

On one occasion in Kanpur it was reported that 10,000 citizens of the community marched in a demonstration protesting the police brutality characterizing the handling of a student demonstration.

College officials' action to discipline individual students, if any, was not reported in the papers. What was reported, however, were 12 occasions on which the colleges were closed for periods ranging from two weeks to the rest of the term.

Government officials at the local level had a problem of maintaining public order. On 8 occasions they invoked Section 144 which prohibits the assembly of more than 5 persons. They called on several occasions for assistance from the state armed constabulary. In one town the officials themselves launched an investigation into police brutality. Two State cabinets called special meetings to discuss the causes of student unrest. The Chief Minister visited two campuses to appeal to the students for the restoration of order. The Prime Minister likewise visited a campus and made the same appeal. Several chiefs of police issued statements blaming the communists for the unrest and violence. A District Magistrate issued a statement blaming the political parties for the problem. High level federal officials met in Delhi and appointed a commission to study the causes of student indiscipline. The home Minister met with the Inspectors General of the police. He also received a delegation of students representing the several all-India and local student organizations involved[11] who demanded the release of all students who had been arrested

[11]Organizations included Delhi Student Union, the Allahabad Student Union (SSP controlled), the Socialist Party (SSP) Youth League, The All-India Youth Federation (communist controlled).

during the month (reportedly nearly 200), and the appointment of a national commission to investigate the causes of
student unrest, one-fourth of this commission to be composed
of students.

There were numerous occasions on which politicians got
into the act, a matter which will be discussed below.

Leadership

During the period of investigation in India, we were able to
confer with 55 student officers of student organizations both local and national. The majority were young men (and two young
women) of considerable energy and self-assurance compared
with other students we met. They were all competent in self-
expression. In only 10 cases did it seem that they were superior,
critical, analytical thinkers when the nature of India's problems
was under discussion or, for that matter, when the subject was
the problems faced by students and the educational system of
India. For the most part, aside from the ten exceptions, they appeared to think in cliches. Their thoughts about and appraisal
of the experiences and problems of students will be discussed in
a later chapter. Those who had some comprehension of the
problems of India and Indian universities were deeply and, we
think, genuinely troubled, pessimistic, and resigned to the difficulty if not impossibility of doing much about those problems. They were most cynical about the corruption of their elders in public life and they acknowledged no heroes among the
nation's leaders.

Nor could we sense any consensus about the role which the
organizations they led should play either in the life of the
university or in the life of India. Their personal role was
usually defined as a "spokesman" for the students. Some few
considered that those organizations could add power to their
spokesmanship, but aside from the possibility of stimulating
a demonstration in support of some of their demands, there
was little conception of how that could be done. Any drawing up of demands, any presentation to and negotiation with
the university authorities (or, in some cases, government
officials) and, in case coercion was deemed necessary, the
arousal of excitement among and participation of large
numbers of students, all are functions which were, in their
view, the task of the leaders, and their immediately associated
henchmen. The objectives of their leadership did not include

making the student association a training ground in democratic procedures for the rank and file.

The number seeking office in the unions varied greatly on the 40 college campuses visited. On four campuses no election had been held for lack of a single candidate to replace those who had graduated. On two campuses we were present on election day, and were handed 20 and 25 name cards respectively, which were the only kind of election propaganda permitted by the college administrators. On four campuses the present leaders reported that becoming elected had been very expensive due to the campaign events and the parties that they had had to conduct in order to meet the competition of such campaign tactics on the part of opposing candidates. Two of these admitted that financial support had come, by an indirect route, from party "sympathizers," in the one case from Communist, in the other case from Congress Party sources.

The reported dividends to successful candidates from the attainment of official leadership are also varied. The sample of 55 leaders on 40 campuses is far too small for safe generalization, but an impression may be recorded as suggestive of the personal advantages associated with that leadership. Six, or 11%, were obviously hopeful that their position would be a way of attracting the attention of political leaders who could pave their way to a political career.[12] Ten others, or 19%, mentioned the opportunity they would have to marshal recruits for participation in celebrations arranged by party leaders for political purposes, and hoped that this cooperation might pay off in "recommendations" for a government job when they graduated. None suggested the opportunity for cooperation with political leaders in support of those leaders' attempts to involve themselves in internal college affairs. A few suggested indirectly, though none explicitly mentioned it, the chance to win friends by virtue of their power to suggest who should be members of delegations,

[12]Contemporary ideas of success in life are heavily influenced by the importance of politics in Indian life. The student can observe many examples of apparent success not based on moral or intellectual attainments. The University Grants Commission in its *Report on the Problem of Indiscipline in Indian Universities*, 1960, says (p. 5) "The politician has tended to become the successful man par excellence because of the prominence he seems to have in public life. Teachers and students, therefore, try to become politicians in their own situations."

appointees to committees and to on-and-off-campus student consultative groups, the recipients of travel grants, etc. The rest, and indeed those already mentioned, appeared to enjoy the prospects of having a task of "student representation" to carry on in a college environment in which few other opportunities are offered for students to have a voice in the management of their own non-academic affairs. Six of these suggested that the activities of their office provided at least a release from the tedium and boredom of their directly educational experience.

The student leaders gave the impression of greater maturity than most of the students we met, but we did not meet any of the "professional eternal students" which some observers have referred to.[13]

External Influences

Anyone familiar with the part played from the begining in India by political parties in sponsoring, supporting, and utilizing youth and student congresses and organizations will not be surprised that most commentators allege that one of the chief reasons for student indiscipline in India is interference in student affairs by politicians. A glance at the record set forth on pages 77ff. above will indicate that every political party has had such a close connection with student organizations and that even the effort to establish "non-political" or "politically neutral" organizations, independent of their status as party appendages, has been sponsored by the parties themselves. The declarations of intent by party leaders to abstain from interfering in student affairs have a hollow ring when announced to those, including students, who are aware of the historical and present-day facts.

It is difficult to understand how any political party interested in the accumulation of the power to rule India (and this includes all of those named) could refuse to interest itself in gaining the support of those most likely to assume public leadership in the future, in marshaling the collaboration of one of the few numerically large groups in close enough personal

[13]The University Grants Committee in the report referred to above says (p. 10), "Usually office bearers. . . are senior students, . . . in the university for 4 or 5 years, but in certain universities there are some union leaders wo have stayed on 9 years or even longer."

association to make organized action at least possible, and in seeking the commitment of individuals from one of the few identifiable groups with the kind of education and training, and, hopefully, the idealism, needed for the transformation of India from an agrarian feudal country into a modern industrialized state.

Given this interest of the responsible party leadership in this entirely legitimate objective, it should surprise no one that those leaders welcome the opportunity to present their views to students from the platform provided by the student unions, that they have their eyes on, and support directly or indirectly the candidacy of, certain seekers of office in student unions, that they seek the organization of mass student participation for political meetings and in the celebrations of anniversaries and of the birthday festivities for prominent national or local politicians, and welcome any interest students show in doing political chores during election campaigns, and that politicians on occasion champion the students' interests.

Relations between the interests of students and politicians are natural in a country in which government plays a large role in the affairs of the universities. Among the areas of political activity in India is the management of the state supported universities and colleges, a management which has an impact on the laws under which the universities and colleges operate, on university finances and facilities, and which includes the appointment, not independent of a political spoils system, of members of the governing boards of the universities and of the vice chancellors, who correspond to the presidents of American universities. There have been numerous occasions reported in which political factions, engaged in backroom maneuverings for achievement of their purposes in such university focused activity, have found the stimulation or encouragement of student demonstrations for or against a particular policy or candidate a useful addition to their personal and functional bargaining power.

Such marshaling of student activism is also present in political moves which are related to student interests but which touch upon issues which are of much wider import. Examples are the demonstrations encouraged in the south against the elimination of English as a link language, and the student support sought by the Congress Party for opposition to certain educational policies of the communist dominated government in Kerala, and indeed for the replacement of that government. What started as a student protest in Orissa against alleged corruption on the part of government officials, and alleged police brutality rapidly developed into a full scale political struggle involving charges that Congress Party dissidents were behind the whole affair and an investigation of the conduct in office of the Chief Minister and his cabinet.

The account of the month's events in North India recorded on pages 94ff. above suggests how minority parties are alert to utilize what they charge is mismanagement of university and student affairs by public authorities associated with the ruling Congress Party, as a basis for political embarrassment of that party and its leadership.

With such an interest of political leaders in university student activities from the point of view of party advantage providing them with an assumption that the campus is a "legitimate" operational field for politically motivated action, it is to be anticipated that such leaders, and lesser politicians as well, will, from time to time, exert personal pressure on university administrations in matters of faculty appointments, promotions, and student admissions or expulsions, and other "internal" university affairs. On occasion student demonstrations can aid such personal objectives.

The situation is anomalous in one respect. In the light of such obvious interest by the politicians in, and the manifestation of their involvement in, association with student affairs, it is strange that the large and important issues bearing on the stability and progress of Indian society, political issues in the most fundamental way, are very infrequently the issues upon which student activism focuses.

Relationship of the Communist Party to Student Activism

The communist influence in the Indian student movement has been concentrated and localized rather than widely pervasive. It has been strong in those areas, particularly in and around Calcutta and in Kerala where the Indian Communist Party is strong. But in other parts of the country the party leaders have faced difficulties and have had limited and intermittent success in developing a strong cadre of youthful leaders able to exert a distinctly communist influence in campus politics, or in stirring the intellectual and emotional enthusiasm of students.

Several reasons can be suggested for this. In the first place the ideological orientation of Communism with its materialistic interpretation of cultural development runs counter to the thoughtways generated by traditional Hindu and Moslem philosophy and religion for those who have had little contact with Western rationalism. Those who have had such contacts, those who for example have been educated abroad, particularly in England, have in many cases been attracted by the Fabian brand of Socialism, but it is an attraction which is not grounded on philosophical premises but on the anticipated pragmatic advantages of that type of economic organization.

In the second place, India has had its own kind of revolution, resembling more that of the United States than that of either Russia or China. Communist theorists starting with a theory which posits a class struggle between an industrial working class and a bourgeois capitalist class have had to wrestle with adapting it to the revolutionary possibilities in underdeveloped agrarian and formerly colonial countries. The time may come when that ideological *tour de force* will have been sufficiently achieved to reduce the intraparty conflicts as to what is the true orthodoxy. The time may come when India's industrial development will have produced the possibility of a working class-bourgeoisie confrontation in traditional Marxist style. That time has not yet arrived. In the meantime the leaders of the Congress Party, and particularly Nehru, early committed India's future to Socialism, which makes difficult the winning of converts by the communists on the basis of their promise to introduce the blessings of socialism as a relief from the exploitation and misery associated, in their doctrine, with capitalism.

Lenin's development of Marxist theory with respect to imperialism might have provided some ideological energy for the drive for independence in the 20's and 30's. But the communists put themselves in the enemy's camp for those committed to India's "revolution" when, during World War II, they refused to join the independence promoting nationalists and instead supported the war efforts of England, against whose "imperialism" the Indian nationalists were marshaling their forces. To some extent, the same impression of confusion about the meaning of imperialism was created in their lack of anti-imperialism fervor (to say the least) in the face of the Chinese Communist offensive on the borders of India in the 1960's.

A further difficulty faced by the communists in a situation in which they are in a minority is that the "boring from within" tactics, potentially effective in such cases, are hampered by the schismatic tendencies which characterize many attempts of Indians at social and political organization. When factions develop within a group pragmatically brought together by an apparently common interest, the tendency is for the dissatisfied faction to disaffiliate. This tendency has been obvious in efforts at student organization on the national level, and there is some evidence it has been present in local situations as well. When communists and noncommunists could not agree, or when one faction lost control of the student organization, each went its own way, and the chance to "bore from within" was sacrificed on the altar of separatist purity of principle. Examples of this tendency will be recalled from the account of the development of student organizations set forth above.

Nevertheless, left wing, if not communist influence has been present since 1920. The chief impetus for the student conferences in the twenties came from left wing Congress men. Socialism provided a propaganda line competing with and at times more appealing than Gandhiism. Communist fellow travelers, stimulated by the Russian revolution were active in campus affairs, their revolutionary predispositions not practically incompatible at the time with the developing nationalist enthusiasms.

The first link of a student group with international Communism was forged when the Congress Seba Dal, originally designed as a politically neutral student organization, affiliated with the Moscow dominated [international] League Against Imperialism in 1928. In 1936, the All-India Student Federation was launched as another national student organization presumably independent of political affiliation, but the organization came increasingly under the domination of activist leftist members, among them communists. In 1940, as reported above, the refusal of the communists to compromise with the nationalistically oriented members on the issue of supporting England in World War II caused the nationalists to withdraw from the organization and form one of their own. The communists were never displaced in their control of the All-India Student Federation. It remains to this day the basic organized instrument of communist influence among Indian students. Although its membership figures have never been published officially it was estimated to have around 5,000 members in

1962. It joined in the attempt by Congress leaders to launch a National Union of Students in 1961, but soon withdrew its support. As an organization among students, the A.I.S.F., it appears, is strongly influential in only two areas of India (Bengal and Kerala) where Communist Party organization is strong.

In India as in other nations the communist influence is fractionalized by the fractionalization of the communist movement itself. There are two formally organized Communist Parties in India, oriented toward the Moscow and Peking party lines respectively, and a group of revolutionary extremists, or "Naxalites". But the involvement of all factions in the students' activism is less an effort to incorporate the students as participants in a domestic or international organized movement to overthrow capitalism and imperialism, than it is the effort to amplify the general unrest, which is a situation favorable to their revolutionary ambitions, or to embarrass the governing Establishment or to demonstrate their support of students in the student initiated efforts to get a satisfactory redress of the grievances which they raise against the educational and governmental Establishment.

While politicians from all opposition parties, including the Communists, as well as those from the Congress Party, have been instigators of student activism on occasion, their role in the great majority of cases has been to "join in" student activism, generated by practical local student grievances, for their own advantage.

Chapter 3
Student Activism in Mexico
and Colombia

The University Reform Movement, launched in 1918 in
Córdoba, Argentina, is usually considered to be the beginning
of student political activity in South American universities,
although sporadic student association and political activity
goes back to the end of colonialism. The resolutions, passed
by the Córdoba students and sent to the Minister of Education, were appropriately directed at grievances related to the
structure and operations of the university. Inadequate educational facilities, poor teaching, authoritarian university government, restrictions on free inquiry, dogmatism, rote learning,
lack of a stimulating and challenging educational experience,
interference from governmental and religious powers, the failure of the university to contribute to the development of a
national cultural identity, these were the foci of agitation for
changes in the university.

The bill of grievances against the university and those who
controlled the university was to become no more important
as a charter for the student movement in coming years than
the vision of the role of the universities set forth in the
Message to Latin American Youth, by Alfredo L. Palacios
which was distributed simultaneously with, and as widely as,
the manifesto itself. That vision furnished succeeding generations of Latin American students with a justification for their
activism that gave an idealistic tone to their initiative. The
changes sought by Palacios were not merely pragmatic modifications in the details of university organization and operations, but a radical transformation in the very nature and
mission of the universities. The university which had experienced such a transformation would be the producer not of
degrees, but of men, a center of creative thinking and spiritual
power. The emphasis in its teaching would be on modern
ideologies and on knowledge relevant to current social problems. Its benefits would extend not only to the *universitarios*

116

but to the masses, and it would establish "solidarity with the soul of the people." It would contribute to a new culture in harmony with the ideals of the Latin race and to the spiritual solidarity of the Latin American people. It would become a political force, even pursuing revolutionary aims. In the framework of student experience provided by such a university, student political activism would be significant and appropriate. Such a concept of the nature and mission of the university was to be proclaimed over and over again to justify a wide variety of student activism as consistent with the high and noble purpose of a university and its students.

The students urged that university reform be made possible by freeing the universities from outside influences and making them truly autonomous, that is, subject solely to the governance of their own administrators, faculty members, and students. The autonomous universities were to be not simply the trainers of professionals, but the active centers for making clearer and firmer among the people the sense of national (and Latin American) identity and culture.

When the granting of their demands was slow, the Córdoba students seized the university, shut the gates, and elected students as Directors of the Schools of Law, Engineering, and Medicine. The government granted by decree their demands for a student and graduate voice in university affairs, optional attendance at classes, periodic renewal of professorships, financial assistance to students, and the independence of the university in determining what was to be taught.

The impact of the Córdoba manifesto and of the students' tactics and victory on the students of other Latin American countries varied. The themes of university reform, university autonomy, student participation in the governance of the university, the role of the university as an instigator of national and continental identity and of social and political change were brought to the attention of student representatives from all Latin American Universities in the first Latin American Student Conference, in Mexico in 1921. Resolutions there adopted included the following:

Establishment of a broader social basis for student admissions

No qualifications for admission except completion of a secondary school

Students to be free to attend lectures of their choice

Students to be graded solely on the results of examinations

The selection of professors on the basis of open competition and periodic review of their qualifications

Students to have the right to repeat a course as often as they wished until they passed the examination

Direct participation of students in the administration of the university to be institutionalized

The Universities to be guaranteed autonomy in the conduct of their own affairs

Eloquent and impassioned speeches were made at the Conference urging that the universities be the instruments of social and political change responsible to the needs of society, and that the *universitarios* become the vanguard of those committed to the development of a sense of cultural community among Latin Americans.

The emphases which have survived as a continuing influence on student activism in Mexico and Colombia are:

The demand for university autonomy

The demand for student participation in the governance of the universities

The drive to politicize the universities as instruments of social and political reform, and the involvement of students in serving as the agents of that reform

The *universitarios* as promotors of national independence and of Latin American unity

The stimulus to student activism from Córdoba and from the South American Student Conference was felt in both Mexico and Colombia, but the two countries were in different stages of their economic, social, and political evolution in 1921. The differences affected the way in which the Córdoba-generated objectives and tactics entered into the traditions of the student movements in those two countries.

Mexico by 1918 had had its revolution (1910) and a new constitution (1917) providing formally the framework for a structure of republican representative governance. Moreover, university youth needed no stimulus from Córdoba to suggest their potential as agents of societal change. The first National Student Congress in Mexico was held in 1910 when the National University, after having been closed since 1858, was reopened. That was just two months before the outbreak of the revolution. Many of the objectives of the revolution were debated and articulated in the student congresses and meetings of this period. The prestige of the university students was high. In fact between 1916 and 1920, the Mexican government appointed student attachés to all its embassies and delegations abroad.

After the consolidation of the revolution and the adoption of the constitution in 1917, and the later move toward nationalization of basic resources and toward giving workers some voice in the affairs of the companies exploiting those resources, and toward making systematic the voice of important economic and social groups in the political structure of the country, the students continued to consider themselves as militant guardians of the Constitution, supporters of the "continuing revolution," and the promoters and defenders of the freedom of the universities from outside interference. And no group in the nation has supported more enthusiastically than the students the efforts of Mexican leaders to develop a national identity and independence. They could be expected to be in the forefront of any public reaction against the infringement of that independence from Europe or from the "colossus of the North", the United States.

The traditions inherited from their predecessors by today's Mexican students, then, suggest the legitimacy of their concern and actions not only with respect to autonomy in the governance of their universities, but with respect to participation in the political affairs of the nation. Yet until recently this concern has not become manifest in major open confrontations with political leaders or the public authorities over matters of national policy or practice save as these affected the affairs of the universities.

On the whole, however, the students were followers rather than instigators. There is, for example, no powerful political figure in Mexico's history whose career began as a leader of student activism in public affairs. Thus, present day Mexican students lack personal symbols to stand for a traditional involvement of students in activism in the political sphere.

Present day student leaders with whom we talked in Mexico, however, asserted that students generally considered themselves the *avant-garde* of the defenders of those objectives of continuing revolution emphasizing concerns for the welfare of all Mexicans and their fuller enjoyment of the economic and social benefits made possible by a modernized and politically stable Mexico. They also considered themselves among the most continuous and consistent critics of political leaders for their failure to move more rapidly toward translating those concerns into realities of life for people throughout the land, and of the self-serving of political leaders in the conduct of their public offices. Such assertions may reflect a mythology, but, if so, it is a mythology which is beginning to surface and manifest itself in a cynicism concerning the dedication of present day political leaders to bringing out into life the proclaimed human and social objectives of the revolution.

The stimulus of the Córdoba manifesto came to the Colombian students in a period when the political and economic control of the Conservatives among the nation's elite, who had dominated the country's affairs since 1886, was being subjected to increasing challenge. Colombia was not well developed economically and socially. Its economy reflected the predominance of agriculture and the primarily rural and local-culture-focused character of the people. World War I and the associated changes in world trade and communications brought Colombia under the influences from a wider world through expansion of its markets and the increasing entrance of foreign capital into its economic life. At the same time, the influence of foreign ideologies, both socialist and liberal, made themselves felt among the young intellectuals. The influence of the revolutions in Mexico and Russia was felt in intellectual and political circles. But the Conservatives among the elite, with their sources of strength in the church, the army, the landlords, and the tradition-predisposed *campesinos* were firmly in power. The Liberals among the political activists who were increasingly to seek a base of power in the functional groups whose orientation was toward the urban, industrial, business culture developing as an accompaniment of modernization, were also of the traditional elite. If they had revolutionary ideas, they were those related to a "palace revolution." In the 20's both the Socialist and the Communist Parties were formed though they were practically effective chiefly in the introduction of ideas challenging to the control of the oligarchs. The political arrangements offered opposition parties little chance for affecting the nation's affairs save through agitation and revolution. Among the common people a deep unrest was becoming manifest, breaking out into the open in peasant uprisings in the banana areas against the United Fruit Company, which had to be put down by the army, and in numerous strikes among workers in the urban centers.

The turmoil was sufficiently disturbing to the ruling elite so that both traditional parties joined in electing a coalition candidate Olaya Herrara in 1930, and in 1934 a Liberal candidate, Alfonso Lopez.

It was in this period of social and political unrest that student activism, at least as an organized movement, became highly visible. Students from Colombia attended the Latin American Student Conference in Mexico in 1921, and in 1923 the first National Student Congress was held, followed by a second National Congress in 1924. It is difficult to know to what degree the tenor and direction of these Congresses reflected the state of mind and predispositions of Latin American students as a whole. Resolutions were debated and passed mirroring the Córdoba manifesto having to do with the reform of the universities, but young intellectuals, who were later to become influential politicians, introduced statements relative to wider societal affairs, some with a positively revolutionary flavor. In the third National Congress held in 1928, resolutions were debated concerning distinctly political issues focused on societal reforms, including those which would give a broader social class base to opportunity, promote the ideological liberation of women, and move toward the nationalization of natural resources.

Colombian students, particularly in Bogatá, participated in, and some say spearheaded, demonstrations protesting the inability of the government and the ruling oligarchy to deal with economic problems and the economic distress of the common people, and to cope with what they contended was increasing economic imperialism from foreign, chiefly American, companies. These demonstrations brought the participants into

confrontation with the police and produced at least one
"martyr," a law student whose death is considered and com-
memorated as a "symbol of the struggles for the transformation of the state." The eventually enacted University reform
bill in 1935, during the administration of President Alfonso
López, seems not to have been passed, however, as a result
of pressure from students. Nevertheless, it provided for token
representation of two elected students on the Directive Council
(of nine members) of the National University of Colombia.[1]

From the beginning of an organized movement in the early
1920's, therefore, it can be said that student activism in
Colombia has been influenced by those who sought to direct
its impact toward political reform if not revolution, and that
students have been involved in demonstrations seeking to make
that impact practically effective.

Stimulus to and Nature of Activism

The kind of student protest activism which attracts greatest
public attention and concern is direct action in the form of
strikes, demonstrations, occupation of buildings, riots, etc.
Actually, however, to judge from the record of student activism
in Mexico and Colombia, a far greater amount of time if not
energy is devoted to less dramatic manifestations of protest,
manifestations which arouse less anxiety among authorities
and less interest from the news media. When one is in contact
with campus life in these countries over a period, he experiences now and then, an on-campus mass gathering, normally
peaceful, to advertise the students' reactions to some university
policy, or some policy or action of a foreign government,
ordinarily the United States (Bay of Pigs, Dominican Republic,
Vietnam war, etc.). Unless these spill over into the streets, they
are unlikely to be reported in the press and their regulation
and control is in the hands of the University authorities. Every
day one is aware of a constantly changing set of posters, open
letters, etc. posted on the bulletin boards or the walls proclaiming the position of one faction or another on some cam-

---

[1]The members of the directive council: Minister of National Education
(as President of the Council), the University Rector (as Vice-President),
two representatives of the national government, a representative elected
by the Deans of the Schools and Faculties, two representatives elected
by the professors, and two elected by the students.

pus or national or international issue. If he sits in the entry room to the office of the Dean of Students or other university officials, he is aware of a succession of delegations coming to negotiate with the officials on matters of interest to the students. Small and large convocations of students are frequent, resulting in resolutions to be publicized on the bulletin boards and in the student newspapers, and on occasion to be presented to the university or public officials, or to the student representatives on the governing Councils of the faculties or schools or of the University.

But not always is the proposal for action directed at the university or public officials. For example, one of the continual sources of protest is the inadequacy of the scholarship funds provided. Resolutions demanding that the government allocate more funds to this purpose are, of course, to be expected. But in 1967 the student societies of the Medical and Engineering Schools in Mexico decided on a campaign to raise funds for scholarships from students, graduates, professional associations and businessmen beyond those provided by the government.

Students with a flair for literary expression, sometimes as individuals, sometimes as spokesmen for student societies or for factions within those societies are frequent contributors not simply to student papers, but to more widely distributed papers and journals. Their message in words is carried to a wider audience in a more fully developed form than is the message in direct action.

This is the underlying day by day activism which only occasionally erupts in mass direct action on campus and infrequently in mass action on the streets. Even in the latter case, the demonstration is normally a march for which permission has been granted, the route and timing and duration predetermined, although the danger of any mass demonstration being transformed into a riot is always present.

The significance of the direct action student protest which does attract widespread public attention is, however, not determined solely by its frequency. Many of the issues which apparently provoke a demonstration or strike are the same as those which are the subject of the more orthodox and less disturbing kinds of activism mentioned above. That direct action, with its dangers to the future careers of students who participate, when resorted to, indicates a depth of concern about those issues among a sizable proportion of students

which is not apparent from the use of more orthodox methods
of obtaining official attention.   It may be a measure of the
inadequacy of the normal university and public mechanisms
for the channeling of protest and for the involvement of
those affected by administrative decisions in the influencing
of those decisions.   The extra-legal methods frequently attending an outbreak of direct action (occupation of buildings,
destruction of property, rifling of files, holding of hostages)
reveals the tenuous hold which respect for mores assumed to
be generally acceptable has on some students. And there is
always present when direct action is launched the possibility
that it may become an end in itself or, under the leadership
of those who are committed to a weakening or destruction of
the established order, an initial mechanism for making progress toward their revolutionary objective.   In any case the
wisdom of experience of those whose personal interest or
public responsibility is associated with the maintenance of
social and political status quo, teaches them that student
direct action can be a spark that lights a destructive fire
fed by causes of unrest existing in the lives of other dissident
groups or of the people generally.   Finally, the tendency of
direct action to spread and to involve the sympathetic activity of students who had no connection with the issue originally stimulating that action, may reveal the development
among students of a class consciousness which can be as
stimulating to mutual support "class" action among them as is
a working class consciousness among the unionized workers of
the country.
    Some examples of recent direct action in Mexico and Colom-
bia will give point to the above observations.

Direct Action in Mexico

    In mid-March of 1966 the students in the Faculty of Law at
the National University in Mexico were dissatisfied with some
of the academic standards set and disciplinary measures taken
by the Dean, César Sepúlveda. The students organized a protest and, when the Dean expelled five students, called a strike
and demanded that the Dean be fired. They surrounded the
Law School and forced it to close. The Rector of the University, Dr. Ignacio Chávez, supported the Dean, and decided to
hold classes off campus. The strike spread to other Faculties
and Schools, as well as to the University of San Nicolas. But

now the demands of the striking students were enlarged to include certain basic reforms such as abolition of the campus security force, greater representation of the students in selection of the Rector and the professors, more dormitories and dining rooms, more scholarships, and a comprehensive medical service.

At the end of April representatives of the law students presented the Rector with these demands. It was alleged that during the interview two students were beaten by campus guards. At least the report of the incident was sufficient to stir a mob to action. The mob invaded the Rector's office and held him captive there until he had signed a letter of resignation. Thirty-five faculty members threatened to resign if the Rector's resignation was accepted, and the Junta (the group responsible for selection of a Rector) refused to accept it, since it was obtained under duress.

Although police and troops are barred from the campus, they surrounded it, and all classes were suspended. When the university tried to resume classes, strikers seized several buildings and drove off anti-strike students with rocks and fire bombs. (Three foreigners and five Mexicans whose student status was questionable were arrested as a result of this melee, and charged by the Attorney General with trying to escalate the student strike into a revolutionary move to overthrow the government).

Dr. Chávez resigned again, this time "voluntarily and irrevocably." This was the third Rector who had been forced to resign in the midst of student agitations since 1930.

Serious unrest again became evident in the spring of 1968. In March a student was run over by one of the buses used to transport students. The students seized 20 of the buses and threatened to burn them unless the bus line paid the injured student compensation of 300,000 pesos.

Later in the spring 1,000 students closed the office of the Medical School Director's office and refused to re-open it until charges were dropped against a student who had stolen over 2000 files on psychological tests run on medical students. The case, however, was already in the courts.

The most violent of all direct action in recent years began in July of 1968 and developed into a strike which continued for four months, completely paralyzing secondary and higher education in Mexico City. The chronology below indicates how a minor incident can escalate into a major direct action disaster.

July 22 -
The spark was a fight between the students of two boys' schools, Vocational # 5 and Ochoterena.

July 23 -
Both of the school groups in conflict, especially Vocational #5, were reinforced by students from other schools, and by "city boys" gangs. The police riot squads were called in and acted "decisively" and, in the students' view, brutally, to "preserve order."

July 25 -
The original contestants forgot their differences and joined in protest against the riot squads' action, a protest in which they were supported by other vocational schools affiliated with the National Polytechnic Institute (IPN), thus bringing university age students onto the scene.

July 26 -
The National Federation of Technological Students (FNET) at the National Polytechnic Institute got permission for a protest rally against the measures taken by the riot squads, and a march of 6,000 vocational students began at 4 PM. The authorities also gave permission for the same hour for a demonstration by several non-student leftist groups in support of Castro. Apparently the *Tricontinentales de la Habana,* a group who were trying to organize a boycott of the Olympic Games, horned in on this demonstration. The FNET leader, José Cebreros, turned his back on the advice of the government department and of his own members to postpone the demonstration on the grounds that the students would be drained off to enlarge the leftist groups' agitation. This is exactly what happened. Cebreros lost control, and the students followed the Castro demonstrators downtown. In the evening, as a march started toward the government offices, the riot squad attacked and the students were pushed back to their schools. In the melee it was reported that 32 students died and many were arrested.

July 27-29 -
Students held protest meetings at the Polytechnic Institute

and in UNAM and demanded the resignation of the chief of the riot squads and other police chiefs, and they enclosed areas with barricades of stolen buses. On the evening of the 29th, 3,000 young people marched toward the Plaza, the police engaged them in battle and by midnight the situation was out of control and the army was called in.

July 30 -

By morning the army had restored order. During the morning the army occupied the Preparatories (associated with the University) and two of the Vocationals to prevent further direct action. By evening 1,400 arrests had been made and 1,000 persons were hospitalized.

July 31 -

The Rector of the UNAM, Barros Sierra now entered the fray, lowered the national flag to half mast in view of 3,000 students and declared, "Today is a day of mourning for the University. Our autonomy is being seriously threatened." Later in the day 20,000 students, professors and university employees gathered in protest against this violation of university autonomy and the Rector declared himself willing to lead a demonstration against the occupation of the University Preparatories by the army. During the day the army left the Preparatories, with the exception of Preparatory 1.

August 1 -

More than 50,000 students led by the Rector, carried on an orderly march 3½ kilometers in length. The professors at IPN supported the students as did the Director of the Polytechnic Institute, though he forbade participation of faculty in demonstrations. The chief of the riot squads proposed a commission to investigate the role of the police, a proposal which was accepted by the Director of IPN and the student organization FNET, but not by the ad hoc student committee which had been formed to direct the total action. By now the student demands were not merely that university autonomy be respected and that punishment be meted out for police brutality, but that the sedition law be repealed and political prisoners freed, and further that the government enter into open debate with the students on all matters.

August 9-11-

The newspapers initiated an attack on all participants. The chief interest of the editors appears to have been putting the finger on the person or the group responsible. Among those speculatively denounced were:

The Communists

Six mysterious French students newly arrived in the country

Politicians who were trying to get a pre-election period advantage over their opponents

An ex-Senator

The CIA and the FBI trying to set up an excuse for American intervention

The military seeking for a situation in which they could arrange for a coup

Businessmen from Detroit which was the likely place to which the Olympics would be moved if the situation in Mexico City made it inadvisable to hold them there

Fidelists

Various Schools in UNAM struck and the strike spread to the interior of the country.

August 13 -

Large demonstrations were held at IPN and UNAM.

September -

The strike continued. The conflicts continued. In September the army occupied the campuses of IPN and UNAM. The Rector of UNAM resigned in protest.

October -

On October 2 the troops opened fire on crowds consisting not only of students and leftist groups, but of un-involved citizens as well. They fired into the apartment buildings surrounding the square where the students were gathering, alleging that sniper fire was directed against them. Official reports listed 28 dead, 80 wounded, and 363 detained. With the Olympic games scheduled for October 12-27, the situation was critical from the point of view of the national reputation. But order was kept during the games and these proceeded without incidents.

November -

The strike continued, but increasing opposition to it was becoming apparent among the students, and division began to be obvious in the Strike Committee. By November 22, the strike leaders decided to call it quits, and on November 25, the students returned to their classes after 4 months of agitation, demonstrations, and strikes.

There is a sequel to the events of the summer and fall of 1968.[2] Eighty-five young men, mostly students, were arrested during the disturbances and have since been imprisoned in Lecumberri Street Prison (the "Black Palace"). Their defense lawyers have protested, to no avail, that their imprisonment is a violation of the Mexican Constitution which guarantees no longer than one year's imprisonment without trial. In December of 1969 the "forgotten 85", as they call themselves, went on a hunger strike. The students took up their cause and launched a major direct action for the first time since 1968. Statements were issued demanding the release not only of the "forgotten 85", but of all political prisoners arrested in the last 10 years. By mid-January the rallies and demonstrations were seriously interrupting the educational process at the National University and to a lesser extent in the provinces. Strikes were called but were of short duration, one or two day affairs. Sympathetic public figures appeared at the rallies, notably Msgr. Sergio Mendez Arceo, Bishop of Cuernavaca. He later circulated a statement which was read by diocesan priests from the pulpits condemning the indefinite imprisonment of the students. This support from liberal Catholic priests was welcomed by the students in the face of the unyielding stand of President Gustavo Diaz Ordaz' government against radical student activities, the lack of active interest on the part of organized labor and the peasants, and of the practical ignoring by the press of the prisoners, their treatment, their hunger strike, and the protests of the students. Students continued their activism chiefly through door to door solicitation of support for the prisoners, though a few have continued to boycott classes.

There is now evidence that the students plan to carry their cause further by organizing a boycott of the presidential elections in July. The PRI candidate, who is assured of election, is Luis Echevarría who, as Minister of Interior in 1968, had a heavy hand in putting down the student activism which resulted in the arrest of the prisoners. The students have once

[2]*Youth Action*, Vol. 1, No. 1, Brussels, Institut Internationale d'Etudes sur l'Education, p. 14.

130   CAMPUS CHALLENGE

more found a common cause which could stimulate a reactivization of the student movement.

Direct Action in Colombia

In May of 1965, Rector Escobar of the University of Antioquia, introduced a set of academic and disciplinary reforms. The student council called a student strike and organized a street demonstration for which they did not obtain the required permit. The police pushed the demonstrators back onto the campus, violating the traditional autonomy of the university. Within a few days, sympathy strikes broke out in various parts of the country and FUN, the leftist dominated National Student Federation, converted the strikes into a demonstration against the United States intervention in the Dominican Republic. Nine thousand students from the National University in Bogotá responded to an "official" strike call by the University Superior Student Council; The Free University in Bogotá furnished more recruits for the action; and the strikes spread to Barranquilla, Bucuramanga, Manizales, and Cucuta. Eleven days of widespread rioting followed. One National University student was killed and many others injured as the police tried to restore order. President Valencia finally declared a state of siege and asked for the resignation of Rector Escobar, hoping to placate the students at the University of Antioquia, who agreed to end the strike if the Rector resigned.

While the issue of University autonomy is nationwide, and therefore a natural incitement to sympathetic action in other universities, an added factor was involved in producing the violent reaction. It was engineered by FUN, the National Federation which had recently been brought under the control of the pro-Peking communist faction when they succeeded in ousting the pro-Moscow communist faction from the executive and the presidency. At the same time, a pro-Peking candidate had been elected to head the Superior Student Council at the National University. It is plausible to interpret the action as a show of strength by FUN whose leaders had been extremely critical of the lack of genuine confrontation with the authorities on the part of the former pro-Moscow communist leadership.

An indication of the way in which demonstrations frequently escalate into serious and violent confrontations is revealed by a report from George Sherman, a reporter from the Washington Star, of a demonstration in 1961 in Bogotá which began as a demonstration in sympathy with the workers at Avianca who were carrying on a wildcat strike against that Colombian airline.

In Bogotá, Colombia, during the first half of September the city center was tied up night after night with students and workers "demonstrating" in support of a wildcat strike against Avianca—the main Colombian airline. On the worst evening 30 military police were wounded, 95 rioters arrested, and 4,000 troops—including cavalry—were on duty around the capital.

Here as elsewhere the movement from demonstration to riot is fairly predictable. During the day pamphlets appear on the streets, notices go up in the university, hasty billboards are pasted on walls, giving the time, place, and main slogans. Everyone is forewarned, including the government. Riot squads arrive and take up strategic positions as the crowd congregates. Shops in the vicinity close a little early, and corrugated steel shields or lattice iron fences clang down over window fronts in metallic unison. If the American Embassy is in the nieghborhood, and it usually is, all employees are sent home early. The building is usually a prime target. When the Embassy happens to be on the sixth floor of a towering skyscraper—as in Bogotá—the mob contents itself with hurling rocks through the windows of Colombian offices below.

Bystanders and curiosity-seekers who pause on their way home to watch the spectacle are a great asset to the fanatics at the core of the crowd. They swell the numbers and confuse police, who have no time to draw fine distinctions between the innocent and guilty, once action starts. This action takes various forms. Egged on by haranguing soapbox orators, the mob burns a parked car, throws itself against a strike-bound office in the center, marches on the American Embassy, or simply drags park benches out into the traffic-bound streets.

Ammunition is limited to sticks and stones. Extensive road-building projects in most major cities provide ample materials. In Bogotá government troops finally had to cordon off the piles of stones laid out for a new expressway through the city. The counter-attack of the troops is swift and coordinated. Because most Latin policemen are poorly paid and their loyalty suspect—in the bloody Bogotá uprising in 1948 they joined the mobs—military police conduct anti-riot operations. Controlled by radio trucks with wire window-nets against rocks, these troops move in with billy clubs swinging and tear gas guns shooting. The cavalry blocks off the danger area, and pistol shots fired in the air add the necessary ingredient of real fear.

The screaming crowd scatters in every direction, chased down narrow sidestreets by troops swinging their clubs without discrimination. Many culprits melt into knots of spectators in shallow doorways or run into open-door cafes. The more persistent filter back to the main streets for another try once the first onslaught is past. The result is more clubbing, more tear gas. This gas lingers in the air for hours afterwards. It produces searing tears which close eyes and nostrils. For part of the evening the city center resembles a gigantic wake where people go about with handkerchiefs to their eyes.

The demonstration and riot usually last about two hours. When they are over, their only visible accomplishment is more human and material wreckage, more broken windows, more cracked skulls, more arrests—and more bitterness. But the instigators on the left look more to cumulative than short-range effects. Their aim is to undermine public confidence in the ability of democratic government to rule. Constant riots and civil strife which disrupts the life of a capital city are a powerful tool.

A later example of concerted student activism in early 1970 began as a protest supported by a strike of the students in the Faculty of Medicine of the National University against the dismissal of some professors by the university authorities.[3] No resolution was achieved, and the Superior University Council cancelled all medical courses for the 1st semester. A student assembly called a general strike. The Superior University Council then closed down all university activities for five months, and the government sent troops onto the campus to prevent any escalation of the disturbances. The protests and demonstrations continued and spread throughout Bogotá and the provinces. On February 28, the demonstrators practically "occupied" the capital. In March a nationwide student gathering was held in Cali to plan a united front against the closing of the National University. The Minister of Education declared that the student actions (now complicated by a general strike of primary and secondary school teachers) was a part of a "general plot" against the Establishment. He was able to withstand the mounting demands for his dismissal for only five days following that declaration, and resigned on March 15.

Two days later a national strike was called in 23 of the Colombian universities, in accordance with a resolution of the Cali meeting, in support for the demand that the closed universities be reopened.

[3]*Youth Action*, Vol. 1, No. 1, Brussels, Institut Internationale d'Études sur l'Education, p. 7.

Objectives

A list of the occasions and circumstances which have sparked student protest and demonstration does not at first glance reveal a framework of continuing objectives. Many of the situations out of which protests and demonstrations develop are unplanned happenings which become escalated when some relevance of the event, or the way it is handled, to what are perceived as "student rights" becomes apparent or is developed into an "issue" by activists who are continuously alert to such issues. Certainly the targets of specific protests and demonstrations do not appear to be suggested by any long range plan or the steps essential to the realization of ideologically relevant goals. Certain types of events, nevertheless, have provided recurring occasions for student agitation and demonstration in Mexico and Colombia. Some are related directly to university life:

Changes in the cost of getting an education, such as a rise in university fees, the cost of food, or bus fares

The dissatisfaction, with or the dismissal of, a professor

The disapproval of, or the appointment of, a Rector

Changes in the entrance requirements or selection process which raise the applicable standards of admission to the University

University discipline of a popular student, particularly a leader

The tightening of regulations and raising of standards with respect to class attendance, to re-registration after failure, to choice of courses, etc.

The occurrence of a demonstration in one university sparking a sympathy demonstration in another

A particularly bitter struggle for power among would be leaders of the student activists and between factions within the student movement itself. Such occasions have been frequent in the sixties between Fidelists and anti-Fidelists

Others are related to relations between the university or its students and the government:

Any violation of the autonomy of the university, particularly by the use of police or troops

Inadequate government financial support for the university

Police or troop harshness or brutality in dealing with student demonstrators

Other government interferences with freedom of speech or assembly

Still others are related to actions of their own or foreign governments which symbolize a policy considered inconsistent with the rights of the people and the independence and dignity of their own nation:

Police or troop action in the case of a workers' strike

The "rigging" of nominations for office or of elections by the ruling party

Any United States intervention in the affairs of Latin American countries or alleged evidence of exploition of Latin American resources by American business interests

The visit of envoys from the United States symbolizing the dependency of their own country upon the "colossus of the North"

It is only occasionally that the issues upon which a demonstration is focused have to do with what adult citizens would consider domestic politics, that is those issues related to the role of the government in taxing, in regulating the operations of business and industry, in the conservation of natural resources, in promoting economic activity and growth, in the provision and management of public services, health, education (other than that related to the universities), and welfare. Even government infringement on the constitutional rights of citizens generally evokes student protest very infrequently.

Recurring Issues

Although the events or incidents provoking a student protest or demonstration have the qualities of immediacy, transiency, and expediency, there are certain persistent basic themes or premises to which the student activism in Mexico and Colombia

implicitly if not explicitly responds. When any situation symbolizes, or can be made to symbolize by a persuavsive activist,
one of the following premises, the situation is full of potential
for producing a protest or a direct action of some sort:

The preservation of the autonomy of the universities

The preservation and extension of the rights of the students
to participate in the determination of university and
societal organization and practice in the light of the impact
of that organization and practice on the opportunities
for and constraints on the lives of students

The freedom to refuse obedience to any authority within
or outside the university which places restraints on the
free exercise of that right

The legitimization of the university as an instrument of
social and political change and modernization, including
its role as a school for leadership for initiating such
change and modernization

The development of the university and of university life
as an instrument and resource for achieving national
identity and independence and a widely shared culture
rooted in Latin American values

A challenge to the centralized authority of a self-perpetuating oligarchy (as in Colombia) or of a monolithic
party (as in Mexico), to control or regulate the economic,
social, and political affairs of the nation

To judge from the past record, however, the specific foci of
each year's activism will be determined by the accident of
events in the universities, the community, the nation and the
world; by particular actions of the authorities in the university
or the nation which the students dislike or feel threatened by,
and which give them the opportunity for criticism and rebellion or self-assertion; by the nature and intensity of the
ideological predispositions of those who happen to be the
current leaders or who desire to be leaders; and by the degree
to which the reactions of leaders to such events are shared
by a sufficient number of students to make responsive direct
action effective.

This is not to say that those who spark the particular
manifestations of student activism in a particular year may

not be deeply in earnest about the issues raised or that
what they do about the issues may not be very significant
for long range university and national development.   It is
only to say that, if their actions do have such significance,
it is usually only by accident and not by design; that is,
not because there is a continuing commitment of changing
leaders to a step by step contribution to the attainment of
any cumulative long range reform, given direction by objectives
defining a concept of the characteristics of the university or
the nation the reforms could produce.

The repeated proclamation of those large and long range
objectives is less an indicator of a plan of action than a
reinforcement and glorification of the action taken.

Nevertheless, the themes and premises set forth above, although not formulated as goals for a planned course of reform
or revolution, such as that embodied in the ideologies and
programs of a labor or a radical political movement, do provide a general sense of direction for student activism in Mexico
and Colombia, an activism which otherwise would appear to
be sporadic, time and place bound, and merely event and
current-leadership generated. It can be anticipated that, whenever events and circumstances and the actions of authorities
within or outside the university symbolize or constitute a
threat to the objectives implicit in those themes and premises,
there will be a readiness of large numbers of students to
protest. Into the complex of forces impinging on the event
or action will be injected an upsurge of student power directed
to the removal of that threat.

It is inevitable that the working objectives of student activism should be short range. The student population is continuously changing, the leadership is temporary, on the whole,
with the exception of a very few professional *políticos* who
return year after year. The program, to the extent there is
a program, is remade every year. With the exception of the
Communists and possibly the Christian Democrats and the
Socialists, there is no well defined ideological guide to appropriate foci of active attention, and even then there is no
certainty that student leaders predisposed to such programs
will be in power more than a year or two. Although it is
commonly alleged that outside political organization is frequently behind those seeking official positions in the student
societies, the candidates do not identify their program of

activities with the action platforms of the political parties which at least do have a general set of changes they are trying to accomplish. They do not seek office primarily in order to promote the domestic or international programs of those parties, though they may get excited at particular times about particular current party efforts. In university affairs they have no long range plans, only some general principles for university reform, many of which are oriented toward making admission to the university possible for a larger number of students. and the task of getting a degree less arduous.

Can the objectives of the student organizations in these two Latin American countries be considered revolutionary?

For *Mexico* the question can be answered in the unequivocal negative. *The* revolution is still a symbolic term summing up the aspirations for a modernized and progressive Mexico. *The* revolution both has occurred and continues. But there is a continuity in the process that in any other country would be called progressive reform. Student criticism of the failure to move faster is frequently and readily expressed, but there is an underlying confidence that progress will continue.

Throughout the sixties, the chief focus of national student Congresses in Mexico was upon university reforms such as the appointment of professors on a competitive basis, the wider distribution of government funds to provincial universities (as late as 1965, one half of the appropriations in Mexico went to the National University while the other 29 public universities were in dire financial need); the increase in scholarships for students with no financial means (in 1964 only 90 of the 47,000 faculty and school students at the National University in Mexico were supported by fellowships); and the administration of admissions tests in a way which did not put those with a poor secondary or preparatory education at a disadvantage.

When the issues upon which activism is focused go beyond the immediate changes which students want made in their student environment, they are related not so much to internal economic or political reform (to say nothing of revolution) but to the behavior of foreign people and governments. The Castro revolution, the Bay of Pigs incident, the "invasion" of the Dominican Republic, the Vietnam War, the Soviet quashing of the Hungarian revolt, the civil rights movement in the United States, police action against students any place in the world (including Mexico), these are some of the issues that stir responses expressed in demonstrations and posters. It is only occasionally that the situation which stimulates activism concerns the problems internal to Mexico or the actions of the Mexican Establishment with respect to those problems. In other words, they are very minimally related to the responsibilities of Mexican citizens for the internal problems of Mexican society.

Can the objectives of the student movement in *Colombia* be considered revolutionary? The resolutions of university student councils[4] and of the national congresses have given that impression from time to time, especially in recent years when extreme leftist groups whose affinity was more with the Chinese Communist Party and with Fidelism than with Russian Communism have from time to time won control of particular local councils or national congresses. Two surveys of student opinion, one in the National University at Bogotá and the other of Colombian students generally, indicated that 80% and 85% of the students respectively felt that a "radical change" in the governance of the country was necessary. Yet the occasions upon which there was a serious threat to the Establishment did not find the students in the role of initiators, although they participated in the disturbances in which the threat became manifest.

The first real challenge to the rule of the elite was sparked by Jorge Eilecér Gaitán who sought a base of power in the support of those previously without a voice in the governance of the nation. He denounced the oligarchy, both its Conservative Party and its Liberal Party members, although he himself had been identified with the Liberal Party. He was of humble origin and had the qualities of empathy and oratorical expression which made him a charismatic figure. His supporters, to judge from the election results in 1946, appear to have come largely from the urban lower classes and the lower middle class.[5] There is little evidence, however, that there was any distinctive student support for him. His assasination in 1948

[4]The student societies are labeled student councils in Colombia. These are not to be confused with the governing Councils upon which students are represented.

[5]Dix, R.H., *Colombia, The Political Dimensions of Change*, Yale, 1967, p. 103.

was followed by a spontaneous outburst of rioting in downtown Bogotá, in which students are known to have participated. But the riots were more the manifestation of the
frustration and anger of non-elite classes who had lost their
spokesman than of adults or students bent on revolution.

The next event with which student action is identified was
the overthrow of the dictator Rojas Pinilla who in 1953 had
usurped the Presidency with the backing of the army. The
response to his coup was enthusiastic at first. His period of
rule had many similarities to that of Perón in Argentina with
its establishment of a National Secretariat of National Assistance under his daughter, harassment of his enemies including
the use of police and the armed forces to put down demonstrations (in one of which several students were killed), the
granting of large favors to the military, public works, social
welfare schemes, taxation on corporate dividends and profits,
higher assessments on land, and efforts to maneuver himself
into another term as president in 1957. In that year the opposition forces finally were felt, and in May there was let loose
a wave of student demonstrations and riots which were a popular manifestation of the disenchantment which had come to
dominate even among the traditional elite, the church, the
business associations, and the military leaders. The students
who participated in the violent street demonstrations were not
just those who normally would be expected to take part, that
is those from the public universities, but also those from
Javeriana, the Catholic University, and other private schools.
The overthrow of Rojas Pinilla was engineered, not by the
leaders of the masses, but by the members of, and those
closely associated with, the traditional pre-Rojas Establishment.
But the event is recorded in the traditions of the student movement as a symbol of the devotion of that movement to liberal,
if not revolutionary, ideals.

Nevertheless, there is little evidence that the student movement in Mexico and Colombia has played an *initiating* part
in promoting direct action which has had a decisive impact
on *national* politics. Rather it would appear that student
activism on such occasions is a part of activism on the part
of other forces or movements which find it advantageous to
allow the students to take a prominent part for the time
being. It is therefore difficult to disentangle the particular
impact of the student movement from that of the other forces

which are operating simultaneously.[6]

Following the downfall of Rojas Pinilla the leaders of the Liberal and Conservative Parties joined in a pact providing that for the next 12 years there would be a uniting of both parties on a single candidate for President, the parties to alternate in power. Opposition to this political arrangement has been expressed and in some cases activated by the youth organizations associated with the Communist Party and of the *Movimiento de Recuperación Liberal* (M.L.R.), the latter of which was an extreme leftist faction of the Liberal Party, led by Alfonso Lopez Michelsen. Maoists and Fidelists are found in these groups but there is no widespread predisposition toward other than a verbal *revolutionary* challenge to the Establishment among the students, or generally among the student leaders. The few who are convinced that this is the only way for the future, go over to the guerrillas as Father Torres did. But neither is there any positive evidence that the continued rule of the oligarchy will promote the progress they desire either for themselves as students and graduates, or for the nation and its people.

"Revolution" is a word used to express a felt need for a radical change away from oligarchical rule. It is not the label for an action program to which students are committed, for the overthrow of that rule.

Organization

Student activism in Latin America differs from that in the other countries under investigation in the degree to which student participation in the formal governance of the universities is institutionalized. We must keep in mind, therefore, two aspects of that activism. The one comes to a focus in the organization and activity of student societies or councils in each faculty or school, and in the university as a whole. This aspect corresponds roughly to the organization and activities of student unions in India and the student self governing associations in Japan. Also similar to student activism in these other countries is the attempt to federate the local student societies on a national basis and to associate

[6]cf. Economic Commission for Latin American Education, *Human Resources and Development in Latin America*, United Nations, 1968, p. 160.

these national federations with one of the several international associations. Periodic efforts to achieve an all Latin American organization representative of the societies in the several countries are also evident, although these efforts take the form of occasional conferences rather than of any ongoing formal organization. These student societies are the students' affair and, although the university administration may aid their activities, particularly those which have cultural or educational objectives, the societies are basically of, by, and for their student members. They have no formally recognized role in the governance of the university. They may, and do at times, perform as pressure groups seeking to influence school or university policy, but they occupy no formally recognized and legally sanctioned place in the administrative structure of the university. That is the first aspect, one that is to be found in all countries.

The second aspect is more distinctive of Latin American student activism. It is the inclusion of student representatives, elected by the students, on the governing Councils of the faculties and schools, and on the governing Boards of the universities. The tradition of such participation is rooted in the Bologna concept of the university as a corporation of students who hire the teachers. This concept survived as a pattern for university governance to colonial times only in Spain. Although in Latin America the universities were not originally founded by students, the Spanish tradition of student participation in control was given new life by the Córdoba (Argentina) student initiated movement for reform of the universities in 1918 and, in survival form, influences arrangements for governance in the public universities and even in some private religious and secular universities. The title of the "autonomous university", of which the public universities in Mexico and Colombia are so proud, is operationally and practically defined as one whose internal affairs are governed, free from interference by the State and the Church, by the administrators, the professors *and* the students.

There is sometimes an overlapping in student personnel involved in the two aspects of the student activism, since leadership of the student societies, either those identified with each of the faculties (Law, Medicine, Engineering) or schools (Economics, Humanities, Architecture, etc.) or with the whole University, or with a national federation is likely to indicate

the capacity for participation on the governing Councils of
the Faculties, Schools, or the University. Also there is always
the possibility, if student proposals for action on the governing Councils are not accepted by the entire Council, which
includes faculty representatives and administrative officers as
well, that the student society leaders will attempt to mobilize
members of the societies for direct action in support of student
representatives on the governing Councils.

The system of *cogobierno* or of student participation in the
governance of the faculties, schools, and the university is
highly institutionalized in *Mexico*. The access to the center of
power and controlling decision making, which students in non-
Latin American universities are demanding, the Mexican students have.

Each faculty and school in the university has a technical or
governing Council on which the students are represented by
two members. These members are elected by a sort of "electoral college." The electoral college members are elected directly by the students in each generation class. Say the course is
a five year course, then the 1st. year, 2nd. year, 3rd. year, 4th.
year, and 5th. year students each elect a member to the electoral college. Those members then choose two students for two
year terms to serve on the faculty or school Technical Council.
They of course are in a distinct minority since the remainder
of the Council is composed of faculty representives from each
of the disciplines in the school or faculty (elected by the instructors) and the Dean.

The function of the Technical Council is to be advisory
to the Dean on matters of academic policy and practice. It
approves programs of study, the introduction or elimination
of courses, additional degrees, graduate work, and other
matters normally coming before the Board of Permanent
Officers or Faculty Senates in American universities. The
functions are defined in public law for UNAM, and other
Mexican public universities normally follow that pattern.

For the university as a whole, there is a University Council
(*Conséjo Universitario*) on which the students are represented.
Their representation on this Council is equal to that of the
faculty. The faculty and the students of each faculty or
school elect two representatives to the University Council.
The students from the 9 campuses of the university administered University Preparatory School have also two repre-

sentatives for the entire school on the Council. Only students who are regularly registered and whose grade standing is 8/10 or better, are eligible for election.

The students, although equal in numbers to the faculty are in a minority since the Council also has as members, the Deans of every faculty and school, the Directors of the research institutes, the Director of the Extension Division, the Rector, the General Secretary of the university, and a representative of the employees of the university. However, not only the students we interviewed who had served on the Councils but administrative officers of the university as well indicated that the faculty, students, and Deans on the Council did not form separate "blocs", since those from a particular faculty or school normally found they had more interests in common as representatives of their faculty or school in matters of high university policy with which the Council deals, than each group had with its peers.

On the table of organization this Council is related to the other agencies and organs of university administration by a broken line indicating a relationship not of line authority, but of coordination. The Council does have however, real powers, e.g. approval of the study programs recommended by the Technical Councils of the schools and faculties, and approval of the university budget giving control over the distribution of funds to various uses.[7] The University Council has committees on curriculum, grading, admissions, etc. which report to the whole Council. At the present time, the Council as a whole is considering reforms in the whole structure of the university. The students are present to make their influence felt in the exercise of these powers and responsibilities.

Formerly, the University Council on which the students were represented had the power of appointment and removal of Deans and Directors of research institutes, and of the selection of the Rector himself. By the law of 1945 these powers are now lodged in another body (*Junta de Gobierno*) composed of prominent persons (including former Rectors, Deans, etc.). The Junta is composed of 15 members one of whom is replaced each year by vote of the University Council.

It is clear that, legally, the student societies to be presently discussed, have no formal role in the governing of the uni-

[7] The University receives its financial resources from the government, but is autonomous in the allocation of these funds.

versity. The possibility is always present, however, that they might exert extra-legal power through strikes or demonstrations to reinforce positions taken by student members of the Technical Council of a faculty or school or the general University Council. That eventuality was not looked on with favor by most of the students who were Council members with whom we spoke in 1962 and in 1968 because of the realization that it might endanger the whole system of student participation in university government, as well as their position of accepted status within that system.

The possibility of the usurpation of powers not legally theirs by the leaders of the student societies was evident, however, in 1966 when the leaders of several societies imprisoned Rector Chávez in his office until he agreed to resign. Moreover, as indicated above, it happens on occasion that an officer of a student society is also elected to membership in the Technical Council of the faculty or school or even in the University Council, thus establishing a personal link between the formal university governing arrangement and the independent student societies.

Participation of students in formal governance of their university in *Colombia* has never been as extensive as it has in Mexico. Student representation on the Councils of the faculties is of the token variety, and representation on the Governing Council of the public universities is very much a minority representation. By the Organic Law of the National University of Colombia of 1935, two students could be elected to the University Council which included seven other members: two elected by the faculty, one by the Deans, two representatives of the National Government, the Rector, and the Minister of National Education. After an unfortunate incident in which student opposition to the then (1969) president Lleras was made obvious, the President abolished elections for student representatives in university government.

The public university student societies or councils in both Mexico and Colombia are normally the students' own affair. The basic unit is the society of a particular faculty. The students in each faculty and school elect officers annually and elections are frequently hotly contested. Cliques of students present and support a slate of particular candidates and, in some cases, the unifying factor is an ideological orientation of the members of the clique. Platforms are announced by the candidates which are in these cases perceived by the students less as a program of probable activity, than as a revelation of the candidate's ideological orientation. The cliques, however, do not identify themselves by party labels used in the national politics. In Mexico, for example, if their orientation is leftist they are "red", if conservative they are "green." Students, moreover, make assumptions as to what political party, or political interest group (and in Mexico, faction within PRI) is "back of" a particular slate.

Since there are no dues, it is difficult to know how many students could be considered "members" of these societies. Theoretically all students of the faculty or school are members. Some societies have membership cards, but their significance is unclear since they are distributed fairly liberally by the officers. Probably the best indication of the numbers of students considering themselves actively interested is the number voting in the annual election for officers. This varies from time to time. No records are available for Colombia. In Mexico, estimates by informed persons concentrate around the proportion of 10% in Architecture, 20% in Engineering and Science, and 30% in such Schools as Political Science, Economics and Philosophy, and in the Faculty of Law.

How are the societies supported financially? The university contributes funds for their social, cultural, and sport activities. University facilities are available for meetings they may desire to hold, but, on the whole, the University administration keeps hands off the meetings. Political subjects whether domestic or international, are not taboo. Announcements of meetings to protest certain policies and practices of the faculty, school, or university, were prominently displayed on walls of the universities. Officers themselves sometimes contribute, or solicit contributions from students for particular activities especially when they are directed against university or faculty policy or practice. Allegations are not infrequent that factions within the ruling political party and opposition parties make "contributions" which hopefully will keep power in the hands of student leaders oriented in their direction. It is clear that, lacking a war chest from dues, the expensive ads taken in papers or printed wall manifestos must be paid for by some source, and the most frequently voiced assumption is that the source is a political party, interest group, or faction.

The need for funds arises chiefly from election expenses, from the preparation of wall or demonstration posters, from newspaper and leaflet printing, and from travel costs for gatherings, demonstrations, and delegations to student Congresses.

Traditionally, each university had an all university student society in addition to the separate societies for each of the faculties and schools, and there was a representative National Student Union bringing together representatives from the several public universities. Since 1966, in both countries it has been impossible to picture such a neat hierarchy of organizations constituting the student movement. The faculty and school societies have gone their own ways, one sometimes trying to obtain the support of the other societies in the promotion of an action of primary interest to the first society. Some of the separate societies attempt to claim that they speak for all the students at a particular university, but the claim is not acknowledged by the members of the other societies. Even when an all university society does exist (as in the case of the Polytechnic Institute in Mexico City), factionalism weakens it, and the legitimacy of its leadership as spokesmen for the entire student body is questioned.

The same thing is true on the national scene. In Colombia no authentic national federation of student organizations has existed in recent years, though a number of attempts have been made to maintain one. The National University at Bogotá and, indeed, Bogotá itself do not dominate the national educational scene to the same extent as is true of the National University in Mexico City and the Federal District in which it is located. Initiatives originating in Bogotá, for example, do not necessarily coincide with sectional interests of those students in the universities located in Medellin and Cali. A strong Catholic influence opposes that of the communists in promoting student activism and organization. And the Communist youth themselves have experienced the bitter conflict between the Moscow oriented and Peking oriented positions. The result has been a series of claims of different organizations to national spokesmanship and a constant struggle for power among the factions within those organizations.

The first national student federation, the Federation of Colombian Students (*Federación de Estudiantes Colombianos,*

FEC) grew out of the 1922 student Congress and continued until the mid 1950's. During that period students participated in public demonstrations, but so far as the scanty records indicate, were not the primary initiators. Most of the activity centered upon local education issues. But by the mid-fifties FEC had become communist dominated and stress was placed upon political activism. At this time two organizations were claiming the status of a true national union, the FEC and a Catholic oriented organization *(Federación Universitaria Colombiana,* FUC).

FEC was an active participant in the overthrow of Rojas Pinilla, while FUC appears to have accepted Rojas. After his fall, FUC declined in importance and FEC became the National Union of Colombian Students *(Union Nacional de Estudiantes Colombianos,* UNEC). This organization at first attracted students of varied political positions but was soon under the influence of the communists, as FEC had been, and by 1960 it was merely a paper organization.

In the early sixties, another nominally national organization, the CEUC *(Confederación de Estudiantes Universitarios Colombianos)* and the Student Council of the University of Atlántico called a national Conference to establish a nationwide student organization representative of all students, which UNEC had ceased to be since being taken over by the communists. CEUC, which was Catholic oriented, proclaimed itself non-political, and sought to gain wide support from non-communists.

The National University Federation, *Federación Universitaria Nacional,* FUN, came into existence in 1963, at a student congress organized by the communist dominated Superior Student Council of the National University in Bogotá. It quickly sprang into prominence by organizing opposition to the army's occupation of the Industrial University of Santander. For two years it was controlled by the communist JUCO or JCC, the youth wing of the Communist Party. But a pro-Peking group constantly challenged the leadership, and finally in May 1965, a majority of the executive group were the candidates of the radicals. But the victory was short lived, and in October the JUCOCO (pro-Peking Communists) lost out to the original sponsors.

FUN's effective support was limited to the Superior Student Council at the National University in Bogotá and some student councils at the Free University of Bogotá and at Santander. It could not lay claim to being truly national, although recognized as such by the two communist oriented international organizations, with which it has affiliated. In August of 1964, another nominally national union, CEU, was formed by a congress of representatives from all the six principal universities in Bogotá, and a program was launched to bring students of other Colombian universities into the organization. In contrast to FUN, CEU proposed to focus its activities on matters relevant to a better educational environment and facilities for students.

Both FUN and CEU were invited in September, 1964, to appear before a Parliamentary commission considering education legislation. The CEU spokesmen were physically attacked by members of FUN after giving their testimony. In their October conference of that year FUN laid plans for scholarships, seminars, and a literacy campaign, obviously intended to counter the appeal of CEU. By 1966, FUN had not deviated from its proclaimed "revolutionary" role and from its emphasis on violent tactics. Communist control was not only admitted, but flaunted. Its activities were concentrated on fomenting student strikes and riots. The only plank in its platform remotely connected with student interests in their educational experience was a campaign for nationalization of the 14 (out of a total 28 Colombian universities) which are private.[8]

At FUN's third convention in 1966, however, one speaker after another rose to admit the failure to win its "battles" and to win the widespread support of students. The high water mark of FUN's confrontation politics was reached in August 1966. In that month Carlos Lleras Restrepo, a Liberal, took over his duties as President of Colombia and announced his intention of restoring order to the campuses. Among the other things done to fulfill that promise, he issued a decree requiring students to attend 80% of their classes and ordered that days lost because of strikes were to be counted as triple absences. FUN challenged him by threatening to take over the universities. On August 26 he met with the leaders and declared he would not recognize FUN as having any authority. The subsequent strike called by FUN received little

[8]*Youth and Freedom*, Institute for International Youth Affairs, Vol. VIII, No. 3, p. 18-20.

support from the students. One by one, the member student organizations began to withdraw from membership.

In October the army occupied the National University in Bogotá after 150 students attacked the President as he entered the university. At the end of October the government, by decree, dissolved the National University's communist controlled Superior Student Council. The influence of the communists in both the guerrilla and the student movements was severely weakened in March, 1967, by the arrest of virtually the entire leadership of the Colombian Communist Party including a number of student leaders. At this writing no leftist youth organization has risen to replace the Superior Student Council at the National University in Bogotá or FUN on the national scene.

In Mexico, in which traditionally the dominance of the National University in Mexico City was so great that the university society there could, with some justification, speak for the students in all Mexico, the lack of an authentic national student organization is equally obvious. There is no agreement that the CNE (*Confederación Nacional de Estudiantes*) is performing this function of national spokesmanship at present. In 1961, representatives from universities in all but three of Mexico's 20 states attended its 25th Congress. The Congress undertook a study of many university problems and of university autonomy and the possibility of closer relations with the national student organizations of other countries, chiefly in Latin America. No major ideological conflicts occurred. Financially CNE was supported by a number of outside sources including business men. By 1965 a coalition of democratic leftist groups placed 16 of their numbers on the 25 man executive council thus taking over effective control from the previous right wing leadership. For the first time the Social Christians appeared as delegates to the organization's National Congress. The Marxists however, did not attend the Congress and the *Movimiento Universitario de Renovadora Orientación* (MURO), the extreme rightist group, had only one delegate. Although the leadership had moved to the left, there was little attention given to political problems external to the universities.

By 1967 the lack of funds (due in part to the drying up of contributions from businessmen when the organization's leadership turned to the left) had forced a drastic curtailment in CNE activities.

The lack of strong and stable national student organizations in Colombia and Mexico becomes evident in Latin American Student Conferences and in relations with international student groups, as different factions associated with different organizations vie for the right to be the authentic voice of the students in the two countries.

Anything resembling a national student movement action in these two countries is likely, therefore, at the moment to be an effort initiated by a strong local or factional leader able to marshal a large following. Under the circumstances, the impact of student action is likely to be felt as a pressure for local change within the several universities. It can be anticipated that impact on the national educational system, or upon the social and political institutions and values of the country, will be minimal.

This lack of institutional stability and strength at the national level is mirrored in the comparative evaluation made of the student movements in the several Latin American countries by *Boletin*, a publication of the Coordinating Office of Latin American Student Movements (an organization under the auspices of the Organization of Latin American Catholic Universities). With respect to the dimensions of development with which the evaluation was concerned, a rating of 1 was highest and 10 lowest. The student movements in Mexico and Colombia were rated as follows:

	Mexico	*Colombia*
Institutionalization	6	6
Ideological & Intellectual Maturity	8	7
Syndicalist Activities	6	6
Political Importance	8	8

Leadership

Campus politics in both Colombia and Mexico is largely an operational field for a nucleus of activist leaders in the national or provincial public universities. Students in general participate periodically in the election of the officers of the local student societies and in the demonstrations which are occasionally instigated by the *políticos* to advertise or promote an issue concerning which they have determined to take action. Very little information is gained by an investigator from students who are not involved in the plans and actions of this nucleus of *políticos* about the structure and dynamics of the student organizations and the political maneuvering which is a major focus of thought and action for the latter. Student politics, like national politics in these countries, is a function of leadership, not of mass participation. Any interpretation of the student movement must therefore begin with an understanding of the characteristics and motivations of those who initiate the action identified with that movement.

There is no more reason to assume that those who seek political office in student societies or "free lance" political leadership, are "normal" in their motivation than are those who seek political office or leadership in the community or nation. Student leaders, or would-be leaders, may experience, along with those whose support is necessary for implementing any action they desire to lead, a number of problems suggesting to them and other students the need for corrective effort. But in political life, a shared need does not lead inevitably to activism. Initiative is required, and that initiative is not provided by the "normal" student or citizen.

What stimulates the initiator? Usually observed to be characteristic of the leaders interviewed in Mexico and Colombia were the following: a desire for personal prestige and power, a high degree of self-confidence, a strong predisposition to self-assertion, unusual physical energy, a mind that is constantly seeking alternatives to present arrangements, a mental curiosity that has reached out to explore such alternatives, a sense of mission as an instrument of change, an intense desire to be a leader and to avoid the need to adapt to initiation by others, a predisposition to talk rather than listen, and the capacity for quick and lively and colorful verbalization.

Note that not all of these are essential for one who seeks his leadership role in sports or drama or debating or student religious or social clubs. Where student activism is operationally defined as the activity of student autonomous societies, particularly activity involving protest and demonstration, these characteristics are to a high degree essential. If they are present in some students on the campus, if events conspire or can be manipulated to provide the occasion, if the event involves factors affecting the interests or values of a critical mass of students, student activism may take the form of mass action. If the last factor is not present, student activism among the would be leaders will be like an underground current of lava seeking for a cleft or a weakened surface through which it may erupt with volcanic force.

In the public universities the opportunity for giving active expression to the qualities named is to be found largely in the leadership of the student societies or in participating on faculty, school, or all-university governing councils. The highly varied interest group organizations found typically on residential campuses in some countries, do not provide the opportunity for leadership among Mexican and Colombian students, the vast majority of whom live at home or in off campus quarters, and commute to the universities.[9] (Incidentally the importance of transportation to most of the students is at the root of the fact that dissatisfaction with the bus service or a rise in bus fares appears periodically as the issue which sparks student demonstrations).[10]

Student leaders are quite frank in acknowledging the personal advantages which accompany their activities. Rectors and deans and professors are well aware of the ability of the *políticos* to initiate action among the students which can help or hinder the former in the performance of their functions. Although denying that they personally had been the beneficiaries of favoritism from university administrators or faculty members, student leaders in both Mexico and Colombia stated that student leaders were known to have received sinecures from deans, jobs that paid them a stipend for which they did very little work. In two recent elections to office in the student societies, one in Colombia and one in Mexico, an issue raised by the candidates seeking to replace the incumbent officers was that the latter were well known to be "Dean's men." It was commonly assumed that professors aware of the potential which student leaders had as troublemakers, went easy on them in class, and a common saying had grown up, "The *políticos* always pass."

Student leaders are highly visible among the masses of

[9]In 1964 at the National University in Mexico City, of the 46,932 students in the faculties and schools, 19,411 were living in the family home, and 25,862 were living in rented rooms, apartments, own home, etc.

[10]In 1964, 62,781 of the 71,595 students (including the preparatory students) at the National University in Mexico City used public transportation to get to the campus.

students at the public university and have thus the chance to attract the attention of politicians and employers outside the university. Even though the leader does not desire an active political career beyond the university, his reputation will attract the attention of employers in government bureaus and in business, industry, and the professions whose successful operations are frequently dependent on "fixers" and liason men between themselves and the politicians. The student leader who has gained a reputation for political know-how and has, while a student, made contacts with politicians in the community and nation can be a valuable asset to such employers. Experience as a student *político* may therefore be as great a contribution to establishing a career as the knowledge acquired in the course of study.

While non-*político* students can provide very little information concerning the structure and dynamics of the student movement, they are clear about what characteristics of the student leaders are likely to gain the respect and support of students generally in elections and in seeking to involve students in participation in the action stimulated by the leaders. Chief among those characteristics is the readiness for, and the daring to undertake, the manly dramatic heroic deed in a situation where most students hesitate to act. This is particularly true when the situation is one which the students interpret as threatening to their rights or interests or can be persuaded that such is the case. To the capacity for decisive action is added the willingness to "go to bat" for the students. Those *políticos* who have the greatest chance of winning the students' respect are those who appear least concerned and timid about protecting their personal reputations with the university authorities or with citizens generally. They are usually the ones who can suggest the immediate course of action for a group of students who, although sensing that something ought to be done, are puzzled about what to do. A capacity to dramatize these qualities by ready and satiric wit and by demagogic oratory is a great help.

A widespread popular assumption held by a number of commentators on Latin American student movements is that the leaders of the movements are normally older students, in fact professional *políticos*, who are students in name only. According to those who make this assumption, the possibility of repeating courses and moving from one faculty

or school to another, amplifies the possibility of making a
career out of being a student leader. As evidence of this
situation in Mexico it was pointed out that one of the
reasons for student *político* opposition to Rector Chávez in
1966 was that he proposed and initiated a move to tighten
up on admissions requirements, a limitation on re-registration
for failed or incomplete courses, and on movement from
one faculty or school to another, all of them measures which
would make a career as a perpetual student leader more difficult. However, the testimony from students and faculty members and administrators confirmed this assumption with respect
to very few leaders. There were known cases, and those which
were cited involved student leaders who had been prominent
over a period particularly in the activities of the national federation of student societies. The belief was also widespread
that such continuing *políticos* had been "planted" and supported financially in the universities to carry on activity advantageous to political parties and factions outside the university. This belief is plausible given the handicaps faced by
the weak opposition parties and factions in both countries in
developing a constituency and in recruiting membership, and
the predisposition of student leaders to stimulate agitations
among students, agitations and demonstrations which in the
past have sparked widespread popular protest against the ruling Establishment. But the evidence obtained from interviews
with those most closely associated with the realities of student
life and activism was not adequate to serve either as a confirmation or denial of the fact that such "planted" partisans had
a significant role in influencing the character or direction of
student activism.

The general impression gained from the resolutions passed
at student conferences, from posters, and from the speeches
and proclamations of student leaders is that the most persis-
tently active among the leaders are ideologically motivated and
are oriented toward the left. Their rhetoric is certainly colored
by revolutionary phrases such as "capitalistic and imperialistic exploitation", "the ruling and working classes", "bourgeois civilization", "bourgeois hypocrisy", "confrontation",
etc. Conversations with the leaders creates the impression that
their leftist ideology is phrase deep, and not a source of either
goals or premises for thought or action. Their ideology appears to be a set of categories and abstract terms into which

such things as "causes" and "results" and "governmental policies", domestic and foreign, can be thrown. The charge that
the choice of their targets for action, the kind of action they
initiate, the tactics they use, or the tone and character that
their leadership gives to the student movement has its source
and guide in their ideology, is questionable. The substance of
the phrases they use is not thoroughly, and certainly not critically, examined. With few exceptions, these leaders appear not
to be widely read in history, the theory of history, or social
science. Consequently they have a limited conception of what
it takes to change the institutions of a society and particularly
its governing arrangement.

Their understanding of Marx, Engels, and Lenin, Mao,
and the Popes' encyclicals is impressionistic and superficial.
The terms and theories of social science and philosophy are
used to describe problems rather than to analyze them. There
is consequently very little in the thought-ways characterizing
the student leaders to indicate that the potential contribution
of students to the solution of the problems of the university
or society will be more rational than that provided by the
present members of the Establishment.   Their contribution to
change, or what some of them refer to as "revolution", is to
agitate for it, to sponsor student gatherings which pass
revolutionary resolutions,[11] to make the established authorities
in the universities and the governments aware of an underlying
discontent with their rule, and to create in their minds an
apprehension of the possibility that student activism could
light the fires of a widespread rebellion or revolt.

The activists lead the students into periodic confrontations
with the authorities of the Establishment.   But when they
attack the authorities in the universities or in the State, when
they engage in a direct confrontation with the police or the
army, it is because "they are there," standing in the way of
some change the leaders wish to accomplish, some freedom of
action they wish to maintain, or some declared student right
they wish to defend.   If disagreement with, active opposition

[11]"The more emphasis there is on mere statements and the less there is
on actual participation, the easier it will be for leaders to count, if not
on support, at least on the acquiescence of the bulk of the student
body". Economic Commission for Latin America, *Education, Human
Resources, and Development in Latin America*, United Nations, 1968,
p. 161.

to, and confrontation with the established authorities marks student leaders as leftists, then there is ample basis for characterizing a very large number of them in this way. But the source of such leftism in action is not, for the great majority, the kind of ideological commitment which could sustain a continuous and cumulative series of actions toward revolutionary goals.

In the sixties, however, there have appeared student challengers of the kind of leftist leaders described above, in both Mexico and Colombia. These challengers declare themselves committed to the kind of revolutionary doctrines manifest in Maoism and Castroism or Fidelism. When they have won control by election to office in the student societies and federations, as they have on a number of occasions, they have steered student activism toward greater emphasis on direct action, intransigent demands, and uncompromising positions. They have also been inclined to transform student activism stimulated by local issues into demonstrations opposing what are labeled examples of Yankee imperialism.

The major impact of that challenge, however, has been to introduce schism into the student movement, a schism mirroring that among radical groups in the society at large. In both Mexico and Colombia, the youth wings of the Communist Party as well as the communists among the students, have split along lines of the Moscow-Peking controversy. The regulars are Moscow oriented. The dissidents direct the same charges of revisionsim, apathy, and compromise toward the regulars as Peking directs against Moscow. The result is a contest for power within the leftist dominated student organizations locally and nationally and a consequent greater devotion to that internal struggle for power than to a program of effective reform or even revolution in the universities or society.

Interaction with Other Political Groups

Since the universities are objects of public support and policy, what happens there is very naturally the concern of the politicians. The victories they win and the defeats they suffer on issues related to the support and structuring of the universities and to the appointment and removal of university rectors are important to political careers in the same way as victories and defeats on issues related to commerce, foreign

trade, labor, public health and welfare, etc. But student
activism at the universities can be an important factor in
success or failure with respect to educational policy. Moreover, in countries like Colombia and Mexico in which students have traditionally affected political events and the for-
tunes of politicians, the latter are aware that student reactions
can be either a threat or a great help to the viability of their
hold on the reins of government. The students are a constituency which cannot well be neglected either by the members of the governing Establishment or by those who seek
to take over from them the management of public affairs.

Furthermore, the campus *políticos* are an important source
of supply in the recruitment of personnel for party or factional
activity. Party or factional strength can be increased by the
support of former campus leaders who can recall with gratitude the help given them by a particular party, faction, or
politician during their career as campus leaders. Moreover,
as we shall indicate in a later chapter, student activism, which
challenges government policy always holds the possibility of
igniting general unrest, unrest which is not only disturbing to
the public order, which it is government's responsibility to
preserve, but can be a threat to the continuing power of the
current leaders of political life and of the existing government
itself.

Politicians in order to protect their own partisan interest as
well as to discharge their public responsibilities, therefore
establish personal relations with student leaders whose activities might prove advantageous or disadvantageous to them.
And the allegation is seldom denied that these relations are
supportive, both in an advisory and in a financial manner, of
some of the student leaders.

There are a number of political action groups in Latin
America who are potential recruiters of student support; but
not all of them exert any significant influence on the student
movement in Mexico and Colombia. In Mexico, political
action is dominated by the monolithic PRI, the Party of the
Institutionalized Revolution, the Continuing Revolution. The
political activity of the major interest groups is integrated
within the party. There is no representation of the students
as such, although should a student seek some influence within
the party, he might do so as a member of the Confederation of
Young Mexicans.

In Colombia, the Liberal and Conservative Parties, both of which are heavily representative of the traditional elite oligarchy, are at the moment working under an agreement by which the two alternate in forming the administration. There are of course, a range of factions within the two parties, but not even the farthest left faction in the Liberal party can be considered to be oriented toward anything approaching revolutionary change. The traditional parties have given small attention to any attempts to organize the students as a group. The extreme left faction of the Liberal party, MLR, did, however, have a youth wing, though it was not limited to a student membership.

In neither country are the opposition parties either of the right or left of any numerical significance. In neither country is there a Social Democratic Party on the European model. Nevertheless, there are political groups and politically minded individuals, oriented to a position of opposition to the dominant political Establishment, which seek contact with the students.

Both Russian and Chinese communists are active, the former through operations centering in the Embassies. Russia offers scholarships to students from Latin American and in 1960 it was estimated that 15,000 students from the continent were studying in communist countries in Europe and Asia. In Mexico and Colombia the themes of communist effort which most frequently coincide with and influence student activism, are opposition to support of the United States in its cold war effort and Vietnam activities, and opposition to economic and allegedly imperialistic exploitation of Latin American countries by the United States. Anti-Yankee demonstrations in the two countries are usually attributed to Russian or Chinese communist initiative. One soon gains the impression from discussions with even the more conservative students, however, that little outside influence would be necessary to stimulate such demonstrations when an occasion was offered. The feelings of nationalism and Latinism, coupled with the perception of historical interference of the United States government or private business in Latin American affairs, and the awareness of the need for accepting financial and market dependency on the United States resources is strong enough to arouse anti-Yankee predispositions to active expression at the slightest opportunity.

The testimony of those student leaders we interviewed who

were active at the time of the Cuban revolution is that the
initial effect of that revolution was to strengthen the influence
of those in the student movement who were committed to
revolutionary activism. At first, Castro was popular among
the latter. He had done what some of them would like to
have done, but which, in the light of the strength of the
established governing powers in Colombia and Mexico, seemed
difficult if not impossible for them, that is, carry through
a revolution. Both among the students and the leaders of the
small opposition parties the possibility of a genuine revolution and the role of students in effectuating such a revolution
appears less than realistic. Nevertheless, at the first Latin
American Youth Congress in Havana in 1960 and the first
Latin American Congress for National Sovereignty, Economic
Emancipation and Peace in Mexico City in 1961, the Cuban
revolution was the central focus of interest. The liberal minded
Mateos government in Mexico was forced to take steps to curb
a stepped up pro-Castro program in 1961. Not only Mexican,
but other Latin American students who attended international student conferences or Soviet financed "visits" regularly
stopped off in Havana on their way home. They returned to
their countries loaded with Cuban propaganda leaflets including detailed instructions for carrying on terrorist activity
and reportedly in one case, plans for the organization of a
communist revolution.

Fidelist groups were formed among the students in both
Colombia and Mexico. Among them the possibility of revolution, Cuban style, enhanced the importance of radicalizing
the students and other potential "soldiers" of the revolution,
of attention to ideological commitments particularly to Marxism, of the utility of guerrilla and other organized violence,
and of the possible support for conspiratorial underground
movements which Castro was obviously willing to provide.
Fidelists among the student leaders competed with other student leaders for control of the student societies and of the
federations, striving to be the authentic spokesmen for all
the students of the two nations.

Although there is much talk of the necessity for "revolution"
among student leaders in Colombia and a growing dissatisfaction among student leaders in Mexico with the domination of
PRI in the governing of their country, and although from
time to time those leaders most committed to destroying the
power of the existing governing class join the guerrillas, the

carrying through of an actual revolution, Cuban style, provided for most of them less of an operational meaning for
the term "revolution" than activities directed to "substantial
change". The eventual impact of Fidelism was, however,
to divide the leftist oriented student leaders.

Moreover, the example of what Castro did about university reform ran counter to many of the specific targets of
traditional student activism in Colombia and Mexico, as well
as in other Latin American countries.[12] University autonomy
was attacked as a bourgeois disease. Failing students were
flunked out to make room for more deserving students, and
those who didn't attend 70% of the classes were not eligible
to take exams. Entrance requirements in addition to graduation from secondary school were introduced. In Cuba,
university structure emphasized control over teaching and
research by disciplines, rather than by faculties or schools.
Student participation in university administration was not
tolerated.

At the same time that Fidelism was introducing schismatic
influences into the Marxist student leadership in Latin American countries, it posed a communist threat in a form visible
and serious enough to provide an activating stimulus to the
Catholics and to the politically concerned priests within the
church. More in Colombia than in Mexico, but in both
countries, the social implications of the Papal encyclicals
furnished an ideological orientation in opposition to that
of Marxism for a number of student activists. Prior to 1959
Catholic action groups among the students appear to have
been more interested in leadership training and in retreats, and
in social service projects among the students than in winning
campus student society elections, and they could be characterized as conservative. After the Cuban revolution a number of
priests involved in student counseling have become more political action conscious and a significant number identify themselves less with the support of the Establishment.[13]   In

[12]cf. "Learning and Politics in Latin America", by John Harrison in
Proceedings, Academy of Political Science, XXVII, p. 339.

[13]Catholic social action activities in Latin America are coordinated
through the Latin American Bishops Council. Students engaged in
Christian Democratic activities are kept in touch through a regional
congress sponsored by the Organization of Latin American Christian
Democratic Youth Groups.

Colombia the story of the activities of Father Camilo Tores is often repeated among the students. He was a chaplain at the National University, a sociologist, and a socialist. He tried to organize a new opposition party, The Peoples United Front, but found that impossible. He eventually left the priesthood, joined the guerrillas in 1966, and was killed in an engagement between the guerillas and government troops.

In Mexico the Catholic church as an institution has long been excluded from overt participation in political affairs and the church officaldom must guard carefully what freedom of operation it has. An organization, *"Corporación"* under the leadership of a Catholic priest, "Don David" has however, for some years interested itself in student affairs. Many of its activities of a social nature are in the open, but claims are made that the good Father has had a large part in steering members of his own choosing into positions of student leadership in the several important faculty and school societies at the National University, into the pre-1966 all-university society, and into the all-Mexican federation. His operations in student politics have been as indirect and as devious (and, it is alleged, over long periods as successful) as those of the communists. His influence has been exerted, according to those who would like to see the student movement more militant, on behalf of restraint; and those who make this judgment consider his efforts responsible in a major way for the reputation of Mexican student activism for a low degree of radicalism, compared with students from other Latin American countries.

There may have been radical rightist student organizations in Colombia, but they were not visible. At the National University in Mexico City, however, a fascist-like organization, MURO, formerly secret, has come out into the open and is active whenever the opportunity arises to express active anti-liberalism. MURO is not adverse to the use of physical violence.

There is little doubt that the opposition political forces in both Mexico and Colombia have interested themselves in making contact with the students. Both the communists and the Catholics have sought, and with marked success, to influence the students. Moreover the impression among students and faculty, as well as among citizens generally, is that the Communist Party and the Catholic Church have used their contacts with students to encourage and support the candi-

SECTION III
COMING OF AGE

Coming of Age

The interpretation of student activity such as that described in the preceding section is aided if consideration is given to the stage of life at which the individual student is seeking to discover and be sure of himself as a person in relation to those others with whom he associates or anticipates association.[1] This approach to the interpretation of student activism is particularly relevant when the experiences through which the country is passing introduce uncertainties and unexpected and unprepared-for complexities into the role of citizenship for all citizens. How can one sense self-confidence that he is making progress toward achieving an adult role which is itself unclear? This condition characterized all the countries visited in the post World War II period. Youths were not facing the problem of "adopting" an adult role the general if not specific nature of which was well established. They faced, along with most other citizens, the task of "creating" an adult role consistent with the requirements for life and work in a rapidly changing world, full of uncertainties and unpredictable developments whose continuity with past and present developments is puzzling.

This has always been true, but 20th century youth is living in the midst of unprecedented radical changes in a pattern of life and work and of personal and national values resulting from the impact of accelerating scientific discoveries and their technological applications, from urbanization, from the demands of the common man for a more meaningful participation in the governing of his own affairs, from the uneasy maneuvering for power advantage within and among nations, and, above all from the overhanging threat of the nuclear destruction of all mankind.

[1] The possibilities concerning the sources of student activism presented here and in the introduction to Section IV are essentially those discussed in Chapter 2, "Roots and Soil of Student Activism", by E. Wight Bakke, in *Student Politics*, Lipset, S. M. (ed), Basic Books, 1967.

The adaptive response of the people and institutions of a nation to these developments has an impact on the essential character of the nation itself and on the image held by its people of the unique wholeness and character of their homeland. This impact is significant for the process of maturation because a youth's conception of what he is and is to become must incorporate as one of its major ingredients the fact that he is a Mexican, a Colombian, an Indian, a Japanese, an American. And what that means is inseparable from the image he holds of the unique wholeness and character of his nation which we have referred to in other writings as the nation's "organizational charter."

In all the countries studied, as well as in the United States, but for different reasons in each country, that organizational charter lacks clarity and dependability at the present time as a touchstone by reference to which a youth may test the adequacy of the institutional facilities provided, of the values and standards by which he is judged, of the expectancies to which he must respond, of the personal requirements imposed upon the mature individual, of the quality and authenticity of the available adult roles, and of his own self-conception. That concept is so central to the process of maturation, and hence so essential to an interpretation of student activism in these countries, that it is desirable to amplify here the nature and function of a nation's organizational charter. The following description is adapted from an earlier book, *Revolutionary Democracy, Challenge and Testing in Japan*.[2] It was in connection with the investigation of student activism in Japan that the relevance of the state of the nation's organizational charter to the radical emphases in student activism became obvious.

> To put it briefly, the organizational charter of a nation is what the name of that nation stands for in the minds and hearts of the people. It is defined by the widely shared concepts of the nature, function, and mission of the nation in relation to its citizens and to its international environment; by the major goal or goals toward the realization of which its resources including its people, are legitimately employed; by the major policies, directed toward fulfilling this function and realizing these goals to which the nation's leaders are committed; by the major characteristics of the

[2]Bakke, E. Wight, *Revolutionary Democracy*, Archon Books, Hamden, 1968. pp. 9ff.

reciprocal rights and obligations governing relations among the nation's people and between that nation and other nations; by the central value premises legitimizing the functions, goals, policies, and system of rights and obligations; and by the symbols and traditions used to clarify, focus attention upon, and reinforce such concepts and gain acceptance for them from people inside and outside the nation. Efforts to maintain the orderliness and integrity of the nation, efforts to meet both internal and external crises, as well as to conduct daily and routine affairs harmoniously, are given direction and are reinforced when the organizational charter proves a widely acceptable, successful, dependable, tradition-sanctioned, and stimulating guide to and reinforcement for public and private action.

Internalized by individuals as their heritage, the organizational charter also provides a powerful ingredient in their conceptions of themselves and gives significance and purpose to individual effort and life. Individualistic as the people of a nation may become, very few can find a meaning for their personal lives by disassociating themselves from the perceived purpose and destiny of their own nation. For the vast majority of us the importance and dignity of our life is amplified and made secure by the worth and honorableness of our family, of the institutions of which we are members, and ultimately of our native or adopted land. The organizational charter of these groups and/or organizations is the ultimate foundation for estimating that worth and honorableness. Respect for and love of country is not simply an expression of patriotism advantageous to maintaining the group solidarity of its citizens. Such sentiments are an important basis for the confidence of the individual in himself.

That these sentiments shall be supported by a national organizational charter which is dependable and a source of pride is particularly important for the youth who are trying to find themselves, to develop an image of themselves which is consistent with and integrated with that of a world larger than that inhabited by their family and circle of friends in the community, the world of adult opportunities and responsibilities. A young man or woman is in a transition from a self whose nature and meaning has heretofore been integrated with the character of family and school, to one which now must somehow be related to, and hopefully consistent with, that of the larger society and the nation. The familial and school-related elements in the concept of one's self are not "thrown away" or ignored; but these elements will now appear in a different light. To the extent that they remain a part of the self, they are part of a self to be integrated with the societal entity, the nation. If the organizational charter of that nation is a hazy oblong blur, integration is most difficult.

The experience of finding and knowing oneself as an adult in relation to a widening group of associates in a widening area of living is one which is common to all youth. The student's experience is differentiated from that of a non-student in his age group only by the ambitions which stimulate, and the peculiar circumstances, opportunities, and problems that advance or constrain his efforts to incorporate in his concept of himself the characteristics of a *student* and to play a role in society appropriate to one who has succeeded in those efforts, and from the relative freedom accorded him as a student. This problem is the subject of Section IV.

The student shares with all young people, however, a process of maturation in which he interacts with and receives clues to his identity from the reactions of his family, his intimate peers, and the wider public and from the meaning given to their lives by the organizational charter of the societal entity of which they are all members. The observation that adolescence is that stage in life to which the person is being transformed from being predominantly a member of a family to predominantly a member of society is related to this changing emphasis. It has also been noted that at the time of this basic transformation the importance of the peer group is heightened.[3] Indeed it often appears to those of college and university student age, whether or not they are students, that it is in reaction to their peer group, in gaining a status within it, in being involved in its activities and associations, in trying to comprehend the society and its institutions and the nation itself in terms verifiable by reference to that group's experience and observations, and in measuring themselves by peer group standards, that they find the most reliable clues to their personal identity and to a role for them to play at the present time and later in an experienced society. It is not that they are not members of a family or of a larger society. But the familiar actions and relationships and codes within the family are no longer sufficient as an operational field for the assertion of their changing and growing conception

---

[3]The degree to which the style, the folkways, and mores of the peer group constitute a subculture, or are perceived as constituting a subculture by youth or others varies in the several countries here under discussion. It is greatest in the United States and least in India. Cf. an excellent discussion of the differences between the United States and India, both among youth generally and among students, in J. R. Gusfield, "The Academic Milieu," in Altbach, P. G. (ed.), *Turmoil and Transition*, Basic Books, 1968.

of themselves as near adults. Yet they have not experienced a widely ranging interaction in the affairs of adult society and, indeed, they are not recognized fully by their elders as participants in it. It can accordingly be said that the young person is passing from dominant association with the members and culture of his family, through association with the members and culture of his youthful peer group, to association with the members and culture of the wider adult society. But the clues to the evaluation of what he has been and to what he aspires to become, as well as to what he now is, as a unique person, are furnished predominantly by the ideas coming from his peer group.

The consciousness that this is exactly what is happening to him, and that he is capable of and on the verge of entering, but is not yet accepted as a full member of, adult "society," is the major common characteristic of the students in all the countries we have studied. The actions both of initiation by student leaders and of response by their followers, appeared to be their announcements and assertions, first of all to themselves, then to their intimate peers, and finally to their families and to the public at large, that they felt they had arrived at that point in their development when they were capable of taking their place as thinkers and critics and actors among the adult members of society.

The degree of certainty and security in this conviction varies as between countries and as between individual students in all countries. The nature, stability, and dependability of what is required of adults varies. The degree to which traditional adult role models are perceived as consistent with the needs of the present and future society varies. The degree to which the socialization process in family, community, and school has conditioned them for acceptance of or rebellion against the status quo varies. But the variations are those of circumstances within which the basic and universal process of maturation becomes manifest.

That process appeared to us to be one (a) of "coming of age," (b) of clarifying, and gaining certainty in, a conception of their selves that was relevant and significant in the affairs of society they faced, (c) of integrating that self with their familiar peer group and with (or at least inserting it into) the adult world of people, institutions, and affairs, (d) of expressing and symbolizing that "arrival" in action, and (e) of assuring themselves, and also gaining a recognition, first of all from their peers among students and then from all adults, that such self-assertion was legitimate and a right to which they were entitled, a right which they were prepared to make manifest in deeds as well as in words.

The manifestations in action of this search and of self-assertion are reinforced and intensified by the sheer animal vigor and the awareness of constant increase in physical competence characteristic of youth at this age. They are psychologically intensified by the excitement about the widening horizons of discovery of what is new to them about their environment, about other people, and about themselves.

The distinctiveness of their identity with *youth* is sharpened by the observation that the adults with whom they are becoming more closely associated present certain contrasts to themselves, at least from their point of view. Those adults, as perceived by youth, reveal a degree of animal vigor and skills which are reaching, if they have not already reached, a plateau. The making of *new* discoveries and the widening of interests appear to youth to be much less characteristic of adults than of themselves and their peers. Any eager examination of and experimentation with anything which is not normal, customary, and safe has, in the opinion of youth, been dulled for adults by personal experiences and the repeated compromises with and adaptation to things as they are. Likewise the adults they know, with few exceptions, seem incapable of unreserved commitment to anything that savors of uncompromising idealism. Moreover, the behavior of adults appears to them to reveal a considerable departure from the ideals of conduct and aspiration and faith which those same adults proclaim in words to be the fundamental premises of a good and responsible life.

It is not surprising, therefore, that youth, in their search for identity, should resist adopting as their own the adult roles they observe in the behavior of the adults around them. It is not necessary under these circumstances to posit a generational *revolt*, or a rebellion against parental authority, to interpret the unorthodox and different reactions of youth to the world they face. Their discovery of a unique personal individuality must be consistent with the qualities they feel they have more of than do adults: increasing animal vigor and skills; eyes open to new discoveries and widening interests; eagerness to examine and experiment with the abnormal, the non-customary, and that which is dangerous enough to test their mettle; commitment to absolutes rather than compromises; and the desire for harmony between ideals and behavior. Those things differentiate them, they believe, from adults.

Moreover, the launching of that self into a world of affairs must be adapted to their perception of the present and future reality of those affairs, uncolored, they insist, by the interpretive stereotypes, prejudices, and preconceptions produced by experiences out of the past, so characteristic of most of the adults they know. They are of course impatient with those adults including their parents, but even with their own peers, who measure their present behavior and attitudes by the standards of traditional orthodoxy. But it is possible that the most relevant clue to that behavior and those attitudes will result from considering their impatience a manifestation not so much of negative revolt or rebellion as of a positive search and self-assertion.

Difficult to explain by reference to any factors other than those internal to the organism of the individual youth himself, is the appearance of particular youths who have an abnormal urge to initiate action and to carry their fellows with them in the direction they are predisposed to take. That urge to leadership among the few will be tempered by experience with foot-dragging associates over time, but during the student years there is ample opportunity for optimistic experimentation in recruiting followers among the members of their peer group. It is these activist and frequently aggressive individuals who normally "launch" and give focus and direction to student activism.

The biological and psychological factors which produce the drive to stand out as a leader will have to be interpreted by scientists who have made such phenomena the objects of study. From our own investigation we would report one observation which may be relevant to that study. A common characteristic of all the student leaders with whom we came in contact was that they were in some repsects "lonely" persons, lonely in the sense that some peculiarity of social heritage, socialization, personality, or character, set them apart from their fellows, and made it difficult for them to experience, without special thought and effort, a natural affinity with the great majority of their fellow students, even though that majority sensed no difficulty in considering them acceptable members of the peer group. We shall return to this clue to the explanation of student activism in Section V.

The chapters which follow explore some of the major experiences which the lonely ones and the masses of students have in common and which provide would-be leaders with the opportunity to challenge a significant number of students to activism of the kind reported in the previous Section, an activism which in their judgment, furthers their progress toward coming of age.

Chapter 4

Coming of Age in Japan

The hypothesis that student activism is in part a response to frustrations encountered by youth in the process of maturation, that it is a form of *self*-assertion in the attempt to experience a secure adult identity, is useful in interpreting that phenomenon in Japan. The problems encountered by youth in coming of age in Japan are not identical with those observed in India, Colombia, Mexico, and the United States but the evidence for the generalization was clear. The plausibility of the hypothesis was revealed in both individual and group interviews. The interest of Japanese students in establishing their unique identity as adults was disclosed in discussions on many subjects which at first glance would appear unrelated to the matter. Also revealed were the problems they faced in finding a meaningful place for themselves in a very confused social, political, and economic adult world at home and abroad. The question was raised, for example, in connection with the following topics:

Japan's future: "How can we know what we are to do and be until the place of Japan in the world is clear and we develop the kinds of government at home that make it sure what part we can play?"

The nature of democracy and freedom: "How can we set up democratic relations in the universities, in industry, and in the country if the folks who are to be related that way aren't sure of them*selves*?" "Do you think a man can be free *in himself* regardless of how he stands with other people?" "It's beyond me what freedom really can mean in a big country like Japan, or the United States, or China, or Russia. So I just try to think what it could mean in my family, but most of all what it would mean for me to say *I* am free."

The degree of social conformity in the United States (and

in Russia): "How can a man claim he is an *independent soul* when he lives like that?"

Foreign authors: The popularity of Albert Camus and Jean Paul Sartre and of existentialist authors generally.

The negro problem in the United States: "I think I know how they feel when they are excluded from *being themselves* like other men can be."

The "new" religions: "I know a young man who has recently joined Soka Gakkai. I couldn't do that because it's a short cut to finding a personal security that's all emotional. How anyone who thinks with his head can do it is more than I can understand. But I will say he doesn't seem to feel lost anymore like I do."

American Western films: "Now *there* are people who are what they are no matter what, and no matter what other people think. They are almost always *sure of themselves.* If they don't like the way things are and their life doesn't suit them, they go out and make one that does. They don't change themselves."

Japan's defeat: "Why do *I* feel ashamed when I think of how Japan failed so badly after so many years of success? I wasn't even born when it all started. What does it have to do with *me?* Maybe I'm just *part me and part Japan.*"

Student demonstrations: "In a way its like being drunk while it's going on. Those people are wrong who say one loses himself in a crowd like that. I never feel more *myself* — at the time that is. You feel that you're really an important part of something big and important. But then the next day, when you're back at all the daily things that you have to do, you wonder, was that really *me*, and, if so, why don't I feel as good today? I've never felt so much like what it must be like to be an important individual and so free of doubts about myself as I did that few days [of mass demonstrations] in 1960. I don't feel that way when I'm alone. But that doesn't make sense, does it? I sometimes wonder who and what *I am* anyway."

Things they are anxious about in college or at the university: Responses to such an opening almost invariably emphasize first of all the prospects for a job and the kind of life they will be able to lead when they graduate. But then come responses that indicate they are concerned about the meaning of living and how they can make friends and maintain friendships in an as yet unexplored adult world while continuing to be themselves.

This personal impression is substantiated by a survey conducted among 600 Japanese students from all parts of Japan by the Research Institute for Student Problems at Tokyo University. Students were asked to circle those items among 139 presented to them which caused them anxiety or concern. Among the 20 items circled most frequently were four (ranked 1, 2, 6 & 14) concerning their outlook for making a living. Nine of the twenty (ranked 3, 5, 8, 9, 10, 11, 13, 16, 17) were concerned with the establishment of one's self as a real person in harmony with other people and with the universe. Only three of the twenty, [ranked 4 (politics), 7 (war), and 15 (injustice)] were concerned with the state of society.

Another evidence was that in 1963, seventeen out of forty-two semifinalists in an English language oratorical contest in the Tokyo area spoke on the theme, "What am I?"

We were also impressed with the frequency that the subject arose in student discussion groups of the ethics of the "about face" (Tenko) which was expected to occur when one graduated, namely, that their decisions and actions would no longer be made on the basis of "principle" but on the basis of "common sense."

Alienation

One concept which has become a frequently used generalization among Japanese students in discussing matters related to the difficulties in realizing themselves as near adults and of coming of age was "alienation." We are aware that this is a term much used by psychologists and sociologists in their explorations of the problems of youth in all countries. The meaning of this term when used by the Japanese students whom we interviewed, seemed to cover many of the difficulties they experienced in developing an awareness of, and a confidence in, themselves as adult individuals in relation to other people and to the world in which they were living. What they were speaking about when discussing their condition of "alienation"

may or may not be consistent with the content psychologists
and sociologists give to this term. Since it was the term used,
we shall also use it in the sense we believe they did, that is, "a
state of not being able to understand, and to experience as
secure, the fact of one's individuality as in harmony with and
integrated with other people and with the adult world and the
universe in which one lives."

From the direct statements of the students and from plausible
inferences which could be drawn from their descriptions of the
circumstances related to the experience they labelled as "alienation," it would appear that the six types of factors discussed below are causally related to that experience. The factors have to
do with:

> The cultural guidelines to adult human relationships
>
> The dynamic changes taking place in the structure and
> character of societal relations and in the "National
> Identity"
>
> The relevance of the training and predispositions of Japa-
> nese youth to the achievement of personal identity
>
> The opportunity for making respect-producing contribu-
> tions to the group and to society
>
> The disregard of traditionally shared values
>
> The superficial experience with new group shared values

The Guidelines to Adult Human Relationships

Traditional Japanese culture provides certain guidelines to
appropriate interactions among people assumed to aid an individual in coming of age. The problem faced by postwar students however, arose from the fact that these guidelines were, in
many respects, irrelevant to the achieving of an adult role as an
independent and equal individual, the kind of a self-image and
role consistent with the democratization of Japanese society undertaken after 1945 by Japanese leaders and urged by the allied
Occupation forces.

We shall in connection with several problems have occasion
to comment on the difference in the Western and the Japanese
concept and experience of becoming and being a distinctive
mature person. In both cases, of course, one becomes the particular person he is in interaction with others and with groups,

that is with what has been referred to as the "human nexus or matrix," of which he is a member. But in Western culture the person is conceived of, and experiences himself, as a relatively autonomous human unit, whereas in Japanese culture he is conceived of as inseparable from and fused with that human matrix (especially his family and ancestors). The Western concept of an individual ultimately free and responsible, answerable finally only to his God or to all humanity or to universally valid principles of living, and in this sense equal with all other individuals, is a working concept only among Japanese Christians or among those who have "adopted" this basically Western philosophy. It is not a concept indigenous to Japanese culture.

There are many consequences of this group-fused concept of the person for the attempt to establish and maintain democratic institutions in Japan.[4] At this point our interest is in noting its consequences for the efforts of a person to establish his adult identity and simultaneously to seek integration with others and his world. It goes without saying that the character of both that identity and of the role required for functional and spiritual integration with others must be consistent if the individual is not to experience what he may call "alienation." The partial irrelevancy of the Japanese cultural guidelines to appropriate concepts of the autonomous adult self and of proper interactional behavior among the individual members of the society made necessary both ideological and action-oriented search and experimentation producing, hopefully, guidelines that were relevant. For some, student activism was the form taken by such search and experimentation.

A person's perception of his identity, his self-image, can of course involve all degrees of relatedness to others from a completely-group-fused man to an anarchist, and such variations are found among Western people as well as among the people of Japan. Practically speaking neither extreme is possible. Biologically a person is a separate entity, and his mental and emotional characteristics are governed in part by that separateness. Socially a person is in constant interaction with other

[4]All of these developments can be seen not only in the postwar student movements in Japan, but also in the reactions of people involved in the attempts to establish parliamentary government, political parties, the many "new" religions, trade unions, local autonomy in educational and police affairs, a "free enterprise" business system, and an individual ownership oriented land reform.

people and with organized society and nature. His mental and emotional characteristics are influenced by, and grow in part as, responses to the experience of such interaction. But when the emphasis in the traditional culture (as in Japan) is at a point on the spectrum close to the first extreme, that is to the concept of the group-fused person, the actual expected customary interactions and interdependencies of a person with others complicates his efforts to define the nature and boundaries of his distinctive individuality. For such a concept is not a mere abstraction. It is made operational by ritual and etiquette and by reciprocal obligations and rights governing the relations of each person to the others. One cannot even define intellectually his adult identity and individuality without being influenced by his familiarity with, and the constraints on *self*-development imposed by, such operational meanings. And unless he completely isolates himself from all association with his fellows, the actual manifestation of his real self will have to approximate to a consistency with the commonly practiced ritual, etiquette and commonly observed rights and obligations among his associates. Otherwise he will become hopelessly entangled in the incompatibility of his concept of his self with the societal opportunities for, and constraints on, its actualization.

The students who were so troubled by the effort to answer the question, "Who and what am I?" seemed to us to be experiencing this entanglement. That experience must have been the lot of those at all periods of Japanese history who sought a definition of their selves characterized by a greater degree of individual autonomy than that consistent with the traditional Japanese culture. But the students, and indeed all Japanese of the postwar era, faced this difficulty in exaggerated form. Why?

The answer is related to the combination of two postwar circumstances associated with defeat and Occupation policies: first from the disturbance to confidence in that traditional culture, and second the emphasis on the establishment of new institutions and ways assuming personal freedom to choose and to speak and to act, and assuming the legal and political equality of all men. These two circumstances touched with amplified impact the lives of a very large number. Among that number were most of the students we interviewed. Their search for the answer to the questions "Who am I?" and "How can I maintain a unique adult individuality in relation to others and to my world?" was no mere academic exercise in response to intellectual curiosity. It was not *merely* a desperate search for a substitute concept of self to replace that which had been weakened and, to some, made irrelevant by the course of events. It was both of these, but more. It was a search for a self-image which would have to be expressed through new and unfamiliar kinds of active relationships and institutions.

It was apparent that something called "individualism" was a premise of those new relationships and institutions. The meaning of individualism as such a premise was not clear, but it obviously was related to the individuality and the meaning of life for particular persons, themselves included, and to their relationship with other particular persons. It was natural and inevitable that they should not only *think* and *feel* about this problem, but should *act* and *experiment* with ways in which their adult individuality would have a chance to express itself under postwar conditions of life.

Moreover, the aspect of their self-image reflected in the awareness that "I am a *student*" acquired enlarged content. As students they were those with the opportunity, if not the obligation, to think about and to experiment in action with ways of making and expressing themselves. That effort, quite naturally, was associated in their minds not only with self-assertion but with making that self-assertion symbolic of the proclaimed principles of the new order such as freedom, equality, and democracy.

Another feature of the traditional Japanese guidelines to appropriate interaction and interdependency among people, both young and adult, is that these shall basically and primarily take place within a vertical hierarchy of relationships. Within such a hierarchy one can identify himself by reference to others as a subordinate of "a" and a superior of "c." In prewar Japan a person had been conditioned to rate his obligation to yield to the control of superiors and his authority to control those in subordinate positions by reference to the distance of the two positions from one directly in contact with the source of all authority, the Emperor. Within such a vertically oriented framework even one's horizontal associates are identified as a group or class or caste occupying a similar hierarchical position. That, of course, is a perfectly possible mode of personal identification, as long as it is widely accepted in the society as appropriate.

To some degree and in some aspects of life that hierarchical mode of relationship survives and becomes manifest in all cultures. This occurs even though the foundation concept of relatedness is that of horizontal equality. The ideal of all men being created equal is, of course one to which those who rank as superiors must pay homage and by reference to which they are constrained and by which the legitimacy of their governing is evaluated. Unless, however, a culture emphasizes as *primary* and legitimate that horizontal relationship of equality, provides encouragement to the solving of both individual and group problems through the action of formal and informal associations of "equals," and legitimizes the power exercised by such associations, the self-making and identifying process operates under a number of constraints. Several such constraints rooted in the traditionally hierarchical ranking of individuals were evident among the students of Japan.

In the first place the degree of opportunity for self-expression and hence for putting to the test a person's concept of what he believes he is or can be if he is given the chance, is determined for each subordinate by his superior, for a child by father or elder brother, for an employee by employers, for a bureaucrat by department and section head, for a soldier by officers, for a student by faculty, administration, and the Minister of Education. Even when he forms horizontal associations with his peers, which he does, the habitual pattern of relationship he is accustomed to accept without serious challenge may cause him to seek and to follow a leader in that association. Hence even the horizontal associations, student associations, political parties, tend to assume a hierarchal pattern internally in which the policies and actions are initiated and directed by the leaders.

Traditionally in Japan, the code of relations of persons to each other in the family, in the army, in the firm, in the political party, in the university, in the community, and of course in the nation provided that a person received his identity by reference to his nearest superior and subordinate associates. When the hierarchical principle was disrupted, by the negation of the sovereignty of the Emperor and by the purging of many of those close to him in the hierarchy, the whole structure became confused and undependable. Individual people found their position and consequent identity was, at best, in a state of unstable equilibrium, since the positions all down the line had traditionally been rated by reference to the distance from that of the Emperor. Students shared with many other Japanese citizens this disturbance to the traditional patterns of relationships, although the others may simply have perceived as an "unclear status" that experience which students referred to as an aspect of "alienation." But the students were in the process of coming of age. What the others had lost as an understandable social framework for their personal identity, the students were seeking and had not found.

The destruction of the dependability of the hierachical superior-subordinate system is not followed immediately and inevitably, however, by dependence on the establishment of relations consistent with a horizontal equality principle. It may more likely lead to exaggerated confusion, dissatisfaction, and loneliness and the feeling of having been cut off or cut out from dependable relations, and to a reassertion in any substitute organization of societal arrangements of the more familiar hierarchical pattern. Or it may lead to another result, not admittedly incompatible with the ones just named, of exaggerated self-assertion on the part of some who thereby seek escape from confusion, dissatisfaction, loneliness, and alienation. All three results were revealed in the testimony of student activists.

A complicating factor is that, after all, the hierarchical principle of the organization of human relationships appears, at least superficially, to the person whose generalizations about life are from the data of immediate observation, more compatible with the reality of variations in the human capacities of people than the principle of horizontal equality. Before the latter principle can continuously and effectively act even as a corrective of the former, generations of thought, devoted to the debate as to the rights and obligations of man in association with man, are required. The experience of many generations is necessary to make possible the integration of the principle that "all men are created equal" with the folklore that some men are born to rule other men, and with the common sense conclusion, reflecting common experience, that some men have the capacities for governing themselves and others, and that others do not.

Not only generations of thought are required, but also generations of experimentation in the establishment and perfecting of working horizontal associations which effectuate and bring the assertions of principle out into life.

Uncomfortable and as disturbing to orderly societal governing, and even as inept and egotistical, as the experimentation with direct action of the students may have been in their response to their enforced alienation from the traditional and formerly dependable principle of hierarchally governed human relationships, their experiments must, we think, be numbered among those essential to the reconstruction of human relationships in Japan if those relationships are to exemplify more thoroughly in the future than in the past such characteristics as freedom, equality, democracy, the dignity of the individual.

To be sure there are dangers both to the individual and the society in such experimentation. Lack of understanding of what action is appropriate for the promotion of either group or the public interest can lead to chaos and even desperate violence and disorder. Lack of experience in, and confusion with respect to, the ways of obtaining consensus in ideas and interests and cooperation in effective action may lead to a reenactment in these groups of the domination of the strong and the confident, as was the case in the traditionally hierarchical groupings. In either case the way is opened for these groups to be used by demagogues or by conspirators of the right or the left.

But without the experimentation of such groups, leading to the successful establishing and maintaining of such horizontal equality oriented relationships, the hope that particular persons can develop a working concept of an adult self in a democratic society which is at once independent of, and interdependent and integrated with (that is, not alienated from) the people, institutions, and other realities of their world, remains a Utopian dream. Such a working concept of self is a product not merely of thought but of experience.

Changes in the Structure of Societal Relations

Compared with the situation in prewar Japan, there was a relative lack of coherence and integration among the several societal groups and strata in postwar Japan. In the earlier period, the strata represented by the Emperor's Household, the Genro, the Cabinet and their ministries, the military top command, business, educational, and religious establishments and their managements, were related to one another by overlapping of membership, a sort of "interlocking directorate" which helped to hold the whole together. Those who found themselves at the base of the structure, students, workers, government employees, shrine members, soldiers, were able to know, by reference to the position of their superiors, where and how they fitted into the whole pattern and how they were related ultimately to the Emperor himself. In the postwar years, integration through "interlocking directorates" was no longer so characteristic, and new arrangements, rules, and instruments had to be developed to facilitate interaction and integration. These have not yet been stabilized, and they do not provide Japanese society with the same degree of coherence as the former arrangement, a coherence which can be reflected in the self-image of those who live in such a society. Moreover, the codes of relationship which can act as a binding-together cement among people and groups in a society were appropriate to the old pattern. The working out of new codes takes time. Lacking that binding cement, the society of people is like a building built with mortar or plaster or concrete which is mostly sand. It doesn't stick together.

Commented one student leader about the problems faced by students in experiencing purpose, harmony, and coherence within themselves in an adult world, "There can be little coherent order and integration within when it is not supported by order and integration without."

Another difficulty, suggested by the comment above, in the development of a stable and dependable adult self, at once independent and interdependent, arises when the institutional environment, in interaction with which that self is formed and tested, is itself unstable and undependable. The sense of alienation under such circumstances does not result from isolation or lack of contact, but from confusing and unsettling contact with an environment which does not mirror the order, stability, and dependability an individual desires to experience as characteristic of himself. In the first decade after the war, the character, structure, and dynamics of Japanese institutions lacked purpose, coherence, focus, and dependable continuity with the past and the future.

Personal purpose is an important organizing element for an individual. If one wishes to have his own purpose consistent with and contributory to those of the society and nation of which he desires to be a significant part, he must know what those latter purposes are. He must be able to answer with respect to the areas of activity in which he is engaged, "Education for what, political action for what, personal hard work and national economic progress for what?" Japanese students found it difficult to answer those questions with a degree of certainty in the postwar era. The dogmatism and absolutism with which they proclaimed the answers and the patterns of self-assertion in word and action made manifest in student activism was explained by several "alumni" of the student movement as a response as much to uncertainty as to certainty.

Continuity in the elements of one's environment is also an

aid toward establishing and evolving a consistent adult self. The postwar period was one of revolution, not continuity. Hence there was a discontinuity of the past and the present. The lessons of the past, valuable in finding or establishing one's adult self, lessons which were the common heritage of all Japanese people, were relatively poor guides for carrying out that process in the present and the future.

Moreover, there was a great distrust, not only of the former principles of personal honor and human mutuality, but of the leaders who symbolized those principles. The past principles had failed. The leaders of the past had failed. But new principles had not yet evolved, and new leaders had not yet arisen.

We shall not soon forget the comment of a student older than most, in his late twenties, which reveals the problem faced by the students related to the discontinuity in guidelines. "When you have no faith in your leaders, which is what we Japanese have had in the past, you have to do *something*, for example, storm the barricades. And when you are doing something, you feel like you are *somebody*. You are somebody just for the day. Even when you are getting successful results with that kind of action and feel very important as an actor, you know that can't continue. There has to be some future way more constructive that is related to, but not the same as, the past. When we finally failed after we reached the peak, although we got Kishi to resign, many of us realized that we deserved to fail because we had thought of ourselves as destroyers of the old, not builders of the new. At least our actions and plans for action were consistent with thinking of ourselves that way."

The Destruction of the National Identity

In the introduction of this section, we have emphasized the importance to the process of coming of age in any land of the existence in the minds and hearts of youth of the image of their nation, its "organizational charter." If that image of the unique wholeness of their nation, its essential character, its continuing system of values, the bonds of institutional relationships which weld a people together into a unity cemented by reciprocal rights and obligations, and the nation's status and role among nations, are clear and widely accepted, that image is a major touchstone by reference to which a youth can guide himself in the process of coming of age. For among the pred-

icates of "I am . . ." none is more basic than that which identifies a man as a "a Colombian," "an American," etc. On the other
hand, if that image is unclear, uncertain, undependable, or in a
state of disintegration or disarray, an essential source of self-
identification is missing. Under such circumstances, a youth is
like a "man without a country" in the sense that he has no sure
concept of this own land which he can incorporate with pride
into the concept of what it means to be himself.

Up to and during the first stages of World War II, Japanese
youth knew what it meant to be People of the Rising Sun.
Japan's organizational charter was embodied in the Meiji
Constitution, the Code of Bushido, the Emperor's Imperial
Rescript on Education, the doctrine of *Kokutai* or the National
Identity,[5] and by a system of education and governance and
religious practice which provided a firm and consistent concept
for the people of Japan of the essence of their country's
nationhood. It provided them with a seldom questioned set
of expectancies as to their relations to each other and to
their country and its Emperor: loyalty, devotion and sacrifice.
The experiences of the last days of the war, the shame-producing
defeat, and the efforts of the occupation to revolutionize
Japanese polity and institutional structure destroyed central
features of this organizational charter, and what was not destroyed was clouded by doubt and uncertainty.

Defeated, worn out, confused, and depressed in spirit, the
Japanese could find few dependable and familiar premises
upon which to base a reconstituted sense of their national
identity. And, before they had a chance to recover any emotional,
intellectual, or behavioral equilibrium, the land was occupied
by armies and agents of the conqueror carrying with them,
and insisting on the immediate adoption of, a whole new set
of premises on which they were told the good society not
only could but must be built, premises like individual freedom,
democracy, sovereignty of the people, peace, and the like, none
of which were firmly rooted in the traditions and values and
practices of the great majority of the Japanese people. Indeed
these were nearly the opposites of the premises upon which

[5]For a fuller description of this central foundation stone of Japan's
prewar nationhood see *Revolutionary Democracy, Challenge and Testing in Japan*, Archon Books, 1968, pp. 12ff and references cited. The
following discussion is adapted from that source. The term *Kokutai*
was written in Japanese by two characters meaning "nation" and
"substance."

life had been built for most Japanese up to the moment of defeat.

As was to be expected, the premises were interpreted and used not in terms of the action implications of their positive substance, but as suggesting the legitimacy of opposition to practices experienced before, during, and after the war, including those of the Occupation forces. Individual freedom was freedom *from* compulsion, regulation, thought control. Democracy was escape *from* autocracy, centralized decision-making, government by oligarchy. The sovereignty of the people was release *from* dependence on a relatively weak popular assembly, an aristocratic upper house, a bureaucracy, and the absence of real electoral choice. And especially was peace the escape *from* war, the shame and disgrace of defeat in war.

The last named premise was of particular significance because it provided the first breakthrough for many Japanese, including the students, revealing the possibility of a central theme around which the image of their nation could be rebuilt. Its meaning was embodied in the Preamble and in Article IX of the Constitution:

> Preamble: We, the Japanese people, desire peace for all time and are deeply conscious of the high ideals controlling human relationships, and we have determined to preserve our security and existence, trusting in the justice of the peace-loving people of the world.

> Article IX: Land, sea, and air forces as well as other war potential will never be maintained. The right of belligerency of the State will not be recognized.

From the volume of active protest, spontaneous as well as organized, which arose at every evidence of an official Japanese or foreign (chiefly United States) move which would endanger the implementation of this commitment, we are, we think, justified in concluding that, up to the present time, more than twenty years after the tragic experience of war and defeat, the great majority of the people of Japan have made adherence to seeking peace a dominant ingredient in the organizational charter by which they wish their nation to chart its course and mission. If we were to eliminate from the record of protest demonstrations, student and otherwise, the number involved in demonstrations against U.S. military bases, revision of

Article IX, resumption of nuclear tests, the H-bomb testing, the Peace Treaty providing for continued U.S. military bases, the renewal of the Security Pact with the United States, the extension of the U.S. airfields, and the visits of Polaris submarines, we would reduce the numbers involved, certainly in student demonstrations before 1968, to the point where they would scarcely have attracted world-wide attention.

The first glimmer of light coming into the darkness of despair and confusion was the possibility of dedication to a revived mission for Japan, of becoming the first nation completely committed to peace, the leader of all nations toward that form of civilization in which men would beat their swords into plowshares and study war no more. General MacArthur contributed his eloquence to transforming a psychological revulsion against war into a positive hope that peace, as a firm principle of Japan's relations with other nations, would be a central premise of Japan's nationhood that arose from the ashes.

Hardly was the ink dry on the new "Peace Constitution," however, when this hope was dashed by the conqueror who had been so insistent on Japan's renunciation of war and so eloquent in asserting the promise of that policy as a basis for a new dignity and glory of Japan among the nations of the world. The Korean war and the need for Japanese bases and production of munitions for a foreign war-wager's use, once more embroiled Japan in the war making which had led to such disastrous results, not now as an independent nation, but as a dependent ally, involved in a world wide military power struggle. And Japan was being propelled into that struggle by the military leaders of the very nation which had urged it to find its destiny in being a peaceful nation.

Once more the image of their nation was beset by uncertainty, their search for identity as a people and as individuals attended by frustration and doubt, and by a renewed sense that once more they had been betrayed by their leaders, and in addition by their conquerors. The second great betrayal, within a few years after the first, created not only confusion and protest, but anger, and sometimes ugly anger, as well. The Mutual Security Pact and the military base and occupation arrangements took on a new and frightening meaning. That meaning was intensified by the uneraseable memory of the horror of the nuclear holocaust at Hiroshima and Nagasaki, and by the awareness of the way in which such features of Japanese life as compulsory military service, police and thought control, and autocratic government had been inseparably bound up with the waging of war.

Accompanying the sense of the disintegration of the traditional organizational charter was the active and intense search for a new image of their nation reflecting viable objectives, a viable polity, a viable mission, reflecting a wholeness and unity of the Japanese people. Students joined in that search.

But the search was a troubled one and made without a dependable map. It was a revolutionary enterprise and subject to all the uncertainties and confusion and disputations characterizing revolutionary times. The only agreement among the searchers was that the new Japan must be truly independent and powerful and that the national identity must be grounded in truly Japanese values. But what kind of international economic and political arrangements and what kind of resources and instruments for self-protection would guarantee that independence? Powerful? Yes, but in what ways, and power for what? What actually were the *essential* Japanese values in the light of the recent traumatic experiences? The answers were not clear.

We have stressed the state of confusion and bewilderment which attended the realization that the traditional principle of national life and the traditional concept of the National Identity had been seriously weakened because we are convinced that this state of affairs produced not only the context for the volume, intensity, and violence of student activism in the postwar years, but created the chief issues actual and symbolic which gave to that activism its revolutionary and anti-Establishment character. When the nation's organizational charter is in disarray, as it was in Japan during that period, when the essential identity of the nation is as confused as the confusion of tongues in which it is being debated, the achievement of a satisfying mature individual identity is difficult if not impossible. The charge that by violent protest and disruptive tactics, the students were undermining the stability and orderliness of the nation has little impact on those who can sense no stability and orderliness in the nation's identity. The charge falls with little constraining effect on the patriotic loyalties of those who have no firm concept in their hearts and minds of the essential character and identity of the nation toward which such loyalties could be directed.

Making Choices

Other difficulties blocking the way to arriving at a clear, stable, unalienated conception of their adult selves are related not so much to the alienating factors in their environment as to inadequacies within themselves. One of the ways in which one becomes aware of himself is in experiencing the process of choosing between alternatives. In a sense he stands apart from the objects among which choice is made. He is a *chooser* among possible friends and associates, among possible modes of behavior, among different fields of work, among different places to live, among different fields of study, among different ideological foundations for the kind of human relations and societal organization desired, among different political and economic systems to which to commit himself, among different objects of loyalty.

Either too few or too many alternatives is a handicap to becoming self-confident as a chooser. If the alternatives are too few or non-existent, there is little opportunity to view oneself as taking independent individual voluntary action. If they are too many, one is simply overwhelmed and confused. What is *too many* is of course relative to the number of choices a people are used to and hence with respect to which they have gained their experience of making choices. It is our impression that for many students in Japan after the war the number was overwhelming in contrast to the range of choice to which traditional cultural guidelines were relevant. As a result they felt unable to choose and, thus through commitment to their choice to become aware of themselves as choosers.

And they gained little help from their customary intimate associates in the family, from their teachers and professors, or from any spiritual advisors. These were as unfamiliar as were the students with the new criteria for choice. From these previously helpful guides they could receive little help. It was easy under such circumstances to mistake a lack of capacity to help, for a lack of concern, and to come to the conclusion that young people were adrift in an incomprehensible world, and that no one cared. The advice which did come from such sources, and in addition from editors, politicians, the leaders of the new religions, the Communists and the sponsors of the "Occupational Revolution" was so varied that it could only add to the confusion.

The number, range, size, and complexity of the choices that

faced the Japanese people after the war, plus the discrediting of the set of shared values by reference to which choices had traditionally been made, lies, we think, at the root of the desperate search for some dependable clue to the nature of the adult self in relation to all this confusing world of people and problems. The variety of the things students were clinging to as clues was large. What they had in common was the intensity and dogmatism with which they bolstered their confidence (at least for the time being) that the clue they had hit upon was a trustworthy one. These clues were ideological positions of both the right and left, loyalty to which some found rewarding. Others focused on participation in faith and action with their fellows in Zengakuren, Soka Gakkai, and less prominent formal or informal associations. Others found in dedication to Japan's reconstruction as a significant member of the society of nations a clue to the meaning of their own lives. The bases for that significance ranged widely from envisioning Japan in the vanguard of the nations committed only to peace, to Japanese neutralism, to Japan as an interpreter between East and the West, to Japan as a front runner in economic development and expansion, to, in some cases, a resurgence of Japan as a mighty military nation. Many students were just looking forward to the time when they could organize themselves and their adult energies around their *jobs*. But the closest and most readily available means for students to find, at least for the time being, an organizing element that gave significance and importance to their selves in relation with others was quite obviously the student movement and involvement in its periodic and emergency "struggles."

Predispositions

One may experience alienation because the predispositions of the individual discourage or inhibit a rational approach to a fusion of the adult individual and his world consistent with the realistic nature of both. It must be left to others to analyze the role played by such psychological characteristics in producing the difficulties Japanese students faced in discovering or developing a stable and an emotionally and rationally satisfying concept of their unique selves in relations with others. In particular we do not wish to make generalizations about "Japanese psychological tendencies" which might be cited as "reasons" for the kind of activity students engaged in in the postwar era, and for their feelings of alienation and inadequacies of self which in turn caused them to seek solutions through association in direct action.

In the first place such "reasons" related to "Japanese" predispositions would logically cause one to expect *all* Japanese students to act as only *some* did. The fulfillment of that expectation could not be verified by empirical evidence. In the second place we do not desire to set forth as data for our conclusions any that are not at least strongly suggested or supported by our own contacts and observations.

There is ample suggestion from Japanese commentators that Japanese tend to be emotional and sentimental, that they are extremely sensitive to personal injury or insult, that they are stimulated to corrective action more by a sense of shame, in the face of the evaluation of others, than by a sense of guilt at having violated principles of ideal conduct. It is tempting to indicate the ways in which such predispositions could inhibit the development of an adult self-concept geared to successful verification in the midst of experiences which students were undergoing in the postwar years, and the ways in which such predispositions could contribute to the experience of alienation so frequently reported. Moreover indications that the predispositions of some students could be so characterized were not absent from our experiences with them. But they did not appear to us to be more widely present among Japanese students than they are among American students with whom of course we are better acquainted.

There were, however, several predispositions which we did observe among the students which could have the inhibiting effect named above. It is not necessary to say that they are "uniquely" Japanese in order to report that they were present among those students who spoke about their experiences of an insecure adult selfhood and of alienation.

The first was their tendency to be more concerned about a mass of specifics than about *inductive* generalization *from the data*. It is not that they do not generalize, but that the specific data and the generalization appear to live in different corners of their minds. The two frequently appeared to be only distantly related. Now the image of the adult self is a generalization about the relationship and integration of various specific aspects of a person. The nature of other selves and the character of society and the universe, to which one is related must also be perceived as generalizations from specific evidence if one is to arrive at concepts in a way consistent with their reality.[6]

A second predisposition was to tire of analytical effort. Frequently before analysis of a problem (including their experience of alienation and insecure adult selfhood) had even approximated to a conclusion, they would leave the uncompleted analysis and spring to something resembling an intuitive conclusion. One should not of course ignore the possibility that an intuitive conclusion may resemble the truth more closely than that arrived at by inadequate analytic and synthetic processes. But if one is ambitious to understand matters like the adult self in integration with other selves *rationally*, it is understandable that the abdication of "thinking the problem through" at a halfway point creates a sense of defeat.

Another observable predisposition was a tendency to *suggest* rather than to *define* where human relations or matters of the spirit are concerned. This predisposition, which one is tempted to describe as a preference for suggestive poetry rather than for expository or definitive prose, may be an approach most likely to arrive at truth under certain conditions, particularly when the hard cold facts of life surrounding the relations or matters of the spirit are stable, dependable, and have a continuity and coherence. These facts of life were not so characterized in postwar Japan. To be sure of one's self and to be meaningfully integrated with other selves and with the confusing society of postwar Japan in a realistic way required more than suggestion, poetic or otherwise.

There was a further predisposition to think in terms of the extremes of possiblities rather than in terms of a middle way. This was most obvious in case of the discussion of alternatives of social organization, or ideological arguments, on the part of student leaders. But it also characterized their evaluation of themselves. They appraised themselves as stable or unstable, confident or despairing, secure or insecure, competent or incompetent, loyal or disloyal, free or unfree, independent or dependent, a champion of justice or a slave, etc. It also characterized their evaluation of their relations to others and to society. They appraised themselves as either integrated or alienated. In

[6]Incidentally this predisposition was also evident in the unrelatedness of their specific data to their generalizations about "capitalism," "Communism," "imperialism," "peace," "neutrality," "the Consitution," "the Emperor System," "freedom," "democracy," "racial purity," "Japan," "Americans," etc.

the face of the obstacles to the realization of the first of each
of these alternatives at any time and place, and in particular
in postwar Japan, students with such predispositions to black
or white thinking must inevitably have accumulated a volume
of frustration in their attempts to understand and to be *themselves* in relations to others, frustrations which required some
kind of release.

And finally in a combination of the last two predispositions
there was a predisposition to "suggest" the meaning of these
characteristics of the adult self in terms of the most immediately
appropriate *action*. The "stable" person *followed* the appropriate ritual and etiquette. The "confident" person *asserted*
himself and even *imposed* his will on others. The secure person
acted in defiance of consequences. The competent person *took*
the leadership in group action. The loyal person *stuck* to his
friends. The free person *opposed* all authority. The independent
person *went* his own way. The champion of justice *led* a revolution in opposition to all purveyors of injustice. One can observe
these predispositions finding expression among the leaders of
the student movement in Japan. Such active expression was
consistent with, if not caused by, their efforts to find a significant and satisfying meaning to the phrase, "This is what *I am*
or *will be* in relation to my fellows and the issues of my time.
What I am is what I *do*."

Other Sources

Three other sources of the perplexities about the personal
meaning of coming of age may be reported more briefly because
their meaning has been underscored in the foregoing discussion.

The individual may experience doubts because he feels that
he does not have anything to contribute which is significant
to the large and important concerns of the group and society,
and which could make him, therefore, deserving of the acceptance and respect of the adults of that group and society.
In a nation in which human relations have been traditionally
governed by a reciprocity of obligations, this opportunity
to put the group in one's debt is an important basis if not
guarantee of being accepted and respected by, and hence,
in one sense, integrated with the group.

The major difficulty here is that in postwar Japan the "large
and important concerns of the group and society," in relation
to which one might make a contribution, extended far beyond

the boundaries of the limited affairs about which students, and indeed most Japanese, had any firsthand knowledge. They were extensive, complicated, and imperative to a degree not before experienced. "What can I as an individual do about them?" became a perplexing and to some an unanswerable question unless the answer was, "Nothing."

Yet among some, such an answer was an intolerable denial of their own future worth and an unacceptable ingredient of their adult self image. That some of them sought the support of numbers in undertaking a leadership in action which they believed was a contribution to their society is understandable.

One may experience anxieties about his ability to fit into adult society because he has removed himself from the group or been ostracized by the group, as a consequence of disregarding or renouncing the traditional values and codes he could have shared with others in his society, and of embracing replacement values and codes which others will not, or cannot, share. This type of self- or societal-induced alienation could have been overemphasized by commentators from among the older generation in Japan, although a foreigner must in all good conscience yield to the judgment of those who are in daily and continuous contact with the students of Japan. One can only report that among those interviewed there was an all but universal predisposition to insist that those values and codes by reference to which they became a unique adult self and according to which their relations with others were governed should be uniquely Japanese, and that these values and codes should be consistent with everything of lasting worth in the ways (and frequently they used the word "soul") of the Japanese people.

Yet among them there is a vague haziness, when there is not disagreement, about what is of lasting worth. There is however, a search for new values better suited to finding themselves and becoming integral parts of a Japan capable and strong in the presence of today's and tomorrow's problems. Both elders and youths can be excused if they interpret such seeking tendencies as a desertion of commonly shared values and codes and the adherence to those which are new and strange.

This sort of alienation is not unique to the youth of Japan, though it was no doubt exaggerated by the events and confusion of the revolutionary period through which they have been passing since 1945.

Finally as a basis for the experience of alienation of those students we interviewed in the 1960's, it should be noted that they were, for the most part, born during and after the war. Hence they had not lived long enough with either the traditional or with replacement values as guides, for those values to become properties of themselves, capable of providing a strength and harmony within themselves. And since there was no agreement among students, and certainly not between students and their elders, as to what was of lasting worth in past values and as to what values were relevant and trustworthy for the present and future, commitment to a set of commonly shared values could not act as a bond of relationship with others. Note that this must inevitably produce an experience of alienation or aloneness with respect to the members of their own age group as well as with respect to the older generation. Among the problems, therefore, to the solution of which association and unity in action with one's fellows in the student movement might well be relevant was not merely the "conflict of the generations" but the need for a bond of consensus among the members of one's own generation as to the values by reference to which one could establish a harmony and wholeness within himself and simultaneously experience himself as at one with his fellows.

Contribution of the Student Movement

In the midst of the confusion and difficulties of finding, understanding, and being their selves under the circumstances existing in postwar Japan, the student movement performed for many of those who were seeking both adult identity and integration an important service. It provided at least one definite operational field unquestionably relevant to the reconstruction of the Japanese nation and society in which the action of each person was significant, in which the ideological foundations of that action could be debated, and in which the role of each in that action could be developed in accordance with his own demonstrated capacities.

Moreover, these efforts were carried out in relationship to the members of a horizontal group, equal at least for the time being in their common status as students, among which the relationships were minimally restricted by the specific hierarchical, superior-subordinate principles of status related to traditional Japanese society. Though, as we have seen, leadership and followership, the relationship of loyalty and dependence, did develop in the student movement also, one could find his place in such an action group by virtue of his personal competence and strength in relation to the issues to which the action was directed, and by his capacity to play his part in a joint effort.

Furthermore, the student movement provided a field of experiment and experience on a grand scale in which individuals could seek an identity and relationship among their fellows geared not so much to traditional patterns as to the requirements for action in the face of current circumstances. The results were no doubt often as painful as rewarding. But it was a result for which they themselves were, on the whole, responsible and from which they could learn not only the opportunity but the responsibilities, not only the objectives but the consequences of being *themselves*.

Participation in the student movement was also, in the ways indicated, a maturing experience. It provided an opportunity for self-assertion and for integration with one's fellows in relation to activity focused on a number of the most important issues faced by Japanese of all ages. But also, in revealing to them the shortcomings and weaknesses of this form of social action as a model for continuing successful advancement either of their own or the public interest, they were made aware of the necessity to bring into a workable relation the need of the individual for self-realization and the need of both in individual and society for order and institutional effectiveness and stability. Such an experience, though short in duration, is a prototype of that through which a whole people must pass over many generations in order to understand the opportunities, the responsibilities, the objectives, and the consequences which are the substance of the kind of individualism which is the foundation for a democratic and free society.

Chapter 5
Coming of Age in India

Student activism in India is more puzzling and confusing than that in the other countries visited. It is practically impossible even to describe that activism systematically, to say nothing of interpreting it. It blazes up in unexpected places in response to a host of unpredictable situations which, for the most part, appear peripheral to any continuing and central personal or group objective. The variations in numbers involved and in the violence of the actions bear little relation to the relative significance, to any save those immediately involved, of the apparent initiating circumstances. Organizationally that activism is all but formless on any continuing basis. It is only obvious that the students are trying to say something in action which they do not make explicit in words. But what are they trying to say?

One possibility is that they are announcing to themselves and the world that they no longer want to be considered children who have to put up with the way things are handled by the adults responsible for the universities and the society in which they find themselves, and certain aspects of which they don't like; that their behavior can, in part, be interpreted as an attempt to express or assert in action a growing conception of themselves as persons about to become full participants in adult society.

If that is the case, then the age at which many of them reach the university would indicate that large numbers have not had the opportunity to develop the self-discipline and self-control, the experience in responding to new unfamiliar, and frequently frustrating situations, or the capacity to manage a freedom from parental or community controls essential for the manifestation of that self-assertion in an orderly and restrained manner. The students enter college or the university normally at the age of 16, but some as early as 12.[1]

[1]Saiyidain, K.G., and H.C. Gupta. *Access to Higher Education in India*, UNESCO, 1956.

But even in the case of those who approximate more closely, after three or four years, to a chronological coming of age, the confusing and unpredictable nature of their activism may be a reflection of the confusion and unpredictability in their minds as to what it means to be an adult in today's Indian society.

Traditional Guidelines Inappropriate or Irrelevant

Growing up in India today is a perplexing business. India is in the throes of becoming a modern nation for participation in which the historical experience of her people is an inadequate preparation. Finding or developing oneself as a youth on the threshold of adulthood in a way adapted to life in today's and tomorrow's India receives little guidance from the traditional objective and process of growing up in the India of yesterday. Any effort to interpret student activism by reference to the specific character of current student life becomes realistic only when it takes account of this basic circumstance to which all Indian youth are subjected, whether or not they are students. It is desirable therefore to consider the ways in which this circumstance is manifest in the experience of Indian youth.

Lack of Clarity of Adult Roles

In any society, coming of age is a process which includes preparation for, and incorporating into one's concept of self, one or more roles appropriate to living as an adult in that society. If the character of those roles is well defined, then the objective is well defined and the process of transition from childhood to adulthood has at least a definite point of reference for testing the appropriateness of the behavior of youth to the objective sought. But the status and role of an adult in modern India is unclear because the present and future nature of life, and the institutional organization of life in modern India is not clear. Neither the role nor the institutional life of the society in which it is to be expressed is sufficiently stable and dependable to provide a firm point of reference enabling youths to develop a viable and satisfying concept of themselves as near adults, a concept which can be tested for its consistency with the actual opportunities and restraints of societal reality. Growing up into man's estate is doubly difficult for Indian youth today because it is a process carried on in a society which itself is in process of transformation, a transformation that must necessarily result in redefining of the status and role of adults, and which consequently introduces new and unfamiliar opportunities, requirements, and restraints into the process of maturation.

The normal conception of coming of age is that a minority, that is the youth of a country, uncertain about and inexperienced in what is expected of them as adults, cross over into a world of adults (and their activities and institutions) whose members have long become accustomed to and are experienced in the functions and problems of adult living. The minority youths slowly learn from experience in working with their elders what adulthood means, and adapt their self-conceptions and behavior to what they learn.

But in India today the elders themselves are subject to changes which make inadequate their wisdom of experience. It is often remarked that the indiscipline of the young in India is rooted in and takes its example from the indiscipline of their elders. If "discipline" is the word, it would be more appropriate to say that both the indiscipline of youth and indiscipline of elders are rooted in the same cause, the rapidly changing requirements of living related to order and discipline at a time when the attempted modernization, industrialization, and democratization of the society is making irrelevant many of those familiar requirements which were adpated to life and work in the days that have gone.

In considering the confusion generated for Indian youth by the irrelevance of traditional roles to contemporary and future life in India, one is tempted to suggest that some of those traditional roles with which the parents, faculty, political leaders, indeed all adults in today's India are most familiar, and which have deep hold on their emotions, are not only inappropriate and irrelevant, but anomalous and destructive in an independent self-governing nation. We are referring first to all, to the role of the pre-independence revolutionist whose function was to embarrass, downgrade, disobey, attack, and eliminate the authorities and governors of orderly life. Those who played that role in India's struggle for independence were not just ruffians and swashbuckling opportunists, but highly respected native leaders in all walks of Indian life, and even saintly leaders to whom nationalism was not only a political but a religious object of commitment.

The present generation of Indian students was born and has been reared during the twenty years since the exemplars of that revolutionary role in action, both orderly and undisciplined, both individual and collective, made effective in 1947 their challenge to the constituted authority. Anything which embarrassed the governors (including student strikes and attempts to boycott and shut down the English sponsored universities) was popularly considered legitimate. The role was heroic. Its behavioral manifestations were those in which not only men of outstanding ability and character, but the least competent and lowly, could participate.

While rational judgment can recognize the anomaly of such a role in the India of today, emotional predispositions produced by a generation-long period of hero worship cannot be wiped out overnight. Suggestions for undisciplined, self-assertive, and antagonistic action to accomplish one major and popular objective may continue to influence the pattern of behavior when no major objective other than self-assertion and the expression of antagonism is apparent.

What Does it Mean to Be an Indian?

It was suggested in the introduction to this section that the most basic of all touchstones by reference to which a citizen of any nation can measure the authenticity of his own self-image and of the role he plays in life is the image he has of the unique wholeness of the nation itself. Both the reality and the perception of nationhood in India, are in the early stages of growth. Indian youth, and indeed Indians generally, have no clear conception of the unique wholeness of their nation, of India's organizational charter. The confusion is reflected in the oft repeated statement that India is not a nation but a continent.

Indian leaders are not unaware of this obstacle to nation building. Their speeches are replete with eloquent references to the Indian "soul", to the role of India as a non aligned mediator between the East and the West, to India as an examplar to other Asian nations of "democratic socialism." Their pleas for a united India are continual. But these words do not translate themselves meaningfully for youth, or indeed for most adults who were interviewed, into a clear concept of what it means to be an Indian. This does not mean that students and Indians generally have no point of reference for developing a concept to themselves as members of a social entity. They can discuss what it means to be a Parsee, a Sikh, a Hindu, a Muslim. They know what it means to be a member of one of the 14 distinct language groups, or of a state whose boundaries have been drawn to encompass population which communicates in the same language. They know what it means to be a member of a particular caste or subcaste. They know what it means to be a Communist, although this is blurred increasingly by the antagonisms between the warring factions within the party. In the early years following the winning of independence from England it was fairly clear what it meant to be a Congress man, but schisms within the party are rapidly clouding that meaning. In other words, there is lacking a consensus with respect to national values, national objectives, national traditions, national policy, even a national language which would provide youth with an understanding of what it would mean to come of age as an Indian. When they are brought together at a University which is not established for the benefit solely of one such sub-group, the communal and caste differences are a frequent source of conflicts which escalate into major cases of riotous activism.

It is a hopeful sign that many students with whom we discussed these matters were convinced that the pluralistic character of Indian values and loyalties was inconsistent with the growth of India as a modern nation and that they were seeking not only for an adult role as Indians, but for a set of national values, objectives, and patterns of relationship, and in some cases for a kind of education and governmental system, which would make that role dependable and secure, one with a future.

Students Without Counseling

If the only certainty about the adult roles in India's present and future is that they cannot be patterned on the roles in the performance of which past generations of Indian youth have realized a degree of personal identity, if changes in the organization and conduct of Indian life have made less relevant any wisdom of experience elders might pass on to youth, if both old and young are confused about what it really means to be grown up in today's India, one would not expect counsel from the elders to be effective in aiding the young to *find* themselves.

This is particularly true of college students who live, not only in a new society with which neither they nor the adults they know have much experience, but in a specific area of that society, the university, about which many of their parents know nothing. Moreover, even the faculty and administrators hastily assembled to man India's burgeoning number of universities and colleges are only now learning about the opportunities for and constraints on maturation provided by experience in the academic area of social interaction.

Parents of large numbers of the students are unfamiliar with the problems of student life in general and in many cases uninformed about what is going on at the college attended by their young people, or specifically about their own offspring's behavior and standing there. Communication between students and parents about such matters is reported by many students to be difficult if not impossible. "They don't understand. We live in different worlds." Communication between college authorities and parents is, on the whole, lacking, and in some cases feeble attempts have been abandoned in the face of the students' objections that such reporting was an infringement on their privacy. Relation between students and faculty members is so limited and on such a formal basis that few opportunities for help are offered from that source, even in cases in which the latter might be able to help.

Some of the mission colleges and two of the government colleges we visited are trying out a system of weekly small seminars in which students prepare papers for discussion on subjects which could open up the possibility of faculty-student discussion of "what's on the student's mind." Student evaluation of these seminars did not always substantiate the high hopes of the Principals who initiated them, but they are a response to a serious inadequacy in the educational methods for bringing students and faculty closely enough together so that they can share ideas, and they are a serious attempt to remove that inadequacy. The respect for and confidence in their teachers, however, is at such a low ebb that such factors scarcely provide the students with any incentive or desire to seek counsel or to receive it from that source.

Administratively arranged student counseling through Deans of Students or student counselors is infrequent, and even where it is provided, there are difficulties in making it effective. Counseling as a profession for which the functions are clearly delineated and understood and for which specific education and training is provided is as yet undeveloped. What formal preparation for the counseling profession exists must depend on research materials on the problems of adolescence and educational psychology made in a different culture (chiefly England, Canada, and the United States). In a field the factors in which are culturally determined, this reduces the utility of research results suggesting an approach to the young people of India. Under those circumstances it is probably wise that counseling is, where it exists, chiefly concerned with administration of college rules, rather than with delving into any maturation problems of the students.

Cormack reports from her investigation of Indian student unrest that one of the most serious and organized experiments in setting up a student counseling office in the Department of Educational Psychology at Baroda University has had disappointing results. The office she says "is as yet unvisited by students" who distrust an arrangement "designed for those students who need psychological help and admit knowing it by coming to seek it."[2] Counseling with relation to the nature of, the requirements for, and availability of vocations would have to be made without helpful and up-to-date research based information on these matters, and, in the light of the traditional and current process of determining the choice of a vocation, would in any case be largely irrelevant.

Advice and counsel in matters pertaining to maturation in most colleges is limited to that which can be obtained from one's classmates, who are themselves as confused and poorly informed and troubled as the one seeking advice and counsel. And the paucity of hostel facilities reduces the range even of that "bull session" form of mutual aid.

What a modern Indian youth makes of himself will have to be developed mainly by his own effort with little if any helpful advice or support from his family or religious leaders, with little understanding guidance, other than exhortation, from his teachers and political leaders, and few aids to self study in the literature written in his mother tongue. Even the acquaintances and friends of his own age group are as perplexed and troubled as he is.

These circumstances make highly significant another feature of the way of life and thought in India which must inevitably intensify the problem faced by young persons in attempting to realize a concept of self adapted to a rapidly changing society in which many aspects of traditional concepts of self are inappropriate if not irrelevant.

[2]Cormack, M., *She Who Rides a Peacock: Indian Students and Social Change*, New York, Praeger, 1961, p. 196.

*Lack of Emphasis on the Individual's Responsibility for
His Own Development*

In all societies, at any time, the achievement of adulthood
by particular persons results from an interaction between the
efforts expended through societal arrangements and institutions
and those carried out by the individual himself. Both kinds of
effort are guided, constrained, and motivated by the traditional
expectancies, and the philosophy of life which support these
expectancies, as to where the responsibility lies primarily. Do
those expectancies and that philosophy suggest to the person
that he take or accept an assigned role, or do they challenge
him to *make* of himself a person capable of filling an achieved
role? In developed and truly modernized societies, the second
emphasis is primary, and a great reliance for societal progress
is placed upon the individual initiative, inventiveness, self-
discipline, and self-generated ambition and energy, which are
by-products of the activization of that emphasis. Societies in
transition must necessarily make this second emphasis manifest
both because they require the by-products of achievement-
oriented personal effort and because the traditional roles
available for assignment are poorly adapted to the kinds of
functions required for societal development.

At least that large portion of India's half a billion people
nurtured in the Hindu structure of expectancies and philosophy
of life have received from their experience and traditions a
minimal stimulus to *self* making in this sense. But increasing
numbers of Indians, and particularly students, whose opportunity is greater than it is for many of their countrymen to
be aware of the demands placed on individual persons by a
modernized society, are experiencing the problem of meeting
the challenge of self making while simultaneously developing
the guidelines for that achievement. It is becoming increasingly
obvious to them that the new order of economic and political
life to which India's leaders say they aspire, has a relatively
smaller place than the old for the kind of individual who
accepts the standing and function into which he was born.
Increasingly the need is for the kind who takes his destiny
into his own hands, creating a self which is individual and
unique. The first kind of individual fits uneasily into the
dynamic society being produced by the efforts of India's leaders
to create a modern industrialized nation with a democratic
political structure. But the Indian traditions relevant to self-

realization offer poor guides to the development of the second kind of individual. Nor do those traditions generate high motivation to effort in that direction.

If the question is put to an Indian student, "What are you going to make of yourself?" the normal reaction is a request for clarification. This does not mean that he is unconcerned about the kind of person he *becomes*. It means, we think, that the content given by their culture to the words "you," "make," and "yourself" in that question is not the same for Indian as for Western young people. The content given by Western culture to such words emphasizes personal striving and mobility, the possibilities for getting ahead in competitive relations with one's fellows, the acceptance of personal responsibility for one's success or failure, the disciplining of one's self to acquire the knowledge and skills required for continuous growth in capacity to work and live effectively, and a general respect and admiration for the person who is willing to work hard enough to make use of his varied opportunities and break out of hampering constraints imposed both by societal and his own inadequacies. Such a path to selfhood is not immediately obvious to Indian young people.

Among the growing number ambitious to *make* of India a modern democratic nation, the relationship to that achievement of what men make of themselves beyond that to which their fate has destined them, is clear. It is obvious to those Indians who have come into contact with Western civilizations (including Russia) that one essential wellspring of the industrial, political, and social processes labeled as "modern," is the initiative and creative contributions of persons who historically and traditionally were considered incompetent to make such contributions. The need for such initiative and creativeness by unique individuals is becoming more relevant and clear because, not only are the traditional securities provided for persons by caste, family, and local community influence disintegrating in India, but also because adaptation to such securities does not assure the nation of a dynamic leadership capable of solving the problems of a modern, changing, industrialized country. The need is becoming more relevant because its satisfaction is necessary in order to make realistic the hopes and aspirations of those groups in the population, traditionally considered as low class or caste and fated to live lives of resigned desperation, who today have sensed new possibilities in the declarations of intent by India's leaders to create a democratic and socialist society.

The recognition of this need has not been introduced into Indian life just since independence in 1947, but it has been highlighted and emphasized. Recognition, which before that date was limited to a relatively few, has become a factor in the motivation of a rapidly increasing proportion of the population including most of those who are determined that their young people shall have the advantages of a higher education, and certainly into the motivations of many of the students themselves.

Yet the hand of the past is still heavy. Also influential are the predispositions, implanted by centuries of living in at least that portion of Indian society dominated by Hinduism, in which a person is considered not the *primary* determiner of his own fate, not the primary maker of himself, but one whose greatest possibility and destiny lie in fulfilling the duties, with patience and resignation, of the station in life into which he was born. Such a predisposition supports a motivation with a residue of traditional expections which have not completely been removed.

Other Culturally Implanted Predispositions

There are a number of other inconsistencies between predispositions implanted by traditional culture and ways of thinking and those which a growing number of Indians sense are present among other peoples who have behind them many years of progress toward the kind of economic and political (if not the social and spiritual) institutions Indians are ambitious to build. It is not asserted here that one set of predispositions is better or worse than the other in any moral or philosophical sense. The point that we are making is that the young person in India who is seeking a self-identity which will enable him to live satisfactorily as an adult in the India of today and tomorrow must somehow reconcile, in his own person, predispositions implanted by a traditional way of life and thought with predispositions he senses are necessary in a "modern" society, but which are different from, if not incompatible with, the old.

For example, the very attempt to seek a unique identity for one's self is not legitimized or conceded to be highly important for an individual by traditional Hindu philosophy, by the simplified versions contained in the oral traditions and myths available to the non-literate, or in the commentaries and literary interpretations available to the literate. The emphasis in all three is on the transcendental reality of the universal Being, and on the faith that the path of highest wisdom and happiness is to achieve assimilation with that Being. The particular and the individual are de-emphasized if not ignored. In such a philosophy, the more life is particularized and individualized in its manifestations in the world of here and now, the less it reveals of, or shares in, ultimate reality.

This tendency toward the de-emphasis on the significance and importance of the particular and individual phenomena in the world (including individual people) in comparison with the true ultimate reality, is reinforced by a lack of conceptual distinction between the specific and the general. Nakamura, in his excellent discussion of the Indian approach to life,[3] points out that even the Indian languages indicate a lack of clarity in the relationship between the universal and the particular or individual phenomenal manifestation. "Indian languages had no pronoun equivalent to 'each and every' which was distinguished from 'all,' so they used the singular form of *sarva* (all) to express 'each and every'."

Now it is true that this attainment of assimilation of the individual with the universal is not a matter of possible experience for Hindu *youth*. It is a final stage of life. But as an ultimate life goal it decreases the moral legitimacy of any effort of youth to "find himself" as, or "make of himself," a real individual in his own right (who then can voluntarily *associate* himself with other similarly autonomous individuals competively or cooperatively).

Now if the nature of that universal were comprehensible and readily perceived as applicable and pertinent to the affairs of this life where real choices have to be made between "worse" and "bad" and "good" and "better," between active people, acts, things, and institutions, for example, the problem would not be so acute. In communist countries, for example, the emphasis on the submission and devotion of the individual to the State is not incompatible with the development of a concept of individuality for a youth who then chooses to submit as a real person to the overriding interests of the State. The "universal" (in this case, the State) is a worldly and definable, not an other worldly and amorphous thing. Its interests are com-

[3]See Nakamura, H., *Ways of Thinking of Eastern Peoples*, compiled by the Japanese National Commission for UNESCO, 1960, for an extended discussion of the Indian stress on the reality of the universal.

prehensible and operationally definable. Its requirements of its
members are for positive acts involving choices and decisions
about practical worldly matters. "Submission and devotion"
are active and positive expressions of real individuals to a
real and understandable societal entity.

In Summary

Indian students are conscious, then, that their adult lives
are going to be carried on in a society which is radically
different from that which their fathers experienced, and to which
their fathers' concepts of responsible adulthood were related.
Students vaguely sense, consequently, that their problem is not
merely to "adopt" or "acquire" the characteristics of adulthood
but to "create" those ways. The role they play will certainly
differentiate them from their elders, their parents, their teachers,
their political governors, but just how they are not sure. Since
there is no consensus existing (even among their peers) as to
this role, each person is forced to figure out for himself what
he is to become, and how this self will be expressed. At the
very time this urge to conceive of himself, if not as an individual differentiated from others in his peer group, at least as
a member of a generation of youth differentiated from the generation of his elders, he is increasingly aware that the emphasis
on individual selfhood is an essential feature of the "modern"
society into which he would like to see his own country
develop. The pressures impelling him to discover his unique
identity are therefore even more insistent, at the same time
that they are more confusing than they are for young people
in countries in which that search and discovery are a tradi-
tion-guided part of the experience of youth on the threshold
of adulthood and in which one culturally supported end in
life is to develop a unique individuality.

Under these circumstances it is not strange that the tendency
of those students who seek to become persons in a modernized India in which individuality, however constrained by the
forms of organized effort, is a cornerstone of outstanding vocational achievement and general political participation, is
toward self-assertion in any way that suggests itself and in
connection with any issue or incident which gives them a
chance to think of themselves as distinctive persons. The issues
and incidents closest at hand are those in which a young
person can discover his own identity by differentiating himself

from his elders. And the first operational field many have known in which that differentiation can be actively attempted is the university.

While his behavior in this effort may be interpreted as a *negative* revolt against adult authority, it'is more meaningful, we believe, to interpret it as a *positive* assertion of what he is reaching for but has not yet attained, a conception of his own self as an adult person, hopefully suited for life in a world neither he nor his elders have ever known.

Unsupplied with any wisdom of experience as to practicable ways to achieve this objective, and, if a Hindu, brought up in a tradition which deemphasizes the importance of the particular and the individual, and which discourages any hope that individuals can challenge their fate and make something of themselves after their own desires, he can either give up and let himself be absorbed into and swept along by the disintegrating forms of group identity suited to an earlier time; or he can assert himself in any way that offers to give him hope that he is becoming a person in his own right prepared for life and work in a modern India.

We met and discussed their problems with both types. The second frequently were ones who found their opportunity for self-assertion as activists in what is referred to in India as examples of student indiscipline.

The foregoing possible interpretation of student activism will be criticized as more rational than any interpretation made by the students themselves is likely to be. While in agreement with that criticism, it can be said that every point made was suggested by comments made by the students, and that our contribution has been merely to organize those suggestions into a systematic presentation.

Opportunities to Grow up

There is one interpretation, however, which requires no assumption of rationality on the part of anyone. If we start with the premise that the student's preparation to conceive of himself as an adult and to act responsibly in that role is a function of learning *from experience* during adolescence what it means to be an individual who can be related to and integrated with other members of society in the work and life of society, then several observations can be made about the learning possibilities provided children and adolescents in India.

The Limitations on Individual Choice

First of all, an Indian young person has experienced that a very great many things which in other societies are matters of choice for individuals (and therefore contributory to self-building) are regulated and determined for him by the rules and ritual of the caste or communal (Hindu, Muslim) group into which he is born. What he shall eat and with whom, who shall prepare his food, whom he will associate with, what work he will do, his chances for position and promotion, in some cases the school and college he will attend, often for whom he will vote, whose authority he will recognize outside his own family (as well as within it), whom he can marry, in all of these matters an individual must, even today, when such caste and communal regulation is being weakened, take into account that regulation, or attempt at regulation. Even if he is independent and daring enough to discount or ignore such a framework for his "personal" decisions he is aware that he is a maverick among the multitudes who submit their choices (though in decreasing degree) to such constraints.

So extensive are the areas of decision-making in which caste and communal traditions and regulations play a role that it has been said by knowledgeable and thoughtful Indians that, if by some miracle they were removed as guidelines to conduct for the whole population, the result would be chaos and anarchy.

The indications, particularly in urban communities, are that the years of survival of these customary ways of keeping life and work orderly and dependable in India are numbered. But the present generation of Indian students has been reared in a society offering relatively few chances for expanding the area of effective personal choices, and for making decisions by reference either to their own desires or to operationally definable rules of conduct more universal than those sanctioned by their caste and communal groups.

Interaction as a Means of Achieving Self-Awareness

Another way in which children between, say, twelve and twenty could conceivably develop gradually a sense of selfhood is by seeing themselves reflected in the reaction of others to their attempts to have their own way. This situation could arise, for example, in the relation of children to parents. That relationship is frequently described in Western countries as an adolescent revolt against parents and particularly against the father. It is very uncomfortable for the parents, but it does provide the child with the opportunity to experience the consequences of taking a position and acting "on his own" and getting an evaluation by someone besides himself, of the person who does that. And since he may be rewarded or punished for the behavior that has been an expression of himself, he faces the necessity of deciding whether he desires to continue to be that kind of a person. If there is disagreement with his parents, as there frequently is, he has to decide whether he wants to be the kind of person who asserts his right to independent action, submits to the judgment of his parents, or conforms overtly with all the politeness he can muster, but remains inwardly uncommitted to anything inconsistent with his personal desires. In any case his conception of himself as a distinctive person is tried out in experience and either made more firm or modified.

Another way of achieving this result is in the relations between boys and girls in which each is trying to display the kind of person which will get a desired reaction from one of the opposite sex. Experimentation, success or failure, these are his teachers. Determination, in the case of failure, to shift the campaign to another person or to an attempt to modify one's behavior in order to demonstrate to the other that he or she was "not really that kind of a person after all," is a self-building process. In case of success, to sense the kind of person implied in the experimental action as approved, and therefore worth perpetuating, is an experience in clarifying a conception of a desirable self. Even when no courtship practice is involved, boys and girls, in being together in play or in work, extend the number and kinds of persons in whose reactions they can see themselves reflected and find that conception clarified.

Another major possibility for such experiences and experimentation is in being employed by someone to do work for wages in the doing of which one receives the evaluation and reward or punishment of one who has an interest in him primarily as a doer of a task and in his qualities of skill, discipline, perseverance, etc. related to getting that task done to the employer's satisfaction.

In the affairs of the school and community institutions managed by older people there is potentially an opportunity for experiencing such growth of the concept of self if the arrangements of certain activities connected with such institutions are made the responsibility of the children or young people, thus giving them the opportunity to consider alternatives, make choices, and take the consequences for those choices.

Children may even grow in their conception of self by anticipating that they will soon themselves have to make serious personal and independent choices affecting their whole lives, the choice of a mate; of college or no college; if the former, which college, if the latter, what life work. If the burden of choice and the responsibility for a good or bad choice rests upon them, they have a stimulus to consider alone or in company with their peers or elders the kind of a person they wish to become.

There are of course other possibilities, some of them peculiar to particular cultures. It is, however, we think, worth observing in the case of Indian youth that the chance for self-assertion and self-clarification through the experiences mentioned above are minimal. The respect for and commitment to family solidarity and loyalty raise substantial barriers to adolescent revolt against parents, though the possibility was suggested, in a number of interviews, of overt and polite acquiescence in the parents' wishes without self-commitment thereto. Free relations between the sexes are taboo after puberty, although before that time boys experience the satisfaction of being bosses if they have sisters to boss. Work for wages, and for others than the parents (in rural communities) is relatively absent, and, among many contemplating college, is considered demeaning. The control of affairs in school and community institutions is normally kept well in hand by teachers and administrators, and, though pupil participation in a limited area of activities is being introduced slowly, it has yet to become a regular and widely experienced way for children to begin to develop a sense of responsibility for the management of their own affairs and to incorporate that element of self-responsibility into their concept of self. The part played by elders, not merely parents, but those respected in the larger family, and influential friends of the family in the community in the determination of the important matters of marriage, school, and vocation is sufficiently large so that the individual's range of self-generated choice is considered by the students interviewed to be limited (although expanding in recent times). The opportunity for anticipatory as well as current self-building is accordingly limited. As one student remarked, "You know from the beginning that there is always going to be someone older than you are whose preferences count far more than yours."

Opportunities to Grow Up in College

If to the above named circumstances is added the fact that students come to the college or university normally at the age of 16, but some at the age of 12 or 13, it can be seen that a conception of student activism as the action of young adults suddenly become aware of their approaching adulthood and determined to play the part of adults and make their world over into a better one than the older generation has succeeded in making, must be severely modified in India. The most that can be said is that they are beginners in a process of discovering or shaping their selves as unique persons that in a few years will play adult roles; that they have had little previous experience in asserting themselves as their own decision makers or choosers among alternatives, a meager opportunity to see themselves as others see them by virtue of the others' reactions to their behavioral assertion of their growing personalities; that they have had little preparation in learning how to meet and accommodate themselves to a wide variety of other people, particularly adult people not members of their immediate face-to-face groups; and finally that they have scarcely begun to realize that action arising from self-expression has consequences for themselves and others for which they must personally bear the responsibility. In fact we think it can be said that the biggest personal problem facing the college and university entrants in India is to *begin* growing up.

It should not surprise anyone, if that is the case, that their type of activism indicates that a sizable number have not got on very far with solving that problem.

Some colleges in India have recognized this situation and have introduced measures which take account of it and which correct some of the inadequacies in the pre-college experience noted above. It is more than a coincidence, we think, that, of the colleges we visited, such were the ones which gave evidence of the least student unrest and indiscipline. That is not to say that student activism was absent — far from it. And though for the most part it was of a positive, consistent, and responsible nature, those colleges had occasionally been the scenes of undisciplined activism which was similar to that which has led to such concern among educators and officials.

This is to be expected, for not all the stimulants to student unrest are related to the problem of late maturation, and not all of those which are so related are amenable to corrective action by college administrators. The more general picture, however, is one of the absence in the colleges of arrangements which are designed to aid the student in growing into his role as a self-disciplining adult.

Sex-Linked Segregation in College

We have noted the pre-college segregation of boys and girls and therefore the minimal function this relationship can perform in the development of a person's concept of self. This segregation continues to a large extent in college. With the exception of a number of colleges for women only, colleges in India are co-educational in the sense that they are attended by both men and women. Women are about 1/5th of those enrolled. Neither sex, however, is prepared to profit from any advantage this situation might provide for amplifying their opportunity to develop a broader self-concept as a reflection of the evaluation in the eyes of the opposite sex. Relations are strained, and the normal solution is for boys to associate with boys, and girls with girls. One is reminded of the comment of a former colleague at Harvard (formerly solely a men's college) in announcing the cooperative relation for joint classes with the girls of Radcliffe (a women's college). His comment was, "Harvard is now co-educational in fact only." The relations also remind one of the "girl teasing" type of play characteristic of American primary schools at the age before an interest in "having a girl or boy friend" has developed. Proximity on the college campus is not a sufficient stimulus to a bisexual association which contributes to the maturation process, save that it is symbolic of a trend which at some future time will have resulted in a changed status for women generally in Indian society and hence for a changed role for both men and women, and to which both will have to adapt in becoming mature adults.

Management of Student Affairs

One possibility for providing students with a maturing experience in college is their organization for managing their student affairs for enjoyment, self-improvement, and eventually for self-government. Numerous attempts have been initiated, but in the face of real difficulties. The large proportion of students (over 4/5) do not live on campus so that time and opportunity for such mutual enterprise is limited. Preferences for class and caste similarity in interstudent familiar associations, although being reduced, still inhibit the possibility of mutual enterprise among the members of the whole student body. The lack of practice by pupils in schools in the pre-college years in this sort of mutual activity means that any capacity (or even desire) for it has to be developed for the first time in college. The evidence of student managed events is clearer in reports of campaigns for election of officers and of inaugural assemblies, and in the announcement at such times of affairs that are being planned, than in the actual reports of affairs carried through. University authorities, mindful of the immaturity of students, and what they label the irresponsibility revealed in student strikes and demonstrations, are, moreover, reluctant to sponsor any form of student self-government in which the reins of control in their own hands would be loosened.

The University a Non-Society

There is an even more basic fact of university experience in India which limits the chance for students to come of age. The interactions and relations among the students as peers, among faculty as colleagues, and between faculty and students and administrators do not constitute what can be termed a culturally structured "society" in the sense that a family or a community are societies. The basic reason for this is that relations and activities in the university environment are concerned with a limited range of human interests chiefly concerned with training for and getting a degree, and do not create the possibility for the informal or formal organization of widely ranging relationships and interactions in the course of which opportunities are provided for development of the many-sided facets of the individual personalities of those involved essential to maturation as social persons.

Maturation is not only a personal, but a social process. It involves not only development of the self but an integration of that self with others. That integration would have to be accomplished during college years, as a function of the adjustment of all persons in the college population to each other, not only as individuals working for and providing training for the degree, but as participants in many kinds of mutual relationships and activities in which reciprocal rights and duties, functions and standings, and culturally structured relationships can be developed. In a sense, maturation is a process of developing capacities not only to *adapt* to the requirements of a society but to *contribute* as one among many to the creation and maintenance of a culturally structured society. It is doubtful if such faculties can be developed through teaching and advice from others. Capability for effective balance between adaptation and contribution is more likely to be the product of participation in the creation and maintenance of a society and its culture, of learning the kind of a person one must be and become in order to do that satisfactorily to himself and to others, and of effort to develop oneself into that kind of a person. Those conditions are unlikely to occur for students in a college environment until the interactions and interrelationships among students, faculty, and administrators involve a far wider range of human interests and functions than lecturing from behind a podium and listening from a school bench, commuting back and forth each day for that purpose, and passing an intermediate examination after two years and a final examination after four years.

Is it possible to consider only the officials and the faculty of a college as the members of this society and the students merely as external customers? Or is it possible to think of students as members of this society participating in all of its essential activity processes relevant to their legitimate interests and capacities, if only as *responders* to activities initiated by the officials and faculty, and to view student response as significant in the creation and maintenance of the college "society," as significant as are the acts of the initiators? Is it even possible to conceive of students as genuine participating *initiators* in a number of activity areas where their interests and capacities could be sources of suggestion and task performance in the total life of the college society? In this latter concept of the college as a "society" whose members include the students as well as faculty and administrators, and the culture of which is their joint creation, lies the possibility of creating a college experience contributing to the personal and social maturation of those students. Indian university life does not offer that kind of a self-building and socializing experience to students.

The lack of multiple purpose interactions is not the only factor which restricts the behavioral field for the mutual effort among faculty and students to develop institutionalized facilities, functions, and norms constituting a unitary campus culture. As we have seen there is lacking a commonly shared concept of the essential purpose of a university other than to produce degrees as passports to jobs, and by reference to which the appropriateness of reciprocal student and faculty behavior and relationships can be judged. Even this limited purpose is weakened as a touchstone for the development of structured social relationships between faculty and students on particular campuses by at least two facts: the cloud thrown over the vocational significance of the degree by the well publicized circumstances of the educated unemployed; and the fact that the faculty on a particular campus are not the ones who evaluate the students' examinations. The latter function is performed by the university's board of examiners.

Moreover, the possibility of collaborative relations between faculty, students, and administrators is minimized by the status differentiation between students and teachers based on concepts of superiority and inferiority related to age and to functions as a teacher or learner.

But singleness of purpose and mutual interests among faculty members and students are not the only bases for the development of a culturally structured campus society which in turn could provide a framework within which students may develop a personal and social maturity. If each can create a culturally integrated peer group society, the latter can provide the social resource for such a development. There are high barriers to such a creation for both teachers and students on the Indian college campus. Our interest at this point is in the barriers existing for the students.[4]

In the first place the overall proportion of students living on campus is less than 20%. Although this proportion varies among the more than 2100 campuses, the opportunity for continuous interaction leading to the necessary creation of mutually acceptable arrangements and norms among all students is minimal on many campuses.

But even though all students lived on campus, the barriers

[4]cf. Gusfield, J. R., "The Academic Milieu," in Altbach, P. G. (ed.) *Turmoil and Transition*, Basic Books, 1968 for an insightful comparison of the Indian and American student experience in this matter.

to the formation of a distinctive student subculture would be
high in India. There is first of all the sex linked separatism
to which we have already referred which all but eliminates
this type of relationship from those productive of shared
values. The hold of caste, class, regional, and language indenti-
fications is strong and interferes with the development of a
distinctive nonfractionalized all-student culture. And for Indian
students these identifications are perceived to be as significant
as, if not more significant than, their identification as a student
in determining how they are, and will be, related to adult
Indian society. Moreover, coming to college does not constitute
a definite break with the members of family, caste, community,
and language group in relationship with whom they have been
reared, and upon whom they will continue to depend for jobs,
marriage partners, and other aspects of personal and social
living, as well as for codes of living. Furthermore, there is
in India little reinforcement for any tendency to create a
homogeneous *student* sub-culture by virtue of the existence of
a youth sub-culture in Indian society generally.

Now it is perfectly possible for Indian youth to accept a
particular cultural touchstone of caste, kinship, region, or
language as a reference point for their own self-identity and
social identification. Among large numbers of students whom
we interviewed, however, there is an awareness that such an
identity and identification is not fully consistent with, and is actually incompatible with, the kind of person capable of contribution to a modernizing Indian society. But the alternative basis
for identity and identification is not clear. The result is confusion and frustration, leading to sporadic, unpredictable, and
directionless self and group expression and assertion.

Activism as Indiscipline

The currently customary key modifying adjective employed
by Indians to describe, for the most part critically, the activism
of students is, "undisciplined." It is an appropriate word as is
evidenced by some of the kinds of activity and its motivation
described in Chapter 2. Presumably its opposite, "disciplined,"
would describe the kind of activism that would win wider
approval. We discussed one evening with a group of educators
what activism so characterized would be like. The following
summation of their responses would, we believe, have widespread support from adults:

It would involve respect for, rather than revolt against, the decisions and works of a past and present adult generation.

It would focus on a sincere and humble attempt to find themselves as mature citizens rather than merely to assert themselves egotistically.

It would be consistent.

It would be responsible.

It would be constructive.

Few persons would quarrel with that list. If, as appears undebatable to many, it is desirable to modify student activism in the direction of those characteristics, it is equally desirable to act in the light of what can be expected of students who are experiencing the stage in life described in this chapter, not to excuse any specific manifestations of their activism, but to be clear about the responding and reacting human beings toward which such attempts at modification are directed.

All expectancies with respect to student activism need to be formulated in full recognition of a fundamental fact that a student is in that stage of life in which he feels no one really understands him except himself—himself and those among his immediately present peer group who agree with his own conception of himself. Although he may frequently amplify this attitude by stating that no one *cares* either, that is not the basic reason for his preception that he alone can hope to understand himself. It is simply that what his childhood companions and his parents think of him is not based on currently shared experiences and the chance to observe and judge him as one wrestling with the problems of that experience, problems his parents know nothing about as far as his special circumstances are concerned. As far as other members of adult society are concerned, he has not had sufficient mutual relations with them to be able to depend on their judgment. The only ones fully conscious of what he is trying to do and to be are his intimate peer associates who are having many of the same experiences. Now consider how he and his familiar peer group are likely to respond to any urging to act on principle, respectfully, humbly, consistently, responsibly, and constructively.

To act on principle in the sense used by adults requires reference to principles they, the adults, consider appropriate.

But what do they consider appropriate in today's India? We have noted the irrelevance of many of their behavioral premises or principles to the kinds of functioning required by the India of today and tomorrow. Moreover, the urging falls on the ears of young cynics all too aware of many examples of inconsistency between principles declared and deeds performed among those in the generation doing the urging. As a test of a young person's sincerity among his peers, moreover, action *now* is probably more important than to postpone action and deliberate as to whether the action is consistent with any defensible adult respected principles.

As suggested throughout this chapter, the crux of students' motivation is not the predisposition to revolt against the older generation, but to find and assert themselves as individuals in the face of factors inhibiting and constraining that self-assertion. The older generation (together with all preceding generations) has produced or administered those hampering institutionalized restrictions. It is easy for students to defend their self-assertion as an "attempt to do a better job of creating a better world than you, our elders, did."

Of course that is egotistical; it would be pointless as a declaration of self-identity if it were not. Also, self-assertion is an easier thing to do than to *find* oneself, and the first may even be rationalized as a method through which the latter objective may be approached.

Students cannot be expected to be wholly "consistent." Consistency implies the achievement of a stable self by reference to which the consistency of actions may be maintained. That they have not yet done.

Students cannot be expected to be continuously "responsible" in their actions if by responsible is meant using only those legal and custom-sanctioned methods of stimulating change, methods which have widespread acceptance among adult citizens in a particular society. They have not yet been integrated as adults into that society and become practiced in and committed to those methods.

One should not expect "constructive" suggestions or action to come from a group of students, or even a single student, when they or he are reacting negatively to a disliked situation. Constructive suggestions require a capacity to analyze causes and to evaluate alternative solutions to a problem. These are rare qualities and skills even among those with long experience in dealing with problems.

The chief contribution of student activism in India to the life of the nation is basically student protest against something they don't like. Whatever that is and whatever "undisciplined" methods students use to make their dissatisfactions and frustrations known, they call attention to matters that may conceivably require the attention and action of those charged by society for maintaining order and progress. In the light of the demonstrated normal predisposition of a large number of those who shoulder such responsibilities in society to act according to the customs approved by their generation, consistently, responsibly, and constructively, a predisposition made manifest in actions which can be described as "letting well enough alone" or "letting sleeping dogs lie," this activism and protest of youth could prove to be a major essential stimulus to national development.

Chapter 6

Coming of Age in Mexico
and Colombia

The hypothesis that student activism is in part a function of youthful peer-group-approved self-expression and self assertion in the process of achieving an adult identity is difficult to test in Mexico and Colombia. Studies of adolescent problems and experiences are not plentiful in either country and particularly in Colombia. Studies of the environment and of the process of maturation are mainly anthropological, dealing chiefly with data concerning peasant communities from which very few university students come. Chronological age is an uncertain indicator of adulthood in youthful nations and particularly unrealiable in the case of university students.[1]

More than in other countries studied, the students interviewed in Mexico and Colombia gave the impression that subjectively they considered themselves already to be mature persons as capable as their elders of functioning in the current adult world and, in the case of the student leaders, more competent so far as the future is concerned.

The Road to Maturity

Nevertheless, these discussions, especially among those who were, or had been leaders of student activism, disclosed something of the same perception as that characterizing activist students in other countries, namely that traditional and current adult role patterns, and the values which reinforced them were not entirely consistent with what was required of a mature individual in a rapidly changing world, a situation which, in a sense justified their efforts to create their own roles as agents of change.

We questioned the students we interviewed about their

---

[1] In a report prepared by the National Autonomous University of Mexico, in 1968, 2½% of the students in the Faculties and Schools were 17 and under, 80% between 18 and 25, 13% between 26-30, and the rest over 30 (including 329 over 50 of whom 70 were 61 and over).

conception of what it means to come of age and about their
pre-university experiences which had a bearing on that process.
The immediate response of most of them to the first question
was the simple operational definition of "getting married and
having the responsibility for a family," or "finishing one's
education and going to work (usually expressed as 'entering on
a career')." In accordance with such a definition very few
students have come of age objectively. They are still on the
threshold of that status.[2]

A more subjective meaning of coming of age, for a large
number, was the experience of being characterized in ways
assumed by them to differentiate the senior from the junior
members of society. Revealed in their comments was a conviction that, as students, they should be well on their way
toward, if they had not already arrived at, an adult stage
in life in which they could experience themselves as independent, self-initiating and determining, self-expressing, and equal
(and, in a few cases, superior) persons. Only in relation to
their peers, however, did they have the experience that they
were acknowledged as mature in these ways. They sensed that
their elders considered them as dependent, responding and
conforming, regulated, and subordinate persons.

The factors producing this experience were not perceived by
the students as limited to those relevant to university life. Non-
student youth, the students said, also felt their impact. The
perceived presence of those factors in the general societal
environment can be inferred from the fact that most of the
students saw their elders as persons marked by these last
named characteristics also. One Mexican student remarked,
"If to be an adult means to be that kind of a person [referring
to the above named adult characteristics] then the only time
in your life you'll be likely to be an adult is while you're
a student, and then only in relation to your fellow students."

The desire for such assumed adult characteristics suggests
what psychologists have termed the search for a personal
identity. Further discussion of the pre-university interaction experiences revealed a minimal opportunity to develop such a
personal identity which could be characterized as independent,

[2]In 1964 according to a UNAM report of the nearly 47,000 students
in the faculties and schools in the National University in Mexico,
44,036 were single, 2754 were married, 116 widowed or divorced, and
26 participants in a free union.

self-initiating and determining, self-expressing, and equal or superior to others. There appeared to be little of the give and take in the pre-university experiences, through which, in relationship with others, one can develop a self-concept describable in these terms. There are disagreements with parents, but, at least in middle class homes, confrontation is avoided. They disagree inwardly, but on most occasions are silent.[3] They do not challenge their teachers in primary and secondary school, nor do they normally challenge their professors in the classroom when they reach the university. A majority of the secondary schools, in Colombia particularly, are run by the Catholic Church, normally in a way providing little opportunity to develop individuality in thought and action. Contacts with the opposite sex, at least in middle and upper class homes, are not of the sort which cause one to discover one's self save as a person who conforms to traditional patterns of relationship, patterns heavily influenced by the middle and upper class parental anxieties about and protectiveness toward their daughters. Moreover, the typical inter-sex relation is, more often than not, in groups, so that the necessity for assuming complete responsibility for one's own conduct is minimized. The chance to learn more about oneself in a relationship with an employer and to modify one's self-image in that relationship is limited for many of those who have reached the university by the fact that working and studying are, for the most part, considered by parents, as well as the youth, to be an undesirable combination. "Going to work" establishes a sort of a cut off point in the educational process. Several students commented that to work while one is still young and in school creates a fear in the minds of parents that the youth might get interested in work and in the money that comes from it, and not continue in school.[4] The awareness of self that

[3]Even with respect to peasant homes, where anthropological accounts frequently report a "rebellion" against the father who abandons the family, or is brutal, or is unfaithful to or disparages his wife, the rebellion is seldom described as an outright confrontation in which the son stands his own ground physically or in open argument.

[4]Reference here is to pre-university experiences. The UNAM report to which we have already referred indicated that in 1964, 20% of the students were self supporting, that 684 had registered for work with the university employment bureau (of whom 263 found jobs) and that during the year over 25,000 reported that they had had some gainful employment.

comes from interaction with an employer is, therefore, experienced by relatively few. There is, in studies concerning lower class life, reference to the encouragement given by mothers to a son's opportunity to learn to stand on his own feet, to go out alone, take part in street gangs, stand up for himself in fights with his companions, and in other ways develop and show his "manliness." But the informants from middle class families, from which most of the students come, did not give evidence of such unrestraining permissiveness in the up-bringing of children.

To the point of entering college, therefore, there is lacking any large chance to develop an individuality which can be considered truly one's own. One's identity is bound up with dependency, conformity, regulation, and subordination. The university experience is the first real opportunity to break out of this set of conditions and assert oneself as an individual. But even at the university the identity that is discovered is less that of the self-assured individual and more that of a peer-group-modeled, or even an intimate-association-modeled person. Even those whose inclination, at least verbally expressed, was anarchistic, appeared to conceive of themselves not as *an* anarchist, but as *one of* the anarchists.

A somewhat more objective concept of adulthood implicit, and at times explicit, in the students' discussions concerning coming of age could be phrased as "reaching a secure place in society." To find and perform a recognized role in the political, economic, and social affairs of society was a major objective of the search for identity and the sought-for mark of maturity among the students of Mexico and Colombia as it was in all the countries included in this study.

This is the point at which the thoughtful student begins to perceive an inconsistency between the roles and values and marks of maturity which he assumes are considered appropriate by his elders and those he considers to be consistent with his own function as an adult in a changing world, the point at which his uneasiness readies him to initiate a role of his own as an agent of change, or to respond in support of those who promote an opportunity for activism in which such a role becomes manifest.

In this search for a reality oriented adult identity the difficulties faced by Colombian students appear to be greater than those faced by Mexican students. Within the life span of Mexican students there has been a greater stability and continuity in the development of political and economic affairs than has characterized the experience of Colombian students. It would be plausible to infer that Mexican youth had a greater reason to be confident that tomorrow's pattern of social roles would not place too great a strain on the adaptive capacities of youth. Yet, in differing degrees, students in both countries faced the same problems. In each of the areas of political, economic and social activities and relationships there was an uncertainty and insecurity about roles and the framework of institutions within which these were carried on, an experienced or anticipated discontinuity between their past and present and probable future form, and the absence of established role models among their elders which appeared fully consistent with meeting the problems of the society in which they expected to live out their careers. Moreover, the way in which their elders were performing those roles appeared to many of them inconsistent with their own social values or even with the values proclaimed as important by their elders. Under these circumstances the process of coming of age was for a number of them (usually the activist leaders of the student movement) not so much one of *adopting* or achieving or being assigned to existing adult roles, as one of *creating* roles for themselves which would provide the opportunity for significant participation in the adult world they were entering. Coming of age is not simply the maturation of the person as a self-contained entity, but of the incorporation or personalization (with or without modification) of adult roles, the utilization of societal institutions to which the functions involved in these roles are related, and the internalization of a concept of the nation or of a universal ideal society which gives meaning and significance to both the roles and the institutions. If one of these elements is unclear or confused, the process of maturation is difficult. If all of them are unclear or confused the process is even more difficult and one alternative way is to establish a self-identity by self-assertion.

Towards Political Maturity

The dominant circumstance which conditions the students' perception of their options in present and future political roles, the performance of which will mark them as mature individuals, is that both countries are in the process of developing a widely shared concept of independent nationhood, a unique national identity. Their self-conception as adult political persons is necessarily geared to the political roles appropriate to that process. Moreover what they want to become as persons is necessarily geared to what they want their nation to become. For all youth, but especially for students whose very attendance at the university has launched them onto the national scene, this concept of the identity of their nation held by themselves and others is a highly significant ingredient in their development of a mature self-image. No longer can their personal identity be made satisfactory by identification solely with family, *compadres*, local face to face groups, a patron, by reference to which so many of their countrymen understand who they are as persons. As long as they are students, they are *Mexicans* or *Colombians* in the sense of being members of the whole nation, participants in an institution whose purpose and function is national.[5] Unless, when they leave the university, they slip back entirely into the narrow, particularized, familiar, and localized group relations from which many of them came, they will continue to be Mexicans or Colombians, not only by blood, but by psychological membership in the nation as a whole.

What it means to be a Mexican or Colombian is an internalization of what Mexico or Colombia stands for in their eyes and in the eyes of the world. If they can be proud and confident of their nation's organizational charter, they have a major psychological resource making it possible for them to have a firm reference point for self-identification and to be proud of and confident in themselves. They may, however, feel that the "Establishment" has betrayed or has failed to implement that organizational charter in action, and rebel against the governance by that Establishment, and think of themselves as present or future instruments of change and reform. This is the case in Mexico.

If, however, there is lacking a clear concept of the nation as a whole, or if the substance of that concept, that organizational charter, is inconsistent or incompatible with what they vaguely aspire to have their nation stand for, then at least the most active, the most concerned, or the most visionary among them will think of themselves as instruments of *radical* change, even of revolution. This is the case in Colombia.

In both countries there is a continuing need for nation builders, and the political roles of rebel, reformer, and revolutionist

[5]In this sense they are like members of the armed forces or national public officials, participants in the life of institutions whose operational field is nationwide.

provide alternative ways of performing as such. The first two options are most likely to appeal to the middle class youth of Mexico, the third to the middle class youth of Colombia. What differences in the organizational charters of the two countries account for this fact? The observations set forth below are summations of the comments of students in the two countries.

The key word in the case of Mexico is "The Revolution" or "The Continuing (or Institutionalized) Revolution." The objective events of the Revolution of 1910, of the Constitution of 1917, and of the modifications in the governing and management of the nation's affairs since 1930 are real enough. These latter pragmatic changes, political, economic, and social have been made in sufficient quantity to justify the claim of the elite leaders of groups who determine the policies and practices of the one monolithic political party that they are the Party of the Continuing (or Institutionalized) Revolution.

The features of their country resulting from the accumulation of these objective changes which stand out in the minds of Mexican students are as follows:

Standing among the nations: Independence of influences of both Europe and the rest of North America; leadership in Latin America; Mexico of, by, and for the Mexicans, following a live and let live policy among nations but desirous of international prestige.

National culture: Seeking roots in and identification with Mexico's past and her earlier peoples; concern of writers, poets, dramatists, architects, painters, sculptors, and philosophers with discovery of and proclamation of the "Mexican soul;" major monumental (as well as personal) symbols of Mexican traditions and evolution (National University, National Anthropological Museum, pyramids, Monuments of the Revolution; etc.); acceptance of selves as they are, and proud of the conception.

Civil rights: Freedom of press, speech and assembly; racial tolerance; universal suffrage (but realistic choice limited to voting for candidates agreed upon within *the* Party); National University autonomous; secular authority superior to religious authority.

Social role of government: Heavy reliance on government (rather than private charity) for social welfare; reliance on government planning and initiative to give dynamic and orderly progress to a country heavily steeped in traditional ways and superstition.

Government intiative in industrial development: Government encouragement of private investment from both domestic and foreign capital sources, but maintenance of majority Mexican control; moving rapidly toward technological modernization.

Power structure: Actual governing centered in strong executive supported by representation of major interest groups integrated in the Party of the Continuing Revolution including farm, labor, and public sectors. The latter includes bureaucracy, small business and industry, professions, youth (though not the students as such), career bureaucracy with administrative rather than policy determining functions.

These adjustments in governing and management have not stemmed from any formalized ideology like the works of Marx or Lenin or Mao or Hitler, although various ideological interpretations of the pragmatic moves have been made. Yet the phrase "The Revolution" functions as more than a summary of those practical moves. Some observers have reported that it symbolizes in almost a mystical way the very character and identity and direction of movement of the nation itself, and that if a project or proposal can be justified as advancing The Revolution, it gains legitimacy thereby. This would be an exaggerated description of its hold upon the students we interviewed. Yet among them also The Revolution was still in progress, an indication of the commitment of the Establishment to change and progress and modernization with popular consent and for the benefit of large portions of the people rather than for the maintenance of the status quo and the privileges and prerogatives of an elite few. The Revolution symbolized for them a nation on the march, not one engaged in a rear guard action to perpetuate the past. They, therefore, gave evidence of some sense of hope in and promise of the future at the same time as they were anxious about changes just over today's horizon. But they were restless at, and critical of, the slowness of the progress, and cynical concerning the amount of self-serving on the part of those with political power, and about the exclusion from any real positive participation in governing of those who were not on the inside of the Party councils.

It is plausible to assume that this awareness of and confidence in what Mexico stands for and what it means to be a Mexican is related to the fact that the major thrust of student activism in Mexico has been directed toward modification of the university and student experiences therein, not toward an attack on the Establishment; and that the efforts of leftist leaders to expand the issues related to a student demonstration or strike to include radical criticism of or a confrontation with the nation's political structure so ordinarily meet with failure. The chief foci of stimulation for what might be termed *political* demonstrations are police brutality and an opportunity for expressing anti-Yankee sentiment. Alleged police brutality, or indeed any police action restricting the activism of students is a sure stimulus to increased activism attracting increased student participants in any land. National independence in all Latin American countries tends to be operationally defined chiefly as "independence from the United States."

Students in Colombia had difficulty in formulating any concept of their nation as an integrated and homogenous entity. In the development of their self-concepts, the facts that one had his origin and associations in a particular family, social class, or population group (e.g. Antioquians); was loyal to the Conservative or Liberal Party or one of their factions (which most students were not) or to one of the small opposition parties or no party at all (which most of them were); came from a particular locality; or was preparing for a particular career; was more significant than the fact that he was a Colombian. If one is to trust the perceptions of the students, nation building, in the sense of achieving a working, purposeful, and stable unity among the disparate groups and factions constituting the people of Colombia, is unfinished business. Any nationalism they expressed was emotional and poorly supported either by symbols or substance, save as it became manifest in a negative form as anti-Yankeeism.

The activist students see themselves as agents of radical change, such change meaning chiefly the ending of oligarchical control of Colombian affairs, but with no symbol or substance of nationhood with which they can identify and by reference to which they could rally their energies and hopes or organize their opposition to continued partisan rule of, by, and for the elite. Those who declare themselves revolutionists, are revolutionists without any ideal image of what a new Colombia could

be save in such general terms as more free, modern, and democratic.

The reforms instituted by the elite groups are not seen, as
they are by Mexican students, to be manifestations of a progressive (albeit all too slow) planned movement toward a modernized and new democratic nation, but as reluctant concessions
made to still any popular opposition to continued elite rule
or to take the wind out of the sails of any nebulous counter-
elite movement. The liberal moves made by the (1969) President,
Lleras Restrepo, in recent years have not dissipated this interpretation. He was, after all, in office in accord with a National
Front alliance of convenience between the Liberal and Conservative parties, both of which are perceived as the political
instruments of the oligarchy. Moreover, his clamp-down on the
activism of the students, in their minds at least, marked him as
an unlikely promoter of *their* conception of a more democratic
Colombia.

Their options in contemplating any future political roles for
themselves are to get in with the elite, to try to renew the periodic attempts, that have previously failed, to launch a genuine reform movement within the Liberal Party, to join forces with the
ineffective opposition parties, to join the guerrillas. None of
these options is very promising in providing an opportunity
for effecting the radical change the activists, and large numbers
of their student associates, declare is necessary. In the meantime,
as students, the activists continue to take every opportunity to
declare in resolutions, in the effort to transform strikes or demonstrations rooted in academic issues into politically oriented
confrontations, and in personal assertions, that they are agents
of radical change.

In both countries the tradition that political change is
achieved through revolution is an ever present influence on the
image of what it means to be an agent of radical change. If
nothing else it suggests that the Establishment cannot be trusted
to initiate on its own any changes which would weaken its power
to rule. But the influence does not necessarily suggest a political role for the student as a conspirator working to overthrow
the government or as a participant in a popular uprising.

Even those who applauded the commitment of those who had
gone over to the guerrillas, conceived of the role of those
who had done so as one aiming to embarrass, confuse, and
make governing difficult for, the Establishment rather than to

overthrow it. On the other hand that tradition, plus the evidence that control and management of the nation is closely held with little chance for influence by those not closely related to the "insiders," suggests the ineffectiveness of a role as a participant in the orthodox process of democracy, making use, as an ordinary citizen, of the electoral, legislative, pressure group, and judicial institutions associated with that form of government. While they are students even those processes are not realistically accessible to them.

A role as a protesting demonstrator or striker is, however, both possible and attractive as an alternative to other political tactics from the use of which, as students, they are, for all practical purposes, excluded. Moreover, the long history of the demonstration and the strike as the chief means by which the attention of the rulers may be called to the grievances and aspirations of the ruled, and particularly the long and successful record of the students as initiators or supporting participants in these demonstrations and strikes, cannot but suggest their use and, because sanctioned by custom and tradition, justify that use. Demonstrations and strikes are not limited to the countries we are discussing, but they have a special appeal and sanction in countries in which there is a history of rule by the few, and in which the many do not have realistically available to them stablized "middle way" political institutions through which the voice of the people can be effectively heard, or time-sanctioned ways for developing them through widespread public debate, pressure from organized groups representing a *wide range* of political, economic and social interests, or through issue-centered electoral activity. Where the traditional alternatives in the face of a desire for change are acceptance of domination, the exertion of personal influence on rulers, or revolution, the demonstration has an inevitable and necessary place as a "middle" course of political activism.

Toward Vocational Maturity

Coming of age for youth is a process also of achieving maturity within a given economic environment and adapted to its requirements. The most obvious approach to this achievement is to do exactly what the students are doing, that is to get a degree passport to employment in a job.

But there was an uneasiness evident in their comments about the dependability of that approach in these days. The uneasiness was rooted first of all in their uncertainty as to what changes in vocational abilities would be required by economic and industrial modernization. Already there was apprehension that the professional training and knowledge acquisition available to those in the public universities was inadequate for achieving the vocational competence required by current technology and methods. Their uneasiness was stimulated also by their anticipation of what the impact of modernization would be on the way of life of all Mexicans and Colombians. The operation of foreign owned or managed enterprise on their native soil, and which they assumed to be representative of the efficiency oriented characteristics of what industrial modernization would bring, were perceived as introducing a dehumanized set of values and an intensity of concentration on material values into the relation of people to their work and the relations of people generally to each other, which were incompatible, they felt, with the traditional Latin American conception of the good life.

Incidentally, since much of this foreign enterprise is American, this characteristic is coupled with the charge of economic exploitation for the advantage of foreigners of the country's resources, as a basis for resentment against Yankee "imperialism." The Yankee's single minded pursuit of efficiency and material gain is considered crude and disturbing to those whose traditional conception of business relations is heavily colored by the opportunities and responsibilities involved for human relations among family, friends, and *compadres*.

The point of interest here, however, is not the stimulus to anti-Yankeeism produced, but the stimulus to anxiety about whether the modernization, which they favor in general, will involve them and their countrymen in economic roles governed by values which are incompatible with those traditionally considered to be appropriate and desirable guides to living.

Those student leaders whose ideological tenets or international affinities predispose them to take every opportunity to organize demonstrations directed at "Yankee imperialism" do not have to convince large numbers of students that the United States is imperialistic in the traditional political and economic meaning of that term in order to marshal them for such demonstrations. Students whose aspirations for their country include its modernization cannot very well demonstrate against the development of technological and methodological aspects of business and industry essential to that modernization, and the hoped for expansion of economic opportunity it would mean for the middle classes. But they can find an outlet for their anxieties about the changes in the personal role and the threats to traditional values expected to accompany that modernization by joining in group demonstrations against American businesses or industries, and against anything symbolizing the values associated with the entrance of the United States into the political and economic life of their country.

The problem of coming of age economically is intensified by the fact that the personal economic and political interests and the economic and political structures in both countries are so closely inter-twined. A main source of initiative for economic development is the politician, not the private entrepreneur, the government not the individual enterprise. And even when the stimulus is from private initiative, the regulation of and support for such initiative involves the entrepreneur in intimate association with the political process. In both countries the students are aware of this relationship and assume that decisions on economic policy are governed first of all by their relevance to preserving the existing political system, those who manage it, and those who benefit from it. In Colombia, this relationship is considered so mutually dependent that little hope was held out for genuine economic modernization as long as oligarchical political control persisted.

There are signs, however, of which few students seemed to be aware, that modernization on the economic front is bringing to the fore in the nation's affairs prominent and increasingly powerful representatives of groups whose common bond of interest is primarily economic rather than political, and that these representatives and the functional groups for whom they speak are beginning to exercise considerable influence in the political and social as well as in the economic affairs of the nation. The businessmen of Antioquia (centered in Medellin) were said to be among the main supporters of the National Front coalition of the previously warring Liberal and Conservative parties in Colombia. The leading business and industrial leaders in Mexico are alleged to be exercising increasing influence on the nation's affairs working in close association with the President. The influence of trade union leaders is making itself felt and this influence will probably increase as industrialization proceeds.

It is possible that as economic modernization advances in Mexico and Colombia the great emphasis on the political aspects of an adult role will be lessened and that the concept of the university as a developer of men will stress its role more as a professional and less as a political institution. But even this possibility introduces an air of uncertainty into the perception of students of what role characteristics will mark the man who has come of age.

In any case the set of role models which the present students inherit in the economic, as in the political aspects of life, does not appear to these students as offering a certain and dependable set of role options in accordance with which they can pattern their careers and which they can incorporate into their image of their selves as mature persons. Moreover, the values exemplified in the persons and institutions identified with the present and probable political and economic Establishment in many cases are inconsistent with their conception of the ideal values by reference to which adult life should be ordered. They question whether the nature and process of the education they are receiving as conducted by the current educational administrators prepares them to be effective and satisfying participants, especially as agents of change, in the future political and economic life of their countries. They are consequently readied to respond supportively to their own leaders in an activism which implies that they are creating their own roles, proclaiming their own values, remodeling their own educational process and facilities. They are seeking to come of age on their own terms.

Reference Group Orientation

The last named predisposition arises from an awareness that the "older generation" offers an inadequate set of norms either as to the activity or values by which genuine maturity can be tested. The predisposition is strengthened when they note the social reference group associations from which their elders obtain their standards of successful living and values. Their conclusion is that their elders seek confirmation of their ideas and conduct from their own kind, narrowly defined: the oligarchs from other oligarchs in Colombia, the PRI politicians from the influential managers of the party's organization and policy in Mexico, the business and industrial leaders from other business and industrial leaders, the priests from the ecclesiastical hierarchy, trade union leaders from other trade union leaders, bureaucrats from other bureaucrats, university rectors and deans from other university administrators or the politicians on which they are dependent, and most of their adult compatriots from their intimate associates in the family and the system of *compadrazgo*. The last named focus of reference is particularly unsatisfactory for students who have become more mobile than their parents both physically and psychologically and have every intention of remaining mobile. They seek new references to supplant the traditional ones of kinship and patronage, the influence of which they still feel emotionally, but which do not have the same possibility of becoming operational and trustworthy for mobile youth. Particularly do they regard as superficial and poorly adapted to stimulating progress, the tendency of many members of the middle class, from which most of them come, to set their standards of the good life by reference to upper class folkways and mores. Such reference group evaluations result, the students believe, in the tendency to perpetuate the political, economic, and social status quo and reduce society's capacity to come to grips with the problems and opportunities of a changing world.

Those students who perceive major political, economic, and social change as the dynamic characteristic of an experienced present and of an anticipated future, and who are associated in an experience which emphasizes the nation, and even the world, as the operational field for that change are not so much in *revolt* against the older "mature" generation as inclined to consider that generation's role patterns and values *irrelevant* to the changing character of life and work for the mature individuals they hope to become or, in many cases, believe they already are. Even if counseling were available (which it is not to any large degree in Mexico and Colombia) the distrust among the young of its adequacy and relevancy would be matched by the assumed limited comprehension of their elders of what will be required of a mature person in a world which neither they nor their juniors have yet known. Since youths cannot with confidence turn to their elders for suggestion, by example or counsel, with reference to their patterns of mature living or values, they most naturally turn to their peer group, which in the first instance in the public universities is composed of companionable individuals among the immediate student associates in their faculty or school. But through an expanding system of communication the actual or vicarious or imagined association is extended until the reference group is enlarged and identified simply as "students," in the university, the nation, in Latin America, and, for some, in the world. What amounts to a "student" class consciousness develops.

Students have few ideologists to support and glorify that class consciousness, but they have some traditions and symbols to reinforce its reality; they, of course, contemplate no lifetime identification with those who share that station in life. But for the moment the student "class" is their most real and influential reference group.

Testing the authenticity of their assertions of self against the standards and the approval or disapproval of that peer group is not satisfactory for all of them, for many do not sense the norms of the older generation as irrelevant. Even those who do, of course, cannot be blind to the fact that the irrelevancy of the wisdom of experiences and norms of their elders is matched by the inadequacy of the wisdom of experience of their peers. That wisdom is poorly grounded in either historical or current reality, and it incorporates an estimate of the future constructed by those with no greater competence in prognostication than that of their elders. Their main claim to the superiority of youth's "wisdom of experience" is that it is, as yet, compared with the wisdom of experience of their elders, relatively untarnished and uncomplicated by the necessity for pragmatic adjustment and compromise. For those for whom reference to this peer group is insufficient to authenticate and legitimize their assertion of self and their confidence in their own maturity, there is the possibility of measuring themselves against heroic characters of the past or present, or of measuring the reasonableness and maturity of their concepts of themselves and the world against a simplified version of an ideology like Communism, Maoism, or Christian Socialism, or even against the philosophies of authors like Camus and Marcuse parts of which support their declaration of independence through action.

Once a sense of community with other students, a student class consciousness, has been developed, leaders with a particular reform or revolutionary objective can identify their cause as important for students as a group, and challenge students to maintain solidarity in pursuit of student interests or just to experience the satisfaction of solidarity with the only group with which emotional solidarity is possible for many, their student peers.

Toward Manhood

A number of studies of Latin American student activism, as well as of political activism generally, have associated the frequency and violence of student and popular demonstrations and strikes with character or temperament traits frequently described as peculiarly Latin, particularly the urge to achieve maleness, *machismo*. If a manifestation of such traits is generally accepted in Latin American society as a mark of the mature individual, the association would be a plausible one. A youth in search of a self-image as a mature individual would scarcely ignore the expectancy of his peers and his elders that aggressive, audacious, fearless, disdainful of risk and danger, physically and vocally energetic, heroic and quixotic, self-assured and even ruthless behavior would mark him as a real man, *macho*. Nor can anyone who has observed student demonstrations and strikes in Mexico and Colombia fail to observe that such occasions provide the opportunity for both participants and for the forces of law and order to demonstrate such traits, especially for the leaders, but also in an only slightly lesser degree for "rank and file" participants. It is not difficult for a foreigner who observes other manifestations of the same traits in the bull fight, the fiesta, the uproarious political meeting, the game of *tijo*, in the competition for "position" in traffic on the city streets (as well as on country dirt roads) not only between vehicles, but between pedestrians and vehicles, and in less savory form the deadly serious feuding in the back country, to conclude that student demonstrations and strikes would continue to be popular as another opportunity for the expression of *machismo* even in the absence of other causes.

We would hesitate to make such a conclusion. In the first place it ill behooves a foreigner, and particularly one who is not a psychologist, to make use of a cliche-like generalization concerning "the Latin temperament" although it can be supported by reference made by native Latin American analysts to the character and predispositions of their compatriots.

But there are other reasons for the hesitancy. The same violent and uninhibited student behavior is evident in England, Germany, India, Japan, and in the United States whose people have never been characterized as uniquely moved to exemplify their *machismo*. Equally constraining on such a conclusion is the presence of girls in significant numbers among the student demonstrators, and not simply as admirers of the actions of their male associates, but as active in the same way. What is present as a stimulus to demonstrating and striking may be more a universal predisposition of youth, when the situation in which they find themselves has reduced the normal restraints on uninhibited behavior, to express and assert themselves in the volatile and exaggerated energetic ways observed. *Machismo* may be simply a summary Latin American category for many of the behavior manifestations (at least of youth) which in other countries have not been given such a label.

Moreover, when the full range of the ways in which students, including the most activist leaders, manifest their activism is considered, it is clear that the greatest amount of their time and energy is expended in the kinds of activities which require no explanation in terms of a predisposition to abnormally agressive or violent "male" behavior. The interpretation of demonstrations and strikes and even of riots by reference to such factors would still be an explanation of a small, though significant, part of the activism which constitutes the dynamic substance of the student movement.

Nevertheless even a foreigner may be privileged to observe that many of the artifacts of culture in Mexico and Colombia reinforce the impression that Latin Americans are in comparison with peoples in other relatively modern countries, predisposed to respond to exciting stimuli. There is a vitality and physically stimulating excitement about even classical Latin music. Paintings, with the exception of those of the down-trodden Indian and peasant (particularly to be found in Mexico) are lively and colorful, often riotously so. Very few statues are to be seen which create the mood of Rodin's "The Thinker." Flamenco dance forms, classical as well as folk, provide the possibility of furious, passionate, and often angry expression. Ideas are most willingly and enthusiastically accepted when expressed in action and symbolized by the physical presence of energetic and dynamic persons. The leadership of and participation in the student strike or demonstration does not appear, to those involved, inconsistent with the achievement of a reputation for exemplifying the attributes indicated.

Summary

To the point of entering college the chance for a Mexican or Colombian middle class youth to develop an individuality which is uniquely his own is minimal. University life provides for those who choose it, a first major operational field for the experiences and interactions through which one becomes aware of his self as an independent entity and by reference to which the norms for achieving genuine maturity become more evident. Students also become more familiar with the character of the real political, economic, and social world beyond their childhood environment of the extended family and home community, and with the pattern of adult roles available for "adoption" by one who desires to achieve that maturity in an adult world. His experiences reveal to him more clearly the context of institutional facilities and the context of expectancies and requirements which he will face in coming of age as a man among men.

But at that point he senses an inconsistency between the roles, values, and marks of maturity that he perceives have the approval of his elders and those he believes are consistent with the requirements of a changing world. This chapter has set forth the kinds of interpretations Mexican and Colombian students interviewed made of this situation, and suggests the impact of those interpretations on their predisposition to seek an active role while they are students as agents of change, and the way in which that process contributes to an awareness of themselves, of their personal identity, as those who have realistically come of age, politically and vocationally, by demanding, initiating, and agressively promoting such change.

The inconsistency between the political and economic role patterns, behavior, and values exemplified in the lives of their elders and what is required for coming to grips with the current and future problems which the nation faces or will face is not perceived as intensely by Mexican as by Colombian students. Moreover, the image of what their nation stands for, of what it is, essentially, its organizational charter, is clearer and more stable for Mexican students. They therefore have clearer guidelines and a more definite point of reference for developing a self-conception, for discovering or achieving an identity geared to the world as they find it, than do Colombian students. Yet both nations are in the process of achieving a widely shared concept of nationhood and a consequent understanding of what it means to be a Mexican or a Colombian. And beyond any objective operational meaning of those terms are the ideals which students hold which are inconsistent with the current experienced reality.

In both countries, therefore, there exists among the students and especially among the activist leaders a predisposition to criticism of and protest against many of the institutional forms and activities and many of the aspects of governance in their societal and university environments and to count themselves mature individuals to the degree that they succeed in becoming agents of change, for many of them, radical and revolutionary change. Whatever this may mean career wise when they have finished with the university, while they are students, it legitimizes in their minds a role as an implementor of protests against, challenge to, and confrontations with the existing Establishment.

SECTION IV

BECOMING A STUDENT AND A CITIZEN

Becoming a Student and a Citizen

Student activism is in part a response to the problems of maturation which students experience in common with all others of their age group everywhere. It is desirable, however, to bring such problems into a sharper focus by considering the ways in which the peculiar motives, circumstances, and outlook characterizing students and student life influence the activism of youth. A relationship among three variables appears to be significant: (1) the "image" or concept of the "Student" and his status and role in society, (2) his university experience, and (3) his perception of the opportunities and constraints present in society outside the university in which the student lives and will live in the future.

The Image of the Student

In every country with institutions of higher learning there is a traditional and a developing contemporary image of the Student in society, that is a concept of what it means to be a student. This concept is built up out of the expectancies held by students and others about the rights and duties, the standing and the function of students. These expectancies are stabilized by popular, cultural, and historical reinforcements. The concept involves both the student's image of himself and what society owes him, and society's image of the student and what he owes society. There are common features of this image in all countries, but there are also elements peculiar to each country, and the emphasis among even the common elements varies. Unanimity and complete consensus as to the content of this image of the Student is not to be expected.

245

The evidence upon which the following categorization of the elements in the image of the Student is based comes first of all from our interviews with over 1000 students, 310 educators, and 205 other knowledgeable persons with experience related to higher education, students, and student life, in Mexico, Colombia, Japan, and India. The generalizations have been tested against our own experience as members of university communities over the past forty-four years.

As an example of the variations that can be observed in the specific content given to these generalized categories, let us set down for each of them operational definitions which could be inferred from the comments on the subject among particular national, university, or academic-discipline populations:

Relative to *career advantages,* a Student is variously characterized by different populations as:

A person seeking and acquiring more than average ability and competence in a particular non-manual occupation

The expectant possessor of a degree passport to a (hopefully) permanent and secure white collar job

A person acquiring influential and career promoting contacts

Relative to *freedom* and *self-determination,* a Student is variously characterized by different populations as:

A relatively free person between two periods of life characterized by externally imposed constraints and regulation, earlier by the family and familiar group and later by the work place, social custom, and government

A person unaware of how to use freedom, and therefore inexperienced and unpracticed in the constraints and responsibilities essential for corporate living

A non-conformist

A rebel without a commonly accepted cause

A playboy

A hanger-on, a "non-student"

An escapist

Relative to *prestige* and *standing,* a Student is variously perceived by different populations as:

A successful passer of qualifying examinations

An ambitious and upward mobile person

A symbol and pillar of his family's societal mobility and status

A very fortunate beneficiary of public concern for education

A member of the white collar class

A person on the road to acquiring a prestigeful title or degree

A member (hopefully) of the fraternity of degree-holding, and presumably educated, persons

A member of a *select*, but not necessarily *elite*, social group

An actual or potential leader

A highly eligible marriage partner

A cultured person

Relative to *intellectual qualities*, a Student is variously perceived by different populations as:

A person who knows more about many things than most people

A person familiar with, or in the process of learning about, ideas embodied in myths, dogmas, and theories produced by others

A person becoming capable in dealing with and producing ideas

A person developing analytical and problem-solving ability

A person seeking for and capable of making significant, useful, trustworthy, and objective generalizations

A seeker for (and at times the creator of) ideological foundations for personal and societal action

Relative to *idealism*, a Student is variously perceived by different populations as:

An admirer, if not a follower, of moral and social reformers

A sponsor, carrier, and defender of popular ideals of justice and human welfare for the "people"

A seeker for (although seldom a finder of) general and universal rather than particularistic and familiar-group-bound ideals

A patriot, but on his own terms

Hopefully, a carrier of some residue of youthful idealism and commitment into the pragmatic adaptation to the responsibilities and constraints of adult life

A cynic with respect to what he considers to be private and public hypocritical morality

Relative to *participation in educational and public affairs,* a Student is variously perceived by different populations as:

A critic of inconsistencies and contradictions between ideals and practice in university and public affairs

A critic of, and one ambitious to be a co-determiner of, educational facilities provided by his university

A critic of and an active initiator of change with respect to political and economic policies, practice, and organizational structure

A fighter for national self-determination

A proponent of modernization in social, economic, and political affairs of the nation

A prospective public servant, but not necessarily a servant of the public

A revolutionist

The University Experience

When a youth decides to become a student in order to internalize in his self certain elements of this image, and to know himself and to be recognized and rewarded by others as a student, he enters into a field of experience which is peculiar to him and others who have made the same choice. He does not by virtue of his attendance at a university miss the difficulties and opportunities of "coming of age". Indeed in many ways the difficulties as well as the opportunities are intensified, and in any case are given a peculiar nature and emphasis which cannot be fully understood by those who have not themselves had the same experience or even if they had it at an earlier period in their lives. The character and adequacy of the university experience, its impact on his growing conception of himself and his place and function within his peer society and within the adult society he is about to enter (or considers he has already entered), needs to be explored and interpreted as an influence giving stimulus and direction to the thought and behavior which characterize his activism.

The delineation of the characteristics of the university experience affecting positively or negatively the personalizing of this image of the Student has been exhaustively carried out by a large number of investigators in many countries. Hypotheses pointing to frustrations produced by inadequacies or inconsistencies in various aspects of the university environment, as independent variables creating a predisposition toward student activism, are frequently encountered in the literature.

The Societal Opportunities

The third important variable involved in this approach to the interpretation of student activism is the student's perception of the operational field for self-actualization outside and beyond the university, both current and future. This operational field is characterized not only by the kind of human, social, political, technological, and economic opportunities and constraints on life outside and beyond the university, but by the traditional and aspired-to methods available for modifying these.

Relationship to Student Activism

It is plausible to assume initially, as a framework for organizing one's observations, that there are certain causal relations of these three variables to student activism. One is that the traditional image of the Student itself suggests and reinforces the appropriateness and legitimacy of some of the kinds of activism observed. Another is that inconsistencies and inadequacies in, or incompatibilities among, the three variables create frustrations which ready the students for reactive responses, and at times suggest the necessity for corrective action which it appears to the students they must themselves undertake. A third is that the role implied in the traditional image of the Student may appear to today's students as irrelevant to their potential for such corrective action; and that they are accordingly attempting through their behavior to create a de facto role more consistent with that potential. A fourth is that the circumstances and conditions prevalent in their universities and societies provide the specific occasion, if not the sufficient cause, of action satisfying their predisposition to self-assertion at this stage of the maturation process. A fifth is that their inclination to activism is intensified by the degree of both public opposition and public permissiveness with respect to it.

We turn then to motivations and circumstances, related to personalizing the image of the Student, which *both* leaders and followers may share, albeit in differing degrees, as revealed in discussions with students in each of the countries.

It is not necessary to assume or demonstrate that all of the stimulants to direct action we shall discuss act upon all the students. No one has ever contended that all of the students in the National University in Mexico City, all the students in the National University in Bogotá, all the students in the University of Tokyo, or all the students in the University of Calcutta, take part in such activity. Nor is it essential, in order that a sizable number shall take part, that all who do so shall react to any one or all of these stimuli. If only an unduplicated 1% were to be motivated by the impact of each of the kinds of stimuli, the cumulative number would be large enough, when they are joined by the simply curious and those who "just go along for the ride," to provide a substantial crowd for effective demonstrations or other manifestations of activism. Moreover the evidence is quite clear that all of these stimulants must necessarily be felt to some degree by a substantial number of the students. *The general hypothesis proposed is that these conditions and circumstances, acting singly or together, produce in a large number of students a generalized readiness to act which can be brought into active focus by activist leaders, whenever they tackle a particular issue by direct action.*

Chapter 7
Becoming a Student and Citizen in Japan

In general the same *type* of elements enter into the concept of what it means to be a student in Japan as enter into that concept in all the countries. There are, of course, variations in detail. The image of the Student in Japan suggests that he is:

Relative to a Personal Career:

An expectant possessor of a university degree pragmatically useful in providing vocational opportunity and security; an apprentice to or qualifier for permanent and secure employment in a bourgeois occupation.

Relative to Freedom:

A relatively free person for the time being; a person unaware of how to use freedom.

Relative to Idealism:

A rebel without a positive commonly shared cause; an admirer of intellectual and moral reformers; a loyal but not necessarily obedient subject of the Japanese State; a future servant of the State rather than of the people; one guided by national and familiar group rules of conduct rather than by general and universal humanitarian ideals.

Relative to Participation in University and Public Affairs:

A critic of, and one ambitious to be a co-determiner of, the educational facilities and political institutions and processes established and governed by others.

Relative to Intellectual Competence:

A successful passer of examinations; a learner of ideas and wisdom produced by others; a potential intellectual.

Relative to Prestige and Status:

A very fortunate beneficiary of public concern for education; a person continuing the progress of an upward mobile family and self; a person acquiring influential contacts; a member of a present and future select, but not necessarily elite, group.

Preparation for a Personal Career

Every survey among students in Japan with which we are familiar emphasizes their preoccupation with qualifying for a degree and thereby acquiring the training essential as a basis for a future job which will be secure and rewarding economically, socially, and psychologically. All interviews produced the same impression. A university education and the degree certifying its completion is sought, first of all, for vocational reasons. Traditionally, since the establishment of universities, this vocational objective of a university education has dominated the concept of what it means to be a student.

In view of the fact that employers do their recruiting for the jobs promising the greatest monetary and status rewards among each year's graduates, this function of a university education and degree is reinforced each year. The expectancy that a university degree will be pragmatically useful in recommending the graduate for consideration to the most desirable firms and government bureaus is entirely consistent with the recruiting practices of employers. The degrees from the several universities vary, of course, in the weight and influence they give to that recommendation, and the student has had that in mind in his attempts to come successfully through the "examination hell" of one of the most prestigeful universities. Often he tries again and again to gain admission to one of them, rather than being satisfied merely to "get an education" at a less prestigeful school. We talked with one Ronin (as such try-and-try-again candidates are called) who had just gained admission to Tokyo University after seven annual unsuccessful tries. University administrators in the prestige schools are in general agreement that over half of the applicants in any one year have already applied more than once before.

A general impression exists among students that a degree from one of five or six prestige universities is the most useful passport to the best jobs. A general impression exists that those who do the hiring for both private industry and government bureaus tend to favor graduates from their own schools, so that something resembling an alumni fraternity is a part of the anticipated future working environment. But *some* university degree is essential if the student hopes eventually to join the supervisory or managerial group among whom, in government jobs, there are practically no non-degree holders, and among whom in business and industry there are less than 10% who do not hold a degree. It is clear, therefore, that in a very real sense the student is beginning a lifetime career in some very specific ways when he enters a university. He faces the future with less anxiety and uncertainty about his career than his counterpart in America.

The degree, of course, is not all he is seeking, for a student also is a trainee, apprentice, or qualifier for a permanent and secure employment in a bourgeois white collar occupation. As a university trainee he is not, however, in all cases expected to acquire the specific skills of a vocation, for employers antici-pate they will need to make an investment in further training to suit him for their particular requirements. This of course varies with the vocation involved and is relatively less true of those looking forward to medical, legal, and engineering prac-tice. However, a very large portion of those job skills which he will use are going to be acquired *after* graduation if he seeks employment with a company or government bureau. He can look forward to a "continuation on-the-job apprenticeship" of possibly ten years before he is recognized as a highly important participant in an organization's operations. He needs the de-gree as an admission card to that continuation apprenticeship. But the "content" of his university education is only a portion of his total vocational education. A student is nevertheless con-scious that he is looked upon by his more adult contemporaries as serving an apprenticeship in the acquisition not only of specific skills but of the more intangible qualities loosely and vaguely summed up in the term "an educated man."

To a large number of students seeking such an admission card to a career, however, the motivation to consistent, diligent, constant, and hard-working attention to his studies receives little reinforcement from the direct relevance of the *content* of those studies to being able to *do* vocational tasks. Neglect of his studies in order to participate in the manifestations of stu-dent activism is not too dangerous a choice to make, especially during the first two years of his university career. And it is among the first and second year students that the largest pro-portion of "followers" for student activism is recruited.

The student's future employer will try to ascertain the ap-plicant's qualifications by requesting recommendations from particularly influential men among his professors, from an investigation of his behavior record in the university and of his family and other "connections," and usually by an interview held for the members of each graduating class prior to, or around, the first of October each year.

The student suspects that an important item sought for in the investigation is whether or not he has participated as a leader in student political agitations and demonstrations. Some employers have contended that such activity, far from being a handicap to employment, indicated to them that the job candidate has qualities they very much desire. The willingness to take the initiative and even risks, ability to persuade and lead men, the training in figuring out what to do next in case of difficulties, and even a dissatisfaction with things as they are, these are qualities that can be useful to progressive firms, especially in the light of the observation that once the college years are over, the students are inclined to settle down and, as one employer expressed it, "get into no more trouble." The general impression among students, however, is that in most businesses, and certainly in government bureaus, evidence of such student activism is a negative rather than a positive recommendation. In any case the probabilities are sufficiently strong in that direction to provide a heavy damper on what future employers may consider "irresponsible" behavior. The probability is even stronger today, after the widespread revulsion against the extreme violence accompanying the 1968-69 virtual war between radical student groups and the university and government authorities. The stimulus must be extremely strong to break through the disinclination to take the chance. That disinclination grows stronger as freshmen move through their courses toward their senior year.

A further consequence of the concept of the student as an apprentice, when held by others in society than the students themselves, is that direct action, particularly of the sort evidenced in the early 50's and in 1959 and 1960 is considered to be "inappropriate" for students. They should, in the minds of many commentators, stick to their task of getting ready to become useful citizens. In a country where "appropriate to a relationship" is a major criterion of ethical behavior, such a criticism is particularly telling, and it will be chiefly strong self-willed persons who ignore it, self-willed or conscious that the times and events are so critical that the criterion of "appropriateness" in this case is itself inappropriate to the situation at hand. A consequence of this situation which can plausibly be anticipated is that the great majority of the students will not be inclined to engage in the more unorthodox and violent forms of student activism, but that those who do will be relatively unrestrained by standards of conduct prevailing among the more conservative majority.

Once he has been accepted for employment as one of the recruits of the class of, say 1968, the student perceives his future as relatively secure, particularly if he joins a large and well-established firm. He will be trained by his supervisors on the assumption that he will not change his job, certainly after his early 20's. The universality of employment practices consistent with this permanency of employment principle is questioned by some Japanese economists and sociologists. They contend, on the basis of statistical surveys, that the mobility among Japanese workers is equal to that in certain European countries. Apparently, however, the students are unaware of the statistical evidence, or believe that the statistics which reveal averages for *all* job changes are relatively inapplicable to the managerial jobs they are seeking. For their perception of the future is consistent with the generally held opinion that life-time employment with a single employer is the norm.[1]

The importance of the job extends into many aspects of life besides making a living. The student anticipates that he will be taken into the "enterprise family," as it were, and that his supervisor and even top management will serve as his protector and patron in many affairs of living even outside of the employment relationship. He may expect that this patronage may, for example, extend to service as a "go-between" in arranging a favorable marriage. It goes without saying that the reputation of the firm or bureau for which a prospective husband

[1] A study made of the reaction of nearly 300 major top executives by Yasno Kotapa of Keio University in 1962 found nearly 58% favorable to the life-time employment principle and 36% with serious questions about it. Discussions with a number of employers substantiated the impression that hiring after the age of 30 was a rare phenomenon. The choice of and acceptance by the original firm is therefore extremely important in a majority of cases. A reading of recent reports of management conferences and of articles in management publications, however, reveals a growing inclination of Japanese employers in the face of competitive cost considerations to question the desirability of this life tenure principle of employment.

works is itself an important consideration to the parents of a girl in giving consent to a marriage. The importance of these patronage services, which depend upon the degree of influence of the employer as a person or of the employer's class in Japanese society, plus the probable life-time relation to that employer once the relationship is established, plus the probable permanence of the firm is one important cause of the difficulty American and other foreign firms report in getting any but the "left-overs" of each graduating class. It is also one reason for seeking the security of employment offered by a large well-established firm in preference to that by a small firm even with growth potential.

Once hired, a young man will not be fired except for exceptional misconduct. His promotion with respect to salary and position will be slow. He will move by seniority with his class. It will be from 10 to 20 years before he reaches a major supervisory or managerial position, though there are a large number of deputy and assistant positions in which he may actually be doing the work of a supervisor, who may hold his position more by virtue of his secure seniority than because of his ability. His compensation, salarywise, will move up about 7% to 10% a year along with the salaries of the others in his age bracket. Informal benefits such as recommendations of his managers for membership in a select club, or for both prestigeful and better kindergartens and schools for his children, extra credit cards, help in building a home, introductions to important people, assignments to more interesting and significant work, appointment as representative of the company at conferences, etc., make both him and his colleagues aware that the quality of his performance has been noticed by management or the administration. Above all he may anticipate, granted his record is superior, survival for appointment to one of the increasingly narrow range of top jobs rather than expect to "mature at a lower level."

A break is beginning to appear in this essentially seniority system in certain industries where new methods and techniques necessary for the maintenance of a competitive position are making the "elder statesman" and even top managers more dependent than formerly on the specialized skills of younger men. If he possesses such skills, a young man may be rewarded differentially from the others in his age class by being appointed, for example, to a research and development group of younger people who can prepare reports and recommendations some of which may eventually be accepted.

During the immediate postwar period, Japanese university students were much concerned about a problem frequently encountered in other industrializing countries, namely, the prospect of unemployment. But in recent years and save for temporary periods of recession, that anxiety has been on the decrease. The shortage of available university trained manpower appears to be on the increase. The Japan Labor Bulletin for March 1964 reported that in 1963 the proportion of job offers to job seekers was, for engineers, 7.6 to 1, and for scientific graduates, 6.4 to 1. The imbalance is less for liberal arts graduates[2] but the overall picture is such that the *Japan Times* could report at that time that University graduates "never had it so good." The shortage of manpower for the "middle" technical positions, for which graduates of the junior colleges and technical high schools and other institutions qualify has caused the Japanese Federation of Employers Association to plead for the expansion of such facilities. The hypothesis of the "unemployment" of intellectuals as a contributing cause of student direct action does not help in interpreting such action in Japan at the present time.

With respect then to the image of the Student as a prospective possessor of a pragmatically useful degree which will assure his opportunity for permanent and secure employment for which he is a trainee during his student years, there is a consistency between image, the chance to become prepared for employment at the university, and the perception of the conditions of opportunity in employment one will face. There are frustrations connected with certain aspects of the situation, particularly the examination system and the failure of so many to qualify. But for the great majority there is little stimulus to restlessness and rebellion in inconsistency between the image of the Student relative to his appropriate career, the kind of preparation he gets in the university (or lesser schools), and the eventual conditions of realization in his own person of the concept of a Student and an educated man. Possible exceptions to this

[2]The proportions of the graduates in the Humanities (24%), does not produce the same problems of the "educated unemployed" as it does, for example, in India where the proportion is 44%, UNESCO, *Statistical Year Book*, 1968, pp 262 ff.

generalization are the medical and law students.

Should there be a change in the customary stable harmony between the image of the Student as one preparing for a relatively prestigeful vocation, his university experience, and the nature and volume of employment opportunities, a condition favorable to the stimulation of student activism would exist here as in a number of other lands. In Japan that stimulation must be sought for in other circumstances.

Freedom

The image of the Student in Japan presupposes that he is a free person for the time being relative to other inhabitants of the land and relative to his own status before and after his student days. In a later chapter, we shall describe the student years in the Latin American countries as life in an oasis of freedom between the years of authoritarian existence at home and in the community from which they have come and those to be spent in the world of vocational and political endeavor into which they soon will go. A somewhat modified characterization can be made of the life of students in a Japanese university. The picture of one free from the normal restricting arrangements of before-and-after university life is not as dominant in the traditional Japanese image of the Student as is the case in Latin America, but its influence on their readiness for unrestrained action cannot be ignored. Especially after the ascendancy of the military powers to governing positions in the late 20's and 30's of this century, did the exercise of thought control, "moral education," police espionage, and public control extend its influence into the life of university teachers and students. Immediate face to face contacts with family were, however, loosened for students away from home, and the regulations of adult societal relationships were not yet relevant, so that days in the university were in some respects comparatively freer than other stages of life. But the controlling hand of the Ministry of Education and the police was always in evidence.

Although it is probably inaccurate to characterize the present-day Japanese family as authoritarian, the testimony of students indicates that it demands the loyalty of members, that traditional control by the male head is still strong, that mutual obligations are owed. These features, among others, do make the family a constraining influence in the experience of youth. Moreover, the constraints of custom and ritual, at least in the familiar relationships, are relieved only periodically by festivals and letting oneself go in physical enjoyment. Furthermore, those in their late teens and their 20's at the time of the most severe student disturbances around 1960, could remember the freedom-restricting privations of wartime and postwar poverty which left them few resources to be free with.

Concerning the future, the resigned attitude with which almost all the students we talked with accepted the probability of little freedom of action once they were embedded in the bureaucratic regimentation of government or business employment was noteworthy. They had no illusions about a life of free choice after they got their degree. A Japanese proverb "It is better to be bound by a long rope than to try to cut it," expresses their mood in part. As far as the opportunity to be innovators is concerned, they well know it will be many years before their chance to experience such opportunity will come.

Postwar experience introduced students to the concept of freedom, not so much as the special privilege of students, as the right of all citizens. Yet because they were the least involved in societal activities where restrictions on personal freedom are a normal and necessary condition of ordered procedures, and because they were of an age when restrictions of free thought and action are most resented, students especially welcomed, and exaggerated the implications of, and carried into action, that concept of freedom.

The tendency to activism was not so much supported by the tradition of students as free, or freer, persons, as it was stimulated by what appeared to them as a sudden and unexpected falling away of the restrictions by which students and others in society had formerly been bound.

At this particular revolutionary period in Japanese history the exhilarating stimulus arising from release from an authoritarian and restrictive background and future was especially strong. The unanticipated and almost startling experience of a conqueror removing the personal and institutional symbols of authoritarianism, such as the freeing of those who had in the past suffered oppression at the hands of the Establishment, the transfer of land from landlords to peasants, the declaration of intent at least to liquidate the Zaibatsu, the effort toward decentralization and toward local autonomy in many public

affairs including police and school systems, the encouragement
of trade union organization, the unquestioned undermining of
the authority and regulative powers of the police, and the reit-
erated emphasis on freedom and the sovereignty of the people,
all of this was initially exciting. Set against the severe restrictions of free expression and action following upon the ascendancy of the military authority in the 20's and 30's, and the
totalitarian controls of the war years, and even seen in the light
of normal conditions of regulated life in the whole history of
Japan, this evangelistic fervor of the Occupation authorities,
enthusiastically supported by liberal and leftist elements among
the Japanese, for free expression and actions and institutions,
was a heady experience.

At the same time that freedom and self-determination were
being emphasized, the former system of police regulation was
decentralized and weakened. The police were no longer able
to maintain public order in the only manner for which they
had been trained.

The traditional relations between the students and police
deserve special comment, for to embarrass the police and to
undermine their power was a constant objective of student
leaders in the planning of their direct action. In a country
where educational status is so closely related to social status
and privilege, a natural antipathy existed on both sides rooted
in the fact that the police were recruited from those who did
not enter the university.

The police were, moreover, the traditional visible symbols of
totalitarian regulation of life in all its aspects. They were the
investigators, the providers of information about all extremist
tendencies in a country in which "extremism" was used to label
many forms of behavior that would not have been so labelled
in Europe and America. The police were the keepers of records
about students' conduct. They were the shield and protectors,
not so much of the people, as of the rulers of people. One
student leader, commenting on his deliberate intention to plan
demonstrations so that a confrontation with the police was
unavoidable said, "They were a main target of our action
because we realized that without them the rulers would be
naked." The police were the enforcers of the system of thought
control, and their iron hand restricted the physical freedom of
those who violated the rules established by the restricters of
intellectual and spiritual freedom. They were the makers of

regulations governing the assembly and group demonstrations of those whose only opportunity for self-expression in opposition to laws and orders which were intolerable to them was to assemble, speak their mind, and demonstrate.

When the Occupation authorities, in the effort to remove these aspects of totalitarian government, reduced the power of effective action by the police, the consequence could have been anticipated. Even when the ultimate object of student demonstration was to influence the action of their own governors or those of foreign countries, the police were the visible defenders of the policy and practice of those governors. And there were scores to settle with them simply as police, not merely as defenders of higher authorities.

The students took full advantage of the situation and took pride in testing the limits of the area of freedom permitted and finding ways to embarrass their traditional enemy. When, after a few years, things began to get out of hand, particularly in the academic and labor organization field, the measures taken by the Occupation authorities to restore order and control stimulated violent reactions to the infringement of freedoms which had been enjoyed for so short a time.

Moreover by projecting the emphasis upon free speech and free action into the future, it was possible for students to hope that social institutions and relations into which they were to go after their student days need not be authoritarian, and that their efforts as students, if receiving widespread popular support, might contribute to a more just and free society.

This realization stirred not only the activists, but even the more conservative and reluctant students. Even those who believed that resurgence of an authoritarian social structure was all but inevitable and were willing to let well enough alone, were stimulated by the expectation that these university years brought them their last chance to be relatively free. For the time being, they considered that they had exchanged a situation of regulation without freedom for one of freedom without regulation.

As was indicated in Chapter 4, however, the Japanese student has not been prepared by his culture for thinking of himself as a free and autonomous *individual*. The group-fused person better describes what he is predisposed by the impact of that culture to become. For such a person, without group support,

the experience of freedom is likely to be merely an escape to
nothing, rather than the opportunity to develop a strong and
secure individuality capable of voluntary and meaningful association with other free individuals. Thrown into a situation
providing the opportunity for freedom, such a person is not
likely to develop into a "loner," or an individual anarchist.
It is more likely that the urge to seek encouragement and
support from his peer group will be intensified. When the rules
for living with others in personal freedom are poorly developed
and the culture has implanted a predisposition to fusion with
an intimate group, his behavior is even more likely to be that
which will be consistent with his effort to "stand in with"
rather than to "stand out from" the group. Relationships among
students in Zengakuren can be so characterized.

One gains the impression that the substance of freedom to the
Japanese student has less to do with personal individual expression than with freedom of association and of joint action
in association. The evidence that Japanese students are simultaneously seekers of freedom and of group support can be
observed on every hand. One who comes into contact with them
for the first time is impressed with the hundreds of voluntary
associations which claim the time and attention and absorb the
energies of the students on nearly every campus. The focus
of interest in these groups ranges from sports to culture and
science. The latter two are frequently correlated with the students' fields of academic interest. Yet discussions with student
participants produced an awareness that the groups are valued
chiefly for the friendships and group support and for opportunity for group activity. Actually many of them are approximately fraternal in their eligibility requirements for membership, in their perpetuation through selection and election of
new by old members, and in the inculcation of a group loyalty
which a member hesitates to betray especially by leaving or
deserting the group. In these groups, students reported, there
develops an approximation to brotherhood which is absent
from the relations in general with other classmates. Some of
the groups have permanent meeting quarters in student union
buildings or other places set aside for the purpose by the university administration.

The lack of student extracurricular activities and associations
and the opportunities they provide for expression and realization for those with leadership predispositions and ambitions

has frequently been pointed to by observers in other lands as a cause stimulating such would-be leaders to initiate direct action efforts among their fellows. There is no lack of such opportunities which would suggest the applicability of such an explanation to student activism in Japan.

The student self-government associations, which are the local units of Zengakuren, are in addition to these many voluntary associations. They provide another focus for satisfying the interest in group support. They undertake, as we have seen, the protection of students from acts of the authorities which appear to them contrary to the freedom and well-being of the students, and give students a sense of group activity in doing something about major public issues, domestic and foreign. Committees of these self-government associations can be seen meeting in tents or on the lawns or in student union rooms in seemingly endless consideration of what to do about something or other. On one campus where a dispute was in process about who was to administer the newly built student union building, the students were insisting on complete control. One of them said, "Unless we do have complete control we will not be permitted to hold all night sessions." They had been deadlocked over that issue for several months while the new building remained unoccupied and the students appeared to be in almost continuous session in the striped tents they had set up before the administration building.

Surveys of student attitudes and anxieties reveal the relatively large number who place problems connected with the search for companionship and comradeship high on the list of their concerns.

One hesitates to ascribe this tendency to groupness to any psychological trait in the Japanese student.[3] But one has only to visit the shrines and other public places in Japan to observe that the predisposition toward such identification of self with the group has a chance to grow and be sustained

[3]Dr. Robert Lifton from the vantage point of a psychiatrist and on the basis of firsthand observation of student thought and activity during the most widespread and active "struggles" of Zengakuren in 1960 has written most perceptively about the psychological problems experienced by Japanese students. See especially, "Youth and History" in *Asian Cultural Studies No. 3*, International Christian University, Oct. 1963, and in Erikson, E. H. (ed), *The Challenge of Youth*, Anchor, 1965, pp. 260ff.

264 CAMPUS CHALLENGE

from their earliest school days. Marching in twos or threes, with their class, in uniform, behind identifying flags, frequently chanting, they early acquire almost a physical preparation for marching and demonstrations, and one would suspect that they grow in this experience of becoming and being a part of a student "body."

The resulting predisposition to groupness, it should be recalled, however, is characterized by a trust in the group's leader to define the objectives and role of the group. Identification with the group is all but synonomous with confidence in and loyalty to the group leader.

One suspects that participation in student demonstrations is a manifestation for many of a desire to melt into and to become a part of the fellowship of their peers. Many students in conversation offered the parodoxical observation that they never felt so free and independent as when they were engaged in a locked arm, chanting, swaying, snake-dancing group of fellow students demonstrating for or against something they felt to be of critical interest to students, the universities, the people, or the nation. Particularly for the first and second year students, who, we gather, form a major portion of the demonstrators, does this comradeship in an exhilarating and frequently dangerous enterprise offer compensation for the loneliness many of them feel when away from the intimacies of their home life.

The freedom experienced by Japanese students in the challenges they make to the Establishment is, then, a freedom heavily tinged by the predisposition to seek its expression in association with, and under the strong leadership of the most persuasive among, their peers.

Idealism

The interpretations of the activism of students in every land are liberally sprinkled with such phrases as, "The idealism of youth," "Unselfish idealism," "Determination to produce a better world than their elders have been able to do," etc. Commentators on the postwar activities of the Japanese students, especially those from other lands, point to such motivations. Japanese interpreters, and even the students themselves, however, lay less stress on this factor than do those in other lands.

It is, moreover, not always clear what content is given to

the concepts "idealism" or "ideal" or "idealistic" in such interpretations. The connotation is not always laudatory. In many cases one senses that the meaning is simply "impractical," "theoretical," or even "crackpot." If this is the meaning, then the use of the term "idealistic" has little relevance to our present purpose of defining the image students have of themselves and of their role in society. It simply is an adjective descriptive of behavior deemed undesirable or foolish by the commentator. In other cases, however, the terms seem to imply that the students have a concept of a good, or at least a better, society in which the chances for happiness, justice, and peace for all are more prevalent, and to the creation of which society they desire to commit some of their thought and activity.

Even though we invest the word "idealistic" with the latter meaning, it still is necessary to give it specific content if we are to suggest what is to be expected of those students who may conceive of themselves as idealists. For the results of the dynamic operation of idealism are products not of idealism in the abstract but of the operational meaning it has and of the specific direction it gives to idealistic behavior and of the character it gives to idealists.

The idealist in a less than perfect world must, at a minimum, view the status quo with dissatisfaction. Never once in our interviews with Japanese students did we find one who was satisfied. To that extent they had taken the first step to becoming and considering themselves to be positive idealists. Their leaders were more than dissatisfied. They were in varying degrees of rebellion *against* what they described as the many "contradictions" in Japanese society. These were contradictions between the actual character of Japanese institutions and life on the one hand, and the vaguely understood notions as to the requirements for human happiness on the other.

Note that "requirements for human happiness" is not in this statement given specific content. For it is just the indefiniteness and variety of the concept of what those requirements are that makes the characterization, "Rebels without a positive commonly shared cause" possible.

Japanese students are more definitely certain of what they are *against* than of the positive things they are *for*. When asked to state why they are opposed to something which has been alleged to be the focus of their written or vocal or

active protests, they respond by naming a variety of desirable
societal conditions which the thing they are opposed to is
presumed to make difficult of achievement. They are opposed to
highly centralized and powerful bureaucracy. That appears
to them to be in contradiction with such varied objectives as
a powerful and effective popular legislative system, with the
maintenance of equal opportunity, with realization of the
sovereignty of the people, with the elimination of special
privilege, with the maintenance of academic freedom, with the
opportunity for revolutionary spirits to have their day, or just
with something envisaged as Democracy. They are opposed to
high degree of monopolistic concentration of private industrial,
business, and financial power. That appears to be in contradiction with the achievement of a "people's democracy,"
the opportunity for small businessmen and industrialists,
the equalizing of incomes of people in large and small businesses, the avoidance of Fascism, the avoidance of control
through money of political policies and practice. They are
opposed to the Mutual Security Pact with the United States.
That appears to them to be inconsistent with the maintenance
of an independent Japan, of "racial autonomy," with a progressive peace mission for Japan, and the avoidance of colonialism and of atomic war. They were opposed to the presence in the
government of those identified with prewar policy and practice.
That appears to be in contradiction with the creation of a
democratic Japan or the avoidance of a return to the old
Japan, or just the opportunity for the younger generation to
introduce their progressive ideas into a society controlled by the
older generation. They are opposed to, or rather, are extremely
critical of, the apathy of the small farmers and fishermen.
Such apathy appears to be inconsistent with the achievement
of a progressively liberal political system, an overthrow of the
forces of reaction, or equality of economic and political opportunity for both agrarian and urban people. The dominance
of the Liberal-Democratic (Conservative) Party they feel may be
incompatible with an increasing voice of the non-elite in public
affairs, an avoidance of entanglement with the foreign policies
of the United States, and the possibility of Japan following
its independent course, or with the gradual achievement of
more democratic and corruption-free government. The centralization of the control of educational affairs appears to them to
be inconsistent with the maintenance of academic freedom,

with the opportunity of students to exercise an increasing power in control of university affairs, or the opportunity of intellectuals to exert forward-looking leadership in the training of the young and the criticism of traditional myths. The revision of the "Peace Constitution" and the growth of "self-defense forces" appears to be incompatible with the maintenance of a mission for Japan as being in the vanguard in the progress toward a warless world and with the avoidance of the return of military conscription and other accompaniments of militarism.

The examples could be extended. There are in the minds of Japanese students obvious dissatisfactions with things as they are and a great number of ideas about a more ideal world. The point that becomes increasingly clear as one listens to them discussing these "contradictions" is that there is greater agreement on a definition of what needs to be opposed or removed, than of the positive and specific nature of the world better-than-what-is which they desire to bring into being. Not only are the objectives of reform varied; in some cases they are incompatible.

Many of the student leaders with whom we talked considered themselves to be revolutionists. There is a negative and destructive objective of revolutionary fervor to which they could give fairly definite operational meaning. But they had, on their own admission, little common concept and vision of the more ideal world to replace that against which they were in rebellion, a vision which could stir and challenge them or anyone else whose support they would need, to positive, creative, and orderly efforts, to say nothing of stirring and challenging the masses whose numerical strength is required for any but a palace revolution.

It did not require the anti-capitalist and anti-imperialist and anti-American propaganda and revolutionary gospel of the communists to make even conservative students aware of these "contradictions" in the society about them. Any sensitive and thoughtful person could observe and experience them. Had there been no Communist Party in Japan, it appears to us likely that Japanese students in the post-world period of destruction and disorganization would have been in rebellion against what they saw and experienced.

What was needed in order to make such rebellion more than protest was something more than a hazy dream about the achievement of such abstract values as democracy, freedom, independence, popular sovereignty, peace, neutrality, etc. What was required was a vision of what these abstract values mean when translated into societal institutions, and into ways of behavior and human relationship.

To state that the students' conception of such objectives was indefinite and hazy is not to criticize the students, but merely to record a circumstance which makes it likely that the function of student activism is to *attack* what they consider obstacles to sound and desirable public policy rather than to initiate and support basic positive policy and practice. A vision of positive objectives, which becomes effective operationally in efforts at the reconstruction of a society *evolves* in the course of generations in the trial and error and success of a whole people to build a progressively more satisfactory society. It does not spring full blown from the brow of Marx, or the Utopian socialists, or the Supreme Commander of the allied forces, or Albert Schweitzer, or Fukuzawa, or Franklin D. Roosevelt, or Gandhi, or Yoshino. Such prophets influence the content of that vision which becomes operationally effective when it is grounded in the action and thought and emotional predispositions of the participants in that reconstruction, whether that reconstruction follows an evolutionary or revolutionary course. That vision was not the common property of rebellious spirits either among students or others in Japan in the early postwar years.

Where there is no vision of the positive aim, but only a dissatisfaction with the far less than ideal, there can be only rebellion, there cannot be either evolutionary or revolutionary reconstruction. Negative oriented idealism is a natural encourager of action *against* rather than *for*. And that was the character of student activism in postwar Japan.

It is true that some of the student leaders make no secret of the fact that their intention was to set in motion a people's or a worker's revolution. But at the height of their success in the role of rebels, it became clear that their idealism lacked a specific concept of a better world which could be shared with the "people" or "workers" whose collaboration would be necessary to the realization of that ambition. They were concerned about removing what they considered "evil," they had no program for establishing the "good," or indeed little commonly shared concept of what the "good" would be save in such slogans as freedom, democracy, peace, protection of education, racial equality, etc., which became popular after the war. But these terms were used by them chiefly for justifying their acts of rebellion, not as specific-content-filled objectives of the kind of a society they were setting about to establish.

This statement is made with no intent of passing judgment on the *degree* of idealism as an element in the image of the Student in Japan, but only to indicate that it is likely to be expressed more often in protest than in positive creative effort, and is unlikely to provide a permanent and stable foundation for persistent reform efforts throughout life, continuously renewed even in the face of the failure of protest.

One character trait which is frequently contrasted with idealism is selfishness or self-serving. The students gave evidence of concern for serving more than their own interest and of achieving something beyond their own well-being. This was evident in their concern about the probability that a personally secure future, after their university days, would demand action governed by what they called "common sense" rather than "principle." That this issue of guidance by principle or by common sense was very much in the center of their attention was indicated by their raising it spontaneously in discussions we had with them individually and in groups, by articles they wrote in their student papers, in topics we saw listed for student discussion groups, and in the frequent mention made of men whose devotion to principle they very much admired, men like Schweitzer, Gandhi, and Lincoln. It was also evident from the reasons frequently given by some students for their participation in the spring and fall "struggles," namely, that they felt ashamed not to be "doing their part" in removing the obstacles to the building of a Japan better than that which they had inherited. Such attitudes were very similar to those which among American students would be defined as "a desire to be of service." In Japan it is closely related to obeying "a sense of obligation." This "sense of obligation" which appears frequently in the descriptions of the Japanese character seemed to us to have certain characteristics among the students which were relevant to an explanation of their postwar activities. Those characteristics suggest certain additional aspects of the image of the student as an idealist.

There can be little question that, in comparison with students in the other countries visited, the Japanese student considers himself to be a person with great obligations to his extended family and to those who are his benefactors.

The concept of obligation to family, past, present, or future, however, did not need to be clarified in abstract terms by assertions made by students. Its nature and degree of vitality could be inferred from their revelation of specific responsibilities which they had for their parents and for specific members of their immediate and larger families, and from their discussions of the actual practical impact of these responsibilities on the plans they could make and were making for their future.

Much has been said about the breakdown of filial piety which has been considered a traditional and notable feature of the Japanese character. The disintegrating effects on family relations attendant upon the movement from an agrarian to an urban environment, and, in particular for this generation, the destructive impact of the disorganization of living accommodations and movement into war industries and military service, as well as the newly prominent emphasis on the freedom of the individual, are said to be eating away at the sense of obligation to family which so long in theory and practice characterized the life of the Japanese.

To judge from the concerns of the many students with whom we talked, this disintegration has not proceeded so far as many commentators declare it has. Weakened as it may be as an element in the image of the Student in Japan, it is our impression that it is far more meaningful and consistent with reality in Japan than in the United States to assert that the image of the Student, even as a person seeking freedom and self-determination, is thoroughly modified by the aspect of that image which indicates he is a person with continuing and life-long obligations to his family.

Another aspect of the larger than personal, if not totally unselfish, present image of the Japanese student is, that he is a loyal but not necessarily obedient subject of the Japanese State. In prewar days it was appropriate to say, "A loyal and obedient subject of the Emperor." Though discussion with a foreigner about the status of the Emperor was very reluctant, one sensed that the traditional attitude of filial piety and loyalty as it related to the *whole* Japanese Family was still strong, although the inclination to *absolute* obedience has disappeared along with the compulsive requirement of such obedience. In the minds of students, "loyalty" and "obedience" in the Japanese code were no longer synonymous.

Being a loyal subject in prewar Japan required severe restrictions on the achievement of any significant degree of self-determination. In any organized society, even the most liberal and free, the latter achievement must be disciplined by some constraints imposed in the interest of group and national harmony and unity. The idea of the nature and extent of loyalty owed by the student to the nation helps to define the meaning of his idealism, for it is a loyalty to something beyond the individual self.[4] Its expression was manifest in the alleged objectives of many cases of student activism.

The quite obvious direct challenge of the activists among the Japanese students in the postwar era to their governors has been characterized by Japanese commentators as evidence of the decay of the attributes of loyalty and obedience to the Fatherland. Active and vigorous protest against the actions of national leaders it certainly was, as well as disobedience to the orders given and regulations established by the police. But "disloyalty" is scarcely the word for the attitude toward Japan as a nation among the former and present leaders of Zengakuren, even the most revolutionary, with whom we talked, or among those whose attitudes have been reported by other investigators. And certainly it is completely inappropriate as a description of the predispositions of the many students who supported the challenge or ignored the challenge made by the activist leaders.

Indeed loyalty to Japan appeared to us to be a basic ingredient of their motivation even for much of their violent attacks upon the actions of those Japanese governors and bureaucrats whom they considered betrayers of the Japan they hoped to see established. Even though the definite character of the new Japan was not clear, they were willing to take great risks and expend much time and thought and energy in the effort to remove obstacles to its establishment.

A dedication to the prevention of a resurgence of those

---

[4]The folklore which is an early influence in the shaping of Japanese character places great emphasis upon loyalty, although the loyalty which is praised has a feudal quality of loyalty to a person rather than to an organized collectivity like a nation. It is easier to be clear about the object of loyalty when that object is embodied in a person.

public policies and practices both domestic and international, which had brought disgrace and defeat to a great and proud nation, can scarcely be interpreted as disloyalty, unless the Japan envisaged as the object of that disloyalty has no other potential character than the Japan of the prewar years.

A negative reaction to men like Premier Kishi, who not only symbolized but actually was, one of the "old guard" implementers of those prewar and war policies and practice cannot be labelled as loss of respect for, or a denial of one's obligation to serve, Japan. Disobedience to public authority is a dangerous and disturbing instigator of disorder which must be kept under control by the governing authorities, but it is not necessarily motivated by disloyalty to the nation or any lack of patriotism.

A major difficulty which contributed to the restlessness and the predisposition to direct action among student leaders and followers in the postwar period was how to bring to life the image of the Student as an idealistic, patriotic, and loyal person, when the perception held of the essential character of the Japan toward which an idealist could work and toward which patriotism and loyalty could be shown, was so confused. What was clear, however,. were two concepts of a very *unideal* Japan which had no claim to their loyalty, namely, the old prewar autocratic and imperialistic Japan, and any contemporary Japan that occupied a position which they interpreted as one of near colonial dependency upon a conqueror or a dominator of Japanese policies. Opposition to the promoters of a Japan with these characteristics was not inconsistent with the assertion of either idealism or patriotism. Especially strong and emphasized in the image of the Student in postwar years, then, was the idea that the Student is: a loyal but not necessarily obedient subject of the Japanese State.

The word "State" in this statement reflects an emphasis which becomes even more clear when the next characterization related to idealism is noted, namely, that the Student is: a future servant of the State rather than of the people. The general traditional character of what may be called "public" responsibility or obligation among the Japanese, is political rather than social. That is the "public" as *people* is of less concern than Japan as a nation among nations. In the traditional effort to create an awareness among the ordinary Japanese of their "public" obligation, little appeal was made to sympathy for the "underdog," to the unfortunate in the population generally. Books like Charles Booth's *Life and Labor of the People of London,* Riis' *How the Other Half Lives,* Sinclair's *The Jungle,* the Swedish labor movement's *Stockholm Back of the Facade,* or *You Have Seen Their Faces,* and a host of what is called "proletarian literature" played little part in arousing and sustaining the social conscience as an ingredient of public responsibility in Japan. Their sense of obligation beyond the human beings to which they were most closely related, was to the State and formerly, even more specifically, to the Emperor, rather than to Japanese people in general. There is, to be sure, a very marked sense of obligation in Japan to family and to particular people to whom a person owes certain advantages in life or to those who have done favors for him. But we did not sense among the students any great and widespread concern for people in general, even for those who are underprivileged or exploited.

The idealistic ingredients of the image of the Japanese Student lacked what might be termed "humanitarian" concerns. The conditions of the Okinawans, South Koreans, the Burakumin or Eta, the temporary workers, and the many socially, physically, and mentally disadvantaged sometimes appeared as the objects of organized group action but seldom of the kinds of student activism we are here discussing. The condition of the workers as such was of concern to the student leaders because such conditions might contribute to the workers' inclination to support their revolutionary ambitions. They were the "proletariat," the instruments of revolution and the beneficiaries of the new system which the revolution would introduce. But the sense of "public" responsibility as an element in the idealism of these student leaders seemed to us to be more probably relevant to opposition to those hindrances to an independent, autonomous, and unexploited Japan as a *nation* than to the promotion of the human well-being of the individual people of Japan or the individual "workers of the world."

In this probability lies the possibility that a fascist leadership could attract a following among Japanese students by an appeal to their "public responsibility" idealism as readily as could the "new look" communist leaders with their emphasis on the realization of nationalistic aspirations.

A closely related characteristic of student idealism can be

noted. The image of the idealistic Student is characterized not only by greater emphasis upon the concept of a public obligation and responsibility to Japan as a nation than to the Japanese public as people, but by his attention to ideals which are more particularistic than universal. The definition of the image of the idealistic Student would include the statement that a Student is: an inheritor and implementer of ideals of human conduct and relationship more particular to a specific familiar group than to a universal humanity. Such ideals when referring to life within a familiar group, the intimate family, the clan, the firm, the student group, or even in relationships between persons whose relative status is well understood, is governed by rules of conduct operationally defined by familiar ritual and etiquette, by mutual respect, and by an understanding of what each owes to the other. But when relations with those beyond the familiar group are involved, the operational definition of ideal interaction and conduct are weak or non-existent and therefore provide little guide to idealistic behavioral expression.

The uninhibited and violent incivility characteristic of student activism in the postwar period could well be, in part, a function of the absence of ideal ethical guides to relations with those outside the familiar group. Those whose activity the students were challenging and opposing were "out-groupers"; consequently no firm rules of conduct or etiquette with respect to them were ready to hand. The unfamiliar ones included military conquerors and foreign advisors, as well as Japanese political leaders, bureaucrats, and *locally* organized police. Moreover, even those with whom at times the students sought cooperative or collaborative relations in mounting their protests were not known as members of a familiar group to which traditional rules of relationship were clearly applicable. Such people were labor leaders, *organized* workers, women with a newly acquired freedom, and radical reformers and particularly communists recently freed from imprisonment for political agitation.

Even students and faculty, while coming into contact with each other in the classroom in traditional and familiar ways, experienced each other as unknown quantities in relationships relevant to the newly opened operational field of student self-government and the arena of political action.

Now this problem of developing appropriate ideal and work-

able codes of conduct among those brought into a new relationship, or into a substantially changed relationship, has happened
again and again in the history of the human race. Witness the
difficulties of transition from "master-servant" to "employer-
employee," to "organized management-organized worker" relations in every industrialized nation. Witness the difficulties of
transition from "master-slave" to "economic-political-and-
social equality" relations between whites and colored people
in the United States. Witness the difficulties of transition from
"caste-governed" to "social-contract-governed" relations among
the people of India. But if the ideals of human conduct have
been established among a people predominantly by reference
to appropriate relations among or between particular familiar
groups, and there is minimal or no concept of appropriate
relations to *all* humanity by which each of the particular set of
relations is to be judged ideally, and to which one owes a superior allegiance, the creation of a concept of new ideals of relationship with formerly unfamiliar persons is doubly difficult
and confusing.

From discussions with Japanese students we gather that this
was and is a difficulty which they share with others of their
countrymen. The unpredictable, disorderly, belligerent and often
violent conduct toward those who found it necessary to oppose
or try to reason with the leaders and rank and file of the student
movement in the postwar years is subject to many explanations.
Among these none is more important than that more predictable, orderly, respectful, civil, and reasonable rules of conduct for the Japanese pertain primarily to people within the
familiar group or among those participating in well-established
relationships involving mutual obligations. Those with whom
the members of the student movement dealt were unknown to
them in the kinds of relations they were involved in. They were
in a real sense, "out-groupers" with whom "anything goes."

Participation

The scope of university and public affairs with which the
student movement concerned itself in the twenty years following
the war was very broad. The students of Japan made the
alleged objectives of their activism very clear. The students
used their new found freedom to take a hand in the administration of their universities, to pressure the university and
public educational officials to devote more resources to the

improvement of educational facilities and to reduce the control of university and public authorities over teachers and students. Their campaigns or struggles also involved them in massive participation in public affairs, especially in those concerning international policy and practice. Their activity focused the attention of the public and the nation's rulers on student dissatisfaction with certain of those policies and practices and on their demands for a change. Among some of the student leaders was the clear assumption that they should participate in public affairs by spearheading a more purely Marxist movement than that manifest in previous communist movements, a movement which would begin in Japan and become worldwide.

The image of the Student implicit in the nature and purposes of student activism clearly included an affirmation of his role as a major and influential participant in such affairs. It cannot be said, however, that this affirmation was firmly rooted in the traditional role played by the students in Japanese society, as is the case in Latin America. This is not to say that historically the students had played no part in such affairs as for instance during the abortive agitations for liberal and socialist reforms in the 20's and against the policy and practice of the militarists in the 30's. But such activity was not prominent in the traditional behavior which society expected of students or that they expected of themselves.

It would not have occured to anyone prior to the end of the World War II to name extensive participation in university or national governance as a normal part of the concept of what it meant to be a student. University affairs were in the hands of university authorities, and overall policy and program and financial support was in the hands of central government agencies. The latter circumstance had the effect, however, of symbolizing for students their national community of interest, suggesting, when they did act, action on a national basis. National affairs were the concern of political leaders and the bureaucrats.

After the war it became clear that the students were determined to make effective their role as *critics* of, and as those ambitious to be co-determiners of, the governance of their universities and their country. This determination ran head-on into opposition from both university and government authorities. The frustration of their efforts provided the excuse for many of their demonstrations. Their occasional success fanned their confidence in eventual establishment of their right to "have a say." But they were creating a new image of the Student rather than perpetuating a well-rooted historical image.

Particularly is the concept of the Student as a participant in governing university affairs so new, so contrary to the traditional image of the Student as an acceptor of the kind of education and educational facilities offered by the Ministry of Education and the university administrators, and teachers, that it really provides no guide to specific appropriate behavior. It provides only a stimulus to experimentation to test the limits of action which will be tolerated. Those limits in the minds of the Education Ministry and of university administrators are considerably narrower than those in the minds of the student leaders. We may refer to this aspect of the Student image then as an aspiration of certain student leaders as to their role, which aspiration is not yet acceptable to educational author- ities or indeed to adult citizens generally.

Unlike the concept of the Student in Latin America, there is no content to the Japanese concept of the Student suggesting that a student has a *right* to participate in the determination of who administers, teaches, and controls academic matters.[5] Since the war, however, his autonomous associations and organizations engaged in carrying on extracurricular activi- ties in the university (and even in some secondary schools) have been relatively independent of faculty or administrator interference. Under initial encouragement from the Occupation authorities (later withdrawn), this increase in student self-gov- ernment has been waxing. It extends beyond a large number of activities in the administration of which they had always played a part: sports, literary, scientific, social and club activ- ities, some of them closely related in interest to the major sub- jects of instruction, others heavily political despite the policy of the Ministry of Education, and in many cases the policy of the college administrators, to maintain "political-neutrality" on the campus. It has also extended to the insistence on having a voice in the administration of university buildings and facili- ties used in part for student activities, and even in some cases to the selection of university officers and adminstrators. It has

[5]There was, in the higher schools, a tradition of students carrying on what amounted to self rule in dormitory life, but this is a different operational field than that involved in the determination of academic matters.

been particularly vehement when directed against infringement by university administrators and especially by the Ministry of Education, on the academic freedom of faculty and students. And at times students have joined with the Teachers Union in efforts to wield a more powerful influence in educational and public affairs.

University students have exercised this new opportunity under the direction of student leaders with greater interest in extending the areas of student control than in perfecting cooperation in spheres of action for which student skills are appropriate. As might be expected in a non-traditional operational field, their activity could not be guided by any well-established appropriate rules of conduct in relations between students and university and public authorities in the effecting of any shared or autonomous control.

It was probably inevitable that in the search for ways of participation both in the affairs of strictly student life and in off- and on-campus political affairs, conflicts should arise over the proper operational field for such action by students. For there was being incorporated into the image of the Student a fresh element which was incompatible with the other traditional image of a youth being trained for a vocational career in a way deemed suitable by the government, the Ministry of Education, and the university administrators. It was also inevitable that those students seeking such an expansion of their field for effective participation should interpret official resistance, on whatever grounds, to be a denial of the new image they were trying to create. It was understandable, if not inevitable, that in the early years of the movement, after the students had tried first the method of petition and negotiation only to meet with failure, that they should turn to direct action. For direct actions such as demonstrations are ever the resort of those who are not recognized by the authorities as those having the right to significant and determining participation in the ordering of affairs that concern them. Neither the university authorities nor the Ministry of Education could accept as appropriate to what was expected of students their demand for the right to what amounted to collective bargaining.

This evolving aspect of the image of the Student continues, and will continue for some time, to be a source of disturbance in student, and indeed in all academic, affairs.

There were ample occasions for protest oriented activism which grew out of situations in the postwar years. The traditional pattern of governance of education and educational institutions, and hence to a large degree of the activities, if not the thought, of educators, pupils and students, had been that of centralized, national government control. The decentralization and local autonomy insisted on by the Occupation authorities began almost immediately to break down, and government-initiated re-centralization set in. A half dozen government bills seeking the reassertion of control by the Ministry of Education, some successfully, and other unsuccessfully, opposed not only by students through Zengakuren, but by the half million strong Teachers Union and other interested groups, have provided burning issues between those who live in the academic world and those in the governmental educational bureaucracy. A recent Supreme Court decision involved a case concerning the forceful ejection by students of police from an on-campus play to which they, the police, had come and were taking notes. The judicial decision set forth an interpretation of academic freedom which widened the field in which the police, in the interests of protecting the public and national interest, have the right to interfere.

A militant leftist Teachers Union and the student movement can be expected to continue resistance to increasing central government control of education. They will find support from those leftist and liberal educators aware of the degree of freedom and autonomy necessary if the universities are to be the wellspring of progressive ideas and the promoters of that aspect of the public welfare that depends upon intellectual vitality in the production of ideas. And as the students seek opportunities to bring out into life their present conviction that freedom means release from the control by authorities, and that democracy means the right both to vote and to oppose by direct action any disliked decisions affecting them, there will be ample opportunity for occasions disturbing to the orderly conduct of university affairs until the time, if ever, when student activism finds outlet in regularized institutional form.

The image of the Student as a participant in collective effort to influence the course of public affairs is also an evolving concept rather than a well-established traditional concept. At this stage the public affairs attracting their interest

are largely associated with international rather than internal
national affairs. This is natural because the postwar events
which provide the most exciting and critical occasion for their
entrance into the public arena involved Japan's activity and
position in relation to other nations and the power bloc
relations of those nations to each other. Whether the evidence
from many surveys that the large majority of students consider
themselves socialists [rather than liberal-democrats (conservatives), communists, or rightists] indicates an eventual interest in
the socialist emphasis in the reconstruction of *domestic* affairs,
is questionable. For the chief emphasis of the Socialist Party in
Japan, to this point, has been upon foreign affairs rather than
domestic socialist reconstruction.

It took no very astute prophet to predict, however, that
another great upsurge in student activism would occur in
1970, when the relations of Japan to the United States, and to
the international power struggle in which both are involved,
would be critically focused on the renewal or abrogation of
the Mutual Security Pact. Twenty years had elapsed since
that first pact symbolizing Japan's dependence on the United
States, and her inevitable involvement in the power relations
with the rest of the world. Sufficient continuous activism had
been manifest in relation to that issue to have fixed firmly
in the present image of the Japanese student the expectancy
that he would be an active and probably violent participant
in public affairs on that occasion.

The impact of this aspect of the image of the Student
(as a participant in and determiner of university and public
affairs) on the massive and violent activism in postwar Japan
was not, then, the consequence of intensifying a type of
behavior consistent with a traditional student role. The impact
stemmed from the fact that that role was being created, and
that the encouragement to its creation in some quarters was
matched by a determination that it be held within narrow
bounds in others.

Intellectual Competence

The conversations and interviews we had with Japanese professors, other professional persons, leading businessmen, editors,
some government officials, and a number of students provided
an exciting and stimulating intellectual experience. The challenge arose initially from the difference in Japanese basic

premises for, and modes of, thinking from those customary in the West. If the attempt is made to understand their basic premises and thoughtways, the experience is a rich one in dealing with and testing ideas and their relevance to the world of affairs.

We had come to anticipate such an experience from teacher-student relations with graduate students from Japan with whom we had come in contact during 40 years of teaching. These persons were the products of Japanese universities, and the inference must be that a native ability to think had found opportunity for deepening and sharpening in the university experience of their homeland. Our impression is that any Japanese student who is ambitious to become intellectually competent in a creative sense can find the support and discipline he requires to fulfill that ambition in the major Japanese universities.

Certain of the premises and thoughtways of the Japanese persons, particularly the students, with whom we conversed, provided difficulties, however, to what Westerners would call "rational and objective" problem-centered thinking. We suspect that all foreigners get this impression in discussions with people of other lands, particularly when those people are forced to express their ideas to the foreigner in a language which is not their own. Nevertheless it would be our conclusion that Japanese students who have the opportunity to come into mind-to-mind contact with many of their professors would find themselves in an atmosphere in which the search for truth is respected and intellectual laziness is abhorred. They would find themselves under the tutelage of those capable of improving the exploratory, critical, analytical, and generalizing capacities of their minds. Moreover the Japanese student lives in a society in which the intellectual is highly respected and is expected to demonstrate the qualities associated with that status in public affairs.

We introduce the discussion of this aspect of the image of the Japanese Student as an intellectual with this testimony, because it must be reported that, on the evidence from discussions with all but a few of the students involved in activism, a dedication to becoming intellectually excellent and to the hard work it requires did not seem to be widely prevalent among them. Many of the student leaders with whom we talked had obviously profited by the aforementioned contacts with intellectually able teachers who were interested in developing and perpetuating superior intellectual competence in their students. Moreover it was clear that one of the features that distinguished their leadership from that in the other countries we visited was an urge to base their programs and actions on rationally defensible ideational premises. But that urge did not appear to extend to the rank and file outside that circle of leadership.

The meaning of "intellectual competence" for the general run of students was much more limited. For many it meant simply being a successful passer of examinations. This is no easy status to achieve in Japan. At the end of each stage in the educational process, and especially at the end of the primary and the secondary school periods, the pupil must qualify for admission to the next stage by a stiff and demanding examination set by the school or university he desires to attend. The death rate is very high (sometimes literally so, upon failure). Particularly difficult is entrance to "prestige" high schools from which entrance to a "prestige" university is highly probable. In fact, entrance to one of these preparatory schools is, for those looking forward to being a prestige-university student, the really big hurdle. The frustration which attends a failure to pass the examination is all the more painful because during the primary school period, a child has never been "held back." He passes along with his class, one might say, regardless of the quality of his performance. Failure would shame him and disgrace his family!

The experience of examination for admission to a university has been described as "examination hell." More than twice as many apply as can be admitted, and the proportion of rejectees is even higher at the prestige universities. The examinations, so to say, separate the men from the boys, and whatever other judgment is made of a student, he is looked upon as a respected successful passer of the series of examinations.

Such an achievement, while an immediate and continuing source of pride, has, however, its shortcomings as a source of permanent self-respect. Examination passing is a taxing, tiresome, non-creative and non-self-expressive engagement of a limited number of one's mental abilities. It is a continuous reminder of one's subordinate status and clear evidence that the many are subject to the evaluation of the few, and that those few do not include one's own age group contemporaries.

A further consequence of this emphasis on the examination for specific universities is that teaching in the secondary schools, with very few exceptions, is to a considerable extent governed by preparation for examination passing rather than the requirements of a truly liberal general education. Memorization and rote learning within the framework of a fairly rigid syllabus provide little opportunity to develop early an analytical and creative and selective mental disposition and ability.

The final qualifying examination and appraisal to which the student will be subject lies still ahead, that which will be given by the firm or the government by which he hopes to be employed.

But once admitted to the university, a student is able, unless he is intellectually ambitious, to take things relatively easy; and many are so inclined. The opportunity for intellectual growth is just that, an opportunity. It is neither a stiff requirement nor a necessary achievement. For those for whom the opportunities requiring hard mental labor are not especially attractive, there is ample time for the activities associated with the student movement. A number of student leaders declared that, in their case, being a student leader came so close to being a full time job that they were retarded in getting their degree for several years. Yet their position as students was not disturbed. Their playing of the role of successful exam passers was simply prolonged.

The ability to pass examinations is, of course, a very inadequate definition of intellectual competence. The student is expected by his fellows and by people in society generally to be a learner of ideas and wisdom produced by others. Perhaps we should better say *reader* and *absorber* of ideas produced by others.

The zeal for learning, for reading, and for absorbing the ideas of others which characterizes the Japanese student is noteworthy. It was encouraged and rewarded among the nobility in clan schools before the Meiji Restoration. Its promotion was made one of the cardinal principles of public policy in the Meiji Charter Oath in 1868 which stated that "Wisdom and ability should be sought after in all quarters of the world for the purpose of firmly establishing the foundations of the Empire." Its encouragement among all the people was given sanction by the Imperial Rescript on Education, an encouragement that was implemented by a rapid expansion and extension of all forms of education from primary school through technical and teacher training colleges to university.

To be sure, that which was learned was rigidly controlled, especially in the later years, in the interest of solidifying the national unity and devotion to country and to the Emperor, and of carrying out in other ways the purpose stated in the Charter Oath of "firmly establishing the foundations of the Empire." To be sure, the learning process laid heavy stress on memorization and rote practice rather than on analysis and critical thought. It is true that the effectiveness of teaching relied heavily on the authority given and the respect accorded the teacher, the *sensei*. But to search after knowledge, to read, to learn, became a generally admired quality which strengthened the respect for and made a highly privileged group of students whose particular occupation for a few years was to profit from the availability to them of a voluminous literature for reading, and, if they desired, thoroughgoing study.

One has only to visit the numerous bookstores in Japanese university cities and to observe the crowds of students who frequent them, to find evidence that this tradition is a living one. (The Russians incidentally have made good use of this predisposition for reading widely, by supplying cheap Japanese translations of Russian materials).

The earliest forms of spontaneous Japanese student organization were study circles, many, if not most, of which seem to have focused their attention on Marx and other socialist writers.

If all that was involved in becoming an intellectual was to be a voracious reader, the Japanese students could lay great claim to that status on the basis of their "learning."

It would appear, however, that, for most, it was not a kind of learning which increased the capacity for independent choice, or for intellectual discernment, invention, and initative. To be satisfactorily consistent with the generally held image of the Student it is only necessary for a youth to be widely read and to be able to quote or refer to what he has read. Such consistency is not judged lacking if he is unable to think comparatively and critically about what he has read. We listened, for example, to many fulsome and enthusiastic and confident *expositions* of Marx, but only as long as we raised no critical comparisons or objections for mutual exploration. To acquire the ability to lay the thoughts of two minds alongside each other for comparative and critical appraisal, to say nothing of their integration, seems to be not a normal feature of what is considered learning among Japanese students.

When it is said, then, that the Japanese image of the Student characterizes him as a "learner" it means that he is the *receiver* of the spoken or written word from his teachers, including his fellow students, of an exposition, not, under normal circumstances, a *participant* in a critical exploration.

In most college classes, we were informed by the professors, there is little discussion to provide training for mutual evaluation of each other's ideas. The student is told; he does not ask; and he is not asked. This does not imply that he agrees. But his acceptance or non-acceptance is not facilitated by the art of dialogue. If he disagrees with his teacher, he can seek another. But he is reluctant to show openly his disagreement. He may display critical tendencies among his peers, among fellow students, but not in the presence of the *sensei*. Does this suggest that student associations may have a vital role to play in an educational process whose ultimate aim is to produce intellectual excellence in students?

The popular image of the Japanese Student which embodies society's and his own expectancies, however, is held very widely to number him among the *potential* "intellectuals." Now the normal connotation of that word implies that a person to whom it applies has a philosophical bent, that he is capable of ascertaining meaningful relationships among data, relationships which are empirically or logically verifiable, that he is capable of making significant generalizations and, at least on occasions, generalizations which are relevant to widespread human experience.

Student leaders especially had their eyes focused on this expectancy. Moreover they were attempting to exemplify the qualities presumably associated with being intellectuals in thinking about their own activism. One characteristic of the leaders of the student movement which distinguished them from the leaders of the movements in the other countries we visited was, as we have already suggested, their effort to give their movement a sound "intellectual" foundation. That foundation they sought in Marxist ideology. Indeed one frequently got the impression in talking with these students that being an intellectual was practically equivalent to being a student of Marxism. That tendency has roots in the establishment of the student study circles in the late 19th Century after Japanese translations of the works of Marx and Engels and other socialist thinkers became available. Those study

circles continued during the first quarter of the 20th Century.
Today's leaders do "think" in Marxist terms; but we would
characterize the results of their thinking as a "framework"
rather than as a "foundation" for the activism they display.
The impact of that Marxist orientation is revealed as much
by the mode of the leaders' intellectualizing as by the content
of Marxist dogma itself.

We hesitate to impute particular attributes to that intellectualizing, for discussions with students were either through an
interpreter or in a language which was not their own. We are
aware of the misinterpretations which can proceed from that
fact. Nevertheless, our original basis for conclusions concerning
the characteristics of the students' thoughtways was our own
observation, and we have cited the conclusions of others only
when they help to interpret those observations.

The philosophical framework student leaders are seeking,
they insist, must be truly Japanese and consistent with basic
Japanese values. For the most part this ends as a declaration
of intent, for if one is to integrate one philosophical structure
of ideas with another, the ideas in both must have been
clearly defined and made available for critical examination in
literary form. Japanese values have had a limited definition,
systematization, and exposition by Japanese philosophers.
The chief *philosophically elaborated* truly Japanese values
were those embodied in the Emperor system and in the concept
of the National Entity, a system of values which student
leaders declare they do not wish to see reasserted. There are
basic Japanese values which are not necessarily dependent upon
their being woven together in that traditional "Japanese
philosophy of life." They stand on their own feet as the
wisdom of Japanese experience. But in attempting to
formulate a Marxism which is consistent with those values,
the student leaders are trying to do what Japanese philosophers
have not succeeded in doing. It is interesting in this connection to note that courses in philosophy, and particularly
social and political philosophy, in Japanese universities are
presentations of philosophies originating in other lands.
The development by Japanese of a systematic philosophy which
might be critical of or tend to undermine the Emperor
System and the concept of the National Entity was not
encouraged.

What results from this attempt to "translate" Marxism into

a truly Japanese version is a set of illustrations of the way in which Marxist categories are exemplified in the developments in Japanese history. This makes Marxism plausible as a way of *talking about* Japan's problems, but not necessarily for *analyzing* them and seeking clues to their solution in the face of contemporary facts.

A second observation is that the "thinking" of the student leaders tends to involve the application of ready-made categories rather than the inductive formulation of generalizations from empirical evidence or the examination of the relevance to empirical situations of the operational contents of those ready-made categories. Once a pattern of action had been labelled for example as "imperialism," "class struggle," "feudalism," "free enterprise," "individualism," etc., empirical evidence challenging the appropriateness and accuracy of the label tended to be ignored, or put to one side. "Rational thinking" as applied to such a process appeared to be a term descriptive of the process of eliminating from a set of empirical data all those that would disturb the categorical ordering of those data. We observed a disinclination to complicate discussions of Marxism by coming to grips with the specific empirical content which might be given to emotionally toned categories like imperialism, capitalism, class consciousness and loyalty, class struggle, feudalism, bourgeoisie, people's democracy, dictatorship of the proletariat, etc. This was equally true of emotionally toned terms related to Liberalism such as individualism, personal responsibility, freedom, democracy, free enterprise, open opportunity, the sovereign people, mutual consent, etc.

One cannot label this tendency as *peculiarly* characteristic of a Japanese way of thinking, for there are too many evidences that many people and students and presumed intellectuals in America and Europe reveal the same tendency. It is relevant to point out, however, that Japanese commentators have themselves observed that Japanese literary language (aside, that is, from that of mathematics and natural science) and customary ways of thinking are more useful for the presentation of intuitive, emotional, vague, ambiguous, and typological expression than for precise and accurate expression concerning real or abstract relationships among specific phenomena or modes of being. Other Japanese commentators have observed this same tendency in the fact that Japanese art and literary expression take simple, uncomplicated, and symbolic forms, and that they suggest rather than define.

A healthy corrective to this tendency to think in ready-made and simplified, and not in operationally defined, categories in the construction of a Marxist framework for their activism, was supplied by the de-Stalinization movement in Russia and by the Soviet-Chinese controversy. Indeed it became necessary for students to undertake a comparative evaluation of the empirical differences in the Marxism of Stalin, Kruschev, and Mao. They had already been introduced to this problem, which, however, they could continue to discuss in theoretical terms, in the difference between the elaboration of Marxist doctrine by Lenin and Trotsky. This was healthy from the point of view of being a stimulus to empirically oriented theoretical debate. It was disastrous from the point of view of its production of factionalism within the student movement. For the splintering of the unity in the movement after 1960 stemmed in large part from the fact that different student leaders took their clues as to the "purest" Marxism from these several interpreters.

In the case of both the Western and Japanese (as well as the Russian and the Chinese) search for and use of a framework for thinking, this inclination to think in categories is present. It becomes particularly evident and critical when, as was the case in postwar Japan, preoccupation with ideological construction and debate becomes important as a guide to the direction of the nation's development in, and after, a revolutionary change.

In the search for causes of the problems which are present and for clues as to what to do about those problems, categorization tends to be substituted for exploration, analysis, and inductive generalization. If no unusual and unsettling changes are taking place in the life of individuals, groups, or societies this substitution of applied categories for exploration, analysis, and inductive generalization simplifies life. If those changes are revolutionary, as they were in Japan after 1945, such a substitution complicates life. For the suggestions for action from categories which may have represented a not too inaccurate generalization about past facts are unlikely to provide sound guides to problem solving under changing current conditions.

It is at such times that skill in disciplined openminded analysis and abstract thinking becomes imperative. Whether the mode of thinking characteristic of Japanese in general supports the development of this sort of skill is a matter upon which we would not be so bold as to express a judgment.[6] Our impression from discussions with leaders of student activism in Japan was that such skill was not highly developed among enough of them to provide promise that student "intellectuals" will contribute in a significant way to a rational analysis of the empirical character of Japan's problems. And, from their reports on the nature of their university training, that development was not likely from their experience at the university unless they were fortunate enough to come into personal contact with some of the professors who possessed such skill.

The integration of ideas and consensus on action implications is particularly difficult under such circumstances. It is not surprising that debates among leaders in Zengakuren over a difference in the interpretation and exposition of Marx result in schismatic tendencies in organizing among expositor-leaders, and stimulate a predisposition to "choosing up sides" on the part of auditor-followers. Nor is it surprising that negotiations between student leaders and faculty and administrators and Ministry of Education officers are so frequently deadlocked. Such confrontations are occasions not so much for collective thinking, or even for collective bargaining, as for respective declarations of demands. That is a situation typically preliminary to direct action since it is difficult to arrive at a mutually acceptable middle position on the questions at issue.

In spite of the limited scope of this conception of the student as a *thinker*, it is from his numbers that the nation's supply of intellectuals is supposed to come. And it cannot be denied that they do come in sufficient numbers to supply the nation with ideas for development in all institutional areas. The implication of the foregoing observations is not that the university system in Japan lacks the capacity to produce intellectuals. It is that many of the leaders and active followers in the postwar student movement had not taken sufficient advantage of their opportunity for "thinking through" their program and activities to modify severely the normal tendency, which Japanese youth share with youth in other lands, to "think" in deeds more than with ideas.

[6]See article by Masao Maruyama in *Journal of Social and Political Ideas in Japan*, Center for Japanese Social and Political Studies, April 1964, pp. 41ff.

Prestige and Status

In some countries the elements of prestige and status in the image of the Student appear to be predominantly important. They are important, but not predominantly so, in Japan.

The specific characteristics of what can be referred to as the prestige and status of the student in today's Japanese society suggest that a student expects to be and is accepted by others as: a privileged beneficiary of parental and/or public concern. The use of the word "privileged" in this definition can be understood in two ways. It may indicate that university students come from the more well-to-do or otherwise "privileged" families. It may also indicate that all university youth are beneficiaries of the public concern that there shall be a sizable proportion of the population in possession of a higher education, a concern which results in the willingness to expend large public funds on providing the opportunity for education to those able to profit from it. That is, the word "privileged" may refer to the state of being a beneficiary either of parental or of public and governmental concern backed by the financial ability of each to provide the privilege.

Students were conscious of a standing in society established in both ways. They also experienced in the postwar world some difficulties in maintaining that standing.

Higher education is expensive. Hence it is the privilege of those who can afford it. A Ministry of Labor survey of 18,000 university students' costs in December 1961 estimated that it would take the salary of a Section Chief in a government bureau to provide a university education for a son without undermining the financial basis for a "reasonable life" for the family. A White Paper of the Ministry of Education published in November 1962[7] asserts that there are 5.2 times the "relative chance" that an upper class child will go to the university as that a lower class child will do so. (The same paper estimates the ratio in the United States as 3 to 1 and in the Soviet Union as 4 to 1). The basis and the definition of "class" is so open to error in all of these estimates that they can lead to no conclusion other than that they are not inconsistent with the universal

[7]English translation *Japan's Growth and Education*, published in 1963. The other statistics in this chapter are taken from this White Paper and from *Education in Japan*, Ministry of Education, 1959; UNESCO, *Statistical Year Book*, 1968; and *Japan Statistical Year Book* 1968 unless otherwise indicated.

testimony given by every Japanese we interviewed that a higher education is the privilege of those who either have easily available the financial resources to provide that education, or lacking such resources, are so highly motivated, concerned, and able that these qualities together with the necessary effort and sacrifice, compensate for inadequate economic resources.

As we have noted before, this effort does not begin merely at the university level but even at the primary level for those who wish to be sure their sons or daughters achieve entrance to one of the "prestige" universities and who, in order to gain such assurance, try to see that their childrens' primary and secondary education is received in schools whose pupils are most likely to qualify for entrance to such universities. Whether they are the sons and daughters of parents in the upper, middle, or lower income brackets, however, the students are aware, as are their parents and friends, that they are "privileged benficiaries" of a concerned and motivated family. They are also the beneficiaries of the general public concern that a substantial portion of the nation's product shall be devoted to education. One of the clearest characteristics of public policy since the Meiji Restoration has been the emphasis given to providing a universal opportunity for education, and increasingly for higher education. By 1957 (when those students who took part in the demonstrations in 1960 were entering on their studies) there were 231 universities and colleges in Japan, 72 sponsored by the national government (at least one in each of the 46 prefectures), 35 sponsored by local bodies, and 124 under private auspices. In addition there were 269 Junior Colleges, 19, 39, and 211 sponsored by the National Government, local bodies, and private organizations, respectively.[8] Tuition and fees are much higher in the private universities (which catered to about 2/3 of the total number of students in 1960 and 7/10 in 1967) than in the publicly supported institutions, but one half of their research facilities and aid to those in financial difficulties is provided by the government.

The White Paper referred to above shows a more rapid increase in educational capital than in either national income or national wealth in the 20th Century. The relevant index

[8]As of Dec. 1, 1968 there were 377 four year colleges and 468 junior colleges in Japan, with a total enrollment of 1,525,000 students according to Kryoaki Murakami in *Asahi*, Jan. 11, 1969.

numbers from Table I in the White Paper are, with 1905 taken
as 100 in each case:

	National Income	National Wealth	Educational Capital
1905	100	100	100
1935 (prewar)	433	447	831
1960	979	686	2,286

In 1966, Japan was spending 5.7% of its national income on
education (U.S. 6.4%). The record can show that in 1940, just
before the war, nearly 100% of both boys and girls aged 6-11
were in primary schools, nearly 100% of boys and 65% of the
girls aged 12-16 were in secondary or quasi secondary (trade,
apprenticeship, or continuation) schools. Education at least to
this level must have appeared not so much a privilege as a
right. At that time (1940) 6.5% of the boys and 0.8% of the girls
aged 17-21 were attending institutions of higher education. But
by 1950, right after the war, these percentages (now referring to
ages 18-21) were 11.1% and 1.2% respectively, and by 1960 16.4%
and 4.1%. In 1967, 20% of college age youth were enrolled as
students.[9] This still indicated higher education as a privilege
available to a few (1.3% of the total population) selected by
ability or wealth or both, but it also indicates that the public
concern that the benefits of higher education shall be available
for an increasing number is not merely declared, but is being
implemented.

The "privilege" of being beneficiaries of both family and
public concern was not manifest in either the excellence of educational facilities or in a comfortable plane of living for the
generation of students to be found in the universities during
the period of greatest student activism between 1948 and 1960.
The students experienced little in their surroundings symbolizing their membership in a privileged group.

Resources from family for tuition and maintenance and from
both private and public funds for the provision of educational
facilities were greatly reduced by the losses of the war and the
inflation which was on the rampage until 1949. If, as one
head of an old and wealthy family remarked, "These students

[9]Central Council for Education, Japan, *Report on Measures to Meet
Problems Facing University Education in Japan*, Ministry of Education. 1969.

right after the war acted like workers rather than the sons of good families," there were ample opportunities to be motivated to do so. The "arbeit" or working student became commonplace. The problems of the working man, job hunting, the disciplinary relationship of manager to workers, the job insecurity of the "temporary" worker, the inadequacy of income, the fatigue of labor, all these became a part of the living experience of those who worked. These experiences they talked about with their more fortunate fellow students. Actually or vicariously these experiences in a former day would have been absent or, at least, farther away from the center of the interest and attention of most students. Through self-supporting work many students now became familiar with the problems of a portion of the Japanese population they might otherwise not have known. They became also not merely "beneficiaries" whose appropriate response was gratitude, but partial providers of the means for their own education. This role may have suggested to them their right to have a voice in the shaping of the facilities which they were "purchasing" by the proceeds of their own work.

The unquestioned interest in and support by public authorities in providing those who could pass university entrance examinations with the chance to receive a higher education, interest and support taken for granted traditionally, were expressed after the war under great difficulties. Primary and secondary school and university buildings (outside of Kyoto which was not bombed) were destroyed in many cases. Shortage of funds and materials for rebuilding slowed the process of restoration of facilities. Dormitory overcrowding (6-8 to a room) and lack of library and other study facilities (including books) made it difficult if not impossible for the student to view himself as one devoted to serious study, and increased the inclination to diversionary activity. The money costs of education mounted, and successive tuition increases for university students became necessary. Demonstrations by students against inadequate facilities and increased tuition were met by a sternness on the part of the public authorities which, at a minimum, clouded the conception of the student as the object of solicitous public policy, at least in their own minds. The gap increased in the 60's between the rapidly mounting number seeking a higher education and the number who could be provided with adequate facilities and teaching. Coupled with the mounting costs of education, particularly for the increasing number coming from the less affluent sectors of society, the situation became not only frustrating but explosive.

It is little wonder that the students in the postwar period sensed the contrast between their expectancies that students were privileged beneficiaries of parental and public concern for education and the educational inadequacies which they faced. Nor is it surprising that they responded to the call of student leaders to join in protest and a movement for the "rehabilitation of education." Such emphasis characterized the objectives of student activism during the postwar period, and much experience was gained in organizing the students for protest in this area of immediate student concern, which later could be applied to protest in the area of public policy and affairs.

Also related to prestige and status expectancies of the students is an aspect of the image of the Student which suggests that he is a person continuing the progress of an upward mobile family and self. There is literally no road to a higher economic social or economic status for individuals in Japan which does not involve becoming a student in a college or university, and preferably in a prestige university. The opportunities provided by occupational position, social contacts, and a "favorable" marriage are geared to that achievement. Tremendous pressure is exerted on the promising child to assure his ultimate attainment of status as a student. For not only his, but the family's chances for upward mobility ride on that attainment. The "struggle" for the "rehabilitation of education" was therefore a struggle for a repair and renewal of a most important instrument of economic and social prestige, and protest against educational inadequacies gained widespread emotional support for this reason. Moreover it was something about which not only the students but their families had a deeply rooted concern.

A final aspect of the image of the Student related to prestige and status in a sense summarizes the rest, namely, that a student is a member of a present and future select, but not necessarily an elite, group. They are obviously select among their own age group since only one out of five of the college age youth are attending the universities. They are select in that they are the survivors of the "examination hell." There is, in a sense, a bond of brotherhood resulting from the fact that they have all been through that examination hell together.

When the Ministry of Education in 1945 sought to have the civilian universities assimilate the undergraduates and graduates of the War and the Navy Academies (which were closed), a violent objection was made by the students of the civilian universities, in part because the students from the Service Academies were to be admitted without examination.

Moreover students are select by virtue of the fact that they are the only ones who will occupy the most responsible white collar, managerial, professional, and "intellectual" position in society. They are select in the sense that they will find themselves at home in a world of ideas and experience which will make them feel removed as educated people from the interests of the common people. In several group discussions we held, there was consensus that students found it increasingly difficult to hold extended conversation with their secondary school former classmates who had not gone to the university, and with members of their families who were not university people. Such contacts they declared were dull; there was no one they could really "talk to."

That others in society are conscious that students are a select and differentiated group is indicated by the failure of the student movement's leftist oriented missionary campaigns one summer among the rural population, and by the difficulties they had in finding a welcome as co-sponsors with the trade unions of demonstrations or even as supporters of the trade union "struggles." These reactions of the rural people and the workers were of course stimulated, not only by an awareness of the social distance between them and the students, but because of the formers' disinclination to accept leftist ideas and to get involved in actions consistent with those ideas.

One of the frequent comments of editorial writers and conservative educators with respect to the direct action manifestations of the students was that such action may be appropriate for "workers" but not for "students." (This criticism was also made of the members of the leftist Teachers Union.) In conferences with employers we gathered the impression that it would be difficult for a university graduate to get a job as a production worker in a factory even on a temporary basis.

Students are select in the sense that they consider themselves a special group in society. They, like the intellectuals, are group-conscious about their special indentity as a group. Unlike the intellectuals, they wear a distinctive uniform which visualizes and symbolizes that separateness. (The student uniform is still a dominant aspect of the Japanese scene, although in some universities the wearing of a uniform is being made voluntary.) This group-consciousness is an encouragement to and a support for group action as students, and the action in turn reinforces the group-consciousness.

Students then stand out from the rest of the population as a distinguishable and select group both in their own eyes and in the eyes of others. But this is not to say that they are considered to be, or even on the way to becoming, an "elite" group intellectually, socially, or politically.

Rating as an intellectual elite is reserved for the more mature and experienced man of ideas, the professor, the professional man, the writer, the editor, who must win his right to such recognition. Incidentally, in a country where literacy is so high and at least a secondary school diploma is becoming all but universal, the intellectual does not stand out as distinctly from the general population as he does among less literate and less schooled peoples. Nor is he accorded unusual admiring recognition. In fact he may be considered an impractical "egghead."

Rating as a social elite is still influenced by birth and family, and the increase in the number of university students in the postwar years makes it inevitable that the proportion of those students making use of the expanded and extended opportunity for higher education who come from families recognized as socially elite should be reduced. In 1940, on the eve of the War there were, according to the annual report of the Ministry of Education, 23,044 graduates of universities. In 1958, there were 101,316, over 4 times as many. By 1966, there were 243,146 graduates, over 10 times the prewar figure. (Incidentally the transformation of a large number of colleges into universities after the war has watered down considerably the social prestige of a "university" degree.)

The winning of status as a political elite in a country as advanced in its economic, social, and political institutions as Japan is dependent on the possession of many qualities of leadership not necessarily associated with those acquired as a result of a university education.

As a university student, then, a man is not considered as a current or even necessarily a preparatory member of an elite intellectually, socially, or politically. If there is any identification of "eliteness" associated with having a university education, it is not derived from the fact of being a student as such but of being a student at one of the "prestige" universities. The chance that the student will, after graduation, have opened to him the opportunity for decision-making and action which will make him functionally significant and recognized as such, the chance that he or she will be able to enter into a marriage carrying with it the identification with a socially elite group, the chance that he will, in his chosen field of work, be associated with a clique of mutually supporting influential alumni of his own university, is directly related to his prestige not primarily as a student, but as a student of one of the prestige universities.

Some of the student leaders we met felt this "eliteness" as a student at one of the prestige universities carried with it an "obligation" for leadership. Whether this was a factor stimulating their initiating and carrying through of the campaigns of the student movement it is difficult to say. But it is relevant to point out that the great majority of the "calls" to action, to organization, and to unity, came from student leaders in Toyko, Kyoto, Waseda, and Hitotsubashi Universities, all of which are popularly rated among the "prestige universities."

Summary

The traditional image of the Student in Japan would not in itself suggest the kind of activism students have displayed since 1945, certainly not to the same extent as is the case in Latin America. To be sure individual students have in the past taken part in protest against regulation and militarism, and have joined others supporting socialist and communist movements, just as individual professors, labor leaders, and military officers have negatively or positively expressed their revolt against what they considered to be unjust regulation of their own or public affairs. But the traditional image of the Student established no expectancy in the public mind or in the minds of the students that they were destined, as students, to be outstanding among the promoters of a more liberal and humane and free society, or to be opponents of those who were considered to be obstacles in the way of the achievement of such a society.

For students, as a body of students, the stimuli to the role they performed in postwar Japan must be sought not

in a student tradition from the past, but in the student
experiences of the present. This generalization will not hold
for the image of the Japanese Student from this day forward,
for the activism of the postwar years has created a tradition
for those who will put on the student uniform in the future.
Moreover the expectancy of activism embodied in that current
image is reinforced by the part students are playing all over
the world. The students have become in Japan a class of
persons from whom the rest of society will anticipate action
critical of and influential on university and public policy
and practice. That action may be severely regulated by future
governments, for it has potentially explosive consequences for
public order and for the maintenance of the status quo. But in
the most progressive and well managed societies there are sufficient contradictions between what is and what could be or
might have been to provide issues suggesting the need for initiation of popular activism of the sort which students in Japan
have shown themselves capable of initiating.

There were real frustrations raised for students in the postwar years by the fact that the university experience was accompanied by physical privation and inadequate facilities for
living and for study. These were intensified by the inconsistency of such inadequacies with the privileged status they
expected to enjoy once they became students. Preparation for
organized activism relative to a wide range of issues was
provided by mass protests against these intra-university inadequacies.

On the whole, there is a security-providing consistency between the traditional image of the Student as one who primarily
is serving an apprenticeship for a white collar career, with the
prestige and status and relatively good opportunities for living
that this implies, the training and conditioning for that career
offered by the university, and the readiness of society to receive
and offer opportunities for self-actualization for those who
successfully have become students.   An inconsistency of this
nature cannot be counted among the important stimuli to
student activism in Japan.

The roots of student activism in postwar Japan cannot,
moreover, be found primarily in restrictions related to the
realization of aspects of a traditional image of the Student
related to freedom, idealism, or to his becoming an intellectual. Actually, in all of these aspects the opportunity for
realization was widened and amplified. It was indeed this

very positive opening of opportunity for *creating* a student role related to these dimensions, and the testing of the limits to which they would be permitted to go which was a basic source of and a strong stimulus to their activism. The universal dynamic of youth and their need to find a focus for self-identity, and their predisposition to assert their selves, was given opportunity for expression by the support offered by the Occupation forces to those among the Japanese who had liberal and democratic ambitions for their country's governance.

Moreover, the occasions for such experimentation, and the issues toward which action could be directed were legion, not only for the students but for the whole Japanese people. It is one of the anomalies of history that the policy of the United States played so large a part in stimulating and implementing the general possibilities of free, and idealistic activity by students, and simultaneously created so many of the issues which stimulated the protest character of that activity.

If we do not find the traditional image of the Japanese Student suggesting the kind of activism observed, there were nevertheless factors in the traditional and present action and thought characteristic of Japanese students, which help to explain some of its features. These factors may be briefly summarized.

The tendencies to self-realization through intimate group supporting relations, in loyalty to the group and especially to the leader of the group as the symbol of and representative of the group's entity. These tendencies readied them for collective and even mass action.

The consciousness of distinctiveness of the students as a definable group in Japanese society and the constant reminders, through symbolic uniforms, through participation in collective pilgrimages, and through a uniform national ordering of the educational pattern, of this community of student interest on a national basis. This consciousness reinforced the predisposition to group activism.

The background of prewar and wartime totalitarian restrictions on freedom and of the image of the police as the instruments of those restrictions, coupled with natural antipathies between students and police. The simultaneous removal of restrictions and the decentralization of and weakening of the authority of the police was like breaking of a dam holding back flood waters.

The emphasis in Japanese idealism on public responsibility to the State rather than to the people focused attention on those issues affecting Japan as a nation rather than on those of primary domestic concern to her people. Moreover, loyalty to the State was no longer considered to be identical with obedience to its governors.

A clearer conception of the objective of negative attack than of the goals of positive achievement gave emphasis to the destructive aspect of student activity.

The familiarity with and hold of particularistic ideals relevant to contacts and relations with those in the familiar group rather than with ideals having a universal validity relevant to contacts and relations with all men everywhere (or even all Japanese). Coupled with the fact that many relationships encountered were those with strangers, such particularistic ideals gave few clues to orderly and reasonable behavior when these unfamiliar others were involved, either as antagonists or collaborators.

The characteristics associated with becoming and being intellectual are significant in the light of the student leaders' interest in having a sound ideological and a basically Marxian justification for their revolutionary activism and because the splintering of the student movement after 1960 was in large part attributable to the varying ideological dogmatics of different student leaders and groups:

> Preparation for the status accorded an educated person does not necessarily require intensive, continuous, and disciplined devotion to study. There was ample time available for non-academic activity.

> Learning through reading rather than through exercises in comparative and critical thinking; and dogmatic exposition rather than creative formulation of ideas are considered in Japan enough to mark a student as an intellectual.

> To apply categories or labels to phenomena, even without critical examination of the empirically observable operational content of the categories is a satisfying intellectual process.

> To short circuit, as a clue to action in the face of a problem, the processes of explanation, analysis, and abstract generalization, and to move immediately from categorization to implied appropriate action does not weaken a person's status as an intellectual.

> Dogmatic defense of a position is as much admired as an effort toward integrative consensus (involving the possibility of compromise).

These characteristics associated with becoming and being an intellectual provided students with the possibility of viewing themselves simultaneously as rational thinkers and the initiators of violent action.

Finally, and, in our judgment, the most determinative factor was the amplification in the minds of the students of their role as "participants" in the governance of their universities and of the nation, coupled with the resistance to such amplification on the part of the established managers and governors. The traditional image of the Student placed minimal emphasis on participation. Spurred on by the possibilities opened by the removal of restrictions on individual freedom of expression and association and democratic processes and by the raising of these values to a high place in the hierarchy of national goals, the students attempted to create and legitimize the image of the Student as an effective and forceful participator in the affairs of their universities and nation. To many in the existing Establishment their efforts to test the limits of public tolerance for such a role smacked more of the attempt to control than to participate. Resistance to those efforts led inevitably to confrontations which were difficult, if not impossible, to resolve by orthodox arrangements for change. Mass force and violence appeared to the student leaders the only road open to the achievement of their goal of realistic participation and effective control.

Chapter 8
Becoming a Student and
Citizen in India

Student activism in India can be characterized more as a state of undisciplined unrest than as a student movement. The causes of that type of activism have been extensively explored by Indian educational authorities and observers. Their reports have been frank, outspoken, and extremely self-critical. No observation a foreigner can make could be more comprehensive and critical than those made by concerned Indians. We choose to concentrate upon the situation as seen through the eyes of the college and university students, teachers, and administrators interviewed. Every observation made, however, can be reinforced by references to surveys, reports, and speeches based on official and unofficial observations by Indians. Particularly those who carry the heavy responsibilities of providing India with a system of higher education have not been lax in their attention to the matter. They are fully alive to the impact of student unrest on their high hopes and plans for the social, political, and economic transformation of India from a colonial dependency of Great Britain into a modern independent, industrialized, and democratic nation.

The size of their problem is overwhelming in its magnitude and complexity. Never before in India's history have her governors attempted to bring the advantages of higher education into the reach of more than a very thin stratum of fortunate and privileged people. Even then heavy reliance was placed on sending the few abroad to foreign universities for advanced education. To establish a system of colleges and universities at home that will produce the highly trained manpower needed for modernizing Indian society, that will fulfill the expectations for opportunity and justice of the masses who have been challenged to make their contribution to a new India and cannot make that contribution without the benefit of higher education, and simultaneously to attain high standards of excellence in the facilities provided and in the human product, is a Herculean task. One is reminded of the answer of President Lowell of Harvard to Leland Stanford, when the latter sought counsel about priorities in his declared intention "to duplicate Harvard on the Pacific coast." Said Leland Stanford, "What is the first and main thing that a great university needs?" Replied President Lowell, "A hundred years of history."

Not the mere passage of time, but the development of foundations for excellence which takes time was, we are sure, the meaning President Lowell expressed in these five words. Among the major essentials of those foundations are: (1) a clear and widely held consensus as to the purpose of higher education; (2) a competent and dedicated body of scholars and teachers committed to a life's work in developing the institutions and procedures for higher education and into whose independent hands and minds can be entrusted that development; (3) a body of students seeking above all the improvement of their intellectual capacities as an aid both to self-realization and to public service, and aware that thinking is no leisure time occupation but the hardest work in the world; and (4) sufficient human and financial resources to provide the vision and facilities required for making firm these foundations. No country in the world (even with the benefit of a hundred years of history in developing its system of higher education) has reached even an approximation to perfection in these matters. As an independent nation, India has had only 23 years in which to try.

Even a working consensus among responsible decision makers, to say nothing of the general public, on the purpose of higher education is lacking. The basic reason for this is that consensus concerning the objectives for India itself as a nation is lacking. Her organizational Charter is, both in formation and in widespread acceptance, only slowly coming into being. The purposes of an educational system are integrally related to the purposes of the whole nation of which it is a part. If the national purpose is confused, the purpose of higher education tends to be confused.

We have met and talked in India with some of the most concerned and dedicated teachers and scholars we have met in any country. The contribution of many Indian scholars and scientists to the literature of their academic fields and their stimulating and useful participation in international scientific meetings is welcomed, recognized, and appreciated by their fellow

intellectuals in many countries. We have met and talked with
Indian students, particularly at the postgraduate level, whose
desire for intellectual competence and whose willingness to pay
the price under most difficult circumstances cannot but arouse
respect and admiration. But in the case of both students and
their mentors the numbers are not large enough, in relation to
the total, to furnish, at this time, the yeast of excellence which
could infuse the whole mass. And, either from inclination or
from fear of the consequences, the political guardians responsible for the total affairs of the state do not trust the academics
to run their own show for which in a substantial measure, aside
from tuitions, the State and the Federal governments supply
the funds.

How could it be expected to be otherwise? Consider only
the speed of growth of the institutions of higher learning in
the 23 years since independence and the numbers of students
they are trying to educate.

In 1947, on the eve of independence, there were 18 universities and less than 500 colleges affiliated to or associated
with them.[1] In 1968 there were 75 universities, over a fourfold
increase. In that year, there were 2,163 colleges of arts and
sciences and commerce, more than a fourfold increase from
the number in 1947. If the colleges of physical education and
teacher training are added, the number is 2,897. Although
some of this increase in the number of universities is accounted
for by the splitting up of older universities, the increase from
18 to 75 universities and from 500 to 2,163 colleges of arts
and science and commerce in 23 years must have involved a
considerable diminution in the average overall quality of both
staff and facilities. That it has been necessary, for example,
to staff the institutions with younger people with less educational experience is indicated by the fact that, whereas
before World War II the proportion of professors was 22½%,
in 1963 it was 13.3%.

Rapid as the increase in institutions has been, the number
enrolled has increased even more rapidly, from around 200,000

[1]Facts stated with respect to the quantitative features of Indian higher
education are, unless otherwise indicated, to be found in *University
Development in India, Basic Facts and Figures*, 1963-64, University
Grants Commission, New Delhi; and in India: Ministry of Education
and Youth Services, *Selected Educational Statistics*, 1968-69.

in 1947 to 1,195,276, nearly a sixfold increase.[2] The increase
has been most rapid since 1950, at an average rate of 10% a
year. Even an increase of 2% a year to keep pace with population
growth would result in 5 years to an *increment* to the student
body equivalent to the total college and university enrollment
in Great Britain in 1960. Even this increment to the student
population does not fully represent the problem that must
plague the educational planners as they strive to bring their
supply of high level manpower to a point commensurate
with the needs of a modern industrialized society. The
enrollment, for example, is equivalent to something over
235 per 100,000 inhabitants in India.[3] In the United States
the comparable figure is more than 3,245, and in Japan more
than 1,283.

A student to faculty ratio which would make possible desirable (and desired) improvements making for a better process
of education is hardly to be expected under these conditions
of rapid expansion. In 1963-64, it was on the average 17.3:1.
In only 19% of the affiliated colleges was it less than 10:1.
In 40% it was more than 20:1, and in 15% it was more than
30:1.

Physical equipment and facilities require funds desperately
needed, and in scarce supply, for all aspects of India's development. Classrooms are overcrowded and often drab, poorly
lighted, under-equipped, and ill-ventilated. Faculty office space
is inadequate. The University Grants Commission says it hopes
in the course of the 4th Five year plan to make available
adequate reading room and textbook facilities for at least
25% of the students! Laboratory space and equipment required
for adequate training in the particularly needed (and almost
wholly new) emphasis on experimental science in the engineering, technological, biological, and medical training is inadequate. Even with great attention to the provision of living

[2]This is the number registered for Baccalaureate or post-Baccalaureate
degrees. If those registered as intermediate students are added, as is
done in some statistical reports, the number is 1,570,138 or nearly
an eightfold increase. These figures are taken from India, Ministry
of Education and Youth Services, *Selected Educational Statistics*, 1968-
69, New Delhi, 1969.

[3]UNESCO, *Statistical Year Book* 1968.

quarters for Students only 18.5% can find places in student hostels.

These are stupendous obstacles to the most sincere and urgent desires of the leaders of the new India to provide the kind of higher education which would relieve some of the frustrations students experience.

Image of the Student

For the very large majority of the Indian population, the opportunity to become a student, to have one in the family, or even to have dealings with a college educated person is so recent that a clear image of the Student has scarcely been relevant either to their thought or their behavior. Among those making up the sixfold increment to the student population attending the 1300 or so new and many of the older colleges, therefore, it is not surprising to find many in whose minds the expectancies as to their rights and duties, their privileges and responsibilities in society are unclear and unsupported by anything except their own experience. The image of the Student in modern India as it applies to Indians generally is in the process of being created. It is a product, not so much of tradition, as of current experience of those who have become students. Beyond their numbers and beyond those who have already graduated, the general public has little basis for knowing what to expect of students.

If this group of young people at the universities is at all aware of their country's administrative history, they may realize the traditional significance of being labeled a student and becoming eligible for a *career* post in the bureaucracy, and to a lesser extent as relevant to other white collar job opportunities. The very novelty and uniqueness of the opportunity which has come their way and the relatively small minority of their acquaintances who have a university education encourages the assumption that a certain *prestige* and standing goes with that opportunity. Once they are involved in association with others on the campus they begin to have experiences and share an atmosphere which emphasizes the aspects of relative *freedom* and *idealism* in the concept of what it means to be a student, and they become more specifically acquainted with traditions concerning the part students played in the struggle for independence in their fathers' generation. If they are fortunate to be enrolled in a college whose faculty has high standards of scholarship, concern for their intellectual responsibilities, and a love of learning, they may catch a spark of enthusiasm for the *intellectual competence* aspect of their role as a student, especially if among that faculty they can have a closer contact than that provided by a seat in the back row of a classroom holding 300 students.

It is our impression that this is the order in their awareness of aspects of the concept, Student, certainly among those who are sometimes referred to in India as the "new" students, that is those coming from family backgrounds in which higher education formerly played little or no part. Their proportion of the total is variously estimated as from 3/5 to 4/5. But even among students coming from families where higher education, at least for some of the boys, is traditional, the traditions of student life have developed among so few in the population (less than 125,000 at the outbreak of World War II) and were so heavily influenced by the "preparation-for-junior-posts-in-the-Civil Service" purpose that the image of the Student as anything but the seeker of a passport to such a job is one being created through present experience, rather than one inherited from past generations of students.

Preparation for a Career

For students for whom a college experience is primarily a pathway to an occupational career the ideally satisfying situation would be one in which the framework of manpower needs in the country, and of a job structure and job opportunities consistent with those needs, were dependable, customary, and clear; in which the universities and colleges had geared their offerings in type and quality to preparing youth to do those jobs; in which there are dependable and well-established ways of moving to those jobs once the university training is completed; and in which the respect and recognition given to those jobs accords with their significance and importance in contributing to solving the country's most pressing needs. Lacking these conditions, confusion and frustration are bound to result among students trying to figure out the significance of their academic experience whether for their personal satisfaction and achievement or for their role in society or for the needs of that society.

Few educators with a concept of education as more than a pathway to vocational competence would agree that such a situation leads to an ideal system of higher education. And no such contention is made here. It is only suggested that *if* the primary and dominant image of a student is that of a vocational trainee, as it is in India, such a situation of a consistency among the four variables would minimize much of the unrest, dissatisfaction, and frustration existing among today's students.

These conditions are lacking in India with respect to the areas of study in which nearly three-fifths of the students were enrolled in 1964[4] in Arts and Humanities (43.6%), Commerce (7.8%), Education (2.1%), Medicine (5%), and Law (2.6%). It is these faculties in which most of the unrest and indiscipline is reported to occur.[5]

The situation among the students in the Arts and Humanities in Commerce and in Law (which in 1964 together accounted for over half of the students enrolled and three fourths of the graduates) is exceptionally precarious and anxiety producing. Neither the students nor the faculty are sure about what relation the students' education has to any work available when they have finished. The qualifying marks for acceptance into the faculties of Arts and Humanities, Commerce, and Law are the lowest of all. One has the impression in talking with students enrolled in these fields, that few have any feeling that their educational experience, as such, has any specific relevance to the opportunity for employment other than the vague hope that a degree will be valuable. Many of them are in college simply because they have nothing else to do, in the hopes that something will eventually turn up.

Where consistency exists to a relatively higher degree among

[4]UNESCO, *Statistical Year Book, 1968*, pp. 202 ff.

[5]Bayley in his survey of students' reaction to and participation in direct action in 4 Indian universities found nothing to support the hypothesis that students in scientific and highly vocational faculties (like Engineering and Medicine) are less given to agitation than those in the Humanities. His conclusion was that the incidence of agitation is a function of living arrangements (i.e., on or off campus), of university regulatory policies, and of climate of opinion on particular campuses making agitation the thing to do or to avoid doing on that particular campus. Bayley, David H., *The Police and Political Development in India*, Princeton, 1969, p.336.

the variables noted above, as in preparation for work in the fields of Engineering and Technology (where 5.8% of the students are enrolled), in Veterinary Science and Agriculture (2.6%) there is a minimum of discontent and unrest.

The case of those studying in the Science faculties (30%) is not clear. The logic of the relation of scientific knowledge to the promotion of industrial development is clear. There is, therefore, a presumption of consistency between what they are doing in the university and the gaining of competence for profiting from the occupational opportunities in a developing country. The qualifying grade requirements for admission to Scientific studies is higher than in any field save Engineering and Medicine, so that, presumably, relatively able students are involved. The school work is demanding. But there is a lack of laboratory facilities without which the development of scientific capabilities of any value to society is difficult. The students (and knowledgeable scientists) complain that much of what they learn is out of date in this field characterized by a veritable knowledge explosion. Moreover, industry and government are not organizationally or functionally set up to make use of the talents students have developed. As a consequence many graduates are doing jobs poorly related to the special training they have presumably received. Employers in industry and government assume that Science graduates on the whole are innately more capable, and have had a more disciplined training than those in the Arts and Humanities, but the chances of their being employed at work for which their scientific studies have specifically prepared them are minimal. The job finding procedure for them is no more clear and dependable than for any save the Engineering students and for those who decide to try for and successfully pass the Indian Administrative Service examinations.

Students in all fields save Engineering[6] do their studies in a state of constant anxiety fed by the twin realizations that occupational success is impossible without a university degree passport to employment and that the degree is no assurance of a job. The latter realization not only is reinforced by the awareness of acquaintances who have qualified for the degree and who are out of work, but it is emphasized by periodic official

[6]Unemployment is found, however, among the engineers. *The Times of India* reported that in 1967, 23,000 mechanical, civil, and electrical engineers were registered at the employment exchanges.

and unofficial studies and by editorials, conferences, and articles about the problem of the "educated unemployed." For example, it was reported in *Unemployment, Full Employment and India* that in 1960 there were 6,650,000 educated persons in India (meaning all that had passed their matriculation examination) of whom 2,000,000 were unemployed and that the proportion of university graduates during 1958 who were registered as unemployed at the Employment Exchanges was 26.3%.

Even in the area of scientific preparation, where common sense would suggest the chances for employment are greatest, the news is disquieting. For example, the political leaders of India were properly disturbed about the Indians who had gone abroad for advanced studies in Science, Engineering, and Medicine, and who could not find places where their talents could be fully and appropriately utilized in India when they returned. Two things called for action, the obvious waste of non-used, or only partially used, scientific abilities, and the fact that, in the face of relatively more promising possibilities abroad, many of these students were deciding not to return to India. So in 1956 the Council of Scientific and Industrial Research decided to set up a pool of 100 (later 500) for temporary placement of those returning from abroad with such advanced training, giving them, of course, a presumed additional advantage over those whose training had been received entirely in India. The numbers revealed were so large that in June 1963 it was decided to abolish the ceiling. By January 1, 1964, 2,119 had been selected for the roster, (914 of these with education in the United States and 823 in the United Kingdom). On that date, only 750 of these returned scientists had been placed (half of them in universities and other institutions of higher learning). The possibility of establishing research units in the public sector, better to utilize their skill, was being discussed. The Madras graduate student (who had graduated as a B.Sc., with first class honors in Chemistry) who called to our attention this news appearing in *The Hindu* for February 6, 1964, commented, "What do you think those of us can expect who don't have the chance to improve our competence abroad?"

Warren Ilchman referring to the studies of the Institute of Applied Manpower Research makes the startling prediction that the number of educated unemployed in 1975-76 will not be far short of the total number of educated persons in 1960-61.[7]

[7]Warren Ilchman, "Educated Unemployment in India". *Survey*, Vol. 9, # 10:46.

One thing is clear in all groups of students, and that is that they do not count solely on even their degree, to say nothing of any competence for work they may have acquired, to get them a satisfying position when they have the degree. Particularly if one were to announce that he contemplated a job in the *private* sector, would he be likely to be asked, "*Who* is making it possible?" Even those who have successfully passed the Indian Administrative Service Examination assume that their chances of location in a satisfying job suited to their preparation will be influenced by their fortune in being sponsored by someone with "pull." We heard frequent references to about a dozen colleges in India which have a reputation for excellent graduates and whose students can count on that reputation of their colleges to give them a job opportunity advantage. This advantage is cumulative as the alumni of such colleges gain positions in which they have a voice in the selection of recruits. Since there are over 2000 colleges in India this advantage is possessed by a small minority of graduates.

An additional factor in the job opportunity situation is the impact of the forces emphasizing the provincial limitations of the job market. The tendency to increase the use of the local languages in the universities of a particular state, the movement to substitute Hindi for English as the link language for the nation and for the Administrative Service Examinations (giving an advantage to those whose native language is Hindi, or Hindi related) would, if fully realized, narrow the field of opportunity for the students in a majority of the states, in some cases, to their own state. (This was one major factor in the student riots in some of the southern states in early 1965 when the time arrived for implementing the law making Hindi the sole official language for all-union matters.)

A final set of factors which clouds the perception which students have of the vocational value of their education, is that in two fields (Teaching and Agriculture) and to some extent in a third field (Commerce), where there are tremendous needs for manpower to match the basic needs of the nation in its efforts for economic and social modernization, the status of the occupations involved is low. The exposition of the reasons for this would require a treatise in itself. One consequence, however, is clear, namely, a shortage in numbers seeking occupation in these fields.

The situation of a shortage of manpower for the tremendous and highly important task of bringing even the rudiments of primary education to the masses, of staffing all the in-

stitutions of learning, and of providing medical services in
the rural areas on the one hand, and unemployed educated
people on the other, is an anomaly of the first order. Also
it is clear to most thoughtful people that India's progress
and the welfare of her people must require a coming to grips
with the problems of its agricultural base not only because
of its importance in the economic and human welfare area,
but because it is the home ground of firmly rooted customs
and human predispositions which are inconsistent with the
application of human effort to effect industrialization and
modernization. The villages need, and can use, educated manpower for improving their techniques and the variety and
productiveness of their efforts, for improving the health of
their inhabitants, for organizing mutual aid and mutual effort
in the political and social life of their area, and for the
gradual development of attitudes and aspirations and ways
of thinking which will support, and not be a drag on, India's
progress toward modernization.

It is understandable of course, that in seeking an occupation
which is worth the investment of money and time in obtaining a higher education, undergraduates and graduates should
focus their desires upon those that pay well, are socially
prestigeful, which offer a *sure* chance for the utilization of
the knowledge and skill they have acquired, and incidental
to which they can be surrounded by amenities of life superior
to those characterizing their earlier life. If such opportunities
are offered by the organization of life and work in their
society there is every good reason why they should accept
them. But there have been periods in the life of every nation
when capable people, including highly educated people, have
not been *offered* such job opportunities by their society. Their
choice in such circumstances is to live lives of frustration
and quiet desperation, to rebel and revolt, or to *make* those
opportunities, to their own, and not infrequently, to their
society's benefit.

The growth of the industrial sector in India must in time
create a demand for direct and indirect services immediately
related to and supporting that sector which will require far
more in numbers and in quality of manpower than the present
output of her universities can supply. It will take time. In the
meantime there are jobs to be done and job opportunities
(including those related to basic education) which can be

made in the rural areas and among the masses of the villagers which may well determine in the end whether the hopes pinned on the development in the industrial-urban sector can be realized. And to those opportunities a great deal of what young men and women have acquired as students, is, or could be made, relevant. Among such acquired qualifications in addition to knowledge and technical skill in many vocations are these: a great deal of the capacity for adaptation to strange and unfamiliar situations and people, the broadening and extension of one's horizons as to the possibilities for progress, the very dissatisfactions with letting well enough alone, any increase in one's ability to communicate his ideas, his ability to read and write and figure, and the prestige he would have as an educated person.

The focusing of attention on that aspect of the image of the Student which proclaims him a person better prepared than others for a vocation, then, can and does lead to frustrations productive of unrest and indiscipline when there does not exist in the society a regularized and dependable customary framework of occupations around which work and life in society is organized and to which a higher education is obviously relevant. The tendency to frustration is amplified when the academic process and its facilities are not practically oriented to prepare him for these occupations. It is intensified when his perception of the possibility of finding employment in those occupations negates the dependability of his degree as a job ticket, and alerts him to the necessity of something with which the education does not provide him, a sponsor or sponsors with influence. The situation is all the more conductive to rebellion when and if he shares a current conviction of his time that somebody, in this case the government and educational authorities, *ought* to do something about it, especially when there is nothing government and the educational authorities can do except over a period of time far beyond his span of years as a student, to make the opportunities available.

For some at least an alternative to frustration because of unprovided vocational opportunities is to *make* those opportunities and to find self-realization in the doing of that. One would like, but can scarcely dare, to hope that this alternative would appeal to the most dynamic and farsighted and energetic activists and leaders among the students. Failing such a response, it is only possible to predict a continuance of the stimulus to unrest and indiscipline residing in the inconsistencies and lack of congruency with respect to the expectancies of the students of what is due them, the framework of occupational needs of the country, the degree to which a university experience can provide preparation for meeting these needs, and the possibility of finding a satisfying opportunity for work within that framework.

Prestige

It is natural and inevitable that students should anticipate that their university degree will carry with it a prestige denied those who do not have that degree. Particularly in a land in which the "educated" portion of the population (i.e., those who have passed the matriculation exam, whether or not they have continued their education) is about 1½%, where between .2% and .3% of the population are enrolled in college;[8] where, even with the expansion of education in the 50's only 1½% of the population aged 17-23 entered the portals of the university:[9] and in the late '60's it was only 2½%; that portion is obviously a highly select group.

Those who succeed in acquiring the Bachelor's degree are even more select. Those who weather the Intermediate Examination at the end of two years are 50% of those who enter. At the end of the four years, of 100 who take the Bachelor's Examinations, over half fail.[10] Of those who passed in 1962 only 30% of the B.A.'s, 58% of the B.Sc's, and 23% of the B.Comm. qualified for 1st and 2nd Class degrees which are the really prestigeful ones. It could therefore be estimated that of 100 who succeed in entering a college 50 will be left at the end of 2 years, 25 at the end of four, and that 12 will have 1st or 2nd class degrees. To the extent that prestige is a function of being the possessor of something which only a few have, the assumption that a university education, and especially a uni-

[8]UNESCO, *Statistical Year Book, 1968*, pp. 185ff.

[9]Parikh, G.D., *General Education and Indian Universities*, Asia Publishing House, New Delhi, 1959.

[10]In 1962, 54% of those who were candidates for B.A. and B.A. Honors; 54% of candidates for B.SC. and B.Sc. Honors; 52% of candidates for B.Comm. and B.Comm. Honors.

versity degree, should provide its possessors with such prestige is well-founded.

This prestige is only to a very limited degree associated with the assumption that by virtue of a university education from an Indian university (with few exceptions) a person becomes "a man of learning." The traditional purpose of universities under British rule de-emphasized general and even oriental learning in Indian universities in favor of a vocational education which would provide the English governors with a supply of junior civil servants.

On the surface it might appear that the 43.6% undergraduate enrollment in Arts and Humanities in 1964 would indicate a departure from this English initiated tradition. The concern about, and studies of, "general" education have produced statements by prominent educators that stress the non-vocational aspects of secondary and higher education. Of the 46,082 students enrolled for advanced Arts degrees (43,282 for M.A. and 2,800 for Ph.D.) 16% were concentrating on traditional fields identified with learning for its own sake [history, archaeology, philosophy, fine arts, literature, music, culture (chiefly Indian), etc.]. An additional 19% were concentrating on Indian and Arabic Languages and philology; and 14% on modern languages, chiefly English. It takes many generations, however, to create the image of the universities as "seats of learning" and for its students to receive automatically therefore a reflected personal glory from this reputation of the universities.

Whatever prestige is anticipated from the possession of a university degree is perceived by the students we interviewed as resting on other grounds which sets them apart from those without that degree. They can be assumed to have certain admired qualities; they are obviously successful passers of qualifying examinations which a large majority of their fellow Indians have not dared, or been economically and intellectually able, to take, and which a substantial majority of those who did dare, or were able to take failed to pass. They are clearly upward mobile and ambitious people and symbols and pillars of any upward mobile ambitions held by the family of which they are members. They are also visible symbols that India is, in its possession of universities, earning the right to be considered a modern nation. They are of the small minority of the population who are the beneficiaries of a national

educational development effort considered and proclaimed to
be highly important and significant by India's political leaders.

The chief basis of the prestige they anticipate, however,
resides in the prestigeful advantages in life which it is hoped
will follow from, or at least accompany, the possession of
that university degree. First among these is obtaining a job
which rates high on the scale of popular esteem and respect,
preferably one with the government, especially the Indian
Administrative Service, a career as a doctor or engineer, or a
managerial position with a good firm. To the degree that
this factor of a prestigeful job is a foundation for the prestige
associated with a university degree, the possibility of being an
educated man in a rural and village community is of limited
influence in encouraging graduates to help advance the task of
rural and village development. For these prestigeful jobs are
city jobs, and, in the eyes of the students as well as in the eyes
of many of their parents, work on the farm is not of the
dignity and status worthy of the sacrifices necessary for giving
the young person an education.

Also closely associated in the minds of students and their
families with the possession of a university degree is the
prestige that may come from its advantageous influence in
enabling their families to arrange a marriage for the degree
holder with a "good" family and in raising their "value"
in the eyes of those who are determining the amount of
dowry associated with the marriage arrangements. Increasingly
those who are influential citizens in the business, industrial,
and political as well as social life of the country are holders
of university degrees, and it is assumed that a degree is a
desirable if not an absolutely necessary passport to association
with such important and influential people.

Beclouding, if not frustrating, these hopes for prestigeful
status for students are several factors productive of anxiety
and uneasiness contributing to their unrest and predispositions
to withhold respect from university faculties and administrators.
First is the association with a group of students, at the start
of their university career, 75% of whom will never be able to
relate a degree to those prestige-giving consequences because
they will never get the degree. This is particularly true of those
43.6% who register for study in the Arts and Humanities
faculties, where the entrance requirements are least demanding
and the relevance of whose curricula to any kind of jobs,

to say nothing of the most prestigeful sort, is minimal. Second is the open and widespread criticism of the weaknesses and poor quality of the universities and their faculties, criticism made actual and vivid by their own experience. Third is the apparent fact that many with university degrees are unable to find any work to do, and that even many of those who do, are employed at work which scarcely qualifies as prestigeful. The prospect which hangs over a large number of university students today is that they will have to "demean" themselves and jeopardize their families' reputations by doing work which carries a low salary and brings no special distinction to the doer.

These factors play less of a role in the relatively few colleges and universities generally considered to be first rate both in the education they provide and in the prospects for good employment in prestigeful jobs and for favorable marriages and association with influential friends. But students in that majority of colleges and universities not blessed with such a reputation, are led to value lowly the possibility that their degree carries any such advantages.

The verification during and after their university experience of any prestige elements in the image of the Student is, in other words unlikely for any but a very few.

Freedom and Self-Determination

During the pre-university years, the experience for large numbers of students has been one of family, and caste, and communal regulation. The degree of freedom and self-determination which will follow graduation is an unknown quantity. Marriage and family affairs, they know, will still be matters in which the formal authority of the father and the less obviously, more subtly expressed influence of the mother will assert itself as a constraining framework for any personal preferences they may have. They have few illusions about the individual discretion and amount of initiative which will be permitted to them in a government bureau or in an industrial or business or educational organization. But political control of their activities and thoughts does not appear to many of them to be as much a threat to free expression as was the case for Latin American and Japanese students.

Those who live as students in lodgings and hostels experience a relatively free life in comparison with their life in the homes in which they have been raised and in comparison with the one-fifth or so of the students who continue to live at home while attending the university. The change is not, however, one colored by a surging emotional feeling of resentment against the constraining circumstances from which they have come or into which they will go when college days are finished. There is not the same urgent conviction that "This is our last chance" which was evident in the case of the Japanese and Latin American students.

Cormack's survey on attitudes to authority, reported in *She Who Rides a Peacock*,[11] reinforces this observation. She posed the question to the students that she interviewed as follows, "India has traditionally put authority in the 'head' of the family, the 'head' of the village, etc. I personally respect authority in . . . ." Eighty-three percent responded, "My parents." Sixty percent responded, "My nation's government." Twenty-five percent responded, "My village's (city's) government." Sixteen percent responded, "My religious leaders." There were write-ins of less than 7% for "Political leaders," for "The state government," and for "My teachers." Since this was not a forced choice response, there is of course a considerable overlap in the responses, and the necessity for write-ins must have reduced the proportions indicating respect for the authority of those not named in the formal questionnaire. While 47% responded, "I respect authority in *Myself*," a significant proportion of the returns do not indicate a decided rebelliousness against the authority of parents and the government.

What is the impact of life in college upon this experience of entering a period of relative freedom? In colleges from which come few reports of unrest and indiscipline there are apparent opportunities for self-expression in constructive, character-building ways, through the efforts of student associations and unions to arrange entertainments, social affairs, discussions, and social service projects. But even in some of these colleges the situation existed, which is normal in India, that a faculty member was the "head" of the association and had a most influential voice in the planning and execution of its activities. This situation, however, must be considered in relation to the often repeated observation that, after the election of officers to student unions and associations, which are events often characterized by excit-

[11]Cormack, Margaret, *She Who Rides a Peacock, Indian Students and Social Change*, New York: Praeger, 1961.

ing campaigning, and an inaugural affair, the officers are relatively inactive in promoting extracurricular affairs.

Another factor that reduces the chances for the development of free give and take and the spontaneous growth of student-centered interests and activity is that only 17.6% live in hostels[12] where campus contacts with other students are natural and can lead to an awareness and an enjoyment of the things and thoughts they have in common as students.

The relations between men and women, although most of the colleges are coeducational, are nearly as restricted as in normal village or urban life. Rather than opening up the opportunity for freer and experience-broadening contacts between the sexes, coeducation presents both men and women with a puzzling predicament which is normally solved by voluntary segregation both in the classroom and out. The manner of resolving this predicament for some of the men leads to "girl teasing" which is a frequent initial occasion for student disorders when either other students or faculty members interfere with the activities of the "girl teaser."

The opportunity for the exercise of initiative in the choice of courses is minimal. The unchallenging character of the teaching and learning process which concentrates on covering the syllabus in anticipation of the final examination for the degree does not stimulate many to "launch out on their own" in exploring more deeply the issues raised in the course work which are of particular interest to them.

Nor is there much evidence that any substantial numbers of the students conceive of their "freedom" as an opportunity to achieve a self that is self-disciplined, hard-working throughout their course, facing a challenging and tough assignment every day with only occasional periods of relaxation. It would be hard to support the conclusion that student demonstrations, group indiscipline, and riots were a reaction in which students were seeking freedom and release from study fatigue. Even the "killing of time" at the cinemas and in the coffee houses is not so much a needed relaxation from the rigors of academic work as something to do to fill up unoccupied time and to relieve the resulting boredom.

In the light of these observations one is led to conclude that the alleged "causes" of student activism do not gain their stimulating force to any large degree from the fact that they

[12]In 1966-67. India, University Grants Commission, *Report 1966-67.*

offer a chance to correct *specific* conditions which frustrate
young people desiring freedom as students or citizens. Probably
more important is that the activity itself, whatever the initial
occasion of it, provides a relief from the intolerable boredom
of being free to do something with nothing to do, and from an
undemanding and uninspiring daily contact with academic
pursuits which furnish them with a purposeless leisure which
they have no idea how to use more constructively.

The campus to which they have come is not perceived as
an oasis of freedom opening up to them the opportunities for
personal development that have been in the past, and will
in the after-university future, be denied them. It is a barren
hilltop of formless and purposeless leisure between two plains
on which, whatever the character of the soil and the land-
scape, *work* is being done in which they were and will be
involved. In such circumstances almost any kind of exciting
opportunities for activism, particularly any which furnish a
convenient occasion to assert their temporary independence
of controlling authorities and provide an opportunity for
exuberant heroics in the eyes of their fellows, will provide
a relief from a boring and unchallenging leisure.

It is no part of our purpose to make recommendations, but
one is tempted to suggest that the clue to the correction of
this situation will not be found in filling up the leisure
time with extracurricular activities, but in reducing the amount
of leisure time which *needs* to be filled up by making urgent
and imperative the need for hard, demanding academic and
intellectual work.

Idealism

Of all the students in countries in which our investigations
were conducted, those in India gave the least evidence of any
action-stimulating predispositions which could be labeled as the
outgrowth of a positive, specific purpose-oriented, and deeply
rooted idealism, in the sense of commitment to unselfish and
service-focused action objectives. There was evidence of admiration for courageous and self-sacrificing reformers like Gandhi
and Bhave, but not as models to follow. There were indications of a desire to find guides for living which would enable
one to escape from the confusing and conflicting demands
and standards of a society increasingly laying stress on

material and power rooted success. There were numerous assertions that India's strength lay in her spiritual resources, and that the so-called idealistic protestations of people in Western nations were superficial and even hypocritical for they were, unlike Indian ideals, time and space bound and not rooted in a national "soul." But what this all meant when it came to providing a motivation for specific action was not clear except as it had been manifest in that golden era not so long ago when men and women risked imprisonment, suffering, and death to "throw off the English yoke." Its application to the current over-whelming problems of Indian society was hazy and obscure and provided a basis for dissatisfied criticism of what "they" were doing or failing to do rather than for a commitment of the student's own personal energy and thought and action to meeting the needs of present-day India.

As a foreigner, one hesitates to record such an observation for a number of reasons. One is keenly aware of the gap between intentions and consequences, between words and deeds in his own country. One is aware that, in every nation, those values which are labeled as ideals are largely man-made and bear the mark of the specific time and space limited experiences through which the men who formulate them have passed. One is also aware of what an imperfect vehicle any language is for conveying the reality of spiritual forces at work in the mind and heart of the speaker, and doubly aware of the difficulties under which an informant labors when he must convey such reality to another in a tongue foreign to him.

Furthermore a Western person is accustomed to think of ideals as "good" and as ultimately incompatible with "evil." How unprepared he is to evaluate the degree to which aspirations or behavior are "idealistic" in a culture in which opposites are believed to be ultimately integrated into a comprehensive and perfect whole so that they in reality are not only compatible but identical. For example consider certain lines from a Tamil poet used as the poem to be memorized and spoken in a declamation contest for 10-12 year olds, which we attended in 1964:

"Sentience is God.
O sentience, May thou live long!. . .
Thou art one. Thou art many.

Thou art amity. Thou art enmity.
That which exists and that which exists not art thou.
That which senses and that senses not art thou.
The good and the bad art thou . . . . "[13]

We are also aware of several surveys involving student responses to questionnaires regarding "guides to life and conduct" which apparently indicate "belief in" (whatever action
implications that phrase may have) high moral principles of
personal behavior such as honesty, loyalty, truth, faithfulness,
concern and respect for others, service to country, and the responsibility of Indians to make manifest "their country's
unique spiritual qualities" in a materialistic mundane world.
We have no basis for questioning these results. Neither their
consistency nor inconsistency with objective reality is, however,
incompatible with the observation here made that, even if idealism were to be defined as the possession of such ethical *beliefs*
and pride in India's spiritual heritage, it has very little to do
with either stimulating or regulating the kind of student activism observable in India.

There is evidence, however, which warns that such a generalization is not universally applicable. There are in a number
of colleges, for example, active organizations for planning and
carrying through social service projects and for inculcating
standards of honesty and trustworthiness and unselfish service
in both university and public life which would symbolize
and make manifest idealism in any land, culture, and language.

Yet, with all these reservations, one is led to observe that
the achievement of positive idealistic objectives plays a small
part in stimulating student activism. Moreover, to judge from
the actions and expressions of the students, any translation of
the ancient religious and spiritual attitude toward life and
conduct into meaning for, and relevance to, the arrangements,
relationships, and activities of secular life in modern industry,
business, agriculture, politics, recreation, and education has
not become sufficiently a part of their life and thought so that
it could be considered either a wellspring of, or support for,
the very secular kinds of student activism observed. One is led
further to observe that idealism, to the extent it has anything
at all to do with that activism, is related to it in a negative

[13]From *The Free Verse in Bharathi* by Prof. T. P. Minakshisundaram

way, in that the students are extremely cynical about the adherence of their professors, principals, and university adminis-trators, businessmen, priests, and politicians to anything more "idealistic" than self-service. And this cynicism is accompanied by a lack of confidence in the integrity of adults which makes their pronouncements about, and attempts to control, student rebellious activity and indiscipline, their challenges to student high-mindedness and responsibility, fall on the students' ears as sounding brass and clanging cymbals. It is more accurate to say that their undisciplined activism is encouraged by this cynicism and its accompanying lack of respect for those with legal and moral authority than to say that it is motivated or supported by idealism.

The practical implication of this absence of idealism at work, relevant to the conduct of secular affairs, is illustrated more spe-cifically when we consider the way in which the image of the Student as a participant in the governance of his university and country, is made manifest.

Participation in and Concern About Public Affairs

A major reason for interest in student activism at home and abroad is the assumption that it mirrors the interest of students in reforming, or even revolutionizing, the way in which their universities and countries are run. Even those who are most critical of the students' mode of behavior and most inconven-ienced by the disturbance created will reluctantly admit that it is to be expected that youth will be dissatisfied with the world as they find it. They may even concede that although student actions (in the judgment of the critics) may be misdirected and irresponsible, those actions are among the factors that keep a society from becoming too self-satisfied and unprogressive. Support for this assumption is found in reports that students have taken active part in demonstrations for or against (usually against) university and governmental policies, decisions, and practices, whether or not they have initiated those demonstra-tions. The demonstrations may be labelled by critics as irration-al means to achieve goals which, from the point of view of the evaluator, are irrational and undesirable. But, in general, that the students do have goals for themselves and their country, are concerned about the obstacles to the attainment of those goals, and believe their brand of activism can remove some of these obstacles to reaching them, is seldom questioned.

That picture does not fit the situation in India. A discussion of the causes of student activism *at this time* (but not in the pre-independence era) would place only minor stress upon the intent of students to make specific changes, to say nothing of a desire to introduce a program of constructive changes, in the policies and practices of their universities or their government.

It is not that students there are satisfied with things as they are. On the contrary, even a cursory discussion with them reveals that there is intense dissatisfaction about a host of things: corruption, malpractice and self-seeking on the part of administrators and leaders in both universities and government; lack of adequate facilities for good teaching and living conditions favorable to study for students; favoritism and nepotism in making appointments; endless ministerial and parliamentary debates and discussion and reports on pressing needs of the universities and the country, but failure to act; factionalism and communalism in the conduct of public affairs; slow progress on industrialization and the economic and social development in agriculture and the rural communities; failure of the government to alleviate the problems of overpopulation, poverty, illiteracy, and unemployment; lack of strong and challenging leadership; red tape and inefficiency in the administration of affairs both in the universities and in anything touched by bureaucracy (which is practically everything); confusion and ineptness in the handling of the language problems; failure to preserve distinctly Indian values in the drive toward westernization. But dissatisfaction is different from a concern for, and personal involvement in, corrective action. And neither dissatisfaction nor concern is likely to stimulate *purposeful* activism unless there is at least a faint idea of what somebody, if not themselves, can do.

Those conditions were not fulfilled among any group of students we talked with, and the answer as to what can be done about it given by their political leaders, that is planning a socialist pattern of society, the appropriation of larger amounts of public funds, equality, justice and freedom for all, are too vague to suggest operational steps or to indicate what the students' role, now or in the future, might be.

Furthermore, that they have personal responsibility is not suggested to them by experience in a society where the role of the elders in the management of affairs overshadows the role of youth. Moreover, it will be recalled that students in India are on the average two years further away from adulthood than they are in most western countries.

The basic problem, however, seems to us to be that which characterizes many of the countries where the attempt is being made to modernize on all fronts simultaneously. The problems are so vast and overwhelming, and the changes demanded are so interrelated, complicated, far-reaching, and comprehensive that what any one person can do appears utterly insignificant and useless. If there were a basic core of dependable and well-established institutional life and of political, economic, and social arrangements, the unsatisfactory conditions would likely be found on the margins of a steady state of affairs; an individual could comprehend, or thinks he could comprehend, what the problem is and even sense a possibility for corrective action. Even the pre-1947 problem of getting out from under colonial rule by a foreign power, although of tremendous and far-ranging import, was one on the margin of the total life of India, and the solution was relatively obvious and clear-cut. The part which could be played by ordinary people, although demanding courage and sacrifice, did not require of large numbers the qualities of analysis and planning and understanding beyond the degree of their possession of these qualities. The response of students at that time in the face of a call to action for a purpose that was clear, to a course of action understandably related to the achievement of that purpose, to a task for which they were capable and which was supported by their cultural predispositions, was enthusiastic, focused, and effective.

The problem of building a new independent India, however, requires attention to all areas of national and local life simultaneously, the purpose is not clear, the course of action is consequently not only unfamiliar but indeterminate, the ability and skill for action have yet to be acquired, and the suspicion is persistent that the action will require an uprooting of the habits and attitudes to which their culture and historical experience have accustomed them.

Students report that they find little help from their university studies for bringing some order and clarity and system into that confusing and discouraging situation. Course content, they say, has little relevance to the facts of modern Indian life. Even in the Social Sciences, that content up to this point, is dominated by general theory rather than empirical data. Moreover, the insistence that university education should be politically neutral restricts the inclination of teachers to introduce analysis of current problems all or almost all of which in a nation committed to national and state and local planning have definite political implications. Even were that inhibition not present, the possibility of clarifying discussion is minimal in the large classes which predominate particularly in the Arts and Humanities and Social Science faculties. The speakers who respond to the invitation of the students to appear before their gatherings are inclined to make speeches which "point with pride" rather than stimulate understanding of problems or encourage critical appraisal of alternatives or of results achieved. They exhort the students to prepare themselves for "leadership to bring about the economic, political and cultural transformation which is necessary for our country's dynamic journey forward" without any specification of what that transformation involves, other than modernization, or without analysis either of the problems of accomplishing it or "preparation for leadership" to do that, other than to renounce "indiscipline."

Practice in participation on the campus, through orderly and regularized representative procedures, for calling attention of the college and university authorities to student dissatisfactions, needs, and suggestions, is, with very few exceptions, nonexistent. Those authorities apparently assume that providing the students with the opportunity for such participation would lead simply to an amplification of the inclination to mount undisciplined action, demonstrations, and strikes rather than to the development of orderly alternatives to such types of action.

Neither on the current scene nor in the future are the opportunities for students to have a recognized part in the conduct of *public* affairs very promising. As indicated above, official policy is that education shall be "politically neutral." Just what this neutrality involves in terms of student behavior is not clear. Almost every one giving advice to students, from the Prime Minister and President down, admonishes them to "eschew political activity now, to study political theories now and leave active participation in politics until you have got your degrees." What neutrality means in terms of the behavior of politicians is formally proclaimed and prescribed, and then actually ignored. Party leaders and other politicians are admonished not to agitate or seek support for their interest among students. All parties do that nevertheless. but seldom in connection with political issues that instil in students a conception of politics as a process of decision making and action with respect to the great and pressing problems of the nation. What political neutrality means in terms of faculty behavior is reluctance to discuss issues whose resolution is going to have to involve political action. What it means in terms of the behavior of university administrators is a tendency to lay the blame for student activism on the politicians who "stir up the students for their own narrow political ends, interfere in elections of the student union, etc."

The few students who try to envisage what the opportunity will be for participation as citizens after their "politically neutral" experience as students are cynical about the reality of that opportunity. It is too early in the development of democratic institutions in India for the appearance of a large number of voluntary associations promoting effectively the interests of particular groups in the population and offering an accepted role for those involved as influencers of public opinion and public action. The representative parliamentary system which can catch up the criticisms, proposals, and agitations of these voluntary associations and hammer out a working consensus for the time being and relate it to the public interest and policy is in its infancy. Such associations and a truly representative parliamentary system could open to the average citizen, both during student years and beyond, many opportunities for participation in the political process other than, or in addition to, direct involvement in party politics. The opportunities, however, do not appear very extensive to Indian students.

The essentially one party system makes a political career appear to mean at best the championship of local, communal, and selfish interests and adherence to factional groups sponsoring such interests *within* the monolithic Congress Party. Recent elections give evidence that the tendency to multiparty politics is growing. Even so the opportunity for youth to play a part is perceived as minimal. As one student expressed it, "The ones with reputations for their activity in the freedom struggle have quite understandably climbed to the top, and then pulled the ladder up after them. If a young man wants to have a part, he can either join one of the small and ineffective opposition parties sponsoring for the most part a single or local or communal position, or the Socialists whose program is hardly distinctive from that of the Congress Party, or the Communists who outside of Kerala and Calcutta haven't much influence, or join up with the Congress Party which is dominated by the old men. Not a very exciting and promising prospect."

The one clear and obvious opportunity now and in the future for the ordinary student to participate actively in the governing affairs of his university and country is to join with his fellows in expressing himself in demonstrations, non-cooperation, and outright defiance of and disobedience to authority. If this element in the image of the Student as a participant is important to any of them, and it is to a number of the most energetic and thoughtful, they have to bring it to life in the forms of behavior they perceive as available to them. Chief among these are to hold meetings and pass resolutions, to demonstrate, and to strike.

It is impossible to make any general statement about the effectiveness of these student actions in accomplishing what they set out to accomplish. The chief reason is that a relatively small proportion of the demonstrations and strikes have been launched with any specific purpose in mind. Most of them appear to be incident-rather than issue-stimulated: the tuition is raised; an examination is considered too hard or unfair; a member of one communal group beats up a member of another; a teacher interferes with a case of "girl teasing"; a warden or watchman enforces a university rule which has been ignored heretofore; a room assignment is unsatisfactory; late passes are refused; a popular student is denied the opportunity to take the final exam because of his failure to meet attendance requirements; bus routes are changed; the visit of a particular speaker or dignitary to the campus is resented; a request for a holiday is refused; a particularly bad meal is served in the refectory; a rumor about the misconduct of some teacher or college or university official spreads throughout the student body; word is received that students on another campus have gone on strike; a visiting theatrical troupe gives a poor performance; a candidate for office in student government is accused of vote buying. On occasion such peripheral matters may be generalized during

the course of the agitation and corrective action be set forth
as formal demands. There are a sufficient number of reports
circulating among the students of official capitulation in such
cases to encourage them to think that such tactics have a chance
of being successful.

Some of the grievances which are the alleged causes of walk-
outs or hunger strikes cannot be dealt with to the satisfaction
of the students by the university officials, because they are
outside the jurisdiction of college or university officials, for
example a change in bus fares, a cut in scholarship funds by
the state authorities, state action with respect to tuition fees,
the appointment or removal of a Vice Chancellor, public discipline for failure to pay fares on trains, the occurrence of
police brutality, change in the national language policy, etc.

Another reason that it is difficult to estimate the effectiveness of student activism is that in many cases others (frequently politicians) get into the act, and their behind-the-
scenes maneuvering may affect the outcome more than the
student action itself.

Whenever a student strike or demonstration of serious proportions breaks out, one can anticipate a series of events. The police
will be sent to the scene. A clash will occur. Some students will
be arrested, others injured, and, on occasion, killed. Charges of
police brutality will be raised. Students on other campuses will
strike or demonstrate in sympathy. The police will be sent to
the scenes of the new outbreaks, with more arrests, injuries and
charges of brutality resulting. The university or college will be
closed down. Editors, university administrators, and politicians
begin to "view with alarm." An investigating committee will be
called for and appointed. After many months they will report.
The report will be "taken under advisement" by public officials
and eventually some specific corrective action may be taken. In
the meantime the faculty and administration of the institution
involved will consider, with varying degrees of action-producing
interest and concern, what they might do "to prevent this sort
of thing happening again." Public figures will make speeches,
sometimes to the students, admonishing the students to behave.
The report will be called to the attention of the public. Parts
of it will be picked up by editorial writers and other public
figures and politicians and made a text for a discussion of what
is needed to improve education and morals generally in the
country. A few intellectuals seriously concerned about the whole

330   CAMPUS CHALLENGE

matter of higher education will take the opportunity to use the
widespread interest in the matter generated by the report to attract attention to their ideas about what is needed in order to
perfect the educational system of the country. Others will consider the economic, sociological, psychological, and moral implications of the report in the light of the general theories and
evidence in these areas of study which they are acquainted with.

And so the process of preparation for change continues. In
this process the student activism has had an initiating part to
play. That part of initial stimulus is not reduced in importance
by the possibility that the whole process might have been set
in motion by some other factor, say an inspired and dynamic
public leader or an influential and highly respected educator.

Surveying the scene as a whole, however, it becomes evident
that student activism has had an influence on university and
public policies since independence. First of all it has kept
the student unrest and indiscipline problem before, and a matter
of constant concern to, thoughtful members of the public, especially educational and political officials. On the principle that
"the wheel that does the squeaking gets the grease," and in
the light of a normal tendency of Indian officials and bureaucrats (and probably officials and bureaucrats everywhere) to
postpone action until the need for it is revealed by obvious
trouble, student activism has been an important part of the
decision making process. Lacking the "trouble" produced by
student activism, it is unlikely that the numerous official and
unofficial investigations of the "causes" of such trouble would
have been made. Those investigations have turned up many
empirically verified facts about educational policy and practice
which suggest desirable improvements, not just to reduce the
trouble, but to build a sound and excellent educational system.

There are men of vision and dedication in India, as in
every country, who need no such spur to thought and action
in order to set for themselves the task of positive progressive
reform. But student activism has added an urgency to their
task and stirred out of their lethargy many whose active effort,
cooperation, and power are needed to accomplish that reform.
The significance of the specific reforms which have been made
in particular cases where student agitation played a major role
in awakening responsible officials to the need for such reform
(for example at Banaras, Lucknow, Aligarh) may well be out-
weighed by the significance of the stimulus provided to con-

sider the adequacy of university academic and administrative arrangements and facilities and procedures in all Indian universities.

Acquisition of Intellectual Qualities

Universities historically have performed a number of institutional functions in a society. Only one of these could not be performed by some other institution. Their *unique* function is to provide the organized facilities and arrangements in which ideas may be produced and transmitted, and through which the human capacity to do these tasks may grow and develop. Their primary purpose is to develop intellectual products and to promote intellectual excellence in their creators and users. It is naturally assumed, therefore, that those who choose to spend four or more years as students in such an institution are desirous of, and capable of, becoming intellectually competent in some sense. They may seek other advantages and results as well. But even those other advantages, whether of career opportunities, freedom, prestige, style, actualization of ideals, expanded chances to participate in public affairs, are what they are because the institution in association with which they are provided is considered to be first of all a well-spring, a nourisher, and a guardian of ideas and of the creators and users of ideas. Moreover the advantages are, to a high degree acknowledged as legitimate and worth the costs to society of making them available to a select number of individuals because it is assumed that those individuals will utilize those advantages in ways which exemplify the intellectual competence and excellence they are presumed to have acquired by virtue of their student experience.

In different countries, however, the meaning and content of "intellectual competence and excellence" will vary. The simplest and most primitive meaning views the intellectual as a person who knows more about many things than most people. A somewhat more specific concept views the intellectually competent person as one familiar with or in the process of learning about, ideas and theories produced by others. Neither of these concepts stresses the use to which such knowledge shall be put. Therefore they do not highlight the quality of creative intellectual *excellence,* a quality the true test of which is provided not merely by the amount and kind of knowledge acquired, but by the development of persons who can augment that knowledge and by the character of its use, i.e. not merely by possession but by creation and by performance. Intellectual excellence becomes an integral ingredient of the concept of the Student when he himself and people in society generally become aware of and acknowledge that the stability and progress of society requires intellectual effort; that it depends on the activity of those who are capable of dealing with and producing ideas, those who can bring analytical and problem-solving skills to bear on life's affairs, those who can formulate (and test) significant, useful, trustworthy, and objective generalizations from the multitudinous, complicated, and often confusing details of the life of a society and its people.

An insignificant proportion of the students we interviewed in India had developed and were committed to living out such a concept of themselves. Very few of their teachers conceived of their role as challenging students with that concept and helping them to achieve intellectual excellence. Critics outside the universities of the educational system were concerned about many detailed shortcomings of the universities, but only a few paid serious attention to the failure to come closer to the realization of this *unique* purpose of a college and university experience. There were, to be sure, outstanding exceptions among students, among educators (frequently those educated abroad), and among those in government responsible for, and among those outside of government interested in, the character of higher education in India. But their voices and ideas did not dispel the impression that the generally effective concept of a Student in India, insofar as that concept relates to his intellectual abilities, pictures him as one who knows more about many things than most people, and that he has learned or is learning a content of knowledge, especially theories, produced by others.

The degree to which in any society all of these elements, and particularly those emphasizing intellectual excellence, are present in the image and concept of the Student is a function of several variables. It is a function of time. Or rather it is a function of adjustments and developments which take place over time. It is a function of (1) the appearance among the people of a country of those with sufficient time and energy and ability and resources and opportunity to be able to devote themselves in heart and mind to the search for truth and knowledge for its own sake. It is a function of (2) changes and even revolutions in societal affairs that make fresh and creative thinking imperative. It is a function of (3) institutional and personal awareness of and adjustment to new ideas and actions and the widening area of need for intellectual effort revealed by those changes and developments or revolutions in societal affairs. It is a function of (4) the correction of the inadequacies of earlier concepts of intellectual competence and responsibility in the face of that need. It is a function of (5) the extent to which power groups in society recognize and make secure the condition of freedom to search for and express ideas no matter how unorthodox or challenging to the status quo those ideas may be. It is a function of (6) the degree to which the educational institutions of the society, and particularly its universities and colleges, have incorporated into their purpose the supplying of the country with manpower capable of the enlarged intellectual functions required. It is a function of (7) the positive response of the faculty and administrators of the educational institutions in the development of programs, procedures, and methods (and in the acquisition of personal competence for implementing them) for accomplishing that purpose. It is a function of (8) the acceptance by students of the enlarged concept of what is meant by intellectual effort and their commitment to the hard mental work during their student years required if they are to be able to supply that effort. It is a function of (9) the development of an audience for new ideas in the population sufficiently large to encourage, yes, demand, the creation of ideas and the development of critics of their relevance to the wisdom of experience and the "felt necessities of the times."

These independent variables, when all are present at least to some degree, mutually stimulate and reinforce each other. Yet there is a real sense in which they are cumulative and in which each becomes active in the operations of society only after the activation of the essential preceding variables as foundations for it. Especially is it true that students cannot be expected to hold to and live by this conception of their status and role as one characterized by intellectual excellence until such a conception has stimulus and support from the other developments noted (1) through (7).

The first of these variables was present in India in ancient times but to a lesser extent in modern times. The second is present to a high degree especially since the successful effort to gain independence and self-determination. The remaining variables are present only to a limited degree.

In the ancient intellectual history of India there were creators of ideas that have elicited the admiration and respect of generations of intellectuals in the fields of science and mathematics, but chiefly in the fields of religion and philosophy. There have been succeeding interpreters and expounders (but few developers) of these genuinely Indian ideas. There has been a whole caste of Indians who have used these ideas to give strength and viability to a structure of social relationships and behavior suited to stabilizing a relatively *unchanging* mode and condition of life for the great majority of Indians and their own prestigeful position within that structure. The view of life embodied in these interpretations and expositions was effectively used by a series of dynamic conquerors as a means of control, and frequently exploitation, of the indigenous population. The ideational and cultural resources carried into India by these conquerors, other than those related to control and exploitation of Indians in the interest of the conquerors (and of those Indians who allied themselves as servants with the conquerors), scarcely touched the ongoing existence of the masses of indigenous people.

Over the centuries, however, there were few Indians who were creators of ideas and searchers for truth for its own sake in any area save that of religion or religious philosophy. The secular order was seldom the focus of activity for thinkers. The contribution of intellectual effort to the development of political, economic, social, and educational institutions was meagre, and for the masses of Indians these areas of life were relatively unchanged.

That period came to a challenging end with the beginnings of the independence movement, climaxed by the success of that movement in 1947. In that year India gained the possibility of self-rule, and, under the leadership and prodding of those who had succesfully led her struggle for freedom from England, launched an attempt at political popular government. at industrialization, at the modernization of agriculture, at the reconstruction of the framework of social relationships basically unchanged for centuries, in short at modernization and the effort to place India among the powerful and influential nations of the modern world. The process was revolutionary. The fresh

thinking required, geared to the unfamiliar problems to which
thinking had to be applied, the new ideas, the analytical and
problem solving effort demanded, the capacity to make organized sense out of an overwhelming mass of complicated details
which was necessary to bring order and system into the process,
all of these needs associated with, and a consequence of, the revolutionary change became highly visible to some, but not all,
of the leaders of the new and free India. The challenge was met
by a number of Indian intellectuals who have come to occupy a
highly respected scholarly and scientific status not only at
home but within the world-wide community of scholars and
scientists.

Even today, however, a sizable and politically active strong
minority is more concerned with the threat posed by the consequences of fresh and problem-oriented thinking to the "Soul"
and traditional character of India than with the promise such
thinking offers for constructing the political, economic, and
political institutional framework through which that soul and
character can find expression and influence and even survival in
the modern world.

But it is one thing to perceive the need, and another to manage the institutional and personal adaptations and reconstruction required to satisfy that need, particularly when the human
resources for the task are minimal. And the cry for emergency
actions is so loud and impetuous that there is little or no time
to think about the need to develop thinkers through a reconstruction of the educational, and especially the higher educational, system.

Yet thinking was done, and is being done. The analyses
and reports and proposals prepared by such men and their
associates as Radhakrishnan, Deshmukh, Parikh, and others
provided the statements of objectives and the blueprints for
reaching them which, had they been used as guides to action,
might well have resulted in substantial progress toward creating
a university system directed toward developing in students that
intellectual excellence which all countries, and especially rapidly developing ones, so desperately need. It is not the fault of
these men that the primary need responded to was not the
need to develop in young people intellectual competence and
excellence, but the need to satisfy the demand for greatly
increased chances for all young people to get a university degree.
The satisfaction of the first need requires the establishment of

high quality, a most difficult task. Satisfaction of the second
need requires the mere expansion of facilities, also difficult,
but much less so than the other effort. The facilities were
expanded fourfold in the number of universities and colleges;
the enrollment was increased more than sixfold[14]; the average
quality deteriorated.

The evidences of this deterioration in quality are too widely
admitted and too well documented in government reports and
in commentaries from academic and journalistic sources to need
elaboration here. We want merely to summarize such evidence
as was reinforced by our own observations and interviews and
which has a bearing on the inadequacy of the majority of colleges and universities to provide the opportunity for the realization of the concept of the Student as a creative thinker. It is
only fair to state that we found general agreement concerning
the names of twelve colleges to which the characterizations below do not apply. Surley there must be others among the over
2000 now operating in India.

The root of the trouble we have already referred to at the beginning of this chapter. It is the lack of a clear-cut conception
of the *purpose* of the colleges and universities and the generally
prevalent lack of emphasis among both students and faculty
upon the primary responsibility of the universities to develop
intellectual competence and excellence and the ideational resources needed for the growth and an effective practical expression of such qualities.

Even if such purpose was clear and those in charge were
committed to its realization, certain features of the pattern of
higher education would discourage that realization. There is
general agreement among Indian critics that features of the
system such as reliance on the terminal general examination, a
fixed syllabus, a rigid curriculum, the memorization-of-uncom-
plicated-answers-to-set-questions, give no encouragement whatever to the development of intellectual competence and excellence in the analyzing, problem solving, idea creating aspects
of intellectual activity. Those features, inherited from the past,
have been perpetuated in the vastly expanded educational
institutions. Such features are made to order to eliminate from
the educational experience of students and the educational
efforts of the teachers any stimulus to a broadening and
sharpening of the intellect which does not have direct and

[14]And if intermediate students are included, more than eightfold.

specific bearing on the ability to answer the questions set by the University for applicants for a Bachelor's degree at the end of their 3 or 4 years of study. They are made to order to discourage the direction of readings and lectures toward exploring the personal and social significance of what is being learned and its relationship to other areas of learning. Such understanding is not to be rewarded at examination time, and effort expended on this matter would have to be at the expense of effort that has some chance of "paying off" on examination day. They are made to order for primary dependence on "made-easies," "guess sheets," intensive tutoring a few weeks or months before that final examination, rather than upon the cumulative day by day acquisition of knowledge, the ability to test and criticize it by disciplined thinking, and the capacity to add to it.[15]

Moreover the fact that the thinking at the university level must be carried on in a foreign language (traditionally English, although even Hindi is a foreign language to a majority) reduces the possibility of sharpness and clarity in that thinking. The use of a foreign language is not an impossibility for a few exceptionally able students, and especially those in whose childhood environment such foreign languages were made familiar through conversation and reading. For the great majority of students (and indeed faculty) the terms and concepts and grammatical structure of their home language (there are 15 distinct ones in India) are the only vehicles of thinking in which they would feel sufficiently equipped and secure to dare to think in any sense far beyond the memorization of answers to set questions.

Recognition of this difficulty has led to advocacy of the use of the local languages in some of the newly established colleges and to a de-emphasis on the learning of English in education preparatory for the university career.

But here arises the dilemma. In matters requiring analysis, generalization, and idea creation in modern India there are few if any written resources in those home languages. Even if that handicap were removed, the sharing, debate, mutual criticism, and cooperative intellectual effort required to produce thinkers

---

[15]The University Grants Commission in its *Report on Student Indiscipline in Indian Universities*, 1960, declared that the examination system makes it "possible for many of our students to go through the larger part of a year without opening a book." p. 9.

and ideas capable of dealing with all-India problems would remain. If and when all other obstacles to making the universities and colleges centers for the development of intellectual competence and excellence are removed, the language barrier will remain. For all save the exceptionally able, the learning process must continue for some time to mean the cramming of words rather than the understanding and use of ideas.

It is difficult to see how such obstacles can be overcome unless those who are chiefly responsible for the day-by-day conduct of higher education, the teachers, are equipped to provide the vision and direction and initiative for the focusing of the educational process on its major and unique intellectual task in society. No one who has discussed these problems with teachers in different parts of India can but recognize certain facts: there are a substantial number of professors and junior faculty members who have that vision, sense of direction, initiative, intellectual competence, and are dedicated to the task; there are *far too few of them* to provide the needed human resources for even a majority of Indian universities; they form a majority of the faculty in only a limited number of colleges and universities; they are working within an administrative system for higher education involving appointment procedures, selection of students, curriculum determination, and student evaluation, which, even when not influenced as much by political as by purely academic standards and interests, provides them with minimal opportunity for experimentation and freedom to initiate; they are pessimistic and discouraged about the chances of improvement in their lifetime. They have little faith in the competence and intellectual stature of most members of the teaching profession; the majority see little chance to achieve a satisfying status as intellectuals in their own country to say nothing of such a status among the world-wide fraternity of scholars and scientists in their own field; they have a minimum of zest for their task, and the attitude of most could be summed up as "holding on and doing the best I can."

Even these men freely but sadly assert that in social status and in relative income the teaching profession has been declining in the last two or three decades; that the profession attracts chiefly those who cannot find better and more secure jobs elsewhere (preferably in government); that the large number of teachers, even at the college level, required to fill the vastly expanded posts, are ill-prepared (most have no more than an M.A., at most the equivalent in years of preparation to the Bachelor's degree in the United States, Canada, or England); that creative work and research is no part of their conception of their task and, even when it is, their training for it is poor, and that the library, field work, and laboratory facilities needed are lacking; that for the most part members of the teaching profession are either demoralized or cynical.

The chance of the college teachers developing a pride in the unique intellectual mission of the university and devoting themselves to the enthusiastic carrying out of that mission is small. The basis for this comment can better be understood if we set down what in general, but with notable exceptions, it means to be a college teacher in the Indian system of higher education.

It does not mean:

Engaging in research and making contributions to knowledge

Training young minds to think, solve problems, evaluate, choose among alternatives, mature intellectually

Sharing in joint intellectual adventures with colleagues and students

Keeping one's subject and its presentation alive, up-to-date, and relevant

Engaging in frequent intellectual exchange with scientists and scholars abroad, or even in India

Participating in the building and maintenance of a university or college society and in the preservation of its integrity and autonomy

Enjoying the respect and prestige accorded to intellectuals by a society which places a high value on intellectual achievement and in which it is an honor to be labelled an intellectual or even to be called by a superficially derisive name like "egghead"

Carrying the main responsibility for the building and protection of that sector of societal activities which creates and nourishes and applies the nation's intellectual resources

It does mean:

Giving lectures (under a heavy teaching assignment) which hopefully will aid students to pass the final examinations for a degree set by the university, and which elucidate subjects contained in a syllabus shaped and infrequently revised by a Board of Studies for the subject and approved by a hierarchy of all university authorities

Conveying information at a relatively elementary level to large classes of intellectually unmotivated students

Preparing and distributing, for small additional income, aids to examination passing, such as course notes and, if he is fortunate in contracts with a publisher, question and answer "made-easies"; also intensive tutoring of students for a fee just before the final examination

Correcting of final examinations, if fortunate enough to be appointed for this monetarily rewarding task

Having little intimate contact, either intellectually or otherwise, with students

Being involved, as a member of the university community, in internal intrigues of political, caste, and communal significance and being a seeker for small personally advantageous improvements and perquisites

Being subject to a bureaucratic university administrative organization established to satisfy not merely academic, but also political interests and pressures

Working under the necessity of not antagonizing an immature and frequently undisciplined student body

Being able to place the blame for limited accomplishment on nonacademic powers and interests

Working in crowded quarters, lack of privacy, with inadequate library and laboratory facilities

The demoralized, disillusioned, and cynical teachers who carry on their work under these circumstances do not provide the students who come into contact with them with attractive human symbols of success and achievement for those students who would live out a role to which intellectual activity gives the dominating character.

Now it may be asked, "If the students do not think of themselves as potential intellectuals, if they have not incorporated into the concept of the persons they are or hope to be the characteristics of intellectual competence and excellence, can there be any frustration in failure to find the opportunity for improving their intellectual capacities in their university experience? There can be no frustration in failure to move toward a nonexistent goal." The position is well taken. The cause of student unrest and dissatisfaction which is rooted in the situation described above is not so much that students are frustrated by it, as that it provides them with no challenge which can dominate their interest and motivate their strenuous full-time labors on a task that, for its accomplishment, would require all the energy they could muster. Nor does it provide them with a set of values unique to the institutions in association with which they are investing four years of their lives, by reference to which values that appropriateness and relevance of all else they do during that time can be measured. Lacking such demand on their energies and motivation to utilize them for such a high purpose, and lacking such a standard for evaluating their behavior in non-academic situations, they find their academic pursuits dull, uninspiring, and pedestrian, if not meaningless, save in the sense that they are considered a more or less unwelcome aspect of the four years of life they must spend to get a degree, after which, hopefully, *real* living begins.

To any extent that there exists in youth an impulse to adventure and excitement, that impulse has in India, little chance for fulfillment in intellectual work and achievement. Closer at hand and uncorrected by the recognition that they are students with an intellectual purpose and provided with an excellent opportunity for reaching it, the undisciplined actions in company with their fellows challenging both university, and public authorities, may appear by contrast exceptionally adventurous and exciting.

It would be more accurate to say that the *lack* of, rather than the *frustration* of, attempts to actualize the image of the Student as an intellectual, or even as a thinker, lies at the root of the readiness of students in India for restlessness and undisciplined activism.

Chapter 9
Becoming a Student and Citizen
in Mexico and Colombia

In 1967 there were 35 universities and schools of higher education in Mexico with 154,289 students enrolled, or .3% of the population of the country. The corresponding figures for Colombia were in 1966, 29 universities and schools of higher education, 49,930 students enrolled, or .3% of the population of the country.

The traditional image of the Student in Mexico and Colombia is that of a young man of acknowledged prestige, who is idealistic, free, an influential participant in university, government, and societal affairs, and on the threshold of a respected career.

Prestige and Status

There is little doubt that, with respect to the components related to status and prestige, many university youth were traditionally, and are today, "on the way." In both of these countries, after the abolition of the titles of nobility accompanying independence from Spain, the university degree of "Doctor" became increasingly important as titular evidence of elite standing, as well as the admission card to one of the honored careers distinguishing the "professionals" from the ordinary "makers of a living," from the carriers of water and the hewers of stone. But the degree was frequently sought for its own sake, a mark of the "cultured" gentleman, without reference to the "work" to which it was nominally related. Had, for instance, the sons of hacienda owners or wealthy urban dwellers sought a degree appropriate to their function, they would have studied, for example, agriculture or veterinary medicine, or commerce. But with no intention of practicing law or medicine they registered in the "prestige" faculties providing the doctorate in these fields, seeking above all else the "title."

This function of the university, as a provider of titles[1] and as a finishing school for cultured gentlemen, characterizing the 19th and early 20th century, still persists, and there was no denying among our informants that there are a number of students whose primary aim in attending a university is to attach to their persons the status and prestige resulting from a degree. The title of Doctor is still a cue to the giving of respect and is used as a means of gaining that respect even by some who have only a "pasante" status, that is have not fulfilled the thesis or general examination requirements for the degree.

The highest prestige attaches to the degrees from the traditional Faculties of Medicine, Law, and Engineering. Between 1951 and 1953, 2/3 of the graduates from universities in Colombia had been registered in these faculties. The proportion was less (45%) in 1966 in Colombia and still less (21%) in Mexico. But well over half (56.4%) of the university students in Colombia and nearly half (45.2%) in Mexico were registered in these three traditional faculties.[2] Several of our student informers indicated that students who could not qualify for admission to these faculties felt they must make a second-best choice when they registered in the newer studies in the Humanities, Social Sciences, etc. This fact may have a bearing on the frequent observation that students in these latter areas are more prone to volatile activism than are those in the traditional faculties.

To the degree that the title itself and not the content of training is, for such students at least, the important factor, much of the criticism made of the university studies related to inadequate teaching and academic discipline are largely irrelevant as far as they are concerned. Moreover, he who would stand out from the general run of humanity, from those who must earn their bread by manual labor, has, in his university degree, the only admission card to a widely respected

[1]There is no intention of suggesting here that this was the only function of a university, only that it was one important way the university fitted into and supported the general structure of the social system.

[2]Economic Commission for Latin America, *Education, Human Resources, and Development in Latin America*, United Nations, 1968.

white collar career. The "taxi" professors without a focused
life-work concern for building institutions of knowledge are,
moreover, no handicap to the aspirations of students who seek,
through their university experience, association with *influential
contacts* in the outside world. Indeed in many cases it is an
advantage that the chief place of work and associations of the
professor, which he leaves by taxi to deliver his lecture, is in
the world of affairs.

If the number of students at the universities is considered
in relation to the total population, there is little doubt that
students are a select group. In 1959, for example, a 10 year
educational plan was submitted in Mexico. In analyzing the
problem it was pointed out that of 1460 Mexican children
reaching the age when formal schooling would be expected
to begin, only one ended with a university degree. The process
was presented as follows:

Of 1460 Mexican children, 460 did not enter school.

1000 start and 471 drop out the first year, and 866 drop
out during the first 6 grades. (In 1963 a report of the
Secretary of education indicated an even larger number,
983, dropping out before the end of the 6 year primary
cycle).

59 enter secondary schools of whom 32 drop out before
finishing. 27, therefore could probably go on to post-
secondary education.

9 go on to Preparatoria of whom 3 drop out.

6 get to a faculty or school university training. Of these,
only *one* finishes.

For those whose primary reason for university attendance is
related to the prestige and status objectives, however, a number
of reasons for dissatisfaction are becoming increasingly evident.

In the first place, an increasing number of university administrators are expressing and attempting to implement aspirations
for standards of education, research, and academic contributions
to the public welfare in the best tradition of the concept of the
university as a seat of learning and a producer of able and
learned people for service to the community. Their efforts di-

rected toward raising selection standards, tightening up academic standards and discipline, reorganizing studies, focusing the administration of studies in particular academic disciplines (like Psychology, Mathematics, Chemistry) rather than solely in faculties related to a career, so that standards relevant to the world of science may apply, are encouraging. Such efforts, when successful, set requirements for students (as well as professors) making a dilettante approach to a degree difficult.

It is our impression that this move is welcomed by students whose ambitions are focused on more than the title, but it is understandably frustrating to those whose purpose in becoming a student is chiefly to acquire the title and who, not unnaturally, would prefer the road to be as painless as possible.

Two of the major examples of rebellious direct action recorded in Chapter 3, began as a negative reaction by students to the efforts at such reform by deans and rectors in the National Universities in Colombia and Mexico. In these cases the direct action was concluded by the departure of the rectors involved. Little evidence of this stimulus to student dissatisfaction was found in the newer private universities whose efforts are not so fettered by the traditions of the past. It would not be surprising, however, to find, among the demonstrators against deans and rectors who attempt to enforce higher academic standards, stiffer requirements for admissions and qualifying examinations, rules relating to attendance and vacations, etc., a number stimulated to activism by such "frustrations."

Another change frustrating to those who are primarily status-and-prestige seekers is the increasing number among whom that standing and prestige must be shared. Built to serve 29,000 students in 1954, for example, the National University in Mexico City already had in 1964, 70,255 students, and some estimates place the present enrollment as high as 90,000. In 1962 that university, it was rumored, refused admission to 10,000 who applied (although some of these were later admitted, partly as a result of student agitation). The situation is becoming similar in the National University of Colombia in Bogotá. An increasing number of these applicants for admission are coming from the middle classes who seek, and whose parents, at great financial and security-of-living sacrifice, seek for them, a place on the educational ladder of upward mobility. It is a truism that among those concerned primarily with the status and prestige components of the student image, the satisfaction of membership in an elite is inversely proportional to the number of actual and potential possessors of that status, and to the numbers, whose families do not already have that status for one reason or another, who are potentially able to achieve it by virtue of being students. Nevertheless, in terms of the proportion of﹅ students in that portion of the population who are of college age (4% in both Mexico and Colombia[3]) students from whatever class are a select, if not elite, group.

One adjustment to this situation, available to those who are primarily interested in maintaining the prestige which their families already possess, is attendance at one of the private universities where a tuition fee limits to some degree the entrance of students whose economic resources are small. We do not share the conclusion that these universities were founded by the Church or by private donors chiefly in order to provide a prestigeful education, but they *serve* this purpose for some individuals. In Bogotá there is a recognition among students both in the National and in the private universities that the typical student of the former is middle class. This is not so true in Mexico, for there the private universities have not proliferated to the same extent as in Columbia. There is potential fuel here for the fires of unrest in the hearts of students from all classes of the population to the extent that they are seeking primarily to make incarnate in themselves the status and prestige elements of the traditional image of the Student.

Yet the primary spark for direct action proceeding from this desire for a prestige rating may be expected to be struck in the public universities which are increasingly becoming the ladder of upward mobility for the middle classes. The distinctiveness and unique advantage of a university degree decreases as the number possessing it increases. A very real danger is that only a degree from private universities will come to have the prestige value once conveyed by *any* university degree and that middle class students at the public universities will become sensitive to this and resent it. Students at two of the private universities in Bogotá and of one in Mexico City told us, "We aren't worried about our prestige as students and as degree holders. We already have it as students, and when we finish we

[3]UNESCO, *Statistical Year Book*, 1968

know we'll continue for that reason to have a great advantage."
This expression of confidence is underscored in Colombia by
the frequent assertions in comments of our informants in the
National University, that those who were eventually able to
count themselves as members of or closely associated with the
oligarchical elite, were predominantly graduates of the private
universities.

A further interesting reinforcement of this confidence was
contained in a survey of student opinion at the National University in Bogotá, conducted in 1961 by Professor Williamson
on leave from Haverford College. Asked to rate five Colombian
universities as to their academic standards, Javeriana, a private
Catholic university, nearly as large as the National University,
was rated at the bottom of the group. Asked to rate the same
five universities as to the probability of graduates obtaining
satisfying and important positions in society, Javeriana was
rated at the top. In a society where the middle classes are
already aware of and resentful against a situation of inner and
upper circle rule, this extension into the university system of
an aid to the perpetuation of that rule is packed with social
dynamite.

An interesting example of the possible relation of this increase
in the number of upward mobile middle class students seeking
prestige and status through gaining a university degree to direct
action by students was the agitation over the use of admission
tests in 1962 for students at the University of Mexico. One of
the reasons given by some of the students for opposition to the
tests (and the consequent or concomitant rumored refusal of
admission to 10,000 applicants) was the possible use of the
tests to give the advantage of a university education to those
whose superior economic position already gave them an advantage in the competition for prestigeful positions in society.
In the opinion of students having this reaction, even though
there was no discrimination not supported by test performance,
those students from the lower middle classes, and particularly
from the villages where educational facilities are inferior, would
lose their chance for self improvement and prestige in a society
where a higher education is the only road to that accomplishment. The tests, in their opinion, provided an automatic way
of giving an advantage to the youths already possessing superior
privilege by virtue of the wealth and social position of their
families, and because of the better primary and secondary education available to them. (These students had no illusions about

the capacity of tests to appraise *native* intelligence and promise.)

The foregoing components of the student image related to his status and prestige will naturally decline slowly in importance as the proportion of students and university graduates in the population increases. The next group of components is much more firmly rooted, is very important at the present time, and promises to continue to be so.

Idealism

The next group of components in the Student image defines the student as an *idealist*, that is, as a sponsor, carrier and defender of his own and of popular ideals of justice, human welfare, and people-centered government, and as a spokesman for the underprivileged. We have no way of knowing whether this reputation for idealism is matched by a genuine and deeply rooted commitment to the building of a better world to a greater extent than would be the case in other nations.

But the conviction was widely expressed, by both students and citizens, that idealism was a significant and common ingredient of the student character.

There were some who thought the idealism was superficial, purely poetical, and at best an emotionally satisfying, but ineffective and not a widespread motivation. The lack of any reported student interest in entering or serving the labor movements, the infrequent occasions when student demonstrations appear to have been stimulated by issues related to efforts of or on behalf of the workers and peasants, and the disinclination and actual refusal of labor leaders to seek working relations with the universities, their faculties, and students, is evidence, for example, that one practical expression of this sort of concern for the underprivileged found in many countries, is not widely exploited. One found little *expressed* concern among leaders of the student societies and federations for the plight of the most disadvantaged class of people of all, the Indian peasants, and little evidence of widespread active effort on their behalf.

Since 1960, however, there has been both in Mexico and Colombia a significant movement in which students (a minority of course) have become enthusiastic about volunteer service as week-end campers and longer period volunteers to help repair buildings of primary schools. In Colombia this and other types of service are undertaken by the *Acción Comunal*, or Community

Development Programs, of the Government. Professor Williamson in the study of attitudes of students at the National University in Bogotá, to which we have already referred, found that 87% expressed interest in participating in some type of social assistance of this sort. All this indicates an attitude on the part of students toward physical labor and community service which reinforces idealism in action. Although these efforts are on a small scale they indicate the presence of a spark that could be fanned into a flame.

Certainly in both Colombia and Mexico, students can see all about them evidences that improvements in justice and human welfare need to be made. The conditions of the underprivileged rural and racial groups are clearly evident and widely discussed, although normally with overtones of pessimism and even fatalism that excuse lack of effort to do anything to change matters. Large numbers of students live in the older and poorer sections of the cities, and many of their families have moved to the cities to live in very straightened circumstances in order that their sons or daughters can attend a good secondary school and the university. These students can clearly observe the human problems and social consequences of the great inequalities in wealth and opportunity. Those who come from the lower middle classes can observe, without looking beyond their own families, the frustrating circumstances providing obstacles to upward mobility. The evidence of rapid increase in the wealth of some public men during their term in office is observable and cynically noted. Cyncism is widespread concerning the opportunity for effective democratic participation of ordinary folk in the affairs of the nation and concerning graft and corruption in high places.

What opportunities does their student experience provide, other than occasional participation in demonstrations, to satisfy the social idealism of such students? Mexico University has a separate Social Service Department which manages "internships" in out of the way villages and, which, among other activities, arranges week-end work camps where students participate in learning about the problems of underprivileged people, and in helping them solve those problems. We have already spoken of the *Acción Comunal* in Colombia and its opportunity for participation in community development. Javeriana in Bogotá had an impressive list of opportunities for student participation in charitable activities including participation by students in workers' education, legal consultation for the poor, visitation to and study of jails, Catholic mission and social work assistance, dental clinics, community medical services. But such a program was not widely duplicated, and we were not able to learn the extent of student participation. In any case students who do participate in such activities are not prominent among those who give direction to and organize student activism. In Mexico since the revolution in 1910 and especially since 1929, and increasingly in Colombia (particularly as evidenced by the University of Valle) the concept of the University as a servant of the people (much like Lincoln's .concept of the land grant college) has been, and is becoming increasingly, a significant part of the organizational charter of the public universities. In both countries the medical students spend a substantial portion of their final year carrying medical service to a particular village which lacks such service. Plans are in hand (and in some cases action is being taken) to make this type of "internship" experience a part of the training of students in other faculties. Medical students in both Mexico and Colombia expressed interest in trying to influence students in other faculties to press for the adoption of such an arrangement. The University of Valle is broadening the concept to include teams of doctors, architects, sanitary engineers, etc. who would perform such service as a part of their education.

There is a stimulus to this activism with respect to social service and reform in both Colombia and Mexico in a widely expressed mythology that students have traditionally been the chief champions of the underprivileged and the powerless in society. The tradition is stronger in Colombia than in Mexico, primarily because there are fewer historical torch bearers in Colombia whose reputations are identified with an abiding concern for the welfare of the masses. In Mexico there are a number of honored revolutionary leaders, not necessarily identified as students, with such reputations, for example, Hidalgo, Morelos, Juárez, Cárdenas, Zapata, and others. The PRI itself has been able to maintain a reputation as a promoter of better material and educational conditions for the underprivileged. Students have no monopoly on the role.

Moreover, other groups have increasingly become known for their social service and their interest in the common man, church organizations and a number of Catholic priests, trade unions, cooperatives of the *campesinos,* for example. Moreover, the latter two have a role in the all powerful political party mechanism, and therefore have the chance to make their influence felt where it counts.

In Colombia also certain priests and women's organizations are adding their voices to those whose concern is the underprivileged. But the image of the Student in the minds of the public and of the students still reveals an emphasis on the students as the traditional primary defenders of the underprivileged and the weak.

This injection of the university and its students into the life and needs of the people, carrying with it the opportunity not only for the stimulation and expression of active and latent idealism, but for becoming intimately familiar with the nation's problems and realities at the grass roots, is a concept of an emphasis in education that justifies widened consideration not merely in Latin America but in North America and on other continents, as well. Yet for students generally throughout the Colombian and Mexican universities it is, we think, fair to say that the opportunity for expressing idealism and the desire for social service and social reform is not sufficient to provide outlets for all the social idealism which exists.

There are, of course, other ways. Political as well as social idealism can be noted. The force and persistence as action goals of political unification and nationalism in both countries is evident in the comments of many students. The dedication to or even the declaration of such nationalistic aspirations can quite easily be experienced emotionally as an expression of personal idealism. The search for a truly Mexican national identity has been a prominent concern of politicians and literary figures since 1910. Students were aware of and interested in this search, and that interest is probably one component in their predisposition to use every available occasion to "declare their independence" from both European and United States influence. The pragmatic efforts to integrate the diverse population and functional groups into a workable political party structure and into a comprehensive national unity, especially since 1930, have implicitly emphasized the same drive.

The reaching for a truly national identity in Colombia has faced many obstacles. The violent virtual civil war between the Liberal and Conservative Parties and their adherents in the 19th and the first half of the 20th centuries contributed to the development of national unity only negatively by revealing the dangers to the survival of the oligarchial rule. The uneasy National Front truce between these warring factions made in 1958 involved no widespread inclusion of non-elite groups as genuinely participating members of one nation, but rather sought to make even more secure the hold of the traditional elite on the claim to *be* Colombia. This elite ruler-nonelite subject pattern is not inconsistent with stable nationhood which is acceptable to a sizable number of the students. For others, a viable Colombia, its whole people united in the enjoyment of first class citizenship, is considered essential, but a condition still to be created; and for many their ideal-oriented political role is to be the instrument of change through which such a nation will come into being.

Students in Mexico and Colombia have their idealistic political status and role differentially influenced by the differences in the stage of nation building at which their respective nations find themselves.[4] Mexico has been through a continuous revolution during which the concept has developed of Mexico as a nation among nations in a 20th century context, and of Mexicans as a people. The participation of an increasing portion of the people in the system of governance has been expanded, and the rights of all classes in the population have been clarified by the acceptance of reciprocal obligations of government for their welfare. The task is far from complete, but progress has been made, and the direction and objectives of that progress have produced and have been supported by a degree of popular consensus as to a national outlook and the structure and character of national life. This discourages the idea that a radical political change must be the prelude to a stable and viable eventual integration of all Mexicans into a just system of government, and into a system of production and distribution promising increasing economic and social opportunity and social security. Moreover, Mexicans can perceive their country as a *modern* nation, ready to incorporate into its structure and operations the technology, institutions, and values that fill that term with operational meaning. Furthermore, the industrial, business, and political structure has provided functional, and to a lesser extent policy making, roles for persons from varied social backgrounds which gives them a stake in the maintenance of the *status quo.*

[4]cf. Scott, Robert E., *Mexico in Transition*, Univ. of Illinois, 1964 pp. 84ff, also in *Daedalus.* Winter 1968.

Students move into these roles following their university study. The single dominant political party provides a system of representation for important functional groups in society which creates at least the potential opportunity for their voices to be heard in shaping the character and the activities of the nation. Organizations of workers, peasants, businessmen, industrialists, intellectuals, have provided a training ground to develop spokesmen for the interests of these groups, and these leaders have frequently personified and made their contributions to the national identity as well.

The students are no longer the only group, and certainly not the unique group, providing candidates for leadership in this task of nation building on a modern model. From their members will continue to come the performers of tasks essential to the perpetuation of the economic, political, and social system so far developed. Many of them will be the initiators of changes and modifications in the evolution of that system. But the need for political talents and sophistication is now matched by the need for economic and social as well as political competence.

Such a process is also under way in Colombia, but it has not proceeded so far, nor have the results of the process created the same faith that participation in the maintenance and evolution of *existing* forms of political, economic, and social nationhood is a sufficient role for students to play. Re-building is still considered by many to be the first business of their lives.

The idealistic political status and role of students in any country then will be perceived not only by students, but by others as well, as related to the stage in nation building in which their country finds itself. And the expectancy that the university experience shall be one which gives justifiable emphasis to developing political talents will vary with the same factor. Not only will the students sense this challenge as related to their own life commitments, but those among their countrymen aware of the same national situation will, if their personal or group interests cannot be satisfied without radical change in governing and management of the nation affairs, encourage and support the *politically* oriented aspects of the university's activities, and on occasion seek to make league with the student *políticos*.

It should be noted that, even in a relatively stable political nation, if there is a major disturbance to the public confidence that the structure and character of the nation are in accord with modern needs and aspiration, the challenge of nation *re*building once more emphasizes the opportunities for and the responsibility of *radical* rather than routine political action. The situation producing this loss of confidence could come as a consequence of inaction with respect to changes in the internal and external problems to which a nation must adapt its structure and operations *and* a resulting loss of capacity of the existing Establishment to deal satisfactorily with those problems. Small perceived variations in such capacity do not cause a loss of faith that, in its essence, the nation is sound; corrections can be made by the reform efforts of those capable and inclined to make those efforts. To those who perceive the variations to be large, that faith is deeply disturbed, and radical national restructuring, not merely reform, is called for. This is the continuing case in Colombia. It could become the case in Mexico, or in any nation.

The few comments indicating that such social and political idealism was poetically superficial do not negate the proba-bility that this idealism is perceived by people generally and by students to be an important foundation for readiness to participate in direct action. Nor is it necessary to assume the universal presence of any such stimulant to action among all students.

We shall return to this perception of the student as an idealist later on in discussing the reasons for the influence of the students with rulers and the public when they do in-itiate direct action, indicating how the general belief that much student action is idealistically motivated increases that influence. Here it is only necessary to indicate the probability that for some leaders of, and followers in, some of the student direct action, the idealistic and reform character of such action both stimulates and justifies in the minds of students their participation.

It is possible that, particularly in the public universities, the "orthodox" opportunities for expression of social and political idealism are sufficiently small so that much of the desire for such expression finds a ready outlet in demonstra-tion when the "cause" of the demonstration is related to the achievement of some idealistic, or social or political reform objective. Moreover, many students can very well feel a com-pulsion to take part in such demonstrations, for there is little doubt that a widespread public expectancy exists that the students form one group that can, and probably will, do something about obstacles to justice, human welfare, and people-centered government.

Participation

The image of the Student in Latin America is thoroughly colored by the tradition that he is a participant in the governing of his university. Through a representative system, he has traditionally participated, and still does participate, in the governing of the university. His elected representatives sit on the Councils of the faculties and schools and join with representatives of the faculty and the deans on the Academic Council and the Superior Council which determine all the affairs of the university. Their voice is reinforced by the willingness of the students to demonstrate or to strike to back up their representatives.

We have explored the character of this *cogobierno* system in Chapter 3. The expectancy is strong that, upon becoming a student, an individual becomes a citizen of a free university world, in the control of which he has a voice.

The prospects for the continued extensive realization of that expectancy in the indefinite future are uncertain, at least as far as sharing in university government with respect to truly academic matters (such as curriculum and course development, standards of admission and qualification for degrees, requirements for remaining in good standing as students, election of deans and professors and rectors, and the like) are concerned. The private secular and religious universities, and increasingly the public universities, are under the governance of educators fully aware from experience of the anomaly of the teachers and administrators being so heavily dependent on the good will of the students if they are to build genuine institutions of learning. The former vacuum in concern for professional institution-building which was left by the part-time faculty members, and the lack of centralized university policy and power, is being filled by the increase in full time faculty and by the policy and administrative integration of the separate and nearly autonomous faculties or schools. The increasing complexity of the subjects taught, the impact of extensive research in each field, and in particular the requirements for fulfilling effectively the service functions of a university in an industrialized society, reduce the expectancy that the students can have wisdom and experience enough to make a significant contribution to the overall organization and control of the universities' research and teaching functions. The implications of these developments are so clear that, even in matters where students could be left to a degree of self-rule in matters, for example, concerning student activities and with respect to some aspects of social service, an increasing degree of administrative control is being exercised.

One may expect, however, to witness resistance movements led and supported by students resentful of this perceived encroachment on their traditional role as student governors and directed against what appears to them to be the domination by educational and political leaders in determining the rules of the university game. The need for modification of this controlling relation of students to the university is considered sufficiently clear and critical among the educators with whom we talked so that we sense a danger that the action they are likely to take will have not only desirable, but also undesirable consequences in addition to stimulating student demonstration against such action. In some cases there appeared to be the maintenance of the form without the fact of participation, a sort of paternalistic relation between administrators and student leaders in which the "children" were allowed to *think* they were participating. The other danger is that "the baby may be thrown out with the bath" and that real values in genuine student participation in determining some aspects of university life will be lost. Needless to say such tendencies create unrest and dissatisfaction among many students possessed by the traditional image of the Student, and increase their inclination to use direct action when recognized traditional instruments of student self-government are withdrawn.

Not only with respect to university affairs, but with respect to affairs in society at large, does the image of the Student emphasize a role in influencing those affairs far greater than that exercised in society by their parents or than that which most of them will in fact exercise after they are out of the university. Moreover, this expectancy is bolstered by the record of public affairs action on the part of past student generations. Of all citizen groups, aside from the inner governing circle and the army, the students are most aware of the strength of their collective voice in affecting the affairs of society generally, even to having a significant part in the overthrow of governments. They are also one of the few groups in the country (other than national politicians and the army), who have had the chance to experience in thought and action an identity with their country as a nation. We shall discuss the reasons for this influence on social affairs external to the university shortly. The record of unquestioned success in influencing the course of events is a stimulus to the use of this power and the reinforcement of the image of the Student as a free man privileged and able to influence societal affairs as few in the society can.

When students feel the urge to activate this image of the Student as a participant in the nation's affairs, how do the prospects of fulfilling that desire appear to them, and what is their reaction to that outlook?

In Colombia, there is no place for activity by students in the management of public affairs. Those matters are the province of a traditional elite, a small, relative to the total citizenry, group of politicians sharing their power with members of the middle class only when the requirements for managing the affairs of a country moving toward becoming a modern industrial society make necessary the dependence on those functions which such "outsiders" are able to perform. Although there has long been keen competition, and at times violent warfare, between the Liberal and the Conservative Parties, the ruling members of both come, on the whole, from the same social stratum. (In general it can be said that the Conservative Party's roots are in the older aristocracies of land and church, whereas the Liberal Party's roots are in the aristocracies of the city and modern industry, but there are major exceptions in both cases.) Their political energies have been devoted to the attempt to wrest ruling power from each other. As mentioned before, the National Front established in 1958, whereby one party alternatively supports candidates for high public office, including the presidency, of the other party, is an uneasy temporary marriage of convenience undertaken when it appeared that the fratricidal warfare between the two oligarchical factions would bring down the continued rule of the oligarchs. During the period of that civil strife a transfer of power from one party to the other amounted to a palace revolution, resulting in a change of appointments all down the line until even the peasants in their villages found their friends involved, family loyalties disturbed, the authorities changed.

The limited social reforms proposed and the still more limited reforms introduced, and the limited promotion of industrial and business modernization, have left basically untouched the control of the oligarchs and the virtual exclusion from major decision making in public affairs of all save the inner circle.

It is that arrangement that caused the great majority of our student informants to speak of the need for radical change, which most of them expressed as "revolution," before Colombia could become a truly modern nation and one in which the opportunity for significant participation in political or economic affairs would be enjoyed by those from the middle classes from which most of them came. Their concept of change, whether they labeled it reform or revolution, was not a matter of detailed reforms of the conditions of life and work, but of a change in the locus of ruling power. They have little confidence that any attempt to engage politically in pressures on the two traditional parties would lead to this result. The opposition parties are so small as to be unlikely instruments of effective "orthodox" political action, either while they are students or later.

One indication of this lack of confidence in the existing channels for orthodox political action is contained in a survey of the political associations of National University students recorded in *Acción Liberal* in 1965 and reported by Robert H. Dix.[5] Although 88% responded that their parents were affiliated with either the Liberal or Conservative Parties, only 17% of the students identify with the official wings of those parties, and 1/4 named no party or did not answer the question.

For the determined revolutionaries, there was the possibility in 1966 of joining one of the guerrilla groups whose activities were coordinated by The Revolutionary Armed Forces of Colombia whose leaders are alleged to have been trained in Cuba. A number of students were reported to have done so, but such a move took them out of the student movement.

This lack of confidence in the present governors of Colombia affairs was present not merely among the middle class students interviewed in the public universities, but also among students in private universities like Los Andes and the Catholic University, Javeriana. The present system of political governance was

[5]Dix, Robert H., *Colombia, The Political Dimensions of Change,* Yale, 1965, p. 349.

perceived by them to offer little hope for their participation in a process of orthodox type change. Equally important, that system lacked legitimacy in their eyes.

No philosophy of legitimacy can assure the loyalty to a governing regime of important functional groups, required for dealing effectively with the political and economic problems presented by the process of modernization, if the members of those groups occupy the status of second class subjects. Whether that process involves a changing mode of production and its impact on social and economic structure or a changing structure of power relations among nations, only the involvement of those groups in genuine participation as decision makers will fully legitimize the regime or the system of governance in their eyes.

The students at the moment are not such essential functionaries, but they soon will be. And they know it. Moreover, they come from a stratum of the population, the middle classes, which even their superficial knowledge of the modernization process in other nations tells them produces essential actors in that process. As a group in Colombia that class has been denied effective participation. If the students were few, they might anticipate with hope the possibility of being coopted into the inner circle Establishment as a result of making the right contacts or demonstrating unusual ability, a hope that earlier generations of students appear to have acted on. But they are many, and the positions which will need to be filled are many. In the light of that fact and of the students' lack of confidence in the predisposition of the present political system and its managers to extend the possibility of participation widely enough to modify radically their own grip on the nation's affairs and their dominant control of the life and work of Colombians, direct action is seen by a significant number of students as a logical and rational approach to needed change and to realizing their ambition to be the instruments of that change.

At first glance the political arrangements in Mexico would appear to provide students with greater prospects, at least after they have finished their university course, for participating in the political process. To be sure, they are aware that public decision making is highly centralized in a strong executive which takes account of the group interests represented in the internal organization of the monolithic Party of the

Continuing Revolution. The development of consensus and
its translation into action is a process occurring within the
Party rather than in the legislature, but a large number of
functional interest groups are represented in the party apparatus
or have influential access to the President. These functional
interest groups cover all of those with which any future career
of a student will be identified,[6] whether related to the farm,
labor, or popular sectors.

Students are aware that individuals identified with some
formally organized interest group have at least the prospect
of some representation in the Party's and hence in the nation's
political process although they have no illusions that the intraparty interactions are free from the influence of differential
power statuses among the participants. PRI is not perceived,
however as *dominated* by a traditional oligarchy as in Colombia.
Indeed all of the presidents since 1920 have come from the middle class. Student organizations are not among those included
in the Party structure although as individuals students might

[6]PRI is organized in three sectors giving nominal representation to the
following groups and organizations:
   I Farm Sector
     1. *Confederación Nacional Campesina*
     2. *Sociedad Agronomica Méxicana*
   II Labor Sector
     1. 8 unions affiliated with B.U.O., as well as a number of smaller
       independent unions.
     2. 5 anti-B.U.O. unions.
   III Popular Sector
     1. Civil Servants (Teachers & Bureaucrats unions.)
     2. Cooperative (2 organizations.)
     3. Small farm proprietors (2 organizations.)
     4. Small merchants.
     5. Small industrialists.
     6. Professionals - Intellectuals.
     7. Youth (*Confederación de Jovenes Méxicanos*)
     8. Artisans
     9. Women's organizations (2).
    10. Diversified persons: Large commercial, industrial, and financial
       organizations or dominant individuals in these areas have an in-
       fluence through access to the President.

P.R.I. candidates for office are practically assured of election. It has
been estimated that the proportions of candidates named by the several sectors are, Farm, 40%; Labor, 20%; Popular, 40%.

be members of the Confederation of Mexican Youth, which is included. However much the promise of post-university participation, as students they have no representation in the monolithic Party activities, and since opposition parties have little chance of significant success in electing their candidates to the legislatures (and no chance in the case of the all important executive posts), party activity in the youth wings of opposition parties is not a realistic alternative for satisfying the desire of the activist student for participation in public affairs.

Looking to their future, nevertheless, students can in Mexico see that the middle classes from which they come are represented in the existing political structure. Not only through the representation of organizations with a primarily middle class membership, but through the National Federation of Popular Organizations (an association of many professional and civic organizations and the union of government bureaucrats), the middle class exercises the dominant power in the Popular sector. And, even outside the party organization, private pressure group associations of major elements in the economic area contribute to a freedom from dependence on government. Any student, therefore, concerned with spreading widely throughout the population the possibility of participation in the political process is unlikely to consider a class revolution a necessary prelude to that achievement. Reform of the Party structure is a plausible possibility.

Nevertheless, criticism of the Party is widespread among students. The pragmatic, specific problem-solving approach of Party leaders to change and the slow pace of that change toward the proclaimed objectives of the Revolution excite no enthusiasm among the activists whose concept of needed change is emotionally toned and defined in comprehensive but very simple and almost shorthand terms.

Students are cynical about the degree to which the present Establishment is genuinely concerned to include all groups, particularly *campesinos* and workers, in the decisive processes of government. There are examples of apparently important persons who have risen from the ranks. But that these can really bring the full force of the needs and interests of the groups from which they spring to bear on the decision making process is doubted.

The monopoly of the Party in the naming of candidates for office is frequently challenged, at times by demonstrations supportive of one of the small opposition parties.

Cynicism was also marked concerning the self-serving tendencies and corruption among highly placed influential members of the Party or those who had been placed in positions in which the manipulation of the spoils system could result in personal benefit.

A very significant indication of the low confidence accorded their governmental system by Mexicans generally comes from a several nation comparative study reported in *Political Culture and Political Development*.[7] The survey of citizens' opinions included a question designed to disclose the degree of their confidence that they could expect fair treatment from the government bureaucracy and the police.

> 42% in Mexico responded that they anticipated fair treatment from the bureaucracy. 50% expected unfair treatment. (The comparable percentages for the U.S. were 85% and 9% respectively).

> 32% in Mexico responded that they expected fair treatment from the police. 5% expected unfair treatment. (The comparable percentages for the U.S. were 85% and 8% respectively).

> 30% of the Mexicans indicated they were proud of their political system. (85% in the U.S.).

It is our impression from interviews with Mexican students that a similar survey among students would indicate an even lower degree of confidence than that expressed by the general population.

Several characteristics of Colombian and, to a somewhat lesser extent, Mexican society, then, give emphasis to any frustration or dissatisfaction which may exist among students about their chances for significant present and future possibilities for orthodox participation in public affairs. In both societies all aspects of life are mightily shaped and influenced by decisions and actions of a political elite, a situation which highlights the importance of personal influence with and loyalty to, members of the elite. It therefore stresses the importance of

[7]Pye, Lucian and S. Verba (eds.) *Political Culture and Political Development*, Princeton University Press, 1965, p. 366.

the contribution of the university to one's prestige and contacts if one has any desire to influence the course of events or even the success of his own career. It also increases the frustration if the expectancies of this sort are unrealized.

This situation is intensified to the extent that there are few if any, well-established alternative institutionalized ways of influencing the course of events that provide realistic, systematic, and effective ways for an orderly and peaceful expression of the voice of the common people and the implementation of their desires. Although it is not unknown that ballots have played a part in social change, the constitutional provisions setting up an apparent electoral framework for government of, by, and for the people seems, to the realists in these countries, to stand as a lightly placed facade before the actual governing operations of a "self-appointed and self-perpetuating elite." The channel of influence is not the legislature and elected "representatives."

That the proclamation and forms of popular democracy are a facade is even clearer and more widely recognized in Colombia[8] than in Mexico. Yet in Mexico also there was an evident cynicism among students and ordinary citizens about the one party system and the all powerful influence of the elite within the various elements within the Party. The elite leadership of PRI in Mexico is commonly believed to be self-perpetuating. The actual ruling group is sufficiently small in both countries, however, the actual participation of the common people in government is sufficiently weak, so that high level decision making would appear to be more a series of "deals" among the few than a systematic and institution-alized process of problem solving under rules and popularly rooted checks. Whom you know is at least as important as what you know. Personal prestige and contacts and being "on the inside" are at least as important bases for affecting the course of events as the possession of personal ability and the rights and duties of a functional position.

[8]An educator in Medillin, Colombia, is the only one of our informants who was not completely satisfied with this observation. He comments: "The ruling elite in the government and in the industries are changing as I can see it in the last 30 years. The middle class that go to the universities are taking care of the government as the rich people don't take interest in politics. The managers of the big corporations in Colombia were the middle class students twenty or thirty years ago as the children of rich people at that time lacked interest in studying."

We know of no land where personal deals and loyalties do not influence high level decision-making. There are, however, lands where that process, and the implementation of the decisions resulting from it, are influenced, checked, and even countered by a bureaucracy and by genuine popular electoral and pressure group activity, which activity creates a recognized and effective role in influencing public affairs for those who are not a part of or on familiar terms with the "Establishment." Moreover, such a variety of pressure centers provides a "middle way" for influencing the course of events, a way alternative to submission to domination or revolution. In such countries, "His Majesty's loyal opposition" and the multitude of ordinary citizens for whom it speaks, upon whose goodwill it depends, and from whose interests it gets its mandate, are not just obstacles to the decision-making of the governing group. The members of the opposition are genuine participants in that decision-making.

But in Colombia, and in Mexico, if one is not in agreement with the decisions and actions of the governing elite, and does not have a personal influence among them, and cannot personally influence them through recognized institutional channels of popular government, the chief hope is confrontation of the decision makers with a public uproar sponsored and supported by those for whom the rulers have a fear or respect even though those respected and feared are not accepted as members of the governing "fraternity." For Latin Americans the available "middle way" between submission to domination and revolution is public demonstration.

We would not wish to create a picture of a political system so rigidly fixed in the paths of inner circle rule that no chance other than explosive demonstration exists for the effective expression of popular interests. There is a slow growth of institutionalized democracy as a means for accomplishing change in Colombia and a more rapid growth in Mexico. Against terrific odds some leaders in the governments of both countries are trying to move toward universal literacy, expansion of primary education,[9] and toward self-rule in

[9]There is a notable lack of equal emphasis upon the increase in free *public secondary* education, however. Its lack provides a restricting bottleneck for students whose families cannot afford the tuition and residence-away-from-home costs of the existing private secondary education facilities. And the chance for a university education of course presupposes a secondary education preparation. A student leader in

local matters which are essential and necessary bases for a people-centered national government and for experience in using the methods appropriate to its effectiveness, stability, and viability. The development of industrialization and the systematic operations of business and finance, however, require an orderliness and dependability of action and the countinuity of policy that are sometimes difficult to achieve when "popular sovereignty" is the arbiter of public action.

There are, to be sure, those in positions of present power who have much to lose from any change which injects a well understood and widely useable, regularized, legitimate, and continuously effective voice of the people into the conduct of public affairs, and which thereby increases the number of interests which have to be taken into account in the *daily* process of decision making on a widening number of issues. There are warnings that too rapid change could produce chaos and anarchy. The need for strong centralized decision making and leadership of a self-appointed elite is frequently expressed even in Mexico, the land of the "institutionalized revolution." Yet the movement in the development of institutionalized ways of change for the satisfaction of widespread popular concerns and needs is in the direction of providing an increasing number of non-violent and non-explosive opportunities for the expression of popular needs and desires. That growth, however, has not yet reached the stage where it has erased from the memories and habits of the many the utility of popular demonstrations as an influence on the decisions and actions of the ruling few, and as a stimulus to a "turnover" among those holding power among the elite, if not to a change in the system of elite rule itself.

Given the dominant impact of political decisions made by a self-appointed and self-perpetuating (though frequently formally elected) elite on all aspects of life, given the importance ot acquiring personal prestige and familiar contacts with the elite in order to influence those decisions, given the necessary failure of a public university degree to provide all its recipients with that prestige and those contacts, given the absence of

Medillin indicated one significance of this situation in the following words: "If I were a member of the elite interested in reducing the pressure of middle class numbers on positions now held by myself, my sons, and my friends, I would not be inclined to encourage the widening of that bottleneck by a widespread development of free *public* secondary education."

institutionalized methods for popular expression and implementation of lower middle-class desires other than demonstration, and given the lack of confidence that the present
governmental structure operates in a way which is fair and
equitable, we see no reason to believe that large numbers of
middle-class university students will cease to test the limits of
their influence on political affairs and those who rule, if
for no other reason than that it is a necessary procedure for
carrying on their careers; no reason to believe that they will
cease, when directing their attention to public affairs, to use
the only method practically available, namely demonstration.

Freedom

It is accurate to describe the public universities in Mexico and
Colombia as oases of freedom for students in the midst of an
otherwise basically constraining society the nature of social control in which contrasts sharply with that in these oases. Prior
to becoming a student a youth has experienced an authoritarian
familial, political, and religious life. A large number of the
secondary schools from which he comes in Colombia are Catholic schools where the authoritarian atmosphere has been little
changed, to judge from the reports of our informants, many of
whom had attended or who were attending these schools. The
opportunity for self-realization by his own efforts in either
country is minimal, and the constraints are numerous. His
adult associates experience the same lack of opportunity for
free choice at least outside of a small primary group of which
the head, perchance, may be accorded the chance to initiate
action not only for himself, but for others. For the great
masses of people the constraints of poverty, illiteracy, and the
underdeveloped opportunities for popular democracy make even
freedom of protest an aspiration rather than an experienced
principle of life.

From such constraining society the student comes to the
university, and into that constraining society he will return,
hopefully with some increased chance for self-determination.
But as a student, and certainly in relation to the university,
he is a free, or, at least, a relatively free man. Theoretically, the
police are barred from stepping onto the campus. "The University City" is off limits for them. It is a sanctuary for free
men. The administrators, faculty, and students in the National

Universities pride themselves on the addition of the word "autonomous" to the names of these institutions.[10]

That, for many of the students, direct action is more an expression of a generalized urge to be personally free in a generally constraining society than of a movement to make the world over into a freer world for all, is indicated by the almost accidental character of the kinds of things students demonstrate for or against.[11] One thing that most of the nominal objectives have in common is resistance to anything that is symbolic of someone else making decisions about matters in which they feel those affected should have a voice. Anti-Yankee demonstrations, for example, nominally organized for or against American policy, are set off by anything that makes visible any Yankee action or persons affecting them or other Latin Americans, such as the appearance of a U. S. warship or a Vice-President, or a distinguished Presidential representative. Both pro-Castro and anti-Castro demonstrations can fit this pattern. The arbitrary raising of bus fares, reduction of appropriations for the university, the instituting of entrance examinations, the appointment of a new rector or dean of whom some students don't approve, refusal of an employer to bargain with a union, or dissatisfaction with and opposition to dictators, all have furnished the occasion for demonstrations *against* the abridgement of someone's (and usually their own) freedom to have a controlling voice in their own affairs.

Where are the demonstrations *for* the new labor code, *for* a basic program for social reform of the tax system, *for* the extension of secondary public education, *for* the removal of graft in high places, *for* a more just land distribution system, *for* a rational national economic and inter-American affairs policy, *for* a revised tax which would make more of the country's income available for investment in public or private enterprise rather than for deposit in Swiss banks? We would not leave the impression that there are no tendencies for students in general to favor such reforms, but only that

[10]The "autonomy" movement which began in the University of Córdoba in Argentina in 1918 spread through Latin America, and the coalition of students and faculty to secure "autonomy" and non-interference became a formal tradition on a generalized Latin American scale.

[11]See Chapter 3.

these do not appear to be the objectives stimulating demonstrations.

Added, then, to the universally observed tendency of adolescents and young people to throw off the constraints of authorities and circumstance, is the stimulus from the expectancy of having the experience of living for a few years in an oasis of freedom, participating in the governing of that oasis, and wielding effective influence on the surrounding society. Soon enough will the bonds constraining the rest of the population restrain *their* freedom again, unless, perchance, they can get into politics and become intimately related to the small minority which rules their country. It is plausible to assume that a substantial number are stimulated by the expectancy to bring to life that freedom in experience, at least for a few years; that occasions for direct action are welcomed by some, *whatever the issue*, as a symbolic expression of this freedom and self-assertion; and that any threat to the realization of this experience of freedom, or to the freedom of the universities themselves, will stimulate direct defensive action among a number for whom the expectancy that they can for a time be free men is of central importance.

The Reasons for Public Permissiveness

The attempts of the students to seek, through direct action, participation in modifying university and public policy and to realize themselves as free men does not, of course, go unchallenged by the university or public authorities. Since 1960 in both countries many rectors and deans have adopted an increasingly stern attitude toward the disruptive impact of student demonstrations and strikes on the campus. Not only disciplinary action against the activists, but the suspension and expulsion of students who neglected their studies to devote themselves to managing the disruptive tactics have become more frequent. The observed reaction of liberal educators in many countries to student activism has become evident in Mexico and Colombia also: "We recognize your freedom and right to dissent, but not to destroy the freedom and right of all students to continue their education uninterrupted by your tactics." At least two rectors in public universities, one in each country, have been forced to resign by student rebellions originally sparked by such disciplinary measures.

Also in both countries the Presidents have taken a stronger

hand in student demonstrations which spilled out into the streets, and in several cases public authorities have even challenged the sacred doctrine of university autonomy by "invading" the campus with police or troops. Yet there has always been, and still is, a noteworthy reluctance to deal harshly with students even when their manifestations of free action become disturbing to the public order. This reluctance is sufficiently obvious to cause editorial writers and critics to decry the "softness" of university and public authorities in dealing with student demonstrations and strikes, and to propose a "get tough" approach to regulating the direct action of the students. This reluctance was more obvious in Latin America than in the other countries we visited, and justifies a special discussion which will not be necessary in the case of those other countries.

We were talking one evening after our return from Colombia and Mexico, with a lawyer about the active part played by students in educational and political affairs in those countries. "Your analysis of the factors that motivate them," he said, "clears up a lot of things I've been wondering about. But it leaves unanswered an even more puzzling question. Why can they get away with it? Why don't the university authorities and the police clamp down on that sort of thing? Things have come to a pretty pass when a bunch of kids can tell the faculty and deans how they should run their own show. And why the public authorities pay attention to such antics is more than I can see."

Our friend was raising a question which must have occurred to many who read these pages. Why, when Latin American students take things into their own hands by direct action, are they as successful as they are? They don't always succeed of course. But they get results frequently enough so that their success in getting a response from their elders indicates the possession of a power the reasons for which are not self-evident.

The more one ponders this question, the more evident it is that the answer leads us even more deeply into the characteristic features of the factors at work in Latin American life and culture than does any explanation of why students make use of direct action in the first place. If for no other reason, the attempt to work out an answer is an instructive task. When a foreigner undertakes that task, however, doubts arise as to whether the problem presented is essentially researchable. We are dealing with a complex of factors the inter-relationships of a large number of which are felt rather than comprehended even by thoughtful people who have lived all their lives in these countries.

Student success in influencing university and public affairs implies a willingness on the part of university and public authorities and people generally to permit a degree of freedom of action, and even to modify their decisions and actions in the direction of the desires or demands of the students. It would, of course, be possible to ask these authorities and a sample of the population directly what the basis is for such permissiveness on their part. We have done this, but not of course to anywhere near the extent necessary to produce the volume of data needed as a basis for valid conclusions. Moreover, aside from the adequacy of the amount of data, there is the question as to the reliability of the answers which constitute that data. Furthermore, our experience in questioning on this matter is that few people have thought analytically about it, and certainly not deeply. One suspects that the tendency to give ear to the voice of the students is so embedded in the habit patterns of those involved that the answer closest to the truth would be, "It has always been so."

In spite of the difficulties in arriving at reliable answers, however, the question itself is an important one. If one tries to fit together the factors named in discussions on the matter with certain features of the culture and life of people in these countries, he can at least suggest a set of not implausible hypotheses. There are three groups whose reactions have a bearing on the matter; the university faculty and administrators, politically motivated public officials, and the general public, or more precisely speaking, that portion of the public who are related to the students by bonds of family, clan, and friendship. The basis for any tolerance in their response to student activism ranges from sympathy, through empathy and admiration, to fear.

The Case of University Authorities

Implicit in many of the circumstances we have been discussing are suggestions as to why university authorites respond in a way not unfavorable to the possibility that students can experience "success" from their direct action. We can begin therefore by abstracting from the discussion of other areas of motivation certain observations and focus them on this question of the reasons for student influence.

There exists in the very concept of the origin of the public university a place for student initiative and participation. The Bologna idea of the university as a corporation of students, transmitted via Spain, where the idea found its greatest flowering, to South and Central America, has had a sufficient influence to raise an immediate presumption of the legitimacy of student participation in the ordering of the affairs of a university there.

Traditionally the students have played a role in the governing of the universities, a fact which has fixed this role as normal; and this normality is supported by organizational arrangements giving them recognized authoritative representative positions on the governing bodies of the universities. A role embedded in traditional organizational arrangements is difficult to modify even if the utility and appropriateness of that role has been made questionable by changing events and circumstances.

The faculty and administrators have themselves been students living within this governing relationship pattern, and many of them possess both an empathy and sympathy with the students' continuance in activity consistent with this pattern. Moreover, rare indeed is the professor or administrator who did not himself participate in demonstrations in his student days. Their present responsibilities (if they shoulder them) may make such demonstrations an inconvenience and even a serious disturbance to the even tenor of their ways, but the negative reaction which might be expected is not unmixed with an understanding of the students' position.

Some administrators, faced with a division and conflict of forces among their several faculties, their deans, and professors, find in the students useful allies in pursuing their objectives against opposition to their policy and efforts arising from these sources. They also sense at least a possibility that the students' governing role might even be turned to advantage in the governing of students.

Professorial encouragement of, and assistance to, student direct action is not unknown. Now and then, we were told by faculty members themselves, a professor is suspected by his colleagues of inciting a student strike for his own selfish purposes or in support of an educational or political objective which is close to his heart. A student strike is obviously a good device for forcing out an unwanted colleague, or for promoting a reform in which a faculty member as well as students may have a sincere and legitimate interest. There are on record cases of faculty members being removed from their posts for such incitement to student action, indicating both the possibility of the presence of this sort of thing and the general disapproval of it, as inappropriate and unprofessional behavior, by the more orthodox majority of faculty members and university officials.

Many of the students will eventually (and not in the too far distant future) become politicians, with a voice in determining the allocation of national resources to the development of universities and with the opportunity to take other action by which a formally and constitutionally autonomous university is encouraged to operate consistently with the interests of the state and the ruling regime. A reasonable consideration now, by university authorities, of the demands of student leaders will do no harm to future favorable consideration of the financial and material and personnel needs of the universities by those students then become politicians, particularly in a political system in which influential personal contacts play so large a role.

Finally the fracturing of the university into what amounts to autonomous faculties or schools reduces the control and disciplinary powers of the central administration. The official academic and administrative coordination among the faculties or schools is weak and in some cases practically nonexistent. Student activity can move from one faculty to another without ever having to face the combined authority of the entire university staff, or an office of overall university coordination and regulation.

At the same time the occupants of such centralized administrative posts, although possessing in practice little power to handle, as university officials, a matter like student demonstrations, are assumed to possess this power which they often do not or cannot exercise. Nor have the members of the teaching staffs or administrators of the several faculties or schools been assigned specific responsibility or authority in such matters.

The result is the presence of a vacuum in the matter of control of, and discipline with respect to, student action outside of the classroom.

The Case of the Public Authorities

A large proportion of student demonstrations in Mexico and Colombia are directed toward university authorities. Those which attract greatest attention outside the country itself, of course, are those which are occasioned by disagreement with public policy, by opposition to or support of particular factions involved in the conduct of public affairs, by developments abroad considered to affect unfavorably domestic affairs, and by reactions to the acts of foreign companies, governments, or public figures. Such latter demonstrations become objects of concern for the public authorities, as do those having to do with internal university affairs when they spill over into the streets.

Ultimately, to be sure, those responsible for public order must say, "Students go home," and enforce that order. But there are many ways of clearing the streets involving different degrees of persuasion and force, not excluding paying attention to the students' demands if they are definitely focused, and even acceding to those demands. It is not necessary to seek explanations for the employment of force for putting down student demonstrations by the police and the political officials from whom they get their orders. What does call for explanation, however, is the frequent "kid-glove" handling of these affairs, and the evidence that the students' objectives are on occasion realized.

The apparent influence of the students on certain occasions was sufficiently obvious so that a limited number of our informants suggested that the students only succeeded because of aid and encouragement from within the government, politicians giving tacit consent and support to the demonstration itself. Students were "used," these informants said "duped", into believing they themselves had influence they actually did not possess. Such a suspicion would be difficult, if not impossible, to verify. In any case, there are, we think, sufficient other grounds for the attitude of the public authorities toward the students so that it is not necessary to rely for an explanation on the presence of any such cynical and sophisticated tactics by government leaders.

A circumstance which is always present is the degree of autonomy enjoyed by the national universities. The universities have a long history of struggle to be free from domination by the state, which in operational terms meant free from the whims or dominance of colonial governors and domestic dictators, as well as, at times, of the ecclesiastical hierarchy. In Mexico for example the use of the word "autonomous" is proudly pointed to by educators as symbolic of the victory in this struggle. Public authorities are aware of this charter of self-determination, and whatever their need or desire to influence informally the affairs of the university, they need a visible and popularly understood symbol of their acceptance of a "hands off" policy. Two symbols of this fall readily to hand. One is the acceptance of the university grounds as a sanctuary into which the police and soldiers are forbidden to go. In 1961, in the anti-bus-fare-increase demonstration of the students in Mexico City,[12] about 100 buses were taken onto the University grounds, a procedure about which the municipal authorities could do, or did do, nothing because the University grounds were "off limits" for them. A second symbol is the soft-gloved treatment of student demonstrators and what appears to be serious high-level attention to their activated demands.

A second circumstance favorable to the effective influence of students with public officials is the high regard in which the rulers of the land hold the intellectual; the respect, in any case, they have for men of knowledge. In Mexico even the untutored among the revolutionists of 1910 had intellectuals on their staffs. Actually, prominent people among the rulers in both countries take pride in being considered intellectuals and literary figures. Now the inclusion of the students in general in that distinguished and highly respected category may in most cases stretch considerably the connotation of the word "intellectual," but the association of "intellectual" and "man of knowledge" with "student" is at least a contributing factor in establishing the presumption that they are worth paying attention to.

We are told that in former days, when those attending the university were comparatively few, there existed a sort of fraternity among students and former students in government positions which led to mutual friendliness and respect and a

[12]A knowledgeable and responsible observer in commenting on this strike told us, "Several very old buses were burned in the streets, but the students vehemently denied that they participated in these acts of destruction. In fact after holding the buses on campus for over a week and winning the removal of the 5 cent increase in fare which was the original cause of the demonstration, the students called upon the Government to come and accept the return of the buses because the responsible members of the student demonstration began to be fearful that the leftist students who were making more unreasonable demands might begin to destroy the buses and thus negate the gains which had been realized and turn public opinion against the whole movement."

consciousness of class membership which established a readiness for mutual confidence. With the growing number of students, the qualifications for membership in such a fraternity go beyond being a student, but what remains of this assumption of mutual interests and group membership among those who have achieved this status would, we suspect, incline educated public authorities to listen more considerately to a student than to an ordinary man on the street who had equal qualifications otherwise.

Moreover in the midst of the insecurities of a political livelihood, no public official of today can be unaware that he may need political allies tomorrow, and that many of these students, perhaps the leader asking for an audience, will become a potential party or administrative supporter or enemy. Where personal favors loom large as a customary and necessary element in political tactics, the confrontation with the student leaders, who are likely to become politically influential in the future is a situation to be handled with some delicacy.

It is, however, we believe the relationship of the student to the possibility of the current regime remaining in power which accounts chiefly for the influence of student direct action on public authorities. The students wield political power affecting this possibility in at least two ways, their influence with the general electorate, and their potential function as the spark which can set a public demonstration ablaze, an event of which even dictators must be fearful.

We have spoken of the facade of popular suffrage, but the trend is toward the transformation of the suffrage, at least among folk to the level of the increasingly numerous lower middle classes, into more than a facade, a genuine popular basis for legitimacy of the regime in power.

The trend once started toward popular sovereignty through government by ballot is, aside from temporary setbacks or the possibility of a revolution establishing a totalitarian state, an irreversible trend. In Mexico and Colombia we sensed no tendency for political leaders to advocate or promote such a totalitarian state-oriented revolution. If it is granted that leaders of the present ruling class, both those in power and those out of power, seek to have the stability or change they advocate and promote legitimized by the ballot, then the first type of student power is a factor to be considered and respected. If we recognize the hope which appears to be characteristically placed in the student by his family, particularly by middle class families, as the embodiment of their hopes for advancement, the influence of a student on the number of votes cast would appear to extend considerably beyond his own. If to the influence of his blood relatives is added the influence he is likely to have on his godparents and their families, and on his friends unable to attend the university, it would seem to be within the realm of reasonableness and possibility to assume an impact of a student on from 5 to 10 votes. Even taking the lower figure of 5, the 90,000 students in the National University in Mexico City alone would carry some weight with 450,000 satellite votes. No politician can afford to ignore that number of potential votes.[13]

An even greater source of student influence with the public authorities grows out of the nature of the political power struggle in these countries. The situation is more relevant to Colombia, where two traditionally feuding parties exist, than to Mexico where political differences are hidden from the public eye by the incorporation of all numerically important political factions in one monolithic party. Echoes of the uneasy truce of the factions within that party are, however, not hard to hear in the conversation of knowledgeable folk outside the arena of active political manipulations. But certainly in Colombia, any regime which desires to remain in power must be constantly alive to the threat to that desire which exists in the circumstances and the series of chain reactions which have led to the overthrow of governments by palace revolution on so many occasions since the early 19th Century, when Colombia became a nominal republic. And any faction within the one party in Mexico desiring to perpetuate its controlling influence must take that threat into account.

In Colombia, we start with the traditional circumstance of long and bitter feuding between the Liberals and the Conservatives, a feuding which does not cease when one party or faction wins the right either by *coup* or election to manage the public business for a period. Traditionally when the "ins"

[13]Most of the critics of the original draft commented that this was a gross underestimation of the impact of students on the popular and easily influenced votes. Others indicated moreover that any positive government aid in the solution of problems raised by the students having to do with the university, increased for the politicians their power residing in popularity so that they gained both power and votes by this "popular" defense of the student.

were in, the "outs" were out.[14] The slate was wiped as clean as an exaggerated spoils system could wipe it. A recognized and respected participating *loyal opposition* has, in the past, been no part of the arrangements for governing. The result is that the "ins" must be constantly alive to the possibility of a successful *coup* by the army, a demagogue, or a dictator, or a *junta* utilizing the frustrated desire for the restoration to power of the "out" faction as the source of energy for the overthrow of the existing regime. And they must be constantly on guard to prevent the kinds of circumstances which provide an opportunity for that to happen. The situation at the present time is changing, but it is the past which produces the interpretations as to the meaning of present events.

The experience of history teaches rulers that one of the most usual circumstances providing the opportunity for their loss of position is widespread popular uneasiness, restlessness, and demonstration. It is as though a giant bonfire of public readiness for direct action were laid and well sprinkled with the gasoline of accumulated public dissatisfaction and frustration, ready for a spark to set it ablaze that would provide a major circumstance in the midst of which an attack from the *disloyal* opposition could be anticipated.

The experience of history also teaches rulers that, as often as not, a student demonstration is the spark which ignites the general public bonfire. When that spark is cast into the human materials prepared, the public has, in the students, either heroes or martyrs, depending on the way their demands and demonstrations are handled. Although either result is an aid to the enemy and a threat to the continuance of the ruling regime in power, heroes are less damaging than martyrs. It is in the light of this sort of possible chain reaction that rulers, by giving attention to, and by the astute handling of, student direct action, seek to avoid the spark being cast.

---

[14]The temporary truce established a few years ago between the parties by the terms of which they agree to exchange the occupancy of important governing positions including the presidency, appears on the surface to have altered this situation, but signs are already appearing that the extremists of both the right and the left are uneasy about this artificial "brotherhood." It is most unlikely that such an arrangement can long reflect the reality of political interests and forces.

The Case of the Public

A further question arises, however, in connection with this chain of possible events. Why is the spark of student demonstration likely to set off a blaze of supporting public action? What accounts for the influence of the students among a potentially and dangerously active *public*?

Let us first of all realize that students, in a country where from 65% to 70% of the population is under 30 and the average life expectancy is well under 50, are not looked upon as a bunch of immature adolescent kids, not yet dry behind the ears. Most of their actions are taken seriously, not considered to be the pranks of youngsters. Moreover, the respect for the man of knowledge extends widely among the people, and the popular image of the student contains this as an important ingredient.

More important as a basis for favorable public reaction to the direct action of students is the traditional reputation of students as the chief carriers and defenders of the aspirations and ideals of the people for increased welfare, social justice, and people-centered government. They have held to liberal views on fundamental issues. They have been in the forefront of opposition to dictators. They have expressed if not implemented a sentimental identification with the underprivileged and the unfranchised. They have been associated with opposition to the military when the actions of that group have been unpopular. They have been initiators and, if not initiators, effective activists, in the promotion of these causes of interest and concern, and often of desperate importance, to the voiceless people of the land; and the record of their successes is clear for all to hear about even if they are unable to read. If student activists succeeded, the people had their heroes. If they failed, the people had their martyrs. Heroes or martyrs, both helped to create the image of the students as the guardians of the aspirations and ideals of the common people.

Who else or what other group in the land has a consistent reputation for doing that? The church, the women, the army, the parliament, a particular political party, the labor movement, outstanding men of, or spokesmen for, the people in each succeeding generation? Is the image of the Student as the carrier of the aspirations and hopes of the common man, simply a myth supported by a few outstanding events such as the part played in the overthrow of dictator Rojas Pinilla in Colombia?

There were those who suggested as much. But when we put the question, "Who else in the land has traditionally even a mythical reputation for performing this essential task?" the respondents in Colombia were silent, as were those in Mexico after naming a few revolutionary leaders like Zapata and Juárez.

The reputation for such service, whether based on myth or the solid fact of performance, can of course be destroyed by use of the power, grounded in that reputation, for selfish or foolish or socially meaningless objectives. And there are occasions when student strikes and demonstrations must have appeared to ordinary folk as being of that character.

One resident of Mexico City gave an excellent example. He said: "It certainly is possible for the students themselves to destroy their influence by selfish or foolish or socially meaningless objectives. We had an interesting example of this several years ago when the students of the Polytecnic Institute in Mexico City were out on strike for a period of 53 days. At first the public was very much in sympathy with the students since their announced aims or goals were to receive a larger appropriation of Government funds for improved laboratory facilities and other buildings. However, when it was found that the students had included among their demands, 'Vacations with pay' and when the students, themselves, in the course of their demonstrations began to destroy property by breaking into motion picture houses without paying, vandalism in bakeries and restaurants in the course of their marches, etc., public opinion turned definitely against them. During this period of strike the police had been given strict orders by the Government never to interfere in a student demonstration, and therefore the students became more and more drunken with their own power and caused a great deal of damage to private property, which the police, when called, never tried to protect.

"Finally articles began to appear in the Mexico City newspapers recommending that people buy firearms of their own to protect themselves and their property against student vandalism, and public opinion turned more and more against the students. Finally one morning at 5 A.M. the Government gave orders to the Mexican Army to surround the Polytecnic Institute, awaken the students who were sleeping in the dormitories, and notify them that, from that point on, the student dormitories were going to be taken over as Army barracks. This action on the part of the Government was applauded wholeheartedly by the public and the students gave up their strike without any

further results. The dormitories were occupied for over two
years by the army for use as barracks and the students at the
Polytecnic suffered a severe loss in prestige and influence."

Should the radical influence in the student groups increase
the tendency to "carry things too far," this would increase
public disfavor for the students' direct action. Leftist radicals
and revolutionists are not the only ones whose exuberance
for a cause or whose lack of concern for public order encourages
them to actions beyond the common sense tolerance point of
even the man on the street. But the traditional strategy of the
revolutionists at least has a place for disturbance and confusion,
for exaggerated demands, and for "training" in group protest,
whatever the immediate issue, which is conducive to the extension of their tatics beyond that tolerance point.

At the moment, however, we think it can be recorded correctly
that the possibility that student initiated direct action will touch
off supporting public reaction is grounded in the relevance of
student prominence and success to their families' upward mobility, and in the traditional expectancy that the students can
be counted on to support moves which are in the interests of
accelerating the progress of the common people toward greater
justice and well-being, and toward a greater voice in the determination of their own affairs and destinies.

Competence in a Career

The final group of components in the image of the Student is
closely related to the subject of his ultimate impact on industrial development as well as on all other aspects of the social
system. These components have to do with the expectancy that
the student is acquiring, and that in the end he will possess,
those qualities which make him outstanding among the population in his capacity to perform the tasks of a particular professional, occupational, or public service role in society. He is
supposed to be a man of more than average initiative and ambition, a quality he is naturally assumed to possess by virtue of
the fact that by going to the university he has presumably
seized the chance to improve his capacities and opportunities.
But the expectancies as to his qualities are even more specific.
He is assumed to be an actual or potential leader, a man of
intellect, general knowledge, and analytical ability, as well as
a man of more than average ability and skill in a particular

profession or occupation by virtue of the university training he receives.

In the cases of all the students interviewed, the motivation to realize in one's person this vocational and career aspect of the image of the Student was high; indeed it was clearly, for many and perhaps a majority, their primary motivation. The interviews were not, of course, with a random sample, so this observation cannot safely be universalized. But in discussing the structure of the universities with all groups, the words "faculties," "schools," and "careers" were used almost interchangeably. One gains the impression, however, that a "career" is by large numbers often considered to be something quite different from, and superior to, a "job," in the sense of putting to "work" the technical knowledge and skills one acquires through a university education. One gains the impression that ideally one should begin a "career" somewhere near the top, in a position which carries with it the prestige and distinction to which the holder of a university degree is "entitled." It was frequently reported that at least the best of the graduates from Law, Engineering, Economics, and even Medicine frequently were able to realize this aspiration and occupy high positions in government or in private industry as managers, as liason men, assistants to the president, "fixers," consultants, etc. In such positions they would find a minimal constant opportunity for "putting to practical work" any *technical* knowledge and skills with which a university education might have supplied them.

It would be surprising if the tradition of the university as a provider of titles, as the producer of an elite "non-working" class, did not encourage a number of students to underestimate the "preparation for work" aspects of their university experience. Yet the realities of requirements for operating an industrialized society are becoming more evident, and the students interviewed were becoming increasingly aware of these. It would be equally surprising if a substantial number, particularly those from the middle classes, were not aware of these requirements, and if this awareness, plus the realization that the places at the top attainable through influence, prestige, and contacts are limited in any society, did not indicate to them that their only hope of advancement lay in their demonstration of their competence even in white collar work.

The desire to become functionally more competent, of course, need not exclude the desire to have the prestige and the contacts with influential people associated with a university degree and experience, especially when these latter qualifications are so closely associated with vocational success. Indeed in Colombia and Mexico these qualifications can be considered as important *vocational* attributes and their acquisition could well be considered by students as of significance equal to the acquisition of professional or occupational knowledge and skill.

Actually, as is to be expected, the integration of these status and vocational components in the image of the Student has not been achieved. The image is confused at the moment; it hasn't really "digested" the growing and necessary emphasis on the student as highly trained for a particular useful vocation, an emphasis which has come to the fore with the increasing complexity of the occupational structure, and the skills of thought and self-discipline demanded by a modern economy. The hold-over elements from the image of the Student as the possessor of a prestigeful title, one freed from restraints imposed on ordinary mortals, as well connected and important politically, has complicated the existing image as a guide both to the expectancies of the students and the ordering of the educational system.

There are colleges, sometimes called "universities," in both countries resembling the American community colleges which cater almost entirely to ambitious middle-class people, young and old, who wish to rise in their middle-level jobs as accountants, technicians, medical assistants, middle-management, secretaries, teachers, etc. Since their degrees do not have the prestige value of degrees from the older universities, they do not attract many students for whom such prestige is the primary purpose of their investment in an education. The University of Bogotá is a good example. The students at such colleges gave the impression that they were seeking an education *primarily* to improve their working skills and knowledge related to their work. Actually many are already at work, and classes are held early in the morning and in the evening to make it possible for them to continue their full-time jobs. (This is necessary also at the National Universities, in order to accommodate those students who are working their way through.[15]) The reports that there

[15]The Williamson 1961 study of the National University in Bogotá indicated that only 22% of the students were working, 7% at full-time and 15% at part-time jobs. This figure included those who were teaching and serving their internships. The 1965 report of the National Univer-

was any substantial number of students in Universities where demonstrations occur, who were *not* interested primarily in amplifying their knowledge, their problem solving abilities, their possession of functional competence, and their capacity for genuine leadership in society, came, however, from a relatively few informants.

University Centered Frustrations to Career Competence

If the majority are, as we believe they are, genuinely seeking knowledge and training to fit them for a useful and important role in society, and the chance to live out that role, there is a potential source of frustration in the kind of training they receive, certainly in the public universities, a frustration inclining them to respond to leaders urging their participation in direct action intended to modify conditions in the university or in the operational field they hope to work in when they graduate. That frustration would arise from the perceived inconsistency between their opportunity for appropriate learning, training, and useful and satisfying employment on the one hand, and the image of the Student as a qualified leader and the performer of a useful and significant role in society on the other.

What the objective facts are concerning the quality of their education in this repect we would not presume to say on the basis of so short a period of observation. Human reactions, however, are normally made to facts as perceived. Even an *impression* of the perceptions of a sizable number of students and others is, therefore relevant to our analysis.

The perceptions reported below which would provide the students holding them with a basis for dissatisfaction with what their university experience offers them in preparation for a significant functional role are subject to checking against empirical evidence. Research directors in the fields of Education and Sociology could render a real service to the development of higher education by undertaking such studies as corrective to the perceptions of both students and others.

A commonly held and expressed complex of impressions and perceptions of what the university can offer in basic and useful knowledge and training and discipline is not very flattering to the *public* universities. Here are some of the discouraging features of that complex as reported.

---

sity of Mexico indicated that 20% of the students in the Faculties and Schools (i.e. exclusive of the Preparatoria) were self-supporting.

The symbolic term as to the inadequacy of instructors is "taxi professor." It is to be regretted that so colorful, easy to use, and harsh-sounding a word has come to stand for the reality. For it carries with it an implicitly "bad" characterization going far beyond the nature of the reality it is intended to describe. The content of this concept suggests a lecturer who is a "professor" with professional status and competence in name only, carrying on one or more jobs outside the university, who seeks a bit of additional income and the prestige of a university connection by teaching one or more courses. In the midst of his preoccupation with many concerns, he suddenly remembers it is time for his lecture, hops into a taxi, rushes to the university, delivers his lecture, and rushes back to his "real" job or jobs. Or he may not, and frequently does not, show up at all. Of course he is delighted when the students go on strike, for then he has a good excuse for not coming to class.[16] When he does come, he is poorly prepared. The part-time professor does not inspire student confidence in his educational or technical ability but rather in his ability to get ahead in the world outside the university.[17] He has, of course, no time for student conferences or participation in any joint faculty effort to improve the quality of education. His interest in his job is a purely personal one, and he has no time or inclination for building the educational institution. That task he leaves to the faculty representative, of the faculty to which he is attached, on the Academic Council. Research, for this kind of a "professor," is no part of his job.

Such is a commonly painted picture of the most important element in an educational institution, its faculty. Responsible

[16]A picture of this kind could be readily checked by reference to administrative records. Not having such records we checked the attendance of professors at the Law School at the University of Mexico each hour during the days we visited there, by simply walking past the 30 classrooms on the hour, a process that took five minutes. The professors were not present and calling the roll in that first five minutes on the average in less than one classroom of the thirty where students were assembled. What is equally interesting was that we never witnessed the students disbanding because a professor was absent before less than twenty minutes after the hour, and normally they waited much longer.

[17]The Williamson survey of student opinion (4th year) in the National University of Bogotá indicated that less than one-half thought the majority of their professors were performing their work adequately.

educators indicated that this situation was being corrected by increasing the number of full-time professors, but no claim was made that, except in the private universities, these full time people were the "typical" providers of university instruction.

Those educators who desire to encourage this sort of corrective development face great difficulties. Salaries on the whole, even of professors, are considered supplements to other main income, not an amount intended to fully support a man and his family. Amounts are geared to their part time function, i.e. as a supplement. As a main source of income, university salaries are definitely not competitive with those in business, industry, or private practice. They are certainly not adequate to encourage well-trained young men with ambitions of a family nature to make a career of teaching unless they can manage to live on "psychological" compensation. The desire to reward particularly dedicated and competent individuals is normally handicapped by the civil service concept of the professor, a concept which carries with it equal pay and perquisites for all within a specific category. "Full time" has not traditionally meant concentration of one's major working time on academic tasks. It means "holding a monopoly on a chair *from now on.*" "Time" refers to a life span, not a day's work. A professorship is more or less like an honorary degree, and for the one nominated and selected, is frequently the high point in his career, not necessarily the beginning of a long and dedicated period of service to the particular institution, or to the cause of higher education. And frequently it is not the beginning of service to education at all, but a stepping stone to personal fortune or even to political, administrative, or diplomatic posts. In the past, appointment has been at least as much on the basis of family or political in-group membership, or other forms of influence, as on outstanding scientific or scholarly excellence. In one case in which the organization of a new faculty required the simultaneous appointment of a number of professors who were chosen primarily by virtue of these nonscholarly or non-scientific qualifications, it was reported that some of the professors did not know, until the announcement was made, in what field they were supposed to teach.

If this were the complete picture, the universities would long ago have collapsed as educational institutions. We interviewed enough dedicated professors at the public universities (from whom, incidentally, the above comments came) and talked with enough students to know it is *not* the complete picture. Yet even these people were agreed upon the inadequacy of instruction at the public universities provided by "taxi" professors and of the difficulty of raising standards and building for better education without the collective support of a whole faculty whose main interest in life is in that building. Moreover it is clear that the presence of even a minority of the type of professors we have been discussing would provide many students with ample opportunity for experiencing educational carelessness and lack of concern about serious study.

It would be unlikely that such carelessness and lack of discipline on the part of any significant number of the teachers would fail to have its effect upon young students. Students have still to acquire from experience the meaning of real knowledge, the rigorous requirements for genuine learning, the single-minded devotion and discipline demanded in the search for truth and in the acquisition of those capacities for leadership grounded in ability rather than in nepotism and influence. If they do not find this in their teachers, who in a real sense, along with books (which are also in inadequate supply) *are* the university, where will they learn the significance of such attitudes and behavior?

There is a sense in which the apparent anomaly of students telling the faculty what they wish to be taught, on what schedule, according to what standards of excellence for both student and professors, is what should be expected if the professors abdicate or neglect their responsibility for such decisions and action. At least *someone,* and presumably the consumer of education, the student, might be expected to try to do something about it.

If students, however, wished to make a major contribution to the improvement of the universities, they would have to direct their manifestos and demonstrations at those factors which inhibited and those that encouraged a respect for and acceptance of the meaning of the genuinely educated and the professionally, vocationally competent man and the personal discipline required to achieve that status. It cannot be expected, however, that any but a few of the young men and women will be sufficiently experienced and mature to sense or to know these things, and then use their power to participate in the governing of the universities, to insist upon changes directed to providing an educational environment in which such respect and acceptance can develop naturally. Certainly it is expecting the impossible that any large number of students will or can do so if the overwhelming number of their professors do not by their example point the way[18]

The frustration students experience does not appear to stimulate them to direct action *which is educationally purposeful* in these ways. Few examples of direct action of this kind can be found in the records of student action since their support of the Córdoba Resolutions in 1918. Some of these resolutions demonstrated a remarkable insight of the Argentine students who framed them into the nature of the problem of making the universities genuine centers of higher learning and providers of genuine training in vocational performance and leadership ability. They made suggestions and demands for modification of some of the factors discussed above. The suggestions appear to an outsider to be positive proposals directed toward educational progress. And the manifesto aroused interest and support from students all over Latin America at that time. But in the half century since then there has been little evidence that student direct action with respect to improving the quality of their universities as centers either of intellectual or professional preparation has consistently followed the direction then suggested. There are more cases indicating the desire to make academic standards for faculty and students less, rather than more, rigorous.

An inconsistency exists, then, between that aspect of the image of the Student stressing his high level capacity for useful vocational and public performance and leadership with the experience in learning and training provided by his teachers. That inconsistency, however, is not so much a stimulant to positive particular action seeking intelligently its removal, and

[18]There are many factors other than those mentioned which contribute to the difficulties in improving the quality of higher education at the national universities. For example, the autonomy of the several faculties without, until recently, any managerial and genuinely representative system for conducting the academic affairs of the university as a whole; the primary relation of the deans to each other as "horse trading" in the distribution of funds with which to develop their little principalities, i.e. their own faculties; the lack of overall university collaboration in the determination of academic standards and practice; the lack of departmental organization making likely the development of high standards in particular disciplines; the lack of emphasis on research, etc. These matters are outside the scope of this treatise.

focusing specifically on the causes producing it, as it is a producer of general frustration and uneasiness among some students that readies them for direct action stirred up by *any* occasion. And when they are warned by "wiser" persons that their action on these occasions only makes matters worse and disturbs even the presently effective educational aspects of university life, it would be suprising if a number who had had a particularly unfavorable experience would not respond, "What have we to lose?"

We would not leave this set of observations, attempting to suggest some of the reasons for student participation in direct action, without correcting any impression that the reader may have from the foregoing discussion that generalizations made about the universities in Mexico and Colombia unexceptionally characterized *all* their educational institutions. Our only suggestion is that these factors are *sufficiently* characteristic as determinants of student experience in *enough places* so that they provide a stimulant to direct action among *enough students* to encourage the amount of direct action observed.

Particularly did we observe among the private universities in Bogotá, especially Los Andes (particularly in its Center of Studies in Economic Development), Javeriana, the University of Bogotá, and the School of Public Administration; The Tecnologico de Monterrey and the University at Guadalajara (affiliated with the National University) in Mexico; at the public universities in Cali (especially in the Medical School and School of Education) and at Medellin in Colombia; and in some faculties in both of the National Universities in Mexico City and Bogotá, an awareness that many of the factors discussed contributed to student frustration and unrest. We have mentioned several indicators of reform: the increase in the number of full-time professors; the establishing of tighter standards of admission and of stiffer qualifications for degrees; the amplification of student extracurricular activities; the gradual federalization of formerly autonomous "faculties" into a genuine *university* with a central policy and administrative apparatus for its successful implementation; the increasing and practical emphasis on the university as an instrument of service to the community as well as a means of self-realization for individuals. Such developments, of course, are not motivated merely, or even primarily, by the desire to eliminate student unrest. They grow out of the vision and efforts of educators, sometimes as individuals, and increasingly as a faculty group, to build institutions of genuine higher learning and to provide responsible service to the community. Nevertheless, such efforts may have the effect of reducing student unrest. Indeed supporting evidence for the plausibility of some of the hypotheses suggested concerning the "causes" of that unrest came from the observation of the minimal tendency to direct action on the part of students in those universities and particular faculties where such developments and reforms are taking place and have made good progress.

On the whole, in the public universities, the chances for an education characterized by access to a professionalized faculty, demanding high quality academic performance, and suggesting clear cut career futures would seem to be most favorable in the older faculties of Medicine and Engineering, and in the schools and departments providing training in the applied sciences such as Architecture and Veterinary Medicine. The chances in the newer fields of study presumably relevant to carrying out a modernization of the nation such as Business Administration, Social Science, Journalism, and Education, are not as favorable.

The fact remains that these successful and promising experiments in particular universities which modify the factors encouraging direct student action have not yet touched the experience of a critical number of public university students sufficient to alter the *general* prevalence and effectiveness of the stimulants to direct action referred to.

Society Centered Frustration

When the student turns his eyes from the university to the society in the work of which he will seek employment there is further cause for uneasiness for many. The Williamson survey of student opinion at the National University in Bogotá disclosed that nearly three-quarters of the 1st year students and over three-fifths of the 4th year students believed that 60% of university graduates would fail to find employment in the "career" for which they were preparing, during their first year out from the university. Mexican students are somewhat more fortunate in their job prospects due to the longer period over which Mexico has been undergoing industrial development and the accompanying expansion of private and, especially, government operations requiring educated manpower. The occupational opportunities for the educated have become not only more numerous but more institutionalized, and the road to them better marked. Also there were fewer charges in Mexico than there were in Colombia that nepotism and contacts were more important than ability. Not that such charges were absent, however, but there appeared to be a degree of faith among the Mexican students that the political processes giving the common man a chance to alter the political control of occupational opportunities could *eventually* be made effective. Direct action was not the only alternative.

This faith was, however, less evident in Colombia, particularly among public university students. A finding of that survey of student opinion in the National University in Bogotá to which we have already referred, disclosed that in their appraisal of five universities relative to the chances of their students on graduation finding useful, important, and satisfying positions, they placed their own public university at the bottom of the list and two private universities at the top. These findings suggest not only an uneasiness about the employment possibilities in general but a conviction that superior employment opportunities exist for those whose parents have sufficient means to send them to private schools. It was a notable fact that students and faculty members in the private universities insisted that their students were infrequently among the demonstrators on political issues. Their interest in political *change* on the whole appeared less acute than that among students in the national universities.

The case of oversupply of graduates is most serious with respect to the law students. It was commonly stated by informants in both countries that at least half of the law graduates would find a precarious living at best in the career for which they were presumably preparing.[19] It is probably not a coincidence, if this be the case, that the initiative for and promotion of many of the demonstrations, and for the initial support of petitions and manifestos is said to come from the law students. This concentration of initiative and promotion of direct action among law students is reported in both Mexico and Colombia.

The hopes of many students in both Law and the other faculties are geared to government employment in both countries.

[19]Actual studies of employment status of alumni several years out from the university would bring empirical evidence to the correction or substantiation of this widely held impression.

Indeed any expansion in the area of state management would be looked upon as an expansion of the "natural" employment opportunities for students and could therefore be expected to encourage support of socialist political emphasis. If we add to the chances for the bureaucratic type of government employment, those which are primarily political in nature although nominally concerned with enterprise management, and those which are concerned directly with political party affairs, it is clear that the occupational hopes of many students are naturally related, in a high degree, not so much to how private enterprise is developing, as to what is happening in government and politics. This awareness does not provide them with an action program with specific reform objectives, but it does encourage concern with and action with respect to political matters as something touching personal individual occupational interests very closely.

This concern is coupled in both countries, with the perception that the political system gives important occupational advantages to the inner circle members, to the relatives and friends of the "oligarchy" in Colombia, and of influential members of PRI in Mexico. It is coupled with the cynical observation that the actions of public officials are oriented toward selfish rather than public motives, and, even when directed toward the public welfare, involve very little realistic participation of those outside the inner circle. This perception provides a basis not only for interest in politics as related to occupational opportunities for all, but as related, for middle class students, to the need for reforms which would open the door wider to their own opportunities for upward mobility. Ninety percent of the students at the National University in Bogotá, surveyed in the study previously referred to, stated that the social and political structure of their country was in need of *radical* reform. We are convinced that this conviction of the need for reform is stimulated less by ideological premises than by the assumption that political and social reform are essential steps to increased economic and vocational opportunity.

Summary

The foregoing observations illustrate the way in which, in Mexico and Colombia, the relations between the image of the Student, the university experience resulting from the effort of individuals to personalize that image in themselves, and the perceptions students have of opportunities for self-actualization beyond the university, contribute to a readiness for student activism.

Specific suggestions inherent in the image of the Student that activism is the kind of behavior expected of the student are contained in the characterization of the student as idealistic, as a participant in affecting university and public affairs, and as a temporarily free person.

Readiness for activism might well arise from certain frustrations of student life produced by inconsistencies between the status or role anticipated on the basis of the image of the Student, and that realized from the university experience. As examples consider the following. The diminishing prestige value of a university training and degree was disappointing to those for whom the expectation of gaining such prestige was important. The increasing opposition to, and the restriction of the area of, student control of university affairs, and the instituting of stiffer entrance and performance requirements by university administrators produced other frustrations to those who considered important their privilege, as students, to have much to say about such things and to live in relative freedom. But most frustrating of all were the inadequacies of university instruction, curricula, facilities, and faculty for developing career and leadership competence, opportunity, and responsibility. The paucity of intra-university organizations provided inadequate extracurricular occasions for the acquisition of vocationally useful attributes and for giving meaningful expression to idealism and self-determination.

The perception of the opportunities for life work, and for gaining societal influence in a society whose Establishment was so exclusive, appeared to many to be quite inconsistent with the elite status in life envisioned as the consequence of having been a student and having acquired a degree—unless perchance they might make contact with ruling powers in that Establishment through a reputation gained in the arena of student activism. Alternatively, if they dreamed large enough, they might even hope that, through reformist or revolutionary student activism, they could modify the structure of power in their society so as to provide a greater equality of opportunity for economic, social, and political self-assertion and expression for other middle class people like themselves.

Readiness of a sufficient number to act was coupled with the occasion to act when frequent situations symbolic of these frustrations and inconsistencies arose.

Such inclinations were intensified by the permissiveness for student activism stimulated by the disadvantages both to university administrators and to the insecure political leaders of wielding repressive authority as a means of countering the students' direct action. This permissiveness in turn arose in part from the status occupied by the students among their families and *compadre* relations and friends. Moreover, the influence wielded by the students within the increasingly politically important middle class population as voters and among the whole population as stimulators of political unrest is traditional, and currently real. Students are not only potential instruments of, but symbols of, a better, freer, and more self-determining life to members of their families who have sacrificed much to give them an education, and to the members of the *compadre* groups and to friends who will never have the chance to attend the university. The traditional expectations that students are destined to be the chief carriers of ideals and the chief agitators for that better, freer and more self-determining life, reinforce their status in the minds and hearts of their countrymen.

To youth with the predispositions of the maturing of youth discussed in Chapter 6, come the experiences discussed in this chapter. The predispositions to self-discovery, identity, and self-assertion are intensified by university experiences. A readiness for *some* action is developed which can explode into demonstration and direct action when the occasion arises and a persuasive leader suggests, and points to, the way.

Specific occurrences of direct action require that there be initiators and followers and also circumstances that ready each to respond by direct action to any event or authoritative decision or action which can provide the occasion. With respect to the initiators, we suggested, in the introduction to Section II, that demonstration is the primary type of activity in which students have an opportunity to actualize any urge to leadership they may have. Student leaders were considered to be "important people." Success in their role as leaders attracted the attention of political leaders to their qualifications, and in some cases it was the prelude to a political career or resulted in the opportunity to serve directly as an agent of a political party, faction, or movement. Basically, student leaders revealed an unusually high degree of sensitivity to the same frustrations which create, in part, the readiness of other students to follow once they have been given the lead.

It does not seem necessary to posit any single set of circumstances which readies *all* the followers to respond, but rather to assume the probability that, of a multitude of circumstances, each acts to ready a limited number of students for that response, and that the cumulative effect on occasion is sufficient to provide the critical number for an effective demonstration.

Although the circumstances in all universities are not equally productive of these inconsistencies and although modifications in economic and political life are reducing the negative elements in the objective character of the opportunities beyond the university, the positive improvements in both the universities and in society have not touched the experience and perceptions of enough students to change the general situation of readiness to use the tradition-sanctioned method of demonstration, both as an assertion of their dissatisfaction and as an instrument of reform or, in some cases, revolution.

SECTION V

STUDENT ACTIVISM IN PERSPECTIVE

Student Activism in Perspective

The description, in the preceding sections, of student activism in Japan, India, Mexico, and Colombia, and the analysis of factors which encourage and stimulate that activism, enable us to view in perspective the phenomenon as it has recently become manifest in the United States. The sources of data portraying the nature of student activism in the United States are listed in the bibliographical appendix.

It can be expected that differences in culture, history, and current circumstances of political, economic, and social life, as well as in the development and nature of educational institutions and student experience, will be reflected in differences in the particular objectives and character of student activism in these lands. But the similarities in these objectives and character are more than superficial. And when one considers the conclusions as to basic sources of this activism reached by those who have studied the phenomenon in the United States, the similarities to conclusions concerning the general nature if not the specific details of these sources in other countries are striking.

In this section, we have attempted to place the interpretations made by researchers and commentators of student activism in the United States in perspective, first by charting those characteristics of the phenomenon as observed in the United States which are underscored by our observations in the four countries (Chapter 10); second, by undertaking to designate the essential variables and their interaction necessary for the formulation of a theory of student activism, in other words to indicate a model which would, hopefully, provide a framework for the interpretation of that phenomenon in any land (Chapter 11); and third, by suggesting an explanation of the universally observed tendency for student activism to escalate from a mere expression of dissatisfaction and dissent to violent and even revolutionary direct action (Chapter 12).

397

Although we have examined the findings and conclusions of those whose books and articles are included in the bibliography, the objective of such exploration of the literature has not been to summarize or to synthesize those data or to undertake a critique of those findings and conclusions. Throughout, the materials of this book have been basically a report of our own observations and of our interviews with students and other knowledgeable people in the countries named. Reference to the research and writings of others has, of course, suggested issues to be explored; and frequently reference has been made to this research and writing to amplify or support our own observations and analysis. The major objective, however, has been to provide a body of first hand observations and an analysis thereof with which other researchers could compare their own first hand observations, the analysis of their findings, and their generalizations.

Chapter 10

Universal Dimensions of
Student Activism

The worldwide student protests and other forms of activism of the mid-twentieth century are manifestations of student predispositions which have surfaced from time to time as long as there have been universities. Much of this traditional and current activism has been directed at political systems and their governors. Organized students have participated actively in the agitation for change which has preceded every major political revolution of the 19th and 20th centuries. They have criticized and protested against the policies and practices of their political governors, challenged the legitimacy of their rule, contributed to the ferment of ideas, and joined forces with other activists intent on embarrassing and discrediting the existing Establishment. They have supported, and at times precipitated, both successful and unsuccessful attempts to overthrow governments, in France in 1848, in Russia and China at the turn of the century, in Mexico in 1910, in China in 1919, and more recently in India, South Korea, Turkey, South Vietnam, Indonesia, Bolivia, Venezuela, and Colombia. Their potential for political disruption has been recognized and met with strong repressive measures in a number of countries including most South American nations, Japan, Burma, the Ivory Coast, Poland, Czechoslovakia, East Germany, Hungary, and the Soviet Union. They have mounted agitations in England, in Spain, in Italy, and in France as well as in the United States, which attack the competence, legitimacy, and moral integrity of the Establishment. They employ the rhetoric and at times the conspiratorial tactics of revolution.

Protests relative to the policies, practices, and governance of the universities have always been present, however, and in recent times have become the focus of intensified attention. In many cases student concern with educational reform is incidental to a concern with personal freedom, extra-curricular affairs, student living conditions, or with a non-academic social or political problem. Interest in broad and fundamental educational issues and purely academic reform has, in the past, received minor and temporary emphasis. The initial agitation for such reform may be followed by the appointment of a committee on which students are represented for the purpose of "restructuring" that aspect of university arrangements against which protest was raised, and there are reports of valuable contributions from the student participants. But the continuous, time consuming, and often tedious labors connected with participation in the implementing of "restructured" academic arrangements and policies has, at least in the past, appealed to very few. The assertion of the need for specific changes in the governance of educational institutions is chiefly a reinforcement of the charge of misgovernance, not a declaration of intent to volunteer for continuing and laborious service in the management of academic affairs. Primary interest is in those aspects of the governance of both political and educational institutions which provide issues capable of "radicalizing" the students.

At the same time the policies and practices of the university as an institution can be identified with governmental policies and practices so that protest and attack focused on the university can be conceived as an opening battle in the societal oriented campaign for change. Also the changes in the university may be sought in order to make it more effective as a haven from which to carry on political activity or as an actual ally in the attempt to make an impact on political and social problems. This linkage between university and politically oriented activism has been evident in South America since the launching of the "university reform" movement at Córdoba in 1918, in the developing nations since World War II, and more recently in France, England, and the United States. It indicates a consolidation of protests with respect to both educational and political objects by associating the university to the political, social, and economic system as a servant and defender of, and a trainer of manpower for, the latter.

The position taken is plausible enough. It is that each subinstitutional system in a society requires the support of the others, and that the quality of the opportunity for human development provided by each affects the possibility for the achievement of civilized life and the realization of human potential provided by the others.

The issue is frequently defined in terms of the *relevance* of the university and its functioning to the current problems of society. For some, who may be classified as reformers, this perception of interdependence becomes a foundation for a protest against the *irrelevance* to the political, social, and economic issues and needs of the time, of the university's performance and of the students' university experience. Consistent with that criticism is the demand that the university become "more involved", and devote a greater amount of its research, teaching, and public service resources and activities to the exploration and resolution of those issues and to meeting those needs. The criticism is also a prelude to the demand that the university be a haven for those scholars, scientists, and students who desire to be agents of reform in particular public policies and practices. Among the changes demanded is that educational, political, and economic institutions be reformed so as to give more effective recognition to the human rights of their participants, and provide the latter with an experience conducive to the maximum development of their potential as human beings.

The perception of interdependence becomes for others, who may be classified as revolutionaries, the foundation for a protest against what they conceive to be the all too active relevance of the university to the existing societal order. They direct their protest to the defense and support which the university offers the "System" in that it provides its managers with knowledge and techniques adapted to their self-specified requirements and with the manpower trained to their specifications. These activists also demand that the university become a haven for and an ally of those who are trying to effect a radical change, that it become a truly politicized institution. Consistent with this demand is the insistence that the university and its personnel cease their support of and service to those activities of political, economic, and military institutions which, in the judgment of the activists, infringe on human rights, destroy the civilized character of human relationships, and retard the fullest realization of human potential.

It is a truism that any form of social behavior, including student activism, will vary in nature from country to country. From our own and other investigations, however, there appear to be certain recurring features of student activism, at the present time, wherever it occurs. The classification of these common features provides a first approximation to the identification of major dimensions of the phenomenon which a theory of student activism is called upon to explain:

Student protest and activism is a behavioral manifestation among a *minority* of student activists who consider themselves as agents of change.

Five definable groups are to be found among the activists which may be characterized as emigrants, volunteers, reformers, revolutionaries, and reactionaries.

Each group of activists employs implicitly or explicitly a distinctive framework of presupposition for the interpretation of the institutional environment, its managers, their performance, and of their own status and role in that environment, and as a justification of their activism.

The most significant foci of ideological differences in such presuppositions among activists are with respect to:

> Their perception of the nature and significance of the environmental changes experienced
>
> Their perception of the nature of the "System" and its governing Establishment
>
> The allocation of responsibility for unsatisfactory problem solving
>
> Their calculation of the probability of non-forced change on the part of those considered responsible for ineffective or unsatisfactory problem solving
>
> Their confidence in the viability of existing institutions
>
> Their time horizons
>
> Their value referents

These presuppositions correspond to differential strategies and tactics among the several types of activists and their followers.

The type of action taken by the several types of activists is characterized by differential emphases with respect to:

> Initial negativism
>
> A challenge to the legitimacy of the System and the Establishment
>
> The value of confrontation
>
> Power achievement
>
> Acceptance of disruption as legitimate

The value emphases implicit in the activists' behavior are:

Reality of the present and of the present act

Desire-realization as a right

Morally defensible motivations

Community with self-actualization

Equality of the affective with the rational

Adherence to principle and consistency

Independence and freedom

Egalitarianism and anti-authoritarianism

Populism

Romantic idealism

Novel doctrinarianism

The activism is predominantly collective in nature, structure, and tactics.

Activism is not omnipresent, and it waxes and wanes.

The activism has a tendency to escalate from disagreement to protest, to demand, to the employment of orthodox methods of correction, to direct action, to civil disobedience, to violence.

We turn now to an amplification of these universal dimensions of student activism as a first approximation to the definition of what we are solving for.

A Movement of a Minority

Student activism is the product of the behavior of a minority of students, who consider themselves to be agents of change. The activist stimulators and leaders of that activism constitute an even smaller minority than the participants in its overt manifestations. The definitions of "activist," made by those conducting studies which provide the basis for an estimate of their numbers, vary. In the countries which we personally have studied, sample surveys have been made providing the possibility of an operational definition of sorts. The proportions of students who reported that they had engaged in 4 or more demonstrations were, in Colombia, 7% and, in Mexico, 4%. In Japan the proportion reported as devoting almost full time to Zengakuren activities at the peak of student activism in 1960 was 5%. If "fellow travelers" are included, informed observers estimate the proportion would be between 2 and 3 times as large.

Peterson's studies[1] in 1965 and in 1967-68, based on questionnaires to Deans in 849 and 859 United States colleges and universities respectively, would indicate that the proportion of students participating in overt protests was less that 5% in all colleges and universities, all issues considered. His respondents indicated that the proportions varied with particular issues.

[1]Peterson, R. E. *The Scope of Organized Student Protest in 1967-1968* (also *1965*). Educational Testing Service, Princeton, 1968. Peterson's two studies provide the earliest comprehensive reliable data available on the incidence and scope of overt group protest in the United States. The sources of his data are the estimates made by Deans or other personnel officers of 859 colleges and universities (849 in 1965). The estimates are probably less subject to error than the claims of protest organizers or news media reporters. His analysis supports the generalization concerning the minority status of student activism when calculations are made *on a national basis*, although the generalization does not hold when applied to particular issues or the particular campuses. The overall percentages of campuses reporting some organized protest were (1967-1968) as follows (extremes of variations indicated in parentheses):

1. Curriculum inflexibility: 15% (11% of teachers colleges and Protestant colleges to 19% of technical institutions and independent universities)
2. Controversies surrounding a particular faculty member: 20% (7% of tech. inst. to 29% of ind. univ.)
3. Dormitory regulations, parietal hours, etc.: 34% (26% of public liberal arts colleges to 41% of tech. inst.)
4. Alleged racial discrimination: 18% (7% of tech. inst. to 41% of ind. univ.)
5. Insufficient student participation in policy setting: 27% (19% of tech. inst. to 41% of ind. univ.)
6. The draft: 25% (6% of teachers colleges and 15% of Catholic inst. to 55% of ind. univ.)
7. On campus military recruiting: 25% (6% of teachers colleges and 15% of tech. inst. to 42% and 48% of public univ. and ind. univ. respectively)
8. On campus recruiting by C.I.A., or war production firms: 20% (2% of teachers colleges and 4% of Protestant inst. to 60% of ind. univ.)
9. Vietnam war: 38% (21% of teachers colleges to 53% and 68% of public univ. and ind. univ. respectively)

For example 4½% to 10% were the proportions reported for protests against various student-administration-arrangements and relationships (6½% for lack of student voice in policy setting) and 4% to 6% for issues related to off campus affairs (5½% relative to the Vietnam war). On particular campuses the proportions of students involved in particular demonstrations or strikes have been estimated as much higher.

Figures on membership in leftist organizations normally associated with overt protest are most untrustworthy. Even the most optimistic claims by the officers of these radical and liberal organizations would place their membership at between 1% and 2% of all students and their estimates of their "following" at 2 to 3 times that percentage.

The conclusion that student activism is a minority phenomenon in no way diminishes the significance of that activism for the persons involved, for those students and other members of the university community who experience its impact on their life and work and for the general community. The tactics of a very few can disrupt the educational process for all for a time. The settlements made to end the disruptive effects pertain to arrangements and policies affecting, for good or ill, all students. Direct action frequently produces a dilemma for those responsible for maintaining law and order but who are committed to freedom of speech, association, and action. Campus disorders have been known to spill over into streets and to face both university and public authorities with a threat to the very perpetuation of the institutions of which they are the guardians.

The same generalizations can be made of all social movements, and, while we have found reason to avoid the universal characterization of student activism as a student *movement*, the analogy holds in some respects. Like social movements of all sorts, student activism is directed to the achievement of institutional change in policies, practices, arrangements, mechanisms, and priority of values, changes oriented toward the satisfaction of group and collective needs and demands rather than purely personal and individual needs and demands. And whether the social movement takes the form of a labor movement, a pacifist movement, a religious movement, a student Christian movement, a communist or socialist movement, a movement for international cooperation or government, a peasant movement, a moral rearmament movement, a civil rights movement, it is always a behavioral manifestation of a minority. The minority involved may be small or substantial, but all accounts reveal that the minority faces a continuing problem in convincing members of the majority of the relevant population, potentially recruitable for participation, that they should commit themselves to change (which the terms "movement" and "activism" imply) either in themselves or in their institutional environment relevant to the needs of the total population.

If the change is accomplished and gains widespread acceptance, and no other issue takes its place, the movement is finished.

The chief ingredient in the self image of the minority who are overtly involved as activists in the manifesations of student activism (as in the case of those involved in the sorts of social movements indicated above) is that they conceive of themselves as *agents of change*, change oriented to the satisfaction not simply of themselves or the minority of their comrades actively engaged, but of the total population whom they consider to be subject to the same conditions and circumstances of life and work as themselves, although the latter may be unconcerned about and apathetic toward the progress they could effect by becoming actively involved in "the movement."

Five Classes of Activists

The normal connotation of "activism", then, assumes the engagement of a minority, in a given population, who are committed to changing the status quo. The status quo is stabilized and perpetuated by the predispositions of the vast majority to accept, or at least to tolerate, and live in accordance with, traditional arrangements and rules, and to adapt the conduct of their daily affairs to whatever opportunities and difficulties arise from the governance, by the existing managers and governors, of the institutions which give structure and dependability to their lives. This is no less true of the members of a university than of members of a family, a community, a nation, a factory, a trade union, a political party, or a government bureau. Their interest in life is to use the institutional facilities provided for achieving the objectives toward which they have made some progress because of, or in spite of, those facilities.[2] The activists frequently label them as apathetic. As

[2]Not all conforming students have the same objectives, but whether they have come to college to acquire a vocational skill, to sharpen

a characterization of their general predispositions, nothing could be further from the truth. They are apathetic only toward the changes proposed by the activists in the institutional arrangements and relationships which, given their own objectives, are serving them passably well. Our concern in this book, however, is, with those who conceive of themselves as agents of change, the initiators of student activism.

The observation of the activities of students in the countries with which our own investigations are concerned leads us to distinguish five types of students who view themselves as agents of change: the emigrants, the volunteers, the reformers, the revolutionaries, and the reactionaries.

The *emigrants* are persons who choose to disassociate themselves from the existing way of life and work, and, hopefully, of governance, by withdrawing permanently or temporarily into what they conceive to be a self-made society. Their protest is not usually made manifest in the demand to change or remake the institutions of society, but in the demand to be left alone. They will leave those institutions to what, in their judgment, is their state of decay. Their challenge is as radical as that of the revolutionaries, for it raises a protest against the whole set of values which cement the relationships and interactions of the great majority of the population including the students. They inherit the traditions of many generations of alienated persons who have joined with others of like mind to disassociate themselves from the order of life and work accepted or tolerated by the majority and to create an alternative order consistent with their own deviant views of the good life.

The basic change they seek is more intended to make themselves free to order their own lives, than to modify the lives of others. For that reason they are, by most observers, not considered "activists" at all. If the meaning of activism is limited to behavior by which a minority commits itself to changing the arrangements and structure of life for everyone, that judgment is well based. But if activism connotes an unwillingness to accept passively social circumstances, opportunities, constraints, and governance with which they are in disagreement and by which they are frustrated, and by an active effort to create

---

their minds, to expand their knowledge, to participate in a respected social ritual, to have a good time, or to find a mate, they find that the institution has developed arrangements which to a degree satisfactory to most, makes the achievement of the objective a possibility.

separate social circumstances, opportunities, constraints, and governance for themselves, then those who do so are genuine activists. Such activists are to be found in all the countries in which we investigated student activism, although it is largely in the United States that there is a semblance of organization to the manifestations of their activism.

Since their attack on the status quo and its arrangements, human relations, and values is less overt and more subtle than that of the reformers, the revolutionaries, and the reactionaries, they arouse the interest of university authorities more as "oddballs," to be observed and somehow lived with, rather than as challengers whose activities have to be dealt with directly. The chief problem they present, other than the subtle influence their standards of collective living and values exert on those beyond their number, arises from the fact that many of them move back and forth between life in the orthodox university society and their own unorthodox mode and style of collective living, and from time to time they join forces with the reformers and the revolutionaries in activism directed against a particular university or public policy or practice. Moreover, since no individual can completely opt out of the life of a society within whose geographical, political, and economic borders he continues to live, the permanent or temporary emigrants must come into at least peripheral contact with the processes and regulations of that society.

Another group we would classify as *volunteers*. The most prominent of these are those who, observing some aspect or aspects of university or societal arrangements which they believe can be improved by individual or collective social effort, volunteer their services for such effort. Social service projects attract large numbers of students in Mexico and Colombia and to a somewhat lesser extent in Japan and India. Examples of "volunteer" activism are numerous in the United States and have long been an important ingredient in actualizing the element of idealism in the traditional image of the Student. Activities in the Peace Corps, various social amelioratory and "settlement house" projects, activities improving chances for racial equality, tutoring of disadvantaged pupils or students, assistance to ghetto community development, draft counseling, voter registration drives, electioneering, etc. are well developed among them. Participants in student government activities in all the countries studied are frequently motivated to seek such participation as a means of becoming instruments of change particularly at times when such activity is an alternative to less orthodox efforts by activists to effect change on their own terms. Others in the "volunteer" category, although not themselves active in such endeavors, will provide moral and/or financial support for those who are, and also for those who have been disciplined or punished for participation in the less orthodox forms of student protest.

It is the reformers, the revolutionaries, and the reactionaries who have most recently been involved in the kind of activism which causes the greatest concern for the managers and governors of educational and political institutions, and who have aroused the interest of psychologists, social scientists, and moral philosophers, as well as journalists. We shall, therefore, give more specific consideration to the characteristics which they evidence in the countries in which we have conducted our investigations and in the United States.[3]

[3] A number of student organizations are popularly assumed to promote a type of activism attractive to those whose ideological and action predispositions fit these classifications. Thus, in the United States, the campus affiliates of Americans for Democratic Action (A.D.A.), Students Against Nuclear Expansion (S.A.N.E.), American Civil Liberties Union (A.C.L.U.), The University Christian Movement, the Young Christian Students (Catholic), Young Peoples' Socialist League, The Young Democrats, and to some degree, the Young Republicans and Young Americans for Freedom, are frequently assumed to be attractive primarily to *reformers*. Students for a Democratic Society (S.D.S.), particularly the Weatherman faction, the Southern Non-Violent Coordinating Committee (S.N.C.C.), the Du Bois Clubs, as well as the campus affiliates of the Maoist Progressive Labor Party, the Trotskyist Young Social Alliance, and the Marxist Youth Against War and Fascism, are rated by large numbers of observers as primarily attractive to the *revolutionists*. The societies attracting the *reactionaries* normally originate as ad hoc organizations in reaction to local leftist sponsored disturbances, for example the Blue Guards for University Loyalty, and Students for Law and Order. But some efforts are being directed to the promotion of national organizations like the Inter-collegiate Society of Individualists. In its recent 1969 Conference the Young Americans for Freedom laid plans for instituting student sponsored opposition, including direct action, on campuses subject to leftist inspired disturbances.

It is dangerous, however, to make such a categorical classification of student organizations, for the intensity of the commitment of their members to activism consistent with reform, revolutionary, or reaction-

Presuppositions of the Activists

The initial way to differentiate the three types of activists which are here considered is to infer, from the way in which they behave, or from their proclamations, the presuppositions of their world view or ideology with which such behavior appears to be consistent. The three sets of presuppositions are outlined below. All three types of activists perceive essential elements in their environment to be changing, and judge that available personal and institutional problem solving facilities are coping inadequately with those changes. But they differ in their perceptions of the causes, scope, character, and significance of the changes and the nature of the inadequacy of the System and the Establishment to deal with them.

Presuppositions of the Reformers

The failure adequately to meet the problems produced by a changing societal environment results from the fact that knowledge is inadequate and that the problem solving process is weak, because:

Structure and dynamics and interacting facets of the problems are poorly understood and misinterpreted, and hence poorly defined.

Methods of exploration and analysis are imprecise, and frequently irrelevant.

Technical facilities are geared to traditional problems, not the current ones.

Priorities for allocation of scarce resources are inconsistent with the critical importance of the problems.

Communication between analysts and decision makers and administrators is poorly synchronized.

The problem solvers and the administrators of the measures are inept in the performance of their functions.

---

ary premises varies from campus to campus. The best overall views of the organizational situation which we have seen is that contained in Chapter 7 by S. M. Lipset and P. G. Altbach, in S. M. Lipset (ed.) *Student Politics*, Basic Books 1967, pp. 205 ff. and by R. E. Peterson, in *Daedalus*, Winter, 1968.

People generally are not aware of the true character of the problem situations in which they are involved.

The responsibility for this failure is attributable to certain influential groups:

Intellectuals for their failure to define and analyze problems adequately

Politicians for their failure to provide leadership in initiating measures consistent with available and applicable technical knowledge and resources

Pressure group interference with solutions rational from the point of view of the public interest (as defined by the reformers)

Administrators unskilled in their administration of programs and mechanisms intended to be adaptive to changing circumstances

The general population for their self-serving and provincial and emotion-colored exercise of their political functions

The existing patterns of institutional structure and behavior are essentially sound and sufficiently flexible to permit adaptive modification.

The actors who are responsible for the failures are able and willing to modify their behavior when rationally persuaded that this is desirable from the point of view of their own, as well as of the public, interest.

The period for action is long range. Gradualism is the soundest policy.

There is a rational and peaceful solution (by mutual consent) for all domestic problems and most international problems.

The values by reference to which the appropriateness of personal and collective action is measured are universalistic and evolving.

Presuppositions of the Revolutionaries

The failure adequately to meet the problems produced by a changing societal environment is largely attributable to lack of will and moral integrity rather than of technical know-how or available resources.

The responsibility for this failure rests on persons, in the past and present, holding positions giving them the power and responsibility to initiate action, i.e. the Establishment.

The lack of will and moral integrity of members of the Establishment is rooted in a desire to maintain the patterns of institutional structure and behavior in which their own status, role, and prestige have a secure place, and which they and their predecessors have created to further their own interests and authoritative control.

Members of the Establishment cannot or will not voluntarily modify their predispositions, rooted in and supported by such patterns, until the patterns themselves are discredited, radically changed, or destroyed, that is without being forced to change.

Such discrediting, radical changing, or destroying is a positive move essential to the creation of more adequate and less class-biased institutions.

Once this has been accomplished, new agents of initiative, organization, and action with respect to the problems of individual and collective adjustment to changing environmental circumstances will appear.

In the case of some, but not all, this conviction is reinforced by an assertion of the validity, as a pattern for reconstruction, of a particular ideology, Socialism, Communism, Christian Democracy, Participative Democracy, etc.

The time for change is now.

The values by reference to which the appropriateness of personal and collective behavior is to be tested are those to which the revolutionaries are committed.

Presuppositions of the Reactionaries

The reactionaries are such in two senses of the word, neither of which, as we are using the word, has any invidious connotation. They are reacting against the behavior of those whom they consider disrupters of the status quo, and they conceive of the necessary societal change as a reactivation of more stringent governance. Their premises are:

The failure adequately to meet the problems produced by a changing societal environment is largely attributable to intellectual, activist, and "free loader" disrupters of the status quo.

The predisposition to disruption, on the part of intellectuals is rooted in romantic, unsound, illogical, unrealistic and irresponsible thinking; on the part of the activists in uncivil, barbarian, irresponsible and antagonistic personal character: and on the part of both in ungoverned egotism. The free loaders disrupt the status quo by their failure to contribute, by their lack of initiative and self-reliance, and by placing a heavy burden for their support upon those who do contribute.

Aside from a laxity in the instruments for social control of the disrupters, the patterns of institutional structure and behavior are essentially sound.

The time for correction of this laxity is now, before the danger grows any more serious.

The values by reference to which the appropriateness of personal and collective behavior is to be judged are universalistic and fully developed, the sound products of wisdom of experience and common sense.

It would be plausible to list the black militants in the United States as a distinctive group. We have not done so primarily because the objective of this exposition is to indicate the features of student activism in the United States which are also found in the other countries. Moreover, although there is at the present time a trend toward separatism between blacks and whites in the organization and carrying out of student protest, all of the five types of activists listed above are found in both black and white groups of activists. A major difference between blacks and whites, who can be classified in any of the five groups, is attributable to the aim of the blacks to seek redress for centuries of discrimination and exclusion from the main stream of American life, work, and culture, and to provide themselves and their fellow blacks with a culture, with institutions, and with basic rights that support their confidence and pride in themselves as blacks and not as tolerated non-whites. Although, therefore, both black and white activists include those defined above as emigrants, volunteers, reformers, revolutionaries and (to a lesser extent) reactionaries, there is a racially oriented intensity about the characteristics when revealed among blacks which complicates the problem of managing, channeling, and transforming protest both for proponents of, and for responders to, their activism.

Although the racial separation issue is not present in other countries in which we have investigated student protest, something analogous to that separatism does exist in some of them. For example, in India there is a tendency for communal groups (e.g. Muslim and orthodox Hindus) to go their own way. In Japan there is a distinct case of separatism between the secular student organizations and those of the new-religion groups (notably Soka Gakkai), and in Mexico and Colombia, although not to the same degree, between the Marxists and the Catholics.

Summary: Differential Presuppositions

The chief differences in the presuppositions of the three types of activists which can be expected to influence their predispositions to action are summarized below:

Perception of the Nature of Environmental Changes

All three are aware of changing environmental circumstances that necessitate adjustments in patterns of personal and institutional character and behavior.

For the reformers and reactionaries the changes have a continuity with historical circumstances, but the reactionaries perceive less essential difference in the kinds of problems posed now, in the past, and in the future for persons and institutions, while the reformers perceive the changes as those of both degree and kind.

The revolutionaries perceive many of the circumstances as sufficiently discontinuous with historical circumstances to make gradually evolving personal and institutional adjustment to them irrelevant and obsolete.

Allocation of Responsibility for Unsatisfactory Problem Solving

Both the reactionaries and the revolutionaries locate the primary blame for unsatisfactory problem solving on the alleged weakness of others than themselves, but on the weaknesses of different groups. For the reactionaries, these groups are the intellectual, activist, and free loader disrupters of the status quo and by implication the "weak kneed" public authorities who fail to constrain the disrupters. For the revolutionaries, those responsible are the initiating and governing perpetuators of the status quo. The revolutionaries also blame the *structure* of the problem solving process itself, since, by definition, it is organized to satisfy the class interests, and to perpetuate the control, of the present managers and governors and their kind.

The reformers are also critical of the weaknesses of people, including themselves, but place a major blame on the insufficiency of knowledge and on the inadequacies in the operation (not the essential structure) of the system and mechanisms of the problem solving process itself.

Calculation of the Probabilities for Voluntary Change

The reformers assume that there is a flexibility in the character of those criticized for institutional inadequacies that leaves them open to persuasion and voluntary change in perspective, predisposition, and direction of action.

The revolutionaries consider the "devils" of their scenario to be so closely identified with the creation and perpetuation of the institutions, which are themselves at fault, that voluntarily initiated change in their policies and behavior is unlikely. Any concessions members of the Establishment make will be with the intention of "taking the wind out of the sails" of their critics, a calculated attempt to maintain their power through "repressive tolerance." Any modification of arrangements to which they agree will simply be a formal facade behind which the same exercise of unilateral initiative and decision making will be carried on.

The reactionaries apparently have little confidence in the capacity or willingness of the disrupters to change voluntarily since their predispositions are rooted in assumed weaknesses in character. But they apparently have confidence that self-interest will cause the educational and public authorities to yield to pressure to "tighten up" their regulation and control of the disturbers.

Confidence in the Viability of Existing Institutions

The reformers consider the nature, structure, and dynamics of existing institutions essentially sound, possessing serious weakness, but reformable.

The revolutionaries consider the nature, structure, and dynamics of existing institutions class-biased, full of decay, and unsalvageable at least under present management and governance.

The reactionaries consider the nature, structure, and dynamics of existing institutions essentially sound, legitimate and viable if social control is adequate.

Time Horizons

All three types of activists are committed to immediate action, but the reformers have a greater sense of the dangers of precipitous action in a complex societal organism and a greater confidence in the built-in capacity of societal homeostatic processes to restore equilibrium when disturbances occur. They sense the need for, and values of, long range evolutionary adaptation and development in the system of organized life.

Value Reference

The values by reference to which the revolutionaries and reactionaries evaluate their own and others' behavior are particularistic, that is those considered sound by themselves and those who agree with them. The values tend to be considered absolute and not subject to modification and revision in response to adaptations suggested by their apparent lack of applicability to particular situations. The reformers consider values to be relative to the needs and aspirations of particular human groups at different periods of their history, but subject to critical evaluation by reference to superior values considered to be universally relevant. For they consider that the values are in evolution as far as their substance is concerned, an evolution stimulated by growing insights into the nature of man and his universe, and by an expanding conception of men's responsibilities to each other.

Strategy and Tactics

Since the foregoing presuppositions of the three types of students who consider themselves agents of change have been inferred from the empirical observation of their activities, it is a defensible move to reverse the process and indicate the probable characteristics of the direction of their predispositions to action as consistent with those presuppositions.

The classification of tactics by reference to their users should not be taken as an indication that specific tactics are exclusively practiced by the type of agent of change indicated. It is particularly true of revolutionaries and reformers that they utilize often times some of the same tactics, and on occasion join forces, to such an extent, indeed, that popular perception infers that there is no difference between them. Discrimination is, therefore, frequently possible only by reference to the ultimate ends (revolution or reform) for which the tactics are pragmatically chosen means.

Strategy and Tactics of Revolutionaries

The revolutionaries require an extensive but relatively simple action program. The requirements stem not only from their perception of the nature of the environmental circumstances, but of the nature and weaknesses of the institutional instruments and the intransigent defense of the status quo by those in positions to initiate and carry through change; from their complete lack of trust in either the institutions or their governors; from the fact that they are a minority group incapable of instituting change unless they can recruit a following giving them mass power; and from the fact that since they attack the Establishment, the orthodox instruments of change, which, on the whole, are managed by the Establishment, are reluctantly, if at all, made available to them. Hence they must resort to unorthodox tactics.

Revolutionaries will try to radicalize a potential following:

> By seeking to discredit the System and the Establishment by publicizing in all possible ways examples not only of their inadequacy in the face of current and future problems, but of their class bias, self-serving, corruption, and control by insidious and immoral and exploitive forces

> By identifying the interactions of managers of existing institu-

tions as a conspiracy for the promotion of their own interests associated with exploiting non-members of the Establishment

By citing the system of the complex interdependency of these managers and the institutions themselves on each other as evidence of the impossibility of substantial change without radical change in the System itself

By labeling the policies, actions, and interactions of the managers with emotionally charged terms suggestive of lack of concern for the welfare of the people whose subordination they desire to maintain (such as exploitation, hypocrisy, imperialism, colonialism, fascism, racism) and characterizing the managers themselves as exploiters, hypocrites, imperialists, ruling class, fascists, racists, and incorporating all of these labels into the term "the Establishment"

By seeking to create a cynicism concerning the moral integrity of the managers by asserting and illustrating the hypocritical inconsistency of their performance with the values they proclaim as guides to their action and with values popularly accepted as sound

By relating the above named general patterns of Establishment behavior to the particular behavior in some cases which students have observed first hand

By translating any unsatisfactory experiences of students into a violation of their "rights"

By arranging action situations on issues symbolic of the foregoing "case" against the Establishment in which the potential supporters will be actively involved and hence in a sense will commit themselves *in action* to an acceptance of the case

Attaching discreditable and emotionally toned appellations to those who disagree or fail to respond positively (such as apathetic, complacent, Uncle Tom, etc.)

Revolutionaries will plan and organize and lead confrontations with members of the Establishment which have the following value for them:

Widespread publicity for their "cause" and public awareness of their existence, including attracting the attention of the press and T. V.

Focusing of attention on an issue which is symbolic of their perception of the "evils" of the System and of the involvement of its managers in that System's evil characteristics

Hopefully demonstrative of the intransigency of the Establishment and of the inconsistency of their proclaimed values with their performance

Create a situation of confusion and disruption among students in which the need for confident leaders or a leader is obvious

Force managers of the Establishment to "recognize" them as necessary participants in the making of any vital decision with respect to the management of the institutions involved

Produce a shock disturbing to the complacency not only of the members of the Establishment, but of potential followers and the general public (Such a shock effect is particularly likely if their actions are extra-legal or violent, endanger life or property, and create disruption of normal routines for large numbers.)

Embarrass and disrupt the Establishment in its conduct of institutional affairs, thus reinforcing the image they seek to create of the Establishment as characterized by incompetence and lack of moral integrity

Revolutionaries will be uncompromising for as long as possible in their "confrontation" with the managers of the institution involved, insisting on a settlement only on their own terms. "Our terms are non-negotiable" has come to have a familiar ring in reports of confrontations of students with educational and political authorities. Such intransigency, they hope, will lead to one of two results, either of which validates their "case." The managers of the Establishment will capitulate, thus giving the impression that there was justification for the protest and simultaneously reducing popular confidence in the strength of the managers and of the soundness of the policies pursued in their previous management; or, in frustration and exasperation, the managers and governors will call upon the police or the military to assist them in dealing with the disrupters of their institutions, thus verifying the contention of the revolutionaries that the governing authority of the Establishment must be maintained ultimately by force rather than by reason.

Revolutionaries seek to transfer the power of ultimate decision on details of policy and practice from the present managers and governors of institutions into the hands of those whose life and work is affected by those policies and practices, in the first instance into their own hands, and then (for some but not all of them) into the hands of all those so affected, labeling such an arrangement "participative democracy."

Revolutionaries will seek to avoid punishment for their actions by appeal to the orthodox institutionalized devices for protecting individuals from arbitrary action of those in authority, to what are referred to as their "constitutional rights", and to the judicial system and legal aid, or by including "general amnesty" among the terms they demand as a price for ending their confrontation.[4] Whatever the outcome, they win. If they escape punishment they consider their actions vindicated. If they do not, the biased and status quo-protecting character of the Establishment is, in their judgment, demonstrated.

Strategy and Tactics of Reformers

The action predispositions of the reformers are much less dramatic, for the changes they seek are in the institutional policies and practices, not in the basic structure of institutions themselves. They hesitate to challenge openly the legitimacy of the governing role played by the existing managers associated with the Establishment. They consider themselves, if not members of the Establishment, at least as eligible for immediate or eventual membership and able to influence its decisions and operations. While the most self-confident among them may seek to initiate a movement and marshal recruits for the action involved, they propose to promote and lead such action within the framework of orthodox and generally approved patterns of behavior and by the effective employment of the orthodox political, social, and economic mechanisms for effecting change. They may, on occasion, join with revolutionists

[4]The demand for amnesty is conceivably rooted in an objective which goes beyond a craven desire to escape the disciplinary consequences of one's acts. In a sense, the demand calls into question the legitimacy of the institution and its governors. Only a legitimate institution has the right to punish. If the governors, therefore, grant general amnesty, they are indirectly acknowledging their illegitimacy, or so the act could be interpreted by the activists.

in supporting the latter's description of the reality of the process of governance of institutions, and in demonstrations protesting some particular manifestation of that governance. But the partnership with the revolutionaries is temporary, a pragmatic and particularized participation in relation to a specific issue directed to the resolution of the issue itself, not a demonstration against the system or the Establishment whose essential character is presumed by the revolutionaries to be symbolized by the issue. For the most part the reformers are inclined to accept the constraints of existing laws although not always the administrative interpretations and applications of those laws. If, on occasion, they challenge a law directly through civil disobedience, the move is justified, not only as a tactical maneuver, but, more importantly as a declaration of a commitment to an ideal of conscience-governed human conduct superior *in this particular instance* to "respect for any and all law." Their predisposition is to accept, as a constraint on the results they can expect, the inevitability of gradualness, and to lay the foundations for cumulative results by increasing knowledge, giving it wider and intelligible distribution, continuous analysis and criticism of institutional processes, organization for and promotion of additive or even cumulative reforms, reiteration of ideal personal and societal values as goals to be striven toward rather than as descriptive of the character of present institutions and reality.

Strategy and Tactics of Reactionaries

The reactionaries are stirred to action primarily as a response to the tactics of the other two groups of activists. They are predisposed to initiate or support steps to strengthen the process for the discrediting, regulating and controlling, or for quarantining the intellectual and activist disrupters, and for implementing a tough set of constraints on benefits to free loaders. The maintenance of law, order, self-reliance and discipline, patriotism, respect for traditional values, common sense, will be the basis of their appeal for support. They seek institutional stability and on occasion are willing to lend a hand in the forceful control of disturbance and disorder.

The foregoing discussion has not addressed itself to a contrast frequently drawn between student activism in the United States and in the other countries. Student activism in the United States is characterized by some as nonideological whereas in the other countries ideology is assumed to play a prominent part in stimulating and maintaining such activism. Whether or not this characterization is considered accurate will depend on the meaning which the critic attaches to the term "ideology." For some, ideology is practically synonomous with Marxism or Socialism. For others it is equated with doctrines or philosophy of either the extreme political left or the extreme political right. For others any group of whatever political, social, economic, or religious orientation has an ideology, that is, a commonly accepted set of conceptual premises by reference to which they describe and interpret their environment and their relations to it and to each other, and the values they seek to achieve in their interaction with each other.

When we review the evidence in the preceding sections concerning student activism, it is apparent that there are a number of recurring action emphases and value emphases explicitly or implicitly revealed in that evidence. In our judgment these emphases, whether or not they have been formally proclaimed in written documents, perform many of the functions of an ideology if they are understood and accepted by activists as premises of their thought and action. The reader is reminded that we are exploring here these matters as they are manifest in the thought and action of the minority portion of the total student population in the United States, Japan, India, Mexico, and Colombia which has been characterized as activist.

Action Emphases

Action emphases among the three types of activists, corresponding to the predispositions noted in the first part of this chapter, although varying in degree, are found in the activism of students in all the countries in which our investigations were conducted.

Initial Negativism

The *reformers* normally begin their campaigns with negative criticism of the performance of the educational and political institutions they seek to reform, but they also frequently propose specific alternative constructive policies and practices they deem more consistent with the adequate service of the institutions to those for whom the institutions provide both opportunities and constraints. The *revolutionaries* also direct critical barbs at the performance of the institutions, but push their criticisms deeper into the very structure and nature of the institutions. Their negativism persists, and in the end is difficult to distinguish from nihilism. They distrust specific changes which appear within the realm of possibility as simply a shoring up of an essentially unsound structure, and indeed as postponing the eventual necessary radical destruction of the System and the Establishment and the substitution of governance and governors consistent with their own pattern. Yet the structure and operations of an alternative System are infrequently spelled out in detail save that they will be governed in reality by, or at least in the interests of, all the people. The *reactionaries* criticize the regulatory ineffectiveness of existing educational and political institutions, and propose changes which will stiffen the regulatory power of those institutions and reduce the impact on their stability of the thoughts and actions of those whom they consider to be disrupters of that stability.

Although the rhetoric of all three groups stresses the positive development of a more nearly ideal set of arrangements, conditions, and circumstances, the practical action programs are, in the first instance predominantly negative, that is against something or someone. It should be pointed out, since reform as well as revolution requires convincing followers to commit themselves to action, that, unless they are convinced something is wrong with the present set up, there is little reason to make the effort. Reformers, therefore, will often attack the same catalogue of weaknesses as far as Establishment policy and practices are concerned as do the revolutionaries. But the attack of all three types of activists against these weaknesses is launched before positive alternatives have been carefully explored or the potentially unstablizing consequences of negative action thought through.

Challenge to the Legitimacy of Authority

It is an obvious conclusion from the foregoing analysis that the *revolutionaries* are not concerned simply with correcting certain shortcomings in the operations of existing educational and political institutions of our time and in the policies and practices of the Establishment which manages and governs them. Their central challenge is to the *legitimacy* of the system of governance and of the status and role of the governors.

What is not so obvious, but which is becoming more and more apparent, is that a modified version of that same challenge is characteristic of the activism of the *reformers*, as well. There are, however, certain differences. The ultimate challenge of the revolutionaries is to the legitimacy of the governing system and of the governors' status and role, without qualification. The activization of the challenge involves the discrediting, disruption, and replacement of both. The challenge of the reformers is to the legitimacy of a few aspects of the System, for example in those cases in which the managers and governors included in the present Establishment mismanage and make unilateral decisions, initiate action unilaterally, reward and punish unilaterally, that is in accordance with their judgment of what is best for all concerned, including, but not limited to, themselves. The activization of that challenge involves, in one sense, simply a demand for the enlargement of the membership in the legitimate Establishment and a revision of the division of labor within that membership.

Educational and political analysts, leaders, and administrators and many among the more thoughtful and literate of the students have produced much advice on changes by which the expressed dissatisfactions with the way in which university and public affairs are conducted could be reduced and removed by modifying institutional arrangements and procedures. Such changes would not necessarily involve any *radical* restructuring of the institutions. In their judgment, student activism could be reduced to manageable size: if success could attend efforts to provide students with an effective voice in the kind of education they receive, in the evaluation and choice of their professors, in the management of their own living arrangements; if the Vietnam war could be ended, the draft and ROTC abolished, all industrial military research and recruiting forbidden on campus; if non-discriminatory access of non-whites to jobs, houses, schools, and public accommodations were to be transformed from civil rights into actual experiences, and the university education for blacks were to be shaped to make them proud of their distinctive history and culture; etc.

Now many such modifications and others in a similar vein may be desirable in their own right, and are overdue in any civilized society in which they are absent. If grievances connected with them are really the "causes" of the students protests, instead of simply factors contributing to a predisposition to activism, the predicted consequence would appear plausible.

If, however, underlying all of these grievances is a questioning of, and a challenge to, the legitimacy of the System and of its governors unilaterally to shape the policy, initiate the actions, regulate the processes, and motivate their performance, the educational and political problem posed is not simply one of a redress of grievances, but a restructuring of governance within the universities and society, whether that restructuring is labeled revolution or reform.

If this challenge to the legitimacy of authority is not just an ad hoc pragmatic rhetorical device designed to create among a small minority of activists and their potential supporters an amplified sense of the world shaking significance of their activism, if instead it reflects a continuing and basic ingredient of the concept, widely shared by students, of their appropriate and justified role in the university and society, the impact of student activism on university and societal affairs has a basis for greater continuity and intensity than it has had in the past.

Moreover, it provides a basis for a continuing concern with the achievement and redistribution of power and a justification for the disturbing tactic of confrontation, the realization of both of which are not likely to be permitted by the existing or, indeed, any future Establishment without the most strenuous opposition.

And if, as Feuer[5] and others have suggested, questioning of, and challenge to the legitimacy of, *all* authority is deeply embedded in a "generational unconscious" of "Freudian sons," our only hope is in the awareness that such human characteristics have long been with us, and that the task of legitimizing and exercising authority has, nevertheless, not heretofore proved impossible.

The Achievement of Power

There is evidence that the concern with the achievement and distribution of power is fundamental and not superficial among

[5]Feuer, Lewis S., *The Conflict of Generations: the Character and Significance of Student Movements*, Basic Books, 1968.

both the *reformers* (as exemplified by the National Student Association, the Student Christian Movement, and the campus affiliates of Americans for Democratic Action in the United States; the Christian Democrats in Mexico and Colombia; the National Council of University Students in India; and certain anti-Zengakuren organizations, and the least radical factions within Zengakuren itself in Japan); and among the *revolutionaries* (as exemplified by the Students for a Democratic Society, the Student non-Violent Coordinating Committee in the United States; the Mao and Castro oriented communist groups in Mexico and Colombia; the National Student Union in India, and the main stream factions of Zengakuren in Japan). The *reactionaries* propose an increase in the power of that portion of the existing Establishment who are opposed to the widening of the circle of power wielders.

The *reformers* propose an extension of the numbers who share the power to initiate and determine policies and practices, a power however, to be exercised within the existing institutional framework and in the public interest. Their proposals for extension do not necessarily, however, assume an equality of competence among all men to exercise the functions with which power is associated. They envision the allocation of the privilege and the power to participate in the formation and implementation of policy in accordance with the type and degree of capacity of the participants to make particular contributions to those processes. That does not exclude a place for an elite, defined in terms of merit, who initiate action subject to constraints exercised by the rest. The reformers normally consider themselves eligible for such elite status.

The *revolutionaries* propose an extension of power also, but in the first instance to themselves and their supporters in order to have an immediate veto over the policies and practices of the present Establishment, and eventually in order to replace the Establishment. Ideologically they are committed to both of two endeavors: (a) to forge the instruments of, and the widespread capacity for, populist governing, and (b) to exercise elite leadership and management of those processes. The integration and the implementation of the two commitments provide the issues out of which arise many factional disputes among the revolutionaries concerning the authentic party line and its implementation in organization and operation.

Confrontation

In the face of the frequently experienced unwillingness of the existing managers and governors of existing institutions to give ground on such proposals, the tactic of confrontation is not likely to be eliminated from the manual of operations of *revolutionary* groups. Confrontation is a method of testing the limits to which the Establishment will go voluntarily. Confrontation on an issue on which the Establishment finds it difficult to compromise is also, for the *reformers*, a way of testing the depth of the sincerity of any tolerance shown by the Establishment. As we have already indicated, the repressive character of this tolerance is already taken as a given constant by the revolutionaries and acknowledged by many reformers who resent being manipulated.[6]

Confrontation is the key tactic of the *revolutionaries*, for it is the only situation in which they, for the moment, are on equal power terms with their adversary, the Establishment, and in which the latter are tempted to resort to the employment of force as a solution of an impasse and hence verify the charge made against them that the essential basis for their relative strength is their power to compel conformity to their will. Among the revolutionaries in all the countries here considered, confrontation often appears to be what amounts to an end in itself. Even though, in the end, the revolutionaries must give way, the victory is still theirs. One is reminded of Eugene Debs' assertion, "No strike is ever lost." The test which, among revolutionaries, separates the men from the boys is the readiness to seek out and stand firm in a confrontation. Those who shrink from this test are viewed with disdain. In Japan, Mexico, Columbia, France, and the United States, the purest revolutionaries among the students have lost faith in the official Socialist and Communist parties, because of their attitude of pragmatic compromise and coexistence in practice which is inconsistent with the rhetoric of their ideology stressing the replacement of one power wielding class with another, and because they weaken in their determination to maintain the confrontation when what the revolutionaries

[6]Cf. Marcuse, Herbert, "Repressive Tolerance" in Wolff, R.P., B. Moore, Jr., and H. Marcuse, *A Critique of Pure Reason*, Boston, Beacon Press, 1965.

label as "token concessions" have been made by the Establishment. Even if all demands are met, a true revolutionary, they maintain, should perpetuate a situation of confrontation by the simple device of adding to those demands if the original ones have been met.

The Place of Disruption and Violence

The *reformers* seek to steer clear of disruption and violence since order, dependability, and mutual confidence are essential to the cumulative evolutionary changes they hope for, and these are undermined by disruption and violence. Moreover, acceptance of their proposals for change is endangered by a "backlash" stimulated by violent tactics. Reformers are caught on the horns of a dilemma when the revolutionaries or undisciplined activists forcefully and violently disrupt the orderly operation of existing orthodox institutions, because the responding employment of force by the authorities, even to preserve the order and dependability required for their reforms, can undermine the process of mutual consent and consensus formation upon which their hopes for reform are built.

The *revolutionaries* engage in disruption of operations of those policies and practices of educational and political institutions most symbolic of what they consider to be their class biased and exploitive structure, objectives, and management, allegedly as a preliminary move necessary to replace them with others. Disruption which is a negative action from the point of view of conservatives and liberals is, from their point of view, a necessary and positive step in the process leading to a new order.

The *reactionaries* are predisposed to fight fire with fire if necessary and fight forceful disrupters with forceful restraint of the disrupters, a process which almost inevitably results in amplified disruption sooner or later.

Value Emphases

Student activism in Mexico, Colombia, India, and Japan is characterized by several value emphases which are also present in student activism in the United States. It is probable that the similarities arise from the necessities imposed on anyone who would raise an effective challenge to orthodox societal arrangements, folkways, mores, and values which have developed over the years as the evolving adaptations of human beings to the problems of collective work and life and to the obstacles to and opportunities for personal fulfillment. What are those recurring value emphases?[7] The first two discussed below are most difficult to understand for the adult members of any society who are accustomed to viewing the process of both societal and personal development as depending on an essential continuity from the past to the present and into the future. The other value emphases, while expressed in words and revealed in behavior which is sometimes unfamiliar, have their roots in values which have long had at least substantial minority support in all the countries with which we are presently concerned.

Reality of the Present and of the Present Act

In all the countries studied except India, the present and its concrete and familiar incidents of personal experience overshadowed the past and the future as an object of concern and interest among the activists. A number of commentators have applied this generalization to students generally and to large portions of the adult population as well. Our contacts with these latter groups leads us to doubt the validity of the extension, but our research was focused primarily on the activists.

This value emphasis does not imply, as Henry Ford is once said to have exclaimed, that "history is bunk"; rather it is an expression of a belief that the "past" and the "wisdom of experience" it has produced has been developed in response to past circumstances and problems and is, therefore, untrustworthy if not irrelevant, relative to the issues which arise concerning the circumstances and problems in the present, or as a guide to the values to which one might appropriately aspire.

Nor is the deemphasis on the future a denial of the necessity to take into account the impact of present action upon tomorrow's results. The mood is one of anxiety generated by uncertainty. The same rapidly changing structure and dynamics of economic, political, familial, and social affairs and arrangements which are perceived as making the past an inadequate guide to the present are perceived as making the nature of the future a poor direction-giving map by reference to which a present course can be charted. And over all hangs the possibility if

[7]Cf. Black, R., in *Journal of Social Issues*, July 1967, pp. 55-59 Black lists seven "value themes" of the student movement on the basis of his research among American student activists. Several of these are similar to the value emphases here named.

not the probability, of man's nuclear destruction of that future. How can this value emphasis be expressed? The present is here. Its reality need not be explored in tradition and story or imagined in prophecy. If it cannot be understood, it can be experienced. And to personal experience is added the vivid news and television portrayal of the experience of others at the very moment in all parts of the world. Action and thought which conforms to the "tried and tested" experience of the past is perceived as having undependable results when tested by present problems. Action and thought constrained by prudence and foresight in the interests of future achievement, in a future which may not even exist, is perceived as nonsense. The past is for ancestors, the future for whoever may be alive at the time. The present is for me. "I am living now, therefore I am", was the declaration of one Japanese activist whose words could express the mood of many others. "Seize the moment; it is all you have. Commit yourself to action now; your commitment and your self-realization in that action are all you are", was the advice to his peers of an American activist.

These are extreme statements of a value emphasis which in lesser degree was revealed in the words and action characteristics of many activists with whom we came in contact. As previously indicated, we have no evidence from contacts with students generally that it represents any widespread conception of self or "world view" among them. It is, however, a view which activists utilize to encourage involvement of a group of followers among students in forms of activism which, from the point of view of those not dedicated to being world changers, are neither traditional nor prudent.

It would be plausible to relate the writings of existentialist philosophers to the value emphasis here under discussion. And indeed, in Japan, Mexico, Colombia, and the United States, student activists suggested that we refer to Camus, and Sartre (and also to Marcuse) in order better to understand their point of view. Discussion of the writings of these men with those who made such a suggestion revealed, however, a shallow understanding of their thought. It is likely that the authors' words have provided a framework of terms for the attempt of some activists to understand philosophically their own vivid experience and their perception of its meaning, as have the writings of Marx and Lenin for others. But it is also likely that the experience itself is the genuine root of their value emphasis. If that value emphasis spreads among student activists and students generally, it will not be because they become avid students of the existentialists, but because the vivid experiences of the present, the proved untrustworthiness of past tradition and learning, and the undependability of the future continue to recommend a course for which the reality of the present act is a guide sufficient unto itself.

Desire Realization as a Right

The emphasis on human *rights* in the Constitution and traditions of the United States is reflected in the definition applied by American student activists to practically every desire they have and every demand they make for change as something which is due the students or citizens, that is, as a *right*. The list of demands comprehends far more numerous opportunities, freedoms, and securities than are set forth in the Bill of Rights amendments to the American Constitution, but presumably the phrase. "life, liberty, and the pursuit of happiness" in the Declaration of Independence is broad enough to cover any specific item declared to be a right. Japanese, Mexican, and Colombian student activists exhibit the same value emphasis; Indian student activists to a much lower degree.

The frequency with which all desires are put forward as "rights" may indicate that the tendency results from more than an awareness that such translation is an excellent device for raising the level of legitimacy of the demands of the activists, making them appear to be reasonable and valid, rather than mere expressions of something the students would like to have or avoid having, and hence more convincing to those whom the activists are attempting to recruit as a mass following, and more likely to gain concessions from those whose consent to change is necessary. But there is little question that the activist organizers of mass protest are fully aware of the value in these respects of defining their desires and demands as rights.

Morally Defensible Motivation

Observers of the American student scene have found evidence among students generally, as well as among activists, of a growing critical attitude toward certain objectives which have traditionally stimulated effort toward personal achievement. Prominent among these criticized objectives are victory in

competition, the achievement of economic affluence, and a
social status measured primarily by success in relation to the
other two. The value emphasis is frequently stated positively
as the desirability of responding to objectives which are morally
defensible to a higher degree, more fundamentally humane, and
more oriented toward the achievement of harmonious, just, and
understanding relations with one's fellows.

This value emphasis became most evident among the students
whom we interviewed in India, Japan, Mexico, and Colombia
in several ways. It was implicit in the anxieties expressed
that the process of modernization, involving the ordering of
many aspects of life on business principles and the introduction
of business ethics as guides to human relations, would emphasize such objectives to the detriment of more humane motivations which, in their view, had traditionally characterized life in
their countries. It was revealed also in a recurring anti-Yankee
attitude one of whose ingredients was the alleged dominance
of such objectives in the motivational climate of the United
States. But on the whole the overt criticism of these objectives
in countries other than the United States was reserved for
their revelation in the motivations of public figures whose
corrupt and exploitive practices were public knowledge.

There were also marked exceptions in several countries, for
example the Antioquians in Colombia and the Parsees in India,
and in all countries among those whose status was non-
affluent, insecure, and who were clearly economically and
socially and politically ambitious and upward mobile.

This generation of students did not invent this type of
social criticism. It has a familiar ring to those acquainted
with the writings and often the dedicated service of social
critics and prophets of the good society from the earliest
times and in all these countries. That generalization applies
equally to the value emphases identified below. It is not
all of tradition which is perceived, therefore, as irrelevant
to life in the present. A major contribution of student activism
can well be to raise certain prophetic elements in that tradition
to high visibility and to pose the question as to whether
societal and human development could not profit from their
reassertion as values to be achieved in the common life.

It may also be noted in passing that the university is one
of the two major institutions in society, an important mission
of which is to preserve the thought of all those over the

generations who have contributed ideas of a "better than
what is" and have confronted society with the ways in which
its institutions constrain or run counter to its achievement.
Students who come into contact with such intellectual and
spiritual resources are alerted to them, and some can be
expected to take them seriously and identify the good life
for themselves with helping to bring their message out into
life for the many.

Community

There is present in all student activism of which reports are
available a value emphasis which may be labeled "community", an evident desire of the activists for, and their commitment to, the organization of human relationships on a basis
emphasizing the community of interests of those involved in
the relationships, and the desire for mutual support, including
emotional support, of each other in satisfying those interests.
The emphasis has both a positive and a negative aspect. There
is evident a positive seeking by leaders and followers alike
for the warmth and intimacy of "naturally" emotionally satisfying contact with one's collaborating peers and with others
whom they consider to be beneficiaries of their activism. Negatively there is evident a resistance to the restraining impact
of conventional norms and proprieties governing interpersonal
association, which are perceived as out-dated, and to the inhibitions to such communal fellowship imposed by the ritualized
formalities of dress, speech, and manners, and by the imper-
sonal role specifications of a highly technical, rationalized,
and bureaucratic society.

Among activist reformers and revolutionaries the human units
of the fellowship sought include not only their fellow students
and the members of their faculties, but those persons in society
who have suffered the disadvantages of the "system" against
which the students' protest is directed.

This emphasis on community does not run counter to the
emphasis on self-assertion and self-actualization so characteristic
of those about to come of age sociologically and politically
(as they are physically) who are searching for a unique identity
for themselves in an adult world. It relieves the insecurity
and loneliness inevitably associated with self-assertion by providing the experience of support from and the respect of those
similarly inclined to risk the hazards of defying the rules and

values traditionally considered to be important and essential to the good life by norm setting adults in their society. Those who consider themselves agents of change are able to satisfy this desire for community chiefly in association with their peers whose self-images are similar. The desire can be realized in the sense of mutual reinforcement derived from group participation, particularly in direct action, in which they can lose themselves and, paradoxically, according to the testimony of many of them, thereby find themselves.

The sense of community, however, is not easily achieved by activists even among their peers. The organizations conducting student protests and reform or revolutionary activities, in their internal affairs, must deal with the same predispositions to disagreement and dissent and protest among their activist participants as do the managers and governors of established institutions when they are the object of such critical predispositions. When the value emphases among activists to be discussed below (egalitarianism and non-authoritarianism, the insistence on the consistency of deeds with words, and the courage to stand by one's convictions without compromise) are coupled with the demand for freedom to do one's own thing, the combination produces predispositions in a self-assertive individual, self-confident that his conceptions of what is wrong with the world and what to do about it are right, which sets the stage for schismatic tendencies among such persons. That tendency is destructive of the achievement of a working consensus on goals and mode of their achievement, and consequently of the sense of mutual reinforcement and community sought. The tendency of radicals everywhere, old as well as young, to be purists ideologically and tactically is such that differences and factionalism among them are easily developed. The organizational consequence is for a disaffected individual or group to go his or its own way, to splinter or disaffiliate, or for the "main stream" proponents to eject the dissidents. This tendency to schism, particularly among the most radical of the activists, is one of the chief "allies" of the defenders of the status quo. Radical movements have within themselves, in this sense, "the seeds of their own decay."

Equality of the Affective with the Rational

Few students who have experienced university life can be unaware of an assumption which is at the root of the science and much of the scholarship to which they have been exposed, namely that human actions, judgments, and interpretations of man and his world are trustworthy when they are the products of rational thoughtways and less trustworthy when influenced by emotions, feelings, aesthetic impulses and other affective aspects of one's nature. Moreover much of the advice they receive concerning the conduct of practical life both within and beyond the university stresses the importance of systematic, rational, and disciplined calculation of the costs and benefits of any course of behavior to which they are inclined. The normally understood connotation of "disciplined" is that the approach involves a subordination of the affective to the rational predispositions in human nature.

It would not be accurate to say that all student activists with which we were in contact were in rebellion against, or even severely critical of, this assumption and its implications for human behavior and relationships. But many of them, in discussing either their own search for a unique identity or the needs of those whom they insisted were constricted and constrained by social institutions (including universities) emphasized the necessity to give freer play to the potential in human beings for the expression and growth of the affective sides of their nature. And among a few, the reforms they sought in the university and society appeared to have as a major objective what one of them called "the breaking out from the tyrannical prison of obeisance to rational calculation."

While the value emphasis here under discussion became more manifest in the predisposition to trust one's affective impulses than in the tendency to downgrade one's rational abilities, it could well be an element in the apathetic or positively negative response of some activists to the invitation of university administrators, "Come now, let us reason together."

The trust of student activists in the appropriateness of following the leading of the affective elements in their nature in making judgments and interpretations and of insisting that their university and social experience provide opportunity for the development and expression of that side of their natures varied from country to country. In order of the strength of that trust it is our impression that the activists in India would rank first, followed by activists in Colombia, Mexico, and Japan. A number of observers have noted the same tendency among American students, particularly among those we have characterized as emigrants. Our contact with student life over the past forty years and at the present time leads us to assess the tendency among students in the United States as less strong, aside from its proclamation, and as of recent origin. It is tempting to suggest the possibility that the variation in the relative perceived trustworthiness of the affective and of the rational approaches to the understanding and interpretation of life is a function of the cultural environments which lay differential stress on the significance of these factors in human life in the several countries.

Adherence to Principle and Moral Consistency

Closely related to the foregoing value emphases, but different in substance, is the justification of the behavior of activists by reference to absolute principles and their insistence that deeds should be consistent with declared moral premises. Their chief denunciations for non-adherence to such values is directed toward other people, particularly toward members of the educational, economic, and political Establishment for failure to conform in action to the moral premises they profess are the guidelines for human relationships and governance.

Examples of the kinds of inconsistencies between ideals and practices in the political Establishment's behavior frequently cited are:

In all countries:

Ideal: Commitment of managers and governors to being honest servants of the public interest

Reality: Self-serving and corruption in the conduct of their public functions

Ideal: Government both at home and abroad by voluntary consent

Reality: Government at home and abroad by resort to force

Ideal: Reference of public policy to the people and its implementation in their interest

Reality: Professionally managed and special interest dominated public policy

To some extent in all countries, but particularly in the United States:

Ideal: Equality before the law
Reality: Differential access to protection from the law and favoritism in its application

Ideal: Equality of opportunity
Reality: Opportunity proportional to status rooted in differential wealth, education, place of residence, race, source of influence

Ideal: Character as a determiner of acknowledged status and personal achievement
Reality: Success, particularly in the gaining of material possessions or in making influential contacts as determiner of acknowledged status

Examples of kinds of inconsistencies between ideals and practices in the university Establishment's behavior frequently cited are:

In all countries:

Ideal: Declaration of intent to provide opportunity for maximum personal development of individual students
Reality: Routinization of requirements and inflexibility of curriculum to which all are expected to conform

Ideal: Scholars and scientists as free, independent, and fearless critics of ideas and human behavior
Reality: Faculty, with few exceptions, maintaining either a neutrality with respect to social criticisms of non-academic origin, or accepting the status quo in regard to "respectable" ideas, and taking the existing educational, economic, and political premises for granted and without questioning; also occasional punishment of those who deviate from orthodox neutrality in thought and action

Ideal: Declaration of intent to develop in students the capacity for self-management, self-discipline, and community responsibility
Reality: Closely regulated academic and personal activities and relations without participation of students in formulating policy or arrangements for implement-

               ing it, thus eliminating experiences from which the intended personal qualities might develop

Ideal: Declaration of intent to develop leaders

Reality: Assumption implicit in the experiences provided that students are being trained as apprentices to be followers and disciples

To some extent in all countries, but especially in the United States:

Ideal: Commitment of faculty to the development of personal qualities, especially intellectual qualities, in their students

Reality: Teaching and other student-faculty relations as a function having much lower status than research and non-academic pursuits in the hierarchy of faculty interests

Ideal: The university as a community of colleagues, including both faculty and students, engaged in the common pursuit of truth and intellectual creativity

Reality: The university as a place where those who are presumed to know the truth impart it to those who do not

The setting forth of these allegations in no way implies an acceptance of their substantial validity. Nor do the comments which follow carry any personal moral judgment with respect to the observed behavior of student activists. Both are set down merely as examples of the perceptions and predispositions exhibited by a number of activists which support their charge of inconsistency against the educational, economic, and educational Establishments and their allegation that such Establishments are not to be trusted and confidently entrusted with the governance of the institutions in which they serve, because of their hypocrisy.

It would be difficult to differentiate among the activists of the several countries as to the degree of cynicism overtly expressed concerning the hypocrisy of those who manage and govern the affairs of the university and society. And the cynicism is not limited to the activists among the students. The reduction of that cynicism will not be easy in any country. Its source is in the easily observable gap between idealistic proclamations of principle and actual practice. And selective examples of exaggerated difference between the two are easily available to amplify the evidence of daily experience.

The lack of confidence in the integrity of those who manage and govern by those who are managed and governed is a major road block in all these countries to the communication and dialogue many in both camps insist they desire.

The insistence on consistency is frequently coupled with a disdain of a compromise with principle. The art of compromise of course, has a respectable connotation for those with extended experience in learning to live in a world of conflicting values, and accustomed to experiences which reveal great differences between what is ideal and what is possible. A very usual adjustment to being a moral man in an immoral society is to learn to compromise at the moment while maintaining the pursuit of the ideal. The activists are less ready to accept the first aspect of that course as inevitably necessary, or indeed moral.

This value emphasis is normally, but not exclusively, applied in judging the behavior of other people, particularly adult members of the Establishment. What at times makes communication and dialogue between the generations on the issue difficult consists of three tendencies of many activists: their apparent extreme self-confidence, interpreted by many of their elders as arrogance, a judgment which is intensified if the principle is proclaimed in an uncivil manner; the fact that the commitment is to selective values considered by them to have importance superior to those considered essential by others; and the lack of consistency in their own living out of their avowed adherence to consistency, as when their proclamation of their "right" to freedom of expression and action does not inhibit them in the infringement of that right for others when they are in confrontation with those with whom they disagree, or when they accord to the opposition the same animated inattention they contend is an obstacle to understanding when it characterizes the response of their elders (or even their non-involved peers) to their proposals. But the golden rule has never been a prominent "principle" of behavior among student activists.

Independence and Freedom

No concepts are more deeply embodied in the declared

aspirations of people everywhere than "Freedom" and "Independence." Among the students of every country concerning which information is available, these words appear prominently in the declarations of purpose, in resolutions for reform, in challenges to the authorities, in summons to action, in reasoned defense of proposals. Indeed a major portion of the values emphasized by student activists could be appropriately discussed in a book the title of which was *Freedom*.

The operational definition of the term will reflect the peculiar circumstances of life and culture in a particular country, and our discussion of student activism in the several countries has made reference to those particularistic operational definitions.

Since our purpose in this chapter is to indicate universal dimensions of student activism, we shall set down here only four operational definitions of Freedom which are prominent in the declarations, writings, and implicit in the actions, of student activists in the United States, and which were clearly the concern of the student activists we interviewed in Japan, India, Mexico, and Colombia. They are as follows:

Open opportunity for individual expression and creativity in contrast to constraints imposed by bureaucratic procedures in all social institutions including the university and government, and by conformity to folkways, mores, and customary styles of living

Freedom of choice for the individual in determining the types and forms of regulation to which he will voluntarily submit in the interest of maintaining workable group relations and activity

The elimination of coercion or manipulation of an individual's predispositions by other individuals or by social arrangements and agencies

Escape from the depersonalization and formalization accompanying mechanization of arrangements for carrying on interpersonal relations between governors and the governed as students, as employees, and as citizens

The value emphasis, Freedom, is also clearly an ingredient in the following two additional emphases.

Egalitarianism and Anti-Authoritarianism

Closely related to the value emphasis, Freedom, is that of Egalitarianism, or, to state it negatively, Anti-Authoritarianism.

There is evident among activists, both reformers and revolutionaries, in all lands for which information is available, a resentment against arbitrariness, unilateralism, and centralization of power in decision making and the assumed right of a few to initiate and supervise and regulate the thought and behavior of the many.

No collective functioning of human beings has ever been found possible without some system for endowing the few with some degree of authority to initiate action for the many and to direct, motivate, and regulate their activities. The majority among the many, including students, recognize from experience the personal advantages, as well as the disadvantages, in such a system, tolerate it, and limit the expression of their disagreement or dissent to establishing institutional constraints on the abuse of that authority. They do not challenge its essential legitimacy. The record of their achievements constitutes the history of the development of constitutional government, a process which has proceeded further in the political than in the economic and educational areas of life.

The drive of youths toward the achievement of self-identity and their predisposition to self-assertion as a means of such achievement bring them, however, initially into contact with the restraining regulative aspects of that authority. That restraining aspect rather than the mutual protection and the opportunity for self-fulfillment in an orderly and productive society provided by the authority system makes the strongest impression on them. Even within the organizations of activists there is found lively and often disruptive criticism when their chosen leaders become too assertive and "undemocratic."

Even when youth proclaims that it recognizes the need for the avoidance of anarchism, their anti-authoritarianism is evident. It is difficult, however, for the managers and governors of social institutions to define the difference, in operational terms, between the two premises for action expressed in the Port Huron statement of the S.D.S., namely, "not to have one's own way, but a way that is one's own."

Populism

The obverse of the value emphasis stated above is that on Populism, that is the assertion that all who are affected by the decisions of the managers and governors of societal institutions should participate in making those decisions, an approach which has been labeled "participative democracy." The assertion implies that no one should be left out or left behind in access to the goods and services and other benefits which the community and its institutions are able to provide, and that all those affected by the decisions essential to achieving that objective are capable of participating in the making of those decisions.

To achieve this state of affairs, say the activists, there is need for broadly based popular participation *with power* in the governance of all institutions. Such participation and power are necessary in order to counter the hierarchical ordering of authoritative functions, and to eliminate unilateral decision making by the governors and managers of those institutions.

There are few more effective stimuli that the activists can employ in order to recruit a mass following than this, a promise that the voice of each participant will count. No one who is familiar with the internal politics of student activism will, however, be inclined to conclude that its organization, plans for and choice of action, the formulation and enactment of resolutions, editorials, the nomination and election of organizational officers, are expressions of a spontaneous "will of the people." But the proclamation of principle, so far as the university community is concerned, is brought to life and buttressed by the mass meetings, the "mass collective bargaining," the interminable debates on strategy and tactics within occupied buildings, and the mass demonstrations the only qualifications for which are the willingness to be labeled as a protestor, the ability to walk and carry a sign, and to sing or shout in unison with others.

The efforts of student activists in the United States to promote similar populist government relative to the affairs of ghetto communities has not proved highly successful. But the need for the emphasis on local self-government and universal participation of all who share the common problems of life in such areas, as well as on the campus, remains as an article of faith among American activists, particularly the black activists. It has not reached such a clear status among the hierarchy of value emphases in the other countries studied.

Whether the value emphasis is revealed in efforts directed toward the change in educational, political, economic, or social, institutions, however, the principle, "government by the consent of the governed" has the ring of legitimacy. It is supported by the traditional philosophy of liberals even in those countries in which its actualization in practice is clouded by a record of governance which in fact restricts its realization to a relative few, or which has historically in fact excluded certain groups like the non-whites in the United States, the Eta (Burakumin) in Japan, the Indians in Mexico and Colombia, and the untouchables in India, from its application.

Romantic Idealism

In spite of the fact that the foregoing value emphases are to be found in the writings and revealed in the dedicated service of individuals in all of these countries, and in spite of the fact that most of them are set forth in constitutions or in public declarations of intent, their sponsorship by any individual or group, including students, is frequently characterized as romantic idealism.

It is probably consistent with common experience and common sense to accept that characterization and make of it a positive asset. Popular usage may make "romantic" synonomous with "fantastic, extravagant, wild." And it is not difficult to observe words and behavior identified with student activism which can be judged, even by students, to be consistent with that meaning of romanticism. But the word is also identified with characteristics of thought and activity such as the reassertion, against ancient constraints, of the imagination, sentiment, adventure, and unlimited horizons, which have always been held in high regard by civilized people.

It is not necessary to endow "youth" with any special predisposition to idealism in order to explain the romanticism either in its negative or positive connotations, which is observable among student activists in all countries. The idealists who have most effectively inspired generations of human beings to reach for and achieve liberalizing progress in human affairs have included a substantial number over 30 years of age. Whether young or old, anyone who would seriously commit himself to becoming and being an agent of liberal or radical societal change would soon abdicate that role unless he had a goodly supply of romanticism in his character, for the path he must walk is rocky and steep. The societal system resulting from the historical adaptive behavior of human beings is a massive creation deeply rooted in the soil of human experience of success and failure, justified by common sense (which is simply the mirror of common experience), reinforced by traditions and values, and only slightly less resistant to change than nature itself. Unorthodox or deviant aspirations and behavior are not tolerantly accepted and easily integrated into that creation. Student activists who conceive their role as that of an agent of change in the political and university system, must deal with that massive creation as a stubborn reality.

The realization by a youth of his aspiration to be and become a unique self is inhibited by the conventional restraints on free intellectual, behavioral and emotional expression. The desire for pure friendship based on a recognition of and respect for what he essentially *is* faces the rigidity of conventional standards of interpersonal evaluation. The predisposition to sense intuitively the meaning of life by reference to aesthetic experience is considered "off beat" to the degree that the culture in which he lives places a high priority on rational interpretations and explanations of the essentials for meaningful living. To "do one's own thing" is difficult in an organized society of interdependent human beings. Even more resistant to change are the societal facilities and values which, whatever their origins and mode of creation, are the existing social instruments with which the great majority in both the university and general community construct for themselves whatever realistic opportunity and security they possess. The achievement of human dignity and social justice are frequently as much restrained and inhibited as they are aided by those imperfect facilities and the inept or self-serving ways in which they are managed. Factors advantageous to one aspect of life, such as the technology for production of physical goods and their transportation, distort humane values and raise barriers to the life of the spirit. The very laws presumed to bring order and dependability and protection into the life of all are applied and often manipulated by the few in a way to bring disorder and uncertainty and exploitation into the life experience of many. The system, which ideally should expand the field of opportunities for self-realization of all, restricts and restrains that field by certain exploitive aspects of its character.

So, say the impatient ones, away with all of those restraints on the creation of a world more consistent with the heart's desire! The faith that this is possible must appear to be highly romantic, in a negative sense, to those who, over the years, have experienced the same desire for change together with the inhospitality of societal norms and arrangements to its realization.

The student activists make no such interpretation. For large numbers of them the ideal is the real. This attribute of their activism is both the source of their potential contribution to the continued evolution of more humane societal arrangements and values and at the same time a source of frustration of their efforts to transform that potential into actuality. It is a source of their contribution, for it challenges the complacency of those who tolerate the inadequacies in routine life to which they are accustomed and the imperfections in the institutions and their governance which perpetuate those inadequacies.

But certain aspects of their romantic idealism also raise barriers to the realization of their dreams. The utopianism of the student activists, their superficial calculation of the nature of the complex social forces that must be dealt with in order to effect lasting change, their arrogance in proposing to change the System although possessing little knowledge of what is necessary to hold a multitude of people and interest groups together in *any* effectively functioning social system, their naive confidence that once the societal restraints to free human expression and self-realization are removed, a more perfect and humane order will spring forth, such qualities discredit them in the eyes of those whose continuing collaboration and support are essential to any minority hopeful of initiating and carrying through efforts for substantial societal change. Those who are in positions of decision making power and sympathetic to many of the objectives of the student activists and who agree with much of the criticisms they raise concerning the existing System, its impacts on human life, and its governance, are nevertheless disinclined to link forces, except for some temporary purpose, with such "untrustworthy" partners. Trained for, and aware from experience of the difficulties in "practicing the art of the possible," they hesitate to make continuing and collaborative league with those whom they picture as bent upon "achieving the impossible."

The hesitancy to make league with the student activists, on the part of those who are continually or frequently active in opposition to the Establishment, but who possess pressure group influence with which the Establishment must reckon, is no less marked, again with the exception of a purely temporary alliance for the winning of a particular battle. Trade union and farmer organization leaders view the romanticism of student activists as inconsistent with the hard-headed pragmatic measures they have learned from experience are necessary to achieve their objectives. Radical party leaders, themselves not lacking in romantic predispositions, even when they sense the possible utility of student activism to their cause, find difficulty in keeping the student activists in harness. One of the most persistent characteristics of relations of the student activists and radical party leaders in the several countries is the criticism of the former by the latter that the students grossly misunderstand and miscalculate the revolutionary potential in the existing social situation, and that their fantasies of omnipotence frequently not only embarrass but threaten the leaders of the party in *their* efforts to control the forces of reform and revolution.

Novel Doctrinarianism

We may return now to the question with which we opened this discussion of action and value emphases. To what extent can student activism be characterized as "ideological?"

Observers of American student activism frequently contrast it with that in South America and Asia by labeling the American variety as non-ideological. On the basis of the evidence recorded above, the generalization can be characterized as over simplified.

If by "ideological" student activism it is meant that the objects of attack are frequently explicitly declared to be the same as those which Socialist and Communist Party leaders emblazon on their banners; and that those party leaders seek to make league with student activists, to recruit them into party membership, to organize party cells on a number of campuses, and provide advisory and financial support for student organizations, the contrast has some justification. Evidence for such a conclusion is to be found in the reports of internal security and police agencies in Mexico, Colombia, Japan, and India, although in the United States, also, there are allegations from F.B.I. sources that that situation is to be found on some campuses.

Two observations are relevant, however. First a *leftist* ideological orientation characterizes only a segment of the student activists and only a portion of the organizations which take part in the totality of student activism in the several countries, including the United States. Second, and this is the more significant of the two, to limit ideology to *leftist* ideology provides the observer with an inadequate basis for estimating the degree to which an ideology is a significant factor among those which give character and direction to the organized efforts of student activists.

In order to marshal recruits for continuing activism it is necessary for the initators and organizers to enlist the active and committed efforts of a nucleus of faithful supporters who will devote themselves to the organizing and operational tasks involved, whether the purpose of the action is to perpetuate, to reform, or radically to change the structure and operation of institutions. At least an elementary set of ideological premises indicating the need for and justifying such activism is necessary to motivate such activity and to hold the activists together in a working team. The premises may be explicitly proclaimed or implicitly assumed. Particularly, when the purpose is change, either by reform or revolution, the initiators of the action find it desirable to make their ideological premises explicit. Moreover, the larger group of followers necessary to provide the power of numbers for effecting substantial changes in their institutional environment through a particular program of action must be given some reason for interrupting the even tenor of their ways. And once recruited it is necessary to cement their loyalty to the cause and their continued conviction that they have common goals, common values, and a shared faith that their collective endeavors are "on the right track." Moreover, the motivation for and the predisposition to engage in continued activism along lines proposed by the activists is increased by ideologically relating what they are doing to more than the local and immediate problems upon which their operational attention if focused, and hence giving a universal significance to their activism.

These essentials for collective endeavors are relevant to those carried on by all human beings, but are of particular importance among students, that is, among those who have revealed some predisposition to integrate their thinking and their actions by associating themselves with that societal institution whose predominant purpose is to amplify an intellectual comprehension of reality and to train minds capable of doing that.

Activist student leaders in all lands therefore, provide their followers with a set of premises basic to a world view, an analysis of reality, an interpretation of recent events, and, in some cases, of historical developments, and a justification for the kinds of action they initiate, whether or not they elaborate those premises into a comprehensive and systematic ideology or philosophy. The action and value emphases set forth in this chapter are examples of such premises which we have noted as explicitly proclaimed or implicitly assumed in the activism of students in Mexico, Colombia, Japan, India, and in the United States as well. In our judgment, this suggests that there is a definite ideological aspect to student activism in all of these countries, including the United States.

The similarities do not end here, and any estimate of the impact of ideological factors on student activism will do well to take the following similarities into account.

In the first place, the specific choice of targets for, and of the tactics and strategy of, student activism are not made by *continuous* reference to any of the traditional ideologies of the left, right, or center. Such choices are not directly derived from the imperatives suggested by the dogmatics of such ideologies. The targets of student activists are those germane to the satisfaction of the students' aspirations and the reduction of the frustrations they face as students and as near adults about to take on adult roles in an adult governed society. That the targets frequently coincide with those to which organized extremists of the left or right are committed does not undermine the validity of this generalization. The tactics and strategy of student activism are primarily determined by the conception student activists have of their own possibilities of effective action *as students*, subject to the existing system of governance in their universities and nations and their status as student-citizens. Even when some segments of the student leadership are closely related, as they are in Mexico, Colombia, Japan, and India, to leftist adult organizations, their independence in choice of targets and kind of action is frequently embarrassing to the officials of those organizations who are attempting to maintain a tactical mode and direction consistent with the current "party line." Not only leaders of the adult extreme leftist ideologically oriented organizations, but leaders of the extreme right, and of the center as well, have learned to be wary of the embarrassment which their student "associates" can cause them. In Mexico, Colombia, and

Japan there have been cases in which the departure of the student leaders from the party line tactics and strategy were sufficiently extreme so that party officials were moved to "expel" the students and publicly disassociate themselves from student activism.

Not only do all but a limited few of the student ideologists assert their independence from the current leaders of ideologically oriented adult organizations, but they are infrequently the devoted disciples of traditional ideologists. Those students who perform the function of current ideologists for student activism are not disposed merely to regurgitate the political, economic, social, educational, or religious reasoning and dogmatics of those normally considered to be the creative thinkers of the race. When student ideologists do find value in the works of such thinkers, the labels they give to their own ideological constructions are, in accordance with the main thrust of their thought, a *new* leftism, a *new* liberalism, a *new* conservatism, a *new* syndicalism. Even those whose starting point is the thinking of the most universally known and influential of the philosophers of radical change, Karl Marx, aspire to the development of a new, a *pure*, a more modern Marxism.

Orthodox ideological conservatives, liberals, and radicals are hard put to it to come to terms with these young Turks who insist that they intend to think for themselves. As in action, so in thought, the latter are predisposed to "do their own thing."

How then, it may be asked, account for the prominent and repetitive use of terms traditionally associated with historically prominent ideologists: capitalist exploitation, imperialism, class struggle, colonialism, war mongering, etc. among the revolutionaries; freedom, equal opportunity, representative democracy, the dignity of man, the rule of law not men, among the reformers? The first answer is that these are not the only terms employed, as should be evident from the foregoing discussion of the action and value emphases in student activism. Yet such terms are used. Not only are such terms used in the rhetoric of students in all the lands with which we are familiar, but they are used in the same way. Aside from the few intellectuals among the students (as well as those in adult society) who are exhilarated by, or feel a responsibility for, systematic thinking, the majority of leaders of student activism simply employ such terms as slogans which are tactically useful in marshaling human resources for the activism to which they give leadership. The terms are employed not as logically related components in a systematic interpretation of social processes, but as a set of categorical short hand labels for observed actions of the Establishment to which the activists object or those which they declare it is the purpose of their activism to make actual in societal life. The terms are used by those students committed to changing the status quo in the same way as they are used by students and older citizens alike who are committed to resisting such change, that is, as clichés filled with whatever content they consider appropriate for justifying their own particular brand of activism.

The above generalizations do not imply that "doctrine" or ideology is of little significance in the promotion and conducting of student activism; quite the opposite. But they do imply that doctrine plays a role in the activism of students in the United States as well as in South America and Asia; that what doctrinarianism is present does not reflect an uncritical discipleship; that the premises to which reference is made although selective, do not exclude those which characterize the cultural values held generally by people of the nation of which they are citizens; and that the premises are employed as a tactical device in marshaling and organizing a following, by leftists, liberals, and conservatives alike, and by all of them as categorical clichés rather than as the ingredients of a systematic ideology or philosophy.

Whether, however, the ideological emphasis in student activism manifests itself in the explication of premises, in sloganeering, or in justification of activities engaged in by students, whether it is manifest as a device for organizing students for efforts toward specific goals, or for attacking the managers and governors of educational, political and economic institutions, the emphasis has one characteristic that is universally observable. It is the insistence that the ideology be expressed in deeds as well as in words. The recurring challenge which student leaders pose for themselves, for their followers, and for those toward whose position and practice their activism is directed is a ringing demand, "Don't just stand there and say something; *do* something!" And usually the challenge is amplified, "Make what you do consistent with what you say."

Student Activism as a Collective Phenomenon

An important question to ask in the effort to explain student activism is, "Why do some individuals participate while others remain aloof from participation?" Much of the most valuable data we have on the subject was produced by those who addressed themselves to that question. Such data will necessarily be interpreted, however, in the light of the fact that the student activism, to which the individuals are or are not attracted, is a collective phenomenon and that collective activity presents problems the interpretation of which amplifies the insights gained from the individual predisposition approach.

The personal interests and grievances which ready students for activism are for the most part common to large numbers of students and in many cases pertain to students as a definable group. The overt expression of protest and the strategy and tactics employed are collective, and the activity is normally organized formally. The stimulators of activism make continuous appeals to student group solidarity, appeals which are made effective by virtue of a group, almost a class, consciousness rooted in a community of interests among students not only on a particular campus, but over the entire nation and the world. The requirements for organized effort among students subject them to many of the same constraints to which they object when experienced in other organized relationships. The maintenance of commitment in action to group activity necessitates the sharing of group values. The nature and the progress of the activity itself is understandable only when analyzed as a manifestation of group, organizational, and even crowd behavior. As indicated in the foregoing pages, the proposals for change place heavy emphasis upon development of collective, and even populist, forms of participation in decision making and self-governance. The reports of students in every country for which data are available stress the values to them, even as individuals, of the sense of community and peer group reinforcement developed through the interaction with large numbers of their fellow students.

The first two of these characteristics are self-evident.

That there exists a group consciousness among students everywhere is not a generalization merely inferred from the existence of nation-wide and world-wide federations of student organization.[8] Those organizations are frequently the instruments of minority groups of students. They serve interests which, as often as not indicate an identity of their organizers with a minority faction among students rather than with all students. Those who have been closely associated with student activism in many lands, however, report a growing underlying sense of affinity of students, activist and non-activist, with each other as students. This contributes to their predisposition to group solidarity in support of the objectives of, if not of the specific modes of action employed by, student activists whether or not known to them personally.

A number of factors contribute to the amplification of this tendency toward a widening of empathy among students.[9] The very nature of their current involvement in acquiring an education provides them with many basic experiences shared with students everywhere. They are faced with similar problems in achieving an adult role in their several societies and in responding to the kinds of opportunities and constraints supplied by universities everywhere, however those universities may differ in their particular objective structure, operations, and management.

For the period of their college attendance, students, particularly those who live on campus, are more frequently engaged in interaction with each other than with any other class of individuals. But even commuting students have frequent contacts with each other. The extension of the period of study for graduate and professional work in recent years increases the length of that experience of interaction. Even before they come to the university, there is a focusing of interest of pupils in secondary and preparatory schools on anticipated student experiences for the increasing number of those who expect to "go on to college." In anticipation they already consider themselves a part of

[8]See Altach, P.G. "The International Student Movement," in *Comparative Education Review*, October 1964, pp. 131ff.

[9]For perceptive comments on the trend toward the awareness of common interests among students see Bell, D. in *Public Interest*, Fall, 1968 pp. 89f.; Shoben, E.J., Jr. in G. K. Smith (ed) *Stress and Campus Response*, Am. Assoc. for Higher Ed., 1968 pp. 135f.; Keniston, K. in *Social Issues*, July, 1967 pp. 130f.; Altbach, P.G. in S.M. Lipset, (ed) *Student Politics*, Basic Books, 1964 pp. 78f.; Lifton, in E. Erikson (ed) *The Challenge of Youth*, Harper and Row, 1963; Gusfield, J.R., in Altbach, P.G., (ed) *Turmoil and Transition*, Basic Books, 1968, pp. 93ff.

the student world. Communications with each other, and in a commonly understood language, are easier than communication with any other kinds of persons, including their instructors. For the kind of risky and unorthodox behavior which sets them apart from those satisfied with the customary routine of living, they have greater freedom, and are inhibited less by responsibility-imposed restraints, than their elders or than their non-student peers.

The universalization of contacts among students has progressed with accelerating rapidity through inter-university and international visitations and conferences. Student newspapers and journals, widely distributed, have multiplied. Mobile promoters of student activism have increased the acquaintance of students on many campuses and in a number of countries with the nature and tactics and spirit of student activism on particular campuses and in particular countries. Students in any one place are front row T.V. viewers of world-wide student activism and auditors of commentaries on that activism almost simultaneously with its occurrence.

Analysis by non-student writers and speakers of "student" problems and behavior and their comments upon "the generational revolt," "student protest" and "student politics" not only indicate to students that *as students* they are a major center of public interest, but that the explanations offered by the analysts and commentators are normally highly generalized appraisals of factors in the experience of students everywhere. Not only in their self-generated appraisals of themselves, but in the appraisal by non-students, therefore, there is an implicit or explicit recognition that students constitute something roughly analogous to a social class, whether or not those appraisals are favorable, unfavorable, or neutral toward the overt manifestation of the predispositions and behavior of the members of that class. The traditional image of the Student varies from country to country, but in every country there is a set of expectancies of what society owes the students and what the students owe society that makes students and non-students alike conscious that in many essential respects students are more similar to each other than to non-students.

Added to these factors is the overhanging sense of an uncertain future which awaits the students, (as well as all youth) in all universities and in all countries, from the threat of nuclear war and from the possible universal destruction, not only of traditional patterns of living and work and the values that support these, but of life itself, for those who have little of life behind them and hopefully most of life ahead of them. Never have the youth and students of all lands had so common an interest in the elimination of the threat of war and in protesting the aspects of societal organization and governance which make such war all but inevitable.

In the United States and to a considerably lesser degree in Mexico, Colombia, Japan, and India the development of what has been called a "youth culture" reinforces this "consciousness of kind" among students the great majority of whom feel the impact of that youth culture as well as do their non-college attending peers.

Given these factors which not only symbolize, but provide the experience of, a community of interest among youth, and especially students, everywhere, the chance for success of the appeal of activists to those whom they wish to recruit for collective activism to demonstrate group solidarity is understandable.

The managerial difficulties faced by the leaders of student activism and organizations described in the foregoing chapters on the characteristics of student activism in the several countries are ample testimony that what happens on the campus or in the streets is not simply a function of the activation of the predispositions of individual students, but of the way in which those predispositions are channeled by the organizational efforts of the leaders and managers of student protest. Their efforts to make it clear what the organization or the movement stands for, to establish its legitimacy in the eyes of all concerned, to counter the centrifugal forces that arise within the group, to adapt tactics and strategy to changing problems, to keep control of the processes they have set in motion, and to foresee and prepare participants for what lies ahead, are similar to those necessary for the leader or organizer or director of any collective effort.

The antipathy of many vocal student leaders to centralized decision making (in their own organizations as well as in society generally), the emphasis on the capacity of all individuals to decide for themselves what is in their best interest, the insistence on the freedom of each person to do his own thing, and their egalitarian oriented attacks on hierarchical relationships have led a number of commentators to see in student activism a drive toward a pure individualism and anarchy.

These tendencies are more observable in the United States than in the other countries, but even in the United States the evidence does not dependably support such a conclusion. The drive of both revolutionaries and reformers is toward participative democracy, a system of decision making in which no one who is affected by the decision is left out or left behind in the process. That drive is toward a system of collective governance based on the consent and participation of the governed. "Let the people decide, not the elite" is the slogan. Mass meetings reminiscent of town meeting democracy and mass bargaining are preferred mechanisms of decision making at least as an addendum to or a support for the nuclear leadership conference. This indicates no denial of the need for organized governing. It is carrying of collective governing to an extreme stage, that is, the inclusion in the process at some level of all the governed. It may be criticized as a retrogression to a form of primitive democracy to which evolving alternatives have had to be found as numbers increase and societal problems become more complex. It certainly is a challenge to the idea that the existing governors have a monopoly on wisdom and skill in governing. But it is not a drive toward anarchy, but rather toward an inclusive collectivism. Were it not that all present and previous governors are by definition identified by some activists as members of a discredited "Establishment", they might even find an appropriate slogan for their concept of the collective governance of their brave new world in the phrase, "Government of the people, by the people, and for the people."

Finally, as an indication of the collectivist nature of student activism are the reports from student leaders and from many fellow travelers of the "fierce joy of group involvement," of being caught up in the mass expression of common needs and common aspirations, of feeling an ineffective self buoyed up by the support of the crowd. Such collective experiences are sought not solely in demonstrations, but in the more orthodox gatherings for discussion and dialogue, and in the search for all sorts of interactions which will amplify the awareness that the students partake in the life of a true community, a community whose membership, for many, includes not only the students, but the faculty, the employees of the university, and the citizens of the community, particularly the disadvantaged groups whose welfare is the genuine concern

and action target of many of them, a welfare which they believe
the university should seek to advance.

To the foregoing universal dimensions of student activism
may be added two others which will be considered more in
detail in the following chapters. They are dimensions which
pose particularly significant problems for the theorists of student
activism. Briefly they are as follows:

Student Activism Is Not Omnipresent, and It Waxes and Wanes

Student activism of the sort which we have been discussing is
not observed on all campuses, although many of the factors
identified as stimulating or encouraging such activism are
apparently as present in places where the activism is absent
as in places where it occurs. It is as important that a theory
offer an explanation of the negative as of the positive case.
The same generalization applies to the non-occurrence or occurrence of student activism in particular time periods.

*Student Activism Has a Tendency to Escalate Toward Violent
Expression*

That feature of student activism has long been evident in
Europe, South America, and Asia, and it has characterized
student activism in the United States in recent years. There
is a tendency for disagreement and dissent to escalate into violent
direct action. Whether the dissent takes the form of negative
objection to something the students don't like, or a demand
or proposal for a positive change, the expression of that
dissent frequently manifests itself successively in publicly
advertised protests, followed by the delivery to the authorities
of petitions and the demand for negotiations between them and
"representatives" of the students, followed by direct action,
followed by violence. This cycle of events is not necessarily
inevitable, and indeed the reports made available by investigators who have focused their attention on both historical and
current student activism in a number of countries indicate that
violent demonstrations and strikes are a small part of the
total amount of student activism. But the importance of the
escalation, when it does appear, is not measured solely by its
frequency of occurrence, but by its impact whenever and
wherever it appears.

Chapter 11
Roots and Soil of Student Activism

The explanation of student activism has, in the past decade, become the preoccupation of an increasing number of psychologists, social scientists, historians, and philosophers, as well as of university administrators, government officials, and a host of journalists. The managers and governors of educational and political institutions sorely need explanations as initial guides to the responsive action they must take to maintain the stability, development, and viability of the institutions they manage and govern. The scientists devoted to individual and organizational behavior have found in the activism on campus a ready made laboratory for the exploration of the dynamic impact of institutions and culture on individuals and of individuals on institutions and culture.

The scientists are reluctant to label their present explanations as more than hypotheses, and with good reason. With the addition of each new body of evidence from a new campus where activism has or has not taken place, or from a country where the phenomenon has not previously been investigated, the task of developing an overall and universally verifiable theory of student activism becomes more complicated, and the hope for a definitive theory is further postponed. Equally puzzling is the non-occurrence of student activism where and when many of the independent variables observed to be frequently correlated with its occurrence are clearly present. If one seeks an explanation through identifying the characteristics of persons who participate in, or of universities which have been subject to, student activism in contrast to the characteristics of non-participants or non-involved universities, he finds certainly a difference in proportions of such characteristics present in the two cases. But the proportion of cases in which some of the characteristics are absent is not insignificant. Nevertheless such analysis is an essential step in the development of an explanation for student activism.

Interpretations of Student Activism

The approaches by American researchers to the explanation of student activism have been of six general sorts:

1.   The interpretation of activism as the overt expression of personal predispositions and characteristics which are observed to a greater degree in activists than in the non-activists and which can find expression in student activism.

2.   The interpretation of student activism as a function of the socialization experiences to which students have been subjected in home, community, and university.

3.   The interpretation of student activism as an expression of deeply rooted predispositions in human nature, particularly in youth.

4.   The interpretation of activism as a protest against, or frustration with respect to, certain perceived inadequacies and inconsistencies in the institutional environment.

5.   The interpretation of student activism as the consequence of the immediate presence of factors, persons, or events which activate latent predispositions to such activism.

6.   The interpretation of continuing and/or escalating student protest as the result of reinforcement and support from a number of circumstances and persons.

This classification is based upon an exploration of the materials listed in the section, "U.S.A. and General" in the bibliographical appendix, many of which were published after our field work in Japan, India, Mexico, and Colombia had been completed. Not all of the variables named in that literature were observed to be present in these countries. But most of them were far from unique to the United States.

It is our purpose in this chapter, first, to set down only those variables, considered to be influential in the causation of student activism in the United States, which to a greater or less degree appear in our data concerning those other countries. Then we shall suggest a syndrome of these factors which have been present in every case of overt student activism which has come to our attention, one or more of which was absent in those universities we visited which to that point had not experienced such overt activism.

Personal Characteristics and Predispositions of Participants

We have first to consider a number of personal characteristics noted among the initiators of activism and to a less, but still marked degree among those who join with them in that activism. Those characteristics observed in studies of American activists which we observed also to be characteristics of the activists in the several countries in which our studies were conducted are set forth below.

Our own appraisal from contact with students who could be identified as initiators of student activism as well as of the appraisal of first hand observers of the scene, characterized them as persons with an unusual amount of physical and mental energy; with a marked desire for personal prestige and influence in relation to others, particularly their peers; with an intense desire to be an initiator rather than a follower; with an inclination to risk taking and to valuing the process of achieving equal to or greater than the achievement itself; with the predisposition to use deeds as well as words as tools of communication; with a high degree of self-confidence and a strong predisposition to self-assertion (frequently interpreted as arrogance); with a curiosity which reaches out to explore alternatives to existing arrangements; with an impatience with things as they are, frequently, but not always, with overtones of idealism; with a sense of mission as an agent of change. Discussions with both activist and non-activist students concerning their appraisals of these activist leaders suggested that many of the latter had the following additional qualities: a capacity to verbalize thoughts in a dynamic way, utilizing language that is both colorful, rich in similie, metaphor, and irony, and geared to the customary mode of speech of his auditors or readers; usually the possession of some outstanding ability or record of achievement which makes him respected by those whom he seeks to activate. It is also to be observed, in Mexico, Colombia, Japan and the United States, that, in every case of overt student activism for which there is adequate reporting, there is present one or more leading activists who are capable of giving heightened significance to the present issues by placing them in a more universal setting, and hence making action with respect to them appear to be more justified than would otherwise be the case.

A most important characteristic observed among the nucleus of initiators and their most active collaborators was a consciousness of being, in some respect, socially or personally separated or deviant from the general run of students, making integration with them in satisfying fellowship difficult, coupled with a desire for peer group support in efforts toward self-actualization. They were in this sense lonely persons. We shall lay stress on this factor in setting forth the syndrome of factors that are in our judgment at the root of student activism.

But the initiators alone do not constitute the body of activists, and their behavior does not constitute a movement. Recruits must come from that portion of the students whose predispositions ready them for responding favorably to the call to action. The evidence is clear that additional predispositions are present among a substantial number of students, both initiators and their followers, on every campus we visited where overt activism had occurred. Our notes are rich with evidence that the following additional predispositions were widely present. Many students were rebellious against the actual or perceived obstacles which obstruct their progress toward achieving, and being recognized as having achieved, a mature identity. The attitude was intensified by resentment or at least disappointment at failure to experience the freedom, anticipated as students, from regimentation and authority in pursuit of that aim. The predisposition was widespread to seek new, unusual, and exciting experience, and to be bored when this was not forthcoming. They were cynical concerning the wisdom and integrity of those who managed and governed the economic, political, and educational institutions of their society and of adults generally. They lacked faith in past traditions and in the future. They gave evidence of positive support for most of the action and value emphases described in the foregoing chapter. Finally the perception of a community of interest among students as students referred to in the last chapter was accompanied by a predisposition to group solidarity and mutual aid when the interests, considered legitimate, of any of them, individually or collectively, appeared to be threatened.

It is not necessary to demonstrate that such characteristics and predispositions are found among participants in student activism and are not found among non-participants in order to suggest that their presence is an important pre-condition, though not a sufficient cause of, student activism. Studies indicating that a larger proportion of activists than of non-activists can be so characterized also reveal substantial numbers of non-activists who can be so characterized, but who apparently find other outlets for such factors in their nature. Nevertheless a major condition of student activism is to be found on any campus on which there is present a critical mass of students who have characteristics and predispositions of this sort which can plausibly be assumed to make them protest prone.

Factors Related to the Socialization Process

Another group of explanations of student activism gives emphasis to the kind of socialization process to which the present generation of students has been exposed, and focuses attention on ways in which that process could have produced some of the personality traits revealed in student activists. The studies of present day childhood and adolescence in Mexico, Columbia, Japan, and India, upon which such conclusions might be based, are not adequate to enable us to judge whether the conclusions would hold for these countries. But socialization continues in the university experience, and here the evidence is adequate as a basis for generalization. Where our findings in Mexico, Colombia, Japan, and India provide some support for estimating the impact of the socialization process, we have so indicated.[1]

The difficulties in placing reliance on explanations of this kind are several. First, the elements in the socialization process alleged to be causally related to the behavior of activists are experienced by many more students who are not activists. Second, among the activists for whose socialization experience, in certain respects, data are available, are found those in whose case the alleged causal factors related to socialization are not present. What can be concluded from the empirical studies comparing activists and non-activists is that, since a larger proportion of activists than of non-activists reveal socialization experiences with the following characteristics, a presumption is raised that those experiences, other things being equal (which they seldom are), strengthen predispositions to activism. Following are the elements in the socialization process concerning which the foregoing generalization probably is valid for the United States.

[1]The absence of such findings does not indicate an absence of the fact, but only that the present writers lack information upon which a conclusion can be reached.

Child training in home, community, and early school encourages individualized self-expression and self-determination,
and stresses the desirability of minimal external discipline and
maximum permissiveness.

A myopic interpretation of the cycle of life, and of the process
of living and problem solving results from segregation by age
group particularly in an urban society. The primary association
with a nuclear rather than an extended family, is an added factor. The small opportunity to observe the continuities between
past, present, and future provided by intimate familiarity with
persons of several generational statuses limits the growth of
time horizons giving perspective to the present moment.

Early and continuous exposure to T.V. commercials encourages unrealistic and superficial suggestions of relations between cause and effect and creates exaggerated and present-ori-
ented appetites. The T.V. programs also reveal a number of
harsh realities of life which cannot be explained away. Among
these harsh realities is the extensive use of force and violence
by dissendent groups all over the world to achieve their objectives, and the equally forceful and violent response of the established authorities. This includes the vivid portrayal of violent student activism at other universities and in other countries. For some, such a factor in their socialization may, in the
light of moral values they have acquired, result in revulsion
against violence. For others it may result in a predisposition toward imitation. For all it provides a vicarious experience suggesting that the achievement of objectives through confrontation, force, and violence is not an abnormal aspect of current
social and political folkways. (Relevant to all countries)

Assuming that a report of religious background by activists
indicates a religious *training* influential in developing political
attitudes, it is relevant to note that several studies indicate
that the largest proportion of activists in the United States
come from Jewish and liberal Protestant homes. But religious
attachment is so frequently correlated with other relations of
parents to the social order that the assignment of a particular
kind of socializing influence to one such variable is questionable.
This caveat is applicable, of course to all of the specific
socializing factors here considered.

Liberal or radical parents provide models for emulation. The
political inclinations of activists and their parents, whether to
the right or the left, have, in those studies which investigated
the matter with respect to both, been revealed on the whole

to be in the same direction. The activists may be more extreme in their positions in some cases, but the general coincidence is marked. The conclusion suggested by these studies is that any alleged generational revolt of the activists cannot be operationally defined in terms of a revolt of youths against the political predispositions of *their own* parents. A far more plausible conclusion would be that they are living out in their own time the political tendencies of their parents in a way adapted to their perception of what modern circumstances demand of those motivated to do so. Such a conclusion is not of course inconsistent with the possibility that some of the activists are making manifest in their behavior the political values which their parents express but do not actively implement. (Chiefly U.S.A., but some evidence that this situation holds in Colombia and Japan also).

Encouragement to dissent is provided by liberal or radical traditions of a particular university or college, or even a particular school or faculty within a university. This factor is amplified by the fact that such institutions, because of their reputation, attract applicants who have activist tendencies or who, at least, are intellectually dynamic and the seekers of extended frontiers for their knowledge and action. The result is that, not only do they form a critical mass on that campus, but other students are exposed to the kind of "socialization" influence which association with them provides. (Relevant to all countries)

The impact of contact with liberally oriented teachers, scientists, and scholars, and curriculum content, particularly in non-specific vocational, cultural, and social-system oriented subjects is stimulating. Even though not "liberalizing" in a political sense, such socializing agents, at least in secular institutions, may increase the predisposition of students to dissent by virtue of their tendency to encourage students to think comparatively and for themselves, to question, and to be critical. (Relevant to all countries)

The availability of modern philosophical, psychological, and social science literature which provides a logical structure to unsystematic "gut" perceptions of students critical of the status quo, encourages the belief that these perceptions are universally valid generalizations. Not only in the United States, but in the other countries investigated, authors like Sartre, Camus, Kirkegaard, and Marcuse have provided intellectual respectability to the predispositions of students to reckon as, not only desirable, but as legitimate and truly "authentic," their emphasis upon personal commitment, responsibility, the creative importance of the present act, inner conviction, and the making of choices that are freely willed. This factor is also included below as one of the strong reinforcements for student activism.

Since such socializing influences enter into the experience of many who are not involved in student activism as well as of those who are, they cannot be considered inevitably productive of student activism. But their probable impact on the developing personalities and character of youth is consistent with the production of the predispositions and characteristics noted above which ready large numbers of students for the kind of overt behavior characterizing student activism.

The Influence of Deeply Rooted Predispositions

Some of the most thought provoking analyses of student activism have sought to consolidate the multiple factors which encourage student activism into one major factor, particularly the surfacing of creative or destructive predispositions in human nature. These analyses interpret that activism as the result of deeply rooted predispositions in youth which ready them for rebellion against the status quo. Student activism is characterized by such terms as: "a manifestation of generational revolt," or "the opposition to the authority of fathers or projected father figures by Freudian sons," or "the integration of students into a new version of class struggle," or the "emergence of protean man committed to fluidity," or "the quest for symbolic immortality or transcendental reality," or "the search for meaningful personal identity," or "the craving for fidelity."

Such explanations or interpretations are thought-provoking for several reasons. They raise the discussion of student activism to an intellectual plane challenging the participants to relate their ideas to concepts more timeless and universal than those normally employed. They warn against the inadequacies in the tendency to be satisfied with the most easily and immediately observable phenomena associated with specific examples of activism. They suggest historical continuities maintained by fundamental characteristics of human beings. They intimate that student activism is grounded in human tendencies which are not solely the properties of youth. They build an intellectual bridge between science and philosophy for those who are competent in both. They reduce the intellectual frustration which plagues the attempt to assimilate and bring order into a multitude of variables, such as those named in the foregoing pages. Moreover, when the specific variables are related to some underlying and allegedly basic "cause," some significance of a specific variable may be suggested which is not apparent when it is considered apart from such relationship. Those who gather data with respect to the multiple variables are thereby alerted to the desirability of adding new dimensions to the information they seek with respect to some of them. Moreover such comprehensive hypotheses suggest the need for types of validating data which, when obtained, are helpful in interpreting the observed manifestations of activism, quite apart from their relation to those hypotheses.

Those who are seeking for a guide to practical responses they can make to student activism in the fulfillment of their responsibilities for managing and governing educational and political institutions receive, of course, little help from such generalized hypotheses, other than to become aware of the magnitude of the problem they face. The roots of the factors emphasized lie deeply implanted in the past history of the race, in the historical conditioning given to generations of human beings, developing in youth basic predispositions one surfacing of which takes the form of student activism. If it is desired either to encourage or to discourage the extent or kinds of activism occurring, or to profit from or to escape the negative consequences of that activism, such hypotheses provide a limited set of clues for those desiring to take such action. The contemplation of such a "cause" for student activism may, of course, comfort those who have to deal with it for their failure to do anything constructive about it, since that activism is considered to be rooted in an evolving human nature the means for the changing of which are beyond their control. Assuming the possibility that the hypotheses reflect reality, however, the governors of institutions can, in their exploration of the possibility for adaptive response recognize the limitations imposed on that response by the reality.[2] In view

[2] A further difficulty which some of us engaged in the study of student activism experience is the lack of professional and scientific qualifications and skills for defining the variables involved in such generalized hypotheses in operational terms, and for observing, detecting, and analyzing them. We are, therefore, inclined to leave both the explications and validation of such hypotheses to those possessing those

of the above named positive contributions of this approach to the interpretation of student activism, to criticize its limited aid to immediate practical problem solving is scarcely relevant.

One difficulty of both the "socialization influences" approach and the "deeply rooted human predisposition" approach is that they are more useful for suggesting an explanation for the presence of student activism than its absence. The characteristics of human personality and the elements in socialization and social relationships involved are so widespread in their presence and impact that it is difficult to see why, if they result in student activism at one time and in one place where it does occur, they do not result in student activism continuously and in all places, in most of which it does not occur. And if the response to this difficulty is that the difference is in the presence or absence at particular times and places of *other* factors, the simplicity of the explanation by reference to the generalized variable evaporates, and the analyst is once more faced with the task of bringing explanatory order into a multitude of variables.

Institutional Inadequacies or Inconsistencies

The foregoing interpretations have focused on factors relevant to the human agents whose behavior constitutes the substance of student activism. Those who stress such factors normally join with other interpreters in pointing to environmental circumstances experienced by such protest prone students the reaction to which, or frustration with which, heightens, the intensity of such proneness and stimulates its expression in critical dissent and in action oriented protest.

The similarities between the reported perceptions of these environmental stimulants to student activism by student activists in the United States, and those by the student activists in Japan, India, Colombia, and Mexico are striking. The specific manifestations of these features of the societal environment in the several countries are, of course, the products of the particular structure and dynamics of societal arrangements and resources in each country. But the general categories for classification and the character of the phenomena included in these categories are strikingly alike.

---

skills and qualifications, and rely for our own hypotheses upon the types of data for the observation and analysis of which professional training has prepared us.

The single most important feature is a lack of definiteness, clarity, and wide spread consensus concerning the essential character and mission, the organizational charter, of the university and/or the nation of which the students are members. Lacking such a point of reference by which to judge the authenticity of their own self-conceptions as students or citizens, and to judge the degree to which their actions will tend to perpetuate or destroy those institutions, they are caught up in the transitory impact of the events and relationships of the moment.

With similar results they are faced with the rapidity of change in the structure and dynamics of their society and the consequent lack of predictability and dependability in the nature and direction of its future by which social roles relevant to that future can be perceived and acquired. This is particularly the case when the probabilities which are evident are productive of deep pessimism, which was the case in the 1960's. Under such circumstances the present moment is perceived as the only reliable reality and immediate action as the chief available means of integration with that reality.

Increasing the confusion concerning the essential character of their university and nation and the unpredictability of the future are certain perceptions of shortcomings in the institutions of their society:

The ineffectiveness or malfunctioning of the university and government in their service to students and citizens respectively

Evidence that the governors of educational, economic, and political institutions are class biased, elitist, manipulative, and inclined to unilateral governance

Evidence that numbers of the managers of educational, economic, and political institutions are incompetent, corrupt, self-satisfied, and hypocritical

The failure to apply assumed available scientific technical knowledge and mechanisms to urgent human and social problems

To the perceptions of inadequacies are added a number of perceived inconsistencies:

The contrast between the scientific and technical problem solving capacity evident in dealing with natural and physical problems and in dealing with human and social problems; and in dealing with production in comparison with distribution problems

The contrast between the generally accepted cultural premise that all problems are rationally solvable and the obvious failure to solve critical societal problems

The contrast between the assertion of reason and negotiation to mutual advantage as a principle of civilized life and the readiness of governments to employ military force in resolving both domestic and international conflicts

The contrast between the foregoing principle and the number of domestic and international situations in which the exercise of coercive power beyond that possible through orthodox methods of civil persuasion and negotiation is effective in yielding results favorable to the interest of the power wielder

Several environmental factors which stimulate students to activism involve perceived institution-centered frustrations to what are considered legitimate expectations:

The arrangements for access to agencies or agents in political, economic, and university life, designed to provide individuals with the opportunity for furtherance and defense of their own interests, are cumbersome and exasperating, and are administered in a discriminating manner with reference to those from certain racial, national, religious, or communal minorities. Also the suspicion exists that preferential treatment is given those with social standing, influence, money, or all three.

Decisions governing one's own affairs in the university and community are made by those having authority without adequate opportunity for the presentation of one's case.

Institutional operations and relationships in the university and community are bureaucratic, hierarchically organized, and esthetically unstimulating, imposing restraints on individual creativeness and self-realization.

Many of the expectations of students with respect to the degree of freedom to be enjoyed and the opportunities for intellectual, vocational, and status improving possibilities to be provided by university life are unrealized.

The expectations of students with respect to being the chief focus of concern for their university professors is frequently unrealized because of the relatively low priority given by professors to teaching, among their several functions.

Such environmental stimulants to student activism which suggests that something *needs* to be done are occasionally accompanied by stimulants which suggest that something *can* be done:

In some universities, firms, and communities in which governance had formerly been characterized by centralized directive hierarchical authority, experiments have been successfully launched to provide opportunity for all those affected by managerial and governing decisions to participate in making them.

Providing another sign that change is not impossible, is the occasional initiation by university or political Establishments of a fundamental change in the structure or process of governing or in the rights and privileges accorded the governed which creates hope for, and the possibility of a break through in, the removal of obstacles to personal development and to self-realization. The consequences of such a breakthrough are to make the remaining obstacles even less tolerable than before and to amplify the stimulation to corrective action before considered difficult if not impossible.

Most of the factors named in the foregoing discussion have to some extent always been present in the experience of some students on some campuses in some countries at some time. The socialization process to which some young people have been exposed has always produced critics of, and rebels against, the circumstances which provide them with whatever opportunities for and constraints on self-realization which they, and those with whom they empathize, experience. Less than perfect socioeconomic-political systems and their mode of governance have always turned up evidence that, in the minds of students, justifies their criticism and rebellion.

The overt expression of such predispositions has frequently troubled the great majority of those who accept the status quo and make the best of it. They are faced with a disturbance to the even tenor of their ways. Likewise the managers and governors of the institutions constituting the System are faced with problems of social control. Yet the disturbance and the problems only occasionally reach proportions producing results beyond the limits of tolerance for the majority, or basically threatening to the stability and viability of the arrangements and institutions which supply order and dependability to work and life. And the managers and governors of those institutions have usually been able to maintain that stability and viability by one or the other of two types of responsive action. At times they have considered the protests symptomatic of needed modifications in their policies and practices and have taken corrective action with respect to the matters which were the focus of criticism and rebellion, thus actually strengthening probability of the popular acceptance of the institutions. At other times, with the active or passive approval of the majority of the population affected, they have forcefully restrained or quarantined the dissenters and protesters.

The factors named in the preceding pages of this chapter are frequently labeled as the *causes* of student activism. They are causes only in the sense that students so characterized as possessing protest prone predispositions, and experiencing such environmental factors are in a state of readiness for student activism. Whether or not that readiness is transformed into overt action will turn upon the simultaneous appearance of certain activating factors.

Factors Activating Overt Protest

What then are these factors which are able to turn a latent possibility for activism into a living reality, to turn undercurrents of dissatisfaction and frustration into openly expressed protest, to translate critical and dissident verbal comments and discussion into a language of deeds?

The following factors were present in every instance of overt student activism of which we are aware which reached the level of collective direct action. They will be more fully discussed in the last section of this chapter.

There was present one or more capable, dynamic, and persuasive initiators of specific courses of action, possibly, but not necessarily, inclined to demagogic agitation. In the great majority of cases these were local students including leaders of activist student organizations. But initiators occasionally come from junior faculty members, from migrant student or nonstudent agents, or, very infrequently, from politicians, or agents of radical organizations.

But more than an initiating agent was necessary. There had occurred one or more symbolic and triggering events or situations. The events ranged from seemingly minor incidents, such as the refusal of a professor to postpone an exam, to engagement of a nation in an unpopular war. Not the size or world-shaking impact of the event or situation but several essential characteristics of it which will be detailed later, appear to make it an essential activating factor.

Factors Reinforcing Student Activism

Once student activism has surfaced on a particular campus, the probability that it will continue or even escalate is dependent in part upon the continued presence of the stimulating personal and environmental factors discussed above, on the failure to make satisfactory progress in the correction of the policies and practices which have been the object of attack, on the presence of reinforcements which reduce doubts among the participants that their course of action is justified and likely to lead to a realization of their objectives.

A most important reinforcement must come from the organizational and operational adaptability of those who were initially, or have become, the recognized leaders. It is much easier to start an action than it is to manage the continuation of that action as events produce new and unanticipated problems relative to the attitudes and conduct of participants, and to the response of those against whom the action is directed or of uninvolved persons (including those within and outside the university) whose interests are nevertheless affected by the action. Many manifestations of student activism have proved to be flashes in the pan, not because the factors producing it cease to be strong, but because the student managers have been confused or inept in their adaptive strategy and tactics in the face of such changing developments.

But assuming the managerial skill of the student leaders is equal to their task, the study of observed and recorded cases of continuing and escalating student activism discloses a number of reinforcing factors which singly or in combination appear to have contributed to maintaining its momentum. We shall merely list here those factors which have been observed in Japan, India, Mexico, and Colombia, as well as the United States, reserving detailed discussion for the next section of this chapter:

Moral or financial support from other student or non-student groups was frequently forthcoming.

The action response of the university or public authorities, in accordance with its nature, appears to have potential both for reducing and for increasing continued overt activism.

The popular cultural climate was in certain respects supportive of the declared or implied objectives and value priorities of the students.

The success of some of the methods used by students when employed by other population groups was frequently cited as justification for those methods.

The support of persons with a respected social status frequently bolstered the morale of the activists.

A Framework of Essential Factors

Are there a number of these many factors, in some manner related to the encouragement and stimulation of student activism, which are essential to its occurrence at any time and place, and which, if absent, would make its occurrence highly improbable? We would now like to review the findings of the previous chapters and attempt a first approximation to a positive answer to that question by indicating in the remaining pages of this chapter only those factors which have been observed to be present *in every case* of overt activism which has come to our attention in the literature or in personal experience in the United States, Japan, India, Mexico, and Colombia.

The structure of this analysis is related to a number of generalizations concerning the dimensions of student activism.

That student activism has been reported ever since universities were established, and that it is characterized by many similar dimensions and features in a number of countries with differing histories, cultures, economic, political, and social institutions suggests the presence of universal elements in the personal and social situation of students everywhere that can produce reactions which ready them for student activism.

That not all students, indeed only a minority, participate as activists suggests that only certain personal characteristics or predispositions which are strengthened by or result from the experience in adapting to that commonly experienced situation ready students for, and can find expression in, student activism.

That student activism is directed toward making changes in the policies and practices of the governors and managers of economic, political, and educational institutions suggests that perceived inadequacies and inconsistencies in the governance and operations of these institutions are necessary preconditions to strengthen, and justify to the student, his predisposition toward, and his participation in, student activism.

That overt student activism is not omnipresent and that it waxes and wanes in both occurrence and intensity suggests two further probabilities. The first is that those elements in the experience which are conducive to, and make some students prone to initiate or join in such activism, vary in intensity at particular times and places. The second is that there are essential activating factors which must necessarily be present if latent predispositions to activism are to be transformed into overt activism.

That some incidents have a short and some a long duration suggests that certain reinforcements are conducive to a continuance or escalation of activism once it has become overt.

The Life Situation of Students

In Sections III and IV, we related our findings in Japan, India, Mexico and Colombia to three aspects of the life situation of the great majority of students everywhere and at all times. Each youthful student is facing the tasks of coming of age physically, psychologically, and socially; of becoming a student; and of becoming a citizen.

The first task necessitates their achieving an image of their selves consistent with the extent and quality of the personal capabilities they believe they possess, and with achieving a meaningful, significant, and secure relationship to the realities of current society as they perceive them or to a more ideal society which they envision, and with the model of mature adulthood provided by the culture in which they have been reared. It also necessitates their finding a mode of assertion and expression of that self which satisfies their desire for uniqueness and personal importance, and simultaneously permits them to interact with others in ways which both they and the others can experience as dependable and mutually satisfactory or tolerable.

The second task necessitates one of two optional courses. The first is the incorporation into their conception of self of the image of the Student prevalent in their society, that is the widely held conception of what a student should be and do. This image is buttressed by expectations held by students concerning the responsibilities of the university and of society to them, and the expectations held by university staff and by people generally of what students owe the university and society. The second is to create through their activity a new image of the Student more consistent with their own concept of what those responsibilities and obligations should be.

The third task necessitates their calculation of the extent to which the realities of the institutional arrangements of their society will enable them to express and assert the self-image they are developing as near adults and students, and the degree to which opportunities and constraints which the societal values, norms, institutional arrangements, and system of governance, as they perceive and interpret them, will aid or inhibit them in that process.

Facing these tasks, which no student anywhere can avoid, students are impressed by certain perceptions they have of the facts of life which become for them of central interest and concern.

The first perception is that the values, norms, and institutional arrangements which are available as resources to them are the products of the adaptation to *past* problems of living for students and citizens, and that their relevance to future and even present problems is, therefore, at least questionable. This conclusion increases in intensity in periods of rapid and accelerating changes in human knowledge, in technology, in human aspirations, and in a period of uncertainty as to the consequences of shifting power relations between groups within a nation and between nations. Such a time is now.

The second perception is that the student and adult roles available for ascription or achievement are likewise adaptations to past and present problems of living, and therefore are also suspect as being inappropriate and, at best, untrustworthy as reliable career opportunities for those whose major portion of living lies in the future. If new roles must be created who shall set the functions and their scope?

A third perception, a correlate of the one above, is that the values and norms by which the appropriateness of their own and others' behavior can be appraised, and the institutional arrangements and roles by which that behavior is ordered, are those created not by themselves, but by previous generations and their elders. The blame for any inadequacies or inconsistencies observed relative to such societal resources is, therefore, appropriately, in their judgment, placed on members of an older generation.

The fourth perception is that the apparent dominant interest of the adult members of society is in perpetuating the existing values, norms, institutional arrangements, role structure, and system of governance, and that those adults give chiefly lip service to the creative modification of such societal resources with reference to the probable character of future societal reality. The governing System which the elders have created and support, is geared chiefly to the perpetuation of the status quo with respect to such societal resources.

A fifth perception, closely related to the last, is that those adult members of society have devised various methods of socialization and social control in family, school, and community, the apparent function of which is to shape the values, character, behavior, and capacities of youth to conform to the presently existing societal pattern, and to produce in them attributes which are unlikely seriously to disturb the perpetuation of that pattern.

A sixth perception is that in *some* families, schools, and particularly universities, their elders provide an example of iconoclasm, creativity, skepticism, and independence which appears to challenge the validity of conformity as a rule for living.

The seventh perception is that the rhetoric with which traditional values are defended is not always matched by faithful adherence to those values in the behavior of adults, and especially of those adults who manage and govern societal institutions. The inference is drawn either that those values and norms are practically unadapted to life as it is, or that their proclamation and defense is hypocritical. A derivative of the latter inference is that the governors and managers cannot be trusted.

An eighth perception, a plausible inference from the other seven, is that the behavior of students in their efforts to come of age as students and citizens is subject to a system of rules and laws in the formulation of which they have had no part, and that they are subject to the governance of those in whose choosing they have had no voice.

The ninth perception is that they are not accepted by the adults of their society and by the Establishment which governs its institutions as those who have reached a stage of maturity and competence enabling them to exercise significant power within the established orthodox processes of governance.

For the most part, it will be noted, these perceptions pertain to the inadequacies and inconsistencies in the societal resources available for individual use in the processes named of coming of age, becoming a student, and becoming a citizen, and to the constraints imposed upon their efforts by the past-oriented orthodox societal values, norms, institutional arrangements and system of governance within the bounds of which they are expected by the adult members of their society to solve those personal problems. More concern is evidenced by students concerning the inadequacy of societal resources than concerning any inadequacy of their own capabilities to use these resources satisfactorily to themselves and others.

One consequence of the combination of these perceptions by students of their life situation is the conclusion that a possible option in solving their tasks of coming of age and of becoming a student and citizen is to change in their university and society the societal resources indicated above to conform to present circumstances, anticipated future probabilities, and to their own personal needs and aspirations. Another consequence is the conclusion that, in the face of resistance to change on the part of those in control (the Establishment) and to student participation in effecting change, a plausible option would be bold self-assertion and "taking things into their own hands" through direct unorthodox action. Not all are attracted to a choice of such options, but those who are have made a choice which readies them for student activism.

Another consequence is that any inhibitions to unorthodox activity and to attack on current institutions and rules of the game, rooted in respect for the accomplishments of past generations, are reduced. These consequences are not the causes of the extremes of self-assertion observed in many student activists, but they minimize restraints on those extremes.

Characteristics and Predispositions Expressed in
Student Activism

It is difficult to see how any university or society could remain sufficiently stable to operate at all, let alone operate effectively, if *all* youth and students were impelled to conduct suggested by the foregoing options. It is apparent that the great majority adapt to the perceived situation, sketched above, in ways that do not seriously disturb the existing pattern of university and societal operations or governance. The results of the interaction of personal attributes with the processes, arrangements, and resources for socialization and social control are such that only a small proportion of youth and students become predisposed openly to challenge the System or its governance, and actively to engage in either individual or collective efforts to change it. The great majority opt for adjustment to the arrangements, processes, and governance by conforming to the requirements for adult approval. It is not necessary to assume complete satisfaction of individual needs or aspirations on the one hand or unavoidable coercive pressure on the other to account for this result.

We must, however, leave the explication of these differential results in the acquisition of characteristics and predispositions which later are given opportunity for expression through student activism to those whose field of study is socialization and social control in childhood and adolescence.

Our contact with student activists occurred at the stage when these characteristics and predispositions are finding expression in student activism. At the beginning of this chapter we listed a number of such characteristics and predispositions which have been observed to predominate among activists more than among non-activists in the several countries. Five of these were present among the activists, both initiators and their closest collaborators, in every overt manifestation of activism which we observed or concerning which we have the relevant information. Briefly stated those possessing such characteristics and predispositions were in some respect separated and lonely, but in search of integrated fellowship with their peers, skeptical and cynical, bored with many aspects of university and community life, inclined to communicate through their deeds as well as their words, and unbelieving and time bound.

The Separate and Lonely

Our observation is that both the initiators and their closest collaborators are in some respect separate, and at times alien and lonely individuals in relation to the great majority of their fellow students. The characteristics of these individuals which, in a sense, set them apart from the members of that majority and make integrated and satisfying fellowship with them difficult, are many and varied, and of course do not all apply to a particular individual. But anyone who has had the experience of college life will be aware that, on the campus on which that experience was gained, there were a number of individuals who, for some reason related to their heritage, their socialization, their personal capabilities, their predominant predispositions, or their personal preferences, did not initially quite fit in comfortably in the company and intercourse of the general run of their fellow students. Some were left out or left behind. Some were left alone. Some were left ahead.

Students so characterized formed the body of personnel from which every student activist leader, and a large proportion of their followers whom we interviewed, had come. Their separateness and distinctiveness would take one or more of the following forms.

They were dedicated absolute idealists among pragmatists. They were committed humanitarians among the unconcerned or self-centered. They were seekers of revenge among those inclined to reconciliation. They were politically alert among the politically uninterested or apathetic. They were religiously devoted among nonbelievers or vice versa. They were pacifists and conscientious objectors among those who accepted military service as a personal responsibility and military force as a necessary and legitimate instrument of foreign policy. They were challengers among the satisfied. They were creative intellectuals among those satisfied with average academic performance. They were of the elite among common folk, or of the common folk among the elite. They were from privileged and affluent backgrounds among the disadvantaged, or from disadvantageous backgrounds among the privileged and affluent. They were members of a racial or communal minority group among those who were members of a racial or communal majority group. They were communists among conservatives or conservative liberals. They were splinter group radicals among "main stream" radicals. They were Jews among Gentiles. They were rebels among loyalists. They were aggressive among the relatively phlegmatic. They were self-confident among doubters and the insecure. They were predisposed to self-expression in action among those predisposed to expression in words, predisposed to confrontation and intransigency among those predisposed to dialogue and compromise. They were self-righteous among those whom they considered transgressors. They were enamoured of the "creative joy of destruction," or at least radical change, among those satisfied with or tolerant of the status quo. They were anarchists among cooperative or competitive collectivists.

Whether or not a student can be characterized as separate or even alien in any of these ways, his achievement of self-identity and of self-confidence is dependent on his being accepted by, and finding a respected role in some group of his fellows. For identity has a double meaning. It refers to the identity *of* an individual and his identity *with* others.

Acceptance as "one of the gang" and mutually satisfying fellowship is possible for most students because they are the same kind as all the others in essential respects. Voluntarily recognized leadership is normally accorded to those who demonstrate their possession of the *common* admired characteristics *to a higher degree* than the rest.

But if they are characterized by important differences such as those named above, and they wish to be accepted, they face a choice critical to their developing image of themselves. They can in some cases, but obviously not in all cases, remove or cover up their distinctiveness and become conformers; *or* they can seek the comradeship only of their own kind that is, those separate, distinctive, and lonely in the same way; *or* they can seek, to a certain extent, to make the members of the larger group over into their own image, that is to develop a following.

All three alternatives are paths toward maturation for youth who are distinctive or alien in the sense indicated, alternatives providing paths to self-discovery and the progress toward coming of age. The first alternative of conformity is not likely to appeal to those in whom pride in their distinctiveness and/or the urge to realize themselves as initiators and leaders is strong; the second alternative, to seek fellowship with those characterized by the same distinctive or alien characteristics, is a commonly made choice in the case of several of these groups, and is evidenced by many small familiar associations and even organizations among students past and present. But the operational field for leadership offered by this alternative is limited. The effective realization of a status as initiator and leader in

accordance with the third alternative, that is by recruiting followers from among those not necessarily having the distinguishing characteristics of the "alien ones," is the most attractive course for those whose escape from loneliness or the intense desire to be "number one," cannot be adequately satisfied
in association with the limited number who are distinctive or
alien in the same way as themselves.

The Skeptical and the Cynical

The experience of difficulties in coming of age, becoming a
student and citizen, and of adjusting to the norms, values, arrangements, and governance of the university and society does
not lead inevitably to the demand for change and attack on the
System and the Establishment so characteristic of student activism. If the indivudal in difficulty is inclined to blame his
own shortcomings or has a degree of confidence in the ability
and integrity of those who govern and manage the affairs of
the university and society, he is inclined to accept and put up
with and make the best of the situation. The widespread skepticism and cynicism among student activists concerning that
ability and integrity of their governors, however, encourages
among many of them the belief that change will not occur unless pressure and coercion is applied to those who manage and
govern. It is not a great step from such a conclusion to the
conviction that change will be made only when they, the activists, take things into their own hands.

The Bored

If it were possible to arrange the conduct of family, school,
community, and university affairs so that the human reaction
of boredom was eliminated from experience, a basic stimulus
to student activism would be greatly reduced. Any attempt to
do so, however, would be plagued by the fact that boredom is
one product of the interaction of the objective environment with
differential needs and aspirations of individuals. What to one
individual is dependable, consistent, stimulating, and meaningful strikes another as repetitive, tedious, dull, and meaningless. In few aspects of life is the saying, "One man's meat is
another man's poison," so applicable as in the search of youth
during college years for new, exciting, challenging, creative,
and meaningful experience.

Whether it is possible so to order the contacts of students with the resources of science and scholarship and with their teachers, the extracurricular affairs of college life, and other educational experiences so that they contribute zest, excitement, and opportunity for meaningful creative experience to that search, rather than a disappointing sense of living in a barren world and being bored with it all, or with important aspects of it, is not certain.

What is certain is that the ordering has not succeeded in doing that for a number of students who have sought for an alternative way to relieve their boredom in student activism.

This characteristic of being bored with some or all of the aspects of the normal experiences of university life is clearly present among some initiators of every manifestation of student activism which we have observed. Discussions with other activists who joined in, strongly suggests that the promise of satisfaction of the desire to escape from boredom is one of the most potent implicit appeals available for recruiting a substantial number of participants. Student activism is far from a dull, tedious, repetitive, and meaningless business at least for the students, although it may become so over time.

The Action Oriented

The characterization of an activist as one who has the inclination to communicate in the language of deeds as well as words appears to be a redundancy. The risk of being redundant must be taken, for the predisposition to act in ways which convey a message even more strongly than do words is not only a recurring characteristic of initiators but of followers, and one for the overt manifestation of which student activism offers peculiar opportunity. This is not to suggest that initiators of activism are more highly gifted in communicating in action than in words. It is to suggest that words, however accurately descriptive and persuasive, are not for them sufficient. The language of the deed is not only needed to support the verbal declaration and to amplify its potency and urgency, but is an effective and necessary language in its own right. The conviction that ideas are not authentic and "real" until expressed in deeds was never absent from the activists with whom we came in contact.

In a real sense this predisposition is reinforced by the others.

No fellowship in merely verbal dialogue relieves completely the experience of separateness, dissociation, and loneliness. Cynicism concerning the lack of integrity of governors and managers is stimulated by the observation that their deeds do not match their words. Much of the boredom produced by contact with the educational system in the university is associated with the heavy predominance of communication through the written and spoken word. And action, particularly risky and dangerous action, especially when directed toward objectives considered meaningful, is an excellent antidote for boredom. The changes sought are chiefly changes in the actions of people. One whose own inclination is to make his own communication effective by speaking in deeds is also likely to be sensitive to the shortcomings of mere words in others.

Most of the initiators are masters of the spoken word, an ability not necessarily present in the numbers needed for mass action. But the latter can, through their actions, raise the demands made to a pitch and tone commanding attention and expressing the degree of urgency with which the demands are pressed.

The Time Bound Unbeliever

The introspective reader, contemplating these observed characteristics and predispositions of student activists may well ask, "What is so distinctive about these attributes? Who among us has not, at times, had frustrating experiences in trying to know and be ourselves in the face of life conditions unfriendly to that effort? Who among us has not felt ourselves, on occasion, separate and lonely, skeptical and cynical, bored, and impelled to act now, regardless of the consequences? But we did not allow that mood to dictate a continuing course of behavior, in our personal and institutional relationships, which implied a fundamental lack of trust in our fellows, in our traditions, and in our future. Nor did it lead to our denial of the essential soundness of the institutional arrangements within which life and work are carried on. What have student activists experienced that we haven't experienced which predisposes them to that course of behavior?"

That some students who experience separateness and loneliness, cynicism, boredom, and the compulsion to act now, do, and others do not, overcome the predisposition to let these emotions govern their behavior, is an observable fact. The exploration of the reasons for this fact would require data which we do not possess. But we venture to suggest that one additional observed characteristic of the activists we interviewed, has a clear relevance to the persistence of that predisposition.

They lacked faith in the traditions they inherited and in the future. As a result both their concept of self and their understanding of the resources of their university and nation for progressive change were time bound. The reality of what they were was perceived as manifest in their present thoughts and actions. The reality of the resources of their university and nation for progressive development was perceived as manifest in their present structure and operations.

It is not necessary to challenge the element of truth in these time bound perceptions to indicate that they provide their holders with little inclination to trust any save themselves and those who agree with them at the moment. Nor does it predispose them to discipline themselves by reference to past traditions or to the requirements for civilized personal or societal growth in a future they consider to be uncertain, uncongenial, or possibly non-existent, and hence not worth the trouble involved in getting ready for it.

It is not difficult to understand their mood and reaction at this time. The threat to the survival of civilized life by the destructive employment of atomic energy triggered by national power seeking calculation, miscalculation of consequences, or by accident, has dominated the political and social climate over their whole lifetime. The projection of the accelerating pace of the application of a sophisticated technology to increasing areas of human endeavor and relationships raises the specter of a mechanized future from which have been drained opportunities for the expanding life of the spirit. The measurement of progress for their nations in terms of increasing G.N.P., material affluence, and bureaucratic efficiency is uninspiring to the humanists among them; and there are many who prize that emphasis in their concept of self. The meager results to date in bringing under control the threats to human survival of over population, man-produced environmental decay, and poverty, and the relatively low priority given to removing such threats in the totality of public endeavor, produce little pessimism-relieving hope. It is no cause for wonder that in the perception of many students, activist and non-activist alike, the present provides the major, if not the only, arena for living. Nor is it surprising that they perceive the present, rather than a future of expanding horizons of opportunity, as the time which demands action on their part, possibly the only time available to them.

A knowledge of and a sense for the past would reveal to them that this is not the first time in history that the times have been perceived as out of joint and the future viewed with a pessimistic and jaundiced eye, only to be followed by a period of restored faith in a future of enlarging promise. It would also reveal to them that those who have led revolutionary movements, whatever their distrust of the past and present, and whatever the strength of current evidence validating that distrust, have been able to inspire recruits to the movement with a faith in a better future.

A major requirement for marshaling and retaining recruits for a sustained revolutionary student movement is that its leaders convince those recruits, not only that present university and societal conditions are *in their experience* irretrievably bad, but that the future holds the promise of a world remade closer to the heart's desire. The activists' pessimism concerning, and their lack of faith in, the future dulls that hope.

The romantic idealism noted in the value emphases of many student leaders is no substitute for this lack of faith in the future. For that faith is necessary to obtain sustained commitment to the action required to reach the ideal. If that faith is lacking, it may still be possible for student activist leaders to stir members to immediate action directed against some presently perceived university, economic, or political "evil." It is improbable that they can lead a *revolutionary movement* of radicalized students which is sustained at a high level of activism over time.

Experienced Institutional Inadequacies and Inconsistencies

Student activism has targets the chief of which are the policies and practice of the governors and managers of present university, economic, and political institutions. But attacks implicitly, and frequently explicitly, are also directed at the institutions themselves, at their essential character, and at the values they embody. The experienced relationship of students to these institutions and to the policies and practices of their governors has brought the antagonistic personal predispositions of some of them to a level conducive to overt expression in student activism.

In every case of student activism which has come to our notice the activists had experienced and become acutely aware of two characteristics of their institutional environment which amplified their readiness for that activism. Among the activists there was an action stimulating awareness from personal or vicarious experience that their allegations of the shortcomings and inconsistencies of the university, economic, and political Systems and their governors mirrored reality, *and* they judged these shortcomings and inconsistencies to be inexcusable.

Verification by Personal Experiences

The roster of these alleged shortcomings and inconsistencies has been amply recorded in the foregoing pages, and need not be repeated here. What makes them factors which ready students for activism directed at their removal is not the allegation of their existence but the verification of the allegation by personal or vicarious experience.

Few students can verify from their own experience the allegation that the university System *in general* fails to provide facilities and opportunities commensurate with the expectations and anticipations with which students in general come into the university world. But when the university and the expectations are their own, the verifying evidence, if any, is close at hand.

With the entrance into the university of increasing numbers from economic, social, and racial groups from environments in which the students or their families and close associates have experienced the impact of discriminatory and inequitable treatment at the hands of the agents of economic and political governance, the awareness from personal experience of such matters becomes more widespread. That personally verified awareness is also increased by participation (frequently encouraged by the schools and universities as educationally valuable) in organized or volunteer efforts to aid those who in some respect are disadvantaged, or by association with efforts of workers, relief clients. racial groups, tenement house dwellers and other ghetto residents, tax payers, public school teachers, and electors to bring their grievances to the attention of the univer-

sity or public authorities. Particularly when these efforts bring
those involved into disillusioning relations with the processes
of public administration and justice, are any inadequacies, inconsistencies or injustices in those processes open to their first
hand inspection. It is in such experiences that they also can
observe at close range the irrelevancy, if such exists, between
their education and their preparation for constructive involvement in the duty of responsible citizens to keep their communities on the road to progress, security, and opportunity for
self-development for all citizens.

Even where personal experience is lacking, the data for their
awareness through vicarious experience is ample.

Anyone who is familiar with the literature and activism of
social protest and utopianism provided by those considered
heretics and rebels and revolutionaries of their own time will
find no new themes in the critical allegations, by present day
students, of misgovernance of the universities and other institutions and of the hypocrisy and untrustworthiness of their
Establishments. Nor is the perception of these institutional
shortcomings and inconsistencies limited to the social critics
and their readers and auditors. In any country whose press and
other information media are relatively free (and this applies to
all of the countries here under discussion) news reports are sufficient which, when added to personal experience or the experience of acquaintances, create a widespread knowledge of evidence substantiating the allegations. If the evidence from the
orthodox media does not do this, the underground press, tracts
for the times, radical authors, folk singers, and traveling student movement delegates supply additional data, not, of
course, considered trustworthy by all.

Inexcusable Evils

Yet all this validating evidence does not *cause* mass activism
directed against the educational, economic, or political system
and its governors among the population or among students in
general. In order that even the validating evidence from personal or vicarious experience shall ready students for activism,
those who become aware of it must add to that evidence the
value judgment, "Such things are inexcusable."

The great majority, even when the evidence is clear, find
some basis for excusing the shortcomings and inconsistencies of

the System and especially of its agents. Most feel no urge to explain their tolerant or grumbling acceptance of the institutional environment as they find it. But the words of those who do give voice to that urge have a familiar ring. "Those abuses refer to the conduct and character of a small minority." "The system itself is sound though exploited for personal advantage by a few." "The case is overgeneralized from isolated and occasional instances." "That's the way it is; you have to make the best of it." "Who am I to tell them how to do their job? They are doing the best they can. I could do no better." "When the present situation is compared with that in the past, real progress is evident." "Rome wasn't built in a day." "There is no progress without pain." "The university and the nation have experienced this sort of thing before and lived through it; this also will pass." "My university or nation, may they ever be right; but my university or nation, right or wrong."

What makes the shortcomings and inconsistencies in the policy and practice of university and public governors inexcusable, if not intolerable, for those whose personal or vicarious experience suggests that they are actual and not just the allegations of agitators? Discussions with both activists and non-activists indicate that this judgment is applied to policies and practices perceived to have the following characteristics:

Policy and practice reveal the university or political governors as lacking in *credibility* and *trustworthiness*. This characteristic can ready students for activism even in the absence of the other characteristics.

Policy and practice do not measure up to the declared intentions and proclaimed values of those governors. In other words the differences in word and deed indicates *hypocrisy*.

Policy and practice reveal those governors as *self-seeking and inconsiderate* of the legitimate needs and aspirations of the governed.

Policy and practice *violate some claimed rights* possessed constitutionally or by custom and usage by those whose lives are affected by that university or public policy and practice.

Policy and practice reveal an attempt on the part of the university or political governors to *manipulate* the governed into acceptance of consequences for them of current policies and practices, particularly when forceful or persuasive coercion is employed.

Policy and practice result from decisions made behind closed doors by a university or political governing elite on the basis of data not open to public scrutiny and by a process of decision-making not in reality influenceable by current popular action.

We noted in the foregoing pages that the activists' lack of faith in the future made it improbable that they could lead a sustained revolutionary student movement. The necessity that students shall verify in experience the activists' allegations that the present university and national Systems and their Establishments are irretrievably bad, or sufficiently bad to justify commitment to sustained revolutionary activism, raises the same improbability. For the actions of the governors of the university and of economic and political institutions which give experienced reality to such a conclusion vary in intensity and vividness from time to time and from place to place, and at certain times and places suggest an opposite conclusion. The level of student activism, whether for reform or revolution, can, therefore, be expected to wax and wane in accordance with the variations in the presence, the intensity, and vividness, of the evidences of mismanagement and inconsistency in the policy and practice of the governors of the university and other societal institutions.

Given the presence on a particular campus of a critical mass[3] of students (a) who have chosen, as a clue to their self-identity as mature individuals, as students, and citizens, to adopt the

[3]What constitutes a critical mass? It is no aid to predictability to infer after the event that there *must have been* a critical mass. But neither our own investigations nor those of others suggest a reliable answer to that question. The estimates of *proportions* of activists in the student population as a whole or even on a particular campus are probably less instructive than some absolute number. The responses of student leaders to our question, "How many committed activists on your campus do you consider necessary to radicalize enough students to assure effective direct action?" varied from 25 to 50. There was no significant correlation of these numbers with the size of the student body. The numbers obviously referred to an inner core of initiators and their closest collaborators rather than to the number of students who were thoroughly radicalized. But on the basis of present studies, most of which were conducted after, rather than before the event, the question must lack a reliable answer; and we must acknowledge this lack as a weak link in our chain of reasoning and of our interpretation and explanation of student activism.

role of a changer of their university and/or political system through self-assertion and direct unorthodox action, (b) who know themselves as separate and lonely, skeptical and cynical, bored, inclined to communicate in deeds as well as words, and lacking faith in past traditions and the future, and (c) who have, through personal or vicarious experience, verified the allegations of inexcusable shortcomings and inconsistencies in the policy and practice of the governors of their university and society, the students on that campus are ready for overt activism challenging the authority and trustworthiness and even the legitimacy of their university and/or political governors.

The Condition of the Organizational Charter of the University and Nation[4]

Overt challenge, however, is not inevitable. For most individuals, reaction is tempered by their awareness that they are members of a university and a nation which have unique identities. The name of that university or nation stands for a particular character and system of arrangements and values. The university and nation have organizational charters which distinguish them from other universities or nations. That awareness may or may not fill them with pride. Nevertheless they sense that the authenticity of their own self-image and of the system of relations existing between themselves and other members of their university and nation demands a high degree of consistency with the organizational charter of their university and nation. This awareness imposes restraints on their own self-assertion and provides an important guide to the avoidance of anarchy and antagonistic conflict in the behavioral adjustments they make in relations with other members of the university or political community.

The factor in the institutional environment experienced by students in universities and nations where activism, characterized by extremes of self-assertion and conflict generating behavior has occured, is that such restraints and guides are in disarray. There is an experienced lack of definiteness, clarity, and widespread consensus concerning the essential unique character, i.e. the organizational charter, of the university and/or the nation by reference to which the individual can establish his iden-

[4]See introduction to Section III for a more detailed discussion of the nature of this exceptionally critical factor.

tity as a student and/or citizen, can validate his developing concept of self, and can evaluate his conduct as a responsible participant in these institutional entities.

Lacking a clear and widely accepted concept of the essential and central mission, values, goals, and other identifying indicators of the character of the university, the idea of what it means to be a student and of the opportunities and responsibilities associated with that role is in a state of confusion. Lacking a clear and widely accepted concept of the character of the nation, the idea of what it means to be a citizen, an American, an Indian, a Japanese, a Mexican, a Colombian, and of the opportunities and responsibilities associated with that role, is incomprehensible. A youth in quest for a concept of self as mature individual, which must necessarily incorporate such roles, is left without a touchstone by reference to which he can authenticate his perception of what it means to be his self in relation to these societal entities. Moreover, even though he senses that, practically speaking, a high degree of consistency is required between a reliable and realistic and authentic concept of self and the essential character of these entities, the test of consistency is difficult or impossible to apply if the character of these is confused and unclear.

Since the leadership, operation, problem solving, conflict resolution, and governance in the university and the nation are difficult unless both the governed and the governors are in fundamental agreement on the essential character of these societal entities, the arrangements and processes of living for all involved are experienced, when the understanding of that character is in disarray, as unsatisfactory, and as lacking in dependability, direction, purpose, and meaning. The confidence of the governed in their governors is undermined by what appears to the governed at best as ineptness and vacillation, and at worst as inconsistency and hypocrisy. It is only a short step from making such a judgment to challenging the legitimacy of their status as governors. Equally significant as a result of lack of clarity of, and broad concensus with respect to, the organizational charter of the university or nation, is that a most important basis for resolution of internal schisms or conflicts is missing.

If, on the other hand, the organizational charter of the university and the nation is sufficiently clear and widely accepted to provide students and citizens respectively with a sense of confidence and even pride, and with the assurance that they are participants in a collectivity sure of its mission, values, goals, essential character, and future, the intensity of protest against the remaining factors would be greatly reduced. And the possibility that corrective action with respect to these factors can be anticipated within the present governing structure of the universities and the nation would appear more reasonable. The necessity to "take things intò our own hands" would appear less imperative. Moreover a common point of reference and mutual concern would be available, suggestive of a standard against which to measure the appropriateness and viability of any adjustment sought or reached in regard to differences and conflicts between students and the university and political Establishments.

Such is not the case at the present time. Student activism seeking changes in the structure, operations, and governance of the university is encouraged by the uncertainty as to the essential mission, values, and future of the particular university involved, as well as of universities in general. Where student activism challenges the major policies, practices, and governance of a university, that challenge and the response to it reveals a lack of consensus among the activists, students generally, the administration, and faculty members as to what that university stands for. Its organizational charter is in disarray. The resolution of that challenge and the modification of university policy, practice, and governance to meet it creatively in a way which preserves the integrity and viability of the institution is difficult, and may, in some cases, be impossible. The parties to the resolution and modification hold no mutually agreed upon concept of what a university essentially *is* and *can become*. They lack consensus concerning the university's organizational charter by reference to which their differences can be resolved.

Moreover, the *national* organizational charters of Japan, India, Mexico, Colombia, and the United States are in a state of disorder and disarray. There is widespread uncertainty of what the essential national goals, values, and standards of civilized domestic and international policy and practice really are. And the differences among those who claim to be certain about such matters are so great that no general consensus exists. The people of these nations are members of a house divided against itself in their perception of the essential character of the nation. One gathers from the available evidence, that the same generalization applies to other countries in South and North America, Europe, Asia, and Africa, in which student activism has, in recent years, occurred with increasing intensity.

The student activists did not create this lack of consensus. They inherit it, and are trying to find themselves and their appropriate place in a university and nation the members of which are unsure and in disagreement about what the university and nation in reality stand for. Continuing and possibly increasing manifestations of their activism can be anticipated, as long as this generalization holds, whenever the activating factors discussed below come into operation, whatever reforms are instituted to correct specific "evils" against which student protest is raised.

Essential Activating Factors

But readiness for activism does not lead inevitably and automatically to overt activism. Essential for the transformation of potential protest of students against the structure, policy, and practice of established universities and other institutions, directed at their managers and governors, are two activating factors which push the relationship between students and those managers and governors beyond an acceptable level of tolerance, and which provide a critical number with the confidence that there is a viable alternative to passive acceptance. In the first part of this chapter were listed a number of such factors all of which have served to spark overt activism in all of the countries investigated and in the United States.

In the absence of two of these factors, a dynamic instigator and a triggering event or situation, we would predict that no overt activism would occur, whatever the degree of readiness for activism of a substantial number of students produced by the encouraging and stimulating factors named above.

Dynamic Initiator or Initiators

The absolutely essential factor is the presence of one or more capable, dynamic, and persuasive initiators of a specific course of action. Those who performed this essential function were usually perceived by those who were aroused to activism by their leadership to have several attributes. They were able to state the need for and objectives of action in clear and uncomplicated primitive terms designed to generate emotional enthusiasm for action. They were quick to suggest a course of action. They were self-confident. They were willing to take the risk of making the first move, and apparently disdainful of consequences damaging to themselves. They understood crowd psychology and were skilled in its manipulation. They understood the motivations and predispositions of that portion of the student population which they sought to marshal for action, and had the capacity to transform predispositions into a commitment to action. Moreover, as we have suggested, those initiators with whom we came in contact and their closest collaborators were liberally endowed with the characteristics of separateness and loneliness, with skepticism and cynicism, with boredom, with a predisposition to consider words unauthentic unless translated into present deeds, and with a time bound distrust of both past traditions and the future.

To assert the necessity for the presence of this human activating factor is to question any hypothesis of spontaneous combustion among students of predispositions which can find expression in overt activism. Without the dynamic and persuasive taker of the initiative, the readied students are like a dynamite bomb without a percussion cap.

The Triggering Event or Situation

Equally essential to the overt manifestations of student activism is a triggering event or situation which brings into focus, as a cause for action and as relevant to the interests of large numbers of students, one or more of the experience-verified allegations of institutional shortcomings and/or inconsistencies referred to above. The variety of events or situations observed to perform this function is great. What in their nature gives them the power to trigger overt student activism? In all cases of which we are aware, several, and usually all, of the following characteristics can be observed.

The event or situation dramatically and vividly symbolizes and provides specific verifying evidence of the perceptions of activists concerning particular objectionable characteristics of the university, economic, or political institutions, concerning the way in which the Establishment manages and governs these institutions, and particularly concerning the degree to which their managing and governing run counter to the life interests of the people involved. The event serves to verify in a plausible manner the "case" the activists advance against the managers and governors particularly that they are lacking credibility and trustworthiness. Even though the "case" may be a derivative of an ideological interpretation of societal reality, it gains strength to stimulate the students' inclination to "do something about it" when reinforced by one or more symbolic immediate events. The characteristics of the institutions to which they object, the objectionable consequences for the life interests of the people involved (including themselves), and their exclusion from the highly centralized governance of these institutions are more likely to stimulate action when made manifest in specific recent behavior of those to whom they can direct overt protest and the demand that such behavior be changed. Recruits, even more than the initiators, require vivid evidence that the case is "real" if they are to commit themselves to an active attack on the alleged evils.

The second essential characteristic of the triggering event or situation is that it shall have a negative impact on the personal aspirations and life expectancies of the majority of students or is intricately associated with some event or circumstance which has such a negative impact. A substantial number of students are made aware that their personal problem of coming of age, of becoming a student, and of becoming a citizen, is vitally affected by the behavior of the Establishment or institution which the event or situation symbolizes. Such a characteristic is certainly likely in the cases of an event or situation symbolizing objectionable features of university life and governance, but is frequently present in those symbolizing objectionable features of economic and political policy and practice. If it symbolizes both simultaneously, it is all the more powerful in its activating impact.

A third and related essential characteristic, conducive to activization of larger numbers than would otherwise be the case, is that the event or situation co-joins the interests of several of the groups of students we have characterized as separate and lonely, and who are seeking integration and fellowship with their fellow students by developing a following in a cause which has widespread appeal. When such an event or situation, for example, co-joins the interests simultaneously of absolute idealists, humanitarians, political radicals, racial or communal minorities, and intellectually dynamic individuals, the possibility for a coalition of the several groups of initiative-prone individuals is present. These several groups of initiators, united even temporarily and for different reasons, will be able to stimulate the commitment to action by a number who are willing to stand by any one of them, but who are unimpressed by initiators with different objectives in mind.

Examples of events and situations which had all of the three named characteristics in the countries under observation are as follows: In the United States, the Vietnam War, the draft, the civil rights movement, the killing of four students at Kent State by the National Guard; in India prior to 1947, the "quit India" and civil disobedience campaign against English rule, and, at the present time, the proposal to eliminate English as a link language, leaving Hindi as the only link language between the several states, several unpopular incidents in the political maneuvering of the Congress Party in the attempt to perpetuate its dominant role in governing the country, and the police brutality accompanying the handling of several demonstrations; in Mexico and Colombia, the "invasion" of university grounds by the police in violation of university "autonomy," particularly obvious efforts by an inner circle elite group to perpetuate themselves in power and to limit the expansion of political participation for those not associated with that group, the action of a foreign government (chiefly the United States) interpreted as a threat to national autonomy and self-determination, and the "successful" Cuban revolution; in Japan, the renewal by political leaders of the Security Pact with the United States carrying with it the potential involvement of Japan and its youth in military operations of the United States, the visit of American nuclear submarines, events demonstrating the continuing subordination of Japanese aspiration for independence and autonomy to the interests of a foreign power, legislative or administrative moves promoting the increasing centralization of educational and police authority in the national government.

Given that the event or situation has these three characteristics, the roster of possibilities is extensive. Any list can only be suggestive. Some of the most frequently named relevant to life within the university are: the refusal of the university faculty or administrators to grant requests or demands for student participation in university governance in general or with respect to a specific issue interpreted as violation of student "rights"; the reduction of the scope of such participation previously per-

mitted; the failure of such participation, when granted, to result in an immediate modification of university policy or practice satisfactory to the students involved. Typical of the specific
issues are those related to the quality or system of instruction,
the evaluation or grading of student performance, treatment of
a particular popular professor by the administration, the regulation or censorship by university authorities of student expression or restriction of their freedom to invite visiting speakers,
the availability of university facilities for student activities,
particularly those considered "dangerous" or "inappropriate
for student involvement," regulations of the students' non-
academic affairs considered to be an invasion of their private
lives, a rise in tuition charges, university admissions policies
and practices, the management of student unions, the disciplining or suspension or explusion of a popular student or
group of students, particularly those who have initiated and
organized student protests, university involvement or non-
involvement in support of, or opposition to, certain public
policies or community centered projects.

Other activating events have their incidence in the activism
of students on other campuses to which students on a particular
campus are moved to give support or to imitate.

The event or incident has frequently involved the relation of
the university to the public authorities, as when the actions of
central government are perceived as an infringement on academic freedom or the autonomy of the university, or when public regulation of admission standards to professional practice,
for which a university education is a preparation, are stiffened,
or when public financial support for university operations or
students is severely curtailed, or when the university authorities
collaborate with government projects considered "immoral" by
the students (e.g. the draft, military training, military research,
investigations of radical activity)

The activating event frequently has its incidence in public
policy or practice or disturbances initially unrelated to student
experience. Such events are the exercise of what is considered
to be privacy-destroying espionage or brutal police power in
the control of a workers' strike or of the angry demonstrations
of a dissatisfied minority or student groups, the conduct of
international affairs perceived as immoral particularly when
coercive military power is employed, the seizure of power by
individuals, particularly those identified with the military and

suspected of dictatorial ambitions, the passive response of one's own government to interference by another government in the former's domestic affairs.

Anyone acquainted with the general literature of social protest can multiply many times the volume of specific "evils" of the university, economic, and political institutions and their governance, and the events and situations which symbolize them, to which student emigrants, volunteers, reformers, revolutionaries, and reactionaries could direct their attention and against which they could protest. But a relatively few of these are included in the "case" against the economic, political, and educational Establishments on the basis of which the initiators attempt to marshal a following to effect a change, and which trigger overt action. The reason is not difficult to discern. Very few students can be stirred from the normal tenor of their ways to participate in any but marginal changes in their life circumstances unless they experience a definite negative impact on their personal lives, values, and aspirations for living of those values, norms, and institutional arrangements and governance, for the changing of which student activism provides the opportunity. And that negative impact must be sufficient to outweigh the positive experienced benefits to the students of other aspects of university and societal values, norms, institutional arrangements and governance.

Reinforcement for Student Activism

In the first section of this chapter were listed several rein-forcements for student activism which have been observed to contribute to the maintenance of its momentum. It is not possible, as we have done in the case of the other explanatory factors, to pick out for special emphasis those which have been present in *every* case of overt student activism of which we are aware. None of them can lay claim to that distinction. But one or more of the following were always present to support the maintenance of that momentum when it was, in fact, maintained.

Support from Other Student or Non-Student Groups

Reinforcement for continuing or renewed student activism has come in particular cases from moral or financial support from other student or non-student groups. Leaders must be wary

of the latter form of support, for the discovery that it is forthcoming from certain sources, particularly political parties or
groups of the extreme right or extreme left, can alienate some
participants whose continuing involvement is essential, and
lead to a stiffening of resistance by university or public authorities.

Response of University or Public Authorities

The action response of the university or public authorities
has potential both for reducing and increasing the continued
overt activism. Unfortunately no definitive guidelines for their
response appear certain from a study of particular cases. It is
clear that an absolute refusal to enter into negotiations with the
activists, undue delay in responding to them, or treating their
suggestions or demands with animated inattention produces
an irritation among present participants likely to intensify their
efforts. Moreover, such a negative response can be counted on
to enlist many for overt action as a response to that evidence
alone. The stronger and more summary the negative, the larger
the number inclined to support the activists, though they may
have remained unmoved by the original challenge of the initiators. For particularly in the culture of interpersonal relations
of a university, respectful attention and reasoned response to
the expressed interest of each member of the community from
all others, and especially from those who govern, are considered
the basic norm. That one should receive that attention or response borders on, or is actually considered, a right. And when
a response or a lack of response is perceived as a violation of a
right, the fat is in the fire.

Two observations concerning circumstances associated with
the occurrence of student activism appear initially to run
counter to the above generalization concerning the activating
role of a hesitant or negative Establishment response to student
demands for change and for significant participation in effecting
change. The first observation, which pertains primarily to the
United States, is that some of the most noteworthy examples
of student activism have occurred at universities whose administrations and faculties have long promoted student involvement
in university governance and are noted for their attempts to
make the educational experience of students relevant to current
societal problems. The second observation is that even immediate

and generous response of university authorities to particular student demands does not always result in a reduction of student protests, but, on occasion, in an amplification of the demands made.

We have no desire to defend an hypothesis .which, when challenged by an exception, is proved invalid. But are we faced here with an actual exception? It will be recalled that, in discussing the factors which created a readiness among students for activism, there was included the factor of unrealized student expectations with respect to the degree of freedom and other benefits to be derived from university experience in general or at a particular university. Also included among the factors encouraging readiness for activism was the presence on the campus of a critical mass of protest prone students.

Now if a university faculty and administration has instituted the liberal arrangements suggested above, two consequences can be expected to result. The first is that the level of expectations of the students with respect to the willingness of university authorities to respond positively to their requests for more of the same will be raised. What is interpreted as *undue* delay or refusal, under such circumstances is not the same as the interpretation in case delay and refusal are, from past experience, to be anticipated. The second consequence is that the reputation of that university will have drawn to the campus those who seek such an educational environment, many of whom can be expected to be amply supplied with protest prone characteristics. A critical mass of such students is almost assured.

A possible explanation of the second apparent paradox is that the particular leaders of the activism involved may have as an objective, not the correction of the "evils" against which the protest has been launched, but the continuing harassment of the Establishment and the System or even its eventual destruction. In that case the tactics reinforcing continuation are those of the repeated raising of new issues, even when some are resolved, in order that the confrontation may be maintained at a high level of conflict. Leaders so motivated who wish to maintain a mass following are aware that there are limits to such tactics, for the great majority among that following are not committed to the objective which suggests the tactics. If leaders persist beyond the limits of tolerance of their followers, their options are to desist or to join with others so inclined to carry on their efforts through conspiratorial and guerilla methods. If the latter option is chosen, they in fact have dissociated themselves from the student movement and opened themselves to forms of social control reserved for other undeniably anti-social and criminal elements.

It is always possible that the response of those in the university or government will be sufficiently swift and powerful in suppressing the overt activism that total defeat for the activists is the outcome. We do not here discuss that possibility, for every evidence available indicates that such "victory" and "defeat" are, in the long run, superficial. And even in the short run, unless such suppressive police action is comprehensive and complete, it frequently has been noted to feed or fan the fire rather than put it out even for the time being. The calling in of extra-university police or troops provides an additional issue to the original ones which arouses a predisposition to support the activists from among students and faculty members previously not concerned, and indeed increases recruits for activism itself.

Disciplinary procedures, though obviously called for, can infrequently be applied to a mass of students, and the discriminatory selection of those alleged to have varying degrees of responsibility for culpable acts, themselves vaguely defined, can easily result in charges of discrimination which also increase the recruits for activism, resentful of such discrimination. Unless such selection and the disciplinary action is wisely and justly administered, the charge of violation of due process becomes an issue stimulating continuing and even amplified protest. The administration of justice by university students, faculty, or administrators is subject to the necessity of making it consistent with the humane values the interpretation and perpetuation of which is a major mission of the university. The administrators are, therefore, faced with the dual problem of maintaining an orderly climate for university operations while not violating the humane values the perpetuation of which justifies those operations.

In the absence of a clear warning of what discipline is to be anticipated for what specific offenses and through what process, and of a willingness to negotiate in good faith and considerable patience when issues are raised, and of unvacillating but fair administration of the discipline about which prior warning was given, the unplanned *ad hoc* reactions of university and public authorities (whether excessively passive or active) to student overt action has, almost without exception, produced a reinforcement to amplified activism. Few students will initiate activism which goes beyond the bounds of orthodox tolerance. Many more will defend their right to do so. Additional persons will join with the first two when active repression of that perceived right occurs, particularly if coercive force in the form of the police or troops is employed.

Support from Significant Others

A most important reinforcement for student activism comes from the support of significant (to the students) others. Expressions of sympathy and approval as well as support in the councils of the university and, on occasion, actual participation in direct action by some faculty and other public figures is so important that some observers in all the countries here under discussion have asserted that student activism would be seriously weakened without that aid. Paradoxically the violent verbal castigation of student activism by public figures believed to be influential in the councils of the Establishment, and whose reactionary positions, on the very issues to which the students are seeking a more nearly idealistic resolution, are public knowledge, fans the fires of student unrest. The writings of widely respected intellectuals sympathetic to, or just understanding of, student needs, predispositions, values, and actions however, provide a rationale for many of the declared or implicit premises of student activism, making it appear intellectually and morally respectable. The support of significant others is particularly important at a stage in the activism when the initial enthusiasm generated by new and exciting experience has begun to die out in the less than fully dedicated, and when the actions of the group, in the judgment of some participants, are "getting out of hand" and going beyond the borders of civilized conduct to which they normally are predisposed to conform.

Supporting Cultural Values

Equally important is the reinforcement obtained from traditional and/or current popular cultural climate supportive of the declared or implied objectives and value priorities of student activists, and from a widespread popular expression of anxiety about, or revulsion against, the same "evil" characteristics of governing arrangements, policies, and practice, to which students object. When the proclaimed traditional ideal values of the society are the same as values which students contend they are seeking realistically to renew or make actual, that reinforcement is amplified.

A review of the value emphases of student activism discussed in Chapter 10 will indicate the degree to which students may, with some justification, contend that they are actually the defenders of, not the heretical destroyers of, the traditional faith.

Evidence of Success of Unorthodox Methods

The same claim can not be made for the *action* emphases which characterize much of student activism. Even peaceful demonstration is on the borders of traditional orthodoxy, and when sit-ins, violence to persons and property, non-negotiable demands, confrontation are added, the activists receive no reinforcement from a conviction that their actions are in accord with traditional civilized morality. Yet they do turn for justification, when the morality of such actions is challenged, to the evidence that there is, at the present time, an increasing successful utilization of some of these coercive methods by groups in society who had infrequently used them before, school teachers, junior faculty, public servants, tax payers, racial groups, priests, as well as students, and that these groups have won apparent victories denied them by the employment of more widely approved methods. An even more telling argument expounded by some is that the very governors who decry the students' use of coertion and violence, employ such violence as an instrument of national policy in coercing "uncooperative" foreign nations as well as dissident groups of their fellow citizens.

The principle that success in achieving justified ends vindi-cates the use of unsanctioned means may not rate high as a moral premise. It is severely criticized by student activists when employed by the university and political Establishments in vindication of *their* acts. This does not prevent its use by activists as a reinforcement for their own activism when that activism goes beyond the borders of generally acceptable methods.

Summary

The foregoing factors, then, have been present in every case of

overt student activism which we have observed or of which we
have knowledge in the United States, Japan, India, Mexico, and
Colombia. One or more of them were not present where that
activism was absent. We infer therefore, that they suggest necessary, if not sufficient, reasons for student activism. They are as
follows:

1. There is present on a campus a critical mass of students who,
having experienced universal elements in the life situation of
youth and students, and the processes of socialization and social control which affect their efforts to come of age, to become
students, and to become citizens, have acquired certain personal values, characteristics, and predispositions which ready them
for, and which can find expression in, student activism.

2. The most relevant of these characteristics and predispositions are: (a) they have chosen, as a major clue to their self-
identity as mature individuals, the role of a changer of their
university and/or political system through self-assertion and
direct unorthodox action; (b) they know themselves as separate
and lonely, but simultaneously seeking the integration and fellowship that could result from developing a following in pursuit of a popular cause, skeptical and cynical, bored, inclined
to communicate in deeds as well as in words, and lacking faith
in their inherited traditions and future; (c) they have verified
through personal or vicarious experience the allegation of, to
them, inexcusable shortcomings and inconsistencies in the policy and practice of the governors of their university and nation.

3. There is lacking a clear and widely shared consensus concerning the essential mission, values, and character, that is the
organizational charter, of their university and nation by reference to which the authenticity of their self-concepts as responsible members of these societal entities can be measured, and by
reference to which disagreement and divisions among themselves and other members can be resolved in a way preserving
both their personal dignity and the stability and viability of the
university and the nation.

4. There is a coincidence of these factors, which ready students
for student activism, with (a) the presence on the campus of one
or more dynamic, able, and persuasive initiators liberally endowed with the characteristics and predispositions set forth
above, and (b) the occurrence of a triggering event or situation
which simultaneously, dramatically, and vividly symbolizes and

makes specific the inexcusable experience-verified shortcomings
and inconsistencies in institutional policy and practice, *and*
makes clear the negative impact of that policy and practice on
the students' personal lives, values, and aspirations.

5. The student activism, once it is launched, is reinforced by
a number of factors among the most important of which are:
(a) a negative response on the part of the university and public
authorities, particularly when police or military force is employed; (b) the support of significant others; and (c) the realization that the values which they are striving to make actual in
their lives and in the life of their university and society are
essentially the same as, although more absolutely defined than,
those which are claimed to be the humane and civilized foundations for policy and practice in the university and political
community.

Chapter 12
From Peace to War

Student activism in any form is a challenge to the governors of the university and the community. At a minimum, the dissent and protest expressed in orthodox ways warn them that all is not well with the mode and results of their governance and that there is room for improvement. The transformation of individual verbal dissent into active collective protest is always a potential threat to the university or public order. In its most violent manifestations, that threat is to the very stability and viability of the institutions they govern. It is the possibility of escalation of student activism from orthodox and widely approved ways of dissent to violent and revolutionary direct action which troubles and angers the governors, as well as those students and citizens generally, who find life tolerable and even satisfying amid the existing arrangements for life and work on the campus and in the community.

Yet some dissatisfaction and dissent from the participants in any economic, political, social, military, or educational institution is anticipated. In all organizations some degree of overt expression of dissent is tolerated if not welcomed. In all organizations orthodox ways for channeling that overt dissent and protest have been institutionalized, the object of which is to maintain the stability and viability of the organizations. These include various ways in which an individual may openly express his personal dissatisfaction and dissent in thought or deed and seek modifications in that aspect of the system to which he objects, subject to the condition that he violates no laws, or even if, moved by conscience, he does so as an individual, that he does not "conspire" with others to effect such a violation. But collective dissent is also tolerated, if not encouraged. Orthodox institutionalized channels and mechanisms for its expression and for the correction of objectionable aspects of the system have been developed. In addition to these orthodox and widely approved ways are those that are on the borders of orthodoxy, involving peaceful direct action, and those that clearly go beyond that point, involving civil disobedience and violence and revolution.

Some of the most frequently employed methods of implementing dissent may be classified by reference to their increasing levels of unacceptability in the judgment of the great majority of students and citizens as well as their governors.

Level 1. *Orthodox legal expressions of dissent and protest:*

> Individual expressions
> Individual or collective petitions
> Request or demand for negotiations
> Volunteer and voluntary association service
> Collective institutionalized reform efforts
> Electoral and legislative activity
> Appeal to courts and other agencies established to provide legal justice

Level 2. *Peaceful direct action:*

> Mass meetings
> Teach-ins
> Mass "advertising" demonstration or picketing
> Mass bargaining
> Legal strike or boycott

Level 3. *Civil disobedience direct action:*

> Collective rule or law violation
> Coercive interruption of institutional processes and of the operations of institutional personnel
> Sit-ins
> Illegal strike or boycott
> Deliberate police confrontation

Level 4. *Violent direct action:*

> Incidental violence and vandalism accompanying other forms of direct action
> Physical restraint of or attacks on persons
> Planned damage to property

Level 5. *Conspiratorial guerilla and terrorist warfare.*[1]

[1]We do not include this form of activity among the manifestations of *student* activism which we have sought to interpret. Such activism,

An inference which might be drawn from recording these forms of dissent in this way is that a sequential process of escalation is involved. Such an escalation can be observed in specific instances in which the activists, intent on effecting change, begin by employing the orthodox methods (Level 1) and, failing to achieve their objectives, adopt the methods of peaceful direct action (Level 2), and, again experiencing failure, move on to tactics appropriate to Level 3, and so on. It is not necessary, however, to posit such a sequential escalation, to note that the classification does indicate a progression in the forms of student activism from that which is widely accepted as within the rights of free citizens to that which is definitely excluded, by all but universal consent. from acceptable and permitted social behavior.

Why do students, who are as aware as anybody of this fact, not confine their activism, as they are frequently advised and urged to do, to those forms which are safely within the bounds of socially accepted behavior, thus making firm their status as

---

to be sure, poses an extreme threat to the university and social order and to civilized life. But those who employ the typical methods of guerilla warfare, arson, bombings, sniping, kidnapping, and assassination have no need of mass support from students in order to carry out their conspiratorial designs, no need to radicalize large numbers of students. Indeed the success of their diabolical schemes is best achieved by a small, tightly knit, secret, and underground band of conspirators. It is true that some student activists in Japan, Colombia, Mexico, and the United States have been converted to such criminal tactics and have associated themselves with terrorists to whom such wholly destructive tactics are a way of life. It is even possible that such converts have personally committed themselves successively to activism characteristic of the several levels indicated, and, in desperation at their failure to effect the changes they seek through such methods, have cast in their lot with the terrorists. We had no contacts with such persons, and therefore have no data upon which to base any conclusions. But in any case the decision to associate themselves with those dedicated to achieving results through such criminal methods is one which dissociates them from the mainstream of student activism and brings them into association with like-minded criminals whose objectives and motivations and predispositions have no necessary roots in the experience of university students. Their individual and collective activity is the field of study for criminologists not for the analysts of student experience and behavior. Moreover, the control of their behavior requires mechanisms of correction and of penology which are far beyond the mechanisms of social control available to university authorities.

"reasonable, responsible, law abiding citizens?" Why, well knowing the risk they run of moral condemnation and of censure from the majority of their fellow students and citizens, do they participate in actions which are clearly beyond those bounds?

We shall, for the most part, leave to the pychologists and psychiatrists the explanation of such behavior as generated by individual personality traits and predispositions. Our major approach in this chapter will be to analyze the advantages and disadvantages of the behavior at each level for achieving the changes in those university and political policies, practices, and governance, the unsatisfactory nature of which is at the root of the students' predisposition to dissent and protest.

We can, of course, recognize, at the outset that there are student activists whose manual of strategy and tactics, derived from radically revolutionary objectives and ideology, stresses the pragmatic necessity for a planned and continuous offensive disturbing to the operations and the established order of the universities and society, and who are disdainful of the employment of either orthodox methods or of peaceful direct action measures as being ineffective in the attainment of their revolutionary objectives. Moreover, we can acknowledge that it is not an uncommon assumption, made by many persons, that such "agitators" are the "cause" of any form of active dissent beyond that implemented by the orthodox approach.

If the identification of such revolutionary activists were patently clear, and their activity was clearly unrelated to that of those utilizing less violent and destructive methods, the forceful elimination of their threat to the stability and survival of current institutions would probably have wide-spread approval among the great majority of less activist participants in those institutions the destruction of which the revolutionary activists threaten. But this is not normally the situation faced by those participants in, and the managers and governors of, those institutions. The "good guys and the bad guys" are usually intermixed in any manifestation of student activism which stirs the university or public authorities to attempt the "restoration of law and order with justice."

Moreover, in no country in which we have observed student activism were such committed revolutionary activists (aside from the terrorists), either within or outside the ranks of the students, numerous enough to mount an attack on those institutions, with the anticipation of destroying them, without recruiting a substantial number of allies and supporters from among those normally opposed to such attack. Any reasonable prospects for such recruitment involves moving a sizable number of students from the predisposition to make marginal changes in the institutions with which they were dissatisfied to the predisposition to bring down the governance of those institutions or to accept the alternative model of governance apparently favored by the revolutionaries. That sizable number would have to be recruited from among those who, although dissatisfied and even inclined to overt dissent, still have a personal stake in the existing system. And when the reactions of the even larger number of students who experience real benefits from the system and who demonstrate little interest in change, and of adults who control the instruments for protecting the system against radical change, are taken into account, the road to successful revolution clearly is strewn with human and organizational obstacles of major proportions.

Under such circumstances the advocates of violent direct action are divided between the absolutists who consider, in spite of evidence to the contrary, that the only successful tactic is to carry on minority supported guerrilla acts forthwith and those who, daring the charge from the absolutists of "revisionism" and "ideological treason", seek to "radicalize" the student body by involving them in a commitment to thought and action in escalating modes of protest and pressure for change. Toward that end they initiate and join in with the others in whatever form of tactics for which the degree of "radicalization" of the latter makes them ready. That they do this while striving to promote that escalation and to intensify the "radicalization", presents those responsible for maintaining the vitality, stability, and survival of existing institutions with a difficult problem. They must deal with the direct action protest of the radicals without destroying the constructive value which the dissent of less radically disposed students may have for moving institutional structure and operations forward toward a greater actualization of their potential for serving the long range needs and interests of all their members.

The presence of revolutionaries dedicated to the radical reconstruction of the System must be considered as one catalytic agent in any formula producing escalation in the mode, style, and institutionally destructive results of student activism.

We talked with student activists in every country we visited who conceived of themselves in the role of such catalytic agents, and could validate their self-conception by reference to the tactics they claimed to employ.

But, if it would be naive to ignore the presence of this ingredient in the formula of escalation, it would be equally naive, either to accord to it a *determining* function in producing the escalation from orthodox dissent to violent revolution, or to ignore the opportunities for reducing the passage of any critical number of students from one level of activism to the other. The key to that opportunity is the fact that, up to level four, a common objective moves the majority of those who engage in the several types of activism. That objective is to reduce the social and political restraints on self-expression and self-assertion consistent with one's own values, and to amplify the individual and collective power of one's own voice in the development of aids to what is perceived as a successful and satisfying life.

The several forms of activism are initiated and employed as experiments in the achievement of that objective. They are all, in essence, forms of political action on the part of people who consider themselves rightfully participants in such action. They are experiments in government at the initiative of, and with the consent of, the governed. They are all expedients being tested for their survival value in the evolution of ways for making popular sovereignty a reality.

Let us turn then to a consideration of the shortcomings of each stage which make it unsatisfactory as a way of accomplishing the desired objective, and the perceived advantages of the next stage, the inclination to turn to which may be either a normal predisposition or one stimulated by student activists.

From Level 1 to Level 2

The critical progression is from Level 1, i.e. orthodox legal expressions of dissent and protest, to Level 2, i.e. peaceful direct action. In every institution, including universities, and in every nation, there are legislative, administrative, judicial and other institutional arrangements and procedures providing the governed as individuals with a means for expressing dissent and for seeking "redress of grievances." These institutionalized arrangements and procedures are so familiar that there is no need to record them here. Also familiar to those living in any particular culture are widely approved, but less formalized, opportunities for individuals, alone or collectively, to express their satisfaction or dissatisfaction with the mode and results of the governance they experience, and to change the features of governing policy and practice to which they object. Familiar examples are: writing letters to the editor or to one's representatives or spokesmen, signing and presenting petitions, making speeches or just expressing one's point of view in conversation, participating in the preparation of position papers, joining or organizing and working for parties or pressure groups or voluntary associations set up to improve or reform some feature of the university, political, or social system. All are well recognized and widely approved procedures. More conducive to the predispositions of many is engagement in voluntary individual or collective services as a testimony to one's refusal to accept things as they are, hopefully with the result that one's contribution will effect a desirable change. The arrangements and procedures are recognized by the relevant Establishment, as well as by the populace generally, as the legitimate orthodox ways available to those who, although dissatisfied, find those ways tolerably adequate in most cases for dealing with the problems which arise in their relations as the governed with their governors, and who wish to be considered normal, respectable, and respected persons. The evolution of democracy is recorded in the continuous experimentation with new ways for removing inadequacies in the mode and results of governing developed to that point, and for including in the process of self-government those who for some reason have been left out, left behind, or forgotten as influential participants in that process. The declaration by student activists of their objective of achieving "participative democracy" is not merely a slogan. It is a declaration of their action oriented identification with generations of activists who have brought the governing process one step closer to the ideal of government of, by, and for the people.

In the light of the historical record of changes in that process, it would be unreasonable to assume that present orthodox legal provisions for channeling dissent toward changing the policies and practices against which dissent is raised will prove adequate and satisfactory to all the people all the time. What are inadequacies of those currently widely approved legal orthodox arrangements and methods?

Shortcomings of the Orthodox Means

The orthodox arrangements for expressing dissatisfaction and dissent and for modification of institutional policy and practice are not equally available to all members of a given population. These arrangements are societal constructions which have been developed over time, often at the urging of, and to serve the needs and aspirations of, particular groups in the total population; and the bargaining power and skill of these groups have varied greatly. Eligibility for access to these arrangements for voicing dissent and seeking corrective measures, is, in some cases, subject to de facto differentiation by reference to age, sex, race, residence, economic resources, social status, or demonstrated ability. The criteria upon which these differentiations are made are sometimes embodied in rules governing the conduct of those who manage the ports of entry to the several social, economic, political, and educational statuses, but also in preconceptions of these managers of what are necessary requirements for dealing with people of different sorts. The individual members of any governed group vary in their possession of qualities which recommend them to the governors as "worth listening to" and in the degree of their resources for, and skill in, utilizing the orthodox arrangements presumably equally available to all. Ideal declarations of the equality of all men and equal opportunity laws notwithstanding, the arrangements for dissent and for modifying the object of dissent and disatisfaction are, for all these reasons, more available and more operationally effective for some than for others. And actually and realistically some of them are not available at all for some people. Those who turn from utilization of such orthodox and widely approved arrangements to direct action include large numbers who have been left out, or left behind, from the company of those for whom orthodox arrangements for transforming dissent into structural and behavioral change, relative to the issue about which they are concerned, are readily and realistically available.

Universities vary considerably in the extent to which their governing arrangements have provided opportunities for the communication of student approval or tolerance of, or dissatisfaction with, the educational experience to which they are exposed, or their ideas about ways in which their perceived needs could be better met. Even when the arrangements provide formally for such communication as well as for involvement of students in the initiation of change, the opportunity for that involvement is subject to variations along the dimensions pointed out above. The same generalization applies to their opportunities for self expression and self assertion with respect to community and national issues.

Another weakness of the orthodox arrangements for the registration of dissatisfaction and dissent is that some of the actions to which objection is raised are those of administrators and bureaucrats who carry on their tasks under very broad constitutional or legislative mandate or under delegated but limited authorizations from superiors. The general mandate may have been the product of representative popular deliberations, and may be subject to periodic public review. But even if this is the case, in the meantime, and so far as its impact on the governed is concerned, the law or rule is what the administrators, by their interpretations and by their deeds, say it is. And the actions of the administrators are in many cases more or less insulated from direct correction by the governed. Even when those actions are perceived as arbitrary or going beyond the limits of legislative intent, the dissenters, if they utilize the orthodox arrangements, must be tolerant of long delays in receiving an effective response to their dissent, and are frequently treated to an exasperating and frustrating experience of buck passing.

A frequent circumstance stimulating dissenters to turn to tactics of an unorthodox sort, is the refusal of governors to negotiate about or even discuss the problem at issue on the grounds that it is not a problem to which the application of joint negotiation between governors and the governed is appropriate or practicable. The list of problems included on the agenda considered by the governors to be appropriately dealt with through such joint negotiation is not fixed for all time. At any particular moment, the items on that agenda have grown from past experience in seeking a resolution of the specific issues with respect to which the community of interest of the governors and the governed has become so apparent that no resolution other than by mutual consent is workable. The agenda is, and always will be, incomplete, to be added to as new issues are perceived to be characterized by such a community of interest.

But if, at any moment in time, a matter in which students have a vital interest is not on the agenda for consideration in orthodox ways they will request or demand that it be placed there. Failing to achieve that objective, the employment of unorthodox ways to promote the inclusion of the issue on the agenda or to force a consideration and a resolution of the issue on their own terms, is to be anticipated.

Two tendencies on the part of student dissenters with respect to their efforts to get non-traditional items onto the agenda for negotiation between the governed and the governors amplify the difficulty. These tendencies do not reveal an inadequacy in the orthodox arrangements as such, but only with reference to their use for particular purposes. The first tendency is for the dissenters to expand a specific operationally definable issue into one which is highly generalized and even abstract. The orthodox arrangements and procedures for transforming dissent into institutional change assume the existence of an identifiable structural or behavioral object of dissent, the character of which can be modified by negotiation and mutual consent resulting in a particularized change in institutional structure or behavior. The alleged unjustified suspension of a negro student is conceivably amenable to negotiation by the use of orthodox institutional mechanisms; the elimination of racism in general is not. The refusal of tenure to a popular professor is conceivably negotiable; the professional and social prejudices of the members of the professional and administrative appointment agencies are not. The elimination of R.O.T.C. or defense contracts is conceivably negotiable; the abstention of the university from any and all relations with "the military-industrial complex" is not. The abrogation of or censorship of a student publication or dramatic presentation is conceivably negotiable; the alleged puritanical and totalitarian evaluating premises of a university faculty and administration is not. The correction of alleged unethical or illegal conduct of one or more among governors or governed is conceivably negotiable; the creation of universally ideal standards, by uncompromising adherence to which all conduct will be governed, is not. The restructuring of *the* governing system of the university to provide greater representation of, and participation by, those currently excluded from representation and participation is conceivably negotiable; such issues as the elimination of *any* governing system, or a restructuring which provides that the right of *ultimate* determination of *all* policy and practice shall rest in all individuals in the population *solely* on the basis that they are affected by decisions made, and ignoring the differential capacities to contribute to viable decisions, are not. The development of modifications in curriculum, teaching methods and resources, student and faculty recruitment and evaluation are conceivably negotiable; the testing of the power of one group to enforce those modifications on the other without their consent, is not.

Actually the expansion from a specific to a generalized or abstract issue is designed to publicize rather than to settle the issue, and for this purpose the adoption of one or more of the forms of direct action is a more effective move, from the point of view of the dissenter.

A somewhat similar difficulty in utilizing orthodox arrangements and procedures results from the "hidden agenda" in the mind of the dissenter and sometimes in the mind of the responder. Orthodox methods for channeling and responding to dissent assume that both the responder and the one seeking response are focusing, chiefly if not exclusively, on an object of dissent and on objectives of the parties known to each one. When this is not the case, and either party is in the dark as to the real agenda of the other and of the other party's real objectives, the probability of a successful resolution of the issues through negotiation is remote. Actually the hidden item may be of the type not amenable to negotiation referred to above. At times the inference drawn from the intransigence of one or the other of the parties to the procedure is that the major item on the hidden agenda is actually the destruction of, or at least serious disturbance to, the institution on the one hand or on the power of the dissenter to realize his demands on the other. If that is the case, some form of direct action appears to the dissenter to be a procedure more applicable to the purpose at hand.

The very term "orthodox" suggests to the minds of many dynamic individuals, with predispositions to seek new and exciting experience, a further shortcoming, from their point of view, of governing arrangements and procedures so characterized, namely that they are routine and pedestrian, and would involve them in more disciplined hard work than in exhilarating relief from the boredom they experience in other "orthodox" aspects of their daily lives. Moreover, since the orthodox arrangements and procedures are already set up, the dissenters have not had the chance to shape them in accordance with their own hearts' desire. These are not necessarily objective shortcomings from the point of view of the purpose for which the arrangements and procedures were established. They are perceived shortcomings from the point of view of those motivated to seek a more direct action approach to achieving their personal objective of exhilarating self expression and self assertion.

Another circumstance which makes success in the use of the orthodox methods, which assume the possibility of rational problem solving, difficult, is that, while both the dissenter and the responder are negotiating directly with each other, they are, in a sense, each negotiating indirectly with others for support, not only with respect to the particular issue, but with respect to the maintenance of their individual status or that of the group or institution which they represent. These indirect negotiations frequently become so important that the direct negotiators "talk past each other," and the resolution of the specific issue between them is made well nigh impossible.

Finally it should be noted that the orthodox arrangements and procedures for responding to and the channeling of dissent into constructive remedial action have little chance of success in resolving six kinds of interests or motivations of the parties: the supplanting of one set of values or ideals for another; the demand of one party for decisions and actions from the other which, under the orthodox rules of organization and procedure to which the latter are required to conform, do not lie within their area of discretion; a demand for a shift in the right and power to govern from one party to another, in other words a demand for revolution; the desire of one party to "test the limits" to which the other will go in tolerating such a shift in relative power; the preservation of the mission, the significant uniqueness, the legitimacy, and the viability of the institutions or group for whose policy, practice, and survival the negotiators are responsible; the loss of confidence in, and a challenging of the integrity of one party by the other. The orthodox arrangements and procedures we are discussing are developed for problem solving involving the channeling of dissent under conditions in which the governors and the governed know themselves as approximating to a sharing of common values and ideas; the assumption that the objectives of both parties focus upon achieving a mutually advantageous accommodation; the acceptance by each party of a result consistent with the area of competence and

discretion within which the other is constrained to act; an acceptance of the necessity for only marginal and evolutionary modifications in the balance of governing power; a common acceptance
of and commitment to the preservation of the unique wholeness
of the institutions or groups with which both are associated; and
a mutual confidence and trust in the integrity of each other.
When these are lacking, which they frequently are in confrontations between governed and governors in the universities and
in the community or nation, successful resolution, by the utilization of orthodox arrangements and procedures for channeling
dissent into "constructive" action, is unlikely.

Furthermore if the orthodox arrangements and procedures
are themselves under challenge, their utility in providing ways
to answer that challenge is plausibly in doubt.

The Advantages of Direct Action

The dissenter or dissenters who raise directly or implicitly
such issues will almost inevitably turn to direct action in the successful carrying on of which the constraints named above are not
so limiting. Peaceful direct action involving mass meetings,
mass demonstration and picketing, teach-ins, and mass bargaining avoid some of the limitations on dissent oriented *self* expression and assertion and, on occasion, has positive values for the
achievement of change.

Being on the borders of orthodoxy, such tactics for making
dissent and dissatisfaction dramatic hold the dangers of the
backlash of conservative students, faculties, administrators, and
citizens generally, who consider only widely approved orthodox
tactics as legitimate. If the inadequacies of those arrangements
and procedures discussed above are pointed out, their answer is,
"This is a free country. You can change those orthodox arrangements and procedures to make them more effective by utilizing the orthodox arrangements and procedures for that
purpose."

As long as the direct action is peaceful, however, and no
major disruption is effected in the routine processes of living,
activist students are inclined to consider its advantages greater
than its disadvantages, particularly if they have not obtained
satisfactory results by use of the orthodox ways. What are those
advantages?

When mass direct action is launched, those members of the

governing Establishments whose decisions or actions the activists desire to influence are presented with a vivid image of the "people" who have been left out of the process of orthodox decision making. The evidence of large masses of people, normally excluded from such decision-making, raising their voice in protest through demonstration is a visual reminder that here are human beings that somehow must be included in the concept and reality of "the people," and that their negative or positive reactions must be taken into account. Such demonstration cannot suggest the "people's" ultimate operational role in the perfecting and maintenance of government of, by, and for the people, but it declares in no uncertain terms that they are there, they exist, and that they have interests and a voice that somehow must be incorporated into the university's or the nation's policy and practice.

Protest, even mass protest, is a natural and understandable preliminary stage in the emergence of the "people" as an influential participant in government. Lacking success through alternative institutional facilities for effective representation, such protest takes the form of demonstration.

Another advantage of peaceful mass direct action is that the requirements for participation in such action are those which can be met by large numbers of people with widely varying abilities or with no special abilities to speak of. Unlike many of the alternative orthodox methods for expressing dissent, little talent or special capacity and no respected reputation or influence is required. Institutionalized orthodox decision-making requires abilities or resources which great masses of people do not possess. At least this is the assumption, whether or not it is well based in fact. Maturity, and a certain degree of rational discrimination, it is believed, are required for even the periodic minimal participation of voting for or against candidates or proposals submitted to the people. Youth below a certain age are excluded, and other criteria of eligibility for becoming a voter result in the disenfranchisement of certain groups. The writing of articles, petitions, letters to the editor, open letters, or personal communication to influential university officials or politicians are possibilities for the occasional person with some literary skill. Influential contacts aid greatly. Paid advertisements in the papers require not only skill for their preparation but the money which is the price of publication. The organization of or even effective membership in a reform or pressure group association requires organizational skills of both initiation and response, as well as an inclination to use leisure for that purpose, qualities possessed by a limited number. Participation in the activities of a student government or a political party require not only a variety of personal abilities not possessed by all, but a predisposition to accept the give and take of organized associational activity. But other than the unwillingness to participate, the inability to walk, or the lack of a wheel chair with a cooperative companion, or insufficient strength to carry a placard, or feeble vocal cords, there are practically no hindrances to participation in a mass demonstration.

Another major advantage of mass direct action is that its message is immediately heard by those at the top of the governing hierarchy. Convinced that the only real corrective answer to their dissent is at the top, the activists involved in orthodox methods are restless and impatient when dealing with those at lower echelons to whom those at the top normally delegate "preliminary" and sometimes "final" negotiations. They seek to get to the place "where the buck stops."

Moreover, demonstrations and other forms of mass activism are difficult for top rulers to ignore. Although most of the leaders of such mass actions have no plan as to how an aroused public is to have its emotion channeled into university or public policy and action, the visible evidence of large numbers of people being drawn into the demonstrations is counted on to bring heavy pressure on those in the centers of power. It is not only a method of public opinion formation but a method of exploiting and focusing that public opinion in order to influence high level action.

Mass action has obvious advantages for advertising the fact that large numbers of students are interested in the issue to which such action is directed. It is a highly visible form of human activity and is bound to be widely reported. There is no guarantee that the issue claimed to be at the root of the action will be any more clearly understood even when, as in the case of a teach-in, an academically respectable name is applied to the method. Nor is there any assurance that the kind of action required to remove the object against which dissent is raised will be stimulated. Nevertheless the issue is called to the attention of a wide range of people who otherwise would ignore it. Advertising and publicity are provided free.

Thus, a demonstration has shock value to arouse those who would normally remain unconcerned. Activists are convinced that a major road block to the effectuation of change is the apathy and lack of concern of large numbers of people, including policy makers and administrators, with the effects on any save themselves of the policies and practices against which objection is raised. Whatever the impact of peaceful direct action on the Establishment's decision makers, student leaders of direct action count on such tactics to arouse even non-participating students and people generally out of their insensitivity to the problems, the critical nature of which these leaders feel they perceive more clearly than others. This shock value, of course, is even greater when non-violence turns to violence. And there are frequently present among the activists, as we have noted, those who are not very concerned that disorderliness, uncivil conduct, and even violence will turn student and public opinion against them. Demonstrators want people to be shocked, for that shock they feel is necessary in order to destroy apathy. Steady pressure and education are too slow and ineffective. What is needed is the explosive stimulus that anger and emotion give. But activists with concern for the steady growth in the effectiveness of their protest in achieving cumulative results are aware that public shock is a two edged sword, when that which produces the shock is the method used and not the nature of the situation against which protest is raised.

No chronicle of the advantages of direct action would be complete which did not point out the release from boredom which it provides. Mass action is an exhilarating experience of escape from daily routine, from the constraining task requirements set by others, especially when those tasks are perceived to lack relevance either to the development of an understanding of one's self or the involvement of one's self in the "really important" issues of life, an escape from the competitive "rat race" and the calculating attempt to win rewards from others, an escape from the limits to self assertion imposed by "playing it safe."

Nor would that chronicle be complete without a recognition of the reports from participants in direct action of the sheer joy of being caught up in the experience of mingling emotionally and physically with a crowd of one's fellow demonstrators and of escaping the loneliness which accompanies the effort to "stand out from" the crowd. In the moment of mass action the participant senses the breaking down of many of those barriers between himself and fellow participants which in the ordinary course of life, prevent their immediate and unquestioning acceptance of each other as equals, as fellow human beings. If that which has brought them together has permanent moral significance for themselves or others, the spiritual value of the experience is amplified. If the stimulus to their mass action does have such moral significance, the experience adds paradoxically to the sense of their *self* importance and to their self-image as one who is unafraid to join with others in speaking out when the apathetic majority is silent. But whether or not this is the case, the togetherness in action itself is fun, physical and emotional fun.

For those activists who seek to "radicalize" an increasing number of students, thus making them more inclined to support the activists' efforts to make radical changes in the university or society, mass direct action has other advantages over the orthodox ways. These activists are well aware that a declaration of interest and commitment in action rather than merely in words lays the best foundation for increasing genuine interest and commitment. Moreover, action brings to the participant a more direct and vivid revelation of continuous action stimulating reality than discussion and thought. Direct action also often raises the issue of the right to dissent in more exaggerated form than does an orthodox method. A very large number who would remain overtly unconcerned about the merits of that issue when resolution is sought through action of an orthodox character, will be roused to the defense of the right to dissent when they have expressed dissent in direct action.

Very few students or people generally will deny the right to dissent as long as it is expressed via orthodox arrangements or procedures. Questions are raised in quarters high and low when direct action is employed. But many who, themselves, will not turn to direct action will defend the "right" of others to do so, certainly as long as the direct action is nonviolent. Thus those who are being "radicalized" receive along the road of that process, the support of significant others should doubts about the wisdom or appropriateness of their commitment to continuing protest creep in.

If the protester is a deliberate and dedicated revolutionist, mass direct action has another advantage. Any gathering to-

gether of large numbers provides him with a forum and at least
with the possibility that, should order and discipline in the
crowd break down, its energies could be directed toward disruptive tactics leading to loss of confidence in the managers and
governors of the university and community. Such loss of confidence is a well recognized stage on the road to revolution.

The Impact of Direct Action

The escalation of overt dissent from Level 1 to Level 2 has an
impact both on the governance of institutions and on the students who are participating. The shift in methods presents no
major unsolvable problems to the governors of the university
and the comminity as long as the direct action remains peaceful.
They are aware, of course, that the non-violent character of the
meetings or demonstrations may suddenly be changed, and that
they must be prepared for a more violent kind of activism. But
governors who are genuinely desirous of knowing the needs
and aspirations of the governed and of having a feedback on
reactions to their own governing can receive useful clues from
peaceful direct action.

With respect to the impact on participants, however, the
shift from the utilization of orthodox and widely approved
methods for expressing dissent and promoting institutional
change, to peaceful direct action is a critical stage in the
escalation of protest. Those who do so have acknowledged to
themselves, and announced openly to others, that the institutionalized orthodox methods and mechanisms provide students
and citizens with an inadequate opportunity to effectuate change
in the processes and results of governance on matters which
are of deep concern to them. By their overt activism they
have revealed a lack of confidence in the institutionalized
orthodox channels for the expression of popular dissent and
for the effectuation of popularly desired change. To that
extent their confidence is clouded that the system of governance
is legitimate, so far as legitimacy is dependent on responsiveness
to the popular will. That experience is an important factor
in readying the participant in peaceful direct action for direct
action which not only goes beyond the borders of orthodoxy
but is actually anti-orthodox in character.

As the turning to peaceful direct action becomes more frequent, however, it tends to become so customary that it is
considered to be an almost normal and widely accepted institutionalized orthodox way of expressing dissent and of pro-

ing educational campaigns concerning the need for change save as a first step in achieving the change sought. And they frequently are insistent on making that change *now*.

Those for whom an operational definition of power is the ability to retain the initiative and to force other parties to accept the terms they demand or offer find the method of peaceful direct action, as well as the more orthodox methods for expressing dissent and promoting change, ineffective in demonstrating that kind of power. The arrangements in both cases provide procedures which, while extending the *power to influence*, simultaneously restrict that extension and protect the existing system of governance and its governors from usurpation by others of the *power to control*. If, through the interruption of university processes or the occupation of buildings, the activists can force the governors and managers of the university to bargain with them to a settlement not otherwise probable, their power to hold the initiative and to control results has been amplified, and this is quite clearly demonstrated. If, in desperation, those managers and governors turn to the courts or the police for aid, the demonstration that the power of students is greater relative to that of the authorities, when both are considered solely as members of the same institution, is implied, since the latter must call on *outside* force to bolster their right to manage and govern.

The "message" delivered by a peaceful demonstration, or even a resolution adopted by a mass meeting is, moreover, subject to that response from those to whom it is directed which activists define as "repressive tolerance." By acknowledging the right of the governed to free expression, by expressing their willingness to listen to and consider carefully demands of the demonstrators, by their expressions of gratitude for the frank and forthright criticism of their policy and practice, or even by making what the activists label as "token concessions," those who are the objects of criticism and of the demands can cause a split in the ranks of their critics, the protesters. The tolerance of the authorities renews in some of the direct activists a confidence that those authorities are, after all, reasonable men genuinely devoted to meeting popular needs and satisfying popular aspirations. Possibly then, they infer, the governors and managers can be counted on to take all practical steps to respond in action in the positive direction sought by the demonstrators. The subtle value of tolerant and apparently favorable attention to

expressions of dissent and protest has the effect, in the judgment of the power-seeking activists, of developing among many
of those whom the latter have stimulated to peaceful direct
action an allegiance to the Establishment. That weakens the
predisposition of followers to continue in such direct action
until the objectives of the leaders are fully realized.

Unless the university and/or political Establishments are
faced, therefore, with a kind of activism of which they *cannot*
be tolerant, the kind of activism which provokes them to a
negative response, preferably an angry response, they have it
within their power through a tolerant reception of peaceful
and legally permissible direct action, to deflate the pressure
which the activists are trying to bring to bear on them.

In order to prevent such tolerance from draining off the
numbers supporting their "cause," and in order to maintain
the momentum of their activism, the activists find it necessary
to force the members of the Establishment into overt and
clearly evident opposition by escalating peaceful and legal
direct action into a more provocative sort which ranges from
verbal and physical abuse to defiance of orders or law, actions
which cannot be tolerated.

From the point of view of generating an activism sufficiently
continuous, persistent, and sufficiently supported by group
solidarity to achieve any major institutional change, demonstrations, picketing, teach-ins, and mass meetings reveal another
source of weakness. For large numbers of participants in such
peaceful direct action, the value of the experience is not predominantly the resolution of an issue. Its value is, for many,
very personal: the escape from boredom, the exhilarating involvement in an exciting and unusual event somewhat more
dangerous than routine behavior, the release from loneliness
produced by "rubbing shoulders" physically and emotionally
with one's fellows, the focusing of physical energies on an objective of greater significance than getting ready for a test or
playing a game of touch football or bridge. Such participants
have not "enlisted for the duration," and tend to return to a
more customary pattern of living when their personal satisfaction level or fatigue point has been reached.

The Process of Radicalization

If, however, the activism in which they are engaged breaks

with a major taboo, as in the case when it escalates to civil disobedience or to incidental or planned violent direct action, they have committed themselves in deeds to a serious involvement. It is difficult to withdraw from that involvement without losing face with their fellows, without renouncing the idealistic premise which appeared to justify violating the taboo in the first place, or without laying themselves open to personal punishment which may possibly be negotiated away in the final resolution of the confrontation if they persist and do not break ranks.

Group solidarity and continuity of effort directed toward structural institutional change is not stimulated, however, simply by such fears and by the obstacles to withdrawal from active participation when self-centered personal motives have been satisfied. Continuing group solidarity and effort are assured only when participants have become ideologically, tactically, and strategically "radicalized" to a degree that they cannot be turned aside from dedicated and untiring collective protest and radical change-effectuating efforts. That point is reached when they become convinced *from emotionally toned experience,* and not merely from intellectual analysis, that the reforms satisfactory to them are impossible given the existing structure and processes of governance in the university and society, and that nothing save a continuing and escalating attack on the university and political Systems and the Establishment will produce the fundamental change they seek. That experience is partially provided by frustration at the inability to obtain result-achieving attention to dissent and protest by the employment of orthodox methods and peaceful direct action. Partial success reduces the intensity of the conviction. When, however, protest escalates, or can be made to escalate, to the levels of civil disobedience or violent direct action, the process of radicalization is accelerated, for those at least who do not drop out entirely. The "men are separated from the boys," that is, the daring from the timid, the absolutists from the compromisers, the dedicated from the merely interested, the ruthless from the considerate. Also those who are unconcerned about the impact of specific changes in institutional governance, policy, and practice on the stability and viability of the institution as a whole are separated from those who *are* concerned. This leaves a smaller number of activists available for what the leaders envisage as a continuing struggle, but it is a determined and even dedicated number. If they come face to face with governors who are prepared from experience to meet the challenge of such a minority group with effective protective devices called "a system of internal security," their impact can usually be kept at a minimum. Operating within the university system, the interaction of whose members is premised on mutual confidence and trust, the appeal to reason, and a community of intellectual and moral interests, such a group finds the university exceptionally vulnerable to its disruptive tactics.

Ideological radicalization of students involves convincing them that the university, the community, and the nation cannot or will not be governed by the free consent of all the governed, but only by the exercise of force-supported authority of the governors. Tactical and strategical radicalization of the students involves convincing them that the governors are willing to modify their policy only when forced to do so under the compulsion of unrelenting pressure from those who dissent. If the latter can force a confrontation by initiating civil disobedience or violent direct action, that conviction is dramatically tested, and, if verified in experience, becomes an exceptionally influential factor in the radicalization of the students. The assumption of the radicalizers is that such verification will result whatever the response of the university Establishment to the confrontation. If the members of that Establishment yield under duress, the conviction that the governors acknowledge and act upon dissent only when the governed force them to do so receives some confirmation. If members of the Establishment hold fast to their position and refuse to yield, and the confronting students can hold out until the governors must use force to restore the university to a functioning institution, the conviction that their authority to govern rests ultimately on the employment of force and not the consent of the governed receives some confirmation.

To radicalize a sufficient group of students to make civil disobedience and violent direct action a sustained and effective procedure for achieving major institutional changes is, for activists, a task of no small proportions. To activate that group and to sustain the momentum of forms and styles of their activism which are uncivil, illegal, and violent, is an even greater task. All the factors, previously discussed in this section, which encourage, activate, and reinforce student activism at any level, including that of orthodox methods and peaceful direct action, contribute to their success. But the deliberate promotion of civil disobedience and violence requires special planning, the presence of particular kinds of activating persons and issues, and reinforcing support, frequently unanticipated, from personal and situational sources.

There is always the possibility that recruits will backslide in their commitment to action as it becomes less socially acceptable. The hold on students of values rooted in the wisdom of experience has to be broken, for those values brand some kinds of actions right and some kinds wrong. Among the latter are stepping on the toes of innocent bystanders, uncivil conduct, infringement on others' rights, unwillingness to modify one's position in the interests of achieving a working consensus, and disrespect for law. But those are just what civil disobedience and violence usually involve. Some plausible ideology has to be developed, some image of the character of the System and its governors has to be developed, which justifies a departure from those values, and provides premises in the light of which the kinds of normally unacceptable kinds of action appear reasonable and right.

It need not be expected that the activists' choice of and presentation of ideological premises and characterizations of the System and the Establishment will more than superficially mirror empirical reality, for the immediate purpose is not rational intellectual conversion but the unleashing of emotions to a pitch which will destroy confidence in the traditional values which inhibit unorthodox and illegal behavior, and which will make that behavior appear acceptable if not respectable in the eyes of the actors. Cliches serve this purpose better than reasoned sentences or paragraphs. The use of simple categorical words for very complex societal phenomena (like "imperialism," "working class," "exploitation," "racism," "Establishment," "System," "the older generation," "youth," etc.) is more effective than critical exposition of the phenomena. "Pigs," "hypocrites," "stooges," and other defamatory, inflammatory, and frequently profane names transmit the desired emotion-toned image of "enemies of the people" more dramatically than balanced descriptions of their conduct. It is, moreover, exceptionally important to stress the physical and psychological "violence" employed by the members of the Establishment whose policy and practice is the object of protest, in order that the students' violence can be justified as a response to allegedly even greater violence. Any accommodation the members of the Establishment make to the demands of the students is characterized as part of a clever manipulative strategy to reduce the intensity with which those demands are made. Uncompromising continuation of the "confrontation" until the ugly face of anger and force shows itself in the behavior of the Establishment is deliberately sought, for only then do revolutionary activists judge they have really "got through," not only to the Establishment, but to the students whose mass support they seek.

One aspect of the strategy to win radicalized recruits for sustained unorthodox activism is the inclusion of "full amnesty" for all participants in the roster of demands. Freedom from punishment is not so important for the most extreme activists for whom "martyrdom" is, on occasion, a welcomed means of increasing their prestige with their followers and their own sense of self-importance. But to large numbers of their followers the escape from severe personal consequences of their activism is important. The inclusion of that issue is also practically certain to prolong the confrontation and make settlement more difficult. As we have previously noted, if amnesty is granted, there is a sense in which the Establishment has, in the opinion of the activists, weakened its claim to legitimacy. For they have renounced the right to punish, a right possessed only by legitimate governors.

An important element in the manual of tactics for sustaining continuing activism characterized by civil disobedience and violence is the interpretation of the action taken and its objectives as being part of larger and more significant movement, for example, "One day in the history of freedom."

The evidence that the escalation to civil disobedience and violence is not always just a "natural" process is contained in the manuals of operations for launching and sustaining confrontations, guerrilla, and revolutionary campaigns. We found such manuals of operations in the possession of some student activists in Mexico, Colombia, Japan, and in the United States. These vary in the sources from which the strategy and tactics set forth are derived. Some are based on an analysis of descriptive, theoretical, and hortatory revolutionary literature, others on an analysis and evaluation of successes and failures of particular populist and syndicalist oriented movements in the past and of student activism at the present time.

Throughout this book, the essential role of the dynamic and

forceful initiator and instigator of direct action, peaceful or otherwise, has been stressed. When that action involves violence, even more essential is the presence among the activists of one or several individuals who, by stimulating and exciting oratory and by daring, risk-taking personal example, can raise the emotions of a crowd to the point at which the normally restraining hold on individuals of predispositions to reasonableness, civility, and self control are loosened. It is possible that a single individual could perform this role, but we have observed no instance of this. The launching of such a challenge to "law and order" on a sustained basis was in every case the work of a closely knit and usually organized group of fellow conspirators to whom the achievement of an all but irresolvable confrontation with the authorities, stimulating them to strong-arm tactics was an objective in itself and a mark of success.

Stimulants to Escalation

Student activists seeking to launch or sustain the momentum of unorthodox action often receive unanticipated aid which reinforces their planned activities. The recent success of direct action of this sort on the same campus or other campuses encourages repetition. The evidence that other groups in the nation, or that nations themselves, make successful use of such tactics in achieving their objectives not only encourages imitation but, to some extent, reduces moral inhibitions among students to using the same tactics. Support, not only for the objectives, but for the unorthodox tactics themselves, by significant others outside their peer group in the university or the community furnishes encouragement. Such assistance is most welcome to the activists. Particularly welcome is assistance coming from members of the faculty either in outspoken support for the institutional changes or action sought by the activists or in hesitancy to deal quickly and in a determined fashion with any of their methods involving the violation of university rules and a disregard for the normal canons of civil behavior.

Certain other factors, which can be called situational, frequently play into the hands of those who desire to escalate student activism toward civil disobedience and violence. Some such factors, of course, have been known to stimulate escalation even though student leaders prefer to contain it and restrict the activism to peaceful and legal procedures. In other words, the situational factors can aggravate unruly predispositions until the "situation" gets out of control.

It would be hard to overestimate the pressure toward escalation, toward violence, exerted by one of these situational factors, the crowd itself. It is seldom that "a hush falls over the crowd." Anyone familiar with the expositions of crowd or mass behavior by such writers as Le Bon and Ortega y Gasset can see revealed in the direct action of students, the tendencies those writers have discussed. The degeneration of the behavior of all to the level of those with the lowest standards of conduct is frequently evident. The weakening or elimination of restraining self discipline when the individual is lost in the crowd is quite clear. The erasing of boundaries to acceptable behavior, the growing sense that "anything goes", once the boundary lines have been blurred, becomes manifest. The sense of personal guilt, if such should arise, is attenuated and dissipated by the awareness of common and shared culpability.

Should the participants in a mass meeting or a peaceful demonstration experience confusion and indecision as to what to do next, a confident and eloquent activist among the students or from non-student groups, has the opportunity to give direction to activity.

Confusion and indecision and delay in response on the part of the authorities, against whom the unorthodox action is mounted, permits the escalation of unruly and violent crowd behavior. The arrival of the police or troops to "restore order," particularly when physical injury is inflicted on demonstrators is almost certain to provide an issue which draws into the extreme forms of activism participants who heretofore had remained aloof.

Added to these factors is one which all responsible leaders, even of illegal activism, learn to fear, the coming into the crowd of outsiders with personal and group interests different from, and even antithetical to, those of the student leaders. These outsiders then employ the tactics of crowd manipulation to steer its activity toward the accomplishment of their own objectives. There is also an ever present risk that individuals, whether in-groupers or out-groupers, will, in the heat of excitement of crowd activity, commit acts of vandalism or physical violence, and that such behavior will prove contagious.

All of these situational factors can be counted on to stimulate an escalation of student activism, at any stage of direct action, into open and stubborn confrontation and conflict between the Establishment and the direct-action dissenters.

In Conclusion

During the past 10 years the attack of students on the status quo in many countries as well as in the United States has been undeniably and often times brutally severe. But the severity was not just a superficial characteristic of their overt behavior. At the root of their behavior was not merely criticism of and dissent from the actions of managers and governors of educational and political institutions. They raised a challenge to the very legitimacy and morality of both the institutions and their governors. That is serious business in any society and particularly in a democracy. We have recorded the nature and intensity of that challenge to widely held popular beliefs concerning the essential mission of educational and political institutions, concerning the appropriate mode of their mutual relations, concerning the custom sanctioned reciprocal rights and duties of those who govern and those who are governed, and concerning the canons of legitimacy and morality which have traditionally justified these rules of the game and the usages of civility which made them tolerably workable.

It is these latter challenges which heighten the significance of the protest from the campus and which stimulated the authors to try and get a clearer perspective on the activism through which the challenge became manifest. Particular outbreaks of student activism can be expected to wax and wane in scope and intensity. The issues raised by the predisposition to such outbreaks, however, remain central to the maintenance and progress of educational and political institutions, as well as to the achievement of individual freedom and responsibility within a stable and viable society.

We have attempted to gain that perspective first of all by exploring both the common and peculiar features of student activism and its alleged causes in four other countries. We sought a more fundamental perspective, however, by examining the factors which are plausibly instrumental in creating in students a state of readiness to become activists in these countries and in the United States, and which turn that latent readiness into overt rebellion. We have in the light of that perspective explored questions such as the following: What disturbances to satisfying experience encourage a sizeable minority of students to a rebellion against, and at times renunciation of, the traditional values, arrangements and ways of action characterizing their own university and nation? What circumstances, social

arrangements, and cultural guidelines condition and constrain
and at times frustrate the efforts of young people in these countries to find and know themselves as mature adults, as students,
as citizens? How dependable are the aids which society furnishes
them for developing in each individual an awareness of himself
as a significant and responsible participant in the world of real
affairs? What dissent encouraging perceptions and interpretations of that world and the way in which it is governed are derived from that experience? Which of these stir in youth the predisposition to be, and the commitment to becoming, an agent of
change? What kinds of events intensify these stimulants and why
are they effective? What recurring combination of factors is essential in order to bring these predispositions to a head and to trigger overt mass activism? What accounts for the tendency of such
overt activism to escalate from forms which, if not fully approved, are at least tolerated, to forms which cannot be permitted by responsible managers and governors of educational and
political institutions?

The data on which the answers to such questions are based
come from the authors' field work observations and interviews
in the several countries, supplemented by an exploration of the
available documents. The guidelines for analysis and interpretation are provided by forty years of teaching, research, and public
service to which the social and psychological sciences are relevant.

Briefly stated, the major thrust of the explanation of student
activism focuses on the ineffectiveness of a most critical and
necessary process in all social organizations, in this case universities and nations, namely the *fusion process*. That is the essential process by which a resolution is normally effected between
the simultaneous effort of an organization and an individual
participant respectively, each to use the other in order to achieve
its own mission and unique identity. The organization seeks to
achieve its own mission and unique identity by making an *agent*
for this objective of the individual participant, that is by making
him over in the image of the organization. Simultaneously, the
individual seeks to achieve his personal purposes and identity by
making an *agency* of the organization for this objective, that is
by making the organization over in his own image. That process
of resolution is bound to be ineffective when there is no widespread consensus among governors and the governed concerning
the appropriate and meaningful image and identity of either the

534

university and nation on the one hand, or the individual on the other.

The Major Obstacle to Peace

While a mutually acceptable and peaceful integration of the personal and organizational identities is not impossible, it is most difficult at times when and places where the members of the university and the nation are not in essential agreement on the essential goals, the mission, the central values of the university and of the nation. For a working agreement on those elements in the organizational charter of the university and the nation is the foundation for achieving a consensus concerning how relations within those institutions are to be ordered, and concerning what objectives and processes of governance are appropriate and legitimate in the light of that consensus. We have emphasized that the lack of clarity and dependability of, the absence of widespread agreement on, of a respect for, and of pride in, the organizational charter of the universities and the nations is the most important factor encouraging and reinforcing student protest. That lack is also the most important factor making difficult the transformation of student activism into a means for making those institutions stronger and better adapted to serving the needs of all involved. It is a major obstacle to the resolution of conflict and confrontation at any level of dissent, and particularly when the activism has escalated to an extreme, uncivil, violent, and destructive level. When disorder has reached that stage it is obvious that those charged with the responsibility for perpetuating the stability and viability of the universities and the nation must act to restrain and deactivate the activists. In the university and in a democratic nation the objective is to do this in a way that results in a solution closer to one mutually acceptable to all concerned rather than one in which the will of one is imposed on the other.

The measures of restraint and control can do little more than serve as temporary holding actions, until such a mutually acceptable solution is possible. But until the essential goals, mission, and central values of the universities and the nations are sufficiently clear and dependable, and widely enough shared and respected to provide a consensus-strengthened touch-stone for testing a solution which is more creative than the mere restraint of attacks on policy and practice, the attacks will con-

tinue. They will wax and wane with the swings in the occurrence and intensity of events or circumstances the response to
which indicates indecision and confusion, on the part of governors and the governed, about the essential character and nature of a university and a nation. The stability and viability of
either is assured only when there is agreement between the
governed and the governors on what the name of that university and nation basically stands for, and a mutual conviction
that a university and a nation with that character is worth their
joint efforts to preserve.

Appendix

Subjects for Interviews and Documentary Research

I. The character of student activism.

   A. Classes of initiators, their characteristics, socialization experiences, self-image, aspirations, ideology, status in the university community.

   B. Classes of rank and file activists: same as A.

   C. Types of activities, strategies, and tactics (together with advantages and disadvantages of each to the several classes of activists).

   D. Operational field and orientation of issues (e.g., related to educational or political affairs within or beyond the university).

   E. Objectives, explicit or implicit.

   F. Organizational charter of the student movement: traditions, declared values, symbols, ideology.

   G. Organizational structure and internal problems of stability and viability.

   H. Relation to federations of student organizations, national and international.

   I. Relations to non-student pressure and action groups.

   J. Examples and record of achievements and failures.

K. Reactions of non-activist students, of university faculty and administrators, of the public, of public officials, and of police.

II. Problems faced by youth in coming of age.

A. Concept of adulthood and cultural guidelines to adult human relationships in the specific society.

B. Character and stability of adult roles.

C. Processes and agencies of socialization including those experienced in family, school, community, religious institutions, peer groups, the university.

D. Culture, value emphases, and self-image of youth.

E. Points of generational conflict and mutuality.

F. Opportunities for and constraints on individual development, self-expression, and participation in self-governance, pre-university, university, post-university.

G. Stability, clarity, and dependability of the nations's organizational charter.

H. Perceived inadequacies in institutional resources relative to achievement of a dependable self-identity.

III. Image of the *Student* and problems of its realization in individuals.

A. The traditional expectancies held by students and others about the rights and duties, the standing, and function of sutdents within and outside the university. The historical and cultural reinforcements for this image.

B. Current redefinitions in process.

C. Factors in the university experience and training which support or which are inconsistent with individual realization of A or B.

D. Perceived probabilities in the beyond-university experience which appear to support or to be inconsistent with A or B.

E. Particular attention to university factors affecting, favorably or unfavorably, (a) career prospects, (b) freedom and self-determination, (c) prestige, (d) intellectual competence, (e) idealism and moral values, (f) satisfying participation in university and public affairs, and which encourage or discourage a predisposition toward activism.

F. Stability, clarity, and dependability of the university's organizational charter.

G. Types and nature of events which have triggered overt activism.

IV. Reasons for effectiveness or ineffectiveness of student activists in achieving objectives from point of view of:

A. Other students

B. Faculty and university administrators

C. Governing persons and groups

D. General populace

V. Facts, relevant to producing a positive or negative predisposition with respect to activism, concerning the country, its history, its institutions, its political structure, its governance, its people, their culture and way of thinking.

VI. Facts, general to the educational system and specific to particular universities concerning their history, organizational structure and governance, source and adequacy of financial support, political and religious orientation, degree of subjection to exterior religious and political influence and pressure, which encourage or discourage a predisposition to activism.

Bibliography

U.S.A. and General (Books)

Adams, J.F. (ed.), *Contributions to the Understanding of Adolescence,* Boston: Allyn and Bacon, 1968.

Altbach, Philip G., *Student Politics and Higher Education in the United States; A Select Bibliography,* United Ministries in Higher Education and Center for International Affairs, Cambridge: Harvard University, 1968.

American Association of University Professors, U.S. National Student Association, Association of American Colleges, and American Association for Higher Education, *Joint Statement of Rights and Freedoms of Students,* Washington, D.C.: AAUP, 1966.

American Behavioral Scientist, Kruytbosch. C. E. and S. L. Messinger (eds.), Vol. II, No. 5 (1968).

American Council on Education, *The Student in Higher Education,* 1965.

American Scholar, issue "Revolution on the Campus," Vol. 38 (Autumn, 1969).

Anderson, Albert T., and B. Biggs (eds.), *A Focus on Rebellion,* San Francisco: Chandler, 1962.

Avorn, Jerry L. and Robert Friedman, *Up Against the Ivy Wall,* New York: Atheneum, 1969.

Axelrod, Joseph, et al, *The Search for Relevance: The Campus in Crisis,* San Francisco: Jossey-Bass, 1969.

Barton, A.H., *The Columbia Crisis,* New York: Bureau of Applied Social Research, Columbia University, 1968.

Bell, Daniel and Irving Kristol, *Confrontation: the Student Rebellion and the Universities,* New York: Basic Books, 1969.

541

Brown, Michael, *The Politics and Anti-Politics of the Young*, Glencoe Press, 1969.

Canadian Youth Commission, *Youth Challenges the Educators*, Toronto: The Ryerson Press, 1946.

Center for Study of Democratic Institutions, *Students and Society*, Center Occasional Paper, Vol. I, No. 1, Santa Barbara, California, 1968.

Cohen, Mitchell, and Dennis Hale (eds.), *The New Student Left*, Boston: Beacon Press, 1966.

Coleman, James (ed.), *Education and Political Development*, Princeton, New Jersey: Princeton University Press, 1965.

Coles, Robert, *Children of Crisis*, Boston: Little, Brown, 1969.

Cornell, Richard, *Youth and Communism*, New York: Walker, 1965.

Comparative Education Review, Vol. 10, No. 2 (June, 1966).

Daedalus, Youth: Change and Challenge (Winter, 1962).

_____, Vol. 97, No. 1 (Winter, 1968). (Articles by M. Lipset, M. Glazer, M. Shimbori, R. E. Scott, R. E. Peterson.)

Dennis, Lawrence E. and J.F. Kauffman, *The College and the Student*,. Washington, D.C.: American Council on Education, 1966.

Douglas, Bruce, *Reflections on Protest*, Richmond: John Knox Press, 1967.

Draper, Hal, *Berkeley: The New Student Revolt*, Introduction by Mario Savio, New York: Grove Press, 1965.

Ehrenreich, Barbara and John, *Long March, Short Spring*, New York: Monthly Review Press, 1969.

Eisenstadt, S. N., *From Generation to Generation*, Glencoe, Ill.: The Free Press, 1956.

Emmerson, Donald K. (ed.), *Students and Politics in Developing Nations*, New York: Frederick A. Praeger, 1968.

Erickson, Erik H. (ed.), *The Challenge of Youth*, New York: Basic Books, 1963.

_____, *Identity and the Life Cycle*, New York: International Universities Press, 1959.

Evans, Stanton, *Revolt on the Campus*, Chicago: Henry Regnery Co., 1961.

Feuer, Lewis S., *The Conflict of Generations: The Character and Significance of Student Movements*, New York: Basic Books, 1968.

Foote, Caleb and H. Mayer and Associates, *The Culture of the University*, San Francisco: Jossey-Bass, 1968.

Fortune Magazine, Louis Banks, Managing Editor, *Youth in Turmoil*, Time-Life Books, 1969.

Foster, J. and D. Long (eds.), *Protest! Student Activism in America*, New York: William Morrow and Co., 1970. [Excellent recent symposium and bibliography].

The Free Society Association, *The New Student Left*, Washington, D.C.: The Free Society Association, 1965.

Harlem Youth Opportunities Unlimited, *Youth in the Ghetto*, New York: Harlem Youth Opportunities Unlimited, 1964.

Hoffer, Eric, *The True Believer*, New York: Harper and Brothers, 1951.

Hoffman, A., *Revolution for the Hell of It*, New York: The Dial Press, 1968.

Hofstadter, R., *Anti-Intellectualism in American Life*, New York: Vintage Books, 1966.

Hook, Sidney, *Academic Freedom and Academic Anarchy*, New York: Cowles. 1964.

Howe, Irving (ed.), *Student Activism*, Indianapolis: Bobbs Merrill, 1967.

International Institute of Intellectual Cooperation, *The Future of Graduates*, Paris: International Institute of Intellectual Cooperation, 1940.

Jacob, Philip, *Changing Values in College*, New York: Harper and Row, 1957.

Jacobs, Paul and Saul Landau, *The New Radicals*, New York: Harper and Row, 1957.

Journal of Social Issues, XXIII, No. 3, (July, 1967) [Edward E. Sampson (ed.). Articles by C. Bay, D.R. Brown, J.L. Craise, R. Flacks, K. Keniston, E.E. Sampson, J.W. Trent.]

Katope, Christopher and P.G. Lolbrod (eds.), *Beyond Berkeley: A Source Book in Student Values*, Cleveland: World Publishing Co., 1966.

Katz, Joseph, *The Student Activists: Rights, Needs and Powers of Undergraduates*, Washington: U.S. Office of Education, 1967.

——————, and Associates, *No Time for Youth*, San Francisco: Jossey-Bass, 1968.

Keniston, Kenneth, *The Uncommitted: Alienated Youth in American Society*, New York: Harcourt, Brace, and World, 1965.

—————————, *Young Radicals*, New York: Harcourt, Brace, and World, 1968.

Kennan, George F. (ed.), *Democracy and the Student Left*, Boston: Little, Brown and Co., 1968.

Kerr, Clark, *The Uses of the University*, Cambridge: Harvard University Press, 1963.

Knorr, O.A. and W.V. Minter (eds.), *Order and Freedom on the Campus*, Boulder: Interstate Commission for Higher Education, 1965.

LeBon, Gustave, *The Crowd: A Study of the Popular Mind*, London: T.F. Unwin, 1910.

Leites, N.C. and C. Wolf, *Rebellion and Authority*, Chicago: Markham, 1970.

Lenin, V.I., *The Young Generation*, New York: International Publishers, 1940.

Lipset, Seymour M., *American Student Activism in Comparative Perspective*, Washington, D.C.: U.S. Department of Labor, 1967.

—————————, *Student Politics*, New York: Basic Books, 1967.

—————————, and Sheldon S. Wolin (eds.), *The Berkeley Student Revolt: Facts and Interpretations*, Garden City: Doubleday, 1965.

Lunn, Harry H., Jr., *The Student's Role in College Policy Making*, Washington: American Council on Education, 1957.

Mandel, Ernest, *Theory and Practice* (A Young Socialist Pamphlet), New York: Merit Publishers, 1969.

Marcuse, Herbert, *Five Lectures*, Boston: Beacon Press, 1970. (Translated by Shapiro and Weber).

—————————, *One Dimensional Man: Studies in the Ideology of Advanced Industrial Society*, Boston: Beacon Press, 1964.

Miller, Michael and Susan Gilmore (eds.), *Revolution at Berkeley*, New York: Dell Publishing Co., 1965.

Milton, Ohmer and E. Shoben, Jr., *Learning and the Professors*, Athens, Ohio: Ohio University Press, 1968.

Musgrove, F., *Youth and the Social Order*, Bloomington: Indiana University Press, 1965.

National Association of Manufacturers, *Thunder on the Campus*, New York, 1967.

Newcomb, T. and Richard Flacks, *Deviant Subcultures on a College Campus*, Washington, D.C.: U.S. Office of Education, 1963.

Newfield, Jack, *A Prophetic Minority*, New York: New American Library, Inc., 1966.

Ortega y Gasset, José, *Man in Crisis*, tr. from Spanish by Mildred Adams, New York: Norton, 1958.

——————. *The Mission of the University*, tr. by H. L. Nostrand, Princeton: Princeton University Press, 1944.

——————, *The Revolt of the Masses*, New York: W.W. Norton, 1932.

Peterson, R.E., *The Scope of Organized Student Protest in 1967/68*, Princeton: Educational Testing Service, 1968.

The Public Interest, No. 13, Fall, 1968. [Articles by N. Glazer, D. Bell, S. Lipset, T. Parsons, J. Bunzel, S. Lubell, R. Starr, M. Crozier, W. Letwin, R. Mayntz, and N. Tarcov.]

Rapoport, Roger, and L. Kirshbaum, *Is the Library Burning?*, New York: Random House, 1969.

Requelme, M.A., *Student Movements in the U.S. and Latin America*, U.S. National Student Association, 1963.

Sartre, Jean Paul, *Existentialism and Human Emotion*, New York: Philosophical Library, 1957.

Sasajima, Masu, Junius A. Davis, and Richard Peterson, *Organized Student Protest and Institutional Climate*, Princeton: Educational Testing Service, 1967.

Sherif, Muzafer and Carolyn W. Sherif, *Problems of Youth; Transition to Adulthood in a Changing World*, Chicago: Aldine Publishing Co., 1965.

Silvert Kalman H. and Frank Bonilla, *Education and the Social Meaning of Development*, New York: American Universities Field Staff, 1961.

Simmel, Georg, *Conflict and the Web of Group Affiliations*, (trans. Wolf and Bendix), Glencoe, Ill.: The Free Press, 1955.

Smith, G. Kerry (ed.), *Stress and Campus Response*, San Francisco: Jossey-Bass, 1968.

Spender, Stephen, *The Year of the Young Rebels*, New York: Vintage Books, 1969.

UNESCO, *New Trends in Youth Organizations*, New York: 1960.

UNESCO, *Statistical Yearbook*, 1968, New York: 1969.

Wallace, Walter, *Student Culture*, Chicago: Aldine Publishing House, 1966.

Wallerstein, Immanuel, *University in Turmoil,* New York: Atheneum, 1969.

Williamson, E.G. and John Cowan, *The American Student's Freedom of Expression,* Minneapolis: University of Minnesota Press, 1967.

Wolfenstein, E. Victor, *Revolutionary Personality,* Princeton: Princeton University Press, 1967.

——————, *Violence or Non-Violence,* Princeton, New Jersey: Center of International Studies, 1965.

U.S.A. and General (Articles)

Abrahams, M.H., "Student Protests: A Phenomenon for Behavioral Sciences Research," *Science,* 161:20-23 (1968).

Altbach, Philip G., "The Future of the American Student Movement," *Liberal Education,* Vol. 52:313-324 (Oct., 1966).

——————, "The International Student Movement," *Comparative Education Review,* Oct., 1964, pp. 131ff.

Astin, A.W., "Personnel and Environmental Determinants of Student Activism," Paper delivered at annual convention of American Psychological Association, September, 1968.

Baird, Leonard, "Who Protests," in Foster, Julian and D. Long (eds.), *Protest! Student Activism in America,* New York: William Morrow and Co., 1970.

Bakke, E. W., "Roots and Soil of Student Activism," in S. M. Lipset (ed.), *Student Politics,* New York: Basic Books, 1967.

Bay, Christian, "Political and Apolitical Students," *Journal of Social Issues,* 23:76-92 (July, 1967).

——————, "Student Political Activism," *Our Generation,* Vol. 5, No. 1:50-73, 1966.

Bell, Daniel, "Columbia and the New Left," *The Public Interest,* No. 13, (Fall, 1968), pp. 61-101.

Black, Jeane, Norman Haan, and M. B. Smith, "Activism and Apathy in Contemporary Adolescents" in J. F. Adams (ed.), *Contributions to the Study of Adolescence,* Boston: Allyn and Bacon, 1968.

Bettelheim, Bruno, "Individual and Mass Behavior in Extreme Situations," *Journal of Abnormal Psychology,* 38, No. 4:417-452 (Oct., 1943).

Braungart, Richard G., "SDS and YAF: Backgrounds of Student Political Activists," Paper presented at the Annual Meeting of the American Sociological Association: August, 1966.

Bronowski, J., "Protest-Past and Present," *The American Scholar*, Vol. 38, No. 4, 535-547 (Autumn, 1969).

Brown, D.R. "Student Stress and the Institutional Environment," *Journal of Social Issues*, 23:92-108 (July, 1967).

"Campus '65: The College Generation Looks at Itself: A Newsweek Survey," *Newsweek*, March 22, 1965.

Clark, George, "Students for a Democratic Society," *Our Generation*, Vol. 3:30-39 (May, 1966).

Committee of Fifteen (Harvard University), "The Crisis at Harvard," *Minerva*, Vol. VIII, No. 1 (January, 1970).

Crouch, Colin, "The Chiliastic Urge," *Survey*, Vol. 69:55-61, (October, 1968).

"Each Against All?" Comment on *Report of President's Commission on Campus Unrest, Saturday Review*, (October 17, 1970) p. 64.

Erikson, Erik H., "Youth: Fidelity and Diversity," in E.H. Erikson (ed.), *Youth Change and Challenge*, New York: Basic Books, 1963.

Ferro, Marc, "Emancipation of a Generation," *Survey*, Vol. 69:41-43, (October, 1968).

Feuer, Lewis, "Rebellion at Berkeley," *New Leader*, (December 21, 1964).

──────────, "Patterns of Irrationality," *Survey*, Vol. 69:43-51, (October, 1968).

──────────, "The Student Left in the U.S.A.," *Survey*, Vol. 62:90-103 (January, 1967).

Flacks, Richard, "The Liberated Generation: An Exploration of the Roots of Student Protest," *Journal of Social Issues*, 23:52-75 (July, 1967).

──────────, "Social and Cultural Meanings of Student Revolt," *Social Problems*, 17:340-57 (Winter, 1970).

Foster, J. and D. Long (eds.), "Activists and the History of the Future," in *Protest! Student Activism in America*, New York: William Morrow and Co., 1970.

Glazer, Nathan, "Student Politics in a Democratic Society," *American Scholar*, Vol. 36. (Spring, 1967).

Goodman, P., "The Black Flag of Anarchism," *New York Times Magazine*, July 14, 1968, pp. 10-12.

──────────, "Thoughts on Berkeley," *New York Review of Books*, Vol, 3:5-7 (January 14, 1964).

Gottlieb, D., "American Adolescents in the Mid-sixties," (with bibliography), *Journal of Marriage and the Family*, Vol. 27:134-303 (May, 1965).

Gusfield, Joseph, "Beyond Berkeley: High Noon on Campus," *Transaction*, Vol. 2:3-7, (March-April, 1965).

Halleck, S. L., "Twelve Hypotheses of Student Unrest," in G. K. Smith (ed.), *Stress and Campus Response*, San Francisco: Jossey-Bass, 1968.

Hayakawa, S.M., "The Bored Student is Social Dynamite," *Wall St. Journal*, 176:8 (August 3, 1970).

Hechlinger, Fred, "Student Targets: Professors Are Next," *Change Magazine*, Vol. 1:36-40 (January-February, 1969).

Hinkle, Warren, "A Social History of the Hippies," *Ramparts*, Vol. 3:5-26 (March, 1967).

Hook, Sidney, "Academic Freedom and Academic Anarchy," *Survey*, Vol. 69:62-75, (October, 1968).

Isaacs, Harold R., "Students and Revolution," *Survey*, Vol. 69:70-79 (October, 1968).

Jameson, John and R. M. Hessler, "The Natives are Restless," *Human Organization*, Vol. 29, No. 2:81-95 (Summer, 1970).

Kahn, Tom, "The Problem of the New Left," *Commentary*, Vol. 42:30-38 (July, 1966).

Katz, J. and N. Sanford, "Causes of the Student Revolution," *Saturday Review*, December 18, 1965, pp. 64-67.

Keene, S., "How One Big University Laid Unrest to Rest," *The American Student*, Vol. 1:18-21 (1966).

Keniston, Kenneth, "American Students and the Political Revival," *American Scholar*, Vol. 32:40-65 (Winter, 1962-63).

——————, "The Faces in the Lecture Room," in Robert Morison (ed.), *The Contemporary American University*, Boston: Houghton Mifflin, 1960.

——————, "Social Change and Youth in America," in E. Erikson (ed.), *The Challenge of Youth*, Garden City: Doubleday Anchor, 1956.

——————, "Sources of Student Dissent," *Journal of Social Issues*, Vol. 23, No. 3:108-138 (July, 1967).

——————, "Youth, Change and Violence," *The American Scholar*, Vol. 37, (1968), pp. 227-245.

Kosa, John, L. D. Rachiele and C. O. Schommer, "The Self-image and Performance of Socially Mobile College Students," *The Journal of Social Psychology*, Vol. 56:301-316 (1962).

Labedz, Leopold, "Revolt or Revolution?", *Survey*, Vol. 67 (July, 1968).

Lifton, Robert J., "Youth and History," *Daedalus*, Vol. 91, (Winter, 1962), pp. 172ff.

Lipset, Seymour M., "The Value Patterns of Democracy," *American Sociological Review*, Vol. 28, No. 2.

——————, "The Activists: A Profile," *Public Interest*, No. 13, (Fall, 1968).

Lulves, John, "Is There a Student Conservatism?", *National Review*, 18:530-31 (May 31, 1966).

Lynd, Staughton, "The New Radicals and Participatory Democracy," *Dissent*, Vol. 12:324-33 (Summer, 1965).

McCormack, T.H., "The Motivation of Radicals," *American Journal of Sociology*, Vol. 56:17-24 (1950).

Marcuse, Herbert, "Repressive Tolerance," in Robert P. Wolff, Barrington Moore, Jr., and Herbert Marcuse, *A Critique of Pure Reason*, Boston: Beacon Press, 1965.

Monypenny, P., "Toward a Standard for Student Academic Freedom," *Law and Contemporary Problems*, Vol. 28:625-35 (Summer, 1963).

Muston, Ray, "The Concept of Student Participation in Governance Becomes Formalized—Gains Momentum," *College and University Business*, 48:12 (March, 1970).

Myerhoff, and Larson, "Primary and Formal Aspects of Family Organization vs. Adolescence," *Journal of Marriage and the Family*, Vol. 27:213-17 (May, 1965).

Myerson, Martin, "The Ethos of the American College Student," in Robert Morrison (ed.), *The American University*, Boston: Houghton Mifflin, 1966.

Neugarten, B. L., "Age Norms, Age Constraints, and Adult Socialization," *American Journal of Sociology*, Vol. 70:710-17 (May, 1965).

Newfield, Jack, "The Student Left: Idealism and Action," *The Nation*, Vol. 20:330-33 (November 8, 1965).

Orbell, John, "Protest Participation Among Southern Negro College Students," *American Political Science Review*, Vol. 61:446-56, (June, 1967).

Parsons, Talcott, "Youth in the Context of American Society," *Daeda-*

lus, Vol. 91:97-123 (Winter, 1962).

Reisman, David, "The Uncommitted Generation," *Encounter*, Vol. 15: 25-30 (November, 1966).

Sampson, Edward E., "Stirrings Out of Apathy," *Journal of Social Issues*, 23, No. 3:1-33, July, 1967.

Schiff, Lawrence, "The Obedient Rebels: A Study of College Conversions to Conservatism," *Journal of Social Issues*, Vol. 20:74-96 (October, 1964).

Shaffer, Helen B., "Alienated Youth," *Editorial Research Reports*, (October 12, 1966) pp. 747-64.

Shils, Edward, "Charisma, Order, and Status," *Sociological Review*, Vol. 30:199-213 (April, 1965).

Solomon, F. and J. R. Fishman, "Youth and Peace: A Psychosocial Study of Student Peace Demonstrators in Washington, D.C.," *The Journal of Social Issues*, Vol. 20, No. 4, 1964, pp. 54-73.

——————, "Youth and Social Action," *Journal of Social Issues*, Vol. 20:36-45 (1964).

Starr, Roger, "The Case of the Columbia Gym," in *The Public Interest*, 13:102-121, (Fall, 1968).

Trent, James, and Judith Craise, "Commitment and Conformity in the American College," *Comparative Education Review*, Vol. 10, No. 2, (June, 1966).

Watts, W. A. and D. N. E. Whittaker, "Free Speech Advocates at Berkeley," *Journal of Applied Behavorial Science*, No. 2, 1966.

Weinert, Richard S., "Violence in Pre-Modern Societies," *American Political Science Review*, Vol. 60:340-48 (June, 1966).

Westby, D. and R. Braungart, "Class and Politics in the Family Backgrounds of Student Political Activists," *American Sociological Review*, Vol. 31:690-692. (October, 1966).

Whitten, N. E., Jr., "Power Structure and Sociocultural Change," *Social Forces*, Vol. 43:320-9 (March, 1965).

Williamson, Robert C., "Toward a Theory of Political Violence," *Western Political Quarterly*, Vol. 18:35-49 (March, 1965).

Yankelovich, Daniel, "Survey of American Youth," *Fortune*, (January, 1969).

Youngquist, W., "Nobody Knows Me," *North American Review*, Vol. 2:31-34 (July, 1964).

Japan (Books)

Bakke, E. Wight, *Revolutionary Democracy, Challenge and Testing in Japan*, Hamden: Archon Books, 1968. (Includes extensive bibliography.)

Battistini, Lawrence, *The Postwar Student Struggle in Japan*, Tokyo and Rutland, Vermont: C. E. Tuttle Co., 1956.

Dator, James A., *Soka Gakkai; Builders of the Third Civilization*, Seattle: University of Washington Press, 1969.

Hall, Robert King and John O. Gauntlett (trans.), *Kokutai No Hongi: The Cardinal Principles of the National Entity of Japan*, Cambridge: Harvard University Press, 1949.

Hall. Robert King (ed.), *Shūshin, the Ethics of a Defeated Nation*, New York: Teachers' College, Columbia, 1949.

Hoar, Francis, *Today's Students, Japan's Tomorrow* (Documentary film by Francis Hoar, on Tokyo and Doshisha U.), Japanese Student News Service.

Jansen, Marius B. (ed.), *Changing Japanese Attitudes Toward Modernization*, Princeton: Princeton University Press, 1965.

Japan: Bureau of Statistics, *Japan Statistical Yearbook, 1968*, Tokyo: Government of Japan, Bureau of Statistics, 1968.

Japan: Central Council for Education, Subcommittee XXVI, *Draft Outline of the Basic Design of the Reform of Higher Education*, Tokyo: Ministry of Education, December, 1969.

_____, *Report on Measures to Meet Problems Facing University Education in Japan*, Tokyo: Ministry of Education, April, 1970, Abridged translation in *Minerva*, Vol. 8:116 (January, 1970).

Japan, Ministry of Education, *A General Survey of Education in Japan*, Tokyo: Government of Japan, Ministry of Education, Printed at the Herald of Asia Press, 1937.

_____, *Demand and Supply for University Graduates*, Tokyo: Government of Japan, Ministry of Education, Research Section, 1958.

_____, *Education in Japan*, Tokyo: Government of Japan, Ministry of Education, 1959.

_____, *Higher Education in Postwar Japan, Ministry of Education White Paper*, 1964, (ed. and tr. by John E. Blewett), Tokyo: Sophia University Press, 1965.

——————, White Paper, English translation, *Japan's Growth and Education*, Tokyo: Government of Japan, Ministry of Education, 1963.

Japan, Ministry of Justice, *Juvenile Delinquency as Seen in the Family Court of Japan*, Japanese Law Pamphlet Collection, Vol. 2, #5 (1957).

Japan, Office of the Prime Minister, *Statistical Handbook of Japan, 1970*, Tokyo: Japanese Government, 1970.

Matsumoto, Yoshiharu S., *Contemporary Japan: The Individual and the Group*, Philadelphia: American Philosophical Society, 1960.

Nakamura, H., *The Ways of Thinking of Eastern Peoples*, Tokyo: Printing Bureau of the Japanese Government, 1960.

Packard, George 3rd, *Protest in Tokyo*, Princeton: Princeton University Press, 1966.

Passim, Herbert, *Japanese Education: A Guide to a Bibliography of Materials in the English Language*, New York: East Asian Institute, School of International Affairs, Columbia University, 1965.

——————, *Society and Education in Japan*, New York: Bureau of Publications, Teachers' College, Columbia University, 1965.

Stoetzel, Jean, *Without the Chrysanthemum and the Sword*, New York: Columbia University Press, 1955.

UNESCO, *World Survey of Education, II*, Paris: UNESCO, 1958.

Uyehara, Cecil H., *Leftwing Social Movements in Japan: An Annotated Bibliography*, Tokyo and Rutland, Vermont: C. E. Tuttle Co., 1959.

Japan (Articles)

Altbach, Philip G., "Japanese Students and Japanese Politics," *Comparative Education Review*, Vol. 7:181-188 (October, 1963).

Bellah, R. N., "Religious Aspects of Modernization," *American Journal of Sociology*, Vol. 64 (July, 1958).

Campbell, Alex, "Sun Up in Asia", *New Republic*, July 5, 1969, pp. 16-18.

Embassy of Japan, "Competition for College Entrance," *Japan Report*, Vol. 13, #4:6 (February 28, 1967).

Etō, Jun, "Need for Identity," *Journal of Social and Political Ideas in Japan*, Vol. 3, #2 (1965).

Feuer, Lewis, "A Talk with the Zengakuren," *New Leader*, Vol. 46 (May, 1960).

Fukashiro, Junrō, "Student Thought and Feeling," (in 4 universities: Nihon, Doshisha, Tokyo and Kyushu), *Japan Quarterly*, Vol. 16, # 2:148-156 (April-June, 1969).

——————, "The New Left," *Japan Quarterly*, Vol. 17:27-36 (January-March, 1970).

Fuse, Toyomasa, "Student Radicals in Japan," *Comparative Education Review*, Vol. 13:325 (October, 1969).

Hani, Goro, "Characteristics of Nippon University Struggle," *Sekai*, January, 1969.

Hayashi, Kentarō, "Postwar Variations" [communist ideology], *Journal of Social and Political Ideas in Japan*, Vol. 3, #2 (1965).

Hirai, Professor, "An Analysis of University Struggle," *Chuo-Koron*, Special issue on student power, December, 1968. (Trans. by K. Wada for this study).

Hirakawa, Sukehiro, "Changing Attitudes Toward Western Learning," *Contemporary Japan*, Vol. 28, #3 (May, 1966).

Kinoshita, Hanji, "Oyoku, the Right Wing of Japan," *Contemporary Japan*, Vol. 27:423 (November, 1962), Vol. 28:116 (October, 1963).

Kyogoku, Jun-ichi, "Changes in Political Image and Behavior," *Journal of Social and Political Ideas in Japan*, Vol. 2, #3, (December, 1964).

Lifton, Robert, "Japanese Youth, the Search for the New and the Pure," *American Scholar*, Vol. 31:332 (Summer, 1961).

——————, "Youth and History," *Asian Cultural Studies*, #3, Tokyo: International Christian University, 1962.

——————, "Zengakuren: a Japanese Case Study," *Sociology of Education*, Vol. 37 (Spring, 1964).

Lynch, James J., "Disorder, Power and the Student," *Virginia Quarterly Review*, Vol. 43, #1 (Winter, 1967).

Minoru, Kida, "Buraku in Japan," *Japan Quarterly*, Vol. 15:323ff., and 472ff. (1968).

Morito, Tatsuo, "The Educational Reforms Reconsidered," *Japan Quarterly*, Vol. 13, #1 January-March, 1966).

Ōkōchi, Kazuo [ex-President of Tokyo University], "Japanese University Problems," *Japan Quarterly*, Vol. 14, #4:429-433 (October-December, 1967).

Pozdnayakov, I., "Japanese Ultras," [right], *International Affairs*, Vol. 41:104 (February, 1965).

Saburo, Matsukata, "The Student Movements," *Japan Quarterly*, April-June, 1960.

Shimbari, Michiga, "Comparison Between Pre- and Post-war Student Movement in Japan," *Sociology of Education*, Vol. 37:60 (Fall, 1963).

_____, "Zengakuren," *Sociology of Education*, Vol. 37 (Spring 1964).

"Some Controversial Characteristics of Tokyo University," editorial comment, *Asahi Journal*, November 11, 1968, (trans. by K. Wada for this study).

Suzuki, Shigenobu, "Education in Japan," *Journal of Social and Political Ideas in Japan*, Vol. 3, #2 (August, 1965).

"Student Power in Japan—an Overview," *Freedom*, December, 1968.

Taguchi, Jiro, "Obsession of Zengakuren," *Contemporary Japan*, Vol. XXVI, #3 (May, 1960), p.527.

Takahashi, Masao, "The Intellectuals in Japan and America," *Japan Quarterly*, Vol. 13:319-27 (July-September, 1966).

Takeyama, Michio, "Tradition and Japanese Youth," *Japan Quarterly*, July-September, 1960.

"The Last Stage of Tokyo University Struggle," editorial comment, *Asahi Journal*, December, 1968 (trans. by K. Wada for this study).

Toyomasa, Fuse, "Student Radicalization in Japan: A Cultural Revolution?", *Comparative Education Review*, Vol. 13:325-42 (Oct., 1969).

Tsurumi, Kazuko, "The Japanese Student Movement, (1) Its Milieu," *Japan Quarterly*, Vol. 15, #4 (October-December, 1968).

_____, "The Japanese Student Movement (2) Group Portraits," *Japan Quarterly*, Vol. 16, #1 (Jan.-Mar., 1969).

"University Strife: The Asahi Shimbun Public Opinion Survey," *Japan Quarterly*, Vol. 16, #2:157-165 (April-June, 1969).

Usami, Shō, "Zengakuren," *Japan Quarterly*, Vol. 15, #2:233-244 (April-June, 1968).

India (Books)

Airan, J.W., T. Barnabas, and A.B. Shah, (eds.), *Climbing a Wall of Glass*, Bombay: Manaktalas, 1965.

Altbach, Philip G. (ed.), *Turmoil and Transition*, New York: Basic Books, 1968.

Bayley, David H., *The Police and Political Developments in India*, Princeton: Princeton University Press, 1969.

Bureau of Social Science Research, *The Indian Student Movement,* Washington, D.C.: American University, 1955.

Chakrabarti, A., *India Since 1947: Allied Problems,* Bombay: 1967.

Chandra, Prabadh, *Student Movement in India,* Lahore: All-India Students' Federation, 1938.

Cormack, Margaret Lawson, *She Who Rides a Peacock; Indian Students and Social Change,* Bombay and New York: Asia Publishing House, 1961.

Curran, Jean A., Jr., *Militant Hinduism in Indian Politics: A Study of the RSS,* Institute of Pacific Relations, 1952.

DiBona, Joseph E., *Change and Conflict in the Indian University,* Durham, Duke University, 1969.

Dongerkery, Sunderrao Ramrao, *University Autonomy in India,* Bombay: Lalvani Publishing House, 1967.

Hart, Henry C., *Campus India: An Appraisal of American College Programs in India,* Ann Arbor: Michigan State University, 1961.

Humayun, Kabir, *Student Unrest: Causes and Cure,* Calcutta, 1958.

India: Ministry of Education, Education Commission, *Education and National Development,* New Delhi: 1967.

——————————, *Report, 1964/66,* New Delhi: 1966.

India: Ministry of Education, *Report on Educational Developments in India, 1965-1966,* New Delhi: 1966.

India: Ministry of Education and Youth Services, *Selected Educational Statistics, 1968-69,* New Delhi: 1969.

India: University Grants Commission, *Annual Report, 1967/68,* New Delhi: 1969.

——————————, *Centres of Advanced Study in Indian Universities,* New Delhi: 1964.

——————————, *India Pocket Book of University Education,* New Delhi: Bahadur Sha Zafar Marg., 1969.

——————————, *Report for the Year 1966/67,* New Delhi: 1969.

——————————, *University Development in India, Basic Facts and Figures, 1963-64,* New Delhi: 1965.

Inter-University Board of India and Ceylon, *Universities Handbook of India and Ceylon,* 1969, New Delhi: Privately printed, 1969.

Mani, Dr. R.S., *Educational Ideas and Ideals of Eminent Indians,* New Delhi: New Book Society of India, 1965.

Mathur, Dr. S.S., *A Sociological Approach to Indian Education*, Agra: Vinod Pustak Mandir, 1966.

Meland, Bernard E., *The Secularization of Modern Cultures*, (Barrows lectures in India, 1964-65), Oxford and New York: Oxford University Press, 1966.

Parikh, G.D., *General Education and Indian Universities*, New Delhi: Asia Publishing House, 1959.

Ram, Mohan, *Split Within a Split*, Delhi: Vikas Publications. (Review, *Indian News*, August 26, 1970, p. 3.)

Ross, Aileen D., *Student Unrest in India*, Montreal: McGill-Queens University, 1969.

Reddy, M. Muni, *The Student Movement in India*, Lucknow: K.S.R. Acharya, 1947.

Rudolph, Lloyd I. and Susanne Hueber Rudolph, *The Modernity of Tradition*, Chicago and London: The University of Chicago Press, 1967.

Saiyidain, Khwaja G. and H.C. Gupta, *Access to Higher Education in India*, New Delhi: UNESCO and International Association of Universities, 1962.

Sarkar, Chancal, *The Unquiet Campus*, New Delhi: 1960.

Sen, N.B. (ed.), *Development of Education in India*, New Delhi: New Book Society of India, 1966.

Shils, Edward, A., *The Intellectual Between Tradition and Modernity: The Indian Situation*, The Hague: Mouton, 1961.

Smith, Bradford, *Portrait of India*, Philadelphia and New York: The J.B. Lippincott Co., 1962.

Weiner, Myron, *The Politics of Scarcity: Public Pressure and Political Response in India*, Chicago: University of Chicago Press, 1962.

India (Articles)

Adiseshiah, Malcom S., "Unemployment of Engineers in India," *Impact of Science on Society*, UNESCO, Vol. IX, #1:63 (Jan.-Mar., 1969).

Airan, J. W., "Tensions in Universities," *United Asia*, Vol. 18, #1 (Jan.-Feb., 1966).

Altbach, Philip G., "Bombay Colleges," *Minerva*, Vol. 8, #4 (Oct., 1970).

_____, "The Transformation of the Indian Student Movement, *Asian Survey*, Vol. 6:448ff. (Aug., 1966).

Banerjee, Reba, "Indiscipline, a Survey of Students' Opinion," *Journal of Psychological Researches*, Vol. 12:1-6 (Jan., 1968).

"Central Board of secondary schools announced a 3-language formula," *India News*, August 7, 1970, p. 3.

Cormack, Margaret, et al, "Symposium on Higher Education in India's Asian Drama," *Asian Survey*, Vol. 9, (October, 1969).

DiBona, Joseph, "Indiscipline and Student Leadership in an Indian University," *Comparative Education Review*, Vol. 10, #1, (Spring, 1966).

Gandhi, Rajnikants, "Conflict and Cohesion in an Indian Student Community," *Human Organization*, Vol. 29, #2:95-103 (Summer, 1970).

Gusfield, Joseph R., "Educational Institutions in the Process of Economic and National Development," *Journal of Asian and African Studies*, Vol. 1:129-146 (April, 1966).

Haldar, M.K., "Education for Frustration," *Thought*, October 22 and 29, 1966.

The Hindustan Times, February 12, 1968.

Hindu Weekly Review, Madras.

Indian Institute of Public Opinion, "The New Look of Indian Students," *Monthly Public Opinion Surveys*, Vol. 14, #1 (Oct., 1968).

Institute for International Student Affairs, *News Features*, December 19, 1967.

Jain, S. P., "Religion, Caste, Class and Education in a North India Town," [U.P.], *Sociology and Sociological Research*, Vol. 53:482-489 (July, 1969).

Lynch, James, J., "Disorder, Power and the Student," *Virginia Quarterly Review*, Vol. 43, #1 (Winter, 1967).

"Medical Education," *India News*, July 6, 1970, July 17, 1970.

Mukerji, S. N. "Qualitative Improvement of Higher Education," *Indian Education*, Vol. 7, #1 (December, 1967), #2 (January, 1968).

Ranganathan, A., "The Language Problem in Indian Education," *Texas Quarterly*, Vol. 9:10-17 (Spring, 1966).

Reddy, P.N., "Indian Student Youth and Identity Crisis," *Education and Psychology Review*, Vol. 8:135-148 (April, 1968).

Sarkar, Chancal, "Crisis on the Campus," *Seminar*, No. 44, (April, 1963).

"Selected Indicators of Economic Development: Education," *India News*, August 14, 1970, p. 1.

Shah, B.V., "Students' Unrest—a Sociological Hypothesis," *Sociological Bulletin*, Vol. 17:55-64 (March, 1968).

Shils, Edward, "The Academic Profession in India," *Minerva*, Vol. 7:45-72 (Spring, 1969).

Tata Institute of Fundamental Research, "Survey of Ambitions of Students." News item in *India News*, September 25, 1970, p. 2.

The Statesman

The Times of India

Verstraeten, A., "Nationalization of Education in India," *Modern Review*: Allahabad: Indian Press, #119:414 (January-June, 1966), Calcutta, Modern Review Office.

Wright, Theo. P., Jr., "The Muslim League in South India Since Independence," *American Political Science Review*, Vol. 60, #3 (September, 1966).

Latin America (Books)

Alexander, Robert J., *Today's Latin America*, Garden City, New York: Doubleday, 1962.

Benjamin, H.R., *History and Aims of Higher Education in the American Republics*, New York: McGraw-Hill, 1965.

Brandenberg, Frank, *The Making of Modern Mexico*, Englewood Cliffs, New Jersey: Prentice-Hall, 1964.

Chávez, José María, *La Reforma Universitaria en Colombia*, Bogotá: Ediciones ABC.

Colombia, Ministro de Educación Nacional, Vol. I, Posada, Dr. Jaime, *Una Politica Educativa para Colombia;* Vol. II, Llevas, Presidente, *Un Proposition Nacional;* Vol. III, Posada, Ministro Jaime, *La Revolución de las Escuelas;* Vol. IV, *Problemas y Soluciones,* presentación gráfica; Vol. V, *Plan de Extension de la Escuela Primaria;* Vol. VI, *La Reforma Universitaria.*

Dix, Robert Heller, *Colombia; the Political Dimensions of Change*, New Haven: Yale University Press, 1967.

Gill, Clark C., *Education in a Changing Mexico*, United States Office of Education, Institute of International Studies, Washington, D.C.: U.S. Government Printing Office, 1969.

Herro, Santacruz, Carmen de, *Contribución al Estudio de la Delincuencia Infantil y Juvenil de Colombia*, Universidad Javeriana, Facultad de Fil y Lettras, Bogotá: 1965.

Houtart, Francois and Emile Pin, trans. Gilbert Barth, *The Church and the Latin American Revolution*, New York: Sheed and Ward, 1965.

International Research Associates, *A Study of Opinions of Students in Mexico*, Mexico City: International Research Associates, 1964.

International Student Conference, *Struggle in South America*, Leiden: Coordinating Secretariat of National Unions of Students, 1958.

Institute for International Youth Affairs, New York: *Youth and Freedom*, Vol. 8, #3:18-20.

James, Preston E., *Latin America*, [3rd edition] New York: Odyssey Press, 1959.

Johnson, John J., *Continuity and Change in Latin America*, Stanford: Stanford University Press, 1964.

Johnston, Marjorie C., *Education in Mexico*, Washington, D.C., Department of Health, Education, and Welfare, 1956 Bulletin #1, Government Printing Office, 1956.

Littig, David, (ed.), *Latin American Student Affairs*, Prepared by the International Commission of the U.S. National Student Association for the 18th National Student Congress, August 22-September 2, 1965, University of Wisconsin, Madison.

Mac-Lean y Estenós, Roberto, *La Crisis Universitaria en Hispano-América*, México, D.F.: Universidad Nacional, 1956.

Magisterio, Agosto-Septiembre de 1964.

Navarro Palacios, Enrique, *La Reforma Universitaria en México*, México: Universidad Autónoma de México, VI.

Nicholson, Irene, *The X in Mexico*, London: Faber and Faber, 1965.

Pan American Union, *Education in Latin America: A partial bibliography*, Washington, D.C., 1958.

Petras, James, and Maurice Zeitlin, *Latin America, Reform or Revolution?* Greenwich: Fawcett, 1968.

Pye, Lucian W., *Aspects of Political Development*, Boston: Little, Brown, 1966.

Pye, Lucian W. and Sidney Verba (eds.), *Political Cultures and Political Development*, Princeton, New Jersey: Princeton University Press, 1965.

Ramos, Samuel, *Profile of Man and Culture in Mexico*, Austin: University of Texas Press, 1962.

Requelme, Marcial A., *Student Movements in the United States and Latin America*, Philadelphia: U.S. National Student Association, 1963.

Scott, Robert E., *Mexico in Transition*, revised ed., Urbana, Illinois: University of Illimois Press, 1964. (Also in *Daedalus*, Winter, 1968, pp. 84ff.)

Silvert, Kalman H., et al., *A Report to the American Academic Community on the Present University Situation*, Austin, Texas: Latin American Studies Association, 1967.

Spencer, David E. (ed.), *Student Politics in Latin America*, Washington, D.C.: U.S. National Students' Association, 1965.

Statistical Abstract of Latin America, 1968, Los Angeles: Latin American Center, U.C.L.A., 1969.

Tepaske, John J., and S.N. Nettleton (eds.), *Explosive Forces in Latin America*, Columbus: Ohio State University Press, 1964.

United Nations Economic Committee for Latin America, *Education, Human Resources and Development in Latin America*, U.N.: 1968.

——————, *Statistical Bulletin for Latin America*, Vol. 6, 1, 1969.

UNESCO, Bowles, Frank H. (ed.), *Access to Higher Education, I and II*, New York: Columbia University Press, 1965.

United States National Student Association, *Readings on Latin American Student Movement and the Rise of the Latin American Left*, Philadelphia: U.S. National Student Association, 1965.

U.S.A. Office of Education, *Education in Columbia* (Bulletin 1946, #6), Washington, D.C.: Federal Security Agency, U.S. Office of Education, 1946.

Vernon, R., *The Dilemma of Mexican Development*, Cambridge: Harvard University Press, 1963.

Williamson, Robert C., *El Estudiantě Colombiano y Sus Actitudes*, Monografias Sociológicas #13, Bogotá: Universidad Nacional, Facultad de Sociológica, 1962.

Latin America (Articles)

Albornoz, Orlando, "Student Opposition in Latin America," *Government and Opposition*, Vol. 2:105 (October, 1966-January, 1967).

Bakke, E. Wight, "Students on the March: the Cases of Colombia and Mexico," *Sociology of Education*, Vol. 37 (Spring, 1964).

Barton, Robert D., "The Militant Latin Campus," *Nation*, 193 (August 12, 1961).

Brandenberg, Frank, "The Relevance of Mexican Experience to Latin American Development," *Orbis*, Vol. 10, No. 1 (Spring, 1965).

Castellanos, Ruben, "The October Revolution and the Communist Movement in Latin America," *World Marxist Review*, Vol. 10, No. 6 (June, 1967).

Chávez, Dr. Ignacio, Rector de Universidad Nacional Autónoma de México, Dr. Francisco Larroyo, and Lic. Alfonso Briseno, "Reforma del Bachillerato Universitario," *Magisterio*, Agosto/Septiembre, 1964, pp. 42ff.

Chiapetta, M., "Philosophy of Education in Latin America," *Phi Delta Kappan*, 214, 1964.

Culhane, Eugene K., "Red Pocket in Colombia," *America*, Vol. 102: 701-04 (March 12, 1960).

Donahue, Francis, "Students in Latin America Politics," *Antioch Review*, Vol. 26:94 (Spring, 1966).

Einaudi, Luigi, "Rebels Without Allies," *Saturday Review*, (August, 1968), 45-46.

Fals Borda, Orlando, "Basis for a Sociological Interpretation of Education in Colombia" in A. Curtis Wilgus (ed.) *The Caribbean: Contemporary Colombia*, Gainsville: University of Florida Press, 1962.

Germani, G., "Política y Sociedad en una Época de Trancición," reviewed by H. G. Martins in *British Journal of Sociology*, Vol. 15: 274 (September, 1964) and by R. and J. Hopper in *American Sociological Review*, Vol. 30:141 (February, 1965).

Gomez, Pedro, "Our Position Among the Students," *World Marxist Review*, September, 1961.

Harrison, John P., "Learning and Politics in Latin American Universities," *Proceedings*, Academy of Political Science, Vol. 27, #4: 331-342 (May, 1964).

_____, "The Confrontation with the Political University," *The Annals*, Vol. 334:74-83 (March, 1961).

_____, "The Role of the Intellectual in Fomenting Change: The University," in J. J. TePaske and S. N. Fisher (eds.), *Explosive Forces in Latin America*, Columbus, Ohio: Ohio State University Press, 1964.

Havighurst, Robert, "Latin American and North American Higher Education," *Comparative Education Review*, Vol. 4 (1961)

Holmes, Lula T., "Educating Mexican Masses," *Mexico*, #94, 1952.

International Student Conference, *Report*, "La Reforma Universitaria en América Latina: Análisis y Documentos"in *Part I, Universities and Colleges*, Leiden: Secretariat of 8th International Student Conference, Leiden, 1959.

Labedz, Leopold (ed.), "Students and Revolution," *Survey*, July, 1968.

Lewis, Oscar, "Medicine and Politics in a Mexican Village" in Benjamin D. Paul, *Health, Culture, and Community*, New York: Russell Sage, 1955.

Moreno, Frank J., "Latin America: The Fear Within," *Yale Review*, Vol. 55 (December, 1965).

Nasatir, David, "Student Action in Latin America: The University as Training Ground for Careerists and Revolutionaries," *Transaction*, Vol. 2, #3, March-April, 1965, pp. 8-11.

Quirk, Robert E., "Aspects of the Religious Influence in Modern Mexico" in William V. d'Antonio and Frederick B. Pope, *Religion, Revolution, and Reform*, London: Burns and Oates, 1965.

Roque, Dalton, "Student Youth and the Latin American Revolution," *World Marxist Review*, Vol. 9 (March, 1966).

Scott, Robert E., "Government Bureaucrats and Political Change in Latin America," *Journal of International Affairs*, Vol. 20, #2:289-308, 1966.

——————, "Mexico: the Established Revolution," in Lucian Pye and Sidney Verba (eds.), *Political Culture and Political Development*, Princeton: Princeton University Press, 1965.

——————, "Student Political Activism in Latin America," *Daedalus*, Vol. 97, part II, 70-98 (Winter, 1968). (Excellent bibliography.)

Taborsky, Edw., "Soviet Strategy and Latin American Students," *Social Science Quarterly*, Vol. 50:116-127 (June, 1969).

Walker, Kenneth N., "A Comparison of University Reform Movements in Argentina and Colombia" in S. M. Lipset (ed.), *Student Politics*, New York: Basic Books, 1967.

——————, "Determinants of Castro Support among Latin University Students," *Social and Economic Studies*, Vol. 14, March, 1965.

Williamson, R. C., "Toward a Theory of Political Violence," *Western Political Quarterly*, Vol. 18:35-49 (March, 1965).

——————, "University Students in a World of Change: a Colombian Sample," *Sociology and Social Research*, Vol. 48:397-413 (July, 1964).

Index

378.198
B

14,580

378.198   14,580 ✓
B
        Bakke, E. Wight
        Campus challenge

DATE DUE

FEB 6 '73			
MAR 1			
MAR 15 '73			
MAY 15 '73			
MAY 26 '73			
JUL 29 1982			